► **RELIGION IN SOCIOLOGICAL PERSPECTIVE**

▶ **ADVISING EDITOR IN SOCIOLOGY**
Charles M. Bonjean
University of Texas–Austin

▶ THIRD EDITION

Religion in Sociological Perspective

Keith A. Roberts

Hanover College

Wadsworth Publishing Company
I(T)P™
An International Thomson Publishing Company

Belmont ● Albany ● Bonn ● Boston ● Cincinnati
Detroit ● London ● Madrid ● Melbourne ● Mexico City
New York ● Paris ● San Francisco ● Singapore ● Tokyo
Toronto ● Washington

Editor: Serina Beauparlant
Editorial Assistant: Jason Moore
Project Management: Carlisle Publishers Services
Copy Editor: Cindy Trickel
Permissions Editor: Jeanne Bosschart
Print Buyer: Barbara Britton
Text Designer: Leigh McLellan
Cover Designer: Sandy Drooker
Compositor: Carlisle Communications, Ltd.
Printer: Arcata Graphics/Fairfield

COPYRIGHT © 1995
By Wadsworth Publishing Company
A Division of International Thomson Publishing Inc.

I(T)P   The ITP logo is a trademark under license

Printed in the United States of America

For more information, contact:

Wadsworth Publishing Company
10 Davis Drive
Belmont, California 94002
U.S.A.

International Thomson Publishing
Berkshire House 168-173
High Holborn
London, WC1V 7AA
England

Thomas Nelson Australia
102 Dodds Street
South Melbourne 3205
Victoria, Australia

Nelson Canada
1120 Birchmount Road
Scarborough, Ontario
Canada M1K 5G4

International Thomson Publishing GmbH
Königswinterer Strasse 418
53227 Bonn
Germany

International Thomson Publishing Asia
221 Henderson Road #05-10 Henderson Building
Singapore 0315

International Thomson Publishing Japan
Hirakawacho Kyowa Building, 3F
2-2-1 Hirakawacho
Chiyoda-ku, 102 Tokyo
Japan

The credits section for this book is on p. 465, and is considered an extension of the copyright page.

1 2 3 4 5 6 7 8 9 10 99 98 97 96 95

Library of Congress Cataloging-in-Publication Data

Roberts, Keith A.
    Religion in sociological perspective / Keith A. Roberts.—3rd ed.
        p.   cm.
    Includes bibliographical references and index.
    ISBN 0-534-20466-X (alk. paper)
    1. Religion and sociology. I. Title.
BL60.R58 1994   94-17307
306.6—dc20   CIP

 This book is printed on acid-free recycled paper.

Contents

Preface

Religion is a complex phenomenon. It involves a meaning system with an interrelated set of beliefs, rituals, symbols, values, moods, and motivations. Each of these interacts in diverse and complex ways with one another, sometimes being mutually supportive and sometimes conflicting. Religion is also a structural system with established statuses, organizational patterns, and even bureaucratic dilemmas. This structural system is itself diverse and multifaceted, characterized by both conflicts over self-interests and strains toward coherence and integration. Finally, religion is composed of a belonging system, with friendship networks, group boundaries, and informal norms that may be quite independent of the formal structure or official meaning systems. These three subsystems of religion are themselves *interdependent*, forming a larger system that is in some ways coherent and in some ways in tension and discord. Further, religion is part of a larger social system, and as such it both affects and is affected by this larger system. It is precisely this complexity of religion, including the complexity of its relationship to the larger society and to the world system, that we explore in the following pages.

This book is designed as an introduction to the sociology of religion. My intent has been to present and illustrate the basic theories sociologists use to understand the social dimensions of religion. First and foremost, I seek to help students understand the *perspective* from which sociologists view religion. By the time students have finished this book, they should understand the central theories and methods of research in the sociology of religion, and

they should have an idea of how to apply these analytical tools to new groups they encounter. The goal of this text is to be *illustrative* rather than all-encompassing. Insofar as it is adopted as a text in a university or seminary course, I have assumed that it will be complemented with monographs or anthologies that explore the specific groups or specific processes the instructor chooses to emphasize.

Theoretically, the third edition continues to draw on a wide range of perspectives. I seek to help students recognize the contributions of various theoretical perspectives and the blind spots of each. Conflict, functional, and interactionist theories are used throughout the text, but discussion of specific processes also calls for a wide range of other perspectives, ranging from cognitive theories to rational choice models. But despite the effort to introduce many perspectives, I have also made an effort to enhance integration of the text by using one paradigm more consistently in each chapter. That perspective, which stresses both structure and dynamic process, is open systems theory.

I have also tried in this book to provide students with an understanding of the relationship between research methods and findings. Without belaboring the issue of methods, I have attempted to make students aware of the relationships between accurate data, operationalization of ideas, correct use of the language of causality, and support of one's generalizations. My hope is that students sense that doing research really can be exciting work.

Each chapter of the first two editions of this text was student-tested for readability and clarity among nonsociologists. This practice was repeated for all new material in this edition, and all revisions were made with an eye to making the material ever more accessible to the nonspecialist. While I have made every effort to enhance clarity and to illustrate abstract ideas, I have also tried to resist appeals from some quarters to lessen the theoretical sophistication of the text.

Many of the changes in the text are matters of updating data and including recent findings. Moreover, during the ten years since the publication of the first edition, the "hot issues" in sociology of religion have changed. This is reflected in new topical coverage. Televangelism was incorporated into the second edition, and globalization in the third edition. Additional cross-cultural illustrations have been added elsewhere in the text as well.

I have tried to make the text adaptable to the particular teaching interests of the instructor. For example, the part on conversion and commitment involves two chapters. Chapter 5 deals with theories that have traditionally been identified with sociological literature, while chapter 6 looks at the same phenomena using psychological perspectives—cognitive developmental and cognitive re-creation approaches. This dual treatment enriches the theoretical base of the book, and allows for comparison of different approaches. On the other hand, the reorganization into two chapters will make it possible for each instructor to make choices about whether to include such psychological approaches in his or her course.

There is substantial value to texts that have interchangeable chapters, for they allow the instructor flexibility in designing the course. What a text gains in flexibility, however, it often loses in cumulative application of theory. While it is possible to vary the order of the chapters in this text, the text is designed to be cumulative. Later chapters are more complex in their analysis than earlier ones and attempt to stretch students to greater levels of analytical sophistication. If an instructor does choose to use these chapters in a different sequence, I recommend that the first four chapters be covered first as a foundation, with other chapters assigned as wished.

While only one name goes on the book cover, a project of this nature is enriched by the labors and support of many people. I am deeply appreciative of the assistance offered by the librarians of Bowling Green State University (especially Will Currie and Sherry Gray) and Hanover College (especially Larry Baerveldt). My reviewers for all three editions deserve special comment for their incisive analysis, their helpful criticism, and their encouragement in this project. These reviewers were James D. Davidson, Roger Finke, Sharon Georgianna, John W. Hawthorne, Richard Malchalek, Perry McWilliams, Edgar W. Mills Jr., Wade Clark Roof, John S. Staley, Tom Kearin, Frank Sampson, Harry LeFever, Les Kurtz, and Charles Bonjean. While all of these persons have contributed to the finished product, they are certainly not responsible for its flaws.

Finally, I must express my appreciation to my wife, Judy, and to my family. Judy has been enormously supportive and has offered helpful comment and criticism. My three children have contributed in two ways: through their ability to provide delightful interludes away from the intensity of the project and through their patience on all those occasions when Dad was at the word processor rather than playing ball or otherwise being attentive to them.

Keith A. Roberts
Hanover, Indiana

Introduction to the Sociology of Religion

Before we delve too deeply into analysis of our topic, we must establish some common assumptions and understandings. The reader need not agree with the author, but at least the reader should know how the author is using key concepts and approaching various topics. That is the purpose of these first two chapters; we are laying the groundwork for a shared investigation.

In chapter 1 we will explore what we mean by religion—what is included or excluded as "religious" and why. Then in chapter 2 we will examine what it means to take a sociological approach to the study of religion, including unique perspectives and methodological assumptions.

What Do We Mean by the Term *Religion*?

W e begin our venture together with a difficult and complex problem: the definition of our topic of study. To students who have never studied the sociology of religion, the definition of religion may seem clear. Certainly, everyone knows what religion is! Let's get on with more important matters! But we dare not be so hasty. The way we define a subject provides boundaries for what are and are not legitimate topics or groups for discussion. Some definitions are so narrow and specific as to exclude Buddhism as a religion. Other definitions are so broad and inclusive that many social behaviors may be considered forms of religion—including patriotism, systematic racism, or any other core set of values and beliefs that provide an individual or community with a sense of worth and of meaning in life.

Your basic assumptions about what religion is may differ from mine. We must begin our analysis, then, by exploring the question of what it is we intend to study. What, after all, is religion? The following discussion shows some of the ways in which social scientists have defined religion.

Substantive Definitions

Many sociologists employ what has been called a substantive definition. This approach hinges on identification of the "substance" or "essence" of religion. Edward B. Tylor used this approach in 1873 when he defined religion as "belief in Spiritual Beings" (1958: 8). For most of us a reference to God or gods does seem to be an essential element in religion. The reason Tylor used the term *spiritual beings* is that many nonindustrialized people worship and/or fear their deceased ancestors. They have little or no concern about gods, as such, but their world is peopled with many unseen beings. Hence, spiritual beings seemed to Tylor a more inclusive term than belief in gods. Some contemporary scholars have reaffirmed Tylor's insistence that religion involves a belief in a Being or beings that are not encountered in normal empirical processes (Spiro 1966).

Trying to define the essence of religion is a difficult task, but it becomes more difficult if our definition is to be applied cross-culturally. In the Western world, we tend to feel that religion is essentially a matter of belief. In fact, some social scientists have attempted to measure the religiosity of people by determining how orthodox they are. (An orthodox person is one who believes the traditional doctrines of a church.) But as R. R. Marett suggests, in many cultures religion is "not so much thought out as danced out" (1914: xxxi). That is to say, ritual and emotion are primary to religion, and belief is only secondary.

Sam Gill's study (1982: 62) of Native American religions has convinced him that these faiths are expressed through dance, ritual movement, and religious objects, not creeds, dogmas, or theologies. And scholars studying Orthodox Judaism have rather consistently pointed out that a focus on behavior, rather than on beliefs and attitudes, is characteristic of that faith (Cohen 1983; Moberg 1984; Sklare and Greenblum 1979). Anthropologists studying other cultures have also insisted that emphasis on belief is a bias of the Western world that causes investigators to miss the underlying thrust of many non-Western religions (Kluckhohn 1972). For example, several observers have insisted that any concepts of a deity or superhuman beings are peripheral to official Buddhism (Benz 1964; Zaechner 1967). On the other hand, most common folks in Burma who identify themselves as Buddhists do believe in superhuman beings (Spiro 1978). So a definition that emphasizes a belief in superhuman beings leaves doubt about whether Buddhism is a religion. Strictly speaking, many Buddhist gurus (who are not concerned with superhuman beings) would not be considered to be practicing religion. Does religion refer only to those who hold a specific kind of belief?

Another definitional approach that tries to capture the essence of religion, but that avoids the requirement of a specific belief, was first suggested in 1915 by Emile Durkheim. Durkheim was fascinated with the cleansing exercises and the change of attitude that in many cultures were necessary before one could enter into religious ritual. He maintained that a recognition of the division of life into sacred and profane realms allows us to identify religion in any culture (1965: 50–62). People around the world seem to undergo a psychological shift when encountering holy objects or engaging in religious ritual. This shift involves a sense of awe, a feeling of fear and majesty. The attitude differs from anything one encounters in the everyday life of these people.

Durkheim recognized that not all experiences of awe or sacredness are religious in character. Religion, he maintained, is a communal activity. It involves a social group: "In all history we do not find a single religion without a Church" (1965: 59). The sacred attitude must be fundamentally a group experience if it is to be identified as religion. Durkheim's formal definition, then, is: "A religion is a unified system of beliefs and practices relative to sacred things, that is to say, things set apart and forbidden—beliefs and practices which unite into a single moral community called a Church, all those who adhere to them" (1965: 62). Since the late 1950s, Mircea Eliade and his students have reasserted the importance of the sacred-profane distinction in defining religion (Eliade 1959).

This approach is helpful in a great many cases, and it avoids the problem of deciding which specific belief is intrinsically or inherently religious. But social scientists who have used this approach have often implied (if not asserted) a dualistic world view. That is to say, life has a religious dimension and a nonreligious dimension. For example, Durkheim insists that

> the religious life and the profane life cannot coexist in the same unit of time. It is necessary to assign determined days or periods to the first, from which all profane occupations are excluded.
> . . . There is no religion, and, consequently, no society which has not known and practiced

this division of time into two distinct parts (1965: 347).

Mircea Eliade concurs with this and writes regarding space:

> For religious [persons], space is not homogeneous; he [or she] experiences interruptions in it; some parts of space are qualitatively different from others (1959: 20).

While it is true that many people organize their life experience into separate categories, not all do. The United Society of Believers in Christ's Second Appearing (the Shakers) attempted to sustain an attitude that all of life is sacred. More recently, a deeply religious utopian society called the Bruderhof (with communes in New York, Pennsylvania, and Connecticut) has also attempted to make *all* life hallowed and has de-emphasized sacraments and rituals. All of one's life is to be lived in the spirit of worship, and the community works to sustain this attitude. Benjamin Zablocki writes, "The Bruderhof is concerned with bearing witness in the simple, everyday acts of

In Islam the inside of the mosque is holy ground, and Moslems recognize this extraordinariness and sacredness by removing their shoes when they enter. (UPI/Bettmann newsphoto.)

living. . . . There are no activities, however trivial, that cannot be permeated by the divine spirit" (1971: 31). This community even refuses to erect a church building lest religion be identified with a distinct time and place. Groups such as these do not seem to bifurcate life into sacred and profane realms.[1] In fact, Kingsley Davis (1949) has suggested that while this distinction is useful in studying nonindustrial societies, it erects a false dichotomy in contemporary society and religion.

Andrew Greeley has employed this criterion of sacredness as a defining characteristic of religion but has avoided the dualism of many writers. Greeley suggests that any being, social process, or value that gives meaning and purpose to life tends to become a source of reverence or profound respect (1972: 10–18). When Greeley refers to a sacred attitude, he suggests that it is not totally unlike a secular outlook but is a matter of intensified respect. Hence, Greeley's reference to a sacred attitude does not entirely preclude the study of nationalism, worship of the free-enterprise system, or any other example of profound loyalty as a form of religion. However, he does insist that not all experiences of transcendence or profound reverence are religious. He does not say how one distinguishes religious transcendence from nonreligious transcendence, but the distinction appears to pivot on the degree to which the object of awe is supernatural.

An underlying question in this whole debate, then, is whether religion by definition includes only that which has an otherworldly or supernatural dimension. What about the person whose ultimate value and deepest commitment is to the United States of America? He or she has a deep sense of loyalty to the flag of the United States and will even give his or her life to defend it. The American

Way of Life and the American Dream provide a sense of meaning, purpose, and value in life. National holidays are celebrated with devotion, and a tear is shed when the national anthem is played. This individual may belong to several organizations for the preservation and promotion of patriotism and the glorification of America. The person loves this country above all else, according it highest value and deepest loyalty. Is this religious behavior? Can nationalism be a form of religion? It is not otherworldly, and it is not essentially supernatural (although the belief structure may include a God who overlooks, blesses, and judges the nation). Certainly the individual feels a sort of sacredness toward the nation and its primary symbol, the flag. But this sacredness does not involve the fear and trembling that Rudolf Otto (1923) and Durkheim (1965) describe as part of the sacred attitude. How does the feeling of awe and reverence toward a nation differ from the awe and reverence toward a supernatural being or realm? Is this difference significant enough to call one experience religious and the other not? These are not easy questions to answer. Some scholars feel that nationalistic behavior as described above is religious in character and that a broader definition of religion is appropriate.

The major criticism of the substantive definitions is that they tend to focus the researcher's attention solely on traditional forms of religion. Some writers feel that people in complex and changing societies such as ours are religious in new ways. The substantive definitions are felt to be too narrow and too tradition-bound, hence blinding researchers to these new modes of religiosity.

A Functional Definition

Milton Yinger has offered a more inclusive definition of religion (1970: 1–23). He suggests that we focus not on what religion essentially

---

[1]Anthropology studies of world views seem to support this view. Exclusive categories of thought are not universal. For example, see W. T. Jones (1972).

is but on what it does. He proposes that we define a social phenomenon as religious if it fulfills the manifest function of religion.[2] He follows Max Weber in asserting that meaning in life is a basic human need (although the nature and intensity of that need will vary among individuals). The theologian Paul Tillich (1957) has described religion as that which is one's "ultimate concern," and Yinger also draws on Tillich's treatment in developing his own definition. The underlying conviction is that a fundamental concern of human beings is to understand the purpose of life and the meaning of death, suffering, evil, and injustice. In line with this conviction, Yinger writes, "Religion, then, can be defined as a system of beliefs and practices by means of which a group of people struggles with these ultimate problems of human life" (1970: 7). Religion helps individuals cope with these perplexities by offering an explanation and by providing a strategy to overcome despair, hopelessness, and futility.

Using this type of definition, the range of phenomena that we consider under the heading *religion* is considerably expanded. Yinger insists that nontheistic and even nonsupernatural systems of belief and practice can be appropriate social patterns for the sociologist of religion. "It is not the nature of *belief,* but the nature of *believing* that requires our study" (1970: 11). Wherever one sees a closing of the gap between fact and hope, wherever one sees a leap of faith that allows a person to assert that suffering and evil will somehow, someday be defeated, there one sees the manifestations of religion. Even a secular faith that science and technology will ultimately solve all our problems is, by this definition, a religious or quasi-religious phenomenon. Yinger writes, "A term that already includes, by common

consent, the contemplations of a Buddhist monk and the ecstatic visions of a revivalist cult member, human sacrifice, and ethical monotheism may have room in it for science *as a way of life*" (1970: 12). Intense faith in nationalism, in capitalism, and in many other objects of deep loyalty may become grist for the student of religion if the object of loyalty and belief is expected eventually to solve the ultimate human perplexities over the purpose of life and the meaning of death, injustice, and suffering. Yinger argues that if a narrower definition is utilized, one may misunderstand and misidentify religion in a society, particularly in societies undergoing cultural change.

This definition assumes that, to some extent at least, all people are religious. Yinger writes, "To me, the evidence is decisive: human nature abhors a vacuum in systems of faith. This is not, then, a period of religious decline but is one of religious change" (1970: vii). The assumption underlying the functional definition of religion does not really invite the question of whether a society is becoming less religious, but rather asks what new forms religion is taking.

This assumption is similar to that adopted by some theologians. Richard Niebuhr, for example, writes:

> It is a curious and inescapable fact about our lives, of which I think we all become aware at some time or another, that we cannot live without a cause, without some object of devotion, some center of worth, something on which we rely for our meaning. . . . If we do not wish to call this faith religion, there is no need to contend about the word. Let us say then that our problem is the problem of faith rather than of religion.
>
> Now to have faith and to have a god is one and the same thing. . . When we believe that life is worth living by the same act we refer to some being which makes our life worth living. We never merely believe that life is worth living, but always think of it as made worth

---

[2]Manifest functions are the *conscious* and *intended* functions of a social pattern or institution. Latent functions are unconscious and unintended.

living by something on which we rely. And this being, whatever it be, is properly termed our god (1960a: 118–119).

Hence, Niebuhr agrees that nationalism and science and many other belief systems are religions; he differs from the social scientist in that he makes a moral judgment about those systems being inferior. According to Niebuhr (1960b) and Tillich (1957), the major threat to Christianity has always been idolatry (belief in a "false god," one that is not really ultimate) rather than atheism. Atheism was never a concern of biblical times; the challenge was the false gods of Baal (sex and fertility as ultimate fulfillment) and Mammon (worship of money).

Yinger, without making judgments about the truth or falsity of belief, is also suggesting that all people have a god or gods that give meaning to life (although the intensity of the need for meaning and the relative consistency of belief patterns vary widely among individuals). The task of the social scientist is to discover what it is that gives meaning to people's lives, for that is their religion. The majority of sociologists who study religion would probably agree that most humans are more or less religious. Some, like Clifford Geertz (1968), think that the assumption of an intrinsic and universal need for meaning is not justified. Social scientists differ, then, in their judgments about whether there is an innate religious tendency in humans.

Another issue that emerges is whether private systems of belief are to be called religion. After all, many individuals have patterns of belief that solve the ultimate meaning issues for them, but that are not necessarily shared with others. Yinger insists, as do most sociologists of religion, that religion is a "social phenomenon: it is shared and takes on many of its most significant aspects only in the interaction of the group" (1970: 10). Privately held patterns of meaning may have religious aspects,

but they are not religion per se. We might well use the vocabulary of Niebuhr here by referring to the individual belief as faith and the social manifestation as religion. Hence, religion is a community of people who have a shared faith.[3]

One problem is that religion often becomes concerned with less-than-ultimate issues, as in the case of faith healers who draw their congregations largely on the basis of a concern for physical health and well-being. Furthermore, "ultimate concern" is a difficult phenomenon to identify and is even more difficult to measure.[4] Nevertheless, Yinger is asserting that any system of belief and action that fails to address the fundamental questions of meaning in life is not a religion.

Some scholars have argued rather persuasively that a supernatural dimension to the belief system is a fundamental characteristic of religion (Stark and Bainbridge 1979). They argue that if religion is not limited to beliefs with a supernatural dimension, the term *religion* may become so inclusive that it is virtually meaningless. Yinger rejects the idea that a supernatural dimension is necessary.

Consider your own presuppositions: Is a belief in the supernatural necessary when you

---

[3]The faith of individuals, even if not celebrated in a group context, is also of interest to sociologists of religion. Such individualized faith systems are sometimes referred to as *invisible religions* (Luckmann 1967). These will be discussed in chapter 16. However, individual meaning systems will be referred to henceforth as personal religiosity or as faith; religion will be defined as a social phenomenon.

[4]Paul Deats has suggested that we probably need to account for the difference between the ultimate concern and the primary concern of individuals, depending on their circumstances. A person who lives on the raw edges of starvation in an impoverished country may be primarily concerned about a mundane issue: the source of his or her next meal. Philosophical issues of meaning of life or the nature of the universe may be of secondary concern at any given time. Because ultimate concern and primary concern may be different, how does one measure or identify the former?

use the term *religion?* Or is it the quality of one's convictions and the depth of commitment that is essential?

Having discussed Yinger's approach to defining religion, it is appropriate to conclude with his full definition:

> Where one finds awareness of and interest in the continuing, recurrent, *permanent* problems of human existence—the human condition itself, as contrasted with specific problems; where one finds rites and shared beliefs relevant to that awareness, which define the strategy of an ultimate victory; and where one has groups organized to heighten that awareness and to teach and maintain those rites and beliefs—there one has religion (1970: 33).

A Symbolic Definition

The anthropologist Clifford Geertz has developed a symbolic definition of religion that is somewhat more detailed in describing what religion does. **Symbols**—objects, behaviors, or stories that represent or remind one of something else—are powerful forces in human behavior, and they are central to religion. Given the abstract nature of the focal point of religion, symbols become its indispensable medium. Symbols include objects (the cross, the Star of David), behaviors (genuflecting before the altar; baptizing a convert; touching the mezuzah on the doorpost of a Jewish home before entering; or kneeling, facing Mecca, and praying five times a day), and myths or stories (the creation story, the story of Jesus washing the disciples' feet, legends of ancestors). (Myths and rituals will be treated as symbols in chapter 4.) Geertz is impressed with the way in which various levels of meaning can be communicated through symbols. Moreover, symbols are more accessible to observation than a subjective experience of "ultimate concern." Hence, he uses symbols as the starting point for his definition of religion. Not all

symbols are religious, of course. A handshake, a kiss, and a wave of the hand are all symbolic behaviors, but they do not normally have religious connotations.

Religious symbols are distinct from nonreligious ones in that the former are macrosymbolic. **Macrosymbolic** symbols are those that help one interpret the meaning of life itself and that involve a cosmology or world view. Because they serve this important function, they tend to acquire a sense of sacredness or profound respect. Many nonreligious symbols are **microsymbolic,** that is, symbols that affect everyday interaction with others and that enhance daily communication and cooperation. Microsymbolic symbols do not claim to explain the purpose of life and do not suggest values and beliefs that claim highest priority in one's life.[5]

Geertz's definition is so fully and carefully developed that it deserves a close examination. He writes,

> Religion is (1) a system of symbols which acts to (2) establish powerful, pervasive, and long lasting moods and motivations in [people] by (3) formulating conceptions of a general order of existence and (4) clothing these conceptions with such an aura of factuality that the moods and motivations seem uniquely realistic (1966: 4).

Religion is a "system of symbols which *acts*" in that the symbols provide a blueprint for understanding the world. These symbols provide a model of the world by helping people understand what the world and life really are. Many people believe, for example, that life is actually a testing ground in which God determines one's fitness to live in the heavenly kingdom. These individuals live their lives with reference

---

[5]Geertz does not stress the macro and micro difference, but this distinction is implicit in his discussion and seems to me to be more helpful than distinguishing "sacred symbols" from "nonsacred" ones.

to this understanding. Other religious perspectives offer alternative views of what life really is. But these symbols not only suggest a model *of* the world, they also propose a model *for* the world. The symbol system describes what life is and also prescribes what it ought to be. Not only do many Christians assert that life is a testing ground, but they claim access to the answers that will help them pass the test.

This system of symbols, Geertz continues, acts to "establish powerful, pervasive, and long lasting moods and motivations" in people. In other words, acknowledgment of the symbols affects one's disposition. Religious activity influences two somewhat different types of dispositions: moods and motivations. Geertz suggests that **moods** involve *depth of feeling*, whereas **motivations** provide a *direction for behavior*. Moods vary in intensity, and they affect our total outlook on life, but they are not aimed at any particular goal. One simply experiences a mood; one does not gain a feeling of obligation about a specific goal to be attained from a mood. "If one is sad, everything and everybody seems dreary; if one is gay, everything and everybody seems splendid" (1966: 11). Some born-again Christian groups emphasize that to be a Christian is to be joyful, even in the face of adversity. The emphasis is on a pervasive mood that is to characterize the believer, regardless of the specific circumstances.

Some religions may emphasize moods as primary (in Buddhism the focus is on mystical experience), while other religions stress motivations and a system of ethics (the Unitarian-Universalist society illustrates this latter focus). Nonetheless, Geertz suggests that in all religions the symbol system produces moods that intensify commitment and motivations to act in specified ways. In another context, Geertz refers to the moods and motivations together as the "**ethos**" of the religion (1958).

Not only do the symbol systems enhance a particular disposition, they also act to "formulate conceptions of a general order of existence." A distinguishing characteristic of religion is that it provides a **world view,** a cognitive ordering of concepts of nature, of self, of society, of the supernatural. Religion creates not only intense feelings but also establishes a cosmology that satisfies one's intellectual need for reasonable explanations. Geertz emphasizes that not all intense feelings of awe are religious. One may be overwhelmed by powerful emotions (moods) in viewing the Grand Canyon, but such feelings may be aesthetic rather than religious. Moreover, one may be motivated to adopt a lifestyle of asceticism (self-denial), but the goal may be to reach nirvana or to lose 25 pounds. If no explanatory perspective or overview of the meaning of life is involved, the experience is not religious.

Geertz properly points out that religion involves an intellectual ordering. Some people claim that their religious experience comes from a walk in the woods rather than from going to church. Geertz is suggesting that a religious sense of awe must include a reaffirmation and commitment to a particular view of the world, a particular mode of interpreting the meaning of suffering, pain, death, and injustice. A walk in the woods may be refreshing and may involve an intense aesthetic feeling, but in most instances it does not change the way one thinks about the world or conceives of the overall purpose of life.

A man may indeed be said to be "religious" about golf, but not merely if he pursues it with passion and plays it on Sundays: he must also see it as symbolic of some transcendent truth. (Geertz 1966: 13).

There are three major challenges which seem to belie the meaningfulness of life, and it is these that a religious world view must resolve: a sense of coherence and reasonableness of events of life, a sense of meaning in suffering so that it becomes sufferable, and a sense of moral order in which evil will be overcome and that virtue, goodness, and justice will somehow, someday, prevail.

Symbol systems, then, attempt to "account for, and even celebrate, the perceived ambiguities, puzzles, and paradoxes in human experience" (Geertz 1966: 23). The world view represents an intellectual process by which people can affirm that life makes sense, that suffering is bearable, and that justice is not a mirage, that in the end, good will be rewarded.

Geertz continues his definition by attempting to answer the question of how a particular world view or set of concepts comes to be believed. The symbols act to "clothe those conceptions in such an aura of factuality that the moods and motivations seem uniquely realistic." How is it, he asks, that despite common sense, everyday experience, and empirical evidence, people will come to believe irrational and unsupportable things? What compels a Christian Scientist to deny the reality of illness, even though the person experiences the symptoms of influenza? Why does a Mormon believe that a new revelation was written to Joseph Smith on golden plates, even though no one could read them but Smith? Why do members of the Unification Church assert that their leader,

Religion is communal in character and often involves intense emotional experiences. The photo depicts a worship service among charismatic Christians in California. The intense emotional experience acts to clothe the religious concepts in a mystique that makes them seem uniquely realistic. (© Hiroji Kubota/Magnum photo.)

the Reverend Sun Myung Moon, is the Christ, even though other observers see him as a rather unexceptional man? Why do Christians continue to affirm that Jesus is the son of God who ushered in God's kingdom, even though he died in the manner of a criminal nearly 2,000 years ago? Geertz points out that religious ritual often creates an aura in which a deeper reality is said to be reached. Truths are experienced or understood that are more profound than everyday experience provides. Indeed the New Testament boldly insists that the wisdom of this world is folly and that Christians must become fools in the eyes of the world (I Corinthians 1: 18–25).

As we will see, Geertz describes a very important aspect of religion. He points out that religion is able to provide a foundation for social values that has its authority outside of empirical verification, and therefore cannot be invalidated (Geertz 1968). Values and perspectives come to be enshrouded in sacredness and unquestioned certainty. We will explore this issue in detail in chapter 8 in the section on plausibility structures.

Many students have difficulty understanding Geertz's heavy emphasis on symbol systems (which are discussed in more detail in chapter 4). Let it suffice here to say that meaning is commonly "stored" or encapsulated in symbols. They are powerful factors in the lives of people. They are also more concrete and observable than an "ultimate concern."

Geertz's definition is long, abstract, and quite elaborate. (His explanation of the definition runs forty-six pages.) This makes it difficult to translate it into concrete research procedures. However, his definition does offer a contribution to the debate over what it is that distinguishes religion from other cultural phenomena. The central contributions are that religion must have a macrosymbol system that acts to reinforce both a world view and an ethos, and has a built-in system of believability or plausibility.

Researchers who like to employ the participant observation method of research find Geertz's definition useful, for it identifies the general properties of religion and helps the observer know what to observe. Yet, it does so without specifying the content of religious beliefs. Those researchers who engage in quantitative studies, such as sample surveys, find Geertz's generalizations so broad and encompassing that his identification of religion is unhelpful. How does one quantify (turn into countable units) a world view or an ethos? The broadness and inclusiveness of Geertz's treatment is frustrating to those who seek unequivocal precision in categorizing types of behavior, but it is this same generality that attracts those who undertake cross-cultural investigations. Geertz, it should be noted, is an anthropologist.

Geertz's analysis is really more than a definition. It is an essay on how religion "works" to reinforce itself and on what religion "does" in the society. Because of this focus on what religion does, the symbolic definition may be considered as one type of functional definition.

Implications of One's Definition for Research

One's definition of religion is often related to one's research strategy. To begin with, some definitions are more conducive than others to certain types of research designs (as we have seen in discussing Geertz's definition). More important, the definition one uses affects the types of questions one asks in doing research. Perhaps the importance of the difference in definitional approaches will become clear if we view the ways in which religiosity has been "operationalized." When we operationalize a concept, we simply translate abstractions into specific questions or statements that can be measured or observed. Let us turn to the issue of how religiosity is operationalized for research purposes.

Some survey research has attempted to study differences at the broadest levels of generalization. Large categories or groups have been compared and contrasted in terms of prevalent attitudes. Church members have been compared with nonmembers in terms of divorce rates, racial attitudes, and other factors. While some interesting differences have been discovered, the category "church member" is extremely broad, placing Episcopalians and members of snake-handling churches in the same general category. Furthermore, it makes church membership the sole criterion of religiosity. It ignores both those who may have an unconventional meaning system and those who may pray regularly but who never officially join a church.

A number of survey studies have taken a similar approach by asking people about their religious affiliation. Again, some interesting correlations have been discovered. For example, Gerhard Lenski found that in Detroit, 54 percent of white Protestants, 30 percent of white Catholics, 13 percent of black Protestants, and 3 percent of Jews were Republicans (1963: 139). He also found that 11 percent of Jews, 34 percent of white Protestants, 38 percent of black Protestants, and 66 percent of white Catholics felt that divorce is always or usually wrong (1963: 166). These figures provide interesting correlations of social variables, but we must remember that such figures are crude. Such categories as "Jew" or "Protestant" include a broad range of theologies and religious organizations. Still other surveys have been more specific by assessing the differences between specific denominations. In these studies the extreme difference between Unitarians and Southern Baptists (both of which are Protestant groups) can be demonstrated. One may discover that Unitarians and Reform Jews are very similar in their views on certain questions, even though the national sample may show a wide difference on those issues between Protestants and Jews.

Identifying the denominational affiliation of people provides more specific information than do the general categories of "church member" or "Protestant." But knowing the denomination of a respondent still does not tell us much about that person's religious orientation. For one thing, there is a wide variation of theologies and world views within any denomination. Although Christianity has traditionally asserted that Jesus was both wholly God and wholly man, 29 percent of the Congregationalists surveyed said that they do not believe that Jesus was any more the son of God than anyone else is a child of God. Some were not sure that a person named Jesus ever existed! Furthermore, 3 percent questioned or rejected the existence of God, and another 16 percent accepted the idea of a higher power but rejected the idea of a personal God (Glock and Stark 1966: 5–7).

This leads us to the second limitation of studies that make comparisons simply along denominational lines: they measure only one's affiliation with traditional forms of religion. Other belief systems that may provide individuals with a system of ethics and a sense of meaning in life are not viewed as religious. The definition of religion is narrow and is operationalized in traditional terms.

The trend in survey research has been to develop more sophisticated instruments to assess individual variations in religiosity. The earliest of such measures were unidimensional, using a single criterion to determine one's religiosity. In some cases, it was frequency of attendance at religious rituals. The assumption was that people who attend services regularly are likely to be highly committed in other respects. Other surveys used a subjective measure; they simply asked respondents, "How important is your religion to you in everyday life?" Still others used a question about the frequency with which the individual prays ("frequent" being defined as daily). And finally, some surveys asked respondents about their beliefs to determine their orthodoxy. (In some surveys only literal interpretations of the Bible were assessed as "religious responses.")

The problem with this unidimensional approach was the assumption that a single index would be an accurate predictor of other religious behavior. This assumption has not been supported by more recent research. For one thing, different churches emphasize different behaviors as signs of faithfulness. The Catholic Church has traditionally insisted that salvation requires attendance at a certain number of celebrations of the Mass per year. Some Protestant denominations have stressed that a tithe of one's income to the church (a tithe is normally 10 percent) is a mark of the true Christian. Others stress prayer and personal devotions. Such liberal denominations as the United Church of Christ have asserted that participation in social action (working for racial and economic justice or in movements concerned about world hunger or international peace) is the mark of the Christian. But beyond group emphases, individuals within the same denomination may find different patterns most expressive of their faith. Hence, most survey instruments developed in the past decade have utilized several measures of religiosity (i.e., they are multidimensional). Box 1.1 provides examples of the types of questions that various scholars have used.

The first major attempt to formulate and measure differences in religiosity was the work of Joseph Fichter in the early 1950s. He distinguished between Catholics based on frequency of attendance at Mass and on overall level of involvement in the life of the parish. He developed a fourfold typology that demonstrated differences between members within the same religious organization depending on their level of commitment (Fichter 1954).

Other measures have been developed since then that have shown even more complex variations within denominations. For example, Lenski studied the differences between "associational" and "communal" involvement. Associational involvement refers to frequency of attendance at church services and participation in the workings of the institution. Communal involvement is a measure of how many of one's close friends and relatives were members of the same religious group. Lenski found that these two indices were not highly correlated and that they tended to have different influences on church members. In fact, communal involvement was a more important influence than was associational involvement in affecting everyday behavior and attitudes. Lenski also studied the difference between doctrinal orthodoxy and devotionalism as modes of religiosity. Doctrinal orthodoxy refers to agreement with the central beliefs set forth by that denomination. Devotionalism refers to a sense of personal contact with God. He measured this by asking about the frequency of prayer and by inquiring whether the respondents sought to determine God's will when they made important decisions. Lenski found that orthodoxy and devotionalism varied independently and that they influenced people differently in economic and political attitudes and in other arenas of everyday living (Lenski 1963). (These findings will be explored in more detail in chapter 10.)

The most elaborate and influential multidimensional analysis is that developed by Charles Glock. His original formulation included four dimensions (1959), but he and Rodney Stark later published several revised versions, eventually specifying as many as eight dimensions (Glock and Stark 1965; Stark and Glock 1968). They sought to operationalize and assess experiential, ritualistic, devotional, belief, knowledge, consequential (or ethical), communal, and particularistic dimensions.

The *experiential* dimension refers to a feeling of having communed with God, an experience one believes to have been a revelation from God, or a powerful experience that convinces one of his or her salvation. A report of some sort of personal experience one considers to be of divine origin or of supernatural dimension is an aspect of religiosity, but it may or may not be correlated with other dimensions. The *ritualistic* dimension involves frequency of participation in corporate worship services. The *devotional* aspect involves faithfulness in private devotions and regularity in private prayer. The *belief* dimension refers to the degree to which the person agrees with the beliefs of the group. This is the same as Lenski's criterion of doctrinal orthodoxy, although Glock and Stark have used somewhat different questions to measure it. The *knowledge* dimension has to do with the extent to which members even know what the beliefs and doctrines of their group are. Several researchers have found that many church members are quite ignorant of the content of their religious scripture and of their church's official doctrines. Glock and Stark insist that people sometimes believe in doctrines which they do not understand. (For example, a substantial percentage of those who claimed to believe in the Ten Commandments could not recite more than two or three of them. One wonders how central such a "belief" could possibly be to one's life.) The *consequential* dimension has to do with the extent to which explicitly religious commitments and behaviors affect attitudes and behavior in everyday life. The *communal* aspect refers to the number of one's friends that are of the same denomination. *Particularism* is a measure of the extent to which one believes that one's own faith offers the only hope of salvation.

Multidimensional modes of analysis tend to measure religiosity in conventional terms. The way in which Glock and Stark operationalized the belief dimension will serve to illustrate. A person who is rated high in religious commitment indicates most of the following:

1. Certainty of the existence of God.
2. Belief in the divinity of Jesus.
3. Belief that Jesus was born of a virgin, actually walked on water, and will someday return.
4. Belief in miracles as reported in the Bible.
5. Belief in life after death.
6. Belief in the actual existence of the devil.
7. Belief that "a child is born into the world already guilty of sin" (Stark and Glock 1968: 22–44).

Each of the other dimensions were also measured with rather traditional conceptions of religion. Using these criteria for assessing religiosity, many people who believe strongly in astrology or in some other nontraditional cosmology would be considered nonreligious. The effect of such operationalization is also to suggest that liberal denominations are less religious than conservative ones (McGuire 1981). This is questionable. On what grounds can a sociologist insist that a devout Quaker is ideologically less religious than a Southern Baptist? And when 94 percent of Congregationalists conform to the position of their church and reject a literal interpretation of original sin, how can a sociologist call them less religious than Catholics? Yet the above set of questions would lead to such conclusions. Certainly the Congregationalist and the Quaker do not think of themselves as less religious. Although Glock and Stark also discuss "ethicalism" as a possible alternative expression of religiosity, they assert: "Supernaturalism, in our judgment, is still the crucial variable in contemporary religious identity" (Stark and Glock 1968: 70).[6]

---

[6]This is in contrast to a national survey in which 86 percent of American respondents agreed with the statement, "The best mark of a person's religiousness is the degree of one's concern for others" (Hadden 1969: 147). For a number of Americans, ethical behavior is the most important manifestation of religiosity.

James Davidson and Dean Knudsen (1977) suggest an approach that overcomes many of the shortcomings of the Glock and Stark model. Davidson and Knudsen insist that because the content of religious beliefs varies significantly from one group to another, questions about orthodoxy are inappropriate for measuring religiosity. They suggest an important distinction between "religious commitment" and "religious orientation." Specific beliefs, tendencies to particularism, ethical applications of beliefs in everyday life, communal involvement,

▶ **BOX 1.1**

Measuring Religiosity

Readers may find it fruitful to design questions that they think would measure the level of religious commitment of respondents. What kinds of questions should be asked? What sort of beliefs or behaviors are indicative of religiosity? The following questions are among those that have been used by various sociologists to identify religious commitment. Which of these questions seem to you to best reflect religiosity? Some questions may seem unusual to you as measures of religion. Why do you suppose sociologists have felt that those questions measure religious commitment? Do you see any unwarranted assumptions about what is religious behavior in any of these questions? Would a highly religious person rank high on all of these, or is it possible to be highly religious and still have low scores in some areas? Are there some on which a person must have a positive score in order for you to consider them "highly religious?"

 1. Which statement comes closest to expressing what you believe about God?
    —I don't believe in God.
    —I don't know whether there is a God, and I don't believe there is any way to find out.
    —I don't believe in a personal God, but I do believe in a higher power of some kind.
    —I find myself believing in God some of the time, but not at other times.
    —While I have doubts, I feel that I do believe in God.

    —I know God really exists, and I have no doubts about it.
    —I don't know.
 2. If you do believe in God, do you believe that God is like a heavenly father who watches over you, or do you have some other belief?
 3. What about the belief that the Devil actually exists? Are you absolutely sure or are you pretty sure that the Devil exists, or are you absolutely sure or pretty sure that the Devil does not exist?
 4. The Bible tells of miracles, some credited to Christ and some to other prophets and apostles.

    Generally speaking, which of the following statements comes closest to what you believe about biblical miracles?
    —I believe miracles actually happened the way the Bible says they did.
    —I believe miracles happened, but can be explained by natural causes.
    —I tend to doubt that the miracles ever happened.
    —I do not believe that miracles ever happened.
 5. How sure are you that there is a life beyond death? Are you absolutely sure or pretty sure there is a life beyond death, or are you absolutely sure or pretty sure there is *no* life beyond death?
 6. Have you ever had the feeling that you were somehow in the presence of God? Definitely; I think so; no, I have not; I am not sure.

and religious knowledge are elements of one's religious orientation. They vary among groups and indicate different styles of religiosity.

Religious commitment (or *extent* of religiosity) is measured in terms of two components: religious consciousness and religious participa-tion. Religious consciousness refers to a respondent's evaluation of the importance of religion in his or her life. That is, it is the extent to which religion is a part of a person's sense of identity—intellectually, affectively, and behaviorally. It is operationalized through three questions:

7. All in all, how important would you say that religion is to you? Extremely important, quite important, fairly important, not too important, or not important at all.
8. About how often do you attend worship services?
9. Do you believe that God answers people's prayers?
10. How often do you pray? Several times a day, once a day, several times a week, once or twice a month, less than once a month, or never.
11. How often do you read the Bible at home?
12. How often, if at all, are table prayers or grace said before or after meals in your home?
13. Do you ever make a point of listening to or watching religious services on radio or television?
    Regularly, sometimes, seldom, never.
14. How much, on average, does your family contribute to church each week?
15. When you have a decision to make in your everyday life, do you ask yourself what God would want you to do? Often, sometimes, seldom, never.
16. If you are married, are you married to someone of the same religion?
17. How many of your close friends belong to the same religion you belong to? All of them, most of them, about half of them, less than half of them, only a few of them, or none of them.
18. On what church committees, boards, or organizations do you serve?

19. How frequently do you attend the meetings of these religious organizations?
    Frequently, occasionally, infrequently, never.
20. Are you, because of your religious commitment, a member of any service organizations, civic clubs, or benevolence societies? Name them.
21. Do you believe that in order to be saved, a person must
    —be baptized?
    —participate regularly in Holy Communion?
    —be a member of your particular faith?
    —pray regularly?
    —tithe (give 10 percent of one's income to the church or the poor)?
    —do good works for others?
22. Do you believe that persons would be prevented from salvation if they
    —never heard of Jesus?
    —break the Sabbath?
    —take the name of the Lord in vain?
    —discriminate against other races?
    —are anti-Semitic?
23. Are you able to recite the Ten Commandments?
24. Name the first book of the Bible.
25. Name two major prophets mentioned in the Old Testament of the Bible.
26. Name the person who delivered the Sermon on the Mount.
27. One person wrote most of the books of the New Testament. Can you name that person?

Religious Consciousness

1. According to whatever standards are important to you personally, how religious would you say you are?
2. Overall, would you say religion is a positive or a negative force in making your life worthwhile?
3. To what extent would you say religious faith helps you in making daily decisions you have to make in life?

Religious participation refers to the respondent's involvement in explicitly religious behavior: ritual attendance, participation in other group-sponsored activities, and devotional behavior. Again, it is measured through responses to three questions:

Religious Participation

1. How many worship activities do you attend in a typical month?
2. How many church organizations or activities do you participate in regularly?
3. Do you ever do any of the following:
   a. Pray privately outside church?
   b. Say grace before meals?
   c. Read the Bible outside of church?

Pilot studies suggest that answers to religious consciousness and religious participation items are highly correlated. Together, Davidson and Knudsen suggest they measure the extent of a person's religiosity.

Differentiating between religious orientation and religious commitment could serve to

---

▶ **BOX 1.2**

Measuring Traditional Jewish Religiosity

Many of the measures of religiosity in Box 1.1 assume a Christian orientation by the subjects. In a study of the Jewish population in the Boston area, Floyd Fowler developed questions to measure religiosity among that religious group. Students may be interested in comparing and contrasting the questions here with those in Box 1.1. Especially noticeable is the lack of questions about what one believes and the emphasis on behaviors. Do any of these items seem odd to you as measures of religiosity? If so, why?

1. Do you take part in a Passover Seder?
2. Do you keep kosher at home?
3. Do you recite a daily prayer or worship service—either at home or at a synagogue?
4. Do you light Sabbath candles?
5. Do you have a mezuzah on your door?
6. Do you usually fast on Yom Kippur?
7. Do you observe special dietary rules for Passover?

8. Do you ever attend lectures or classes of Jewish interest?
9. Have you ever been to Israel? How many times?
10. Do you regularly read any newspapers or magazines of Jewish content?
11. Do you belong to a synagogue or temple?
12. Over the past twelve months approximately how much did you and other members of your family give altogether to various charities (not counting what you gave to a synagogue or temple)?
13. About how much of this was to Jewish causes (not counting what you gave to a synagogue or temple)?
14. Altogether, counting contributions and dues and so on, about how much have you and your family contributed to a temple or synagogue this past year?

Source: Floyd J. Fowler. *1975 Community Survey: A Study of the Jewish Population of Greater Boston.* Boston: Combined Jewish Philanthropies of Greater Boston, 1977: 114–22. Reprinted by permission.

clear up much of the muddiness in recent survey studies. Certainly there is an important difference between the extent and the style of one's religiosity. Davidson and Knudsen's approach avoids the fallacy of defining some theologies as inherently more religious than others. The authors found little correlation between the various elements of a person's religious orientation, and conclude that people's religious orientations are inclined to be highly inconsistent and do not represent integrated wholes. This confirms earlier studies that found the elements of religiosity to vary independently.

On the other hand, the lack of coherence between the elements of traditional religiosity may be evidence that traditional religion is inadequate to meet the meaning needs of modern people.

Yinger (1969, 1977) has suggested that in rapidly changing societies, religion itself may be changing and may "look different." New forms of religion may be emerging—forms that are not measured by traditional questions. Rather than starting with traditional concepts of religiosity and trying to assess its effect on everyday life, functional definitions begin with the consequential dimension. They ask what it is that really provides meaning and purpose in the lives of people, for that is where one finds religion. If a traditional belief system does not affect a person's life, if it does not provide a coherent understanding of life's experiences, then it is not really that person's *faith*. If it is not one's real faith, then the question arises, What is? For those using a functional definition, it is inappropriate to try to assess levels of religiosity by asking only traditional questions.

Using such a functional definition of religion, Yinger operationalizes his research in a very different way. Rather than asking about one's *religion* (a term that brings to mind traditional concepts of ritual, prayer, and orthodoxy for most people), Yinger asks his questions in a nontraditional way. Yinger proceeds by posing certain statements and asking respondents to indicate their level of agreement or disagreement. The following statements illustrate (1977: 76):

> Suffering, injustice, and finally death are the lot of humanity; but they need not be negative experiences; their significance and effects can be shaped by our beliefs.
>
> Somehow, I cannot get very interested in the talk about "the basic human condition" and "humanity's ultimate problems."
>
> A person's most difficult and destructive experiences are often the source of increased understanding and powers of endurance.
>
> Despite the often chaotic conditions of human life, I believe that there is an order and pattern to existence that someday we will come to understand.

Depending on how respondents answer these questions, Yinger feels one has an indication of the basic religiosity of the individual. He then seeks to determine what it is that serves as an ultimate concern for those religious persons by asking some open-ended questions:

> In your most reflective moments, when you are thinking beyond the immediate issues of the day—however important—beyond headlines, beyond the temporary, what do you consider the most important issue humanity has to face? Or, to put the question another way, what do you see as the basic, permanent question for humankind? (1969: 93).

Because Yinger also believes that religion is essentially a group phenomenon, he also seeks to discover what groups the individual may be participating in that support the emphasis on this ultimate concern and that develop a strategy to address it. His follow-up question is this:

> Are you a participant or member of some group, whether large or small, for which the "basic, permanent question" and the beliefs connected with it are the focus of attention and the most important reasons for its existence? If so, please characterize the group briefly (1969: 93).

As one can readily see, Yinger does not presuppose what religion will look like or what sort of beliefs one might have. He uses an inductive method; he seeks to discover what concerns people ultimately and what provides people with a sense of meaning and hope. Clearly, such an approach does not make for neat correlations and computer-run multivariate analysis. At this point, at least, the method has not produced the sort of hard data that some sociologists prefer. The formulation of the questions will no doubt be continually modified and will undergo further sophistication as such research instruments are tested. One study has found that responses to Yinger's questions have elicited traditional religious answers (Roof et al. 1977). Persons who score high on traditional measures of religiosity are also the ones who score high on Yinger's measure. However, another study using Yinger's approach has reported that the procedure was helpful in discovering invisible or nonconventional religions in our midst (Nelsen et al. 1976).

For researchers who define religion strictly in terms of a supernatural dimension, or for researchers interested in the effects of traditional religious beliefs and institutions. Yinger's operationalized questions are less fruitful than those of Glock and Stark or Davidson and Knudsen. For those interested in religion at the individual level or for those interested in religion as an evolving cultural system, Yinger's approach can stimulate new areas of investigation.

The discussion should make clear to readers that one's definition of religion is important to how one conducts research. Furthermore, readers may have a clearer idea of how one's definition of religion can cause individuals to disagree on whether a particular social phenomenon is essentially religious. Of course, in both cases Methodism, Catholicism, Mormonism, Islam, and Krishna Consciousness are all considered forms of religion. Substantial and functional definitional approaches differ primarily on the questions, "Where does one draw the line between religion and nonreligion?" and "How do you measure or discover religiosity?"

The Concept of Religion as Employed in This Text

My own underlying interest is in the way people generate and sustain new systems of meaning in the midst of social change. Moreover, I am interested in how individuals create their own systems of meaning. Usually, meaning systems involve a synthesis of official church doctrine with other cultural beliefs. Rather than dichotomizing religion from nonreligion, I seek to explore anything that provides meaning and purpose in the lives of people. I tend to ask *how* people are religious rather than *whether* they are religious. Hence, the perspective of this book will be most compatible with those of Yinger and Geertz, each of whom was interested in religion as a cultural system. While I incorporate the research and the insights of those who use a more narrow definition of religion,[7] I also address the broader issues of meaning in a changing culture.

Without attempting to offer a new definition, let me synthesize the debate over definitions by simply highlighting my own view of the distinguishing characteristics of religion. First, *religion is a social phenomenon* that involves the grouping of people around a faith perspective. **Faith** is an individual phenomenon that involves trusting in some object, event, principle, or being as the center of worth and the source of meaning in life. I sympathize with Yinger's insistence that the "nature of believing" is probably more indicative of religion than the "nature of belief" itself. Hence, a profound commitment to Marxism, intense

---

[7]Actually, most of the book is devoted to traditional expressions of religion.

nationalism, or faith in science and technology as the ultimate solution to our human predicament could be considered at least quasi-religious phenomena.[8] But religion is also viewed here as a social phenomenon—involving a group of people with a shared faith or a shared meaning system. Beyond being just a social phenomenon, religion has to do with that assortment of phenomena that communicates, celebrates, internalizes, interprets, and extrapolates a faith. These phenomena include *beliefs* (myths[9]), *rites* (worship), an *ethos* (the moods and moral values of the group), a *world view* (the cognitive perspective by which the experiences of life are viewed as part of a larger and ultimately meaningful cosmology), and a *system of symbols* (which serve to encapsulate the deepest feelings and emotion-packed beliefs).

The criteria identified here should be specific enough to distinguish religion from many other cultural phenomena. For example, I have suggested that a world view and an ethical system are intrinsic aspects of religion. A feeling of awe or sacredness is not considered religious in this text unless it includes a cognitive pattern that helps persons make sense out of life and helps explain the meaning of suffering, death, and injustice.

On the other hand, it is hoped that the criteria for identifying religion are sufficiently broad so that we do not miss the religious significance of nontraditional groups. We will be studying Methodists, Baptists, Roman Catholics, and "Moonies"; but this approach allows us to explore scientific humanism, tran-

scendental meditation, and American nationalism as religious or quasi-religious movements.

Distinction between Religion and Magic

When studying religion, social scientists often find themselves investigating a closely related phenomenon—magic. Erroneous generalizations about religion and spurious theories about religion and society have sometimes been set forth because religion and magic have been viewed as one and the same thing. In fact, the two are often found together, but because they serve rather different functions, students of religion should understand the distinction between them.

Many criteria have been used to discriminate between religion and magic. In the listing below, some of the differences are juxtaposed. Various scholars have emphasized one or more of these factors (Titiev 1972).

Religion	*Magic*
1. Sense of a "group" of common believers: a "church."	1. No "church" or "group consciousness" involved.
2. Moral ethos, or a system of ethics to guide behavior.	2. No moral ethos or systematic pattern of ethics.
3. Rites are meaningful: they reinforce patterns of belief.	3. Rites not necessarily meaningful; they are used to cast a spell or make something happen.
4. Rites occur calendrically (on regular basis each week, month, and/or year).	4. Rites occur at critical (crisis) times.

---

[8]For those who reserve the term *religion* for meaning systems that have a supernatural dimension (Stark and Bainbridge 1979), these outlooks are considered *functional alternatives to religion*. Regardless of whether we call them new forms of religion or functional alternatives, they are of interest to the sociologist of religion.

[9]The term *myth* does not refer to a belief that is untrue. Myth refers to any belief that helps people understand and interpret the events in their own lives. It is a macrosymbolic system of meaning.

Religion	*Magic*
5. Functions for both the individual and the structure.	5. Functions only for individuals, not for social structure.
6. Participation is open; leader leads entire group in performance of ritual.	6. Leader is only one to know ritual and how to perform it; others present are passive.
7. Worship of a transcendent Being or Power as intrinsincally worthy of one's attention.	7. Manipulation of impersonal, transcendent power for utilitarian reasons.

These seven distinguishing factors make a nice, neat picture of magic and religion, but in reality the distinction is not so precise. There are many churches in which the members may not find the ritual meaningful. Many members may attend worship only at critical times in their lives (funerals, baptisms, marriages, or times of emotional stress for the individual), and the minister may emphasize utilitarian reasons for belonging (e.g., God's blessing on one's business or promises of good health). Yet the phenomenon hardly seems to be magic rather than religion. Furthermore, the factors listed above do not show a high correlation with each other. The distinction between magic and religion remains somewhat foggy. Nonetheless, one factor seems worthy of our attention.

The primary difference between religion and magic has most commonly been defined in terms of the attitude toward the transcendent: Is it considered of intrinsic or utilitarian value? The religious perspective views the object of worship as being of inherent, categorical worth. It is not worshiped primarily because of favors to be returned for performance of the ritual. God is worshiped in the Christian tradition—or at least is supposed to be worshiped in that tradition—simply "because God is God." In religion the object of worship is the center of worth or the epitome of value.

In the case of magic, the world is believed to be controlled by supernatural forces that control one's destiny. The objective is to get those forces working for you and not against you. Magic involves manipulation of supernatural forces. In a discussion of magic in American culture, George Gmelch (1971) points out that many baseball players will often follow such patterns as rising in the morning at a specific time, eating only certain foods prior to a game, consistently taking the same route to the stadium, getting dressed according to a specific preset pattern (e.g., always putting on the right sock first), and always stepping on third base on the way to the outfield. The players who followed these rituals seemed to feel that they would be jinxed if they break them. Somehow, the unspoken forces of fate would betray them if the proper (nonrational) steps were not taken.

While this may be an unusual example, the world view of expecting supernatural and impersonal forces to control one's destiny is characteristic of what anthropologists have called magic. The supernatural forces are not personal beings to whom one prays or with whom one develops a relationship. Rather, they have no will of their own. They simply represent laws of the universe that must not be violated and that might be used to one's own advantage. Hence, magic in tribal societies is a supraempirical means of controlling one's chances of success in any endeavor. Whenever the desire for success is high but the chances of failure are great, people may look for any means possible to ensure success. Bronislaw Malinowski writes, "Magic is to be expected and generally to be found whenever man comes to an unbridgeable gap, a hiatus in his knowledge or in his powers of practical control, and yet has to continue in his pursuit" (1931: 638).

Some of the functions of magic are the same as those of religion. In a study of water witching (using a forked twig to locate a source of underground water), Evon Vogt (1952) found some important functions being served. In Homestead, New Mexico, the cost of drilling was high, the chance of failure great, and success in finding water critical. Hence, people turned to a dowser (water witch). The persons investing money in drilling were satisfied that they were doing *something* to increase the likelihood of success. Because the water witch had confidence, the anxiety of the people was reduced, and they were willing to invest more in any given drilling site. They agreed to drill deeper because they were assured that water was there. Vogt insists that there is no scientific evidence to support the claim that dowsers can actually find water and that mere chance is actually a more reliable means of hitting water than employing a dowser. Nonetheless, farmers continue to use them because doing so lessens their anxiety. The world view of those farmers is magical in that they assume some supernatural force is at work in helping the witch to locate water. Box 1.3 offers another example of an appeal to magic.

Magic provides a concrete action to *control* adverse events. In actuality, magic serves as a form of primitive technology or as a complement to empirical techniques. If I want to control events, but I do not have at my disposal rational means to do so, then I may turn to supernatural methods. In the case of magic, one looks for ways to manipulate supernatural forces for one's own benefit. One does not have to confess sins or otherwise earn a right relationship with supernatural beings. The twig will work regardless of the moral righteousness of the dowser. Magic has no ethos and no "moral community."

It is true that religion is often concerned with mundane adversities, but the method of resolving the problem calls for moral purification, confession, or some other transformation of the person involved. Faith healing, for example, is usually expected to be effective only after the person is in "right relationship with God." If a person is ill and resorts to magic for a cure, it is believed that healing will come if the words are said correctly and the ritual is performed properly. If healing is not forthcoming, the ritual was not performed correctly. However, if a person turns to a religious faith healer for help and the ailment is not cured, the explanation usually is that the afflicted person or the healer is not in harmony with God.

When studying any one group, the question of whether one is encountering magic or religion may not be as clear and categorical as suggested here. Nevertheless, the primary appeal of magic is to manipulate the world. Science and technology are more rational means of controlling one's environment. As science and technology allow persons to have increasing control over their lives, magic tends to decline. The amount of magic in a society tends to be inversely correlated to the amount of science and technology.[10] As Malinowski says, we do not find magic wherever the pursuit is certain, reliable, and under the control of rational methods.

Magic, I would assert, will be replaced in large part by science, technology, and the modern secular world view. The primary functions of religion, however, are not to manipulate one's environment. There are other functions that are central to religion; explaining the meaning of life and preserving central values and ethical codes in the culture are among those. Technology may help us control our

---

[10]This does not mean that magic is the primitive substitute for science. Anthropologists have shown that even the most simple society has some empirically validated knowledge (Fabian 1992; Malinowski 1948), and technical skill is never replaced by magic. Malinowski writes: "Magic, therefore, far from being primitive science, is the outgrowth of clear recognition that science has its limits and that a human mind and skill are at times impotent" (1931: 637). Only when technology can ensure success in a task does magic cease.

► **BOX 1.3**

Chain Letter Based on a Magical World View

A few years ago a friend of mine, a college physical education instructor, sent me this chain letter:

1. President of the largest steel company
2. President of the largest gas company
3. President of the New York Stock Exchange
4. Greatest wheat speculator
5. Great bear of Wall Street
6. Head of the world's largest monopoly
7. President of the Bank of International Settlement

These should certainly be considered the world's most successful men. At least they found the secret of making money. Now, some fifty years later, where are these men?????

1. The president of the largest steel company, Charles Schway, died a pauper.
2. The president of the largest gas company, Howard Hopson, is now insane.
3. The president of the New York Exchange, Richard Whitney, was released from a hospital, to die at home.
4. The greatest wheat speculator, Arthur Cooken, died abroad insolvent.
5. The greatest bear of Wall Street, Gosabee Rivermore, died a suicide.
6. The head of the world's largest monopoly, Ivan Krueger, the match king, died a suicide.
7. The president of the Bank of International Settlement shot himself.

The same year, 1923, the winner of the most important golf championship, Gene Sarazen, won the U.S. Open and the PGA tournament. Today he is still playing an excellent game of golf and is solvent.

Conclusion: Stop Worrying About Business and Go Play Golf.

This letter originated in the Netherlands and has been passed around the world at least twenty times, bringing good luck to everyone we passed it on to. The one who breaks the chain will *have bad luck.*

Do not keep this letter. Do not send money. Just have your secretary make four copies and send it to five of your friends to whom you wish good. You will see that something good happens to you four days from now if you do not break the chain. This is no joke. You will receive good luck in four days' time.

Put your name at the bottom of the list, leaving the top name off, and mail the original and four copies to your five friends to whom you wish good luck.
[10 names followed]

The letter lacks coherence and is absurd in its presumptions, yet my well-educated friend sent it in all seriousness. When I probed, I found that he had not been granted tenure in his department, his contract was running out, and he had had a job interview scheduled for the third day after he received this letter. With a sheepish grin he commented, "I just wasn't about to take any chances." The presumption of impersonal supernatural forces that may determine one's destiny is characteristic of the magical world view. My friend was afraid to take a chance of offending these forces by violating a ritual requirement: forwarding the letter. He would probably have destroyed the letter, except that he was faced with a task in which success was both important and uncertain. In American culture, a magical outlook tends to emerge at critical times rather than being continuously present. (Because my friend landed the job, his "superstition" is not likely to wane in future times of crisis.)

environment and can make life more comfortable, but it can never explain why life is meaningful in the first place. The function of science is to expand our knowledge; the function of religion is to offer people wisdom.

This is not a defense of religion. Often the "wisdom" offered by a given religion may be bizarre. But wisdom has to do with *values* rather than with *facts.* Science answers the question of why something happens in terms of causality; religion answers the question of why in terms of values and ultimate meanings. Because I believe that religion addresses a common human need (for meaning), I also believe that it is here to stay in some form.[11] This is contrary to secularization theorists who claim that religion is rapidly being replaced by modernism and by scientific outlooks. I believe they have confused religion with magic.

A Final Word about Definitions

One's definition of religion is important, for it specifies what is and what is not appropriate data for study. The discussion in this chapter was designed to help the reader understand the differences in the way religion has been defined by scholars. I hope that the discussion has stimulated you to think through your own criteria for identifying religion. A consensus among us would be convenient, but a lack of agreement need not cause problems. The purpose of this text is not to convert readers to the author's theoretical persuasion but to help them think more clearly about the relationship between religion, culture, and society. Before going further, it would be helpful to have clearly in mind (1) your own assumptions

regarding the definition of religion, (2) the defining criteria used by the social scientists discussed in this chapter, and (3) the perspective of this author.[12] As Yinger has written, "Definitions are tools; they are to some degree arbitrary. . . . They are abstract, which is to say they are oversimplifications. . . . We must relinquish the idea that there is any one definition that is correct and satisfactory for all" (1970: 4). The definition we each use tends to "slice up life" a little differently and causes us to focus on slightly different phenomena as most important. Hence, we have begun by making our assumptions about religion conscious and explicit.

Although there is no consensus on the definition of religion, there is agreement among sociologists that any investigation of religion must be based on empirical methods of investigation. In the next chapter, we explore what it means to take a *scientific* approach to studying religion.

Summary

Definitions of religion are usually one of two types: *substantive* (which focus on the substance or essence of religion) and *functional* (which focus on what religion does). Substantive definitions usually emphasize a specific belief such as in spiritual beings or in a supernatural realm, or they stress the distinction between sacred and profane realms of experience. Substantive definitions delineate the traditional forms of religiosity. Functional definitions identify religion as that which provides a sense of ultimate

---

[11]Notice that I said "common" need rather than "universal." The need for meaning appears to be nearly universal, but at this time we cannot claim universality of the need.

[12]As a suggested study tool, readers might (1) make a list of the factors they think are central to any definition of religion, (2) make a list of the defining characteristics specified by Tylor, Durkheim, Yinger, Geertz, Glock and Stark, Davidson and Knudsen, and Roberts, respectively, and (3) develop specific questions by which they would operationalize their own definition of religion.

meaning, a system of macrosymbols, and a set of core values for life. They invite an investigation of any profound loyalty or ultimate meaning system as a form of religiosity.

One's definition tends to affect one's research design. Those who use substantive definitions can measure religiosity with questions about specific beliefs people hold, their religious affiliation and attendance, and their assessment of the importance of religion in their own lives. Multidimensional measures have usually offered the greatest insights. Those types of questions have generated significant insights into traditional types of religiosity and have usually provided more precision than is yet possible with functional definitions.

Those who favor the latter approach tend to ask open-ended questions that seek to *discover* one's ultimate meaning system—whether it be traditional religion, nationalism, astrology, or some other "invisible" religion. Social scientists who are interested in cultural change and the new forms of meaning that emerge in times of cultural transition tend to favor functional definitions. They view religion as changing rather than as declining.

This text is based on a functional definition but includes material from researchers using both approaches. The assumption is that religion is a social phenomenon that includes the following characteristics: beliefs, rites, an ethos, a world view, and a system of symbols. The assumption is also that religion serves a different function from either magic or science, and that because the functions religion serves are so different, religion is not in jeopardy of being replaced by science or by secularization.

A Scientific Perspective on Religion

A highly respected sociologist once said of religion, "There are few major subjects about which people know so little, yet feel so certain" (Yinger 1970: 2). This seems to be true of both those who are sympathetic to religion and those who are hostile toward it. In light of this, I would suggest two characteristics or attitudes that will be particularly helpful in approaching our topic of investigation: a healthy dose of humility and a corresponding openness to new ideas. No one has all the answers on religious behavior, but by listening to one another, we can each broaden our understandings.

In this text, I will be presenting a sociological perspective on religion and explaining some of that discipline's findings and theories. Sociology does not offer the whole truth any more than any other discipline or perspective, but it does offer insights that can be helpful to those interested in religion—whether they be believers or skeptics. My point is that we seek understanding here; a posture of defensiveness—with each person seeking only to preserve his or her own preconceived notions—is counter-

productive. We seek neither to dissuade believers from their faith nor to convince skeptics of the efficacy of religion. Our goal is to gain a new perspective on religious behavior and thereby expand our comprehension of religion.

Sociology offers only one of many possible vantage points from which to view religion. Perhaps an analogy would be helpful in clarifying the point.

Many people may interact with the same child and yet have quite different perspectives and understandings of that child. An artist may try to encapsulate the child's charm by focusing on his or her unique physical properties such as facial features, body proportions, and shades of coloration in the eyes, skin, and hair. A physician is interested in the physiological needs of the child and the requirements for good health—concentrating on such characteristics as height and weight, immunizations, and the family's history of congenital diseases. A developmental psychologist may study the child not because of an interest in the characteristics of this child but as part of a broader investigation of childhood development. This child is one case out of which a general theory of childhood maturation is sought.

Parents, of course, are interested in the uniqueness and specialness of this *particular* child. Their concern is not one of detached analysis, for their emotional attachment to the child influences their perception. As the persons responsible for the child's social and emotional development, they try to be concerned about the child's overall welfare. But because they are so close to the child, some important patterns of behavior may go unnoticed. The findings of each of the previous observers may be of interest to the parents as they come to a fuller appreciation of their child and a better understanding of their parental responsibilities. Of course, too, the child is a unique self-experiencing individual with his or her own self-understanding.

It would be foolish to ask which of these persons has the "true" understanding of the child. No one perspective is total and complete. In fact, the insights of the psychologist may influence the socialization practices of the parent, or the prescription of the physician (e.g., the child needs to wear a back brace) may affect the child's behavior and experiences. In each case, the "objective" view of an outsider may differ from that of the parent or of the child, and it may lead to changes. But in the long run, those changes may be beneficial.

Just as people from many fields may have unique perspectives on a child—none of which contains the whole truth about that child—so also can religion be understood from many angles. The psychologist analyzes religious experience as a mental and emotional experience of the individual. The concern is not with religion as ideas or beliefs that may hold eternal truth but with the effect of religion on the human psyche. The philosopher of religion approaches the subject by comparing, contrasting, and analyzing beliefs of various faiths, focusing on the ideas of life, death, suffering, and injustice among the many religions of the world.

The systematic theologian formulates doctrines about God and about God's relationship to the universe and to humanity, placing what is believed about God (in a particular tradition) into a logically comprehensive and coherent framework. The religious ethicist attempts to define moral responsibility of religious persons, or at least to clarify moral discourse and identify moral dilemmas for members of a faith. The faithful follower understands his or her religion through yet another lens—that of personal commitment. The person's faith is viewed as a source of ultimate truth and personal fulfillment. Members of the clergy also view religion from a vantage point as committed followers, but they are also leaders who constantly seek understanding of religious processes so they can be more effective in guiding others. Hence, they may use the insights of the social scientist, the philosopher, the theologian, and the ethicist in order to understand more fully both their faith and their leadership responsibilities. The sociologist, as we will see, offers a unique perspective that differs from these others and that can contribute to a holistic understanding of this multidimensional phenomenon we call religion.

The Sociological Perspective

The sociological approach focuses on religious groups and institutions (their formation, maintenance, and demise), on the behavior of individuals within those groups (e.g., social processes that affect conversion, ritual behavior), and on conflicts between religious groups (such as Catholic vs. Protestant, Christian vs. Moslem, mainline denomination vs. cult). For the sociologist, beliefs are only one small part of religion.

In modern industrial society, religion is both a set of ideas (values, beliefs) and an institution (a set of social relationships). We will be looking at both in order to understand how they affect human behavior. We will investigate differences in beliefs, not because we expect to prove their truth or falsehood, but because beliefs—regardless of their ultimate veracity—can influence how people behave and how they understand the world.

Religious institutions, however, can also affect behavior quite independently of beliefs. In fact, religious institutions sometimes entice people to behave contrary to the official belief system of that religion. .

Later in this book, we will discuss the fact that religious organizations may contribute to racism and combat it at the same time. While the belief systems of most mainline denominations proclaim prejudice to be wrong, the institutional structures of the church unwittingly permit it—and sometimes even foster it. Furthermore, religious beliefs themselves can have contradictory effects. While some Christian teachings have maintained that antipathy against others is always wrong, certain other beliefs have contributed—often unconsciously and unintentionally—to racial prejudice, sex bias, and anti-Semitism. Many readers probably did not know, for example, that some first-century Christians believed that women were incapable of being saved—unless they were first transformed into men. These Gnostic Christians reinforced the accepted cultural view of that time that women are defective human beings. We will also find in this book that between A.D. 1400 and 1700, the Christian churches (both Protestant and Catholic) were involved in burning between 500,000 and 1 million women as witches. In fact, two towns in Europe in the late 1500s were left with only one female inhabitant each (discussed in chapter 13). But this massive gynocide[1] was due much less to religious beliefs than to changing sex roles in the society. Secular conflicts (over

the proper role of men and women) were expressed in "religious" activities (burning witches as infidels). Religious behavior can be either a cause or an effect of other social processes.

In short, there are many ways in which religious groups, religious values, and secular social processes can be interrelated. Beliefs are not always at the heart of religious behavior. Social scientists have found that persons sometimes become committed to new religious groups with little knowledge of the group's beliefs. They become committed through group pressures and social processes (discussed in chapter 5). Sociologists are convinced that knowing what a group believes provides insights only into one aspect of this complex phenomenon we call religion. For a fuller understanding, one must comprehend the social processes as well.

Most Americans believe that the central differences between religious groups have to do with their beliefs, but there are many interesting and important variations in style of worship, authority structures, and psychological appeal of religious groups. The short descriptions in Box 2.1 of three religious services illustrate some of the range of diversity.

Sociology, then, focuses on the social dimensions of religion—including the manner in which religion affects society and the ways the society influences religion. Like the developmental psychologist who studies a child to discover the stages of personality development in all children, we will be looking for the common patterns—the general rules—rather than for unique characteristics of each religion. When we do look at unique characteristics, it is to find how those characteristics affect behavior in special ways.

This sociological perspective is characterized by two fundamental principles: reliance on empirical data and objectivity. By reliance on empirical data, the sociologist considers only data that are observable through the five senses. This limits sociological insight because

---

[1]Genocide is the annihilation or attempted annihilation of an entire people (such as the Nazi holocaust in Germany). Gynocide (*gyno* meaning women) is the attempted annihilation of the female sex.

► **BOX 2.1**

Religion in America Varies in Content, Style, and Appeal

Religion is a diverse and multifaceted phenomenon. We can gain some insight into the diversity of American religion simply by observing the religious services of various religious groups. Religion can be big business, or it can be a small-group experience. It can appeal to emotions, intellect, or tradition. It may be geared to an authority figure, may encourage individual autonomy and independence, or may stress corporate responsibility and social action. The worship experience may be designed to create a mood of awe and quiet meditation, or it may be devised to stimulate critical thinking and motivation to join a protest movement.

The following descriptions by William Martin allow us to vicariously attend three very different worship services in the heart of Texas. The first is that of a growing, evangelical Baptist church where thousands take the leap of faith. The second is a liberal Unitarian congregation where members look (and analyze) before they leap. The third description is of Yom Kippur services in a Reformed Jewish temple, where tradition and social responsibility are blended. These glimpses into American religiosity suggest considerable variation, yet these include only a small segment of the entire range. They represent only the more conventional expressions of religiosity in the United States.

Readers may find it instructive to list the various ways in which these religious groups differ in content, style, appeal, and source of authority.

First Baptist: Appeal to the Heart

"This place in the eye of God is more favored than any other. It is from here, from our dear church, that we are all going to heaven." He knows his words are hyperbolic. He also knows he can get away with them, because he is Wallie

Amos Criswell, pastor for 35 years of the First Baptist Church in Dallas, largest in its denomination and the apotheosis of Texas religion.

First Baptist has over 20,000 members, a weekly budget of approximately $135,000, buildings and parking lots that sprawl over five city blocks, a staff of 256, a library of 30,000 volumes, and recreation facilities that include two gymnasia, a skating rink, bowling lanes, racquetball courts, Nautilus equipment, and a sauna. Among its dozens of programs are 21 choirs, 11 mission centers, an academy with a kindergarten-through-12th-grade enrollment of over 600, the Criswell Center for Biblical Studies with over 275 students pursuing two degrees of religious certitude, an FM radio station, and a Fellowship of Christian Truckers whose members minister at truck stops and terminals in Dallas County. First Baptist also produces one of the more notable worship services this side of the 19th century.

I knew the church had a 70-piece orchestra and a 175-voice choir, but I was not prepared for the processional. In a maneuver that is repeated each week, the musicians strolled casually to their places, picking up the strains of "On Jordan's Stormy Banks" as they settled in. Then, as I wondered why they hadn't coordinated things more smoothly, the orchestra was suddenly in place and a steady stream of tan-robed singers poured through four doors and the tympani pounded the cadence and the volume and intensity mounted so that when they reached the refrain—"I'm bound for the promised land"—I felt a tingle and an urge to shout, "Wait for me! I'm coming, too!"

Our spirits thus lifted and charged, we prayed and sang awhile ourselves before hearing Diane Daniels, a stunning young woman with a beautiful voice and professional stage manner, sing "Come, Ye Sinners."

In the fullness of time, the announcements ended, and W. A. Criswell loomed into the pulpit. . . . Resplendent in a ceremonial white suit, with his deep-set eyes sparkling out of a broad face crowned with wavy white hair, Criswell looked like Nelson Rockefeller playing William Jennings Bryan in a fundamentalist pageant. . . . The world is groping for answers, he said; the politicians, the economists, the great literary men have failed to provide them, but there is an Answer and He's coming soon, "to take us in triumph and victory back to heaven [where] there'll be no more funeral processions down those golden streets.". . . Criswell speaks in a compelling measured rhythm, bobbing slightly on key words and punctuating his declarations by drawing down his hand in a controlled tremble. . . . He expands words like "God" and "glory" and "maaarvelous" and fills them with a sonorous vibrato that makes them more than they might have been if left to themselves, and he rolls out phrases like "through the centuries and the ages and the eons" just to revel in their rhe- torical rumble. . . . Criswell made no effort to argue the truth of his sermon, but rested content simply to preach it with authority. . . .

There is, no doubt, some lukewarmness in the veins of First Baptist's body, but it is unquestionably a thriving, vital enterprise, "a going church for a coming Lord." . . . Churches that proclaim, without apology or hesitation, that *"this* is the way, the truth and the life" are growing. . . . Sheep seek direction, not a philosophical discussion of alternative paths, and Pastor Criswell stands ever ready to point the way.

Emerson Unitarian: Appeal to the Mind

In sharp contrast to the weathered stone or freshly painted white clapboard of the picturesque old Unitarian churches in New England, Emerson Unitarian in Houston is a new adobe-colored box that reminded me of a pueblo with a pipe organ. Large side windows, however, let in a great deal of morning light and produce a much airier quality than seems possible from the outside. The small, functional foyer contains a needlepoint sampler of Emersonian scripture—"Nothing is at last sacred but the integrity of your own mind"—and a framed scrap of inconsequential correspondence that serves as a relic from the Concord saint's own hand. On the morning I visited, the foyer also contained the church's minister, Dr. J. Frank Schulman, who not only greeted me warmly but took time to ask if I had ever been to a Unitarian church before and to offer to respond to any questions I might have about Unitarianism. A few days later, he followed this up with a cordial letter that touched on points in our conversation and reaffirmed his offer of assistance. As I entered the sanctuary, I was met by Jack Leatherman, a large, garrulous man who has been lavishly anointed with the spiritual gift of ushering. He commented on what a lovely Sunday morning it was, generously offered me a wide range of seats, suggested one that was "very quiet and peaceful," and encouraged me to attend the soup-and-sandwich luncheon immediately after the service.

Since Unitarianism is nothing if not ecumenical, I was not surprised to see a pulpit cloth bearing the symbols of the world's great religions clustered above a single flame that symbolized their essential unity. . . . In good Unitarian fashion, the readings included a passage from the apocryphal book of Ecclesiasticus and a reflection on primitive religion by anthropologist Sir James Frazer. Overall, the service was well conceived and well integrated, with a skillful and pleasing interweaving not only of major components but of the internal segments of prayers and choral responses as well. When Schulman mentioned in the course of his sermon that he did not like

Continued

BOX 2.1—*Continued*

a sloppy worship service, the knowing chuckles in the congregation led me to believe that the order and precision of the liturgy probably bore his strong imprint.

Schulman spoke on "Religion as an Intellectual Process." His education at the Harvard and University of Chicago divinity schools shone through in a presentation solidly grounded in history, philosophy, and theology and characterized by notable literary style and grace. He chastised fundamentalists for their inattention to the intellectual dimension of religion and affirmed that nothing is so cherished by Unitarians as the search for truth. Religion, he said, is a reaching for something beyond ourselves—"Call it God, call it the Spirit of the Universe, call it the Oversoul." It is not enough simply to do good; we must also *understand* and know what we want to accomplish if we are not to drift aimlessly. . . . Theologians have prepared us well to seek new answers to the enduring problems of religion, and if we will build upon rather than discard their traditions, we can erect theological constructs that will be adequate to our needs and times. The task, he insisted, is imperative: "We must not let the ranks of society close about us so that religion is shut outside."

Schulman's message, of course, was designed for people who have surrendered or never possessed the "blessed assurance" claimed by evangelical Christians. The modest crowd may indicate that such an appeal is limited in a city and state dominated by true believers. But for those who no longer find

traditional theology plausible, [Emerson Unitarian provides a context] for pursuing religious questions in an intellectually responsible and systematic fashion. . . .

Temple Emanu-El:
Appeal to Conscience and to Tradition

The Day of Atonement—Yom Kippur—has long seemed to me the most intriguing of Jewish ceremonials. In biblical times it was the . . . day on which the sins of the Israelites were symbolically transferred onto the head of a scapegoat, which was then led into the wilderness. In October, at Temple Emanu-El in Dallas, [an] enormous crowd flocked to duplicate services, arriving an hour early to get good seats. No goat was set loose on Hillcrest Road, but the High Holy Day still provides ample opportunity to contemplate both commission and release of one's sins. . . .

Yom Kippur is a solemn occasion observed by 24 hours of fasting and several separate services. . . .

Again and again, we read and were reminded by the rabbi and the choir that a multitude of sins separate us from God and His law and from one another. We confessed sins committed under stress or through choice, openly or in secret, in stubbornness or in error. We acknowledged that we had abused power, profaned God's name, shown disrespect toward parents and teachers, exploited and dealt treacherously with our neighbors, been selfish

sociology does not use reports of supernatural influence—except to investigate how such reports influence the subsequent behavior of informants. But the limitation of data to only empirical data is also a strength. The sociologist deals in facts that can be measured, ob-

served, and tested. If a sociologist claims that belief *X* causes behavior *Y*, empirical studies can be set up and data gathered to support or refute the hypothesis. If politicians and members of the public believe that devotees of religious cults are more likely than nondevotees when we should have been self-sacrificing, harsh when we should have been gentle, hard when we should have been kind, thoughtless when we should have been considerate, heedless of our better natures, and open to inclinations to swerve from the paths of purity and right. I soon began to wish we would come to the part about not making graven images, since that is one I have absolutely never committed, even in my heart. It was reassuring to be reminded, also repeatedly, that "the gates of repentance are always open" and that reconciliation with God is always a possibility.

In his sermon for the evening service, Rabbi Jack Bemporad inaugurated the season of repentance by focusing on Big Sin: nuclear war. . . . Buttressed with quotations from the Dalai Lama and Pope John XXIII, Bemporad cited the prophet Hosea, who warned that trust in weaponry is a false hope, a form of idolatry that places ultimate trusts in that which is inherently limited and partial, and thus it violates the first of the great commandments. The impulse to power, long the basic sin of humanity, separates us from wisdom, love, compassion, and understanding, and lies at the heart of war. We have survived its evil in the past, he said, because we lacked the capacity to do the worst; now, with nuclear weapons. . . .

Peace is no longer a luxury, the rabbi insisted, but a necessity. We must recognize that the people on the other side are as human as we, are also made in God's image. . . . We must

recognize, too, that God does not desire the death of His children but wills that all should repent and live, beating their swords into plowshares and studying war no more. . . .

The services on the following day maintained the serious tone of the first, with many similar or identical readings and extensive musical responses by an excellent choir and soloists, who sang in both Hebrew and English. . . . An afternoon service memorialized departed members and relatives of members of the congregation. . . . A concluding late afternoon service extended assurance to worshipers that the forgiveness they sought had been granted. The Shema ("Hear, O Israel! The Lord our God, the Lord is One!") was proclaimed, the shofar (ram's horn) was sounded, and we were told that God had made our sins to vanish like a cloud and our transgressions to disappear like a mist. . . .

I was a bit hungry, a bit tired, and a bit sorry I had sat in a folding chair. I was also more than a little reflective over having been reminded of my shortcomings for the better part of a day. . . . Though fully aware I would inevitably fall short, I truly resolved to do better, not only that what remains of life might be fuller and richer but that from my grave, as the prayer book says, "may spread not the barren thistle but the fragrant myrtle, a blessed memory redounding to God's honor and glory."

Source: William Martin, *Texas Monthly.* September 1979: 260–66; December 1981: 218–24. Used by permission of William Martin.

to be mentally unstable, that hypothesis can be substantiated or disproved through empirical investigation. If members of certain religious groups or persons with particular religious beliefs are thought to be more racially prejudiced than others, only empirical investigation can

establish the validity of that claim. The sociologist is not satisfied with general impressions but seeks concrete, verifiable data to prove or disprove any generalization.

The sociologist also tries to be objective. Objectivity does not mean that the sociologist claims to be above error or to have the whole truth; we have already pointed out that no discipline can claim omniscience. Objectivity means that the sociologist tries to prevent personal beliefs about religion from entering the study. The social scientist is committed to the search for truth wherever that search leads. Although sociologists as private citizens have preferences and commitments, they seek to be open to the data and to avoid prejudgment of any particular group or any particular religious process. A sociologist may not agree with the views of a group being studied, but makes every effort to understand the group on its own terms and to avoid bias in interpreting the processes of the group. For example, the charge by many people that religious cults engage in brainwashing is primarily an attempt to discredit those groups. The charge is based on hostility toward the groups and preconceived notions about what they do to recruit members. Sociologists—even if they do not agree with the activities of the group in question—try to base their judgments only on the data in front of them.

Sociologists seek objectivity as a rule of behavior in exercising their discipline. But this objectivity is not always easy to achieve. A sociologist who is active in a church or is otherwise a "believer" is perhaps more likely to be sympathetic to "believers" than is a sociologist who is a committed atheist. The difference is subtle, but the researcher who is personally active or is a believer is less likely to view religious behavior as irrational. In this regard it may be useful for you to know that your author is an active church member,[2] but one who is sometimes skeptical of religious claims and who re-

mains open to persons with perspectives quite different from his own. Along with Andrew Greeley (1972: 3), I am convinced that being an insider has provided me with insights into religious behavior and religious organizations that I would not otherwise have gained. However, like any other set of experiences, this personal commitment may unconsciously affect my perspectives on religion. Readers may want to keep in mind that I have sympathy for religion. However, my unabashed commitment to the scientific method also requires that I report the data accurately—even when it is an acute embarrassment to those of us who are believers.[3] The important point here is that the first step toward objectivity is to identify as clearly and thoroughly as possible any feelings and biases one might have about the object of inquiry. This is not a simple matter of declaring one's group memberships. It involves an ongoing soul-searching into previously unrecognized feelings and biases and a constant effort to understand each group on its own terms.

Resistance to the Scientific Study of Religion

Many religious people are highly suspicious of any scientific study of religion. The attitude of constant critical thinking and seeking empirical evidence of causality seems contrary to the utter trust that faith requires. Hence, sociological analysis of religion is viewed as a threat to pure faith. Indeed, the sociological method does discover patterns that are sometimes unsettling to the faithful, and sociological theories sometimes offer interpretations of causality that challenge the believer's concept of "revelation." Although the ability to combine

---

[2]I have a theological education (Boston University School of Theology) and was ordained in the United Methodist Church. However, my denominational affiliation has varied depending on the theology, style of liturgy, church programming, and social involvements of the local congregations where I have lived. Over the past two decades I have been active and held offices in United Methodist, United Church of Christ, and United Presbyterian congregations.

[3]Not only am I an active church member, I am also a white, middle-class male. While I will strive to avoid any ethnic, sexual, or class bias, those who are sensitive to unconscious sources of bias may want to be cognizant of this background.

the posture of scientist and worshiper is sometimes difficult to maintain, it is possible. I have personally found that the scientific study of religion can be beneficial in that it forces one to be rigorous in the search for truth and demands logical coherence in the articulation of faith.[4] Of course, it cannot be proved that the scientific study of religion is always beneficial, but I would contend that the maintenance of ignorance about the social characteristics of one's religion—and the continuance of unconscious social patterns that are undesirable—is harmful in the long run. Knowledge is sometimes threatening, but ignorance is even more dangerous. For this reason, I am convinced that believers as well as nonbelievers can benefit from a scientific investigation of religion.

On the other side of things, some nonbelievers (especially in the scientific community) insist that religion is not worth studying because it is of so little consequence. They maintain that religion has little effect on human behavior. Social class is usually identified as the most important influence on social attitudes and behavior. However, Gerhard Lenski (1963: 326) found in a Detroit study that of thirty-five variables studied, socioreligious group was slightly more important in affecting social attitudes than was social class—both in potency and in range of influence. Religion was the most important single variable in predicting the social attitudes of respondents. Of course, religion was in some cases a cause, in some an effect, and in still others a noncausal correlate.[5] However, when other variables were controlled, religion still proved to be a significant factor in shaping the attitudes of people on a large number of issues.

Other studies have also shown religion to be an important determiner of social values and perspectives, but it is not always the same elements of religiosity that are significant. In some cases, there are significant differences between members of different denominations. In other cases, denominational affiliation is relatively insignificant, but social behaviors are correlated with theological orientation (fundamental, conservative, or liberal) or with level of devotionalism (frequency of personal prayer). In still other cases, the extent of participation in the life of the church is the critical variable (including attendance at worship services and/or involvement in informal church friendship networks). Various dimensions of religiosity have been found to be significantly related to such diverse factors as racism and anti-Semitism, attitudes toward divorce and birth control, likelihood of completing a college education, inclination to support the idea of a welfare state, enjoyment of one's occupation, engagement in installment buying, tendency to vote Republican or Democratic, conviction that alcohol consumption is immoral, and likelihood of supporting traditional sex roles in society. Religion is related to larger social attitudes and values but sometimes in rather complex ways. In this study, we explore both external social effects of religion and internal social processes of religious groups that allow some to survive while others die. It is my conviction that the social processes of religion *are* important—or else I would not be writing this book. Furthermore, it is my assumption that readers find the social dimensions of religion worth investigating—or else they would not be reading it.

---

[4]These are qualities that I value in science or in faith.

[5]Correlation means a tendency for two characteristics to occur together. If we say that education and income are positively correlated, we mean that there is a tendency for people with much education to also have a high income. On the other hand, if education and age are negatively correlated, it means that high age and low education tend to appear together (i.e., older people tend to be less well educated than younger people). The tendencies of variables to occur together may be causal (one factor has caused the other) or noncausal (e.g., both factors have been caused by a third factor).

Sociology and the Language of Causality

As in any other science, sociology attempts to identify social processes that cause, or effect, other social processes. To fully understand subtle differences that social scientists make in the importance of one variable in shaping another, it is critical to understand the language of causality.

First, a variable can be a **contributing factor,** which means that it is one of many factors. If we were to explore the variables that cause persons to become juvenile delinquents, for example, we might find that coming from a single-parent family greatly increases the likelihood—the *probability*—that one will become a delinquent.

This does not mean that all children who come from single-parent families will be deviants, nor does it mean that this is the only factor leading to deviance. It simply means that five or six circumstances together may incline one toward this form of behavior and that being from a single-parent family may be one of those factors. But finding that single-parent family membership contributes to deviance is not the same as saying that it is necessary.

A **necessary factor** is one that must be present. It may not be the only factor that may cause a behavior pattern, but if the factor is absent, the behavior will not occur. Some social scientists believe that social instability and unrest are necessary conditions for the rise of a witch-hunt hysteria, but social turmoil is not enough by itself to cause witch-hunts. A statement that a variable is necessary is a much stronger statement of causality than one asserting a variable is a contributing factor.

If a factor is **sufficient** to cause a certain social behavior, then that factor alone can cause a particular behavior. It does not need to combine with other factors. *A* alone is enough to cause *X*. But various other factors may cause

X as well. The combinations of *B* and *C* or of *C, D, E,* and *F* may also cause *X*. Although variable *A* may be sufficient to cause *X*, it may not be a necessary condition. (See Box 2.2.)

The strongest statement of causality is that a factor or a particular set of factors is **necessary and sufficient.** This means that the behavior will not occur unless these variables are present, and these variables will cause certain behaviors regardless of whether any other conditions are present. This is the simplest and most direct statement of cause, but due to the tremendous complexity of the social world, it is extremely rare that a sociologist can assert with assurance that a factor is both necessary and sufficient. Indeed, sociology is often referred to as a *probability* science because it usually points to various contributing factors. Statements about the necessity and/or sufficiency of one factor in causing another are usually made with many cautions and are normally stated tentatively rather than as firm conclusions.

In reading this book or attending to any other commentary on social behavior—newspapers, magazines, textbooks, talk shows, or lectures—students would be well served to be sensitive to these distinctions. Unfortunately, some writers and some speakers assert "necessity" and "sufficiency" when the evidence requires a much more modest conclusion. Scholars must learn early to be precise in their use of causal language.

The conclusions of sociologists of religion are not etched in stone, and we often recognize multiple paths of causality in the formation of any behavior pattern. But the fact that we are very cautious about the use of causal language does not mean that the findings are ambiguous. Indeed, caution allows for greater precision in describing the social world accurately. The unwillingness to make simple and absolute statements of cause is due to the complexity of our subject matter, not to the confusion of sociologists.

Sociological Methods of Studying Religion

The sociologist of religion claims to use scientific methods. It is appropriate therefore to discuss the methods by which sociologists gather their data. Essentially, the methods they use to study religion are the same as those employed in investigating other social processes— historical interpretation, cross-cultural comparative analysis, controlled experimentation, observational studies, sample surveys, and content analysis. The methods used in any given situation are determined by the nature of the topic under investigation and by the predilection of the researcher. However, religion as a topic of study occasionally presents special problems.

Historical Analysis

Some sociologists have used historical data to look for patterns of interaction between religion and society. When sociologists use historical material, however, they tend to have a different emphasis than historians. Historians normally seek to offer a detailed description of historical situations and perhaps to elaborate the specific circumstances that seemed to have caused, or resulted from, a particular set of events. Sociologists are likely to be interested in whether a particular social situation is usually accompanied by or followed by some other "typical" situation or circumstances (Nottingham 1971). The sociologist is normally looking for a pattern—a general rule—in the relationship between social events and religious characteristics. The goal is to develop

---

▶ **BOX 2.2**

Necessary and Contributing Factors

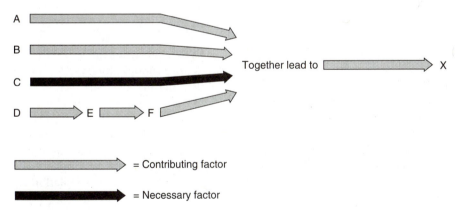

This diagram shows a very simple model of causality depicting several factors that contribute to *X*. The solid line leading from *C* indicates that *C* is a necessary factor. Hence, *C* is necessary, but not sufficient, to cause *X*.

How would the diagram be modified if we want to show that *A* was sufficient to cause *X*? How would the diagram be drawn if *A* and *C* together were necessary and sufficient?

a generalization or theory that explains the relationship—not just in that particular circumstance but in most cases. This approach has led to the development of typologies of religious groups (chapter 9) and to the development of theories about the evolution and decline of religion in modern society (chapter 14). Historical analyses have also been employed in suggesting that Protestant theology contributed to the rise of capitalism (chapter 10) and in exploring religious sexism (chapter 13). Historical analysis can be useful, but the danger is a tendency to impose one's own pattern on the data and thereby distort history. The goal of this method is to recognize and uncover historical patterns that are relevant today, but a nonbiased execution of this method is far from simple to accomplish.

Cross-Cultural Analysis

Another method that can be extremely useful, but that is open to similar hazards of subjectivity, is cross-cultural analysis. By comparing socioreligious patterns in several cultures, sociologists can get some idea of whether a correlation is due to specific characteristics of one culture or holds for all sociocultural conditions. Max Weber tried to test his theory about the relationship between the Protestant ethic and the rise of capitalism by studying religion and economics in India and China. A pattern that supported his hypothesis would not prove its veracity, but contradictory evidence would serve to undermine it. He viewed the lack of negative evidence as support for his theory (Weber 1951, 1958b). Yonina Talmon (1965) used cross-cultural data to discover universal patterns among millenarian movements—religious movements in which the end of the world or a new era of existence is anticipated in the near future (chapter 11). Other scholars have used cross-cultural comparisons to demonstrate that religious witch-hunts correlate with changes in male-female relations in the larger society (chapter 13).

One difficulty with conducting cross-cultural analyses of religion is that concepts of religiosity vary so widely from one culture to another that one can easily get caught in the trap of comparing noncomparable data. And, of course, the fact that a correlation between two variables is not universal does not negate the possibility of a causal relationship between those factors in a specific situation. Cross-cultural comparisons can be useful, but like historical analyses they are sometimes difficult to employ with the precision that scientists prefer.

While historical analysis and cross-cultural analysis are empirical in the broadest sense of the word, the four methods that we discuss next are generally recognized as the primary empirical methods of sociology and allow the researcher to experience the data personally with his or her five senses.[6]

Experimentation

The most powerful tool of the social sciences in terms of ability to control variables is controlled experimentation. Experimental research in sociology has been undertaken primarily by social psychologists. But experimental research on religion—even by social psychologists—has been almost nonexistent. Obviously, one cannot use control groups and experimental groups to experiment on the factors operative in conversion to a new religious organization. (I cannot, for example, experiment on students with several techniques for converting people to the Hare Krishna.) In fact, most forms of experimentation regarding people's religiosity would be considered a gross violation of an unwritten

---

[6]Of course, anthropologists can personally experience several cultures and do cross-cultural analysis. However, most cross-cultural comparisons of religion—like historical comparisons—have been done by using the written reports of other scientists who gathered the data.

social norm. The public would be outraged—and rightfully so. Religion is so intensely personal and deeply felt by so many people that manipulating it for purposes of study would not be tolerated. Research ethics committees (which approve research projects) are unlikely to endorse such a study unless participants agreed to the experiment and were fully aware of its nature. But informing participants of the full nature of the research would bias the outcomes. And even if participants were to be informed, many ethics committees would balk at experimentation in this sensitive area. Thus, experimentation on religious behavior has been limited to only a few areas.

One area is with shamans and seers who claim powers of extrasensory perception (ESP) (Barnouw 1982). In this case, the individuals involved agreed to such experimentation. There are also a few other areas in which experimentation is possible—for example, in evaluating the differential effects of several different modes of religious education. In this case, many religious people are willing to have their children participate in an experiment in the hope that the findings will determine which methods are most effective for religious socialization. Other quasi-experimental designs may also be used if one allows a natural event to be the manipulator of variables. For example, Daniel Batson (1977) suggests that one could do pretests and posttests on psychological characteristics and values of people before and after a revival meeting. While such a procedure would not conform to all of the normal standards of an experiment, it could offer an important means for establishing the validity or inadequacy of certain theories regarding the effects of religious rituals and celebrations. Most people would probably not object to such tests, for the experimenter would not be attempting to manipulate religion directly but only to measure the effectiveness of other "manipulations."

J. M. Darley and Daniel Batson (1973) also conducted a quasi experiment with seminary students in which they tried to measure effects of biblical stories on subsequent behavior. They staged a scene in which they placed a groaning, coughing, sinister-looking man who was apparently in need of help in an alley through which the seminary students passed en route to where they were to deliver speeches. Some of the students had recently read the Good Samaritan story and were to speak on that parable. Others were assigned to speak on the role of theological education for nonpastoral occupations. The purpose was to see whether those who had recently read the Good Samaritan story and were to speak on it were more likely to stop and help. (They were not more likely to help—although other factors of religious orientation did affect the likelihood that the students would help.) In such experiments, the controls on variables are not as strong as in most experimental research, and that is why Batson insists they are only quasi-experimental.

Furthermore, the range of topics that can be explored with quasi-experimental methods is limited.[7] The fact remains that most research on religion must proceed without this powerful tool of the social scientist. Although the lack of much experimentation on religious behavior is fully understandable, it does limit the research tools available to the sociologist of religion.

Participant Observation

A frequently used method in studying new religious movements is participant observation. By participating in the group, a researcher can

---

[7]For discussion of the potential uses and limits of experimentation in the study of religion, see Batson (1975, 1977, 1979); Darley and Batson (1973); John Yeatts and William Asher (1979); and Walter Pahnke (1963).

observe the behavior of people in a religious context. This can be done overtly (with subjects aware that the observer is studying them) or covertly (with subjects believing the observer is a new member). Participant observation has several advantages. First, it allows for observation of symbolic interactions between members of which the actors may be only partially aware. For this reason, observational studies are particularly popular with social psychologists who use symbolic interaction analysis.[8] Second, participant observation is useful when a researcher believes there may be a gap between what people say and what they do. Respondents may verbalize statements that express tolerance of others, yet they may unwittingly say things or behave in ways that reveal anti-Semitic attitudes. Or respondents may verbalize profound commitment to orthodox teachings of a major religion, but their everyday behavior may raise questions about how pervasive that commitment really is.

Several researchers studying religious cults have found that devotees present a front of profound commitment. But after several months, the researchers were able to get to know the devotees well and were interested to find them admit that they had serious reservations about the belief system of the cult (discussed in chapter 5). This brings us to a third advantage of observational studies: They allow more authen-

tic study of nonconformist groups that are very private and that maintain a front with the public. Obviously, no cult is going to admit to the use of brainwashing techniques in recruiting new devotees. Questionnaires and interviews with cult members will not satisfy the public that brainwashing is not occurring. Likewise, interviews only with those who leave the group will not satisfy scientists, for these persons do not represent a random sample of those who joined. It would represent only those who became dissatisfied. Moreover, apostates from any group have a tendency to "reconstruct" their experiences in ways that allow them to save face for having joined—an act they have come to view as foolish. Covert participant observation has been useful in the study of secretive cults to get accurate information about their internal social processes (see chapter 5).

Participant observation allows the researcher to observe subtleties that would not be revealed through responses to a questionnaire or through a one-hour interview. Hence, observation is often referred to as a "qualitative" method of research. The quality of the data is rich, but it is also limited to the researcher's observations. This presents two problems with this research method. First, the data are normally limited to one case (one congregation, a single cult, clergy in one denomination). This limits the ability of the researcher to make generalizations. What is true in this one case may not be true in others. Case studies permit the researcher to go into great depth in gathering data, but breadth is thereby sacrificed. A large number of case studies is needed before generalized patterns can be identified, and then they are often specified by persons who did not have firsthand experience in each group.

A second problem is that the reported data are bound to be somewhat biased by the observer's own "filtering" system. First, not all observers are likely to notice or be interested in the same patterns. Hence, there is the issue of

---

[8]Symbolic interactionism is one theoretical perspective of sociology—especially of social psychology. This perspective maintains that individuals do not respond to the world or to other people directly, but they place a symbolic meaning on objects and behaviors and respond to that meaning. Many times these symbolic meanings and rules of behavior are learned at a very early age and are so thoroughly assumed to be "the way things are" that they are taken for granted by the individuals involved. Clothing, eye contact, distance between people during a conversation, and gestures are examples of phenomena that are often symbolically significant in understanding a culture. These are the types of objects and behaviors that symbolic interactionists use as the basis for their analyses.

unconscious filtering of data. Second, what the observer chooses to write up cannot possibly include all those observations made. The researcher must consciously choose which data are relevant. This provides a second filtering of data. The same sort of filtering process occurs in all research, but in other sorts of research it is easier to identify the sources of possible bias by analyzing the nature of questions asked of informants or by checking other available data. Because it frequently happens that only one person is undertaking participant observation on a group at any one time, that observer's data are sometimes the only written record of that particular phase of a group's development. This subjective element in observational studies is a serious hazard. See Box 2.3 for a discussion of still other interactional issues that can arise in becoming a participant researcher.

Despite shortcomings, the method has proven extremely valuable in the sociological study of religion. In fact, readers may find it enriching to do some participant observation of religious groups different from their own as they read this text. While you will not be trained in participant observation methods, you may find that your observations will provide illustration and/or questions regarding concepts discussed in this book.

Survey Research and Statistical Analysis

Perhaps the most popular form of research design in sociology, especially in the past three decades, has been sample survey research and statistical analysis. The use of this method has also expanded recently in the sociological study of religion. The sociologist sends out questionnaires or conducts interviews with a random sample of a particular population. The more ambitious surveys undertake a sampling of the entire nation, but because such studies are very expensive, most surveys involve a smaller population base: a

sampling of college students at a particular type of institution (such as state universities, private liberal arts colleges, or high-prestige schools), a sampling of residents in a particular city or set of cities, or a sampling of members of a particular denomination. Respondents are asked about their religious affiliation, frequency of church attendance, frequency of personal prayer, knowledge of denominational doctrines, belief in specific religious concepts and other measures of religiosity. This procedure has been extraordinarily useful in demonstrating correlations of specific religious characteristics with particular social attitudes or attributes.

Although historical or observational insights allow for subjectivity in interpretation of data and permit impressionistic guesses as to certain patterns and correlations,[9] survey data allow researchers to identify more precisely the correlations of religious characteristics with social attitudes and characteristics (fundamentalism with anti-Semitism, frequent church attendance with sex-role traditionalism, or denominational affiliation with social mobility and income level). In the absence of the experimental method, survey research and statistical analysis provide us with our best control of variables and most certain identification of correlations.

One difficulty is that although statistical analysis tells us on a large-scale basis which religious characteristics are correlated with which social attributes, it does not reveal very effectively which factor *causes* which. There are ways to control for variables so that the sociologist can make educated guesses, but a great deal of interpretation enters at the point of suggesting causality. The fact that the data are

---

[9]For example, impressions by church officials regarding the relative growth and decline of various denominations have been found to be in error by large-scale statistical analyses in which critical variables were controlled.

characterized by correlations of hundreds of answers to specific questions also means that the interpretations of the meaning of events for the respondents themselves is sometimes lost. Furthermore, the data do not demonstrate the process that an individual goes through; they are static or nonhistorical. They do not reveal, for example, the stages of progression in a conversion experience. Specifying causality requires that one determine which variable occurs first. Most survey data do not reveal this.[10]

A second difficulty is that sociologists sometimes assume that negative responses to certain questions mean that the respondent is "less religious" or "less orthodox" than other respondents. The questions frequently do not allow people to express alternative modes of religiosity and do not account for the fact that what is orthodox in one denomination may be unorthodox in another. The presuppositions of

---

[10]Clearly, the problem of inferring causality is not unique to survey types of research. This is an issue in all research, but any static or nonhistorical method faces special problems—for the order in which variables occur is difficult to establish. Nonetheless, ingenious research designs and modes of analysis have helped to compensate for this potential problem.

▶ **BOX 2.3**

Participant Observation in a Fundamentalist Church

Participant observation is often made difficult by the fact that the people one observes are often trying to figure out who the researcher is and how they ought to respond to this new participant in their group. What statuses does the person hold? What roles will she or he play? Do members relate to this person as a potential recruit? As an "insider" who can be trusted or as an "outsider"? Establishing rapport is not always easy. For Nancy Ammerman, author of an award-winning study of a local fundamentalist church, her position in the church changed significantly for the better when it became obvious that she was pregnant.

> In every social interaction, the people involved respond to each other and the situation. That is no less the case when the social interaction is within the context of "doing research." When I went to Southside Gospel Church, I entered a year-long process of discovering who they were, while at the same time they were discovering who I was—and we were each being changed along the way.

I began with some ready-made knowledge about them. It came from reading books by and about fundamentalists and from my upbringing in conservative (but not fundamentalist) Southern Baptist churches. I knew enough to understand most of what they said, even when they were talking about fairly esoteric biblical references. I knew enough to sing their hymns and behave appropriately in their church. I looked and sounded like an insider, and most people responded to me as if I were.

But they still had to figure out what sort of insider I was. I was coming to church by myself (my husband never even visited with me). But that was not so uncommon; there were other women who came alone, and most just assumed that I had an "unsaved husband." Those who got to know me well enough to learn that my husband was actually pastor of another church had a harder time understanding my church-going habits. For those people, another category had to be called on to explain who I was: I was writing a book.

the researcher (the filtering processes) are sometimes at work in formulating and interpreting the questions. The critical point in this type of research, then, is the objectivity of the questions and accuracy in interpreting the answers. A number of sociologists have shown great ingenuity in formulating questions, as we will see.

One final problem with survey studies is that sometimes what people say is quite different from what they do (Deutscher 1966, 1973).[11] Survey information does not involve a direct study of religious experience itself but focuses on reports of religious experience or,

more frequently, on the consequences of religious experience. It is a truism in the social sciences that people often operate on assumptions and respond to symbols of which they are only partially conscious. Hence, the value of survey information is affected by how "hard" (how verifiable, objective, and

---

[11]For example, in a study of why people switch denominations, Frank Newport (1979) states that there is a strong basis for doubting the reasons people give for their own switching. He insists that the validity of such self-reports is problematic.

Neither of those categories came, for most members, very early in the process, however. By the time they had to think about me as a pastor's wife and book writer, they had already seen me as a hymn-singing, Bible-reading participant in the life of their church.

No matter what the occupational, marital, or church-going category, however, one status was clear. I was a woman. And in the South-side congregation, being a woman means—first and foremost—being concerned about one's family. For most of a year, I was present in that congregation without any apparent connection to the one thing that would make my status as a woman sensible to them. All that changed, however, when I became visibly pregnant. As a woman with a (soon-to-be) family to care about, I was able to enter into conversations previously closed to me. I was accepted as a new kind of insider.

All of these assumptions about who I was—woman with unsaved husband, woman writing a book, insider, woman expecting a baby—shaped the conversations I had with

people at the church. In turn, my evolving assumptions about them shaped those conversations as well. In the early days, the talk about "do's and don'ts" seemed overwhelming. I found myself listening with ears tuned to rigidity and structure. At some point, I saw enough of the genuine care Southside members had for each other to begin to see the strengths of their community. And toward the end, I could see the subtle negotiations that were going on between their professed ideals and the realities of their lives. At each stage of the process, I was able to ask different questions, look for different things.

What I learned, then, was not a simple set of answers to a predetermined list of questions. It was more like an unfolding story, a story about them and a story about me, and a story about how we got to know each other.

Nancy T. Ammerman
Candler School of Theology
Emory University

▶ **BOX 2.4**

Statistical Analysis Employing New Procedures on Historical Materials

Research often utilizes several methods in a single study. Professor Rodney Stark and his graduate students, for example, used sophisticated statistical methods to analyze some very old data in new ways. Professor Stark tells how exciting the discovery of research can be for a scholar—and also reveals the unanticipated way in which a scholar may discover a new line of research.

   One day I was sitting in my office at the University of Washington when Kevin Welch, one of my graduate students, brought me a two-volume set of books, published by the Bureau of the Census, titled *Religious Bodies,* 1926.
   "What do you know about these?" he asked.
   "I've never heard of them," I confessed. "Where did you get them?"
   "In the census section of the library. There are sets for other years too: 1890, 1906, 1916, and 1936."
   As I leafed through the volumes I was stunned at their range and depth. They provided the most extraordinary historical, doctrinal, and statistical information on 256 separate religious bodies, including very tiny ones as well as those outside the Judeo-Christian tradition. As I grew excited about the possibilities the volumes presented, I also grew increasingly embarrassed. I had been publishing studies in the sociology of religion for more than fifteen years and I had

never known such books existed. How could I have been so uninformed? Then I recalled Petersen's paper, which I had read during my second year in graduate school. How could he not have known? How could generations of scholars have remained ignorant of what was clearly a massive census undertaking? Indeed, how could demographers, and especially their graduate students, fail to notice a whole shelf of books of religious statistics located alongside the regular census volumes? In fact they didn't overlook them—the books weren't missed, they were dismissed. I have since talked with many demographers who noticed these volumes while in graduate school, but in each case they were informed by faculty members that these statistics were nothing but junk that the Bureau should never have bothered with. Why? Because they were not based on tabulations of individual responses to a question on the regular census form. Instead, they were based on reports prepared by individual pastors or boards of elders. And, it was claimed, such people were not to be trusted. The figures would necessarily be hopelessly inflated.
   Perhaps these demographers knew little about American religion and never bothered to examine the data with care. Hopelessly inflated statistics are precisely what are obtained when individuals are asked their religious affiliation. Ever since the start of public opinion polling in the late 1930s, surveys

unchangeable) the data are. Statements about the frequency of church attendance over the past two months are based on hard data. In such cases, the answers given to researchers are reliable. But to determine the relevance or the importance of religion to respondents, sociologists sometimes ask, How significant is

your religion to you? or How important is religion in your everyday life?
   The information gathered by such questions is much "softer" in nature than is information about attendance. A person may say that his religion is very significant to him, and may want it to be so, but it may actually have

have always found that virtually everyone has a religion. I know of no national survey in which as many as 10 percent answered "none" when asked their religious affiliation. But the nation's churches cannot possibly seat 90 percent of the population. More careful investigation reveals that for many, their claim to a religious affiliation amounts to nothing more than a vague recollection of what their parents or grandparents have passed along as the family preference. Consider that substantial numbers of students at major universities commit the most unlikely spelling errors when filling out a questionnaire item on their denomination. Can students who think they go the Pisscaple Church have ever seen the word Episcopal? Or what of Presditurians? If one wishes to know which churches have how many members (that is, people sufficiently active to have their names on the membership rolls), one needs to visit churches and count the rolls. Or one can ask how many names are on the rolls. But it takes very careful and elaborate research techniques to calculate membership by summing the responses given by individuals.

Rather than being hopelessly inaccurate, then, there are strong prima facie grounds for thinking that these old census statistics are relatively accurate. But there are strong indications of their accuracy as well. The first of these is that the numbers claimed by the churches are modest. The national rate of religious adherence based on the 1890 data is only 45 percent. Second, the data are extremely stable over space and time. Had there been substantial local misrepresentation, then the data ought to jump around between nearby communities, and they do not. By the same token, there should have been a great deal of inconsistency from one decade to the next, and there is not. Finally, the Bureau of the Census was very concerned with accuracy and provided extensive, sophisticated, and persuasive evaluations of its procedures.

After this rather accidental discovery of these existing sources, Stark teamed up with Roger Finke in a new research project. Applying several statistical procedures to control for errors and to aid in analysis, the two developed a new body of evidence and a fresh interpretation of long-term trends in American religious affiliation (reported in part in chapter 14). Sometimes innovative lines of research are spawned by such chance encounters. Despite their cause, scholars find such moments of insight and opportunity exhilarating. Doing sociological research can be akin to solving a mystery: one starts with a question and seeks ways to solve the puzzle.

Source: Roger Finke and Rodney Stark, *The Churching of America: Winners and Losers in Our Religious Economy.* New Brunswick, N.J.: Rutgers University Press, 1992: 7–8. Reprinted by permission of Rodney Stark.

little influence on the individual's everyday life. Another respondent may report that religion has very little influence, yet her childhood moral and religious training may significantly affect her daily decisions in unconscious ways. Moreover, a question on the "significance of religion"—as one question among two dozen—does not measure the saliency of any specific belief with accuracy. Individuals may say that they do believe in life after death or in the existence of the devil and that they feel religion is very significant or definitely affects their everyday life. But this does not reveal the importance of those particular beliefs. A problem of validity of correlations exists unless the answers are interpreted with great care. Fortunately, any bias or questionable assumption by the researcher is made manifest in the questions and is accessible to other social scientists to recognize and correct. (In other methods of research, the assumptions of the researcher are usually less explicit.)

Surveys and statistical analyses are extremely useful tools for the social scientist and have provided us with a great deal of concrete data. Although there are several pitfalls in the use of this method, the primary arguments usually occur over the validity of particular questions—whether they accurately measure those things they purport to measure.

Content Analysis

A final method used by sociologists is that of content analysis. In this instance, the researcher tries to ferret out underlying religious themes or unarticulated assumptions by analyzing written materials. Attitudes toward women might be identified through analysis of sermons preached by popular evangelists in various decades (chapter 13), or differences in values and outlooks among denominations might be identified by exploring the themes in the most popular hymns sung by each group (chapter 11). One study of the popular religion of Americans involved an analysis of popular religious books (Schneider and Dornbusch 1958). This procedure allowed the researchers to get beyond the official doctrines of the denomination and permitted a study of the religious ideas that appeal to the common person. The assumption is that books that sell particularly well are those that express (or shape) the beliefs of common folks. Often these beliefs are quite different from those taught in the churches. Likewise, the civil religion of the United States (a kind of religion of the nation, which will be discussed in

chapter 16) has been studied by one scholar through a content analysis of the religious references in the Declaration of Independence, the inaugural addresses of various presidents, and other official statements that articulate the goals and purposes of the nation. Content analysis has been useful, but one difficulty is its assumption that the written statements accurately represent the views of the people. Presidential inaugural addresses may or may not reflect the American people's attitudes and values. Best-selling religious books are worth studying, but we do not always know which population within the United States buys which books or which persons fully agree with the authors.

To some extent, the weaknesses of each research design can be compensated for and overcome. However, no one research design is entirely adequate in itself. The variety of approaches allows scientists to check the accuracy of their theories from a variety of data sources. Sociologists often quarrel over which research design is most adequate, and most researchers tend to prefer one approach over others. However, our ability to gather data in several ways provides checks on the weaknesses inherent in any one approach. Together these approaches allow social scientists to substantiate or dismiss various generalizations about religious behavior. Examples of each of these methods of research—except for the experimental method—will be incorporated in this text.[12]

Summary

Sociology offers a unique vantage point for viewing religion and religious behavior. While

[12]Experimental studies of religion have been undertaken on only a very few occasions, and those have dealt with very specialized areas of theoretical interest—areas that we will not be investigating in this text.

sociology certainly does not claim to offer the whole truth about human behavior, it does provide insights that other approaches may fail to recognize. The sociological perspective focuses on religious groups and institutions or the behavior of individuals within those groups and on conflict between groups. While religious beliefs are seen as important, they are not the exclusive focus of sociologists. In fact, beliefs are viewed as one variable of religion among many—and often beliefs are found to be the effect of other social behaviors rather than the cause. Sociology of religion does not attempt to prescribe how religion ought to work. Rather it attempts to describe accurately the social underpinnings of religious groups and to generalize about common patterns and apparent causal correlations.

Two fundamental principles characterize this sociological approach: reliance on empirical data and objectivity. The sociologist is not satisfied with general impressions but seeks concrete, verifiable data to prove or disprove any empirical generalization about a group. And although sociologists have preferences and commitments of their own, they seek to be open to the data and to avoid prejudgment of any particular group or any particular religious process. Such objectivity is not easy to maintain and serves as an ongoing goal for each sociologist.

Sociology is commonly referred to as a probability science because the statements about causality are normally statements about contributing factors. It is important for readers to be cognizant of the language of causality and to recognize that the complexity of the social world makes it very rare to be able to identify necessary and sufficient factors. Our conclusions about the social world are not etched in stone, and we often recognize multiple paths of causality in the formation of any behavior pattern. But the fact that we are very cautious about the use of causal language does not mean that the findings are ambiguous. Indeed, caution allows for greater precision in describing the social world accurately. The unwillingness to make simple and absolute statements of cause is due to the complexity of our subject matter, not to the confusion of sociologists.

In order to gather empirical data, a number of different types of research methods have been employed. Each has its own advantages and disadvantages. Collectively, they can provide checks and corrections on errors that any single method might make. However, due to the nature of religion as a topic of study, some special problems arise. This is especially true in the case of experimentation. Ethical considerations prevent many aspects of religious behavior from being tested and analyzed through controlled experimentation.

The Complexity of Religious Systems: Integration and Conflict

Religion is a complex phenomenon. It plays a diversity of roles in society and is itself composed of an intricate interplay of symbols, myths, rituals, mystical experiences, and social interactions. In chapter 3 we examine the multifaceted relationship between religion and the larger society. To do so, we first need to understand two major theoretical perspectives employed by sociology and how each contributes to our overall understanding of societies and social processes. At the end of the chapter we will explore a theoretical model that attempts to integrate insights from both perspectives. Then in chapter 4 we turn our attention to a micro perspective and to the internal complexities of a religious system. In this chapter we will examine and apply another critically important sociological theory: symbolic interactionism (also called social constructionism.) In both chapters we will discover ways in which religion can serve as a source of social cohesion or as a major contributor to conflict and divisiveness.

CHAPTER THREE

Religion in the Larger Society: Macro Perspectives

The relationship between religion and the larger society is multidimensional and complex. To explore this relationship, we will be engaging in a macro analysis. By **macro** we simply mean an attempt to explain the relationships and dynamics of the society at large. Macro theories look at the structure of societies, the overall patterns of organization, rather than at the minutiae of everyday interaction between individuals. The two primary macro theories used by sociologists in the past several decades are functional and conflict theories. Each of these has rather different perspectives on social behavior and on the primary forces that affect human beings. Although controversy rages between advocates of the two perspectives and although the theories are sometimes viewed as incompatible, these theories can complement each other and together can broaden our understanding. Each tends to focus on slightly different aspects of society and each illuminates certain elements in the relationship between religion and the larger society.

Functional Theory and the Functions of Religion

Our first macro perspective is functionalism. This perspective emerged out of concern by early social scientists questioning why certain social behaviors came into being in one society and not in others. And why, they asked, do a few social patterns exist in all societies? Religion, for example, was believed to be a cultural universal, to exist in some form in every culture in the world. Why is this the case? **Functionalism** sought to explain social organization and behavior in terms of how a particular behavior or belief satisfied human or social needs.

Although functionalism can be first attributed to Emile Durkheim, it was popularized and developed as a systematic method of analysis by anthropologists Bronislaw Malinowski and A. R. Radcliffe-Brown. One principle of their approach was that any social pattern or institution that does not serve a function will cease to exist. Furthermore, any pattern found among all people is believed to have its basis in innate human needs. Before focusing on the functions of religion, let us review the development and controversies within functional analysis itself, especially the divergences between these two theorists.

Functional and Structural-Functional Analysis

Bronislaw Malinowski maintained that all basic human needs or drives must be satisfied in a way that does not cause social chaos. The hunger drive, the sex drive, and the need to relieve oneself of body wastes are all satisfied in ways controlled by society. One cannot satisfy one's sex drive with just anyone and everyone. Certain norms specify which persons are or are not potential sexual partners. Lack of consent by the partner (rape) or close family relationship (incest) are only two of the more common prohibitions societies set down. Similarly, the society as a whole has a stake in controlling how one procures food and where one deposits body waste. Hence, all societies are made up of institutions—regularized patterns for the satisfaction of human need. Human needs or drives are thereby satisfied without creating social conflict or chaos. (See Figure 3.1.)

Malinowski believed that all institutions and regularized patterns of behavior satisfy a basic human need. Otherwise, he believed, those institutions and behaviors would cease. Therefore, the task of the social scientist is to identify which needs, conscious or unconscious, each social pattern serves (Malinowski 1944).

Malinowski maintained that evil and misfortune cause persons to feel helpless. Religion allows one to feel that there is a source of power and hope that is greater than one's own resources. Especially important for humans is the need to cope with the anxiety and personal disorganization caused by the death of a loved one. Although the various religions deal dif-

ferently with death, all religions establish some belief and ritual that functions to reduce anxiety over death.

As Malinowski points out, the intended purpose of religious behavior is not necessarily the same as its function. A social scientist may not be able to determine whether a prayer for a safe fishing trip actually protects the natives from danger (the *purpose* of the prayer); but that prayer can be observed to provide a calming, anxiety-reducing effect on those who pray (a *function* of the prayer).[1]

Malinowski traces the function of religion and that of many institutions to basic human needs, drives, and emotions. In this sense, functionalism à la Malinowski tends to be rather individualistic and psychological in character. The bottom line in understanding many social patterns is the needs of individuals (Malinowski 1944).[2]

A. R. Radcliffe-Brown developed a different approach to functionalism. According to him, the function of most social patterns is traceable not to individual needs but to needs or requirements of the society as a whole. For example, according to Radcliffe-Brown (1939), fear of hell and damnation, and perhaps fear of death itself, would not exist if the teaching of religious groups did not instill such fear. Religion generally functions not to resolve anxiety but to create, foster, or heighten it. He

---

[1]The anxiety-reducing function of prayer may be both conscious and intended; thus, it is a manifest function of religion. But it is still not the purpose of the prayer. This distinction in religion between manifest function and manifest purpose may not exist in other institutions. The purpose of economic activity, for example, is also its manifest function: to meet certain individual and social needs. The purpose of religion, as conceived by believers in many traditions, is to satisfy something outside the realm of normal human experience. This makes religion unique as an institution.

[2]Malinowski does, however, recognize that some needs are social needs and others are derived needs—needs created by the particular social structure. But his treatment of religion focuses much more on individual needs—such as that of coping with anxiety and fear.

maintains that in his own field studies, the subjects were more likely to experience anxiety if a ritual was improperly conducted than they were to turn to ritual procedures when they felt anxious.

Why would religion act to enhance anxiety? Structural-functionalists answer that social stability, especially in simple tribal societies, requires a rough consensus on values, beliefs, and norms. In most societies, formal legal sanctions are not the primary source of social control. In fact, in some societies they may be almost entirely absent. Hence, maintenance of a common world view and constant reinforcement of values and belief patterns are critical if the society is to continue as a stable system. Religious ritual acts to reinforce the belief structure, the values, and the norms of the larger society. Fear of hell, anxiety over offending one's gods, or fear of being bewitched by evil spirits tends to ensure social conformity. Radcliffe-Brown insists that by making one anxious about breaking cultural rules, religion functions to discourage deviant behavior. The function served is not an individual but a societal need. For Radcliffe-Brown the need for social integration and stability is a driving force behind most institutions.

While admitting that some taboos or rites may not have a structural function, he insists that structural or societal needs are usually primary. No society can exist unless individuals are willing to behave in ways that may not serve their own personal desires. For example, sex codes limit the range of persons with whom one can experience sexual satisfaction. Such codes may therefore contradict the desires of individuals; nonetheless many of those codes are necessary if the society is to continue.[3] Because his emphasis has been on the way social patterns meet societal or structural needs, Radcliffe-Brown's brand of functionalism has been called **structural-functionalism.**

Actually, Radcliffe-Brown's structural approach had been used earlier by Durkheim. In 1915 Durkheim maintained that God stands in the same relationship to worshipers as does a society to its members. God transcends the individual in power and scope, is immanent within the individual, and occupies a world that is fundamentally different from the world of the individual. Furthermore, the divine has priority over the individual: human need must always give way to God's demands. Similarly,

---

[3]This is not to suggest that every sex code *is* functional, but many sex codes do serve to enhance social stability. The point here is that a code that seems disadvantageous for the individual's gratification may be advantageous for the social structure.

▶ **FIGURE 3.1**

Satisfaction of Human Needs Through Social Institutions

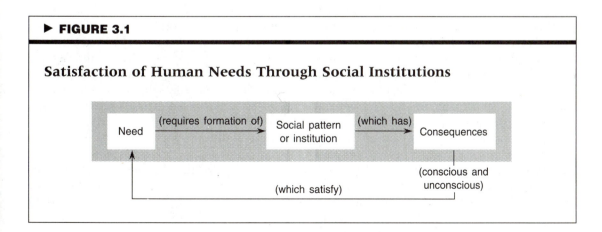

society transcends the individual in power, scope, and longevity. Society is contained within the individual in that each member of society has internalized the values and norms of his or her group. The demands and prerequisites of the society have moral priority over the desires of individuals (Durkheim 1965).

A thoroughly socialized person is one who wants to do that which is necessary for the society to survive. Persons must be motivated to *want* to behave in ways that may contradict their own desires. If the only argument presented to a person for not engaging in extramarital liaisons was that social stability would be adversely affected, most persons would probably not suppress their desires. But when the prohibition is presented as a moral principle that is based on divine command, people will more likely internalize that norm. Similarly, people may not curb their desires if they are simply told that incest is wrong because it creates intrafamilial competition, undermines the socialization role of parents, and confuses the lines of inheritance and authority. These may be the functional reasons for the incest taboo, but many people honor the taboo because incest is an unthinkable sin. It is a moral absolute, the violation of which would seem to undermine the laws of the universe.

Durkheim's approach has been referred to as "metaphoric parallelism" (Winter 1977). He believed that the sacred world is a world that parallels the mundane world. Behavior patterns that would cause social chaos are prohibited by fear of sanction from the supernatural realm. That which is structurally dysfunctional is simply made taboo. According to Durkheim, the term *God* is a metaphor for *society*; worship of God is really worship of one's own society. People are not aware of this projection process, and taboos and moral models become unquestioningly absolute and binding.

Functionalists do not always assume, as Durkheim did, that the belief in God is a mirage. For most functionalists, the existence or nonexistence of God is beyond the capacity of empiricism to prove or disprove. The concern of the functionalists, regardless of the truth or falsity of a belief, is how a belief or ritual operates in the society. What needs does it meet?

Durkheim and Radcliffe-Brown granted that religion may serve some individual function, but they believed the most important functions of religion are structural. Do you find that you tend to identify with the functionalists or with the structural-functionalists? Does religion *alleviate* anxiety about death, or does it *create* anxiety about death in order to assure social conformity? Readers might find it instructive to attend funeral services in several different religious traditions. Notice comments made by the clergy who officiate and listen carefully to the prayers. What emotions do they seem to create? During regular worship services, do prayers and sermons create anxiety about death? If so, how is this accomplished?

George Homans (1941) has offered a synthesis that attempts to avoid the either/or choice, pointing out instead that both processes may be at work. He uses the term *primary anxiety* to refer to the anxiety an individual may feel as a result of loss of a loved one. **Primary rituals** are rituals designed to *alleviate* this anxiety or grief; they serve an individual function, à la Malinowski. **Secondary rituals**, on the other hand, work to *create* anxiety, ensuring that society's members will conform to social norms. Hence, they serve a structural function, à la Radcliffe-Brown. In many cases, a specific religion will have some primary and some secondary rituals. It is also possible for a single ritual to relieve primary anxiety while creating secondary anxiety.

For example, a Protestant funeral service may emphasize that the departed loved one has gone on to the next world and is in the loving care of God. The virtues of the individual are emphasized. The minister may suggest that the bereaved family members will be united with "Grams" (as she was known) when they, too, pass on. "She is with us in spirit," they are assured, and "she wouldn't want us to stop and pine away. She would expect us to carry on. The best way to honor her is to remember the wisdom she offered and to live our lives with faithfulness to the values she taught and lived." Comments that produce fond memories, assurance that the deceased is with us in spirit, affirmation that the bereaved will again see the deceased, and confidence that the deceased is dead only in physical form are all reassuring to the survivors. They help to lessen primary anxiety: grief.

At the same time, persons attending the funeral may be reminded that their own lives have not been as noble or righteous as the deceased. The thought of meeting God and receiving one's just reward may heighten their anxiety. The challenge to remember Grams by living a righteous life like hers may increase the listener's sense of humility and inadequacy: "How could I ever be as generous and wise as Grams?" (One tends to recall primarily the most *positive* qualities of the deceased. Remembrance of faults often seems crass and creates guilt feelings. Hence, the positive qualities of old Grams may be magnified in the eyes of the mourners at that moment.) The funeral service then may remind one of his or her own finitude and may cause one to reflect on one's own life. This secondary anxiety may cause the person to reaffirm conformity to the mores of that religious group. Hence, the same ritual may *reduce* primary anxiety and *create* secondary anxiety. As Homans's synthesis illustrates, the analysis of the function of any institution may be a complex process. The diagram in Box 3.1 may illustrate the complexity of relationships between individual and structural functions, manifest and latent functions, and dysfunctions. Let us turn now to some of the specific functions of religion and see how modern functionalism is applied.

The Functions of Religion

From our discussion thus far, it should be apparent that religion serves a variety of functions. Religious faith and religious organizations serve a number of needs of individuals and the social structure. However, it can be misleading to offer a general list of the functions of religion, for the way in which a religion functions will vary somewhat depending on the social structure, the culture of the society, and the specific characteristics of the religion itself.[4]

For a group that has emigrated to a new country, religion may take on increased significance as a source of identity. For a group experiencing great suffering, religion may offer a supraempirical explanation that makes the suffering bearable. In a society experiencing rapid social change, religion may provide a feeling of security and assurance, and the value-maintenance function is emphasized. For an individual who is geographically isolated from family members, a religious group may provide a sense of belonging. However, without overgeneralizing it is possible to point to four types of functions that religion typically serves: meaning functions, identity or belonging functions, cultural functions, and structural functions.

Before discussing these, I would again emphasize that the functions of religion (even the manifest ones) are frequently not the same as the *purpose* of religion. The purpose of religion is usually the worship or adoration of a being, an ideal, or a set of supernatural principles. Nonetheless, the practitioners of religion are usually conscious of many of the functions or consequences discussed below.

Finally, readers should be warned against the temptation to use functional analysis to

---

[4]To assume that religion serves the same functions in all societies is to fall into a trap that Robert Merton (1968) refers to as "the fallacy of assuming universal functionalism."

"explain away," or dismiss, religion. Sometimes students new to the sociology of religion assume that functional explanations furnish a complete elucidation of religious behavior. This assumption limits rather than broadens our perception of religion. Functional analysis provides one lens for viewing religion. It furnishes important insights, but it does not establish the whole picture.

Individual Functions   Religion functions for individuals in two primary ways: provision of meaning and provision of a sense of identity and belonging.

1. Meaning Functions. The function most explicitly associated with religion is the provision of a sense of meaning in life. Religion provides a world view, or cosmos, by which injustice, suffering, and death can be seen as ultimately meaningful. As Clifford Geertz says, when suffering or death has meaning, it becomes sufferable. Friedrich Nietzsche says the same thing when he insists that "He who has a *why* to live can bear almost any how."

▶ **BOX 3.1**

Model of Functional Analysis

Those social patterns that are functional for the individual may be dysfunctional (harmful) for the structure, and social patterns that are functional for the structure may be dysfunctional for the individual. Because individual functions are more often conscious and intended and structural functions are more frequently unconscious, the heavy line illustrates the general pattern. However, either type of function may be conscious or unconscious, intended or unintended.

To meet the meaning function, however, religion must include more than a set of ideas or notions about the world. Abstract philosophical systems of thought seldom satisfy this function for the masses. Meaning involves both concept (idea) and demand (imperative) (Kelley 1972). The world view must be presented to the prospective believer in such a way that the person seems to be held by the belief rather than voluntarily holding the beliefs. Although religion affects patterns of thought, acceptance of a particular religious cosmology is seldom based on logical argument alone. Philosophical systems of thought may provide a cosmic world view, but they seldom address people's emotions and they are not presented in a way that make people feel they are held by the belief system. There is nothing that emotionally impels them to believe: there is no demand. The communication of concepts through rituals and symbol systems incorporates both affective *and* cognitive dimensions.[5]

The desire to make sense out of the world seems to be nearly universal. People may be willing to admit that their own world view is less adequate than another, but they are not willing to give up their interpretation for none at all. They are simply not willing to say that human events are meaningless. It seems that bafflement (lack of explanation) is an extremely anxiety-producing experience; religion acts to combat it. The religious response to the question "Why?" is answered primarily in terms of values: What does a particular event *mean* in understanding the ultimate purpose or goal of one's life? Another way to say this is that religion locates a specific experience, event, or observation within a larger context of experiences, events, or observations. The larger context is attributed with

ultimate meaning, and the specific event is viewed as having significance because of its relationship to the "big picture" (Wuthnow 1976b).

2. Belonging and Identity Functions. A less often recognized aspect of religion is its importance for the sense of identity of the believers. Andrew Greeley (1972: 108–26) argues that the reason denominationalism is so strong in the United States is because of the function religion has played in the lives of immigrants. Before coming to the United States, many Italians (for example) did not identify themselves primarily as Catholics. Placed in a new environment, however, with different norms and values, many Italian Americans came to identify strongly with the Catholic Church. Many Italian Catholic congregations became community centers that helped members preserve their sense of roots. Similarly, other immigrant groups have shown increased denominational loyalty and intensified religiosity after coming to the United States. The denomination, in effect, became a source of ethnic identity and a bastion of cultural stability for those facing culture shock (Marty 1972). As decades pass, religious services eventually come to be conducted in English, assimilation occurs, and ethnic loyalty starts to fade; religion then becomes the source of identity in and of itself (Warner 1993). Indeed, because of the tradition of freedom of religion in North America, religious groups often serve as a "free social space" under which persons with various agendas can associate and develop an autonomous identity (Warner 1993).

Along similar lines, in Poland, Ukraine, and other Eastern European countries dominated by the Soviet Union, the Roman Catholic tradition became a source of identity and solidarity for those opposing foreign control. In Poland, the church contributed a sense of commonality for people of several ethnic groups and gave sacred sanction to their

---

[5]The affective dimension has to do with feelings; the cognitive dimension has to do with intellectual processes.

resistance to a government that they viewed not as the legitimate Polish one, but as a puppet government controlled by Moscow. Unity of the Polish people—based on a common *religious* identity—was an important component of their survival and ultimate success (Tamney 1992).

But even beyond the cases of immigrants or of victims of colonialism, a sense of religious belonging often affects individuals' understanding of who and what they are. A teenager at a party may forgo alcohol or may refuse to participate in certain activities. The individual may identify herself strongly as a Christian and, according to her definition of what that means, certain activities are unacceptable. Or a young Mennonite, faced with his draft papers for the U.S. Army, may conclude that his identity as a Christian conflicts with his identity as an American. As a Mennonite, he may accept the prohibition against war as categorical. His petition for status as a pacifist may be a profound statement of identity as a Christian. Similarly, many acts of individuals can be understood as responses to their identity as Jews, Moslems, or Buddhists.

The importance of the identity or belonging function will be emphasized in chapter 5 when we discuss conversion and commitment. But it is worth pointing out here that scholars have rather consistently found that emotional ties to members are a primary factor in conversion of new members and in maintenance of commitment in established members. Greeley emphasizes that while meaning functions may be primary (in the sense of being closer to the manifest purpose of religion), the belonging functions may actually be prior to meaning in terms of chronology. He writes,

> With some exaggeration we may say that instead of Americans belonging to churches because they believe in religion, there may be a strong tendency for them to believe in religion because they belong to churches (1972: 115).

When I first read that statement by Greeley, I thought he was mistaken. After doing a good deal of research on the social psychology of religion, I have come to believe that he is essentially correct. In a rapidly changing society, especially in a society with a high degree of geographic mobility, a sense of belonging is a critical need. If one's kin all live 500 miles away, the need for emotional support during a time of crisis can be intense. Religious groups often serve to satisfy this need. This is true for both mainline congregations and new religious movements (McGaw 1979; Roof 1978).

In some societies, religion serves another sort of identity need. As an individual progresses through life, he or she may undergo a variety of rites of passage, celebrations, or rituals signifying changes of status in the community. Before such a rite, a youth may be considered a child; after the rite, the individual is a man or woman. In many tribal societies, such rites of passage are important in defining one's role and the limits of appropriate behavior. This sort of function is deemphasized in American life, but it is part of the religious tradition in many cultures. Insofar as religion does recognize and celebrate role changes, it may contribute to the maturation process of individuals.

Societal Functions   Religion serves the society as a whole by bolstering both the culture and the social structure.

1. Cultural Functions. In most societies, religion functions to sacralize cultural values. As indicated in Box 3.2, generalizations about the relationship between religion and morality, or religion and everyday values, must be cautiously made and must take into account the researcher's definition of religion. They are most accurately made with reference to a specific religion in a specific society. Nonetheless, I would concur with Geertz in asserting that for most individuals in most religions in most societies, religion and everyday morality are closely linked. Geertz writes,

> The need for such a metaphysical grounding for values seems to vary quite widely in intensity from culture to culture and from individual to individual, but the tendency to desire some sort of factual basis for one's commitments seems practically universal; mere conventionalism satisfies few people in any culture. However its role may differ at various times, for various individuals, and in various cultures, religion, by fusing ethos and world view, gives to a set of social values what they perhaps most need to be coercive: an appearance of objectivity. In sacred rituals and myths values are portrayed not as subjective human preferences but as the imposed conditions for life implicit in a world with a particular structure (1958: 426–27).

For most people, a moral code does not seem compelling if it is enforced by nothing more than social tradition. Would the great majority of people refrain from incest if the only argument against it was simply that incest would cause social instability? Possibly not. One of the important functions of most religions, then, is to provide a metaphysical basis for the moral order of the social group and to reinforce obedience to norms. We will be exploring this issue in more depth in chapter 4, but Thomas O'Dea's comment seems to be accurate for most cases: "By showing the norms and rules of society to be part of a large supraempirical ethical order, ordained and sanctified by religious belief and practice, religion contributes to their enforcement" (1966: 6).

By providing a metaphysical foundation for the culture's values, moral codes, and outlooks on life, a religion helps to combat the confusion, disorientation, and deviance that anomie can generate. This, in itself, enhances stability for the culture.

2. Structural Functions. Religion also serves the organizational structure of society.

Durkheim emphasized that religion served as a sort of glue to bond together people who otherwise had diverse self-interests; it helped them to define themselves as a moral community with common values and with a common mission in life. This unifying and self-defining function is especially true of religion in nonindustrialized, homogeneous societies. In the pluralistic society of the United States, no single traditional religion can claim that role. Some

The bar mitzvah is the "coming of age" ceremony for a Jewish boy, at which time he reads publicly from the Torah for the first time. Religious rites of passage such as this symbolize a change of status in the community. (Cornell Capa/Magnum Photos.)

scholars insist that a sense of collective national identity and sense of purpose is critical and that a new form of religion has emerged in the United States to fulfill that function. Referred to as civil religion, this new form of religiosity attempts to define the meaning and significance of the United States in relationship to some transcendent reference. (Civil religion will be discussed in chapter 16.) In any case, religion often serves as a basis for collective identity.

▶ **BOX 3.2**

The Religion-Morality Connection

Some scholars have asserted that religion is not really concerned with secular values and morality, that it focuses on a spiritual plane or otherworldly existence. Is religion related to a culture's system of values and morality? The answer to this question will be affected to a large extent by how one defines religion. Which groups one considers to be practicing religion will vary, depending on the definition of religion that is used. Hence, the empirical evidence for making a generalization may vary from one social scientist to another.

The definitional criteria that I have set forth would suggest that religion is intimately bound with morality. With Geertz, I have suggested that an ethos (or set of moral moods and motivations) is by definition a part of any religion. After all, if religion focuses on that which gives meaning to all of life, then the being or object that one worships must be a significant value and perhaps a source of other values. In fact, the word *worship* itself suggests this emphasis. It actually means "worth-ship," the state or quality of worth. During worship, that which is of central value is lifted up, praised, or recognized. The worshiper re-affirms that this being or entity is the most exalted of all values. In monotheistic reli-gions, all other values are thought to emanate from this central value or being. In actual fact, monotheistic religion often does not affect ev-eryday values as much as its theologians and more devout practitioners would like.

The problem here is partially one of meth-odology. Who and what do we study when we study religion? If we study the religious belief systems and the most devout practitioners, the religious values or center of worth seem to affect everyday values directly. However, sur-veys of Americans, even of those Americans who say that religion is important to them, show that religion has little effect on their ideas of social morality.

Sociologists may respond in several ways to this discrepancy between what religion is supposed to do and what it really does. Some scholars simply assert that the role of the social scientist is to describe the reality, not the prescriptions of what church officials think ought to occur. This, they assert, is the advantage of empirical research over purely philosophical investigations. The fact of the matter is that the religious affiliation of the average American does not significantly affect his or her everyday values. They are inter-ested in whether traditional religious organi-zations and theologies influence everyday behavior.

Other social scientists may take a different tack: the problem may be in the definition of religious faith and in the use of traditional questions to measure the influence of one's religion. Faith has been defined in this text as that which gives meaning and purpose to life. For many Americans, Americanism may be their primary faith. However, faced with a questionnaire that asks for one's *religious affili-ation* an individual immediately thinks in terms of a denomination or religious organiza-tion. The person may be affiliated with the

As indicated above, religion also enhances social stability by sacralizing (making sacred) the norms and values of the society. This persuasive power of religion can have a number of important consequences. If certain behavior

is taboo (so heinous and so dangerous that it is unthinkable), people may conform for fear of the consequences of breaking the taboo. Many Eskimos believe that Sedna, the goddess of the sea, determines one's success or failure in

---

United Methodist Church, but is that organizational membership really indicative of his or her faith? Many people join churches because of the fellowship or the status or the respectability that such affiliation may provide. If an individual's faith or religion is actually the American Way of Life rather than Christianity, his or her verbal response may be misleading. These are complex issues. Does the sociologist accept an individual's self-definition of his or her faith, or does that social scientist probe more deeply into the social psychology of the individual's behavior for definitions? Do I have any right to suggest that your "real" religion is something other than what you claim it to be? On the other hand, do I have a responsibility as a social scientist not to accept statements simply at face value?

Many times people will respond to a question in terms of what they want to believe about themselves. Edward Stevens offers an example. Suppose that we ask a man if he values reading. He may respond that reading is very worthwhile and is important to him. In a forced-choice questionnaire, he may rate reading more highly than television, and he may agree with the statement "Daily reading should be a part of every adult's life." Yet we may find that this same fellow spends two or three hours per evening watching television, and that he has not read a book, magazine, or newspaper in the past year and a half. We might conclude, contrary to his verbal insistence, that he really values reading

very little. His behavior suggests that television has priority on his time. Reading is not so much a *value* as a *velleity*. This fellow would like reading to be a value, but in the actual scheme of things, he does not act on his feeling of ought. Stevens concludes, "A velleity is something I would like, but I'm not prepared to act on it. A value is something I consistently act upon. Action is the acid test of value" (1974: 13–14).

This example is simplistic. Nonetheless, because surveys elicit information based on verbal responses, there always remains the possibility that a gap exists between verbal affirmation and actual behavior. When one claims that religion "is very important to me," does that always mean that religion is an intrinsic part of the person's everyday life? Or can the claim sometimes represent a velleity— what one would like to be the case? And when religion is said to be "very important," what part of religion is important: meaning? identity? belonging? The debate continues over which beliefs and which behaviors are the best indicators of religious commitment. The issue is complex, and I do not expect to resolve it here. But this example may illustrate the difficulty of making generalizations about the effect of religion on any aspect of society. Do note, as a central point, that for those who use a functional definition of religion, religion and moral values are inseparable; for those who use a substantive definition, the relationship is an open question to be answered with empirical research.

hunting seals. Such believers are not likely to risk offending her by violating one of her rules. Hence, no Eskimo kills more than is needed; waste is unthinkable. This conservation ethic is functional for Eskimo society; yet it is enforced by religious rather than legislative sanction. In most societies, religion creates an environment of moral obligation to norms that benefit the social structure.

Although structural-functionalists have often emphasized religion's stability-enhancing characteristics, it can also be an instrument for change. This is referred to as the prophetic function of religion. Biblical prophets, such as Amos, Hosea, and Micah, insisted that God required social justice, and they consistently pressed for change in the interests of a more just social system. They were early spokesmen for the poor. The Radical Reformation certainly played an important part in the Peasants' Revolt in Europe in the sixteenth century. Similarly, the religious faith of Martin Luther King Jr. and of the black community in the southern United States was critical in the success of the nonviolent resistance strategy in the civil rights movement. In the 1970s and 1980s Roman Catholic bishops in Latin America were demanding redistribution of wealth and a restructuring of the social systems in many countries. Numerous other examples in which religion has supported social change could be cited. The point is that change is not only functional for many subjugated individuals but also that it can benefit a social structure. Although social stability offers many benefits to its members, stability is not an intrinsic and universal good. Functional analysis must evaluate the functions and the dysfunctions of both stability and change. Stability is necessary in that human society cannot exist without a fairly stable pattern of norms, roles, and values. Those patterns, however, may become inflexible and fail to meet human needs. Change can be positively functional for the social structure in such a case.

Dysfunctions of Religion and the Diversity of Consequences

A few years ago an agricultural agent from an international organization visited an impoverished country. The people were starving, and the agent hoped to teach them modern farming methods. He was certain that they could receive a better yield from their fields. He had several tractors flown in, and he began to teach them how to use a tractor to plow. The native people immediately protested and insisted that he stop at once. "The Earth is our Mother," they began. "Would you take a knife and stab your mother in the breast? Neither would we so gouge the flesh of our Mother, the Earth, who nourishes us. No, we barely scratch the surface of the ground with a stick and gently place the seed in the small furrow."

The religious world view of these people may have provided them with certainty of values, may have reinforced their social structure, and may have helped them interpret the meaning of their suffering. It may also have been functional ecologically and in preventing the people from being ensnared in an exploitative world system of economic and technological interdependence. However, their religion was at the same time dysfunctional in terms of food production. Note that religion may be both functional and dysfunctional at the same time.

In Western culture, religion has often rejected scientific knowledge. Copernicus's claim that the earth revolves around the sun was condemned as heresy, and Galileo was tried by the Inquisition for asserting that he had proved Copernicus correct. Much later, biblical literalists condemned Charles Darwin's theories and insisted that such heresy not be taught in the public schools. The criterion of truth was the Bible, and alternative theories or ideas were to be suppressed. Such an attitude is certainly dysfunctional for scientific inquiry. More recently, the Roman

Catholic Church has adopted official opposition to artificial methods of birth control. Many demographers who are concerned about the population explosion in predominantly Catholic Latin American countries see this stance as one contributor to world hunger. Our world population is increasing more rapidly than our food supply, they say. Religious opposition to contraception is therefore seen by many social scientists as dysfunctional.

Any institution or behavior pattern is likely to have a multiplicity of consequences in a society. In terms of economic development, a profound reverence for the earth may be dysfunctional. On the other hand, viewed in terms of the ecologic system, such a conservational attitude may be functional. Hence, when one evaluates some social process as functional or dysfunctional, it is important to keep one's criteria in mind: functional *for whom* or *for what*?

The stabilizing function of religion also has more than one consequence. It is interesting that Karl Marx and Emile Durkheim basically agreed on the way in which religion contributes to society. Religion tends to unite people around common values and beliefs. This occurs even when the self-interests of members are contrary. Durkheim admired the way religion functioned for social unity; Marx was appalled by it and referred to religion as the "opiate of the people." Marx claimed that religion unites people under a "false consciousness," a false sense of common interests. By interpreting injustice as meaningful and as being rectified in an afterlife, religion has served to keep oppressed people in bondage. Religious support of the existing social system may benefit the system while being dysfunctional for the disfranchised of that society.

The prophetic role of social criticism can also be functional and/or dysfunctional. Social change in the direction of greater economic equity may be functional for the poor and for

society. But sometimes prophets, seeing themselves as agents of God's will, employ extremism and unwillingness to compromise. This may either constrain the possibilities of change or cause changes that may not be beneficial to the society.

The identity function of religion is important in a heterogeneous and geographically mobile society. The sense of belonging a religious community provides can serve important psychological needs. However, this sense of belonging and this identity function may lead to extreme parochialism, bigotry, and ethnocentrism. Religion frequently breeds narrow-mindedness and strong group boundaries.

Finally, religion facilitates the process of role changes by celebrating the stages in the maturation process. But religion may also encourage immaturity and dependence in people. Many religious groups, including a wide variety of charismatic cults, insist that converts abdicate decision making. Members are simply to do what their leader tells them. The mass suicide of nearly 1,000 religiously committed people in Jonestown, Guyana, in 1978 caused many Americans to question whether religion is always constructive. The fact remains that religion, including many mainline denominations, does not always encourage independent and critical thinking. I would maintain that independent thinking is part of being a mature person and that religion is often dysfunctional in this respect.

The evaluation of functions and dysfunctions involves an investigation of consequences of a behavior pattern for all aspects of society. The important point is that one must be clear about his or her point of reference in using these terms. Furthermore, one must always be cautious about broad generalizations regarding religion. In order to be precise, we must discuss the functions and dysfunctions of a specific religion, for specific individuals, for a specific structure, in a specific society.

Problems with Functional Analysis

Functional analysis is but one lens through which any social process can be viewed and understood. There are, however, distortions in this lens.

1. Functionalism tends to err in the direction of overemphasizing social stability and underemphasizing conflict and change. In so doing, functionalists have often assumed that societies are quite well-integrated systems; the positive functions have been stressed more heavily than the dysfunctions.

2. In stressing functions, one also loses sight of the historical process by which any particular religion established its present character. The new emphasis on historical sociology (or diachronic analysis) in the study of religion is an important corrective to this oversight (Geertz 1968).

3. By emphasizing the critical needs that religion fulfills, one might assume that the traditional forms of religion are indispensable. But much research in the past two decades has been devoted to discovering new forms of religion or "religion surrogates" (Bellah 1970b, 1975; Yinger 1969, 1977; Luckmann 1967; Wuthnow 1976b). Hence, it is important to avoid the trap of thinking that traditional forms are indispensable.

4. Functionalism has sometimes evolved into a social philosophy rather than a tool of empirical research. As a social philosophy, functionalism has sometimes used circular reasoning to posit and then prove a point. Certain basic needs, whether biological, psychological, or social, have occasionally been set forth as basic and inherent to human society. Any existing social arrangements are said to be *created by* those needs and, in turn, to have the *effect* of satisfying them (see Box 3.1). This makes a neat theory because it cannot be disproved. The answer is presupposed in the question; satisfaction of some posited need is both cause and effect!

Most sociologists do not accept many of the assumptions of functionalism as social philosophy, but functionalism continues to provide an important *methodology*.[6] By this I mean that the basic questions of functional analysis continue to guide much sociological inquiry: What individual and social needs does a particular social pattern serve in a particular society at a particular time? How does a social pattern or institution affect the lives of individuals and influence other social patterns and institutions? What are the social forces that contribute to social integration? As a method of analysis, these questions are asked as open-ended queries and with the realization that the amount of social integration in a society is never total and is always subject to change.

5. Structural-functionalists have often evaluated social functions as being primary, while seeing individual dysfunctions as necessary evils. Therefore, some functional theories have operated with a conservative bias. This need not be an inherent problem with functionalism as a methodology, but it has been a tendency of functionalism as a social philosophy. For functionalism as a method of analysis, social order is not intrinsically good or evil, but a variable to be assessed in each society.

As a method of analysis, functionalism has certain common concerns with conflict theory, for both seek to discover the social consequences of a particular belief, behavior, or structure. But many sociologists are interested in issues of change, conflict between interest groups, and inequalities in power. Conflict theory addresses these issues more adequately

---

[6]For a more detailed treatment of the history, criticisms, and logical problems of functionalism, see Jonathan Turner and Alexandra Maryanski (1979). The authors also provide an excellent discussion of the difference between functionalism as an empirical methodology versus functionalism as a social philosophy.

than does functional theory, and it is to this second macro theory that we now turn.

Conflict Theory and Religious Conflict

Marx maintained that the fundamental reality of history and modern society is a conflict between the classes. The haves use every tool available, including coercion and ideology, to sustain their advantageous position over the have-nots. According to this view, understanding modern industrial society does not necessitate an analysis of cultural values and beliefs. The basic issue is economic conflict. Hence, Marx is often identified as the father of modern conflict theory. He maintained that values and beliefs basically operate (after the fact) to justify the self-interests of various groups. Along this line, Marx viewed religion as an ideology that justified the current social arrangements. It served as a tool of the upper classes and helped maintain stability. Marx, like Durkheim, viewed religion as a force for social integration. But for Marx, this had a tragic consequence; religion served to maintain an unjust status quo. Religion acts to unite persons of various classes when, according to Marx, all persons of the lower class should be uniting against all those in the upper class. In fact, the ideology that promised rewards in an afterlife for conformity in this world had as much of a pacifying effect as opium (hence, his comment about religion being the opiate of the masses).

Certainly there are many examples that would lend credence to the Marxian interpretation. The Hindu belief in reincarnation has led many lower caste Indians to conform to the laws of *dharma*. Only by conforming to dharma (which reinforces caste lines) can one expect to be reincarnated in a higher position. Those who violate these laws can expect to be reincarnated in some lower animal form. This sort of belief system tends to undermine any impetus to rebel against the social system. Christian beliefs in otherworldly salvation sometimes act in a similar way to pacify the poor and the disenfranchised (see chapter 11).

Conflict as a Source of Social Disruption

Not all conflict theorists emphasize the integrating and stabilizing function of religion. In fact, a number of them emphasize that society is not well integrated at all. Society comprises interest groups, each of which seeks the fulfillment of its own self-interests. They believe there is no consensus over values and beliefs that serves to unite the society; rather, modern society is characterized by conflict, coercion, and power plays by various groups. When stability does occur in a society, it is because (*a*) a temporary balance of power exists between groups or (*b*) one group has gained enough power to control the others. Stability lasts only so long as the distribution of power remains the same. Sometimes social stability is attributed to economic interdependence of groups—such that overt conflict would be dysfunctional to each. In any case, religious groups are viewed as simply one more set of interest groups in society. Common beliefs are viewed as relatively unimportant in social integration. Hence, Marx's principle—that self-interest is the key factor in shaping social relationships—is a central emphasis of all conflict theory.

Conflicts between Christians and Jews provide a vivid example. Christians and Jews have coexisted in the Western world for nearly 2,000 years. Yet because Christianity has been the dominant religious force in Europe since late Roman times, Christian leaders have often determined the nature of the relationship. At some points in history, Jews have been enticed to come to predominantly Christian cities because they brought needed skills and services. For example, in 1084 A.D. the bishop of Speier attracted Jews to that city because of their professional skills and because they would provide loans, which Christians would not do because they believed that usury (lending money for interest) was immoral. Jews were quite willing to lend money and so provided a needed service for the community. As part of the enticement, Jews were given their own section of the city, a section the Jews called a ghetto.[7] In fact, they willingly purchased a charter and paid a lease for the privilege of having their own ethnic enclave. However, as Christian mores changed and usury became an acceptable Christian enterprise and as Christians moved into the professions Jews had occupied, conflict between the groups began to intensify. By 1555, Pope Paul IV had made the Jewish ghetto compulsory rather than volitional, and Jews became objects of severe persecution (Berry and Tischler 1978).

The record of such conflict is long and consistent. The day before Columbus first set out for America, all Jews were ordered to leave Spain. The same thing had occurred in England in 1290 and in France in 1306 (Berry and Tischler 1978). Although we have not expelled the Jewish population, the pattern of discriminatory treatment continued in this country. Many Christians blame their victims for their plight, insisting that some characteristic of the Jews causes them to be persecuted. But the evidence is overwhelming that the primary cause of discrimination is the desire to gain an edge in a conflict over scarce resources (jobs, the best housing, the best educational opportunities). For many decades in this country, universities and professional schools had quotas for Jews. Only a limited percentage of Jews would be admitted each year, regardless of superior qualifications of Jewish applicants (Belth 1979). Christians

have often used their power as the dominant group to place Jews at an economic disadvantage. Ironically, those same Christians have then labeled the Jews as being the ones who are devious, manipulative, and driven by economic interests.

But, as Box 3.3 illustrates, religio-economic conflict has certainly not been limited to that between Christians and non-Christians. In the United States, Protestants have used their dominant numbers and established positions of power to oppress Catholic immigrants. Because they were here first, Protestants were well established before Catholic immigrants of Irish, Italian, or Hispanic background came to this country. The Know Nothing Party and the Ku Klux Klan are two examples of American movements that were intensely anti-Catholic and that limited membership to white, American-born Protestants. Some analysts (e.g., Gusfield 1963; Wilson 1978) insist that the temperance movement was also essentially an anti-Catholic phenomenon in which Protestants sought to force their own definitions of Christian morality on Catholics and Jews. The Anti-Saloon League, formed in 1896, specifically attacked the symbol of the urban, ethnic, Catholic, lower-class leisure lifestyle. For many Protestants, the saloon was a symbol of the Irish Catholics, recent immigrants who had come in large numbers, were taking jobs, were gaining political power in urban centers, and were beginning to upset the economic advantage Protestants had enjoyed.

According to this analysis, Prohibition was largely an attempt to define ethnic Catholic lifestyles as illegal and thereby to label such persons as deviants. Protestants continued to dominate the top positions in business and finance into the 1950s, with Catholics—regardless of competence or credentials—effectively shut out. For example, Charles Anderson (1970) reports that in that decade 93 percent of the top executives in manufacturing, mining, and finance were Protestant and that

---

[7]A ghetto is not necessarily a poor area of the city. A poor area is a slum; a ghetto is an ethnic enclave. Some ghettos in America are also slums, but the terms are not synonymous.

Protestants held 85 percent of the highest positions in the 200 largest corporations. This was despite the fact that Catholics comprised approximately 25 percent of the American population (Stark and Glock 1968; Greeley

1974). Fortunately, since then levels of anti-Catholicity among Protestants and anti-Protestant sentiment among Catholics have declined. Although some Protestants blame Catholics themselves for their so-called lack of

▶ **BOX 3.3**

Conflict and Coveting: The Norm in Jerusalem's Church of the Holy Sepulchre

Roman Catholics visiting the church of the Holy Sepulchre in Jerusalem are often led by brown-robed Franciscan monks as tour guides. The group may pause at what is believed to be Christ's tomb and offer a short prayer. But they have little time to tarry, for black-hooded Armenian priests are on their way with another group—accompanied by chanting choir boys swinging incense burners. Each group has its turn, and the schedule is rigidly enforced.

Five religious groups "share" the most sacred church in Christendom. But here Christian religions mix "about as well as holy oil and holy water." Every inch of the church is carefully divided between the groups and is jealously guarded. Protestants and other groups get nothing, and those who do "own" a share spend much of their time coveting their neighbor's share. A chapel in the church is built over a mound that some people believe is the historic Golgotha—where Jesus was crucified. The floor in that chapel is made up of tiny marble stones, and each stone can be identified as belonging to a specific group: Greek Orthodox, Coptic, Armenian, Syrian, or Roman Catholic. A priest who polishes a stone which does not belong to his own group may be in serious trouble!

Members of each of the groups have been known to throw stones at one another and to switch the locks during the night so others cannot get into the church. Sometimes the combat is limited to verbal exchanges. According to a *Wall Street Journal* article, highly edu-

cated clergy—who claim to worship the same Messiah—have been fussing with each other for years about their relative portions of a pillar supporting the roof.

On Easter Day, times for services are calculated so precisely that a twenty-one-page booklet is published to inform worshipers *who* may pray, *when* they may do so, and *where* this will occur. But not even this level of cooperation is always achieved. Repairs on the church, which was built during the time of the Crusades, are a serious problem. The groups are unable to agree on how to maintain and restore the church. If one group goes ahead and whitewashes the walls or repairs damaged floors, zealots from the other group may tear up the repairs and even retaliate by destroying some other part of the church identified with the sect that initiated repairs.

Similar conflicts exist in other holy sites. In the Church of the Nativity in Bethlehem, Greek and Armenian monks fought with fists and brooms at Christmas time a few years ago. The fight broke out over who would dust a cornice. Hatred between the various groups of Christian devotees in the Holy Land is sometimes intense, despite the teachings of their master. Forget the admonition to love thine *enemies*; these folks can't stand their religious kinsfolk. And the tenth commandment, which advises that "Thou shalt not covet," is obviously passé—or at least irrelevant when such important issues are at stake!

Source: Rosewicz, 1985.

success[8] (due to a supposed lack of a sufficient work ethic and an inadequate sense of delayed gratification), John Wilson (1978) argues persuasively that the economic differential between Protestants and Catholics is due to discrimination against Catholics. In short, Protestants are an interest group that uses a position of power and influence to ensure an economic advantage.

Outgroup hostility varies in large measure with the extent to which lines of religious affiliation are coextensive with ethnic and class lines. When ethnic ties and economic interests act to create social solidarity, religious differences may serve as one more symbol of differentiation. In fact, apparent religious conflicts may mask other underlying causes of intergroup conflict. The armed combat between Protestants and Catholics in Philadelphia in 1844 was an example of such conflict (Shannon 1963: 43). Similarly, the conflict in Northern Ireland cannot be understood without reference to ethnic and class issues as well as religious ones (McGuire 1981: 166–79).

American society is increasingly characterized by many cross pressures and countervailing forces. Persons may have group loyalties, friendships, and business partnerships that involve alliances with members of other religious groups, social classes, and ethnic groups. Insofar as this is true, the multiplicity of crossed alliances provides the basis for integration and social stability. These countervailing forces tend to weaken the tendency to view members of other faiths as enemies.

This is not to say that religious conflict is eliminated, however. For example, there were 1,730 reported incidents of anti-Semitism in the United States in 1992. These incidents included vandalism to Jewish institutions and property (such as arson and bombings of synagogues or Jewish homes and the painting of Nazi swastikas on synagogue walls) and harassments, threats, and assaults to Jewish individuals (beatings, bomb threats, harassing hate calls on the phone, etc.). These anti-Semitic actions included a doubling of such incidents on college campuses since 1988. (AntiDefamation League of B'nai B'rith 1992). The late 1980s and early 1990s has also seen the rise in the United States of hate groups such as the neo-Nazi gang, "the Skinheads." Christians, especially conservative Protestants, continue to blame Jews for the death of Jesus, and they justify hostile and illegal acts on this ground.

In the late 1970s, there were also incidents of youths attacking Amish buggies, and at least one person was killed—an Amish infant whose skull was crushed by a rock. However, interreligious conflict is less severe in those settings where religious, ethnic, and class lines are not coextensive and where countervailing forces can afford structural integration to the society.[9]

Religion may prove divisive in another instance, that is, recognition of what constitutes proper authority. The central value system of a religion may come into conflict with the secular legal system. In this case, persons must choose which set of values and norms they will respect. Often this boils down to the issue of which value system is authoritative or which leader (religious or political) is attributed with proper authority. In the late 1960s and early 1970s, a number of religiously

---

[8]A disproportionate percentage of the very highest paying and most prestigious jobs are still held by Protestants. But differentials in mean income between Protestants and Catholics are closing rapidly (Greeley 1981; Roof 1979). Table 10.1 provides specific data on the mean income of the members of various denominations.

[9]Note that in this circumstance it is economic interests that provide social integration and harmony. This, of course, contradicts the claim of some functionalists that social consensus regarding common values is necessary for social integration.

motivated individuals violated federal laws in protest of the Vietnam War. For example, two Roman Catholic priests, Daniel and Phillip Berrigan, broke into draft board offices and poured blood on selective service files. They maintained that their Christian conscience would not permit them to remain idle while young men were being drafted for war. Likewise in the 1980s, evangelical Christians were bombing and sabotaging abortion clinics, despite the illegality of the act in the civil law. In these and

other such cases, a person's theological understanding may generate norms that differ from those the civil laws uphold. (See Box 3.4.)

The Amish regulation that their children must not go to school beyond the eighth grade provides another example. When this norm conflicted with state law compelling all children to stay in school until graduation or age 16, some Amish parents in the 1950s and 1960s chose to go to jail rather than obey the law. In 1972, the Supreme Court settled the

The most extreme expression of antipathy against a religious group occurred in the 1940s, when an estimated 6 million Jews were gassed by the Nazi government in Germany. The stated goal of Hitler was to exterminate all Jews. This scene is from the concentration camp at Dachau. (UPI/Bettmann newsphoto.)

issue in *Wisconsin v. Yoder,* ruling that a state is in violation of the First and Fourteenth Amendments to the Constitution if it forces the Amish to send their children to high school (Hostetler 1980: 255–64).

The Mormons also encountered intense conflict with the federal government in the nineteenth century. In this case, the issue was over which authority, the church or the state, would decide how many wives a man may have. The Supreme Court ruled against the Mormons, and later church leaders revised their doctrine in conformity with federal law. However, conflict between the Mormon church and the government had nearly escalated to a small-scale civil war.

In each of these cases, religious norms have conflicted with secular law. The result has been considerable disruption of social harmony and unity. Whether the disruption was good or bad is not our concern here; the point is that religious loyalties sometimes result in discord and conflict in the larger society. Religiously motivated people often march to the beat of a different drummer. Religion, then, may contribute to either consensus or dissension.

Conflict as a Source of Integration

While religious conflict may bring disruption to the larger society, it may also be a source of internal unity for the religious group. Some groups seem to cultivate conflict with the out-group because conflict is functional to the group's internal solidarity. As we will see in chapter 5, groups with high boundaries usually

---

▶ **BOX 3.4**

Conflict between Religious Orientation and Secular Authorities

In September of 1984, Columbia City, Indiana, Circuit Judge Edward J. Myers sentenced a fundamentalist couple to five years in prison for letting their baby die without medical care. Explaining the rationale behind his decision, the judge said his court would "not tolerate child abuse or human sacrifice in the name of religion."

The parents, Gary and Margaret Hall, are members of the Faith Assembly, a religious sect that practices faith healing and rejects traditional medical treatment. Their twenty-six-day-old son, Joel David, died on February 16, 1984, from pneumonia. Medical experts testified that a few dollars worth of medicine could probably have saved the child's life. The Halls were convicted of reckless homicide and child neglect for denying medical care to the baby. The Halls argued that Jesus was their doctor, and acceptance of medication would show a lack of faith in Jesus. The judge told the Halls that their behavior was outside the accepted norms of society of moral and legal behavior.

Mrs. Hall was pregnant with the couple's fourth child at the time of the trial, and the judge indicated a willingness to suspend the prison term for her. But when she was asked whether she would accept medical treatment in the future, the twenty-seven-year-old mother replied, "On the basis of my convictions and fear of God Almighty, I cannot provide medical care for myself or my baby."

The county prosecutor asked the welfare department to take custody of the couple's three-year-old daughter and nearly two-year-old son while the couple was in jail.

sustain stronger member commitment and retention than do those with low boundaries. Some Amish groups shun their deviant members, especially those who marry outside the group or who adopt the lifestyle of the outside. The shunning, or *meidung,* involves a refusal to interact with persons so labeled. In some cases, Amish parents whose child marries outside the group have considered the child to be dead, have refused to speak the child's name, and have refused to acknowledge the child's presence when in the same room. The interesting point sociologically is that those groups that are very strict about practicing *meidung* have greater retention of members than do more liberal groups (Hostetler 1980).

Conflict produces internal cohesion for several reasons. First, repression and hostility by outsiders tend to create a feeling of common plight and common destiny. The more external animosity neighbors direct toward the Amish, the more inner unity is normally created within Amish communities. Second, a common rejection of something helps articulate one's own beliefs. Actually, it is usually easier for a group to agree in the rejection of something than it is to formulate a constructive statement about what its members do believe. A shared disgust at the actions of a deviant member may provide unity for the conformists (Erikson 1966). Likewise, rejection of worldliness or of some other specific group (e.g., satanic cults) may be a significant source of group harmony. For this reason, social conflict and social integration must not be seen as opposites but as different sides of the same coin. One can see the same phenomenon at work at the national level. When the United States was at war with Iraq over Saddam Hussein's invasion of Kuwait, the sense of patriotism in both countries was greatly strengthened. Conflict at one level often creates integration and unity at another. Moreover, the most threatening conflict occurs within the context of a meaningful or important relationship with others. When conflict occurs, it is within a larger system of interrelatedness. Social harmony and social conflict must be understood together (Coser 1954, 1967).

Conflict as a Pervasive Element within Religious Groups

Conflicts exist not only between religious groups but also within each group. Many times these internal processes can be analyzed as part of a struggle for power, privilege, and prestige. In other words, social behavior within the group is often a result of individuals protecting their self-interests.

For example, men have dominated the leadership roles in most denominations. In Orthodox Jewish groups, only male members are counted as part of the necessary quorum for prayer meetings. Until recently, most Protestant congregations excluded women from the ordained ministry or even from lay positions of leadership (such as offices of deacon or elder in Congregational or Presbyterian churches). Some conflict theorists have viewed these practices as evidence that men are an interest group—whose members cling tenaciously to their positions of authority and power (see discussion in chapter 13). Other examples can be cited of groups within a denomination perceiving themselves as "we" and others in the denomination as "they." The regulation in white churches that specified that black Christians must worship in the balcony (and not on the main floor) led to blacks forming their own independent churches (see chapter 11).

There are other intrachurch conflicts as well, such as that between clergy and laity (especially when the clergy get involved in civil rights or antiwar movements) and that between theological liberals and conservatives. (These conflicts will be explored in chapters 4 and 14.) Peter Berger (1981) suggests that clergy-laity and modernist-conservative conflicts are essentially part of a larger class conflict. The conflict is between two elites in American society that are struggling for power, privilege, and prestige. One is the business elite—a class of people managing industrial production and manipulating business enterprise. This group is more attuned to conservative theology, as is evidenced in the conservatism of most laity. Berger claims that conservative theology tends to justify the self-interests of the business elite. The "new elite" are those who manipulate symbols and words and who manage the production of ideas. This group includes intellectuals, educators, members of the helping professions, media people, and various social planners and bureaucrats.[10] Highly educated clergy of the mainline denominations are also part of this group, which advocates federal support of education, social welfare, minority rights, and environmental protection. This new class is highly represented in government-supported work, and its members argue for increased business regulation. Hence, this new elite really seeks its own self-interests. Berger insists that proclamations by the National Council of Churches normally reflect the current interests of this new class. Clergy and modernists are much more likely to support the National Council than are the laity in general and conservatives in particular. Producers of ideas and producers of material objects are viewed as two diverse social classes in a postindustrial society. The conflict between such groups as the New Christian Right and the National Council of Churches is interpreted as part of a deeper struggle for access to power and privilege.

Even the conflict over creationism versus science can be viewed as being, in part, a conflict of self-interests. Christians who are well educated, whose professions are related to scientific investigation, or whose business depends on scientific advances tend to be the ones who dismiss creationism and claim that theology should be reformulated to be consistent with science. In other words, theological modernism can be self-serving. On the other hand, biblical literalism is adhered to largely by the lower- and working-class people—folks whose jobs are sometimes threatened by technological innovations. Furthermore, working-class Americans may be rankled by a perception that many of the persons who occupy high-paying and high-prestige positions—physicians and scientists—are foreign-born. Antiscientific views may be interpreted—through a conflict theory analysis—as veiled attacks on those who threaten the jobs and prestige of lower-class Protestants. Although such an analysis certainly does not tell the whole story, it does raise some interesting questions about the extent to which our behavior—including religious behavior and beliefs—is influenced by our self-interests.

Readers should be cautioned that because a particular position can be shown to be self-serving, it does not follow that the position is fraudulent. The analysis here does not seek to prove or disprove a position but attempts only to show that people are inclined to believe something if it also fosters their own self-interests. This is the contribution of conflict theory to the sociology of thought (referred to by sociologists as the sociology of knowledge).

Readers may find it fruitful to reflect on their own assumptions about the role of self-interests in shaping beliefs.

Conflict as a Source of Change

Conflict is often a source of change, and as we have seen from our earlier discussion of the

---

[10]Berger defends his position that this is a new class: "If a class is defined by a particular relation to the means of production (as Marx, for one, proposed) then indeed there is a new class here" (1981: 197).

prophetic role of religion, change may be good for the society. Clearly, religion is capable of contributing to conflict and to social change. One aspect of religion that most interested Weber was the role of the charismatic leader. He found charisma to be fundamentally contrary to social stability and a major source of change. As a person who is attributed with divine authority, the charismatic religious leader is able to challenge social mores where there is otherwise little room for social and political dissent. (This will be treated further in chapter 7.)

In the eyes of those who defend the status quo, such conflict is disruptive and therefore dysfunctional. Such conflict is indeed disruptive, but disruption is not necessarily dysfunctional for everyone. Religiously motivated abolitionism was assessed as dysfunctional by slave owners. In terms of the interests of blacks and in terms of the structure of contemporary post-industrial society, abolitionism is today viewed as having been a beneficial disruption of the status quo. Religion is capable of disruption because religious values sometimes define social relationships differently from the way the encompassing culture does. If a religious ideology maintains that all people are equal before God and if the society is rigidly stratified, a dissonance may be created for that small group that takes the religious ideology seriously. Christian churches in South Africa are among the most active opponents of that country's racist policies. And as we shall see in chapter 11, the African American church in America has often served as a buffer for blacks and has reaffirmed their sense of innate worth, despite the negative images in the larger white culture. By affirming the innate personal worth of African Americans, the church provided a foundation for many of these Americans to assert their rights and to insist on social change. Whether the contribution is direct or indirect, religion can contrib-

ute to the modification of the larger society, for it can provide an alternative world view and an alternative set of values.

On the other hand, conflict and change in the society can also be a major source of *religious* change. Rapid social change is one factor in the rise of new religious movements. Societies that are stable and highly integrated are not conducive to the emergence and expansion of religious cults, but loosely integrated, changing societies do experience such phenomena with great frequency (Stark and Roberts 1982). Social change may also mean a change in one's socioeconomic standing, and such changes are often accompanied by modifications in theology and world view. As we will see in chapter 11, declines in the socioeconomic standing of a group can significantly affect its theodicy (explanation of the meaning of suffering), and so can a rise in socioeconomic fortunes.

The broad sweep of social change in the direction of secularization has also brought modifications in religion. The advent of rational, scientific, empirically oriented culture has caused changes in the world views of many people. Scientific interpretations of such issues as the origins of humanity have induced liberal theologians to reformulate religious ideas so that they are compatible with scientific ones. This, of course, has involved conflicts between modernists and conservatives within religious bodies. Hence, the growth of science as a major institution in the modern world has led to changes and conflicts within religious groups.

Other cultural changes and social conflicts have also brought shifts in religious behavior. Some analysts have maintained that changes in sex roles in postmedieval Europe—including conflict between men and women over jobs—resulted in a rise of belief in witches and the development of institutionally sanctioned witch-hunts by the Christian churches (discussed in chapter 13). As will be amply illustrated throughout this text, changes and conflicts in the larger society often result in changes and conflicts within religious bodies.

One of the advantages of conflict theory is that it tends to focus attention on issues of change. Religious conflicts can contribute to social change, and social conflicts can cause religious change. Those changes may create social dissension and disruption, but depending on the nature and location of the conflict (external versus internal) they are also capable of contributing to the integration and cohesion of a group.

Conflict theory's tendency to use historical analysis lends it another strength. In so doing, it offers an important corrective to more static theories that ignore the *causes* of a particular social pattern by focusing only on current functions.

Most important, perhaps, conflict theory illuminates the many ways in which self-interests affect perceptions and behavior—including religious ideas and (supposedly) religiously motivated behavior.

Problems with Conflict Analysis

Although conflict theory offers important insights and correctives to functional analysis, it is not without its problems. If functional theory often errs in overemphasizing consensus and harmony, conflict theorists often see only social stress, power plays, and disharmony. Although conflict theory is helpful in illuminating the causes of change, it is less complete in explaining social cohesion and cooperation.

Perhaps the most important criticism of conflict theory—especially by scholars within a religious tradition—is its tendency to view all behavior as motivated by self-interest. For those who believe that religious commitment may call a person to genuine unselfish action, the appeal to self-interests as the ultimate motivator of all behavior is unsatisfactory. The

response among conflict theorists is that appeals to altruistic motives are simply ways of mystifying or hiding the true motives. However, the willingness of deeply religious persons to sacrifice even their lives for others or for their faith raises questions about this unicausal interpretation. Persons may be influenced by a wide range of motives. Conflict theory correctly points out that self-interests can be pervasive and can influence a wide range of behavior and attitudes. However, when it insists that *all* behavior is determined by self-interests, conflict theory commits the error of reductionism.

Another problem with this emphasis on self-interests is that interests are often interpreted only in economic terms. Although economic self-interests are more encompassing than we once realized, other sorts of self-interests can also profoundly affect behavior. For example, a calculation of one's spiritual self-interests—such as a desire to attain a heavenly afterlife and avoid hell—could cause persons to behave in ways that are contrary to their economic self-interests. Religious moods and motivations are, to quote Geertz, "powerful, pervasive, and long-lasting." They are capable of influencing behavior in ways that are insensitive to economic consequences. Conflict theory does not normally take into account such forces.

Conflict theory stresses conflict and dissension, and the role of self-interests in shaping behavior. It de-emphasizes the harmony, consensus, and interrelatedness that functionalists point to. There is no shortage of data on conflict within religious groups, but given all of the conflict that does exist, most groups cohere surprisingly well.

Toward Synthesis: An Open Systems Model

Some sociologists believe that no synthesis of the structural functional and conflict perspectives is possible. And it is true that they offer very different perspectives on society and on human behavior. But one approach to a unified position is promising. That approach is called open systems theory. Variations of systems theory have been used to understand units as small as nuclear families and processes as large as the "world system" of international economic interdependence (Wallerstein 1974, 1984; Shannon 1989). Interestingly, systems theory—especially world systems theory—is often claimed to be an outgrowth of conflict theory, but the systems approach is equally asserted by structural functionalists to be an extension of their favored perspective. Open systems theory is not a panacea; it does not solve all of the problems or discrepancies between the two dominant macro perspectives, but it does offer some overview of how an entire system may be characterized simultaneously by interdependence and by conflicts of interests.

Contemporary systems models stress the idea that societies are both stable and dynamic, depending on whether one focuses on structure or on processes. **Structure** refers to the parts of a society that are resistant to change. The structure can be diagrammed on an organizational chart: statuses, roles, departments, organizational units each in relationship to one another. Religious denominations have stable sources of income, officers who fill certain roles and responsibilities, and clergy who are responsible to bishops or district superintendents. Local churches have commissions and committees that make decisions regarding certain parts of the life of that church: worship, religious education, fund-raising, care of the building, and so forth. These offices or interrelated positions may evolve over a period of time, but generally they remain with similar job descriptions and a consistent set of responsibilities. This is structure.

On the other hand, churches are also characterized by action; nothing is ever fixed or final. This is the **process** dimension of the system. The members of committees change, the ministers retire or move to new churches and are replaced in the old ones, the values and ideas of the church are transformed in light of national events (such as a recession or the AIDS epidemic), international crises (such as a war in which some members are called to serve and others feel compelled to oppose), or local incidents (such as a racial conflict to which some members of the congregation want to respond). Such happenings may change the value orientations of members, bring a shift in perceived interests of various groups, or impel a transfer in the allocation of resources within the organization. While it is true that organizations are somewhat stable, it is equally true that they are always becoming something new as they interact with the larger environment.

Structure and process are both necessary parts of any social unit; they cannot be separated. Structure provides the context for action; but action brings the structure to life. Without process, an organization would wither and die; without structure, action would be disorganized and aimless (Ballantine 1993; Olsen 1978).

Figure 3.2 illustrates one dimension of the systems perspective on how organizations work.[11] Any organization or institution exists within a field of forces, which it tries to influence and which try to influence it. The model provided here is simplified for our understanding, but it is important to recognize that the "organization" in this diagram might be a nation, a national institution (such as a denomination), a local organization (e.g., a church), a unit within a church (e.g., the religious education committee of the church),

---

[11]This model is an adaptation from Ludwig Von Bertalanfly's (1962) general systems theory and is effectively applied to educational systems by Jeanne H. Ballantine (1993).

or a subsystem (e.g., an adult Sunday School class).

One of the first points that we must comprehend is that all organizations have outputs. For schools, the outputs are graduates, new ideas, new skills and ways of doing things, and developing cultural values and outlooks. For religious organizations, the **outputs** or "products" that influence the larger culture include the following: values, attitudes, benevolence or "mission" programs, published instructional materials, broadcast programming, movements to influence the larger society (e.g., peace organizations, anti-abortion groups, and movements to have "creation science" taught in the science curriculum of the public schools). Nearly all organizations want to influence, at least in some marginal way, the larger social environment in which they exist. Their outputs are the means through which they do this. Even if influencing the larger culture is not an explicit goal, religious groups

are bound to have some impact on the secular society around them as these groups struggle for resources necessary for survival. Also, religious groups typically feel an obligation to engage in benevolent acts, or what they interpret as benevolent acts, for those "less fortunate." This requires outputs beyond the boundaries of their own group.

As the diagram suggests, outputs of any organization will enter and influence the environment, that is, the dominant culture or larger society. The extent of influence varies with the goals and purposes of the group and with the amount of power the group wields. Regardless of the intent of the religious groups themselves, segments of the larger society are being influenced by the religious organization and may even be competing with it for resources (including the time, energy, and monetary donations of members) and for ability to shape central values and beliefs of the culture. Therefore, those in the social environment want to

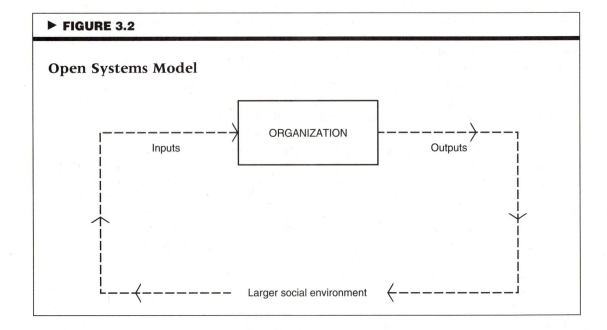

▶ **FIGURE 3.2**

Open Systems Model

influence the religion itself. So the final dimension of the process is **inputs** into the organization: new members, secular values and beliefs (including nationalistic pride, scientific theories, and definitions of morality), attempts by governments to legislate religious groups (such as financial disclosure requirements to prevent fraud), new ideas (e.g., use of the latest business principles to run a church), and even new technologies (including computerization of mailing lists and sophisticated technology to record religious services).

The more the organization is an **open system,** the freer is the flow of both information and resources to and from the surrounding society. In theory a totally open system would have a completely open interaction with the larger society. In reality, in all environments there are some people who will resist influence from the organization because their own interests are threatened. Further, all systems like to control the input from the community. In fact, in order to develop in a controlled manner any organization must maintain an appropriate ratio of input and output. Internal needs of the organization demand some filtering of the flow of information (Olsen 1978).

At the other end of the spectrum, some groups are **closed systems,** organizations that try to nearly exclude outside influence and whose desire to shape the larger culture is minimal. It is as if the group built an enormous barricade around the organization. That barricade is what sociologists call a social boundary. Especially important for some groups is the building of a wall preventing inputs, often to protect the self-interests of the organization. We will see examples of this resistance to input from the surrounding society later on in this book. No organization, however, is totally closed, for all must live in an interdependent relationship with the environment. For effective adaptation to new circumstances, any organization must have some

flow of information into the organization from the environment, but the important point here is that each group is selective about—or at least *tries* to control—what penetrates the organization. Religious liberals and religious conservatives each try to filter the inputs (with varying degrees of success), but both allow inputs of one kind or another.

No one diagram can fully explain all of the complexities of the systems approach. Figures 3.3 and 3.4 illuminate another dimension of the social systems view of society. As Marvin Olsen (1978: 99) puts it, "Organizations overlap and interlock with each other, forming a gigantic social web, the totality of which is human social life." Any organization or system is made up of a number of interdependent parts. A family is made up of the various members who are linked together with a variety of bonds and obligations. Imagine that in Figure 3.3, each dot represents a member of your family and the lines between them represent the bonds of love and concern. If one person is undergoing some stress (e.g., chemical dependency, unemployment or job stress, or poor health), the rest of the family might well support that individual by taking up some of his or her roles, by offering emotional support, and by helping in other ways. This stressor on one person might then cause stressors on other family members as they try to help out and "make things work" during this time of special tension.

Religious groups are also characterized by interdependent roles and statuses, each dependent upon the other for effective functioning. For the religious education committee to do its job, the stewardship committee must solicit enough money from the congregation to meet the budget. But the stewardship committee may not be able to be successful if the worship committee and the minister do not function effectively and everyone finds worship unsatisfying and empty.

But systems are not just dependent upon each other; each system is related to other systems. The family is linked to and dependent upon many other institutions: health care, the workplace, schools, the religious community, the criminal justice system, the banking system, and so forth. If any one of those systems is not functioning properly, the family experiences pulls and tugs on their own life. If the economy is in recession and the workplace lays off family members, or if the agents of law enforcement are harassing members of your ethnic group, or if your local church is wracked with angry conflict and division, the family will likely feel the stress. Likewise, if families are not socializing their children with values consistent with those of the church or are not functioning well at all, or if large numbers of the congregation are out of work and unable to pay their pledges because of local industry closings, the church will feel the stress.

All of these institutions and more comprise an interdependent system that make up the nation. But our nation is only one system that is interrelated to many others: Great Britain, Canada, Iraq, Germany, Russian, Somalia, Pakistan, Israel, El Salvador, and so forth. If we have trade relations or diplomatic concerns with that system (which we most assuredly do), then a malfunction in that country or that region of the world may cause stresses on our nation. If war is declared in the Persian Gulf, stresses are generated on the resources of our country, and they impact families (whose members may be called into combat duty), the economy, the churches (which may have some members advocating peace and others wanting the church to support the war effort), and so forth. Likewise, an economic recession in Europe or Japan can influence trade and therefore negatively impact certain businesses in this country; a destruction of rain forests can have devastating effects on the health care community as certain medicines become more scarce.

Some institutions would be influenced directly and profoundly by stresses in the global

---

▶ **FIGURE 3.3**

Systems Composed of Subsystems

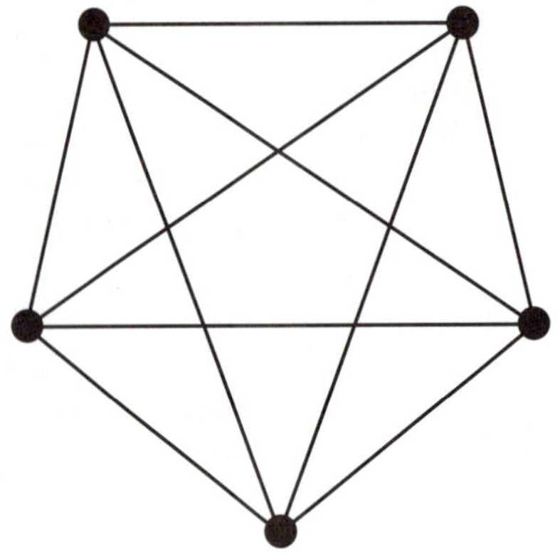

system; others would experience only indirect impact. But the important point is that social systems are interrelated in a variety of ways; this brief discussion greatly oversimplifies the complexity of the ties, but our purpose here is to illustrate the point that social systems are layered. Subsystems exist within subsystems, within subsystems. Sometimes subsystems are parts of two or more overlapping macrosystems (Olsen 1978). One example would be a military chaplaincy in which the chaplain is both an officer in the military (and answerable to that hierarchy) and an ordained member of a specific denomination (and responsible to a bishop and/or to denominational policies and values).

▶ **FIGURE 3.4**

The Interdependence of Social Systems

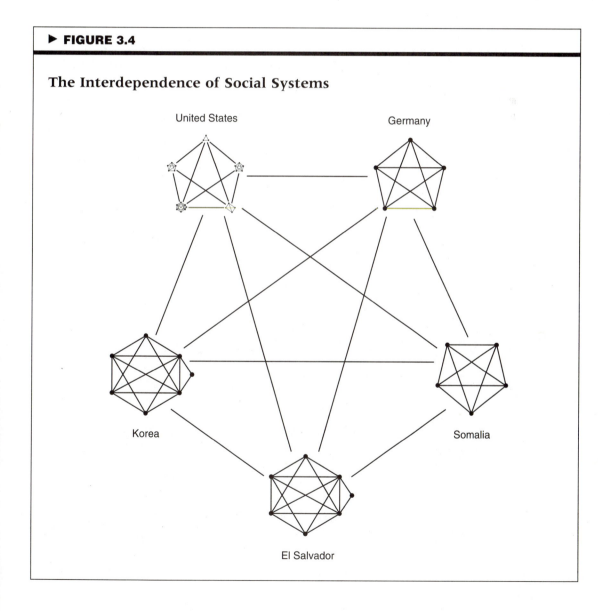

Similar to structural-functional theory, systems models stress the interrelatedness of society. But unlike functional approaches, there is no assumption of harmony and consensus within the system. Indeed, systems often experience conflict and tension as various units pursue their own self-interests. Further, those with power in the larger society are often able to ensure that various institutions (such as religion) serve and legitimate their own positions of privilege. Unlike functional theories, systems models view societies as dynamic and changing. While there may be some forces pushing toward coherence and stability, the model is anything but stagnant. The ties between units may be stressful rather than supportive, and that stress is itself not necessarily viewed as negative. Stress may bring change and enhance the health of the organization in the long run. But at any given period of history, a system may indeed be characterized by fairly high levels of consensus and relative stability. Rather than assuming either harmony or discord, systems models leave that question open to investigation for the specific system and period of history.

One word of caution regarding systems models is in order. Some reaction against general systems theory has occurred because some theoreticians have tried to propose a single theoretical model to apply to a wide range of phenomena, including biological, psychological, cultural, and social systems. While certain common ideas may be applicable across disciplines, my assumption here is that each system being studied needs to recognize variation and uniqueness of that particular type of system. Further, while a systems model can inform our thinking, an overarching model is no substitute for empirical research that investigates the specific relationships within a given social system (Olsen 1978).

Summary

Irrespective of the ultimate truth or fiction of a religious ideology, religion has certain kinds of social effects or consequences. These consequences are what most interest sociologists. Functional theorists tend to focus on the beneficial role religion plays. For example, at an *individual* level, religion may offer a sense of meaning in life, sacralize and give certainty to a system of moral values, and establish a sense of belonging. Religion thereby affects an individual's sense of identity. Furthermore, religion can also serve *societal* functions. By providing a sense of values and beliefs around which a social consensus is formed, religion may contribute to social coherence and harmony. This is especially true for societies in which there is only one religious tradition.

On the other hand, religion is sometimes characterized by conflict—experiencing *internal* discord and/or contributing to conflict in the *larger* society. Dissension itself may be either beneficial or disruptive, healthy or unhealthy. Conflict theorists tend to focus on dissension, disruption, and change. Conflict theorists also tend to emphasize the role of self-interests in human behavior, including supposedly religious behavior.

Conflict and functional theories need not be mutually exclusive. They each offer important insights, and each have blind spots in their views of society. We will be incorporating insights and analysis from both perspectives in this book. No analysis that relies on only one perspective can offer a rounded understanding of the relationship between religion and society.

The central fact to remember is that the balances of harmony versus dissonance and of value consensus versus interest-group coercion will vary from one society to another.

Furthermore, the amount of integration or conflict within religious groups varies significantly. (Baptists have experienced more schisms and have generated far more sectarian groups than have Episcopalians.) Moreover, it is not just the people in the group who may be in harmony or discord. Within any religious group, the various elements of religion themselves may or may not be well integrated.

The systems model of social organization attempts to integrate many of the key ideas of both structural-functional and conflict theory. Systems approaches stress the fact that structures of society tend to be rather integrated and stable, while processes of societies are dynamic and action-oriented. Systems are viewed as composed of subsystems, which are composed of subsystems, with the largest systems being global in nature. This view of organizations stresses the interrelatedness of social units, but it does not presume harmony within the system and does not predict that any one element of the system is indispensable. Religion is viewed from this approach as a complex system, linked to other elements of society in intricate ways and often protecting its own self-interests in relationship to the larger society. Open systems theory will be used to understand the dynamics of religion throughout this book.

In the next chapter we will turn to microsociological analysis, exploring integrity and dissonance among such elements as belief, ritual, symbol, and world view.

CHAPTER FOUR

Religious Experience, Symbol Systems, and World Views: Integrity and Dissonance in Religion

Having investigated the ways in which religion operates in society and in individuals' lives, it is appropriate next to investigate the internal interrelationships of religion's elements. Nonrational religious experience, myths, rituals, symbol systems, world views, and ethos are all part of this complex phenomenon we call religion. Scholars are interested in how each of these facets relates to the others and which one may be primary. The fact is that conflicts between laity and some of the highly trained clergy in the interpretation of myths, rituals, and symbols sometimes occur. The lack of agreement about the meaning of central symbols or myths may disrupt the group.

In turning from the relationship of religion to the larger society toward the internal dynamics of religion, we also move from macroanalysis to microanalysis. Thus, we begin this chapter by exploring another major theoretical paradigm in sociology: *symbolic interactionism.* The sociology of religion is vitally interested in the role of religious symbolism, so this field is especially well suited to application and testing of symbolic interaction theory.

Symbolic Interaction and the Social Construction of Reality

Symbolic interaction theory is based on the view that human beings have a profound mutual impact upon each other. People act toward things on the basis of the meanings that the things have for them. The meanings are derived by individuals as they interact with others. Hence, humans are above all symbol creating and symbol modifying creatures, for **symbols** are those acts or objects that represent something else and therefore have meaning beyond their own fleeting existence. For the symbolic interactionist, symbols are the key to understanding human life, for we go about the task of fitting our actions together because of shared perceptions or shared meanings. Meaning is not inherent in events, but is created by individuals and communicated among them. Through internal manipulation of symbols and interpretation of meaning, we *define situations*—determining what is going on and what type of behavior is appropriate for that situation.

When humans are in ambiguous situations, where the definitions of what is happening are unclear and the expected norms of behavior are clouded, they tend to look to others for a definition of the situation. When people around us behave as if something is normal or true, we often accept that interpretation. This is, as we will see, highly relevant to the study of religion, since understanding the mysteries of life and the meaning of death and suffering are frought with ambiguity. Because of this emphasis on the human tendency to look to others for reassurance of what is "real" or what is happening, this interactionist perspective is sometimes called "social constructionist theory."

When persons create symbols, such as a flag or a new greeting ("give me five"), the process is called *externalization*. Once externalized, symbols come to be *objectified*—they have an existence and importance which is independent of the original creator (Berger and Luckmann 1966). They may long outlive the symbol-maker. Who was it that designed the "Star of David" and gave it meaning? Who determined that an eagle should symbolize the United States? Most people don't know—but they do know what the symbol stands for. They do share with others the meaning of this object. In fact they may feel intense loyalty to the symbol. An entire history of a people may be recalled and a set of values rekindled when the symbol is displayed. This is because other people have *internalized* the objectified symbol. By this process, symbols are created, transmitted, and modified. It is not just the symbol that is transmitted, however. It is also the definition of reality, the concept of what is normal or abnormal, acceptable or unacceptable, true or false (Berger and Luckmann 1966).

Having briefly introduced the basic elements of symbolic interaction theory, let us begin a micro treatment by exploring the roles of religious experience, myths, rituals, and symbol systems and investigating the relation-

ships among them. We also discuss the way in which these specific manifestations of religion are related to the more intangible elements of world view and ethos. Then we turn to an

This Greek Orthodox painting, which appears in the Stavronkita Monastery, is typical of the icons throughout Greece. All Orthodox icons show a rather unusual hand configuration with the thumb and the ring finger crossed, the little finger and the pointer finger pointed almost straight up in the air and the middle finger slightly bent. When I asked a priest about it, I was told that this is the symbol of Christianity. I was told with considerable impatience—as if *anyone* who was Christian would most certainly know that. It's interesting that all icons of Jesus depict his hand in this posture. At this point, no one knows who created this symbol, but it is so objectified and internalized in the Orthodox church that it is inconceivable to Greeks that this symbol of Christ has not always existed. Christ is even thought to have used it as an infant, always with the right hand and often with both hands.

investigation of the conflict between folk and official versions of a religion.

Experience of the Holy

Many social scientists define religion in terms of the sacred-profane distinction. For these scholars, the essence of religion has to do with a unique and extraordinary experience—an experience that has a sacred dimension and is unlike everyday life. According to some scholars, all religious phenomena evolves out of this seminal experience—the experience of the holy (James 1958; Otto 1923; O'Dea 1966). Such an experience is often called *nonrational,* for it is neither rational nor irrational. These **nonrational experiences** are described by those who have them as being outside the usual categories of logical, systematic reasoning. They are not illogical; they are simply nonlogical. These experiences seem to defy the normal categories of language. Whether a nonrational experience is the essence of all religious behavior may be debatable; that such mystical experience is one important aspect of the complex phenomenon we call religion is not. It is appropriate, then, to focus initially on the experience of the holy.

Emile Durkheim in 1915 was one of the early scholars to discuss characteristics of the sacred. Using a broad description of religious experience that he believed would be applicable in all cultures, Durkheim (1965) defined the sacred realm as one that both attracts and repels individuals. The sacred is not only attractive but also repugnant; it is capable not only of being helpful but also of being dangerous. This ambiguity rests in part in the attribution of great power to the sacred; because of the overwhelming power that it possesses, it holds the potential for being either beneficial or harmful. Nevertheless, the attraction of the sacred is not based primarily on utilitarian considerations. The sacred is conceived as a *nonempirical force* that is considered intrinsically valuable. As such, it places a moral obligation on the worshiper and imposes certain ethical imperatives.

Durkheim was fascinated by the importance his nonindustrial informants attached to sacred taboos—rules that prohibit immoral or impure behavior. People do sometimes violate these rules, however, and in doing so they become unclean and unfit for the sacred realm. Durkheim also noted that mere participation in the secular world could cause one to become tainted. Ritual purification before reentering the presence of the sacred was necessary, and this often involved a rather elaborate process. For Durkheim this emphasized the fact that the sacred was radically different than the profane world. Certain places and times were set aside as special and as belonging to another dimension of reality.

Rudolf Otto explored the nature of the religious experience in his classic book *The Idea of the Holy* (1923). In that work, Otto insists that there is a tendency of people in Western culture to reduce the holy to rational concepts about God. By analogy to human life, the holy has been attributed with certain qualities that can be understood, debated, and defended in intellectual terms. Otto's contention is that this intellectual or rational focus is a confusion of the original idea of holiness. He believes that holiness originally had a much larger dimension, a dimension that cannot be entirely reduced to intellectual concepts. Hence, Otto attempts to describe the experience of the holy, rather than describing the holy itself. He insists that the experience of the holy is so unique that one can never fully understand his description unless one has experienced it. Although the experience of the holy is beyond rational or ethical conception, the experience seems universally to bring forth a "creative consciousness." A person is profoundly humbled as he or she senses an utter dependency and unworthiness before the holy (see Box 4.1). Rational and moral

▶ **BOX 4.1**

Personal Accounts of Religious Experiences

I remember the night, and almost the very spot on the hilltop, where my soul opened out, as it were, into the Infinite, and there was a rushing together of the two worlds, the inner and the outer. It was deep calling unto deep—the deep that my own struggle had opened up within being answered by the unfathomable deep without, reaching beyond the stars. I stood alone with Him who had made me, and all the beauty of the world, and love, and sorrow, and even temptation. I did not seek Him, but felt the perfect unison of my spirit with His. The ordinary sense of things around me faded. For the moment nothing but an ineffable joy and exaltation remained. It is impossible fully to describe the experience. It was like the effect of some great orchestra when all the separate notes have melted into one swelling harmony that leaves the listener conscious of nothing save that his soul is being wafted upwards, and almost bursting with its own emotion. The perfect stillness of the night was thrilled by a more solemn silence. The darkness held a presence that was all the more felt because it was not seen. I could not any more have doubted that *He* was there than that I was. Indeed, I felt myself to be, if possible, the less real of the two (1958: 66).

I have on a number of occasions felt that I had enjoyed a period of intimate communion with the divine. These meetings came unasked and unexpected, and seemed to consist merely in the temporary obliteration of the conventionalities which usually surround and cover my life. . . . Once it was when from the summit of a high mountain I looked over a gashed and corrugated landscape extending to a long convex of ocean that ascended to the horizon, and again from the same point when I could see nothing beneath me but a boundless expanse of white cloud, on the blown surface of which a few high peaks, including the one I was on, seemed plunging about as if they were dragging their anchors. What I felt on these occasions was a temporary loss of my own identity, accompanied by an illumination which revealed to me a deeper significance than I had been wont to attach to life. It was in this that I find my justification for saying that I have enjoyed communication with God. Of course the absence of such a being as this would be chaos. I cannot conceive of life without its presence (1958: 70).

In that time the consciousness of God's nearness came to me sometimes. I say God, to describe what is indescribable. A presence, I might say, yet that is too suggestive of personality, and the moments of which I speak did not hold the consciousness of a personality, but something in myself made me feel myself a part of something bigger than I, that was controlling. I felt myself one with the grass, the trees, birds, insects, everything in Nature. I exulted in the mere fact of existence, of being a part of it all—the drizzling rain, the shadows of the clouds, the tree-trunks, and so on. In the years following, such moments continued to come, but I wanted them constantly. I knew so well the satisfaction of losing self in a perception of supreme power and love, that I was unhappy because that perception was not constant (1958: 303).

Source: William James, *Varieties of Religious Experience.* New York: New American Library, 1958; originally published in 1902.

conceptions about religion come only much later, as an outgrowth of the experience itself.

Otto elaborates on the quality of this experience, which he calls the *mysterium tremendum et fascinosum*. He identifies five qualities of the *mysterium tremendum*. First, the individual is filled with a sense of awe and fear. The word *tremendum* itself expresses the tremor or terror that Otto feels is part of the experience. The story of Moses awed and frightened by the burning bush provides an example of feelings a religious experience generates. Second, one feels overwhelmed by the absolute unapproachability of the holy. Durkheim's concept of the sacred as a dangerous force is obviously shared by Otto. The ancient Hebrew prohibition against even mentioning the name of Yahweh because of his absolute power and unapproachability provides an example. One can also see elements of unapproachability in many high churches that allow only the clergy to enter the chancel area. Some Roman Catholic cathedrals and most Greek Orthodox Churches even have a screen that hides the altar from the congregation. To go behind the chancel without proper ritual purification would be to risk death. This leads us to the third characteristic: power, energy, or urgency. Otto claims that in describing the experience of the holy, people use such symbolic language as "vitality, passion, emotional temper, will, force, movement, excitement, activity, impetus." Clearly, the holy has tremendous power, which reinforces its unapproachability and awefulness. Fourth, the experience of *mysterium tremendum* causes an awareness of the "wholly otherness" of the holy. The mystery of the experience lies in its unfamiliar and non-empirical nature. The holy is utterly unlike the profane. Fifth, one feels a sense of fascination with and attraction to the holy. Although it is potentially terrifying, it also elicits a sense of wonder and a feeling of ultimate goodness. Hence, it commands a sense of ethical impera-

tive. According to Otto, this experience of *mysterium tremendum* is the universal foundation and source of all religious behavior. Thomas O'Dea has followed Otto's lead by suggesting that all other forms of religiosity are generated from this nonrational religious experience. We shall return to O'Dea's treatment in the chapter on secularization.

Otto's description of the essential religious experience is corroborated in most respects by other scholars who have studied mystical experience. However, there are many people who consider themselves devout believers who have never had one. The emphasis of many mainline denominational congregations is much more intellectual than Otto would suggest. As a theologian, Otto maintains that the experience of the *mysterium tremendum* ought to be at the heart of religion. Herein lies the problem. Otto has claimed to describe a universal pattern, but he has normative expectations that endorse a particular experience as "more religious" than others. Hence, he makes a value judgment about some persons being less religious because they have not experienced the holy as he describes it.

Some theologians emphasize the immanence (proximity, involvement in human life) of God rather than the transcendence (wholly otherness) of God. Are they less religious? They certainly don't think so. Or to use another example, one does not observe mystical experience as being central (or even common) among Unification Church members (Moonies). Is the Unification Church, therefore, not a religion?[1] By making a value judgment about what one ought to do to be religious, Otto has departed from purely empirical observation. Religiosity is multidimensional. The kind of

---

[1]The assumption here is that loyalty to a charismatic leader is a somewhat different experience than a first-hand mystical experience as described by Otto.

experience Otto describes is vital to religious life for many people, but it is not the only source of religious conviction.

Religious conviction is more than ideas. To influence lives in a fundamental way, religion must have an emotional component, something that makes the ideas or belief systems "seem uniquely realistic."[2] A nonrational experience often provides such an impetus to belief.

Andrew Greeley offers clarity to this discussion of the role of sacred experiences. In his analysis of "sacredness" and the extraordinary quality of religious experience, he grants that the sacred is usually removed from everyday existence. Yet, he writes, "not everything that is extraordinary is sacred." The important point is that the sacred is something that is treated with profound reverence and respect. Greeley capsulizes his argument with an important twist:

> [People have] a tendency to sacralize [their] ultimate systems of value. Even if one excludes the possibility of a transcendent or a supernatural, one nonetheless is very likely to treat one's system of ultimate explanation with a great deal of jealous reverence and respect and to be highly incensed when someone else calls the system of explanation to question or behaves contrary to it. It is precisely this tendency to sacralize one's ultimate concern that might well explain the many quasi-religious phenomena to be observed in organizations which officially proclaim their non- or even antireligiousness. The communist, for example, may vehemently deny the existence of a "totally other" and yet treat communism and its prophets, its dogmas, its code, and its ritual with as much respect as does the devout Christian approach [Christianity] (1972: 9).

Rather than citing an experience of the sacred as the source of all religious behavior, Greeley

suggests that whatever we value very highly, we tend to sacralize (to make sacred). Sacredness, then, may be the *result* of a valuing process rather than the primal *cause* of all other religious activity. Greeley does not suggest that experiences of the holy are always secondary; he merely points out that the relationship between values, beliefs, and the sacred may be more complex than Otto, Eliade, and O'Dea suggest.

Because not all forms of extraordinariness are religious, Greeley offers a clarification. There are two kinds of extraordinariness that traditionally have been called religious. One has to do with the need to make sense out of life, the need for a meaningful interpretation of events. The second has to do with the need for belonging, the need to feel a relatedness to other persons, to humanity, and to the universe. "Sacredness, then, relates to [humanity's] experience of the need for meaning and the need for belonging, as well as the fulfillment of these needs" (Greeley 1972: 16). The sacred experience, then, has appeal insofar as it can help persons make sense of the world and feel a sense of belonging. Greeley's approach reintroduces the rational element that Otto was so eager to de-emphasize.

Greeley's interpretation is also more consistent with a number of empirical studies than is Otto's. Otto had implied that it was difficult, if not impossible, to be truly religious unless one has had a profound experience of the *mysterium tremendum*. Yet Gordon Allport reported that in a study of college students who rated religious sentiment as significant in their lives, only 17 percent cited mystical experience as a major influence in their religiosity. After studying many variables affecting one's propensity to hold strong religious convictions, Allport concluded, "The lesson we learn . . . is that the psychological roots of religious sentiment . . . are very numerous" (1950: 44). He further insisted that there is "no single and unique

---

[2]The reader may recall this phrase from Clifford Geertz's definition of religion.

religious emotion, but rather a widely divergent set of experiences that may be focused upon a religious object" (1950: 5).

Several conclusions can be drawn regarding nonrational religious experiences. First, they vary greatly in intensity from one person to another. Some people have a "strange warming of the heart" while others have an ecstatic, orgiastic type of experience (Neitz and Spickard 1990). Second, nonrational experiences vary in frequency. For some, mystic experience becomes a goal in itself and may even take on the form of a full-time occupation. This attitude is particularly common among certain Eastern religions, especially in Buddhist monasteries in Asia and in Hare Krishna temples in the United States. But some Roman Catholic religious orders have established monasteries in which the pursuit of religious experience becomes the principal goal.

Third, they vary in context. For some people and in some religious traditions, intense nonrational experiences occur to individuals in isolation, as was the case for Plains Indian men who went off by themselves in search of a vision quest. For other people, profound nonrational experiences are primarily social, occuring in a charismatic prayer meeting or during a worship service (Neitz and Spickard 1990). In either case, social norms usually prescribe how to achieve such an experience, the value of such an experience, and what one "looks like" and how to interpret it when it does occur.

Fourth, they vary in content. The Eskimo shaman makes a spiritual journey to the bottom of the sea to visit Sedna and to appease her for violations of taboos (Barnouw 1982). The Lakota (Sioux) holy man experiences a visit by forty-eight horses that approach in groups of twelve from the four cardinal directions (Neihardt 1961). The Christian mystic[3]

may see the Holy Virgin, experience the love of Jesus, or hear the voice of God. The Buddhist mystic may experience "nonbeing" or "utter unity with the universe." The content, or at least the interpretation of the experience, is defined in culturally familiar terms.

Fifth, the people who value and expect a religious experience are those who report having had one. Abraham Maslow (1964) insists that probably everyone has had at least one nonrational "peak experience" but that some people do not value such experiences and therefore dismiss them as insignificant or bizarre or even forget them altogether. Other researchers (Glock and Stark 1965; Hood 1970; Davidson 1975; Wimberly et al. 1975; Straus 1979; Batson and Ventis 1982) insist that people who desire such experiences may cultivate behaviors and attitudes that make it likely that they will have them. This view suggests that social expectation helps cause such experiences. For example, Robert Wimberly and his colleagues found that many born-again commitments were not life-changing events but affirmations of existing values. Further, one's social context (a religious setting) can cause one to interpret a particular nonrational experience as religious or nonreligious. Experimental psychologists administered LSD to people in a supportive environment that included a number of religious symbols and stimuli. Ninety percent reported that it gave them a greater awareness of God, a Higher Power, or Ultimate Reality (Savage et al. 1963, reported in Batson and Ventis 1982). By contrast, a majority of persons given LSD in a context lacking religious stimuli did not interpret the experience in religious terms (Ditman et al. 1962). In any case, a positive

---

[3]Some writers reserve the word *mystic* solely for Eastern religions with their search for spiritual unity

with the universe. Others, following Troeltsch, use the term to refer to any nonrational religious orientation that denies the importance or reality of the social order. However, most writers use mysticism in a broader sense to refer to any nonrational experience that the actors define as sacred.

attitude toward peak experiences (including conversions) is highly correlated with reports of having experienced them.

Finally, a social group's definition of what is normal or desirable influences both the way individual members interpret their own experiences and the kinds of experiences they try to bring about. This is a basic premise of symbolic interaction or social constructionist theory. The theory is useful in understanding and predicting variations in religious experiences between groups. Roman Catholics are surrounded by much visual stimulation in churches (stations of the cross, statues, and stained glass windows). It should not be surprising that Catholics are much more likely than Protestants to have religious experiences that involve visions, while Protestants, whose worship experience is heavily auditory, are more likely to hear voices.

Regardless of variations, some form of nonrational religious experience seems to be at the root of religious behavior for many people. Such an experience gives impetus and emotion to belief systems. However, the assumption (by Otto, Durkheim, O'Dea, and Maslow) that a mystical or nonrational experience is the only source of religious conviction may be overdrawn. As Greeley points out, people have a tendency to sacralize the things that they value most highly and that give meaning and purpose to their lives. Note, for example, the sense of sacredness that accompanies ceremonial handling of the American flag. The directions that accompany the newly purchased flag emphasize a sense of reverence and awe that should be maintained when caring for the flag (see Box 4.2). Such sacredness is not caused by a mystical experience but is created in the presence of a valued symbol. The sacralization of objects or beliefs places them above question; it ensures their absoluteness. Hence, that which we value highly tends to be perceived in reverent or sacred terms.

Anyone who doubts the fact that a firsthand religious experience can be very important need only observe the major surge of born-again and Pentecostal movements in Christianity in the past ten or fifteen years. The emphasis of each of these movements is the assurance and sense of certainty provided by a personal experience of the holy. Furthermore, many of the Eastern religions that grew rapidly in the 1970s placed heavy emphasis on nonrational religious experience. Although an experience of the *mysterium tremendum* may not be the sole source of religious behavior, a sense of sacredness is clearly one important aspect of the complex phenomenon called religion.

Myth and Ritual

When Americans speak of religion, they usually think of a belief system. Indeed, many social scientists have even attempted to measure religiosity by questioning subjects on their agreement or disagreement with certain orthodox religious beliefs. Even the practice of referring to faithful members of a religious group as believers is indicative of this focus. But, as we will see, belief and ritual are quite interdependent, and in the case of some religious groups, ritual is the more important of the two.

Myth

Religious beliefs are usually expressed in the form of myths. By myth, the social scientist does not mean untrue or foolish beliefs. Nor does the social scientist identify myth with legends, fairy tales, or folk tales (Kluckhohn 1972). Myths, as opposed to the latter phenomena, usually carry with them an element of sacredness. As we have seen from the earlier discussion, that which is sacred is normally that which helps one make sense out of life.

► **BOX 4.2**

The American Flag as a Sacred Symbol

The American flag is often treated with a profound respect and reverence, as indicated by the directions for flag etiquette. The mere fact that detailed rules are spelled out so explicitly for the treatment of this symbol and the reality that violation of these rules will infuriate some Americans is testimony to the awe with which this symbol is held. The extreme anger expressed by many Americans over the burning of an American flag is also evidence of its sacredness, though the behavior itself is not the cause of anger. One of the rules of flag etiquette is that a tattered flag should be burned or buried as a sign of respect.

Excerpts from a publication on care of the flag are provided below.

Flag Etiquette

Display the flag only from sunrise to sunset on buildings and on stationary flagstaffs in the open. However, the flag may be displayed at night upon special occasions when it is desired to produce a patriotic effect.

The flag should be hoisted briskly and lowered ceremoniously. No other flag or pennant should be placed above or, if on the same level, to the right of the flag of the United States of America, except during church services conducted by naval chaplains at sea, when the church pennant may be flown above the flag during church services.

The flag, when flown at half-staff, should be first hoisted to the peak for an instant and then lowered to the half-staff position. The flag should be again raised to the peak before it is lowered for the day.

That no disrespect should be shown to the flag of the United States of America, the flag should not be dipped to any person or thing. . . .

The flag should never be displayed with the union down save as a signal of dire distress.

The flag should never touch anything beneath it, such as the ground, the floor or water.

The flag should never be carried flat or horizontally, but always aloft and free.

The flag should never be used as a drapery of any sort whatsoever, never festooned, drawn back, nor up, in folds, but always allowed to fall free. . . .

During the ceremony of hoisting or lowering the flag or when the flag is passing in a parade or in a review, all persons present should face the flag, stand at attention, and salute. Those present in uniform should render the military salute. When not in uniform, men should remove the head-dress with the right hand holding it at left shoulder, the hand being over the heart. Men without hats should salute in the same manner. Aliens should stand at attention. Women should salute by placing the right hand over the heart. The salute to the flag in the moving column should be rendered at the moment the flag passes.

Flag Holidays

NEW YEAR'S DAY, January 1
INAUGURATION DAY, January 20
LINCOLN'S BIRTHDAY, February 12
WASHINGTON'S BIRTHDAY
  (President's Day), 3rd Monday in February
EASTER SUNDAY (variable)
MOTHER'S DAY, second Sunday in May
ARMED FORCES DAY, third Saturday in May
MEMORIAL DAY (half-staff until noon),
  last Monday in May
FLAG DAY, June 14
INDEPENDENCE DAY, July 4
LABOR DAY, first Monday in September
CONSTITUTION DAY, September 17
COLUMBUS DAY, 2nd Monday in October
VETERAN'S DAY, 4th Monday in October
THANKSGIVING DAY, fourth Thursday in
  November
CHRISTMAS DAY, December 25

Source: Annin and Company. Used by permission.

Hence, **myths** are stories or belief systems that help people understand the nature of the cosmos, the purpose and meaning of life, or the role and origin of evil and suffering. Myths explain and justify specific cultural values and social rules. They are more than stories that lack empirical validation; they serve as symbolic statements about the meaning and purpose of life in this world. One sociologist of religion has gone so far as to suggest that all religious symbols (including religious myths) are in a fundamental sense true (Bellah 1970a). He does not argue their literal veracity, but he insists that symbolic systems of meaning are true insofar as they speak to the fundamental human condition. Hence, they need to be taken seriously. Myths have a powerful impact on the subjective (mental) orientation of persons because they communicate and reinforce a particular world view or a particular outlook on life. (See Box 4.3.)

After undertaking an in-depth study of the Hare Krishna, Stillson Judah insists that " 'myth' is actually the highest subjective reality to the devotee. It is the vehicle [which carries one] to inner integration. [Humans] can only live without 'myth' at [their] peril" (1974: 196). Judah goes on to suggest that what liberal religion needs for revivification is not a new theology but a new mythology. "A new theology would only result in a new rationalization. . . . The real need is for a powerful mythic statement about the world" (1974: 196). We discuss the rationalization of myths in the form of systematic theology later, but what is important here is a recognition of the emotional power of which myth is capable. For many persons, logical, systematic, and scientific statements do not capture one's imagination so as to mobilize one's emotional resources. The capacity of myths to do this is precisely the reason they have such power in the lives of individuals.

A Central Eskimo myth may serve to illustrate. Historically, the Central Eskimo believed in the existence of a woman, Sedna, who lived at the bottom of the sea. Sedna was once an Eskimo girl. However, against the wishes of her father, she married a bird and went to an island to live. Her father came to get her, but Sedna's husband caused a violent storm to arise while the father was returning Sedna to her home. The father threw Sedna overboard, but she hung on desperately. To prevent his boat from capsizing, the father chopped her fingers off with his knife, and she finally sank to the bottom of the sea. The pieces of fingers turned into the various sea mammals—whales, seals, and walruses.

Eskimo women in particular were constrained by many taboos or moral prohibitions. For example, when seals were killed and brought home, certain behaviors were prohibited until the seal had been cut up; the skins from the sleeping platform could not be shaken out, women could not comb their hair, and young girls could not take off their boots. After the cutting was complete, products from land and sea had to be cooked in different pots. Many other taboos were related to food preparation, to giving birth, and to menstruation. If any of these taboos were broken, a vapor was believed to emanate from the body of the violator. That vapor sank through the ice, snow, and water, and settled in Sedna's hair as dirt and maggots. Because she had no fingers, Sedna could not comb out this debris. In revenge, she would call the walruses and seals (which were once her fingers) to the bottom of the sea, and the people would face starvation. Salvation came only if a shaman (Eskimo holy man) entered into a trance, traveled spiritually to the bottom of the sea, combed Sedna's hair, appeased her, and discovered who the offenders were. When he returned, all offenders were required to confess their taboo violations openly. The seals then returned (Barnouw 1982: 231–34).

Sedna was not a benevolent deity. She was vengeful and had to be obeyed. She was the cause of much anxiety, fear, and even hostility. The Sedna myth served to create these moods of fear and anxiety in people, which then motivated them toward certain types of behav-

ior (obeying of taboos and prohibitions). This myth reinforced an overall world view that the world is a hostile environment, that the future is fraught with danger and may be jeopardized

---

▶ **BOX 4.3**

Myths Can Create Powerful Moods and Motivations in People

The mythology of heaven and hell and the belief that one who is not saved by God will go to hell are vividly expanded by Jonathan Edwards in this passage. By emphasizing this myth and elaborating on it, he sought to create powerful, pervasive, and long-lasting *moods* (awe of God's power, humility, fear of God) and *motivations* (repentance, change of attitudes, and behavior).

> The God that holds you over the pit of hell, much as one holds a spider, or some loathsome insect over the fire, abhors you, and is dreadfully provoked: his wrath towards you burns like fire; he looks upon you as worthy of nothing else, but to be cast into the fire; he is of purer eyes than to bear to have you in his sight; you are ten thousand times more abominable in his eyes, than the most hateful venomous serpent is in ours. You have offended him infinitely more than ever a stubborn rebel did his prince; and yet it is nothing but his hand that holds you from falling into the fire every moment. It is to be ascribed to nothing else, that you did not go to hell the last night; that you was suffered to awake again in this world, after you closed your eyes to sleep. And there is no other reason to be given, why you have not dropped into hell since you arose in the morning, but that God's hand has held you up. There is no other reason to be given why you have not gone to hell, since you have sat here in the house of God, provoking his pure eyes by your sinful wicked manner of attending his solemn worship. Yea, there is nothing

else that is to be given as a reason why you do not this very moment drop down into hell.

> O sinner! Consider the fearful danger you are in: it is a great furnace of wrath, a wide and bottomless pit, full of the fire of wrath, that you are held over in the hand of that God, whose wrath is provoked and incensed as much against you, as against many of the damned in hell. You hang by a slender thread, with the flames of divine wrath flashing about it, and ready every moment to singe it, and burn it asunder; and you have . . . nothing to lay hold of to save yourself, nothing to keep off the flames of wrath, nothing of your own, nothing that you ever have done, nothing that you can do, to induce God to spare you one moment.*

Readers might find it instructive to attend several different religious services in their communities and listen to the symbolism of the language. What myths are being played upon? What moods do the clergy intend to create with these myths? What motivations are sought? What is the symbolic role of emotionally laden language in these services? Another exercise would be to read sermons from clergy of various theological persuasions to identify the symbolic power of language in creating moods and motivations.

*Source: Jonathan Edward's sermon, "Sinners in the Hands of an Angry God" (preached in 1741). In *Jonathan Edwards: Basic Writings,* edited by Ola Elizabeth Winslow. New York: New American Library, 1966: 159–60.

by human acts, that survival depends on conforming behavior and obedience to rules by everyone, and that negative behavior will always be reflected back to the actor in some devastating form. The Sedna myth served to solidify and sacralize the general Central Eskimo outlook on life. Insofar as this view was consistent with the harsh environmental conditions in which the Central Eskimos live, the myths may have contributed to adaptation and survival.

Ritual

Although Americans tend to think of belief as the central component of religion, ritual appears to be equally important. In fact, Louis Schneider (1970: 23) points out that **orthopraxy,** not orthodoxy, is central to Islam. That is, precise conformity in ritual behavior (e.g., prayers five times a day facing Mecca) is what is mandated for the faithful, not total conformity in theological interpretations.[4] Many scholars have also observed that Judaism—especially Orthodox Judaism—focuses much more on concrete behaviors (orthopraxy) than on theological tenets, beliefs, or attitudes (Cohen 1983; Moberg 1984; Sklare and Greenblum 1979).

A careful observation of human behavior is enough to make one aware of the great attraction of humans to ritual experiences. Consider, for example, the elaborate pageantry and ritual of a Shriner's convention, or a Masonic lodge,

---

[4]Schneider is actually citing earlier observations by Wilfred C. Smith and Gustave von Grunebaum.

Moslems pray to God five times a day at set times, regardless of where they are. They are also required to face Mecca. Conformity to this and other ritual behavior is considered a more important measure of faith than doctrinal orthodoxy. (UPI photo/Bettman.)

or a De Molay installation. Football games always begin with the playing of the national anthem, and colorfully uniformed marching bands perform. Many meetings of secular civic groups begin with a ritual pattern: the pledge to the flag and a prayer. And for many people, marriage is not legitimate unless the couple has been through a ceremony, however brief. Although common law marriage (marriage without benefit of ceremony or marriage license) is perfectly legal in thirteen states, many people still feel the ceremony is what makes marriage legitimate.

The preceding examples do not necessarily involve a sense of sacredness or ultimacy, and I do not suggest that they are particularly religious phenomena. My point is merely that there is something about human beings to

This Russian marriage ceremony in the Central Palace of Festive Events in Kiev illustrates the importance of ritual in human affairs. In the Ukraine, while the antireligion policy of the former Soviet Union was in effect, socialist rites were instituted to replace religious ceremonies. These were not simple civic ceremonies but elaborate occasions that offered a sense of sacredness to the event, while stressing the ultimate worth and sanctity of the state. Elegantly robed officials, usually women, performed various rituals for most of the "rites of passage" (naming ceremonies, marriages, funerals, and so forth) in front of altarlike tables, flanked by a bust of Lenin and an "eternal flame," punctuated by appropriate organ music and sometimes a full choir, and aided by various symbolic artifacts. In the place of appeal to God, all was done in the name of the state and to the greater glory of patriotism and socialism. (1983 Serge Schmemann, NYT Pictures photo.)

which ritual and pageantry appeal. At a time when many denominations are making their worship liturgies *less* formal, many secular organizations seem to be generating *more* elaborate pageantry! Perhaps this is because the myth systems associated with church rituals are no longer capturing the imagination of many people; hence, the formal ecclesiastical rituals seem hollow rather than awe-inspiring. We will return to this issue, but the elaboration of nonsacred ritual at such events as the Olympic Games is quite interesting (or are these rituals and events *really* nonsacred?).

Religious ritual usually involves affirmation of the myths and gives emotional impulse to the belief system. Judah provides an example when he discusses the role of chanting by Hare Krishna members: "The power of this chanting should not be underestimated. The enthusiasm of the devotees leaping in ecstasy with upraised arms before the shrine can be contagious for many" (1974: 95). Not only is the mood contagious; Hare Krishna members insist that complete acceptance and understanding of the belief system is attained through chanting. Judah cites a number of devotees who made comments such as the following: "Although we may not understand something when it is given to us, it comes to us through faith. It's revealed to us through our continuing efforts in chanting" (1974: 169).

Ritual may involve the enactment of a story or myth, or it may symbolically remind one of the mythology of the faith by moving participants through a series of moods. Perhaps a brief analysis of a ritual familiar to many readers will help illustrate the point.

Biblical theology was based on the idea that God had a covenant (or contract) with the chosen people. If they obeyed the commandments and worked to establish a kingdom of justice and righteousness, then God would protect them and provide for them. The scriptures maintain that the Hebrew people got into trouble whenever they broke the covenant, forgot the demands of justice, and ignored the sovereignty of God. In these circumstances, the prophets called the people back to the covenant. The prophets assured them that if they would repent and renew their covenant, Yahweh would forgive them. The New Testament renews this theme, with Jesus calling the wayward to repent and promising God's forgiveness. The most important sacrament in the Christian church is Communion (alternatively referred to as the Lord's Supper, the Eucharist, or the Mass). In instituting this practice, Jesus claimed to be inaugurating a new covenant. Covenantal theology, then, is a basic Christian mythology or belief system.

Many Protestant Christians are not consciously aware that the liturgy (or ritual) in which they participate is based on this theology. In fact, many lay people believe that the order of a worship service is rather arbitrary, that the minister randomly intermixes hymns, prayers, a confession, scripture, anthems, and other liturgical devices. Let us look, however, at a consistent pattern that prevails in many American Protestant liturgies. The sample provided in Box 4.4 will serve as an illustration. This sample was selected because it explicitly articulates the development of the service through subheadings.[5] However, most liturgies are based on a logical pattern that moves worshipers through successive movements or moods. While there is some variation in the order of Protestant worship services, the

[5]Most Protestant services do not have the subheadings printed in the order of worship to show the change of mood. Some that do have subheadings may emphasize three movements—whereas others have four. For example, some liturgies subsume the "service of praise" and "service of confession" under a single heading: Service of Preparation. Regardless of whether subheadings are provided in the bulletin, the general sequence described here is typical for the mainline Protestant churches. The model described here is based on patterns that prevail in several hundred church bulletins from various denominations that I have collected over the past decade.

majority of mainline American churches tends to follow, in rough outline, the themes developed in this liturgy. Let us examine the relationship between these liturgies and the mythology of the divine covenant.[6]

At the outset of the service, the liturgy is designed to create a mood of awe and praise.[7]

---

[6]I first became aware of this basic and recurring pattern through Paul Johnson's book *The Psychology of Religion* (1959). Johnson discusses the psychology of

worship by analyzing several different liturgies from different denominations or faiths. The application of this Protestant liturgy draws on Johnson's analysis, though it is a bit more specific than his earlier work.

[7]Those interested in a symbolic interactionist analysis of behavior in a liturgical setting might want to see Gary Hesser and Andrew Weigert (1980).

▶ **BOX 4.4**

Order of Worship
First United Methodist Church, 10:30 A.M.

Service of Praise

Prelude: "Entreaty" (Martin)
   Our worship of God begins with the music of the prelude. Let us listen to the music. Let us read the words of the hymns we will sing today. Let us center our thoughts before God. Let us be silent, opening our lives to God.

Introit: Senior Choir

Call to Worship

Hymn of Praise: No. 38, "Joyful, Joyful, We Adore Thee"

Service of Confession

Prayer of Confession (in unison)
   Lord, we gather on the Sabbath to worship You and to dedicate our lives to Your service. Yet in the strain and hurry of everyday living, we often forget you. We say the unkind word, or we fail to do the loving deed. We betray the values which we profess on Sunday morning, and we do not remember that you are the Center of Life. Forgive us, O Lord, and renew in us a resolve to live Christ-like lives.

Personal Silent Confession

Assurance of Pardon

Service of Proclamation

Apostles' Creed

The Gloria Patri

Children's Sermon

Anthem: "The Lord's Prayer," John Zaumeyer

Scripture Reading
   Amos 5:21–24
   Matt. 7:21–24
   Luke 10:25–37

Hymn of Proclamation: No. 256, "Be Thou My Vision"

The Message: "Incarnation: The Medium Is the Message"

The Morning Prayer

Service of Commitment

Concerns of the Congregation

Prayer of Intercession and Lord's Prayer

Offertory: "Panis Angelicus" Franck

Doxology

Hymn of Dedication: No. 399 "Take My Life and Let It Be Consecrated"

Charge to the Congregation

Benediction

Benediction Response: The Irish Blessing

Postlude: "Choral Song," S. S. Wesley

The architecture of the church may also enhance this sense. Many church bulletins request that worshipers sit in silence and focus their attention on a rose window, on some other symbol, or on "the presence of God." The prelude is frequently a piece of music that will lift one's spirits. The call to worship draws one's attention to the reason for gathering: to worship and praise God. The congregation then joins together in a hymn of praise, which is frequently a joyful, uplifting song of adoration.

Shortly after the congregation is made aware that it is in the presence of God, the mood shifts. Although most of the worshipers were in the same church dedicating their lives to God just a week before, the liturgy attempts to make them aware of the fact that they have not always lived in a way consistent with Christian values. They are reminded that in the push and pull of daily living, they have said the unkind word or failed to do a loving deed (sins of commission and sins of omission). The values they professed on Sunday they may have betrayed by Wednesday (if not on Sunday afternoon). Hence, the second mood or theme of this worship liturgy is a "service of confession." No one can be loving, just, self-sacrificing, or righteous all the time, and the liturgy leads participants to acknowledge their lack of consistent faithfulness. For this reason, confession is sometimes called an "act of honesty" (between oneself and God). But this liturgical movement does not end on a note of guilt. Confession is followed by "words of assurance," "assurance of pardon," or "word of new possibility." At this point, the congregation is assured by the minister (often through quotation of a biblical passage) that persons "who sincerely confess their sins and who renew their commitment to God are forgiven." The convenantal theme of repentance prior to renewal of the covenant is enacted.

The liturgy then moves to a third phase, an "affirmation of faith," or "service of proclamation." This phase is frequently the major part of Protestant services. The congregation may repeat a creed or covenant, listen to an anthem or other special music, sing a hymn of proclamation, listen to scripture, and hear a message (sermon) delivered by the minister. In this phase of the ritual, the emphasis is on celebrating God's love, remembering and rehearing the Word of God, and remembering the demands of the covenant. Infant baptisms are usually a part of this movement, although churches that practice only adult baptism and view it as an act of commitment may include it as part of the final movement.

The final movement of most Protestant liturgies is a service of dedication. This part of worship calls for a response to God's word by the congregation. The movement is characterized by a monetary offering (a symbolic act of the giving of one's self), concerns of the church or announcements from the pulpit, a hymn of dedication, a charge to the congregation, and a benediction. In some churches, the third and fourth phases of the liturgy (proclamation and dedication) may be merged into one. In this case, some acts of dedication and commitment (such as the offering) may actually precede the sermon. However, the hymn of dedication always follows the sermon. In the more evangelical churches, this hymn may be followed by an "altar call"—a request for members to make a public commitment by coming forward and standing before the altar.

It should not be inferred that all Protestant worship through history has followed this mood sequence. The pattern described here was initiated by John Calvin, who articulated a rationale for an order of worship that corresponds roughly with the pattern and the theology identified here. However, Huldrych Zwingli, another reformer of Calvin's day, felt that the climax of the service should be confession. The rest of the service was to build a sense of guilt in the worshipers until the final act of repentance. This influence can be seen in Puritan liturgies of colonial America. Some denominations continue to be influenced by the

Zwingli tradition in their liturgical formats. Furthermore, some Pentecostal churches and Christian sects do not have a consistent pattern of worship. The rationale for the order of worship is insignificant, for emotion is judged far more important than thought patterns.

It is also interesting that much of contemporary Protestant worship emphasizes proclamation and commitment. The Catholic Mass seems to place more stress on the service of praise. This reflects a fundamental difference in Protestant and Catholic views of worship (Pratt 1964). The Roman Catholic Church has historically taken an objective approach to the Mass. The emphasis was on glorification of God, and the liturgy was designed with that in mind. It was best to have a congregation present at the celebration of Mass, but if no one came, the Mass would go on. On the other hand, a Protestant minister would scarcely think of conducting a full service of worship if no congregation gathered. The more subjective emphasis of the Protestant denominations—especially the ones that have a more informal, low-church tone—is on how the worship affects the worshipers themselves. Hence, the beliefs about worship itself significantly affect the order of a liturgy and the themes it includes.

From the example provided, it may be seen that ritual and belief are often closely intertwined and tend to be mutually reinforcing. That is, they tend to provide an interrelated *system*. It is noteworthy that sample surveys have consistently found a high correlation between regular attendance at rituals and a high level of acceptance of the belief system of the denomination. However, it is also true that many people are unaware of the logical progression of the worship liturgy and of the theological basis for its order. Hence, the liturgy is viewed as just so many hymns, prayers, and scripture readings in random order. Given this fact and given the fact that some people attend church for purely status reasons (as a demonstration that they are good citizens), it

is not surprising that the correlation between ritual attendance and doctrinal orthodoxy is far from perfect.[8]

Relationship between Myth and Ritual

Ritual often precedes myth. Judah, for example, insisted that "chanting is the primary prerequisite" in conversion to the Hare Krishna movement (1974: 170). Some scholars have gone even further by suggesting that, in terms of chronological development, ritual emerges first and myth develops later to justify the existence of the ritual. Franz Boaz particularly emphasized the primacy of ritual and the secondary explanatory role of myth (Kluckhohn 1972).

However, the process may develop the other way as well (Kluckhohn 1972). The Mass is clearly an example of a ritual based on a sacred story. Another example is the Ghost Dance, a religious ritual based on a dream or vision by Wovoka, the Paiute holy man whose trance in 1889 regenerated a powerful religious movement among Native Americans. In this case, the interpreted dream provided both a mythology and a command to perform a ritual (LaBarre 1972). Clyde Kluckhohn emphasizes the complex relationship between these elements of religion:

> [T]he whole question of the primacy of ceremonial or mythology is as meaningless as all questions of "the hen or the egg" form. What really is important is the intricate interdependence of myth with ritual and many other forms of behavior (1972: 96).

In some cases, both myth and ritual may be viewed as factors dependent on a third

---

[8]It is important to keep in mind that the operationalization of doctrinal orthodoxy has tended to rate people higher on orthodoxy if they view scripture literalistically. Hence, the measures themselves need careful interpretation.

component: mystical or nonrational experience. This, of course, was the position of Otto (1923) and, more recently, of O'Dea (1966). Gerardus Van der Leeuw (1963: 49) has also written that awe, "once established . . . develops into observance." The experience of awe may be so fascinating and attractive that a ritual is established to try to elicit or recreate that experience. Furthermore, a mythology is generated to try to explain or make sense of the experience (O'Dea 1966: 24, 40–41). At this point, it seems fair to conclude that no generalization can be made about which of these three factors is primary, for there is wide variation between cultures and even within cultures. For that matter, there may even be variation within the same religion, as each denomination or sect of a faith emerges in accord with its own internal dynamic.

The image presented here of highly integrated ritual and myth needs a word of caution. The discussion of the Protestant liturgy suggested a high degree of integration and interdependence between ritual and belief system. However, that integration is largely a matter of interpretation; that is, this integration is to a considerable extent in the eye of the beholder. The participant *interprets* the ritual and myth as mutually supportive, hence it is mutually supportive for that person. However, many cases have been found in which diverse tribal people practice the same ritual but interpret that ritual as expressing very different myths. Likewise, people holding the same belief system may celebrate those beliefs with very different ritual patterns. In summary, we can say that beliefs, ritual, and religious experience are important components of what we call religion, that they are usually interrelated and mutually supportive, and that the integration of the three is itself largely a matter of interpretation by the believer and the community of which the believer is a part (Batson and Ventis 1982).

As readers attend religious services in their own communities, they may be interested in asking themselves, What is the rationale for the order of this liturgy? How are myth and ritual intertwined and mutually supportive, or is there no apparent relationship? What does the ritual mean to the *members* of this group?

The Importance of Symbols

The reason why myths and rituals normally have a close relationship is that they are both manifestations of a larger phenomenon—a system of symbols. Elizabeth Nottingham emphasizes the unifying function of symbols:

> [It] is not hard to understand that the sharing of common symbols is a particularly effective way of cementing the unity of a group of worshipers. It is precisely because the referents of symbols elude overprecise intellectual definitions that their unifying force is the more potent; for intellectual definitions make for hairsplitting and divisiveness. Symbols may be shared on the basis of not-too-closely-defined feeling (1971: 19).

Certainly, this is one reason that symbols are important. Clifford Geertz emphasizes a slightly different reason that symbols are critically important when he writes, *"Meanings can only be stored in symbols:* a cross, a crescent, or a feather. Such religious symbols, dramatized in rituals or related in myths, are felt somehow to sum up what is known about the way the world is"* (1958: 422, my emphasis). Edmund Leach's research on the symbolic power of rituals supports this view. Leach has studied rituals as "storage systems" that encapsulate knowledge. He maintains that ritual provides an important form of economical thinking among many tribal people. Meaningful information and important knowledge are encapsulated in ritual in a way analogous to the loading of computer chips with information in our culture. Rituals are viewed by Leach as vessels that carry powerful symbols and that authoritatively transmit a world view and an ethos (1972).

A consideration of certain elements in the Catholic Mass illustrates the power of symbols. As the celebrants come before the altar, they genuflect and cross themselves. Although the act may sometimes be perfunctorily executed, making the sign of the cross acts to remind believers of a particular event. The cross has meaning because it reminds the participant of a sacred story, a particular life, and a divine event. The theological interpretation of the event may vary somewhat from one celebrant to another, but with the regularized pattern of crossing oneself, the centrality of Christ on the cross will not be forgotten. The stained-glass windows may have symbols meaningful to the early church or perhaps depictions of Jesus in a well-known scene. These symbolic representations also bring to mind a whole series of events and stories that are part of the sacred myth. When the priest says, "Take, eat, this is my body," another central event is recalled. At certain points in the Mass, the congregation kneels. This act is a gesture of humility and is to remind one of an utter dependency and humility before God. In each case, the entire story does not have to be repeated in detail. If the myth is well known and if the symbolic meaning of the ritual action is understood by the celebrant, then all that is necessary to elicit certain moods and motivations is to introduce the symbol itself. The symbol stores meaning and can call forth certain attitudes or dispositions.

In the Jewish tradition, one can see the same power of symbols in a religious festival such as the seder meal. Even a Gentile cannot help but be moved by the symbolic reenactment of the escape from Egypt. The eating of bitter herbs, which actually bring tears to one's eyes, reminds one of the suffering of the ancestors. The unleavened bread, the parsley, and the haroseth (a sweet condiment) each has symbolic value in recalling a sacred story. This symbolic reenactment confirms in the minds of the Jews where they have been, who they are,

and what task lies before them. A sense of identity and a sense of holy mission is powerfully communicated through the ritual.

Geertz's definition of religion articulates very well the important role of symbols: "Religion is a system of symbols which acts to establish powerful, pervasive, and long-lasting moods and motivations in [people] by formulating conceptions of a general order of existence" (Geertz 1966: 4). The symbol systems are important in that they act in people's lives.[9] Ritual and myth, then, are important as symbol systems. In this text, the concept of religion has stressed world view (conceptions of a general order of existence) and ethos (powerful, pervasive, and long-lasting moods and motivations) as central elements. Hence, the next issue before us is the relationships among world view, ethos, and symbols.

World View, Ethos, and Symbols

World view refers to the intellectual framework within which one explains the meaning of life (including one's cosmology). Myths are specific stories or beliefs, the net effect of which is to reinforce a world view (Wuthnow 1981). A single story may not be sufficient to convince someone that God is in charge of the universe and all is well. However, a series of many such myths may serve to reinforce such an outlook on life. World view is a more abstract concept than myth; it refers to one's mode of *perceiving* the world and to one's general overview of life. In this sense, a world view is more taken for granted and less questioned. Many individuals may not be fully conscious of the alternative types of world views, and many never question the fact that their perception is influenced by intellectual constructs.

---

[9]Those interested in exploring the role of religious symbols further may also want to consult Turner (1967) and Bynum, Harrell, and Richman (1986).

Whether one is optimistic or pessimistic in outlook is strongly influenced by one's world view. (See the passages from Jonathan Edwards in Box 4.2.)

A religious world view is also closely related to a group's *ethos*, as illustrated in Box 4.5. A people's *ethos* is the tone, character, and quality of their life, its moral and aesthetic and mood;

▶ **BOX 4.5**

Native American Ethos: Moral and Aesthetic Style and Mood

Sam Gill insists that the moods and motivations of Native American religion are both critically important for understanding Native American religion and often beyond the capacity of rational discourse to explain or describe. In a discussion of the oral tradition of story telling (myths), Gill comments on the ethos.

> Ordinarily underlying questions of meaning is the assumption that these oral traditions carry messages and that we need to translate these speech acts into their messages so that we too will know what they mean. After spending much time asking Native American people questions like "What does this story mean?" and feeling by their lack of response that it must have been a stupid question—or having gained answers completely incompatible with the story—I have had to seek ways of understanding how these stories bear meaning and how we can appreciate them. . . .
>
> Perhaps we can approach an understanding by certain olfactory experiences. I cannot smell the odor of juniper smoke without experiencing a series of peculiar images and feelings related to experiences I had while living among Navaho people. If you were to ask me what the smell of juniper smoke means to me, I would at first be confounded, for such a question seems inappropriate to ask. The smell bears no translatable message, although it has an emotional impact upon me; the experience is meaningful but has no meaning at all in

the sense of bearing a message. Listening to music evokes similar sorts of meaning by awakening a certain emotion, often a series of images or memories connected with the music through one's personal and cultural history.

> Speech acts in Native American cultures . . . have an emotional impact, a significance much more far-reaching. In their performance, they are not simply streams of words whose full significance lies in the information they convey. They are complex symbols, networks of sounds, odors, forms, colors, temperatures, and rhythms. . . . Consequently any story, any song, any prayer is a stimulus that frees strings of associated images, emotions, and patterns. To ask what they mean and expect a translatable message is often to ask an inappropriate question. Their significance is inseparable from the whole field of symbols which they evoke (1982: 48–49).

The inability to articulate the meaning of a particular myth may be twofold. First, part of why it is meaningful is because of the emotionally laden context in which it is told—the religious ethos. Second, the myth may reinforce a world view that is only partially explicit or conscious to the subject. It is taken for granted. The world view may, for example, assume certain categories of time and certain meanings of the concept of time that are not shared by the interviewer. Without that shared world view, the informer hardly knows where to begin to explain the "meaning" of the story.

it is the underlying attitude toward themselves and their world" (Geertz 1958: 421). Ethos refers to *attitudes* about life (moods, motivations), whereas world view refers to an *intellectual* process (concepts of a general order of existence).[10] Both attitudes and concepts are essential to the establishment of a sense of meaning in life. The world view is confirmed and made to seem objective by the ethos. The set of concepts is placed beyond question and is made absolute by the sacred mood in which it is transmitted. Furthermore, this basic attitude (ethos) is justified and made reasonable by the world view. So in a well-integrated religious system, the ethos and world view are mutually reinforcing.

Symbols, according to Geertz, play the central role of relating the world view to the ethos. Symbols transform fact into value. The function of sacred symbols is to encapsulate, or summarize, the system of meaning and to deliver that meaning system with power and authority at appropriate times. Geertz discusses the symbolic significance of the circle among the Oglala Sioux as an example:

> For most Oglala the circle is but an unexamined luminous symbol whose meaning is intuitively sensed, not consciously interpreted. But the power of the symbol, analyzed or not, clearly rests on its comprehensiveness, on its fruitfulness in ordering experience. Again and again the idea of a sacred circle, a natural form with a moral import, yields, when applied to the world within which the Oglala lives, new meanings; continually it connects together elements within their experience which would otherwise seem wholly disparate and, wholly disparate, incomprehensible (1958: 423).

Thus, symbols have power to bind world view and ethos into a unified system of meaning.

The lack of a consistent cosmology to explain events and to justify one's values and lifestyle can be disrupting and disorienting. Peter Berger asserts that society is the guardian of order and meaning, not only at the level of social structure but also at the level of individual consciousness. Sacred images help preserve order in the structures of society and in the structuring of the individual mind. "It is for this reason that radical separation from the social world, or anomie, constitutes such a powerful threat to the individual. The individual loses his orientation in experience. In extreme cases, he loses his sense of reality and identity. He becomes anomic in the sense of becoming worldless" (Berger 1967: 21).

Durkheim suggested long ago that the experience of anomie[11] can be so unsettling that it can result in suicidal behavior. The feeling of a firmly rooted world view, with certain and definite moral rules and regulations, is a compelling need for many humans. Geertz (1966: 16) insisted that his tribal-society respondents were quite willing to abandon their cosmology for a more plausible one. What they were *not* willing to do was abandon it for no other hypothesis at all, leaving events to themselves.

In line with this emphasis, Mary Douglas has offered an insightful interpretation of biblical taboos. Not all taboos are health-related as was once maintained. Some taboos have to do with protecting the distinction between sacred and profane. Still others have to do with those things that are anomalies (unexplainable phenomenon) to the accepted world view.

In the process of socialization, a child learns to think in terms of categories of language and in terms of theories or explanations extant in a culture. When new information is received, it is

---

[10]It may be helpful for readers to review the material on Geertz's definition of religion in chapter 1. The distinction between moods (which he describes as having to do with depth of feeling) and motivations (which he describes as directional) is elaborated. Both moods and motivations are part of the ethos.

---

[11]Anomie can be defined as a lack of purpose, identity, or ethical values; social rootlessness.

interpreted in terms of those accepted categories of thought. New experiences and new information are assimilated into the present world view. When an experience does not seem to fit into this mold, the person experiences **dissonance** (internal cognitive conflict). According to cognitive psychologist Jean Piaget, one is likely to revise and reorder one's world view when too much dissonance occurs. However, a good deal of dissonant information can be tolerated by certain techniques. This is precisely where Douglas claims that taboos enter the picture. Many taboos have to do with avoidance of those things that violate one's world view (Douglas 1966, 1968).

The food taboos of the Old Testament provide an excellent example. To understand the abominations of Leviticus, we must go back to the creation story in Genesis. Here a threefold classification is presented, with the earth, the waters, and the firmament as distinct realms. Leviticus develops this scheme by allotting to each element its proper kind of animal life. Douglas (1966: 55) summarizes:

> In the firmament two-legged fowls fly with wings. In the water scaly fish swim with fins. On the earth four-legged animals hop, jump, or walk. Any class of creatures which is not equipped for the right kind of locomotion in its element is contrary to holiness. Contact with it disqualifies a person from approaching the Temple. Thus anything in the water which has not fins and scales is unclean (Leviticus 11: 10–12).

Contact with anything that is "contrary to nature" causes a person to be unclean and unfit to enter the temple—for example, anything in the water that does not have fins and scales. Hence, catfish are unclean because they have whiskers and no scales; they violate the principles of creation as spelled out in this world view. Creatures that have two legs and two hands, but that walk on all fours, are unclean. Thus, animals that have handlike front paws (the weasel, the mouse, and the mole) are

explicitly taboo because they violate the law of creation. An animal with hands, but that perversely uses its hands for walking, does not fit into the proper scheme of things. Anything that creeps, crawls, or swarms on the earth is also defined in Leviticus as an "abomination." "Eels and worms inhabit water, though not as fish; reptiles go on dry land, though not as quadrupeds; some insects fly, though not as birds. *There is no order in them*" (Douglas 1966: 56, my emphasis).

Among these pastoral people, cloven-hoofed and cud-chewing animals are the proper sort of food. Wild game is edible only if it seems to conform to these characteristics. But animals that do not conform in *both* respects are unfit as food. The pig and the camel are both cloven-hoofed, but they do not chew a cud. Douglas points out that the failure to conform to these two necessary criteria for defining animals as acceptable food is the only reason given in the Old Testament for not eating pork; no mention is made of pigs' scavenging habits.

Douglas offers a fascinating and well-documented thesis: Many taboos function to protect the culture's world view and to provide a category for those things that don't make sense (anomalies). They are simply abominations that are dirty and to be avoided.[12] Other aspects of order may also be protected or reinforced by taboos. Beliefs about women being unclean during their menstruation and in need of purification functioned to remind them of their inferior social position. The insistence in the New Testament that women cover their head in church served a similar function. Men and women were viewed as fundamentally different. This was symbolically emphasized

---

[12]Another explanation of the abominations of Leviticus, popular among some Jewish scholars and many sociologists, is that they were antiassimilation laws. They forbade activities that were popular among other people in the geographic region and thereby limited interaction with and assimilation to these other groups.

by men keeping their hair short and women keeping theirs long. Anything that threatened this essential distinction (essential to that world view) was an abomination (it threatened concepts of order). Douglas demonstrates vividly that protection and preservation of the world view is very important in understanding much religious behavior.[13]

Sociologist Peter Berger insists that one's world view must seem authoritative, certain, and compelling. In the midst of alternative paradigms and cosmologies, one's world view may become fragile and vulnerable. Hence, the vulnerability of a world view is concealed in an aura of sacredness (Berger 1967: 33). Without a basis in a convincing world view, social values would not seem compelling and social stability itself may be threatened. Geertz came to the same conclusion through cross-cultural analysis of religion:

> ... mere conventionalism satisfies few people in any culture. Religion, by fusing ethos and world view, gives to a set of social values what they perhaps most need to be coercive: an appearance of objectivity. In sacred rituals and myths values are portrayed not as subjective human preferences but as the imposed conditions for life (1958: 426–427).

In conclusion, we might simply point to the complexity of the relationships among the various components of religion. In terms of the integration of these elements into a coherent religious system, we might summarize with the following four points:

1. Ritual and myth tend to be mutually reinforcing as symbol systems.
2. Symbols (including rituals, myths, and artifacts) encapsulate the world view and ethos of a people. Hence they can elicit powerful emotional responses and (by

repetition) help reinforce a general world view.
3. The ethos and the world view are themselves mutually reinforcing.
4. Together they provide a compelling basis for social values (see Box 4.6).

A problem may arise when a religious system is not so well integrated and mutually reinforcing. Geertz has himself described the social and cultural disintegration that can happen when ritual, myth, social values, and social structure do not harmonize (Geertz 1957: 531–43). Some measure of conflict between these elements can be tolerated and is normal. This is the advantage of symbols: they can unify individuals who each adhere to the symbol but who attach alternative meanings to that symbol. However, some scholars believe that the lack of a common, shared world view can eventually become a problem for a pluralistic society. Their argument is that lack of agreement on the big picture, the unifying ideology or outlook, leaves the culture without a unifying core. Barbara Hargrove goes so far as to suggest that public school teachers may be left with no common framework for interpreting data. If this occurs, teachers will only be able to impart "disjointed facts" (1979: 186).

It is a maxim of the social sciences that "facts do not speak for themselves; they must be interpreted." The difficulty in a heterogeneous culture is that there is no agreement on which big theory really makes sense and explains the meaning of life. The overriding, integrating world view, which religion provides for many cultures, is not a uniting and integrating factor in a pluralistic one. For most science teachers in the past several decades, evolutionary theory has provided the big picture, the overriding theory that explains the relationships among data. With the creationist movement, this big picture is being challenged in the courts. Some functionalists view the lack of an integrated culture—with a core of common

---

[13]For a more detailed discussion of the use of taboos to maintain sex roles, color bars, and class lines, refer to chapter 3.

assumptions about the way things are—as devastating to social life.

This cultural diversity, combined with the multiple interpretations of religious symbols, leads us to explore an interesting phenomenon, the development of folk and elite versions of a faith. The theological elite sometimes interpret scripture, myths, and rituals quite differently from the way the common laity view them.

▶ **BOX 4.6**

The Meaning System: The Interrelationship between the Elements of Religion

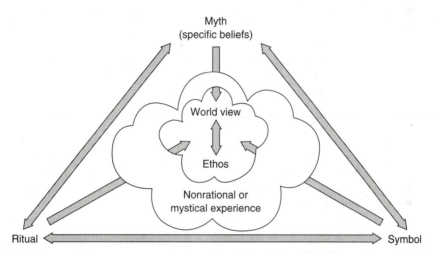

World view and ethos are at the heart of what we mean by religion. Yet these concepts are abstractions from experience; an individual's world view and religious ethos (moods and motivations) are so pervasive and so taken for granted that the individual may not be fully conscious of all their dimensions. These abstractions are made concrete and are reinforced by more concrete expressions of religiosity: ritual, myth, and symbols. Each of these is interrelated and acts to confirm the ethos and world view. Frequently, the entire religious realm seems uniquely compelling because of a nonrational religious experience. Some groups may emphasize some of these elements more than others (e.g., religious experience may be more important than unquestioned belief in the myth). Variations in interpretation of any of these may also lead to considerable conflict within the group. In actual practice, religion always has a good deal more internal inconsistency than this diagram would suggest. Hence, it is important to bear in mind that this model is idealized. It does represent a strain toward integrity that is a very real part of all religion. It is also true that when glaring incoherence in this system and conflict in interpretation of the elements becomes severe, some form of religious change is likely to take place.

Official and Nonofficial Religion

The conflict between Christian modernism and more conservative Christianity has frequently been a conflict between theology professors, professional clergy, and church bureaucrats on the one hand and common folks on the other. Jeffrey Hadden focused particularly on this issue in his book *The Gathering Storm in the Churches* (1970). The problem underlying his study was an allegiance to a common symbol system by two groups of people, but the attribution of entirely different meanings to that symbol system. The two groups were the ecclesiastical officials and the laity of the various Christian denominations.

Gustav Mensching (1964) described several distinctions between the folk religion of tribal peoples and the world religions that attempt to be universalistic. Folk religions preserve the local culture and customs, but world religions tend to evolve a complicated rational theology, a system of ethics based on that theology, a formal cultic ritual, and a professional clergy that protects, preserves, and elaborates the theology, ethics, and liturgy. However, world religions also tend to develop folk versions of the faith. The masses are seldom moved by complicated rationalized theologies, and a localized version of the religion evolves. Hence, most world religions have within them an official and a folk version of the faith that blends with local customs, beliefs, and myths. Sometimes ethnic groups within the nation have their own unique interpretation of a faith. This is another form of folk religion, which may also diverge from the official form of that faith. **Official religion** is the orthodox faith as is presented by ecclesiastical officials, and it usually involves a more systematic theology and a more universalistic application of the faith.

Two central dimensions to the conflict between official and folk religion concern us here. The first has to do with the relative importance of rationality: official religion tends to develop a systematic theology. Theology professors, publications' editors, directors of boards of social concerns, and other clergy in the bureaucratic structure may struggle with the relationship between science and mythos. They may develop rather secularized theologies, or they may develop orthodox theologies that may require mental gymnastics to understand. In either case, the theology is founded on a principle of logical consistency and coherence. (The theology is to be consistent within itself even if it does not relate to everyday experiences and perplexities of lay people.)

Sometimes the theological elite engages in the demythologizing[14] or remythologizing[15] of biblical stories. All the while, the common lay person may not be troubled at all by the lack of logical congruence in the theology. Many people seem to be quite comfortable with a highly incoherent assortment of beliefs and practices. Furthermore, they may be quite satisfied with traditional myths—and find the demythologized or revised versions rather sterile. In fact, the laity of some churches are hostile to the idea of exegesis and biblical criticism. The rise in this century of snake-handling cults and other mystical beliefs among the laity may suggest that secularization is more a phenomenon of the clergy—the elite of trained religious professionals—than of common folks. In fact, the growth of charismatic groups, the rise of biblical fundamentalism, and the decline in membership in liberal churches may suggest that emphasis on myth

---

[14]Demythologizing is reducing myths to logical principles or philosophical statements.

[15]Remythologizing is a process of recasting or reinterpreting myths in a way that is compatible with secular scientific thinking. Berger insists that the demythologizing strategy of dealing with secularization is theologically bankrupt and will ultimately lead to a denial of the existence of any supernatural realm (Berger 1979: 93–113).

and emotion in religion are the felt needs of many Americans. Rationalized theology may be less capable of providing a powerful, pervasive and long-lasting system of meaning for the average person. Systematic theology can offer a logical world view, but it does not normally generate the ethos necessary for a vibrant and alive religion. Greeley argues that conflict over the world view of science and that of religion is not a concern of most Americans.

> To some extent American believers have been able to avoid the conflict between science and religion by simply denying that it exists. Whether this is intellectually honest or not may be questioned, but the point remains that it has been successful; religion and science can go on their merry ways, not conflicting with each other very much, despite the arguments of some elite religionists and elite scientists that they should (1972: 106).

The struggle for logical coherence and consistency in theology is only one aspect of the divergence between folk religion and official religion. A second and equally important factor is the desire on the part of the elite to make the faith relevant to all cultures and all peoples. Hence, the theology and ethical principles of the faith are articulated in such a way that the faith does not appear culture-bound. The desire is to emphasize those principles of the faith that would have universal appeal. The values and attitudes that are specific to one particular culture are downplayed. The folk religion, on the other hand, involves a synthesis of the historic faith with local customs, values, beliefs, and traditions. The myths and symbols of the religion may be interpreted in such a way that they confirm and justify the local concepts of morality. The ethnocentric biases of the community may be so strong that this localized version of the religion may seem to be the only true understanding of the faith. Due to the modification of a religion so that it

is compatible with a particular culture, some writers distinguish folk religion from "true religion" (Southwold 1982). However, the terms *true Buddhism* or *true Christianity* involve unwarranted value judgments. Frequently, official religion is also a modified version of the world view set forth by the founder of the faith. Each usually represents consistency with the original tenets in certain respects and deviation in other ways. Neither official nor folk religion is entirely static.

Folk religion is certainly not limited to the laity nor is official religion restricted to the clergy. However, the religious professionals who have extensive training are more likely to recognize that the historic faith has undergone modifications in different eras and in various cultures. The professionals are likely to seek out the universalistic elements of the faith and to be cautious about identifying local customs as its only legitimate expression. Meanwhile, the abstract formulations of systematic theologians and ethicists may seem sterile and unsatisfying to the untrained layperson. What they seek is an assurance that their own concept of morality is absolute. Therefore, acceptance of elite versions as opposed to folk versions of the faith tends to be correlated with the extent of professional and theological training.

The Moral Majority is an excellent case in point. This group, founded by the Reverend Jerry Falwell of Virginia, is an organization established to restore moral values to American society. It supported many traditional Christian values. However, Christian theologians from Europe and from other parts of the world were appalled by what they considered a warping of Christianity. The Moral Majority had taken many traditional American values and attitudes and presented them as basic to Christianity. Many of these have never been part of Christian theology or ethics, and in fact some of them are antithetical to the historic position of Christian churches.

The Moral Majority[16] took the position, for example, that the only moral and Christian stance is one that favors a balanced federal budget. Although many Americans favor such a position and although there may be good economic reasons for a balanced budget, there seems to be no biblical or theological grounding for such a viewpoint. The Moral Majority also opposed the Equal Rights Amendment and the Strategic Arms Limitations Treaty; it supported the development of the MX missile system and increases in defense spending. Congressional representatives and senators who disagreed were labeled immoral and un-Christian (Berger 1981; Tamney 1992). These moral imperatives did not seem to be based on any biblical or theological foundation, but they are part of the culture, values, and beliefs of many Americans. Some Christian theologians find it inconceivable to claim that Christian morality supports spending money on war-related goods at the expense of feeding hungry people in the world. They claim that this is directly contrary to the historic position of the Christian church.

What we see in the Moral Majority is a powerful folk religion that blended Christianity and Americanism. It endorsed the American way of life, the free-enterprise system of economics, and middle-class American values and lifestyles as central to Christianity. In fact, true believers who made donations to the Thomas Road Baptist Church in Lynchburg, Virginia (Falwell's church), were sent an American flag lapel pin—an interesting symbol to represent faith in Jesus. Falwell's potential for wide appeal was due to his synthesis of two primary loyalties of many Americans: Christianity and patriotism. (Civil religion,

that is, theologizing about the significance of the nation and of the national culture will be discussed in more detail in chapter 16.)

As Wade Clark Roof pointed out, folk religion involves a loose constellation of values, norms, and beliefs—some of which are religiously based and some of which are culturally based. The posture of most official religions is that ethical positions are expected to emanate almost entirely from theological beliefs (1978: 54–55). To some extent, any religion must bend and adapt if it is to have wide appeal in a given culture. The values of the faith must be, at least in some basic respects, compatible with the values of the culture in which it hopes to have adherents. In this sense, all American Christianity is influenced by American values and culture. The official group of trained professionals who seek to articulate a universalistic Christianity is not exempt from this influence. But, while no religion is totally independent from localized mores and outlooks, some do have a more universal appeal than others.

Several scholars have treated the conflict between church officials and the laity as a struggle over power (Berger 1981; McGuire 1981). The trained professionals who work in the national headquarters of the denomination may exercise their authority and come to see the church as the national organization. The laity in the local churches may see the church as the local congregation. The parish minister serves as a buffer between these two views of the church (Hargrove 1979: 266). The conflict is over the ultimate source of authority: Who has the right to speak for the church? Who has the right to act on behalf of the entire denomination?[17]

Meredith McGuire goes a step further in pointing to the controls the professionals in the

---

[16]The Moral Majority gained significant media attention in 1980 and 1984 for its involvement in presidential and congressional elections. Falwell changed the name of the group to "Liberty Foundation" in 1986, but the movement is still referred to in the media and the public as the Moral Majority.

[17]Berger (1981) insists that the conflict is a type of class conflict between those who manipulate economic production (the business class) and those who earn their living by manipulating symbols in our society (a new class of academics, clergy, and helping professionals).

hierarchy establish to ensure the continuance of their power and privilege. (Refusal to ordain women is one such method of control.) She demonstrates that women have been systematically excluded from significant roles in the official religion and have frequently been required to wear head coverings and/or veils as a means of setting women apart and reminding them of their inferior status. On the other hand, women have often had important roles in the emergence of nonofficial religion. Hence, nonofficial religion has served an important function in allowing for religious leadership by very able women (Baer 1984; McGuire 1992). This raises an important point: Not all nonofficial religion is necessarily folk religion as we have defined it here. Hence, we may define **nonofficial religion** as any "set of religious and quasi-religious beliefs and practices that is not accepted, recognized, or controlled by official religious groups" (McGuire 1992: 104).

McGuire's insight is important; she insists that there is more than one process that can lead to the emergence of nonofficial religious groups. For our purposes here, we can distinguish two. First, common laypeople may reject the emphasis on rationality and on abstract universalistic concepts. In place of this systematic, logical theology, they may affirm a localized version of the faith that incorporates many of the local attitudes, values, and customs. Second, nonofficial religion may arise through disenfranchised groups seeking to exert their own leadership skills and express their own religiosity. In this case, emergence of nonofficial religion is largely a result of exclusivity on the part of the official elite. McGuire also points out that official religion has traditionally affirmed masculine values and concepts and the substantial involvement of women in nonofficial religion represents a search for alternative expressions of religiosity (1992).

This line of investigation suggests that more work is needed to understand fully the rela-

tionship between official religion and its various nonofficial forms. Although folk religion may be one type of modification of official religion, other nonofficial variations of Christianity include faith healing, spiritualism (attempts to communicate with the dead), astrology, and stichomancy (the method of receiving a divine message by randomly opening the Bible and pointing blindly to a passage). Hence, nonofficial religion often coexists with official religion. Many people who participate in nonofficial religion or who hold folk religious beliefs are also lay leaders in mainline denominations. In any case, the world view of nonofficial religion is often quite different from the official religion of the trained specialists.

Melford Spiro (1970) pointed out that, in the past, study of the religions of other parts of the world tended to focus on what the religious gurus and the clergy believed and practiced. He felt that the study of the folk religion of Buddhism was much more interesting and important than was the official religion of Buddhism.[18] It is the latter that is more frequently explored in philosophy of religion texts. Likewise, most sociological studies in this country have tended to focus much more on official religion than on nonofficial religion. In fact, the measures of religiosity have often gauged religious commitment in terms of conformity to official positions. Increasingly, social scientists have sought to understand both the religious orientation of the elite and the religion of the common folk. Both forms are important parts of the religiosity of a society.

An understanding of this difference between the theology of the highly trained theologians and that of the common folk can help in understanding intradenominational conflict. The religious needs of these two groups are somewhat different. The felt need among the

---

[18]For a discussion of official and folk Buddhism (including a critique of Spiro), see Martin Southwold (1982).

highly educated (whether clergy or not) is for logical coherence and consistency and for an understanding of the faith that is not bound to one national or ethnic tradition. This is not a felt need for many other faithful members. In fact, many members are looking for a metaphysical grounding for the cultural beliefs and values that they learned as children. The difference in needs within a religious group and the attribution of alternative meanings to the same symbol system are two sources of the variations in styles of religious expression.

The fact that members of the same congregation may interpret rituals, myths, and symbols in light of a very different world view can also set the stage for intense intracongregational conflict. Rather than gathering on the Sabbath to reinforce one's world view and ethos, the religious gathering may be a source of dissonance and stress. This may be so disconcerting to believers that the conflict may lead to schisms, a topic to be discussed in later chapters. The integration of any religious system is never total and always remains somewhat fragile.

Summary

Symbolic interaction theory focuses on microprocesses of human interaction and on the way in which humans make sense of their experiences. According to this perspective, meanings are derived by individuals as they interact with others. For the symbolic interactionist, symbols are the key to understanding human life, for people go about the task of fitting their actions together because of shared perceptions or shared meanings. Meaning is not inherent in events, but is created by individuals and communicated among them. Through internal manipulation of symbols and by watching how others act in certain circumstances, we *define situations*—ascertaining what is going on and what type of behavior is appropriate for that situation. Because of its emphasis on symbols and on the construction of meaning in ambiguous situations, this theoretical perspective has much to offer the study of religion. Clarification of the meaning of life, of death, of suffering, and of powerful nonrational experiences are fraught with ambiguity and require interpretation of meaning.

Nonrational religious experiences, myths, rituals, and symbol systems are all related to the ethos and world view of a religion. Frequently, there is a perceived integrity between these elements, and they are mutually reinforcing. It is nearly impossible to identify one as primary—at least when one is referring to religion as a general phenomenon. However, specific groups may emphasize one or more of these and de-emphasize others. When a religious group begins to undergo change, the relationships between these elements of religion may be less direct. This can be terribly disorienting to members of the group, and they may be quite emotional in denouncing "heretics" who offer a different interpretation of the symbols, the myth, or the ethos. When integration of the elements is threatened, the religious group strains to regain the old unity, strives for a new synthesis, or splits into several groups.

PART THREE

Becoming and Remaining Faithful

The processes by which people become committed to a religious group are of intense interest to sociologists, and the conversion and voluntary bestowal of members' resources on religious entities has generated much research. But beyond an intrinsic interest in these processes themselves, sociologists are curious about the fact that some religious groups prosper and others collapse. Out of thousands of new religious movements that come into existence, only a few survive more than a decade or two. There are a number of factors that determine which groups will or will not persist. Among these are the group's recruitment strategies and the ability to convert new recruits, the depth of the commitment that is engendered in members, the institutionalization of the group, and the ability of the group to mobilize and focus its resources effectively. In chapters 5 and 6 we look at some of the recent research on the social psychology of religious conversion and commitment. In chapters 7 and 8 we address the issues of institutionalization and mobilization of resources.

CHAPTER FIVE

Conversion and Commitment: Sociological Perspectives

In chapter 4 we viewed the elements within the religious meaning system as being relatively integrated and stable. Dissonance and change were viewed as aberrations and unusual phenomena. Yet most religions give considerable attention to the process of personal change or transformation. In this chapter we investigate the change of world views that is expected and even anticipated by religious practitioners. We also turn our attention to another subsystem of religion—the belonging system—and begin to explore how people come to join a religious group and how belonging, meaning, and institutional systems in a religion are linked.

Conversion, Brainwashing, and the New Religious Movements

The term **conversion** refers to a process of "turning around" or changing direction in life. Specifically, it refers to a change of world view. It often is viewed as a sudden crisis event, but the process can also be a gradual one. In any case, conversion represents a transformation in

a person's self image. (See Box 5.1.) The change is often symbolized by a change of name (e.g., Saul became Paul in the Christian tradition, and, more recently, Cassius Clay became Muhammad Ali in the Muslim tradition).

Much of the research in recent years on conversion and commitment has focused on nonconventional groups—the "new" religions. Perhaps this is to be expected. Conversion to a group that affirms the basic values of the dominant society does not seem as mysterious and puzzling to most people as conversion to a cult.[1] Persons who convert from Methodism to Catholicism have not engaged in terribly unconventional or "abnormal" behavior. The individual who departs from his or

[1]The terms *sect* and *cult* will be treated in more detail in chapter 9. For our purposes in this chapter, we define a sect as a new expression (or a renewed form) of a *traditional* religion. We define a cult as the nascent organization of a new religion. It involves a break from the traditional religions in a society and the creation of a nonconventional form of religion (Stark and Bainbridge 1979).

her Episcopal heritage to join a congregation of Reform Jews is somewhat more of a curiosity because the change involves adherence to a different religion and an acceptance of minority group status. However, the person who gives up all of his or her possessions to join a religious commune is even more of an enigma to the average American. Anyone who would shave his head, wear a pink gown, and chant "Rama Krishna" all day is terribly puzzling and somewhat frightening to many middle-class Americans. The charge of brainwashing seems a ready explanation for this otherwise inexplicable behavior.

The public is often attracted to the brainwashing thesis, but most people have little idea what brainwashing actually is. The term has a specific meaning in the language of the social psychologist. **Brainwashing** is usually used to refer to a process by which persons are *involuntarily* caused to adopt a belief system, a set of behaviors, or a world view. To force a person to make such a change, one must have total physical control over the individual. The captors must control all the necessities of life and be able to control life and death itself. The captive

must be in a circumstance in which no alternatives and no other choices seem available. Even in such a total-control situation, only small numbers of American soldiers yielded to the brainwashing techniques of the North Koreans in the 1950s. And most of the acquiescences to the North Korean and Chinese torture procedures were merely verbal. The Americans were eager to return to their previous culture as soon as the total-control situation was alleviated. Only about a dozen men were permanently converted by North Korean thought reform out of thousands that experienced the severe treatment (Farber et al. 1951: 271–72). Clearly, religious cults (in which there is much movement in and out of membership) do not hold the same sort of physical control over members' lives that was experienced by prisoners of war held by the North Koreans or the Chinese.[2]

---

[2]There is some evidence of a near total-control environment, with inducement of utter exhaustion and threats to the lives of individuals and their families in Jonestown (Moberg 1980). Hence, there may be a few isolated cases in which converts experience something similar to Korean brainwashing procedures. This seems to be the exception, however.

▶ **BOX 5.1**

Conversion? Or Intensification?

Part of the problem in understanding conversion in mainline groups is that the rhetoric of religious groups can be misleading. What is sometimes called a conversion is often a ritualized reaffirmation of a world view already held. Many adolescent "converts" at revivals and crusades do not really change their world views. They merely go through an experience by which they publicly affirm the faith in which they have been socialized since infancy. This is a significant experience, but it is not

necessarily conversion as has been defined here. In fact, Billy Graham (who leads many of these crusades) defines conversion as a "change in the direction of one's life to a totally new direction" (quoted by Wimberley et al. 1975: 162). According to the research by Ronald Wimberley and his colleagues, most of those who respond to the crusades are not really converts by Graham's definition. What they really experience is an intensification of their faith.

When most Americans use the word *brainwashing,* they have in mind some form of hypnotic trance or mysterious mind control. The implication is that the new religious groups manipulate the minds of potential recruits so that the latter are unwitting and somewhat passive victims of the process. The actual studies of conversion and commitment suggest otherwise. For example, Roger Straus insists that the recruit to a cult is actively involved in choosing to be converted. "The act of conversion, we find, is not a terminal act. Rather, guided by the principle that the way to be changed is to act changed, the new convert works to make conversion behaviorally and experientially real to self and others. . . It is not so much the initial action that enables the convert to experience a transformed life but the day to day actions of living it" (1979: 163). Rather than a passive victim, the research findings suggest that the recruit is an active seeker who wants the conversion experience and goes to considerable effort to cause it to happen (Staples and Mauss 1987; Straus 1976, 1979; Judah 1974; Balch 1980). In short, the "new religions" have not, by and large, been involved in putting people in a hypnotic brainwashed trance (Beckford 1985; Levine 1984b; Bromley and Shupe 1981; Batson and Ventis 1982; Barker 1984; Stark and Bainbridge 1985).

Why, then, has there been so much talk of brainwashing and mind control? Essentially, the conflict is over resources (Bromley and Shupe 1981). Cults are recruiting members whose time and energy is spent on the new religions. The conventional churches lose that resource. Further, many of the new religions demand such total commitment that recruits have little time or energy to devote to their families. In fact, the religious group comes to be an alternative family unit, with emotional commitments to the group replacing family ties.

Thomas Robbins and Dick Anthony (1978) point out that the brainwashing metaphor is used as a weapon to suppress these nonconventional groups. Anson Shupe and David Bromley (1978) even insist that the anticult movement has so distorted information about the cults that the attacks are actually very akin to the witch-hunts of an earlier era. The same might be said regarding sensationalism surrounding "Satan worship" in the late 1980s and early 1990s (Richardson, Best, and Bromley 1991).

Such attacks by established forces on new and growing religious movements are common throughout history. When Christianity was still a new religious movement, pagans claimed that the Christian movement was a dangerous one because Christians worshiped an ass's head, murdered children as sacrifices, and committed other atrocities (Baroja 1961: 41). As recently as forty years ago in the United States, Roman Catholics were characterized as subversives who committed all sorts of abominations (Bromley and Shupe 1981). The charge of brainwashing is primarily a way of discrediting new religious movements and making them appear illegitimate and dangerous.

Stigmatizing unconventional groups makes them appear more dissimilar from conventional religions than they really are. What we will find is that conversion and commitment processes of mainline groups and new religious movements do differ, but more in intensity than in kind. Religious sects and cults normally demand very high levels of commitment. For that reason, much can be learned about commitment by analyzing the social psychology of these types of religious movements. Many of the examples in this chapter are from those groups that elicit such high levels of commitment.

Chronologically, of course, conversion precedes commitment. However, in terms of understanding the social psychology of the two related phenomena, it is logical in this context to treat commitment first. The ultimate outcome of conversion is to elicit a cadre of loyal and committed members. Hence, we first explore the way in which a group creates and maintains a high level of commitment. Only after we have an understanding of commitment theory do we turn to a discussion of conversion—the process by which one moves from the status of nonbeliever or marginal member to that of highly committed convert.

A Multidimensional Model of Commitment

Rosabeth Kanter became interested in the elements of commitment while studying utopian communities and communes. She wanted to investigate factors that caused some communities to survive while others dissolved. Clearly, living an austere lifestyle with all things shared in common demanded a high level of commitment. The result of her research was to identify a number of dimensions of commitment of successful communities. These seem to apply to a variety of different types of organizations,[3] but the model is particularly applicable to religious movements.

Kanter found that commitment occurs on three different levels: commitment to the organization (instrumental commitment), commitment to other persons in the group (affective commitment), and commitment to the rules, regulations, ideas, and mores of the group (moral commitment). (See Table 5.1.) Any group or institution may elicit one or more of these types of commitment. Although they are interrelated, they are also distinct aspects of social organization that can be analyzed separately, for they are forms of commitment to the institutional system, the belonging system,

and the meaning system, respectively. According to Kanter, each of the three types of commitment involves two mechanisms that enhance commitment.

Instrumental Commitment

Instrumental commitment means the individual must be convinced that continued association with the group or organization is worth the time and effort it demands. Hence, the individual engages in a sort of cost-benefit analysis. At the cognitive (thinking) level, the committed individual must conclude that the profits associated with continued participation are significant and well worth the time and energy expended. Furthermore, if individuals feel that there would be substantial cost associated with leaving the group, the institution stands to gain in its retention of members. Two organizational mechanisms tend to enhance instrumental commitment by influencing this cost-benefit ratio. They are sacrifice and investment.

> **Sacrifice** means that membership becomes more costly and is therefore not lightly regarded nor likely to be given up easily. **Investment** is a process whereby the individual gains a stake in the group, commits current and future profits to it, so that he must continue to participate if he is going to realize those profits. Investment generally involves the giving up of control over some of the person's resources to the community (Kanter 1972: 72).

Members of religious movements are sometimes asked to make substantial sacrifices. Many times a comfortable life has been sacrificed for the rigor of an austere lifestyle, in which numerous popular recreational and social activities are denied. Devotees may be forbidden alcohol, drugs, or coffee, and they may find that card playing, social dancing, and movies are disallowed. For example, Stillson Judah writes of the attitude of the Hare Krishna:

---

[3]Many of the same processes are used in organizations as divergent as Alcoholics Anonymous (in the social service sector) and Amway Corporation (in the business sector of society) (Butterfield 1985).

The devotee must be ready to relinquish anything material for the satisfaction of Krishna. He must be ready to give up something that he strongly desires, while accepting something he does not like. He should concern himself with the material only when absolutely necessary (1974: 91).

Such attitudes of asceticism or self-denial are frequently found among sectarian and cultic groups. Kanter shows that this sacrifice is quite functional for commitment: "Once members have agreed to make the 'sacrifices,' their motivation to remain participants increases. Membership becomes more valuable and meaningful. Regardless of how the group induces the original concessions or manages to recruit people willing to make them, the fact is that those groups exacting sacrifices survive longer. . .The more it 'costs' a person to do something, the more 'valuable' he will consider it, in order to justify the psychic 'expense' " (1972: 76). Sacrifice causes a person not to want to leave because leaving would be to admit that the sacrifices were not worthwhile. Whether consciously or unconsciously, people do not like to admit that they have made foolish sacrifices. Hence, once a part of the group, demands for self-denying behavior act to increase and sustain members' commitment.

The other mechanism that enhances instrumental commitment is investment. Although people sacrifice by not using their time, energy, and resources in activities they might otherwise find enjoyable, they are expected to invest that time, energy, and money in the group. Many vibrant religious movements require at least a tithe (usually 10 percent of earnings), and some require that for full membership the devotee turn over *all* of his or her earnings to the organization. The Divine Light Mission, the Hare Krishna, and the Unification Church are recent examples. If the donation of all one's worldly goods is irrevocable, the investment becomes even more important, for

it deters one from leaving the group later. Most people prefer to continue their association with a group rather than to admit to themselves that they have been rash or foolish.

The devotee may also be required to invest substantial amounts of time in the group. The expectation of the Church of Jesus Christ of Latter-day Saints (the Mormons) that young men devote two years proselytizing, or missionizing, is a good example. Likewise, the hours of public chanting among the Hare Krishna were consciously designed to enhance commitment (Judah 1974).

Research by social psychologists has indicated that the act of making a public statement on any issue is one of the most important factors in solidifying one's commitment. If you were asked to serve on a panel to discuss the benefits your university offers to the community, the likelihood increases that you would be willing to make a financial donation to that university. You would have invested time and energy in defending the school's importance. Furthermore, after you have taken a stand in favor of something, you may tend to perceive any attack on that organization as an attack on you. You don't want to lose face, so you would likely become defensive in behalf of the institution. Likewise, the public chanting of the Hare Krishna, the door-to-door proselytizing of the Mormons, and the airport fund-raising efforts of the Moonies[4] all served to reinforce commitment.

The important factor in understanding retention of members is that a group that requires little investment and little or no sacrifice is likely to elicit little instrumental commitment. Persons may be committed at other levels, but commitment to the organization itself will be low. Because religious

---

[4]This was a major source of income for the Unification Church in the 1970s, but this practice is now replaced by business operations and has been discontinued among the Moonies today (Beckford 1985).

movements bent on radical transformation of the world usually exact a high cost (alienation from family, rejection of opportunities of an affluent life, etc.), they must emphasize the benefits and de-emphasize the costs. Moreover, their major source of recruitment will be among those who do not yet have much invested in the status quo. It is for this reason that youth are the major target of many new religious movements. In conventional religious denominations, the recruitment process need not be so intense and need not be limited to a particular clientele; the *costs* of joining a conventional group are much less severe. Regardless, some measure of instrumental commitment is important for any organization.

Affective Commitment

Affective commitment refers to an emotional dependence on the group. The group's members become one's primary set of relations. Many sects and cults work to become the *only* reference group of the members. But affective ties are important in conventional religious groups as well. In a Detroit study of the relationship between religion and other aspects of social behavior, Gerhard Lenski (1963) found that **communal involvement** (close interpersonal relationships with persons of the same faith) was a more important variable than **associational involvement** (participation in the organization or institution itself). Affective commitment is of central importance in religious behavior. Andrew Greeley suggested that while meaning functions may be *primary,* the belonging functions are often chronologically *prior.* We see this clearly as we explore the commitment and conversion processes in the new religious movements. For example, "warmth and friendship among the devotees" was one of the reasons most frequently cited by members for original attraction to the Hare Krishna movement (Judah 1974: 153–54). It is also noteworthy that the Moonies consciously look for signs of isolation or symbols of

transiency—like backpacks—to identify prospective converts (Bromley and Shupe 1979: 172). Such persons are less likely to have other affective commitments and are more likely to be in need of a group that can offer emotional support.

The affective commitment process involves two mechanisms: detachment, or renunciation, of former ties and communion with the new group. Many of the new religious movements have demanded that new recruits not contact their families for the first few weeks or months. And this emphasis may continue. Among the Hare Krishna, for example, "progress depends on willingness to give up the company of anyone who is not a devotee" (Judah 1974: 91). **Renunciation** of one's former friends, family, and social groups may involve defining outsiders as evil or as insignificant. For example, a Hare Krishna devotee responded in the following way when asked whether he corresponded with his parents:

> No, not really. Sometimes they write me a telegram. They want to know where I am so I tell them, but I am a "sannyasi." We're not supposed to do all these things anymore. Your parents are so temporary. When I speak to my mother on the phone, it's like a stranger . . . What is a father? A father is one who. . . gave me this material body. But what is that relation? It's a relation of bone and stool and blood. That's all it is. . . But Prabhupad . . . told me what to do—how to live like a human being, how to elevate myself. . . My father is Prabhupad and my mother is the scripture (Judah 1974: 179).[5]

Among the Amish, the Bruderhof, the early Christian church, the early Mormon church, and other nonconventional religious groups, we find high boundaries and a tendency to define nonmembers as degenerate, evil, or confused. Hence, contacts with outsiders are limited and are controlled by norms that make

---

[5]Judah emphasizes that this is "the extreme position of the Sannyasis."

those interactions rather formal, ritualized affairs. The experience of being treated as a stranger—and as a rather suspect degenerate stranger—may be confusing and disconcerting to the family member, who can only make sense of the formality and defensiveness by assuming that the devotee is under some sort of trance. Certainly, confusion, hurt, and anger are understandable responses. But it is important for the public to recognize that the process of conversion and commitment to new religious movements has to do with a change of reference groups, not a hypnotic trance.

The second affective mechanism is **communion.** While new recruits are removed from former reference groups, they are warmly embraced and provided with a high degree of emotional support in the new reference group. The Moonies have been very intentional about this process, which they refer to as "love bombing." Particularly for isolated persons, transient people, or loners, this intensity of concern and emotional warmth may be the most significant experience of family that the individual has known. Many communes and religious groups refer to themselves as family, for the group actually becomes a surrogate family for the members. It is also not surprising that many of the early recruits to the Hare Krishna were individuals who were already alienated from their families.

It is not necessary to focus only on cults to see the importance of this process. Most of the more conservative churches with high retention rates have extensive meetings and social events. If a person attends church on Sunday morning, has another worship experience on Sunday evening (perhaps preceded by a potluck dinner), attends the men's prayer breakfast or the women's prayer group on Tuesday morning, goes to Bible study on Wednesday evening, and serves on a committee of the church, he or she has little time or energy for other social commitments. The other persons attending those functions become one's primary social relations. Some of the mainline

churches that do not seem to elicit the same kind of intense commitment are lacking in programs that develop close and supportive interpersonal relationships among members. In fact, Hare Krishna members frequently cited a lack of meaningful friendships in their original religious group as a reason for leaving that faith (Judah 1974: 151). In contrast to this, the communal living arrangements among the Hare Krishna, the Moonies, and many other such religious groups create intense feelings of unity, of brotherhood and sisterhood, of oneness.

Once recruits become a part of the group and begin to identify its members as their best friends, they may come to realize that the group has an internal stratification system. Some people are more highly respected than others. Because one wants to be liked and respected by one's new friends and colleagues, obedience to the rules becomes important. As one receives responsibilities and is recognized for contributions to the group, one has begun to climb the stratification ladder. Having taken a step or two up the ladder, the individual has made an initial *investment* in the group. Hence, affective commitment leads naturally to instrumental commitment. Commitment to the group members and commitment to the organization are intertwined—as indeed, the belonging and institutional subsystems of religion are linked.

Retention of members, especially among cults with world-transforming views, also depends on an ongoing set of primary relationships with believers. Bromley and Shupe report that when Moonie devotees are not harbored in supportive environments, defections are very high (1979: 184). The insistence on endogamy (marriage only to individuals within the group) is one way to ensure interlocking relationships, and the Reverend Moon was quick to recognize this. If one's spouse and eventually one's children are within the faith, then defection from the church will also involve separation from one's family of procreation. By ensuring endogamous marriages, a set of inter-locking and mutually reinforcing relationships are created.

Moral Commitment

Moral commitment refers to commitment to the norms and values of the group, indeed, to the meaning system of the religion. If the group is to develop in a coherent way, members must accept the mandates of the ideology—the world view and ethos—as it is formulated by the leaders. To put it another way, the leadership must be able to control the group in order to direct its development. Because religious groups do not have military powers or total economic control over the entire populous, they are limited in the extent to which they can coerce members to obey the norms of the group. They must depend on voluntary compliance. The control issue is more problematic for groups that deviate from the dominant society, for compliance with the religious group means deviation from the dominant culture. Hence, the cause of the group must seem compellingly true, eternal, and just. There are two mechanisms that can enhance the moral commitment of devotees: mortification and transcendence.

The **mortification** process places heavy emphasis on the willfulness, egotism, selfish-ness, and conceit of people, and this generates a sense of profound humility. This is done by emphasizing that without this group or the faith perspective of this charismatic leader, the members would be worthless degenerates. For example, Oneida was a religious commune in upstate New York that survived for thirty-three years in the mid-1800s. It is a fascinating community but is especially remarkable be-cause it is the only free-love commune[6] to

survive for such a long period of time. One reason Oneida proved so viable is because of a practice called mutual criticism. This involved a public confession of all one's faults, weak-nesses, temptations, and areas of needed growth. Furthermore, the assembled members would add to the confession if the confessor failed to include everything. The founder of Oneida, John Humphrey Noyes, was espe-cially forthright and aggressive in probing a person's inner feelings and motives.

The journals and diaries of members offer a fascinating account of how members of Oneida perceived this process. They uniformly re-ported that after such a session, they felt ut-terly humble and worthless. But the more important emotion (and perhaps the more sur-prising one) was a feeling of utter exhilaration and joy. Kanter writes that "the use of mortifi-cation is a sign that the group cares about the individual, about his thoughts and feelings, about the content of his inner world. The group cares enough to pay great attention to the person's behavior, and to promise him warmth, intimacy, and love . . . if he indicates he can accept these gifts without abuse" (1972: 105). The act of being emotionally naked be-fore others whom one trusts tends to engender ecstatic feelings of intimacy and union with one's associates. But recognizing the feeling of worthlessness and humility is also important in understanding why people follow the lead-ership of the group with such unquestioning loyalty. Any personal initiative, critical think-ing, or alternative explanation of things will be defined as egoistic, self-centered, and self-aggrandizing behavior. Any challenge to the doctrine of the group is a sign of "the Devil at

---

[6]Oneida's system of complex marriage meant that any adult man and any adult woman might engage in sexual relations on a given night. However, there were

many norms that guided these practices. In this sense, the *free love* term, which is commonly applied to Oneida, is somewhat of a misnomer. Oneida defined itself as a biblically based and profoundly religious community. The members did not view their sexual practices as promiscuous (Carden 1969; Parker 1935).

work" in the individual or an indication of a lack of humility. In either case, the person may be demoted in the stratification hierarchy of the group. This demotion may induce humility if the other techniques did not.

Many other groups could be cited for similar mechanisms to induce feelings of humility or individual worthlessness. Regardless of specific variations in the way different cults engender the attitude, a sense of personal worthlessness, sinfulness, and self-centeredness is very functional for the group. When people are convinced that they are truly insignificant as individuals, they are more humble and more willing to obey their superiors.[7] They are also less likely to assert themselves in conflict with peers, and deference to others enhances harmony and cooperation.

This leads to the second process: **transcendence.** Although the person may feel worthless as an individual, his or her life has ultimate and eternal meaning as a member of the group. The group offers a hope of final victory that obliterates the meaninglessness of mundane existence. The group offers the Truth and claims an exclusive hold on that Truth. Nowhere else, members believe, can one gain these insights and participate in this victory! This generates a sense of mystery and a feeling of awe for the leaders and/or for the myths, symbols, and rituals of the group. These processes of de-emphasizing the individual, glorifying the group, and creating a sense of awe about the group's ideology are the foundation stones of moral commitment.

Some of the mechanisms that contribute to commitment in sects and cults are antithetical to many denominations. First, the doctrine of the "priesthood of all believers" in some mainline groups[8] is contrary to the "spiritual hierarchy" of many sectarian and cultic groups. Second, the emphasis on open-mindedness and tolerance of others in most mainline denominations counters the sectarian emphasis that one's group has the whole truth, the only truth, and

---

[7]This mortification process is the process most akin to Chinese thought-reform techniques as described by Robert Lifton (1969). In the cult situation, however, people *voluntarily* undergo mortification.

[8]This doctrine is historically Protestant but is not equally applied in all Protestant denominations nor in all congregations of any denomination. Furthermore, many local Catholic groups incorporate this concept and downplay rigid concepts of spiritual status.

▶ **TABLE 5.1**

Kanter's Commitment Theory

Type of Commitment	Processes That Enhance This Commitment
Instrumental commitment (Commitment to the *organization*)	1. Sacrifice 2. Investment
Affective commitment (Commitment to the *members*)	1. Renunciation 2. Communion
Moral commitment (Commitment to the *ideas* as spelled out by the leaders)	1. Mortification 2. Transcendence

the exclusively held truth. The high boundaries of "us" and "them" have been falling away as the more moderate and liberal denominations have stressed cooperation and ecumenism. Third, and perhaps most important, the more liberal clergy in mainline denominations have tended to emphasize the importance of self-esteem, thereby reversing the sectarian denigration of one's self. They see a positive self-image as essential to mental health and well-being and maintain that religions encouraging dependency are not allowing individuals to nurture their God-given creativity. People who respect themselves and their own ideas are more likely to engage in independent and critical thinking, but this does not enhance commitment to the group's ideology. Hence, liberal churches may have lower levels of commitment because of their emphasis on individuality and personal self-esteem.

Many different types of groups and organizations use one or more of the commitment mechanisms discussed by Kanter. The unique quality of nonconventional religious groups is that they must elicit and sustain a very high level of commitment. The cults and sectarian groups that survive are those that use all or most of the commitment processes discussed here.

Commitment, then, can be commitment to the organization; to the group members with whom one has strong emotional ties; or to the ideology and the moral rules of the group, as they are interpreted by the group's leaders. Often, commitment at one level will lead to commitment at another. Although it is possible for people to be committed at only one level, nonconventional religious groups normally are very intense about demanding commitment at all three levels. This is especially true of groups that expect to transform this world. But even traditional religious groups need commitment at multiple levels, for the subsystems that compose a religion are linked together in ways that mutually affect one another. When any one of the three (belonging, meaning, or organizational structure) is weakened, the others are likely to feel some strain.

This takes us to an investigation of the conversion process. How does one move from apathy to commitment? How is it that people come to the point of committing their lives and resources to these groups?

Process Models of Conversion

For the first six decades of this century, conversion was viewed by social scientists as a single event that brought radical change in the orientation of an individual. More recent analyses have tried to identify a process or series of steps involved in conversion (Richardson 1985). In the first real process model—based on a study of conversion among the Moonies in the early 1960s—John Lofland (1977) identified a sequence of factors that operate to move a person from nonmember status to committed devotee.[9] Lofland's theory is based on the "value-added" model of Neil Smelser (1962), which maintains that a social movement or process may best be understood by identifying "successively accumulating factors." According to this perspective, it is the cumulative effect of many different factors that gives rise to specific types of behavior.

According to Lofland, only persons who experience all conditions are likely to convert to a new religious group. Hence, the experiencing of these conditions helps determine who will convert and who will remain uninvolved. "The sequential arrangement of the conditions may be conceived as a funnel"; that is, they "systematically reduce the number of

---

[9]Sometimes this model is referred to as the Lofland-Stark model because the ideas were first set forth in skeletal form in a jointly authored article with Rodney Stark (1965). Lofland's more elaborated version appeared the following year in book form. Several other sequential theories of conversion have also been set forth by social scientists, but most follow a schema quite similar to Lofland's. Those interested in another example of this sequential model (based on research with the Divine Light Mission) might want to see James Downton (1980).

persons who can be considered available for recruitment" (Lofland 1977: 31). A large portion of the population may experience stress or tension, the first condition. A somewhat smaller portion of the population may adopt a religious problem solving perspective, the second condition. The third condition may apply only to a segment of *that* population, and only a few who experience the first three conditions may confront the fourth. Hence, the number of converts, and who those converts are, is largely a function of the proper combination of events in the lives of individuals. (See Box 5.2.) These conditions are either predisposing or situational factors. Lofland maintains that there are three *predisposing conditions* (dispositions, attitudes, outlooks) that must be present for the individual to be susceptible to cult influence. The predisposing conditions are attributes of individuals that exist *prior* to contact with the cult.

Predisposing Conditions

Tension Lofland writes, "It would seem that no model of human conduct escapes some concept of tension, strain, frustration, deprivation, or the like, as a factor in accounting for action" (1977: 35). Indeed, it is a commonly accepted maxim of the social sciences that personal change is generally the result of some felt need for change. This implies a dissatisfaction with the status quo. "This tension is best characterized as a felt discrepancy between some imaginary, ideal state of affairs, and the circumstances in which [potential recruits] actually saw themselves" (Lofland 1977: 35).

In societies such as our own that undergo a great deal of change, persons often experience anomie or normlessness. They feel that they are without roots. Clearly, this anomie creates a great deal of stress in persons. The tension caused by anomie may be resolved in any one of several ways: suicide or affiliation with absolutistic religious groups are two of the possible responses. But anomie is not the only source of stress that can cause dissatisfaction

with one's status quo. And although Lofland viewed tension or dissatisfaction as necessary, it is certainly not sufficient by itself to cause a religious conversion. Dissatisfaction may be worked out in a psychiatrist's office, in a political campaign designed to change social conditions, or in any one of a dozen different ways.

Religious Problem-Solving Perspective The second personal characteristic is an inclination to solve problems by turning to religious leaders or religious methods rather than to political or psychiatric ones. Only when a person begins to attach religious or spiritual meaning to events does the individual become amenable to the message of religious groups. Otherwise, one will seek political, psychiatric, or other resolutions to problems. James Downton (1979) maintains that young people were not favorably inclined toward the Divine Light Mission and the Guru Maharaji until they first sensed that religion was a viable problem-solving route. Hence, Lofland posits that a spiritual outlook is necessary before a potential recruit will take seriously the message of a proselytizing group.

Religious Seekership Lofland insists that among the Moonie converts there was a dissatisfaction with the conventional religious groups and a feeling of being a religious seeker. Virtually all converts had church-hopped or had drifted from one religious group to another. They had already concluded that the world view of the religion in which they were raised was inadequate. The new converts had identified themselves as seekers of truth. However, not all seekers were converted. There must be a certain amount of "cultural conduciveness" between the world view of the group and that of the recruit. To illustrate, in the nineteenth century the Ghost Dance religion spread rapidly among Native American nations. However, it failed to attract the Navajo. The Ghost Dance religion predicted the rise of the dead, but the Navajo were afraid of ghosts. Hence, rather than celebrating such a future event, they refused to have anything to do with this movement. Similarly, it appears that at least a gross congruence of world views between the potential recruit and a religious cult is necessary.

The Shakers might provide another example. They were able to get both married couples and singles to join their group, although they required absolute celibacy of their members. Success in gaining converts stemmed from the fact that they recruited from a society that already defined sexual relations as debased. Presumably, they would have a hard time finding recruits among a people who practice a fertility orgy. Likewise, Lofland suggested that for a person to be a likely candidate for Moonie recruitment, he or she must already have held some attitudes that are consistent with Moonie theology. Uniform congruence of beliefs is not required, but a general compatibility of outlook seemed to be necessary for a potential recruit to become an actual convert.

Situational Contingencies

If these predisposing conditions are operative, the *situational contingencies* become relevant. Situational contingencies are circumstances that influence the social interaction between a potential convert and a recruiter to a religious group.

Turning Point in Life   The converts to the Unification Church had reached important turning points in their own lives. "Each had come to a moment when old lines of action were complete, had failed, or had been or were about to be disrupted, and when they were faced with the opportunity or necessity for doing something different with their lives" (Lofland 1977: 50). Potential converts had recently migrated, had lost or quit a job, or had graduated from, dropped out of, or flunked out of college. On the other hand, Lofland found that marital dissolution and illness seldom served this turning-point function. Apparently, some types of turning points stimulate the meaning and belonging needs more profoundly than do others. Nonetheless, persons who are not at turning points in their lives are less likely to be responsive to proselytization—especially to proselytization of unconventional groups (Moonies, Hare Krishna, etc.). Turning points are times of new beginnings when investment in the status quo is minimal.

Close Cult Affective Bonds   In Lofland's study of the Moonies, almost all recruits were gained through preexisting friendship networks. The Moonies learned that cognitive appeals to ideology (with a focus on the moral commitment level) did not win converts. As the Moonies became aware of this, they gradually began to modify their recruitment strategy. Lofland emphasizes that they "learned to start conversion at the emotional rather than the cognitive level" (1977: 308). In other words, they learned that affective levels of commitment precede moral levels of commitment.

Weakening of Extracult Affective Bonds Because of migration away from one's family or because of disaffection from it, an individual may experience isolation, alienation, or loneliness. Such a person is more in need of emotional support as he or she faces a turning point than is one who has a close network of friends and family. As I have mentioned previously, Moonies consciously looked for signs of transiency (backpacks, individuals who are alone). The person who has no other immediate reference group is less likely to have someone oppose or intervene in the conversion process. Without another individual or group to offer an alternative interpretation of the group, the individual is more likely to be drawn into that group. Furthermore, without another significant reference group, the process of renunciation of the outside is much less complicated.

Intensive Interaction Lofland maintains that some Moonies were only verbally committed, that is, they were not yet totally committed. This seventh condition solidifies commitment to the group through intensive interaction among members. In this way, "moral-level commitment" is enhanced by providing "communion" with the group. Once the intensive interaction provides a sense of unity and oneness, the devotees actively *want* to believe the ideology. By consciously working on strengthening their faith, they come to believe the ideology, to feel a sense of awe about the leader, and to uphold the group's values. The conversion becomes total, and commitment becomes intense at all three levels.

Critique and Evolution of Lofland's Process Model

For a decade and a half, Lofland's model of conversion was used widely by sociologists studying cults and sects, and was supported as recently as 1988 in a study of a black cult (Singer 1988). However, several scholars have voiced reservations about the applicability of

---

▶ **BOX 5.2**

Lofland's Conversion Model

Tension

Religious problem-solving perspective

Religious seekership

Turning point in life

Close cult affective bonds

Weakening of extra-cult affective bonds

Intensive interaction

One might view Lofland's model as a "filtering" of people. Each step involves a filtering out of some people and a filtering or even funneling in of others. Those who have experienced the first six filters become "verbal converts." They must go through the seventh step as well to become "total converts." Total converts really believe the theology or ideology of the group. Verbal converts feel committed to the members of the group, and they verbally assent to belief, but they are not yet really committed at a "moral level."

this particular "process model" to all groups. The first direct challenge came from David Snow and Cynthia Phillips (1980), who studied the conversion process in an American Buddhist movement. They suggest that several of Lofland's stages may not be universal even among cults. First, Snow and Phillips question whether personal tension is necessarily higher for converts than for the general population. They cite self-report survey data that suggest that tension is high among the entire population and question whether the intensity and duration of stress is really higher for those who join new religious movements. Much of the report of tension may be a retrospective interpretation—reading into an earlier situation something that was not felt to be present or important at that time. The ideology causes a reinterpretation of previous experience. This can be seen in the comments of converts reported by Snow and Phillips in Box 5.3.

It is also possible that religious conversion actually *creates* the increased tension. We discussed in chapter 3 the view of A. R. Radcliffe-Brown that religion sometimes creates tension

---

▶ **BOX 5.3**

Tensions and Personal Problems as Factors Leading to Conversion

Male, Caucasian, single, under 30:
> When I joined I didn't think I was burdened by any problems. But as I discovered, I just wasn't aware of them until I joined and they were solved.

Female, Caucasian, single, under 30:
> After I attended these meetings and began chanting, I really began to see that my personal life was a mess.

Male, Caucasian, single, under 30:
> Now as I look back I feel that I was a total loser. At that time, however, I thought I was pretty cool. But after chanting for a while, I found out that my life was just a dead thing. The more I chanted, the more clearly I came to see myself and the more I realized just how many problems I had had.

Male, Caucasian, married, over 30:
> After you chant for a while you'll look back and say, "Gee, I was sure a rotten, unhappy person." I know I thought I was a saint before I chanted, but shortly after I discovered what a rotten person I was and how many problems I had.

The reports of cult members cited here would seem to support the thesis that tension and unhappiness are factors that contribute to cult conversion. However, these reports may represent substantial revisions or reinterpretations of precult experiences. This involves assignment of motives and use of an interpretive schema which was learned from the cult. Hence, the perception of prior strains and problems may be a *result* of conversion rather than a cause of it. The passages quoted here are generally typical of those made by devotees to cult researchers. However, these statements are chosen because their wording illustrates the retrospective nature of the analysis: "as I discovered, . . . I wasn't aware of them until . . ."; "after I attended these meetings . . . I really began to see"; and "as I looked back. . . ."

Source: Quoted in David A. Snow and Cynthia L. Phillips. "The Lofland-Stark Conversion Model: A Critical Reassessment." *Social Problems* April 1980: 430–37. Used by permission.

and anxiety in order to provide social solidarity. Snow and Phillips follow this line of analysis. They suggest that while tension may well exist in the convert, it may sometimes be a *result* of joining the group and of having a new interpretation of the meaning of events. For example, belief that the world will soon end or that all nonmembers are evil—including one's family members who refuse to join—may cause great stress. Furthermore, it may cause one to redefine one's premembership status as depraved and stressful.

Snow and Phillips also insist that a religious problem-solving perspective was not a prerequisite to persons becoming members of the cult they studied. They point out that ideological congruence was *facilitative*—but *not necessary*—for persons to become active members. Similarly, they found that new members did not always define themselves as religious seekers. Many who joined the Buddhist group they studied had not been active in other religious groups. Some claimed that they had probably always been seeking religious truth but had not been aware of what they really wanted until they found the *Nichiren Shoshu* movement. Again, this revised interpretation of one's previous experience *may* be a function of reading things into prior experience so that present behavior makes sense. Such self-reports must be analyzed with sensitivity to possible bias in the data.

Likewise, the question about whether one was at a turning point in one's life at the time one encountered a religious group is a matter of interpretation. "Whether a particular situation or point in one's life constitutes a turning point is not a given, but is largely a matter of definition and attitude. There are few, if any, consistently reliable benchmarks for ascertaining when or whether one is at a turning point in one's life. As a consequence, just about any moment could be defined as a turning point. . . We again face the problem of retrospective reporting" (Snow and Phillips 1980: 439).

Snow and Phillips also insist that it is not necessary that members have weak extracult affective bonds. They suggest that the necessity of this element may depend on several factors. The extent to which the group's values represent a break from values and perspectives of one's family is very important. If group membership does not involve a transformation of the values one shares with one's family, then alienation from family is unnecessary. Moreover, the tendency toward isolation may be related to the extent to which the group is particularistic (the extent to which it insists that it has the exclusive path to truth or salvation). Finally, isolation of members from extracult relationships may be a phenomenon of groups with a revolutionary, idiosyncratic, or peculiar world view. Weakening of extramovement ties by cults may be a strategy to neutralize the stigma that nonmembers attach to the group. If outsiders are neutralized as a reference group, then their opinions are not a threat to the group. If the cultic group is not stigmatized, then the strategy of alienating members from nonmembers is less important.

An empirical study of conversion among Dutch adolescents reported in the early 1990s has also challenged some elements of the Lofland process model. Kox, Meeus, and 't Hart found that while many of the factors identified by Lofland were present, they seemed to vary independently. They did not appear, in this very small sample, to be cumulative as is suggested by the funnel concept. While the idea of a sequential cumulative process seems to be a fruitful way to think about conversion, with various factors *contributing,* at this point there is no consensus about which factors might be *necessary* ones or what the precise sequence might be that is most typical.

Interestingly, Snow and Phillips did find in their study that both recruitment through affective bonds and sustaining members through intensive interaction were critical. In an analysis of ten case studies of conversion in diverse groups, Arthur Greil and David Rudy (1984) found the same two factors to be indispensable factors, and the Dutch study mentioned above revealed that affective bonds were critical in 80 percent of the cases. Other researchers have also found affective bonds and intensive interaction to be central to conversion (Cornwall 1987; Roof and McKinney 1987; Stark and Bainbridge 1985), and the lack of intensive interaction to be crucial to deconversion or apostasy (Jacobs 1987). Weakening of extracult affective bonds has been found to be critical only in nonconventional religious movements.

Actually, Lofland and a colleague have offered a modification of his original theory. They now suggest that there appear to be several conversion processes and that different types of groups tend to employ different processes. Lofland and Norman Skonovd (1981) discuss six different conversion motifs with each involving a slightly different series of factors. Some conversions are induced by nonrational experiences, others involve a more intellectual process of study, and still others stress affective ties and belonging functions. Lofland and Skonovd also conjecture that different modes of conversion may be more common in different epochs of history. Hence, the heavy emphasis on nonrational experience by William James and Herbert Otto earlier in this century may have been due to the fact that mystical modes of conversion were more common then, while affective modes have been more widely employed by groups in the 1960s, 1970s, and 1980s.[10] It is interesting to note, however, that of the six conversion motifs outlined by Lofland and Skonovd, four emphasize belonging and group participation *prior to* belief. Intense involvement normally precedes total conversion. In the case of contemporary sects and cults, this sequence seems to be nearly universal.

The Convert as Activist: A Rational Choice Model

Historically, most social scientists explained conversion using a rather passive model of human behavior. Conversion was an event that happened to the individual because of unconscious psychological processes or compelling social tensions (Richardson 1985). Certainly, the "mind control" hypothesis is consistent with this perspective. The process models of Lofland and others represent somewhat of a break from this determinism. A series of events are believed to be at work—events in which the participant has some choice and makes some decisions. But several researchers believe that even these models have too much of a passive view of the convert. They feel that even these models depict conversion as the result of various social pressures outside of the individual.

Several social scientists have set forth a view of conversion in which the individual is an active agent purposefully making choices and seeking conversion (Straus 1976, 1979; Balch 1980; Balch and Taylor 1976, 1977; Richardson 1985; Kilbourne and Richardson 1989; Dawson 1990; Finke and Stark 1992; Warner 1993). This activist view—sometimes called "rational choice" theory—stresses that individuals are seeking meaning in life, and they consciously join groups that they believe may fulfill their needs. To give the faith a fair chance, they thrust themselves into the roles and behaviors of the group.

One major version of this perspective focuses on role theory.[11] As people play the role of convert, sometimes they find the role rewarding. They make an investment in the group, they gain

---

[10]A few scholars think that what has changed has not been the types of conversion, but the perspectives and paradigms through which scholars have viewed conversions in different eras. See, for example, Kilbourne and Richardson (1989).

[11]Another model, set forth in its most fully developed form by Finke and Stark (1992) is based on an economic model. This approach views churchgoers as consumers who are out to meet their needs or obtain a "product," and depicts churches as entrepreneurial establishments trying to compete in a supply and demand market. Converts are thus regarded as active and rational agents pursuing self-interests, and churches that grow are those which meet consumer demand.

certain ego gratifications for playing the role well, and they may come to believe in the ideas that justify and explain those roles. In essence, the new recruits convert themselves. However, some who join do not find rewarding roles or find that the faith does not meet their meaning needs, and they drop out. Still others may find the roles fulfilling for a while, then find that as role partners change and the organization evolves the roles become unsatisfying. These people then fall away from the group.

The activist perspective need not be incompatible with the reference group models discussed above; it simply serves as a corrective. It is a mistake to view the convert as a passive participant, who is the unwitting "victim" of social processes beyond his or her control (Dawson 1990). The recruit is a participant in the definition of his or her situation. Most sociologists do not view humans as robots who are totally controlled by outside stimuli. Persons are active agents who help shape their environments. But it is also true that reference groups are extremely powerful forces in any person's interpretation of experience. The individual actively chooses his or her reference group, but the reference group in turn helps the individual define norms and make sense of experience. If theorists lose sight of either side of this dual character of humans, their theories will be simplistic and distorted.

Conclusions Regarding the Conversion Process

The research on conversion leads us to two conclusions. First, for most people conversion is not a sudden and all-encompassing event. It is normally the result of a series of events that lead to a complete change in one's commitments and one's outlook on life.[12] Second, the evidence

seems clear from both new religious movements and more conventional groups that affective commitment usually precedes full acceptance of a belief system.[13] If a religious group is able to establish itself as the primary reference group of an individual, the new member is well on his or her way to full commitment. As one person who experienced the "love bombing" of the Moonies put it, "I wanted to break through my feeling of isolation badly enough that right then it almost didn't matter what they believed—if only I could really share myself with them" (quoted in Lofland 1977: 311).

It is worth noting that many devotees of religious groups sometimes castigate themselves or feel guilty if the belief system does not seem to make sense to them. They already feel a commitment to the religious group or to the role they are playing in the group, and their lack of belief is interpreted by them as a personal fault. These converts want desperately to believe. They choose to belong, and they choose to believe; they are not forced against their will.

Again this must not lead us to a simplistic conclusion that affective commitment is *always* chronologically prior to moral or ideological commitment. The order *may* be reversed. There are many historical examples of persons who have had mystical experiences that changed their lives. For example, in the case of Saint Paul, it certainly appears that ideological conversion preceded any close affective bonds with members of the Christian community.

Any one of the types of commitment (affective, instrumental, or moral) may come first, depending on personality characteristics, the cultural climate, and the emphasis of the particular religious group in question. There is, for example, an understandable difference in conversion experiences between conservative and

---

[12]In chapter 6 we explore cognitive models of conversion, including changes of perspective that occur among mystics, saints, and founders of new religious traditions.

[13]This does not negate the affirmation that the meaning function is primary. The meaning function is primary in that it is closer to the manifest purpose of religion. Chronologically, however, the belonging function seems to come first.

liberal Christians. **Conservative** (or evangelical) **churches**[14] tend to have a negative view of human nature; sin, depravity and egoism are believed to have been innate human tendencies since the time of Adam and Eve. Thus, conversion in the form of a radical break from the past is necessary. **Liberal churches** (which includes "mainstream" or "old line" churches such as Congregationalists, Presbyterians, Episcopalians, Unitarians, Methodists, and Christian or Disciples of Christ) tend to stress the creation myth that appears in the first chapter of Genesis, in which humanity is said to be created in the image of God and is declared intrinsically good. Based on this mythology, humans are viewed as capable of either good or evil, and the critical element is education, nurturance, and growth. The latter involves gradual processes of change, and sudden transformations are simply not emphasized in the theology or required for membership in the group. It is reasonable to expect, therefore, that the nature of religious change and the frequency of reported "conversions" would be different for these groups.

While there are variations, the evidence remains strong that, for the majority of people and the majority of religious groups, acceptance of beliefs is a *late* development in the process of becoming a committed member. As we will now see, some of the same forces are at work when people decide to switch from one conventional denomination to another. This latter type of religious change may—or may not—involve modification of an individual's world view.

"Switching" among Mainline Denominations

Changes in denominational affiliation by Christians have become fairly common in the United States. According to a Gallup Poll, a minority of U.S. residents (43 percent) report that they have remained in the same denomination throughout their lives (reported in Jacquet 1980: 269). Further, the tendency to leave the church of one's childhood is highest among younger adults. So while "switching" from one mainline denomination to another is quite rare in Canada[15] (Bibby 1987a: 132), this behavior is common and on the rise in the United States.

Switching of denominations does not necessarily involve a conversion. It may not involve any change of world view. But it does involve a change in organizational membership and loyalty. In the past two decades, church administrators and social scientists have become interested in understanding why some churches are growing and others are declining and whether switching is a primary factor in the change of fortunes of various religious groups.

Dean Kelley's book, *Why Conservative Churches Are Growing* (1972) was one of the first to explore this phenomenon. Kelley's thesis was that people are attracted to churches that have strict standards of membership and that expect members to invest much of their time and resources in the group. He pointed out that conservative churches (fundamentalist, charismatic, and evangelical) are growing rapidly while liberal churches are declining. Box 5.4 provides the type of data Kelley used. Readers can see the decline in United Methodist, United Presbyterian, United Church of Christ, and

---

[14]Southern Baptist, Missouri Lutheran Synod, Assemblies of God, Nazarenes, Churches of God, and other sects are among the conservative churches.

---

[15]This may be because the big three establishment denominations in Canada (Roman Catholic, United Church, and Anglican) each provide a considerable range of religious expressions. One can find an alternative religious "menu" without changing denominations. Interestingly, conservative evangelical Christianity is not growing in Canada the way it appears to have been in the United States. For example, the percentage of Baptists in Canada has declined from 5 percent of the population in 1925 to 3 percent in the 1980s (Brinkerhoff and Bibby 1985).

Episcopal denominations. He believes people are switching to more conservative denominations (Churches of God, Nazarenes, Seventh-Day Adventists, Jehovah's Witnesses, Southern Baptists, Mormons). The reasons he cites for conservative church growth are basically congruent with Kanter's theory of commitment.

However, Kelley's interpretation of data has been challenged from several sources. It appears that most of the converts to the conservative churches are rejoining after a period of absence, or they are coming from other conservative congregations. The conservative churches actually seem to be growing because of two factors: (1) recruits from other evangelical or fundamentalist groups and (2) a high fertility rate in conservative churches.[16] In one study, less than 10 percent of the new members to conservative churches were converts from outside the evangelical community (Bibby and Brinkerhoff 1973). On the other hand, liberal churches seem to be drawing a much larger percentage of their new members from the more conservative churches. The movement of denominational switching is not primarily from liberal churches to conservative ones, but vice versa (Bibby 1978; Newport 1979; Roof and McKinney 1987).[17] A similar recruitment pattern holds in Canada as well, where conservative churches have been slightly less successful than the more liberal mainline churches in reaching the unchurched. Most recruits to conservative churches in that country are from other conservative groups (Bibby 1987a).

Despite the overall switching trend from conservative groups to liberal ones, many conservative churches in the United States are growing in membership while liberal churches generally are declining. One reason is that most liberal and moderate churches do not *retain* members as well as most conservative churches. We must be wary not to generalize too broadly here. Conservative churches have more commitment mechanisms, and these tend to enhance retention. Jehovah's Witnesses, Seventh-Day Adventists, Southern Baptists, Pentecostals and holiness groups, and Mormons have some of the highest retention rates. However, conservative fundamentalist and evangelical sects, whose members are largely lower socioeconomic class, have some of the worst retention rates (Roof and McKinney 1987). Their poor retention rates are countered by very high birth rates (Newport 1979; Perrin 1989; Roof and McKinney 1987) and by very active recruitment from other conservative sects. There is a great deal of switching between these groups. While they lose many members, they gain at least an equal number from similar groups. As long as their birth rates remain high, they can lose more members to liberal churches than they gain and still grow in absolute numbers.

Hence, the growth of conservative churches and the decline of liberal churches makes sense. The conservative churches in the United States employ more commitment mechanisms, have higher fertility rates, and have more religious training in the home, accounting for better overall membership trends (Bibby and Brinkerhoff 1973; Hoge and Roozen 1979; Newport 1979). On the other hand, liberal mainline churches in Canada have better retention rates than their counterparts in the United States, and are not experiencing as much decline in numbers. One recent study of a mainline congregation in the United States

---

[16]Dean Hoge and David Roozen (1979: 322) report that, over time, birth rates have been the most consistent correlate with growth and decline of church membership. They insist that "contextual factors" (aspects of the larger society that the churches cannot control) have usually had a greater effect on church membership levels than have "institutional factors" (policies or actions within the church itself).

[17]Switching seems to be primarily to the high-status (generally most liberal) and the very low-status (generally most conservative) churches and away from middle-status congregations. Hence, the movement is not entirely in one direction (Newport 1979; Roof and McKinney 1987).

Church Membership Statistics, 1940–1991: Selected U.S. Denominations

The data in this table give an indication of the growth and/or decline of various denominations. Although the numbers are interesting, caution must be maintained in interpreting these statistics. First, these are figures reported by the denominations themselves. While reliability and completeness in statistical reporting were among the criteria used in selecting the bodies, there are differences in reporting procedures. For example, the Roman Catholic Church reported all individuals from the time of baptism. Because Catholics practice infant

baptism, their figures include infants and small children. Many Protestant denominations report only church members. Hence, their figures include only those above the age of twelve or thirteen and who have gone through confirmation. Finally, some denominations remove members from their "active" rolls who do not make financial contributions, attend church, or otherwise participate in the life of the church. (They do this to lower the "per head" tax to the denomination and to keep accurate records of active members.) In-

Denomination	1940	1950
Assemblies of God[b]	198,834	318,478
Baptist General Conference	NA	48,647[c]
Christian and Missionary Alliance	22,832	58,347
Christian Church (Disciples of Christ)	1,685,966	1,767,964
Church of God (Anderson, Ind.)	74,497	107,094
Church of God (Cleveland, Tenn.)	63,216	121,706[e]
Church of Jesus Christ Latter-day Saints	724,401[d]	1,111,314
Church of Brethren	176,908	186,201
Church of Nazarene	165,532	226,684
Cumberland Presbyterian Church	73,357	81,806
Episcopal Church	1,996,434	2,417,464
Evangelical Covenant Church of America	45,634	51,850
Evangical Lutheran Church of America	(3,117,626)	(3,982,508)
Free Methodist Church of North America	45,890	48,574
Jehovah's Witnesses	NA	NA
Lutheran Church-Missouri Synod	1,277,097	1,674,901
Mennonite Church	51,304	56,480
North American Baptist Conference	NA	41,560
Presbyterian Church (U.S.A.)	(2,690,969)[a]	(3,210,635)[a]
Reformed Church in America	255,107	284,504
Reorganized Church of Latter-day Saints	106,554	124,925
Roman Catholic Church	21,284,455	28,634,878
Salvation Army	238,357	209,341
Seventh-Day Adventists	176,218	237,168
Southern Baptist Convention	4,949,174	7,079,889
United Church of Christ	(1,708,146)[a]	(1,977,418)[a]
United Methodist Church	(8,043,454)[a]	(9,653,178)[a]
Wisconsin Evangelical Lutheran Synod	256,007[d]	307,216

Primary source: *Yearbook of American and Canadian Churches, 1987*, by Constant H. Jacquet. © 1987 by The National Council of The Churches of Christ in the USA. Used by permission of the publisher, Abingdon Press. (This data was supplemented with information

from the *Yearbook of American and Canadian Churches, 1993* edited by Kenneth B. Bedell, and from *Where Are the Lutherans?* Minneapolis: Augsburg Press, 1984.)

[a] Statistics listed in parentheses are composite totals for each of the denominations which eventually

actives are held on an "inactive list," but they are not reported in these statistics. Finally, those interested in total numbers of denominational families (e.g., all Methodists or all Baptists) would not get complete figures from this table. Many small sectarian offshoots of each denomination are not reported here.

The pattern to which Kelley points may be seen if readers compare recent membership patterns of the United Presbyterians, United Methodists, United Church of Christ, and Episcopalians with those of the Churches of God, the Nazarenes, the Assembly of God, the Church of Jesus Christ of Latter-day Saints (Mormons), the Jehovah's Witnesses, the Southern Baptist Convention, and other conservative groups.

It is important to remember that these are crude figures of growth and decline. Studies that indicate direction of switching have been based on surveys that asked switchers about their present and former denominations. Obviously, such figures provide more specific data for analysis.

1960	1970	1980	1991
508,602	625,027	1,064,490	2,234,708
72,056	103,955	133,385	134,658
59,657	112,519	189,710	267,853
1,801,821	1,424,479	1,177,984	1,022,926
142,796	150,198	176,429	214,743[i]
170,261	272,278	435,012	620,393
1,486,887	2,073,146	2,811,006	4,336,000
199,947	182,614	170,839	148,253[h]
307,629	383,284	484,276	573,834
88,452	92,095	96,553	42,433
3,269,325	3,285,826	2,786,004	2,471,880
60,090	67,441	77,737	89,648
(5,295,502)	5,650,137	5,373,394	5,245,177
55,338	64,901	68,477	73,572
250,000	388,920	565,309	914,079[i]
2,391,195	2,788,536	2,625,650	2,607,309
73,125	88,522	99,511	99,431[i]
50,646	55,080	43,041	43,087
4,151,860)[a]	(4,045,408)[a]	(3,362,086)[a]	3,778,358
354,621	367,606	345,532	340,991
155,291	152,670	190,087	150,143[i]
42,104,900	48,214,729	50,449,842	58,267,424
254,141	326,934	417,357	446,403
317,852	420,419	571,141	733,026
9,731,591	11,628,032	13,600,126	15,232,347
(2,241,134)[a]	1,960,608	1,736,244	1,583,830
(10,641,310)[a]	10,671,774	9,584,711	8,785,135
348,184[f]	381,321	407,043	420,039

merged to form the group listed here.
[b] Assemblies of God statistics for 1971 and later are full membership statistics.
[c] Data for 1952.
[d] Data for 1939.

[e] Data for 1951.
[f] Data for 1961.
[g] Data for 1989.
[h] Data for 1990.

[i] Data for 1992.
NA = not available.

that *is* growing at a very healthy rate revealed that the key to their success lays largely in a strategy of implementing affective and instrumental commitment mechanisms—small support groups for emotional bonding, eliciting a commitment of time and energy in the organization by new members, and so forth (Wilson et al. 1993).

This entire field of church growth and decline is enormously controversial currently in the sociology of religion. Many books and articles published in the 1990s are devoted to exploring the reasons for the trends and, indeed, the direction of the trends. Some scholars side with Kelley, asserting switching to evangelical churches is occurring and that strictness, absoluteness, and otherworldliness are powerful attractions that cause growth (Finke and Stark 1992; Perrin and Mauss 1991).[18] Others counter the argument with alternative data and interpretations (e.g., Bibby and Brinkerhoff 1992; Smith 1992). One sociologist—using information from sample surveys rather than from denominational reports—has even argued that as an absolute proportion of the population, conservative churches as a whole are *not* growing (Smith 1992). While there are many trends within trends, it does appear that in the United States certain conservative churches are gaining a larger overall proportion of the *church-affiliated population.*

Regardless, switching does occur, and it is important to recognize the predominant reasons for this behavior. The predominating drift from conservative to more liberal churches does not seem to be primarily an attraction to modernistic theology. What happens is that people tend to worship with others of a similar socioeconomic class. As people are upwardly mobile, they often change their denominational affilia-

tion. It is not clear whether the move to a denomination of higher status is usually a planned "image-enhancing" strategy or merely a function of joining a church where one has a friendship network (co-workers and colleagues). In any case, the move to higher-status churches is commonly a move to a more modern or liberal theology, for the high-status churches tend to be more modern in theology. For someone who is in a professional occupation or who has moved up the social ladder, the more modern, more secular theology may be appealing. A world view that accepts the advances of science may provide more personal coherence and meaning to a highly educated scientist than does a world view that rejects Darwin. Further, religions of the have-nots tend to condemn materialism and the accumulation of possessions as signs of depravity. This may be comforting to the dispossessed, but it can be most uncomfortable to those who are affluent. Liberal theology tends to embrace this world more completely. Regardless of reasons, changes in socioeconomic status do seem to be the major source of denominational switching (Hoge and Carroll 1978; Newport 1979).[19]

A second important factor is denominational intermarriage. When a person marries someone of the same religion but of a different denomination, one of the two is likely to switch. This comprises a significant proportion of religious switchers (Newport 1979; Suchman 1992). Hence, the "friendship network" factor is extremely important in this case as well (one's spouse being the "friend").[20] One reason that Roman Catholics, Jews, and conservative Protestants tend to have higher retention rates than do liberal Protestants is that the

---

[18]Perrin and Mauss in a subsequent study distinguished "strictness" (absolutism, conformity, and fanaticism) and "social strength" (commitment, discipline, and missionary zeal), and found in that study that the two vary somewhat independently. (See Perrin and Mauss 1993.)

[19]I should hasten to add that there is not consensus on this point either. Based on trends in the past decade, Stephen Warner (1993: 1077) is convinced that "switching is decreasingly likely to mirror upward social mobility and to represent instead genuine religious change."

[20]Hoge and Roozen (1979) report that marriages in which partners continue to belong to different denominations are highly correlated with religious inactivity.

former are much more likely to marry within their own denominations (McCutcheon 1988).

Newport concludes that "the present evidence argues against the notion that Americans pick and choose their religious affiliation on the basis of some well thought-out and *theologically* based criteria" (1979: 550). He goes on to say that this does not imply a total absence of theological considerations, but that such concerns appear, from current evidence, to be secondary.

It is clear that denominational switching is not the same as an internal conversion experience. Much of the change from one denomination to another is a matter of merely changing organizational membership and a change in world view may not be necessary. But the feeling of belonging—because of friendship networks or because of socioeconomic homogeneity—seems to be the primary influence in this decision to switch. Reginald Bibby's summary of the research on recruitment among Canadian evangelicals seems to apply equally well to American churches of all kinds: "If they are serious about recruiting 'real live sinners,' the best approach is either to befriend them or marry them. For this is how the majority of outsiders are actually recruited" (1987a: 30).

This does not mean that we can simply ignore Kelley's thesis that the growing churches are those that emphasize uncompromising theological principles. First, strictness tends to induce high levels of commitment and retention. Second, it may be that downwardly mobile people are more concerned with theology (answers to questions about the *meaning* of life) and upwardly mobile people are more concerned with social functions—such as composition of church membership (Newport 1978: 538).[21]

---

[21]Such conclusions must be acknowledged at this stage of research as tentative. At least one researcher believes that the opposite is true: Wade Roof believes that meaning functions are more important among liberal cosmopolitans and belonging functions are more critical for conservatives who are oriented to local issues (Roof 1978: 207).

The pattern of substantial growth in many of the very conservative churches is clearly the result of a complex mix of factors: higher birth rates, higher percentages of endogamous marriages, more commitment mechanisms, stronger plausibility structures, and higher overall retention of members. Their numerical success is clearly *not* due to switching of members from liberal churches to conservative ones or to recruitment of large numbers of people from among the unchurched. The old mainline churches in the United States, on the other hand, seem to be suffering from apathy and dropping out more than from massive outmigration to other denominations.

Summary

Commitment and conversion are complex processes, and there is much we do not know. What does appear entirely clear at this point is that the new religious movements are not engaged in brainwashing as was once charged by the anticult movement and by the media.

Commitment may involve one or more dimensions: intellectual commitment to an ideology or a world view (moral commitment), emotional commitment to the other members of the group (affective commitment), or commitment to the organization itself (instrumental commitment). Organizations that require high levels of commitment, such as unconventional world transforming cults, must instill commitment at many of these levels. Although cult conversion has often been treated in the popular press as a manipulated intellectual transformation, the research suggests that affective commitment to other members usually comes first (the belonging system), followed by instrumental commitment (the structural system), and then moral commitment (the meaning system). This sequence seems to hold in the majority of cases for mainline denominations as well. Hence, our conclusion is that belonging functions are prior in religious groups, even if meaning functions are primary. On the other hand, nonrational religious experiences or theological arguments may be the first and foremost elements of commitment for many people. One must be wary of overgeneralization. There are probably multiple conversion processes, some of which are more affective and some of which are more intellectual in nature. We are only beginning to understand these processes and the factors that make one process more or less amenable to certain persons and to particular periods of history.

Switching denominations also seems to be a result largely of affective factors. Friendship networks and marriages across denominations appear to be the most powerful factors, but other factors are at work as well. Interestingly, the conservative churches are the fastest-growing, despite the fact that most switching is toward the more liberal churches (and from liberal to "no preference"). This growth pattern is because birth rates are highest in the more conservative churches and strict membership rules in those churches generally contribute to higher levels of retention. Liberal churches gain more new members from other churches, but they lose members at even higher rates than they gain them.

In this chapter we have used sociological concepts and theories to help us understand conversion and commitment. In chapter 6 we turn to a very different perspective for understanding these processes. By exploring cognitive theories of the same phenomena, the reader will be able to see how different paradigms can lead social scientists to different sets of research questions and different sets of conclusions.

CHAPTER SIX

The Social Psychology of Conversion and Commitment: Cognitive Perspectives

I n chapter 5 we viewed religion from a traditional sociological perspective. We discussed such central sociological concepts as roles, reference groups, and group functions. However, there is another significant theoretical perspective on religion and world views that deserves our attention. This approach is somewhat more psychological than sociological in character, for it has to do with perception and with the development of cognitive processes. But the sociologist would be seriously remiss to ignore this line of research, for it raises some important issues that could alter our understanding of conversion, the development of a person's world view, and the nature of commitment.

Our discussion of cognitive theories includes two approaches: cognitive structural theory[1] and Batson and Ventis's cognitive re-creation approach.

Cognitive Structuralism

The structuralist approach emerged from the research on cognitive development conducted by Jean Piaget and his followers.[2] Piaget (1950; 1954) identified a sequence of steps that occur in intellectual development, steps through which every individual in every culture must progress. He maintains that each stage represents a way of understanding or making sense of experience. Furthermore, he insists that movement through each of these stages is an innate characteristic of the developing human mind. This insight may have important implications for understanding world views. For

---

[1]Cognitive structuralism is so named because it posits an innate developmental structure in the minds of all persons, regardless of cultural background. This school of thought is also sometimes called cognitive developmentalism, structural developmentalism, developmental epistemology, genetic epistemology, or developmental costructionism.

[2]There is another school of structuralism that has emerged from anthropological research. We will be limiting our discussion to the work of Piaget, Kohlberg, and Fowler. Students interested in structuralism may also want to explore the anthropological work of Claude Levi-Strauss, Lucien Levi-Bruhl, and their followers.

example, Ronald Goldman, who applied Piaget's approach to religious education, maintains that a child in the concrete operational stage (seven to twelve years old) is legalistic and literalistic. Hence, the child at this stage will understand biblical stories literally regardless of how they are taught (Goldman 1964: 165). Only when the child enters the formal operational stage of thinking can he or she understand biblical stories as mythical symbols. Each stage therefore represents a kind of world view—or at least profoundly affects one's world view.

According to Piaget, a person does not move to a new stage until he or she experiences cognitive dissonance—an internal, intellectual conflict—that forces one to face the fact that one's present interpretation of experience is inadequate. Change comes about in one's world view as one matures intellectually. Each change of stage, in one sense, represents a sort of conversion. It should be clear that this theory is primarily concerned with changes in the intellectual sphere. Insofar as religious conversion represents a change in world view, structuralist research may offer significant insights.

Kohlberg's Moral Development Model

Basing his research on this structuralist position, Lawrence Kohlberg developed a theory of moral development (Duska and Whelan 1975; Kohlberg 1971, 1980; Wilcox 1979). The implications of the research go well beyond strictly moral decision making; the theory has to do with one's world view. Kohlberg maintains that all persons, regardless of religious background or culture, move through the same sequence of stages. His cross-cultural research suggests that one's formal religious affiliation and one's culture may affect the rate at which one advances through the stages, but not the sequence. Furthermore, Kohlberg and his followers maintain that no one ever skips a stage.

Kohlberg's research is conducted by giving children moral dilemmas in which two values are in conflict (e.g., the right to property versus the value of human life). The child is asked what would be the right thing to do in each situation (see Box 6.1). The specific answer (e.g., whether or not Heinz should steal the drug) is of much less interest to the structuralists than is the *rationale* that is given. The researcher asks, "Why is that the right thing to do?" It is the answer to this question that is critical in understanding one's moral stage, for each stage represents a mode of reasoning and an outlook on life. Only by understanding the individual's rationale can one determine his or her outlook. For example, two people may agree on what is appropriate behavior in the case of Heinz, but one person may be responding to selfish interests while the other is concerned with philosophical reflections about what would be just for everyone. Kohlberg has done longitudinal studies on the same individuals for a span of almost twenty-five years. Based on these extensive longitudinal studies, he has identified three levels of thinking with two stages at each level, six stages in all.

Preconventional Level   A tiny infant has no sense of right or wrong. The infant simply experiences the world. But gradually that child comes to realize that some behaviors result in punishment. Playing with electrical plugs may result in a shout of "No!" from the parents and a slap on the hand. Even before developing the ability to talk, the child begins to sense that some behavior is wrong. The child has begun to enter level 1. At this preconventional level, the person is entirely egocentric in outlook. Right or wrong is gauged strictly in terms of the consequences for that individual. The person's outlook is quite literally "looking out for number one." The person is not able to project into a role other than the one he or she is currently experiencing. Small children are egocentric in their perception, and Kohlberg contends that some adults remain at this level.

► **BOX 6.1**

Examples of Moral Dilemmas Used by Kohlberg

A. Judy is a twelve-year-old girl. She had saved babysitting and lunch money for a long time so that she would have enough money to buy a ticket to a rock concert that was coming to her town. Her mother had promised her that she could go to the rock concert if she saved the money herself. She had managed to save up the $5 the ticket cost plus another $3. Later, her mother changed her mind and told Judy that she had to spend the money on new clothes for school. Judy was disappointed and decided to go to the rock concert anyway. She bought a ticket and told her mother that she had been able to save only $3. That Saturday she went to the performance, telling her mother that she was spending the day with a friend. A week passed without her mother finding out. Judy then told her older sister Louise that she had gone to the performance and had lied to her mother about it.

1. Should Louise, the older sister, tell their mother that Judy had lied about the money or should she keep quiet? Why?
2. What would be the best reason for Louise to keep quiet? Why?
3. Louise thinks about how it would influence Judy in the future if Louise tells. What influence on Judy's future should Louise consider? Why?

B. In Europe a woman was near death from a special kind of cancer. There was one drug that the doctors thought might save her. It was a form of radium that a druggist in the same town had recently discovered. The drug was expensive to make, but the druggist was charging ten times what the drug cost him to make. He paid $200 for the radium and charged $2,000 for a small dose of the drug. The sick woman's husband Heinz went to everyone he knew to borrow the money, but he could only get together about $1,000, which is half of what it cost. He told the druggist that his wife was dying and asked him to sell it cheaper or let him pay later, but the druggist said, "No, I discovered the drug, and I'm going to make money from it." So Heinz got desperate and broke into the man's store to steal the drug for his wife.

1. Should Heinz steal the drug? Why?
2. Which is worse, letting someone die or stealing? Why?
3. What does the value of life mean to you, anyway?

C. In a country in Europe, a poor man named Valjean could find no work, nor could his sister and brother. Without money, he stole food and medicine that they needed. He was captured and sentenced to prison for six years. After a couple of years, he escaped from the prison and went to live in another part of the country under a new name. He saved money and slowly built up a factory. He gave his workers the highest wages and used most of his profits to build a hospital for people who couldn't afford good medical care. Twenty years had passed when a tailor recognized the factory owner as Valjean, the escaped convict whom the police had been looking for back in his hometown.

1. Should the tailor report Valjean to the police? Why?
2. Suppose that Valjean were reported and brought before the judge. Should the judge have him finish his sentence or let him go free?
3. From society's point of view, what would be the best reason for the judge to have Valjean finish his sentence?

Used by permission of Lawrence Kohlberg.

There are two stages at the preconventional level. The first of these is the punishment-obedience orientation. At this stage, the child is concerned first and foremost about obeying superiors in order to avoid punishment. "Wrong" is whatever one gets punished for, and "right" is whatever powerful people want. In a very real sense, the person believes that might makes right. The stage is egocentric because the individual is concerned only with avoiding punishment for himself or herself.

The stage 2 person is still egocentric, but he or she is more calculating in determining right from wrong. The person is willing to risk the possibility of being caught and punished if the potential reward is great enough. A person at this stage engages in a cost-benefit analysis with his or her own needs and desires as the criteria for evaluation of cost and benefit. At this stage, the person recognizes the need for friends and social relationships. The concept of justice or fairness in such relationships is reciprocity. A stage 2 person would help a friend if the friend would reciprocate, but if the individual doesn't think the friend would help in a similar situation, then aid may be withheld. Justice means that "I'll scratch your back if (and only if) you will scratch mine." The bottom line in any relationship at stage 2 is "what's in it for me."

Conventional Level   The second level is the conventional level. At this level, the individual begins to realize the importance of the social group. Conformity to the social group takes on extreme importance, and the individual is willing to sacrifice his or her own needs and desires for the sake of the group. One common definition of the socialization process is "convincing individuals to *want* to do what they *must* do (for the society to survive)." At the conventional level, the person is thoroughly socialized such that social norms and social needs are internalized in the individual. The conventional level

of thinking focuses on reducing egocentrism. On the other hand, the conventional level usually heightens ethnocentrism.[3] This level includes stages 3 and 4.

Stage 3, interpersonal sharing, is oriented toward pleasing significant others or conforming to a reference group in order to be liked. First and foremost, the individual wants to conform to the norms of the group or the expectations of specific other people. Kohlberg sometimes calls this the "good boy/nice girl" stage.

When I was a child, I remember visiting frequently with an older woman. Sometimes her expectations for my behavior were more limiting than the norms in my own home. If she would scold me for misbehaving when I felt I had done nothing wrong, I would question why that behavior was inappropriate. The answer was always the same: "What will the neighbors think?" I have no idea what stage I might have been operating on at that time, but the woman was clearly thinking at stage 3. Her criterion for right or wrong behavior was always what someone else would think. (This reference point was not limited to her conversations with children.) The stage 3 person wants to conform to the expectations of those with whom she or he has a face-to-face relationship.

Eventually, the person is likely to discover that if everyone conformed only to the expectations of his own family and friends, the entire society might collapse. Survival of a society requires laws, and it requires that the citizens obey the laws. Maintenance of the social order at all costs becomes the criterion for "right." The person at this stage (stage 4) is likely to be a great advocate of law and order. Obeying authority is extremely important to

---

[3]Ethnocentrism is the tendency to assume that one's own society's norms, values, and cultural patterns are the only moral standards. It is manifested in a closed-minded and narrow loyalty to one's own culture and a prejudice against other ways of life.

such a person, not because of fear of punishment, but because the social system must be preserved. Again, persons at this stage are very ethnocentric, but the circle of loyalties has expanded beyond one's immediate acquaintances; one's loyalties now include one's nation or ethnic group. The battle cry that one often hears during wartime is indicative of this stage: "Our country, right or wrong." Such a statement suggests that loyalty to country is so strong that moral questions are irrelevant; not even God dare criticize her! What is right is what is good for my country. Furthermore, wrong is defined in terms of the law. A person at this stage is not even particularly concerned with whether the law is just for everyone. Of course, the reference point may be a group other than the country, and the laws may be other than the *civil* laws. The loyalty may be to an ethnic or religious group, and the "law" may be encoded in scripture rather than in civil law.

Principled Level The third level, with stages 5 and 6, is the principled level. Kohlberg maintains that 80 percent of the American population has not reached this level. He also suggests that this level is usually not attained until the person is at least in his or her early twenties. Kohlberg's principled level involves a decision-making procedure that is based on well-defined social and ethical principles. The thinking is more abstract, and one considers many more factors in order to determine a just solution to a problem. At this level, the individual defines morality in terms of fairness for everyone, not just for self or for one's own group. Rather than being egocentric or ethnocentric, the person at this level attempts to develop moral principles that are *universalistic.*

The fifth stage is referred to as social contract thinking. Unlike the person at stage 4, the individual at stage 5 asks whether a law is just before deciding whether it should be obeyed.

The person emerging from stage 4 thinking usually goes through a process of relativism: do your own thing. However, relativism is hardly the material for building a just and stable society. Soon the individual learns that his or her rights are limited by the rights of the neighbor. As the adage goes, one's right to swing an arm is limited by the proximity of a neighbor's nose. Hence, the person begins to think in terms of how to construct a legal system (a social contract) in which the rights of each individual can be protected. Laws are to be obeyed if they are agreed on by the members of the society and if they are indeed fair to all members of that society. Furthermore, the stage 5 thinker is interested in procedural justice and insists that due process must be protected. Maintenance of due process is at least as important as the conviction of any given lawbreaker, for due process protects the civil liberties of the innocent. The framers of the U.S. Constitution were excellent examples of stage 5 thinkers.

Stage 6, the universal ethical principle orientation, emphasizes respect for human personality as a supreme value. Moral decisions are based on well-thought-out ethical principles. These are logically comprehensive, universal, and consistent. They are not concrete rules (like the Ten Commandments) but abstract ethical guidelines for decision making. Mahatma Gandhi and Martin Luther King Jr. are examples of such thinkers, but one could also point to the ethical systems of a number of philosophers and theologians.

Typically, a person is in a given stage for two or three years. It is possible, however, for a person to "freeze" at a particular stage. Some adults, for example, have never progressed beyond the very egoistic preconventional level. Progress in moral thinking, when it does occur, is stimulated by hearing a moral rationale that is one stage higher than the person's current stage at a time when one is experiencing cognitive dissonance. (A moral argument that is more than one stage above the individual's present thinking is said to be unintelligible to that individual. One might as well speak in a foreign language.)

Kohlberg points out that although he has identified a developmental process that humans go through, this does not automatically mean that persons have to go through these stages or that the stage 6 person is more moral. That is a value judgment rather than a description by a social scientist.

Kohlberg's work has been criticized on several grounds, but the most serious flaw in his work was that he used only males in his original studies, and the model of stage development was built on the basis of his early data. One former associate of Kohlberg, Carol Gilligan (1982), insists that the stages of development are rather different for girls and women than for boys and men. Her research suggests that males are socialized to think in terms of individual achievement and of the necessity of laws or rules to govern competitive

▶ **FIGURE 6.1**

Kohlberg's Stages of Moral Development

6. Universal ethical principles	Decision making based on ethical principles that are logically comprehensive, consistent, and universal.	Principled (universalistic) level
5. Social contract orientation	Protect individual rights and liberties; concern with due process. Justness of laws important.	Principled (universalistic) level
4½. Relativism phase		
4. Societal maintenance orientation	Maintain social order for its own sake; "law and order" is highest priority.	Conventional (ethnocentric) level
3. Interpersonal sharing orientation	Desire to be liked; loyalty to in-group.	Conventional (ethnocentric) level
2. Instrumental relativist orientation	Cost-benefit analysis; "You scratch my back, and I'll scratch yours."	Preconventional (egocentric) level
1. Punishment obedience orientation	Avoidance of punishment; deference to powerful people.	Preconventional (egocentric) level
0. No concept of moral imperative	Tiny infant who does not yet have language.	

behavior. Females are socialized to view nurturance, identification with others, and development of community as ultimate goals. Women are much less likely to view rule making as a central method of problem solving. The problem is that stages 4 and 5 in Kohlberg's scheme are oriented toward rules and rule making.

While working with Kohlberg, Gilligan was troubled by the fact that females seemed less likely to reach the higher stages. The problem was not that females were arrested at a lower stage but that there was a bias in how those stages were formulated. Gilligan's work is newer and has much less data available to support her own sequence. In fact, her sequence of stages is less delineated at this point.[4] But she suggests that level 3 thinking for women (universalism) focuses on meaningful relationships and on caring for others (nurturance). Moral thinking for females at this stage is characterized less by the impersonal language of laws and rules and more by concern for constructive interpersonal ties between people. As in Kohlberg's theory, Gilligan believes that at the highest level of moral development, one is concerned with the welfare of *all* persons (including one's self).

Moral development theory focuses fundamentally on role-taking capability. The research is highly relevant to understanding world views. Other cognitive structuralists have begun to explore other aspects of perceiving and thinking as well. One line of research has been on stages of development in faith.

Fowler's Faith Development Model

James Fowler (1981) has developed a model of faith development, which is a further out-

growth of the cognitive structuralist model.[5] Like Kohlberg, Fowler posits six stages. The stages are based substantially on the sophistication of one's understanding of symbolism and on one's perception of authority. All six stages may occur within any of the world religions; the stages refer to the cognitive processing of symbols and myths, not to the content or specific beliefs of a faith.

Stage 1 occurs in children between the ages of two and about six or seven. Called **intuitive-projective,** this stage is egocentric, with the individual unable to imagine that there could be any other perspective on events and experiences other than his or her own. The world is experienced without benefit of inductive or deductive logic; events occur as isolated episodes without any necessary causal links. The world is a magical place in which anything is possible: Santa coming down chimneys, monsters twice the size of the house sneaking into the child's bedroom at night, and a small wooden puppet named Pinocchio being able to turn into a "a real live boy."

The line between reality and fantasy is indistinct. My own daughter, when she was about four years old, had heard the children's story *The Witch at the Window.* Although at bedtime she would clearly state that she did not believe that there were really any such things as witches flying around on broomsticks, for nearly a year she would not sleep in a room by herself for fear of witches. There was for her no logical inconsistency between an acknowledgment of the nonexistence of something and being afraid of that very thing.

The stage 1 child constructs images of God from the symbols and images in the culture. God is viewed most frequently as an older

---

[4]Gilligan suggests three levels that are essentially the same as Kohlberg's: egocentric, conventional, and universal. She does not at this point propose distinct stages at each level.

[5]Fowler used intensive interviews, including hypothetical problems designed to discover the subject's sense of meaning in life, as his method of research. Unlike Kohlberg's work, Fowler does not have longitudinal information gathered from the same subjects over several decades.

man, with white beard and long hair. Although they acknowledge that God is spirit, children at this stage may still wonder aloud where and how often God gets his hair cut! At this stage, children are not able to understand the abstractness of symbols. Religious thinking is largely just a repetition of words and phrases heard from parents or from other significant adults.

Stage 2 is the **mythic literal** stage. Most children enter this stage by about the age of six and remain in it until at least the age of twelve. Some persons remain in this stage throughout their life. In this stage, the person tends to be oriented toward acceptance of whatever authority figures say and are extremely literal in their acceptance of anything in print. This literalism is *especially* pronounced in relationship to scripture. The person has a rather mystical view of the world. Beliefs in Santa and other fairy tales have been shed, but a firm conviction remains in the possibilities of walking on water or of surviving for days inside the stomach of a large fish if one believes strongly enough. Belief itself thus carries certain mystical power—power sufficient to obliterate the laws of nature.

Also characteristic of this stage is a concept of one's relationship with God as being reciprocal. Fowler quotes one woman who views acts of praise to God as efforts to store up God's good favor for use in times of special need.

> . . . everyday I say a Our Father, a Hail Mary, and a Glory be to God. And then when I need it, it's in the bank. And now I have my children doing it when they're walking to class and all, and I say, "Build up your bank account." . . . You just know that if you get in a mess, you have that bank and it will open up and it will help you through the mess (1981: 146–47).

In essence, acts of praise toward God are done so that God will "owe" the person later on. Fowler's religious reciprocity stage is very akin to Kohlberg's interpersonal reciprocity stage. Both are ultimately egocentric, coming down to the issue of "what's in it for me?"

Fowler's stage 3 religiosity is **conventional**, with the primary focus on group conformity (consistent with Kohlberg's stages 3 and 4). Authority is external to the self, residing in the group—what "they" think. Reference group pressures are especially important to persons in this stage of cognitive development according to structuralists. Faith is not rationally scrutinized, remaining more implicit or unexamined. Religious perspective is taken for granted just as all other perspectives of that reference group are taken for granted. And because the particular reference group is so important, the group itself may enhance or retard further growth by encouraging or discouraging independent thought about one's faith.

At stage 3, symbols are inextricably tied to meanings. A symbol, appearing on a record album or a book cover, that is identified as having to do with Satan or with a despised religious tradition has an intrinsic power that is believed by stage 3 persons to seduce the owner or the viewer unwittingly. Wearing jewelry that bears an astrological sign or is otherwise identified with some element of the occult is thought to put one under the power of evil supernatural forces. Likewise, the Bible, bread and wine, or some other symbol of faith may be treated with such sacredness and respect that lack of awe and reverence in the treatment of that symbol may be viewed as blasphemy toward that which the symbol represents. Hence, improper folding of the American flag or failure to salute it properly may be viewed as a highly offensive insult to one's country, and the guilty party may be scolded for lack of patriotism. The symbol *is* the reality.

At stage 4, **individuative-reflective** faith, the symbol is understood as separable from its meaning. The individual understands that meaning is assigned to symbols and that meanings can be reinterpreted or that symbols can change. Meaning is "constructed" or arbitrarily assigned. Therefore, the symbol is not vested with power and intrinsic worth itself. Indeed, there may even be interest in "demythologizing" the myths of the faith and trying to reduce symbols to logical propositions that can be detached from the story or symbol itself.

For the stage 4 person, final responsibility for determining meaning does not rest with the reference group. The individual begins to take responsibility for constructing his or her own system of beliefs that are satisfying. Authority for determination of what is right and wrong, true or false, is transferred from what "they" say to an evaluation process occurring *within* one's self.

Problems for the individual within this stage are twofold. First, the sterile logic and "flattening" of meanings and symbols to intellectual propositions means that the faith may have less motivating power. Demythologizing involves a destruction of much of the ethos, the unique moods and motivations that made the beliefs seem plausible and compelling. Second, stage 4 thinking is still dualistic, caught in either/or dichotomizing and division of the people, groups, and events into good-evil and we-they categories. The perspective remains simplistic and does not account for complexity.

Stage 5 religious perspective, which seldom develops before midlife, is termed **conjunctive faith** by Fowler. At this level, the individual begins to recognize the power of imagery and renews his or her interest in mythology. But myths are clearly understood as rich in symbolism; they are not accepted at face value or interpreted literally. Both the myths and symbols of one's own tradition and those of other traditions are affirmed as carrying wisdom. At this stage, reality is understood as being both complex and interrelated, and the rigors of systematic logic and ideological consistency are viewed as limiting.

Stage 5 faith grants that symbols may have a life of their own, which may be nonlogical; a new openness to nonrational experience allows the individual to affirm the imagery and fantasy that a symbol stimulates. This stage involves a "desire to resubmit to the initiative of the symbolic" (Fowler 1981: 188–89). The individual is no longer in control through reducing symbols to logical theorems. Fowler concludes "The new strength of this stage comes in the rise of the ironic imagination—a capacity to. . . be in one's group's most powerful meanings, while simultaneously recognizing that they are relative, partial and inevitably distorting apprehensions of transcendent reality" (1981: 198). Myths and symbols are appreciated as carriers of truth and wisdom, but unlike earlier stages, those truths are viewed as relative and as less than complete.

Persons at stage 6, **universalizing faith,** often generate new visions, each with unique characteristics and combined in complex ways. Stage 6 faith thus becomes very difficult to describe, for it occurs in so many diverse forms. The element that stage 6 persons have in common is that they are driven by a vision of justice that supersedes the normal boundaries between groups and nations. Universalizers are often misunderstood and frequently die at the hands of those whom they try to change. The commitment to a system of justice for all humanity is so compelling that the individual becomes "heedless of the threats to self, to primary groups, and to the institutional arrangements of the present order" (Fowler 1981: 200). Mahatma Gandhi, Martin Luther King Jr., Dietrich Bonhoeffer (the Lutheran theologian and martyr in Nazi Germany), Mother Teresa of Calcutta, and Jewish theologian Abraham Heschel are examples of stage 6 persons.

The essential difference between stage 6 and stage 5 is that the commitment to one's vision becomes complete (not compromised by the feeling that one's vision is relativistic). But even though the commitment is uncompromising, it is not exclusive (insisting that others can reach truth only by following the path that one has taken). The commitment is both *total* (in the sense of being unwilling to compromise or to be immobilized) and *open* (in the sense of accepting new truths and the insights of other traditions).

Fowler grants that stage 6 faith is vague because it is so diverse in form and is extremely rare in its occurrence. The fact that it also points to religious leaders who have been very liberal or radical in their political and economic positions have caused critics to question whether stage 6 has been formulated in terms of Fowler's own value preferences

and, indeed, whether the sixth stage can be demonstrated empirically to exist at all. Fowler admits to having both descriptive interests (regarding what really does exist) and normative ones (what ought to exist). The question is whether his interest in the latter has interfered with his perception of the former.

This has, of course, left Fowler open to the same criticism that Kohlberg has faced: a judgment of some levels being "lower" or "less adequate" seems to violate the principles of cultural relativism and of disinterestedness in social science research (Richards and Davison 1992). Some researchers advocate a "pluralistic model" (Kwilecki 1988) that defines multilinear

► **FIGURE 6.2**

Fowler's Stages of Faith Development

6. Universalizing faith	Global role-taking; increased ability to understand the richness and diversity of myths and symbols.
5. Conjunctive faith	Complex understanding of truths conveyed via myths and symbols; openness to diversity.
4. Individuative-reflective faith	Demythologizing of myths; "flattening" of myths to logical maxims or propositions; tendency to we-they polemics.
3. Conventional faith	Implicit acceptance of religious tradition; conformity to standard orthodoxy because that is the group's affirmation.
2. Mythic literal faith	Extreme loyalty to whatever "authority" says; literal interpretations of printed Word.
1. Intuitive-projective faith	Magical view of the world; fantasy and reality blend.

paths of development, but so far the empirical evidence to support this model remains thin, at best.

The Significance of Cognitive Structural Models

Structuralist theory presents a slightly different lens for viewing religious change and commitment. It can have significant implications for our understanding by suggesting a different set of considerations. Let me suggest four ways in which structuralist theory might alter the way one views conversion and commitment.

First, the structuralist position raises some interesting questions about one's definition of conversion. Kohlberg and other structuralists are quick to emphasize that the structure of one's thinking is different from the content. One can have stage 3 liberal Christians, stage 3 fundamentalist Christians, stage 3 Moslems, or stage 3 Buddhists. A change from one of these groups to another—with the change of beliefs and practices that are appropriate to members of the new religious group—is what is normally called conversion. Romney Moseley (1978) suggested, however, that such a change might be called lateral conversion. A change of content of religious beliefs occurs, but the individual still operates within the same stage of perception. Moseley reserves the word *conversion* for changes involving change of content *and* change of stage (e.g., from a stage 2 Christian to a stage 3 Buddhist). A number of structuralists insist that change of stage is as important in transforming one's world view as a change of one's specific beliefs.[6]

The importance of stage changes as transformations of one's world view can be illustrated by looking at the differences in interpretations of a religion by persons in different stages. A person in stage 2 interprets the teachings of Christianity in terms of reciprocity. Such a person serves God with the expectation that God will reciprocate, and that individual does unto others so that others will return the favor. A person in the conventional stage of faith development tends to interpret the essence of Christianity as maintenance of the religious system (in unchanged form) and rigid adherence to rules (such as the Ten Commandments). Stage 2 and stage 3 thinkers have very different views of the basics of Christianity. Furthermore, conventional interpretations differ markedly from postconventional ones. Because conventional thinking involves extreme loyalty to in-group norms, persons at this level are likely to be particularistic (believe that only their own group offers truth and salvation). A change to the next level requires a radical reinterpretation of world view to a more inclusive outlook and a more complex understanding of symbolism.

All of this raises the question whether a change of stage, without a change of religious group, can be considered a conversion experience. Some writers insist that conversion involves a significant alteration in one's values and beliefs; a change in the content of one's beliefs is assumed. However, the intensification of a belief system so that one's priorities are reordered has also been referred to as conversion by many scholars. Many converts at revivals and crusades are persons who have undergone a radical alteration in the *interpretation* of their faith, but they have not changed religions. Not all scholars consider a significant reinterpretation of an existing faith to be a conversion experience, but if one does grant that this falls under conversion, then it is also possible to describe a change of stages as a sort of conversion too. I know one minister whose theology has changed drastically over the past

---

[6]Fowler clearly states that he views conversions as changes in content, from Methodism to Judaism or from Presbyterianism to Zen Buddhism. He does not claim that stage changes are conversions. But as we will see in the cognitive re-creation approach, some scholars view the movement to a higher stage as the epitome of transformative religious experience.

twenty years. He has not joined a new religion, nor has he changed denominations. Neither has he had a nonrational experience, which might be called a born-again encounter. Yet, he describes his gradual change as a type of conversion, and he uses moral development theory to explain his transformation.

Kohlberg and other developmentalists insist that each change of stage represents a change of outlook—a modification of world view. For this reason, structural theory raises some interesting questions about our concepts of conversion. Structuralists are not in agreement about whether a stage change is a form of conversion, but it is at least possible, using structuralist concepts, to distinguish several types of conversion: **stage conversion** (same religion, new stage), **lateral conversion** (same stage, new religion), and **diagonal conversion** (new stage, new religion). Sociologists would likely differ on whether a stage conversion is really a form of conversion, unless there is some modification of *social behavior* (either involvement in a new group or intensified participation in a group to which one formerly belonged). Figure 6.3 visually illustrates these three types of conversion.

A second possible contribution of structuralist theory is that it introduces a new factor as the primary inducement to certain types of conversion. Piaget, Kohlberg, and other structuralists stress that stage changes are induced by cognitive dissonance. This suggests that in conversions involving a change of stage (stage conversions or diagonal conversions), intellectual conflict is central. Whether such conflict is also operative in lateral conversion is unclear.[7]

---

[7]Insofar as some people convert to a different religion because the world view of their former religion does not explain the anomalies of life, cognitive dissonance would seem to be operative in lateral conversions as well. Such dissonance would seem to be a factor in the religious seekership element described by Lofland.

▶ **FIGURE 6.3**

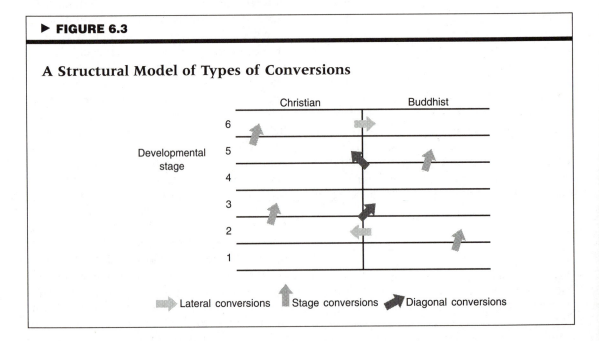

A Structural Model of Types of Conversions

It may be that lateral conversions are more likely to be based on an affective process (belonging and participation preceding belief), whereas diagonal conversions may normally follow an intellectual conversion mode (change of belief comes first). At this point, these are speculations. The role of intellectual conflict in conversions may become clearer as structuralist research on religion continues.

A third insight of the structuralist perspective is that a person's stage of moral thinking may serve as an important conducive factor in lateral conversions. In reading Lofland's study of the *Doomsday Cult,* one cannot help but notice the predominance of stage 2 and stage 3 thinking among members of that group during its early development (1977: 210–11). This raises two interesting questions. Are persons at certain stages more likely to join particular groups? Is an individual's developmental stage a predisposing or deterring condition for recruitment to any one group? If so, perhaps it should be added to the list of factors included in process models of conversion (like Lofland's, discussed in chapter 5). Second, is the conversion and commitment process any different for stage 5 people than for stage 2 or 3 people?[8] For example, are stage 5 thinkers less inclined to affective conversions and more predisposed to intellectual or mystical conversion motifs? Kohlberg, Fowler, and other structuralists stress that those at later stages are more willing to be nonconformists. Hence, it would be logical that they be less likely to be influenced by affective conversion strategies that stress reference group factors. Likewise, are persons at stage 2 or 3 attracted by some conversion strategies but not by others? At this point, we have only interesting speculations that need empirical investigation. Much research is needed to validate and expand structuralist theory and to explore the implications of the theory for understanding religion.

As a project to deepen understanding of theories discussed in this chapter, students may want to list ways in which cognitive structuralist theory is similar to the models of Kanter and Lofland, and specify ways in which structuralism is in conflict with the approaches of Kanter and Lofland. How might these theories complement and correct one another? By addressing issues such as these, students can develop their own skills in comparison, contrast, and synthesis.

The Cognitive Re-Creation Approach

Daniel Batson and Larry Ventis (1982) take a somewhat different approach, but one that also focuses substantially on cognitive processes. Batson and Ventis are social psychologists. Predictably, much of their interpretation of religious commitment and religious experience emphasizes reference groups (and is consistent with the symbolic interaction perspective discussed at the beginning of chapter 4). Batson and Ventis cite extensive empirical research—including laboratory experiments—on the role of other people in shaping one's interpretation of events and circumstances. Especially when we are in situations where the norms of behavior are ambiguous, the evidence indicates that we look around to see how others have responded and tend to accept their definition of the situation as fearful, normal, anger-producing, inspiring, funny, or whatever. Compatible with the emphasis on belonging factors in chapter 5, these theorists stress that a

---

[8]My hunch is that it is. I suspect that a person who thinks at stage 5 would be much less likely to abdicate personal decision making, accept mortification, and passively obey the authorities of a religious group. Stage 5 thinkers value independent thinking too highly to abdicate personal responsibility for their own thoughts and actions.

great deal of religious experience is shaped by the views of one's close associates.

Batson and Ventis also believe that to adhere exclusively to reference group theory is to oversimplify a very complex process. They insist that religious conversion experiences vary considerably and that some people have intense experiences of insight and inspiration that transcend the perspectives of the group. They also believe that, although emotional or affective dimensions are important, the *central* characteristic of religious experience, including conversion, is cognitive.

In trying to understand the intense reality-transforming experience of religious conversion, Batson and Ventis begin with the assumption that the basic psychological processes involved in religious experience also occur in other profound reality-transforming experiences. The experience that is psychologically closest to religious inspiration is the creative experience. Both artistic and scientific creativity involve processes of profound inspiration. While religious experience and creative inspiration are in some ways different, Batson and Ventis believe that the differences are in content. The process appears to be the same.

It is important to note here that Batson and Ventis use a functional definition of religion. They believe that any intense struggle with "existential concerns," with problems of the meaning of life, are fundamentally religious. It is not necessary that such concerns include a belief in the supernatural in order to be considered "religious" (1982: 12).

Creative Inspiration and Religious Inspiration

Batson and Ventis set forth six propositions on the psychodynamics of creativity, propositions that they also believe apply to religious experience. First, they emphasize that *our reality is constructed.* What we view as "real" is in fact data filtered through our sense organs and organized into meaningful classifications or categories by our minds.

> Although we tend to think of reality as something "out there" and quite independent of ourselves, this conviction is based entirely on our experience, experience that without the imposition of meaning upon it by our minds would be . . . a booming, buzzing confusion. To say this does not mean that we can make of our experience what we will; should you have any doubt, try walking through a wall. But the meaning we attach to our experience is what gives it the structure and stability of "reality." And this meaning is very much a human creation (1982: 66).

We tend to notice those things that we have been trained to see and to organize the stimuli that our organs receive into categories that we have been taught to use.

> To illustrate, a civil engineer sees something quite different when looking at a bridge or building than the rest of us do. Equipped with the technical language of stresses, forces, and tensile strength, he or she is likely to see through the surface appearance of the bridge to focus instead on the underlying structure. . . . Most of us just see a bridge (1982: 67).

The ideas and categories provided us by our culture shape the way we experience the world, what we notice or ignore, and how we organize information into meaningful units.

Second, the *reality we construct is based on our cognitive structures.* Batson and Ventis turn here to the work of cognitive structuralists in the tradition of Piaget, pointing out that the stage of one's intellectual development affects how one perceives the world. A person in Kohlberg's egocentric stage 2 (instrumental relativist orientation) perceives social relationships very differently than does a person in the ethnocentric fourth stage (societal maintenance). Only the latter person is readily inclined to sacrifice self-interests for the benefit of the group. Batson and Ventis contend that the way one understands and evaluates life experiences is determined in large part by one's stage of cognitive development.

A third proposition, consistent with the cognitive structuralists, holds that *cognitive structures are hierarchically arranged.* Higher levels of perception are more complex (differentiated) and more capable of dealing with more abstract generalizations. Further, higher levels involve a greater degree of integration, a greater ability to perceive relationships between ideas or concepts. Lower levels of thought and perception are tied to concrete or specific cases and are less able to comprehend abstractions from the concrete experience. "When we are presented with a problem that requires organizing principles at a higher level of conceptual complexity than we have developed, it will appear to be insoluble. Indeed, it is insoluble within the existing cognitive structures" (Batson and Ventis 1982: 71).

This leads us to the fourth proposition, that *creativity involves an improvement in one's cognitive organization.* In short, higher levels are better modes of thought, for they represent more complex problem-solving ability. An "improved" organization or structure of thought is "one that, through greater differentiation and integration, makes it possible to think what was previously unthinkable" (Batson and Ventis 1982: 72–73). With this in mind, creative thought is defined as "the process whereby one's cognitive structures are changed toward greater flexibility and adaptability [because of] greater differentiation and integration" (Batson and Ventis 1982: 73).

Not all change of thinking is creative. Acquisition of new knowledge or new information—through reading or listening to a lecture—does not normally involve creativity. It simply means addition of new content and perhaps some modification within an existing structure. Change can also occur toward simpler organizing structures. And perhaps most important, a process that they refer to as "alternation" involves a shift from one cognitive organization to another at the same level. Creativity involves a change to a more complex and more integrated mode of thinking.

The fifth proposition regarding creative process is perhaps the most important for our understanding of religious experience: *There appear to be four identifiable stages in the creative process.* These stages are preparation, incubation, illumination, and verification. Scientists often go through a period of baffled struggle during which the individual tries to solve the problem within the framework of his or her existing cognitive structures. If the existing cognitive organization is sufficient, the problem may be solved without the need for true creativity. But if the current mode of thinking is insufficient to solve the problem, the scientist continues to struggle and begins to feel frustrated and trapped. The period of "beating one's head against the problem" is the *preparation* stage and is necessary for the emergence of creativity (Batson and Ventis 1982: 77–78).

Exhausted and perplexed, the scientist finally gives up. But "in giving up, one relaxes active use of the existing cognitive structures. This relaxation appears to be necessary if one is to be able to think about the problem in a new way" (Batson and Ventis 1982: 78). This period of disengagement allows for *incubation.* As one studies scientific inspiration among scientific or artistic geniuses, one often finds that brilliant creative insights occur in such places as the bath, the bed, or public transit. Sometimes insights occur as dreams. In any case, one is mentally disengaged; one is not actively pursuing the problem.

This sets the stage for *illumination.* While one has at least temporarily given up the attempt to solve the problem, new and more appropriate cognitive organization is able to emerge. While one is intellectually disengaged from the problem, a flash of inspiration may occur that allows one to see the problem from a new perspective. "This illumination occurs at the level of the unconscious or nonconscious mind. . . . Perhaps this is the reason that the creative process is perceived to be illogical, mysterious . . ." (Batson and Ventis 1982: 78). The flash of insight causes one to view the process as intuitive. Often it is characterized as a gift from God. Box 6.2 provides two examples from the sciences.

▶ **BOX 6.2**

The Creative Experience in the Sciences

The story of Archimedes' (ca. 287–212 B.C.) discovery of the principle of specific gravity is well known. His ruler, Hiero, had been presented with a new crown, claimed by the maker to be solid gold. Archimedes was given the task of determining whether the claim was true, or whether Hiero had been cheated by a crown adulterated with silver. Archimedes' life rested on his success. He could not melt down the crown to determine its composition, because if it were solid gold he would be killed for destroying a priceless treasure. On the other hand, if he said it was gold and it was found not to be, he would be killed for letting his ruler be cheated.

Archimedes knew that silver and gold were different in weight, but in order to test the composition of the crown by weight he would have to know its exact volume. And to determine the exact volume of a crown by measuring the thickness of the metal at each point along its face would be an endless task. While puzzling over this problem, Archimedes went to the baths.

Suddenly, as he stepped into the water, he had it! He noticed the familiar phenomenon that as he entered the pool the water level on the side rose slightly. He could determine the volume of the crown by the amount of water it displaced. Ecstatic, he ran through the streets, nude it is said, shouting "eureka!" ("I have found it!").

The chemist Kekule (1829–1896) presents a fascinating account of his discovery of the benzene ring. He had been working on the problem of the molecular structure of these hydrocarbons for days, without success. Then, one afternoon,

> I turned my chair to the fire and dozed. . . . Again the atoms were gambolling before my eyes. This time the smaller groups kept modestly in the background. My mental eye, rendered more acute by repeated visions of this kind, could now distinguish larger structures, of manifold conformation; long rows, sometimes more closely fitted together; all twining and twisting in snakelike motion. But look! What was that? One of the snakes had seized hold of its own tail, and the form whirled mockingly before my eyes. As if by a flash of lightning I awoke. . . . (Findlay 1948).

The insight for which Kekule had been searching was that the structure of these carbon compounds was not a chain but, like the snake biting its own tail, a closed ring. This insight led to what has been called "the most brilliant piece of prediction in the whole range of organic chemistry and . . . one of the cornerstones of modern science" (Koestler 1964).

Source: C. Daniel Batson and W. Larry Ventis. *The Religious Experience: A Social-Psychological Perspective.* New York: Oxford University Press, 1982: 75–77.

The final stage is *verification*. The scientist or artist returns to the laboratory or the studio to test the insight to see if the new idea really works. Sometimes the flash of insight is a "flash in the pan"; it simply does not work as one expected. For the artist, the verification stage may also include considerable elaboration of the new idea and application of the idea in new ways.

The sixth proposition is that *the creative process outlined may have a physiological basis*. Batson and Ventis, being psychologists, draw on the literature regarding brain-hemisphere specialization. They point out that "the left hemisphere is the seat of logic, language, and of linear thought; the right hemisphere is the seat of perceptual organization, spatial relations, and insight" (1982: 79). They also note Robert Ornstein's (1972) suggestion that formation and maintenance of cognitive structures are right-hemisphere operations, while processing of information *within* the structures is accomplished primarily by the left hemisphere. Batson and Ventis speculate,

> During the preparation stage of the creative process, the individual attempts to deal with the problem in terms of the logical, linear thought of the left hemisphere. During the incubation stage, [the individual] relaxes active processing by the left hemisphere, permitting the less dominant, perceptually oriented right hemisphere to go to work reorganizing the cognitive structures. This reorganization leads to the new insight or illumination. Verification involves a return to the left hemisphere dominance; the individual logically tests the functional value of the new insight (1982: 80).

The suggestion, then, is that the physiology of the way the brain works may help explain why creativity involves the four stages.

Batson and Ventis propose that religious insight or inspiration occurs through a four-stage sequence that closely parallels the creative process. In the preparation stage, the individual goes through a period of dissatisfaction at the existential level. That is, a struggle ensues for a sense of meaning and purpose in life and answers that seem satisfying to the individual are not available. Sometimes a severe illness or death of a loved one may precipitate such a crisis. But often, the vacuum of meaning occurs precisely at those times when all of one's basic physical needs are met and one has the luxury of thinking about the larger issues of life. The inability of existing cognitive structures to provide a sense of meaning in life causes a profound and painful sense of emptiness. The individual feels a bafflement akin to that which the stalemated scientist experiences.

Trying, and failing, to gain a sense of meaning in life from within one's existing reality, one is driven to despair and hopelessness. The response to this existential despair is self-surrender, a response analogous to the incubation stage of creativity. There is a loss of consciousness that typically occurs as part of a meditation state. One's grip on the old way of thinking is loosened as one enters a period of relaxed or disengaged consciousness.

A new vision or some other form of illumination follows the relaxed state of consciousness. A new perspective on the meaning and purpose of life allows one to transcend the old modes of thinking, modes that were based on the old cognitive organization. Those who have had an intense religious experience often make a claim to the effect that "old things have passed away, all things have become new" or that "it was like entering a new world." Indeed, Batson and Ventis believe a new stage of understanding *has* been achieved.

Following the new inspiration, the individual begins to live in accord with the new perspective and with "a new state of assurance." The application of the new vision to everyday affairs and testing its effectiveness in coping with questions of meaning is an important part of the validation process.

Batson and Ventis conclude,

> This four stage model provides our understanding of what happens psychologically during a dramatic, reality-transforming experience. Summarizing, we may say that *religious experience involves cognitive restructuring in an attempt to deal with one or more existential questions.* Consistent with our proposed analogy, the cognitive process involved seems quite similar to that involved in creativity, although the problems at issue are existential, not intellectual (1982: 86).

They also emphasize that emotions are an important part of this religious experience, but they reaffirm their conviction that the religious experience is at its core a *cognitive* transformation. They obviously feel that world view is the central element of religious faith.

This cognitive re-creation perspective views religious experience as analogous to the creative experience in other ways as well. Just as creativity is related to a hierarchical model of cognitive organization, so also religious experience is viewed as creative or uncreative. If religious experience is creative, it "allows the individual to deal more positively and effectively with a wider range of experiences and people" (Batson and Ventis 1982: 87). Like Fowler's faith development model, the cognitive re-creation model views each higher stage as being more flexible and as involving more complex and integrated understandings of existential problems. But some religious change involves flight from everyday life into other-world fantasy or imposition of rigidity through strict and unbending dogmatism.

Although they recognize that religious experience may involve a horizontal move to another religious tradition at the same level, Batson and Ventis treat religious experiences that involve a move to a higher level of intellectual sophistication as the most perfect manifestation of conversion experience. Although many people essentially "switch" religious traditions, the classic *intra-faith* mystical experiences reported by saints and mystics are often creative transformations. They are every much as creative as the inspired flash of genius of the innovative scientist or the gifted musician. This type of religious conversion—the type experienced by the anguished man who came to be known as St. Augustine or by the young Siddhartha—cannot be explained solely by reference group or role theories.

Facilitating Factors for Religious Experience

Batson and Ventis do, however, point to several external factors that can facilitate these creative religious experiences. These facilitative factors are psychedelic drugs, meditation, and religious language.

In religious settings, particularly as employed by shamans in nonindustrialized societies, psychedelic drugs may contribute to religious experience by relaxing the individual's state of consciousness and allowing for free-floating association of concepts in ways that are not restricted by his or her normal cognitive organization. In this way, hallucinogens may contribute to the incubation and illumination stages; they will not, however, lead to religious experience unless one has already been struggling with existential questions.

Part of the capacity of drugs to stimulate religious experience in these settings is explained by social constructionist (or symbolic interaction) theory. A number of social psychologists maintain that many human emotions—love, anger, fear, intense anticipation—result in the same set of physiological responses. Each of these experiences result in rapid heart beat, release of adrenaline resulting in agitation, rush of blood to the head, accelerated breathing, sweating, and the like. A large body of experimental research now indicates that if these physical reactions are stimulated by drugs, with the subjects not informed that the chemicals they received were stimulants, the subjects tend to look around for clues that help them define the cause of their agitation. They use their social and physical environment, including the behaviors of others and the presence of symbols, to construct some meaning of their experiences—to interpret what is happening. If an extremely attractive person of the opposite sex is in the room with them, they may attribute the cause of their arousal to romantic attraction. If other persons in the room display anger or fear, the subjects tend to assign the same cause to their own response (Schachter 1964; Schachter and Singer 1962; Schachter and Wheeler 1962; Walster 1971). If the room is filled with religious artifacts and symbols, subjects tend to define their experience as a religious one (Masters and Houston 1966).

In simple societies in which the religious leader is a shaman, drugs may be used to stimulate religious experience. In the Peyote Cult among Native American tribes and in its offspring, the Native American Church, consumption of the hallucinogenic drug "mescal"[9] is reserved for religious rituals. These drugs are taken in a context that clearly is defined as "religious." It is not surprising therefore that the hallucinations and other altered states of consciousness are defined in religious terms.[10]

Batson and Ventis emphasize that the use of hallucinogenic drugs may *contribute* to religious

experience, but drugs clearly are neither necessary nor sufficient. Further, there is little evidence that psychedelic drugs are more prone to stimulate creative (as opposed to noncreative) religious experience.

A second facilitating factor is meditation. There are many types of meditation techniques, but all have in common the idea of stopping the flow of conscious thought and bringing the mind to a relaxed and receptive state. In so doing, meditation may enhance the incubation stage: the individual is not actively processing information through existing cognitive structures. This creates the condition in which creative free association can occur. Meditation does not create a new vision, but it can weaken the hold of the old one (Batson and Ventis 1982: 119).

A number of studies have been done on meditation and brain waves. Four basic brain wave patterns have been found in the brain: beta, alpha, theta, and delta. The high-frequency beta waves are those in operation when a person is thinking about a problem or processing information. Alpha waves occur when one is relaxed but fully conscious. Theta waves occur when one is dropping off to sleep or just awakening; delta waves predominate when one is in deep sleep. Most scholars believe that the low-frequency, high-amplitude alpha and theta waves are those associated with the incubation stage of the creativity process.

Batson and Ventis (1982: 121–23) cite a number of studies of the brain wave patterns of Zen masters, yogi meditators, experienced Christian meditators, and practitioners of transcendental meditation. These studies consistently indicate that during meditation—at least among experienced meditators—alpha and theta waves predominate. Batson and Ventis think that these findings offer some plausibility to their claim that meditation may facilitate the incubation stage of creativity.

Because meditation serves essentially the same function as psychedelic drugs, the two

---

[9]The scientific name for peyote or mescal is *Lophophora williamsii* (LaBarre 1964).

[10]On the other hand, an experiment with theology students in Boston, conducted by Walter Pahnke (1963), shows that the type of drug one consumes is significant. Students given a psychedelic drug in a chapel setting were more likely to interpret their subsequent experience as an intense mystical experience than were subjects in the same setting who were given nicotinic acid. This latter drug produces tingling sensations in the skin but no psychedelic effects (hallucinations, delusions, or intensified sensory awareness). Some drugs seem more capable of stimulating experiences that are defined as religious, regardless of the social environment.

may be seen as functional alternatives. Either may be found as a facilitator of religious experience; but hallucinogenic drugs and meditation techniques are not normally used together.

The third facilitator of creative religious transformation is religious language. Religious language serves as a metaphoric symbol system that helps define a situation as "religious." We have just seen that persons who are stimulated by drugs may define their arousal as romance, anger, fear, or divine inspiration—depending on the symbolic cues around them. Language can serve as one such cue.

Religious language can operate at three different stages of the religious experience. First, language is an important part of the struggle stage, the period of heightened crisis or preparation. One's general sense of malaise and dissatisfaction may be cast in religious terms because of the predominance of the use of religious language in one's subculture or one's reference group. In other words, if one's primary reference group is one in which religious language is often used, one tends to think along religious lines in conceptualizing any problem. Second, religious language is often operative at the time of illumination. Language may be part of the symbol system by which a new vision is conceived and expressed. Often mystics report having heard a voice, which presumably was saying something both inspiring and understandable. Third, language is important in the verification stage as one tries to test the validity of the vision and apply it to everyday life.

Ironically, religious language may also *reduce* the likelihood of creative religious experience. If religious language is taken as literal rather than symbolic, then the words themselves become the focus. In such a case, religious language may become a barrier to creative religious growth (Batson and Ventis 1982: 131–33).

These three facilitating factors are contributing factors, not necessary ones. Nonetheless,

Batson and Ventis point out that when either the use of hallucinogenic drugs or meditation techniques is combined with religious language, factors affecting all four stages are present. At this point, any conclusion is speculative, but Batson and Ventis believe the combination may be sufficient to trigger a religious experience.

The cognitive re-creation model provides an interesting perspective for understanding intense life-changing religious experiences. It seems to make sense of religious transformations by those saints and mystics who had a conversion experience while isolated from any significant reference group (see Box 6.3). The model also explains the visionary experience of religious men and women who have spawned new religious movements.

But Batson and Ventis's theory also focuses so exclusively on cognitive processes that one wonders whether it is based too much on a white, middle-class experience of religion and not enough on more emotive religious expression, such as the black religious experience. I happen to share Batson and Ventis's perception of religion as fundamentally having to do with world view. And I certainly am not implying that they have used only white, middle-class examples in their analysis. But they, as I, look through the lens of white, middle-class culture, and that lens may be distorting or filtering what we perceive.

I view religion as substantially cognitive (having to do with thinking and perceiving), partially because my own religious experience is fundamentally cognitive. But when I listen closely to what scholars studying the black community are telling me, religion and many other aspects of life are more fundamentally emotive in that context (see Kochman 1981). In the black religious experience and in the Kachina religion of the Hopi in Arizona, ethos appears to be at least as important as world view. Cognitive processes are important in all religious experience, but the claim that intellectual processes are primary in *all* religious experience is a claim that needs further empirical investigation. This is one more way in which we need to be sensitive to the diversity of religious cultures in North America.

The Cognitive Models

Cognitive models are generally not as widely accepted by sociologists as are reference group and role theories, probably in part because sociology as a discipline focuses on group processes as the central determinants of human behavior. But persons new to the field of sociology of religion need to be aware that the variables that influence human behavior are both multiple and complex in their interrela-

tionships. Religious conversion, as one form of human behavior, is certainly no exception. No single theory of conversion can explain all instances. Indeed, no current theory can, by itself, give a total picture of any one conversion. Cognitive processing of information, reference group loyalties and affective ties, role expectations of the individual, and previous investments of time and resources all interact in each case. What is really needed for a comprehensive understanding of religious conversion and commitment is an integrated theory that accounts for each of these variables. At present, we have no such holistic model.

Which variables appear to be most important in the majority of cases? As I have already made clear, I am convinced that reference group factors are the most powerful in predicting

---

▶ **BOX 6.3**

The Transforming Religious Experience

The sequence of events that Siddhartha experienced in his existential quest for meaning in life appears to be the same as the four stages of creative innovation that Batson and Ventis identify.

> Siddhartha, of the family of Gautama, was born a prince of the Sakya clan in India in the first half of the sixth century B.C. He grew up surrounded by luxury and sensuous enjoyment, carefully protected by his father from the sorrows and frustrations of life. Somehow, when in his mid-twenties, he became aware of the sad truths of disease, old age, and death. This knowledge provoked Siddhartha to anxious and puzzled reflection, and finally to determined action. At the age of twenty-nine he left his father's palace, his beautiful wife, and newborn son, and he set out to find a meaningful way to live in this world of

suffering, sorrow, and death. For seven years he sought enlightenment. He consulted hermit sages, but did not find the answer. He tried ascetic self-denial, but found that prolonged fasting and other punishment of the body brought only exhaustion and impotence of mind. Finally, his quest reached its culmination in a long period of meditation under a spreading Bo tree, not far from the present city of Gaya in northern India. When he arose, he knew that he had found enlightenment; it lay in recognition and acceptance of the essential unity and harmony of all life.

Siddhartha's insight has provided direction to millions since. For through it, he had become the Buddha.

Source: C. Daniel Batson and W. Larry Ventis. *The Religious Experience: A Social-Psychological Perspective.* New York: Oxford University Press, 1982: 57.

religious changes for the bulk of the population. I am persuaded by the large body of empirical findings that show that most people remain loyal to a faith or transfer their commitments to another because of friendship networks and other affective ties. Even among those who have "born-again" experiences, these experiences usually occur within a framework of reference group expectations. All this does not deny that some people do have religious experiences that depart from anything one might predict from the individual's primary networks. But such religious creativity is not the norm among the masses.

It may also be the case that persons who are in Fowler's stage 3 thinking are more susceptible to reference group factors than are those in higher cognitive states. Some scholars find the cognitive stage to be the best starting point for building a comprehensive theory.

Rather than simply accepting my conclusions, students should be formulating their own. I encourage you as you read to be an active learner—to think critically and to formulate your own hypotheses. Which models make more sense of your own experience with religion or with religious people you know? Do you have reason to believe that the cases with which you are familiar are typical of religious people in this country? Why or why not? Each of the theories are supported with different types of evidence gathered with various types of research designs. Which types of evidence do you find most convincing? Why? Which combination of contributing factors do you believe are sufficient to stimulate religious change or to intensify religious commitment? Are any of the factors absolutely necessary? Why or why not?

Summary

Cognitive theories focus on the intellectual processes involved in religious conversion and commitment. Because the primary focus is on thought and perception processes, world view is stressed as the most important element of religion. Cognitive structuralists emphasize that the ability of individuals to understand role taking and the complexity of symbols occurs in stages. Cognitive re-creation theorists point to the four-step creative process as a model for understanding the innovative religious experiences of the founders of religious movements.

Both approaches suggest that one can have a religious conversion without changing one's religious affiliation. Cognitive reorganization of one's world view may be considered a profound transformation, even if the transformation involves a new understanding of one's traditional religion. Both models also recognize that such cognitive reorganization will result in changes of behavior as well. Conversion never remains purely intellectual. It is always manifest behaviorally. Behavioral changes may involve transfer to a different religious group or a change of one's understanding of moral responsibility within the traditional faith.

Conversion involves a change of commitments. Such changes may occur because of changes of friendship networks and other affective ties, because of investments of one's time and resources, or because of cognitive reordering of one's world view. Although there are differences between scholars about which of these processes is primary, most conversions probably involve a complex interplay between these factors.

Formation and Maintenance of Religious Organizations

In the previous chapters we have explored two of the three interrelated subsystems that comprise the larger system we call religion. We have investigated the meaning system (the network of myths, symbols, rituals, ethos, and world view) and we have pointed to the importance of the belonging system (the network of friendships and affective ties). We have learned something about the process of why individuals come to join a religious group. The question of how these religious organizations originate and what organizational factors are necessary for the survival of that group will be a central focus of this unit.

We will also be exploring some of the dynamics of the structural system (interdependence of statuses and roles within the organization, along with the generation and allocation of resources to keep the organization functioning). Survival of a group depends on a capacity to keep this dimension of the religious system healthy and vibrant. Each of these three systems depends on the vitality of the other two.

CHAPTER SEVEN

Emergence and Viability of Religious Movements: Charisma and Its Routinization

Maintaining a high level of commitment from members is necessary for a group to survive. Such commitment, however, is not sufficient to ensure the group's ongoing viability. In this chapter we look at the development of any religious group from its beginning as a fledgling cult to its status as an established and stable religion. Ever since Max Weber first developed the proposition that new religious movements generally start out as cults headed by a charismatic leader, much of the sociological work in religion has evolved around the concept of charisma. Therefore, we begin by exploring the concept of charisma. But Weber insists that charisma is inherently unstable; if the group does not institutionalize, it will die shortly after the founder dies. Many cults never make the transition and therefore never develop into viable religious groups. Even if a group does institutionalize, the process of institutionalization is itself fraught with dilemmas, usually causing changes in the religious movement. In this chapter we explore the role of charismatic leaders in the emergence of new religious movements, discuss the importance of institutionalization in the survival of these movements, and examine problems that this institutionalization creates for the group.

Charisma and the Charismatic Leader

Weber was the first sociologist to write extensively on the importance of charismatic leadership. He maintained that new religions generally get their impetus from the attraction of a charismatic leader, a dynamic person who is perceived as extraordinary and set apart from the rest of humanity. Weber writes,

> The term *"charisma"* will be applied to a certain quality of an individual personality, by virtue of which (s)he is set apart from ordinary [people] and treated as endowed with supernatural, superhuman, or at least specifically exceptional powers or qualities. These are such as are not accessible to the ordinary person, but are regarded as of divine origin or as exemplary, and on the basis of them the individual concerned is treated as a leader (1947: 358–59).

The charismatic leader is able to use this power to mobilize followers and to create within them a sense of mission.

Weber insists that charismatic leadership is not to be judged as intrinsically good or evil, for it could be either. The point is that some individuals come to be regarded as exceptional and perhaps even divine by followers or disciples. Although the followers do not necessarily experience the *mysterium tremendum* in quite the way it is described by Rudolf Otto (see chapter 4), they do become convinced that their charismatic leader is a direct agent of God, or perhaps God incarnate. Believers may feel a sense of mystery and awe in the presence of such a leader. The feelings of members of the Unification Church for the Reverend Moon provide one example. He is believed to be the new Christ, God incarnate. Whatever he says is believed to be true simply because he said it.[1]

Later writers, building on Weber's concept, have elaborated the difference between charismatic and ideological leaders. Margrit Eichler (1972) suggests that the charismatic leader's wisdom is considered to be Truth simply because he or she utters it. The ideological leader, on the other hand, is one whose leadership comes from an ability to interpret an existing belief system in a compelling manner. Final authority rests outside the person, but the leader is the primary interpreter. This distinction is consistent with much of Weber's writing about charisma, although at other times he uses the term *charisma* in a broader context and seems to accept many types of leadership as charismatic. Hereafter, we will reserve the concept of charismatic leader for those whose authority resides in their very personhood or in their utterly unique relationship with the deity. What they say does not need to be legitimated or confirmed by some other source. What they say is viewed as truth itself.

One element of charismatic leadership that Weber thought to be especially important was its antiestablishment and revolutionary tendencies.[2] Weber believed that charismatic authority is intrinsically unstable and is antithetical to social order:

> Charismatic authority is specifically outside the realm of everyday routine and the profane sphere. In this respect, it is sharply opposed both to rational, and particularly bureaucratic, authority and to traditional authority. . . . Both rational and traditional authority are specifically forms of everyday routine control of action; while the charismatic type is the direct antithesis of this. Bureaucratic authority is specifically rational in the sense of being bound to intellectually analyzable rules, while charismatic authority is specifically irrational in the sense of being foreign to all rules. Traditional authority is bound to the precedents handed down from the past and to this extent is also oriented to rules. Within the

---

[1]This is a different sort of religious experience than Otto describes. Nonetheless, some elements of this phenomenon are quite similar to those described by Otto and by Emile Durkheim (chapter 4). Although the absoluteness of power and unapproachability are not as pronounced as with the *mysterium tremendum* experience, the charismatic leader's authority is nonempirical, total, and unquestionable. The charismatic person offers the only source to truth or salvation and in this sense has a good deal of power. Hence, the leader has a considerable amount of personal space; that is, he or she may be approached, but not too closely. A second important characteristic of the charismatic authority is that it is specifically outside the realm of everyday routine. Like Durkheim's concept of the sacred, charisma is foreign to the profane world. The experience is based on something beyond the ordinary empirical world. Hence, we might identify this awe in the presence of a charismatic leader as an alternative form of nonrational religious experience.

[2]Peter Berger has shown that Weber's assumption was based in large part on the most recent biblical scholarship of his day. Contemporary Old Testament scholarship based on new evidence and different assumptions, points to the prophet or charismatic leader as a member of the establishment and not as an isolated individual. Although the prophet often was part of the establishment, he did challenge the status quo and in this sense was quite revolutionary (Berger 1963).

sphere of its claims, charismatic authority repudiates the past and is in this sense a specifically revolutionary force (1947: 361–62).

Weber was emphatic in asserting that the Old Testament prophets were not spokesmen for some economic group. Their interests were explicitly religious, although there were social and economic implications to their messages. Weber was interested in the power of ideas in bringing social change. More recent research has focused on why people attribute superhuman powers to others. This line of research has stressed the fact that adherence to a charismatic leader and the development of a charismatic cult is likely when certain social conditions prevail.

Social Processes in the Evolution of a Charismatic Group

Sociologists do not usually accept the theory that charismatic leaders are "Great Persons" who are able to bring change solely by the dynamism of their personalities. In its simplest form, the great person theory suggests that some individuals are so dynamic and magnetic that they could transform any culture. The current evidence suggests otherwise; certain conditions in the society may be conducive or nonconducive to the rise of a charismatic leader. Anthony Wallace has explored this issue and has identified a series of somewhat overlapping stages in the revitalization of a culture. His scenerio describes the process by which a charismatic leader comes to influence a culture—whether it be the entire culture or a particular subculture.

Wallace (1972) approaches the process of transformation as a crisis of meaning. He uses the term *mazeway* to refer to an individual's concept of nature, society, culture, personality, and body image and of the relationship between each of these. He is interested in the process by which a whole culture may change its mazeway, or what we have called its world view. Wallace points out that when one is under severe stress, one's world view provides explanations and specifies actions for the reduction of that stress. However, if one is under stress, particularly chronic stress, and the current cognitive orientation does not provide effective channels for its reduction, the person must choose between tolerating stress and changing his or her outlook on life. Wallace believes that structural stress leads to formulation of a new world view. He even goes so far as to insist that all organized religions are survivals from the mazeway reformulation that occurred at an earlier time of cultural crisis and individual stress.

The first phase in the development of a revitalization movement is a "steady-state" period. At this point, the established cultural processes are able to meet most of the needs of the majority of the population. Varying levels of stress may be experienced by members of the society, but most stress is tolerable. In cases where it is not, deviant coping mechanisms (including psychosis) may be adopted. Some cultural modification may occur but at rates that are sufficiently gradual that social stability is not threatened.

During the second phase, larger numbers of individuals may begin to experience increased stress. Many types of factors can interfere with the effectiveness of the cultural system: political subordination, pressures to acculturate to a larger cultural matrix, military defeat, economic displacement, epidemics, and so on. Although the individual may be able to tolerate some increased stress, eventually a level may be reached that demands a search for alternatives. The system of meaning that justifies social relationships is no longer adequate; cultural norms begin to weaken, and explanations that help people cope with bafflement, suffering, and injustice no longer suffice.

When individuals begin to ignore cultural norms and to explore new behaviors and new ways to reduce stress, the culture may enter a period of distortion, the third phase. The culture begins to "wobble" as it experiences internal distortion: the elements of the culture are no longer related in a harmonious way.[3] This rise of anomie, or normlessness, is itself a source of further stress. As people become aware of the incongruities of the culture and the inadequacy of the current world view, they may experience disillusionment, apathy, and meaninglessness.

Other scholars have pointed out that revitalization movements may be induced by either anomie or by alienation. **Anomie** is the feeling of frustration that results when the rules of the game are unclear. It is frustration due to a lack of consistent cultural expectations. **Alienation** is the feeling of frustration that results when the rules are clear but when

---

[3]Wallace's research was conducted in relatively simple, homogeneous societies in which a single religion served to enhance cultural unity and provided the meaning system.

one feels left out of the social matrix. The norms seem foreign, and the institutions seem beyond one's control or one's meaningful participation. While anomie is normally a result of rapid cultural change, alienation frequently occurs in rather stable societies. In short, persons may experience great stress, and subcultural groups may endure substantial wobble due to either anomie or alienation. Disillusionment, apathy, and meaninglessness are results of both processes (Hargrove 1979).

The fourth phase is the period of revitalization, which contains six steps or substages: mazeway reformulation, communication, organization, adaptation, cultural transformation, and routinization (see Box 7.1). First, one individual experiences some sort of abrupt and dramatic moment of insight that seems to offer an explanation of the "real" nature of the culture's problems. Wallace refers to this as *mazeway reformulation.* This new insight is defined as a revelation or inspiration. Although other scholars seriously question his broad generalization, Wallace insists that the new path to meaning and "wholeness" is almost always based on the hallucinatory vision of a

---

► **BOX 7.1**

The Emergence of a Revitalization Movement with a Charismatic Leader: Wallace's Scenario

1. Steady state
2. Period of increased stress
3. Period of cultural distortion (cultural wobble) as traditional meaning systems break down
4. Period of revitalization
   a. Reformulation of the world view by an individual-inspired by a nonrational experience or "hallucinatory vision"
   b. Communication of the world view to others
   c. An organization emerges
   d. Adaptation or modification of the world view for greater "fit" with existing cultural values
   e. Cultural transformation—as large numbers of people accept this new meaning system
   f. Routinization (or institutionalization) of the meaning system
5. New steady state

single individual. This person usually comes to be seen as a prophet who explains the cause of the cultural malaise and the solution. This solution provides a new world view by which one's experiences in that society seem meaningful.

After the prophet has formulated a new mazeway, he or she communicates that world view by preaching and exhorting members of the society to repent and reform. As new converts are made, the beginnings of organization take shape. A small clique of special disciples provides the inner circle and the nucleus of the campaign for conversion. Hence, there comes to be a hierarchy of members: the prophet, the disciples, and the followers. The leader is held to be charismatic in the sense that Weber used the term.

We may also note that some prophetic messengers fail to gather a following. They remain "voices in the wilderness," and no social movement ever emerges. This usually means the message falls into oblivion.[4]

Many revitalization movements have a revolutionary—or at least antiestablishment—message. Insofar as a group does bear a message that is hostile to the status quo, it will experience resistance from significant portions of the society. To be widely accepted, the group must gain some measure of legitimacy. For this to happen, the original doctrine may be modified or adapted by the prophet. In response to criticisms and affirmations, various beliefs may be played down and eliminated or emphasized and elaborated. Hence, the original vision may be modified so that it has a better "fit" to the personality patterns and cultural assumptions

of the population. If cultural conduciveness is not present at the outset, it may be achieved through continuing revelations of the leader. Those who have studied the Unification Church have commented on the modification of the Reverend Moon's original proclamation of Korea as the chosen land. Once in the United States, Moon recognized a central role for the United States. After all, not many Americans were likely to convert to a religion that glorified another country and assigned only secondary significance to their own country and ethnicity. Continual expansion of any religious movement may be dependent on such adaptation of the world view.

As increasing numbers of people come to accept the new mazeway, or world view, a *transformation of attitudes and behavior* may take place in the entire culture or in a substantial subculture. Theodore Long (1986) points out that the power of the charismatic leader is symbolic or cultural, not structural. Prophecy challenges the existing social order through a revolution in meaning systems. Thus, the resulting social changes usually evolve gradually as the new world view takes effect, rather than suddenly through direct political action. In any case, Wallace insists that the movement that supports the new world view must be routinized, or institutionalized, and a new steady state established.[5]

A number of other scholars have discussed the influence of charismatic leaders and how they come to be viewed as extraordinary. Social psychologists have pointed out that people who are experiencing some sort of stress or anomie are likely to attribute extraordinary powers to someone who offers hope. Attribution is somewhat like projection as a psychological

---

[4]Occasionally, the messages of such prophets survive, even though no new social group is mobilized. In ancient Israel, Amos, Hosea, Jeremiah, and other prophets never organized a movement and were in fact socially marginal. Yet their prophetic visions influenced later religious thought within the tradition. Advanced students interested in the role and social origins of prophecy should refer to Theodore Long (1986).

[5]Wallace was describing this process as a cultural transformation of an entire nonindustrialized society. However, revitalization movements are certainly not limited to homogeneous and relatively simple societies. Barbara Hargrove (1979) is only one of many scholars who treat Christian fundamentalism as a nativistic or revitalization movement in modern America.

process: other people are perceived to have particular qualities because the viewer *wants* to see those qualities in the person. Hence, social circumstances are very important in the development of a charismatic movement. If the charismatic leader were in a social climate that did not have intense cultural strains, he or she would likely be viewed as an ordinary citizen or possibly as mentally deranged.[6]

Nonetheless, once the charismatic leader has emerged and developed a following, it is necessary for the group to undergo a transformation. Charismatic leadership is not only revolutionary, it is inherently unstable. Hence, the movement undergoes a process that Weber referred to as the "routinization of charisma."

The Routinization of Charisma

If the religious movement is to survive for any significant period of time, a stable set of roles and statuses must be established and a consistent pattern of norms generated and adhered to. Hence, the nature of the charismatic authority is transformed.

> In its pure form charismatic authority has a character specifically foreign to everyday routine structures. If this [religious movement] is not to remain a purely transitory phenomenon, but to take on the character of a permanent relationship ... it is necessary for the character of charismatic authority to become radically changed. Indeed, in its pure form charismatic authority may be said to exist only in the process of originating (Weber 1947: 363–64).

The community gathered around a dynamic leader must evolve into one with a stable

matrix of norms, roles, and statuses. This process of **routinization** (developing stable routines) is commonly referred to by sociologists as institutionalization. Any group that fails to institutionalize its collective life simply will not survive.

Institutionalization serves both ideal and material interests of followers and leaders. The ideals of the group can be furthered only if it survives and only if it mobilizes its resources. Hence, institutionalization serves the ideological interests of adherents. But the followers and the leaders also have a material stake in the survival of the group. Insofar as they have invested time, energy, and financial resources in the group, they are likely to feel that they have a vested economic interest in its survival and success. Therefore, the inherent forces working for routinization are strong.

Perhaps the most critical test of a group's routinization is the way it handles the issue of succession. When the charismatic leader dies, the group may quickly disperse. However, many people have a vested interest in the survival of the group and will seek to ensure its viability. But who will provide the group with leadership? And how will that decision be made?

The transfer of power to the next designated leader has important implications for the subsequent evolution of the group. First, the charisma that was once identified with a personality must be associated with the religious ideology and with the religious organization. The group, the body of beliefs, and perhaps a written record (a scripture) become sources of veneration. This more stable source of authority in itself changes the character of the group. Second, a decision-making process itself becomes sacralized as the divinely appointed method of choosing the successor. This method may involve the designation of a successor by the original leader, some form of divinely sanctioned and controlled election, the drawing of lots, a hereditary succession, or

---

[6]Long points out that social distress is a contributing factor, not a necessary one, for the emergence of a prophet. Occasionally prophets arise in times of relative stability, and they sometimes provide expressions of social solidarity (Long 1986).

any one of a number of other procedures. In any event, the followers must recognize the new leader(s) as the legitimate heir(s) to leadership. Otherwise, the group may be torn by schisms as various splinter groups identify different persons as the rightful leader.

The new leader or group of leaders is not likely to possess the same sort of unquestioned authority that was vested in the personhood of the original leader. Some of the awe and respect will have been transferred to the teachings and to the continuing organization itself. The rules and values of the group must be attributed with transcendent importance in and of themselves. Commitment is now to the organization and to the ideology of the movement, and the authority of the *new* leader(s) may be restrained by these stabilizing forces. No longer are the sayings of the leader taken as true simply because that person said them. They must be evaluated in light of what the original leader said and did. In short, the new leader is usually an ideological leader rather than a charismatic one.

Another issue of routinization has to do with provision of a stable economic base. If some members are to devote full time to the service of the leader and the movement, then a continuing and consistent source of income must be provided. This may come from some obligatory payment to the organization by members who are employed in secular positions (a tithe), from members begging or soliciting (as some new religious movements in contemporary America have done), or from the establishment of some industry sponsored by the organization (as in the Bruderhof production of Community Playthings or, in the mid-nineteenth century, Oneida's production of steel traps). However accomplished, this provision of a stable source of income is a critical part of the routinization process. Without this financial base, there can be no full-time clergy, administrative staff, or other regular employees. If there are no career opportunities within

the organizational structure, instrumental commitment may begin to wane. Furthermore, some type of full-time administrative staff may be necessary if the group is growing and expects to continue expanding.

Sometimes routinization is a slow process that occurs largely after the death of the leader. After the death of Jesus, his disciples were a band of frightened and discouraged individuals. Through a series of experiences they became convinced that Jesus had risen from the dead and their faith was renewed. However, it was the new convert, Paul (previously known as Saul of Tarsus) who was responsible for the expansion of the group, for he universalized the faith and recruited Gentiles on an equal basis with Jews. Paul also established organizational links between the various congregations. He collected money from his Gentile converts, which was given to the parent organization in Jerusalem, and he traveled from one congregation to another forging a bond between them and creating a loyalty to himself. In fact, the parent group often sought to undermine his authority, and Paul constantly had to work at maintaining his position of leadership. (By most accounts, Peter and James, leaders of the Jerusalem church, were not adept at organizational matters. However, in the early period they felt that Paul was wrong to allow Jew and Gentile converts to eat together and to be treated as equals.)

Paul established norms and expectations that were spelled out in his teachings and in his epistles. He often "corrected" local congregations because they had begun to follow norms that had emerged spontaneously out of the group. He assumed authority and was sought out as the person to resolve conflicts and to define customs and mores (e.g., whether women could worship without a head covering, and what format the love feasts should follow). He also authorized teachers at various churches. In fact, in his later epistles, he even referred to bishops and deacons.

These officials appear to have been local ones at the time, but eventually the roles expanded to be more centralized, with broad supervisory functions. The routinization process was by no means complete by the time of Paul's death, but it was well under way. It is clear that Paul was the organizational genius who initiated the institutionalization process; it was his organizational initiative that eventually resulted in that bastion of European religious life, the Roman Catholic Church.

So in some cases, a later organizer initiates institutionalization of the faith after the death of the charismatic founder. In other cases, the charismatic leader also happens to be an excellent organizer. In any event, the routinizing function must be performed.

Perhaps the most important test of the routinization of charisma is that of determining leadership succession. However, normalization of roles and statuses, establishment of relatively stable norms, and provision of a stable economic base usually have to be addressed long before succession becomes an issue. If routinization does not occur, the viability of the group for any substantive period after the death of the original leader is unlikely.

Weber did not believe that charismatic leadership was limited to religious groups. For example, many political movements are initiated and guided by charismatic figures. However, Weber did imply that virtually all new religious groups are formed around charismatic leaders. Weston LaBarre (1972) insists even more strongly that *all* religions begin as charismatic cults. Scholars are not in agreement on this.[7]

It does seem safe to say at this point that most religious groups that seek to establish a new religion (as opposed to a new denomination of an existing religion) are founded by charismatic leaders. (Such groups are called *cults* or *new religious movements*.) In sectarian movements (religious groups that seek to reform or renew the traditional religion), a charismatic leader is not a prerequisite. Sectarian movements may take place without members becoming utterly dependent on the authority and inspiration of one person. For example, scriptural literalism may be the basis of a religious reform movement. One person may be the primary interpreter of scripture, but what the individual says is not considered true simply because he or she said it. This is an example of an ideological leader as opposed to a charismatic one (Eichler 1972).[8] Regardless, if a new group is to prosper and survive, it must undergo a process of institutionalization. Its extent and form will vary from group to group, but some routinization must take place.

---

tually convert" each other to the group's world view through a series of many small steps. They also insist that sect—a more traditional religious group—that is faced with hostility may gradually emerge into a cult. The problem with the Stark and Bainbridge proposal for our uses is that many of the "cults" they studied were not religious, including most of those that were created by subcultural evolution. Because we have defined the cult as a fledgling organizational stage of a new religion, most of the spontaneously created groups that they describe would not be considered cults by our definition. If subcultural evolution—without a charismatic leader—is possible for a cult, it is a rare phenomenon. Certainly the sect-to-cult movement can be documented, but the only sects that undergo this transformation seem to be those that have charismatic leaders.

[8]For an example of a sectarian group with an ideological leader (rather than a charismatic one), see discussions by Eberhard Arnold and Emily Arnold (1974) and Benjamin Zablocki (1971) on the Bruderhof. The Bruderhof is a Christian communal society with settlements in New York, Pennsylvania, Connecticut, and several places in Europe.

---

[7]This will be discussed further in chapter 9. For an analysis by two scholars who do not think a charismatic leader is necessary, see William Bainbridge and Rodney Stark (1979). They believe that a cult can gradually emerge as a process of subcultural evolution. Individuals may gradually create a "deviant" subculture through group interaction processes and may "mu-

But institutionalization itself creates new problems or dilemmas.

Dilemmas of Institutionalization

As Thomas O'Dea puts it, "religion both needs most and suffers most from institutionalization" (1961: 32). Although institutionalization is necessary, it tends to change the character of the movement and to create certain dilemmas for the religious organization.

The Dilemma of Mixed Motivation

When the enthusiastic band of disciples is gathered around the charismatic leader, there is a single-minded and unqualified devotion to the leader and to his or her teachings. The followers are willing to make great sacrifices to further the cause, and they willingly subordinate their own needs and desires for the sake of group goals. However, with the development of a stable institutional structure, the desire to occupy the more creative, responsible, and prestigious positions can stimulate jealousies and personality conflicts. Concerns about personal security within the organization may cause members to lose sight of the group's primary goals. Mixed motivation occurs when a secondary concern or motivation comes to overshadow the original goals and teachings of the leader. Conventions of clergy sometimes debate pension plans and insurance programs more heatedly than statements of mission (O'Dea 1961).

It is important to recognize the dilemma in this process. Religious institutions do need to provide for the economic security and well-being of their full-time professionals if they expect them to maintain high morale and commitment. Likewise, if those professionals are to be satisfied and fulfilled by their work, they need to feel that they can really use their creative talents and abilities. These secondary concerns are important to the individuals in question. The problem for the organization is that these secondary matters can take on primary importance for some members and subvert the original sense of mission.

Such secondary concerns may come to the surface while the charismatic leader is still alive. For example, at the time of the Last Supper, Jesus' disciples got into an argument over who was the most important and who would have the most exalted position in the Kingdom of God (Matthew 18:1; Mark 10:37). However, such self-oriented motivations can be rather easily overcome by a simple command of the charismatic personality. Mixed motivation is more likely to develop when the group's sense of security is institutionally based rather than charismatically based. Later generations are much more likely to belong to the group for reasons unrelated to the teachings of the charismatic leader.

In the 1960s, one American inner-city congregation voted to spend tens of thousands of dollars to air condition the sanctuary and sandblast the building's facade. The church was located on the edge of a black ghetto where poverty, unemployment, and inadequate health care were rampant. The congregation chose to use its resources to make the sanctuary more comfortable when it was very hot (on four or five Sundays per year) and to beautify the building so that it could be "a symbol of prestige and grandeur in the community." Prestige and personal comfort would seem to be a wide mark from the unselfish sacrifice and service called for by the founder of Christianity: "the least of you shall be the greatest." In this congregation, where social status became a primary goal in church decisions, mixed motivation would seem to have taken its most extreme form.

Mixed motivation may also involve a more subtle form of goal displacement. Max Assimeng

(1986) studied six millennial and Pentecostal Christian mission groups in Africa, which began with a goal of converting people to their own faith.[9] Their focus was otherworldly and theological.

But to attract converts and to demonstrate their concern for people, some groups started schools; others established hospitals. While the religious message itself was not always well received, the hospitals and schools were enthusiastically embraced. Indeed, promises of offering such this-worldly services were often necessary before the government authorities would allow the group to proselytize in their country. It is natural, one might suggest, for people to repeat those behaviors that are successful and well received. The enthusiastic and warm response to this-worldly benevolent aid was an enticement for missionaries to focus more and more of their energies on provision of those services. Goal displacement began to occur in the allocation of time and resources because the areas in which success did occur provided ego gratifications for the individuals involved. Such goal displacement did not occur equally in all groups or in all regions of Africa; for a variety of reasons, some missionaries were more effective than others in resisting goal displacement. But the original goals in many mission stations were displaced. Success can be intoxicating and alluring and can cause one, consciously or otherwise, to redefine one's goals.

The Symbolic Dilemma: Objectification versus Alienation

In chapter 4 we explored the importance of symbols in religion. For a community to worship together, a common set of symbols must be generated that meaningfully express the world view and the ethos of the group. However, this process of projecting subjective feelings on to objective artifacts or behaviors can proceed to the point that the symbols no longer have power for the members. "Symbolic and ritual elements may become cut off from the subjective experience of the participants. A system of religious liturgy may come to lose its resonance with the interior dispositions of the members. . . . In such a case the forms of worship become alienated from personal religiosity" (O'Dea 1961: 34).

We have already explored the fact that variant interpretations of a symbol in a religious community can have divisive effects (chapter 4). But according to O'Dea, symbols may also become utterly meaningless to members of the religious community. Many Christian churches have stained-glass windows that depict a fish. This was a powerful symbol to the early Christians. In Greek the first letters of each word in the phrase, "Jesus Christ, Son of God, Savior" spelled the word fish. The fish came to be used as a coded symbol of insiders: a drawing of a fish identified one as a Christian to other believers without giving one's Christian identity away to Roman soldiers. Hence, a representation of a fish became an important symbol of solidarity and conviction for Christians, a highly persecuted group. Most modern-day worshipers do not know the origins of the fish as a symbol of faithfulness, and the symbol does not enhance the worship experience. In this case, the symbol is treated with indifference rather than with hostility. In any event, the fish is no longer a powerful symbol that acts to solidify the group, create powerful moods and motivations, and reinforce the world view.

At the Last Supper, Jesus gave his disciples a cup and told them that it represented the "new covenant." He asked each to drink from the cup. A short time before this, he had told

[9]Assimeng's study examined the development of the mission programs of the Seventh Day Adventists, Jehovah's Witnesses, Plymouth Brethren, Pentecostalism, Moral Rearmament, and Salvation Army as they operated in central and western Africa. Millennial groups are ones that expect the second coming of Christ and the end of this world very soon.

the disciples that they could not drink the "cup" from which he must drink; a few hours after the supper, he prayed, "Take this cup from me." In each case, the concept of drinking from a cup had a symbolic reference to accepting an obligation or responsibility.

At that Last Supper, the act of drinking from a common cup may have been as powerful a symbol to the disciples as its contents. The ritual was substantially an act of commitment. Because sharing a common cup is not a symbol of a contract or covenant in our society, much

of the original symbolism is missing for the average Christian. The communion service is still a powerful ritual enactment for most Christians, but at least part of its symbolic meaning may have changed over the centuries. Many churches focus exclusively on what is *in* the cup, and few congregations share a single chalice. (See Box 7.2 for an example of forgotten meanings of symbols in the Greek Orthodox tradition.)

In other cases, the symbols may come to be seen by some as a barrier to communication

---

▶ **BOX 7.2**

Official Symbolism and Actual Behavior in the Greek Orthodox Church

In the Greek Orthodox Church, when people cross themselves they are supposed to use the thumb, the middle finger, and the index finger pressed together to represent the Trinity. The other two fingers are to touch the palm of the hand and stand for the two characteristics of Christ: human and divine. The interesting thing is that when Orthodox Greeks cross themselves, they are supposed to touch their heads (representing the fact that the faith affects their intellect), then they touch their hearts (representing the fact that the faith is to affect their emotions) and then they are to touch their right shoulder and then the left shoulder (to indicate that the faith is to also influence their limbs, their activities). As I watched Greeks cross themselves in Greek churches I noticed that few of them touch their head and then their heart; most touch their throat and then about three inches below that, and then move a couple of inches to the right and a couple of inches to the left. Nor were their hands usually held in the way prescribed by orthodox manuals. So the intended meaning attributed to this symbol—faith in Christ influencing intellect, emotions, and behavior—appears to be lost on the people. The "official" meaning of the symbols

is less powerful than just the kinesthetic activity of making a sign of the cross.

Review the hand symbol of Christianity in Greek Orthodox icons as illustrated on page 83. This symbol is always made with the right hand and is used by priests for blessings. The index finger is supposed to be straight, forming an "I"; the middle finger is slightly bent forming a "C." The little finger is slightly bent (also forming a "C"), and the thumb and ring finger are slightly crossed, forming an "X." The "I" and "C" of the index finger and the middle finger are the first and last letters of the Greek name of Jesus. The "X" and the "C" of the remaining fingers stand for Christ (Elias 1984).

Especially interesting in this symbolism is the fact that in many of the icons, the index finger is bent in the shape of a "C" instead of being straight to form an "I." Furthermore, in most of the icons of Jesus the thumb and ring finger—which are supposed to cross—often simply meet at the tips to form a circle. So again, there is symbolism that has obviously gotten sloppy over the years and is very much lost on most of the people, including some of the priests.

with the transcendent. The antisymbolism of the Puritans, who rejected stained-glass windows and identified Roman Catholic stations of the cross as "idols," provides an example. In the minds of these people, visual symbols had come to symbolize an overbearing bureaucratic organization rather than a transcendent experience. Such alienation from established forms, symbols, and rituals can lead to either apathy toward religion or radical revolt and reformation of the faith.

The process of developing objective, observable symbols that express a deeper subjective experience is part of the process of institutionalization. Symbols are necessary to bind a group together and to remind them of a common faith, but that very objectification of experience into symbols may eventually create problems. If the symbols lose their power and meaning for members, the group must either create new symbols or it will face internal problems of meaning and belonging.

The Dilemma of Administrative Order: Elaboration of Policy versus Flexibility

As a religious group grows and enters the process of institutionalization, it may develop national offices and a bureaucratic structure. In so doing, a set of rational policies and regulations may be established to clarify the relationships between various statuses and offices in the organization. Like the federal government or any other bureaucratic structure, these rules and regulations and the plethora of interrelated departments and divisions may create an unwieldy and overcomplicated structure. Ecclesiastical hierarchies are no less susceptible to red tape than any other bureaucratic structure. And as O'Dea points out, attempts to modify or reform the structure may run into severe resistance by those whose status and security in the hierarchy may be threatened. Resolution of the dilemma of administrative order may be impeded by the existence of mixed motivation. Many persons within the hierarchy may view reorganization as a threat to their own security or positions of power and prestige.

Again, the dilemma must be recognized as such. Students sometimes see unwieldy organizational complexity and excessive rules and regulations as silly and unnecessary. However, people in complex organizations frequently feel a profound need for guidelines for decision making. The search for concrete policy in the face of some new problem is common in any large, formal organization. If no policy has been clearly established, people look to the resolution of similar cases in the past. The precedent often then becomes an unwritten rule. The development of elaborate and sometimes overly complex policy is a natural outgrowth of the desire of people to know how to solve problems and deal with unusual cases. People at lower levels in the organization do not feel comfortable making decisions without the sanction of those with more authority. Yet, this felt need for clearly articulated policy can mean that an organization is run entirely by rigid rules and regulations. Not only is this uncomfortable and frustrating but it also greatly reduces flexibility.

A group of clergy appointed to a committee to screen candidates for ordination and ministry may not feel authorized to establish their own standards for ordination. They want to know what guidelines have been set by the denomination as a whole. If none are available, they would likely seek to have some guidelines formally approved to help them make decisions. (In the absence of formally approved policy, their own decisions may take on the authority of official policy.) The guidelines that are adopted may specify a college degree and a seminary education from an accredited university and theological school, respectively. However, years later an ordination-screening committee may encounter a case in which an individual brings impressive experiential credentials and enthusiastic letters of reference but holds degrees from nonaccredited institutions. Does the committee have the authority to waive the national guidelines in this case? Whatever the members decide, their decision may be seen as a binding precedent for future cases. Policy continues to be elaborated, but it may also restrict a group in its ability to be flexible with new circumstances.

John Fry (1975) believes that the United Presbyterian Church, U.S.A., has been caught in this dilemma of administrative order in recent years. In the late 1960s, the United Presbyterians, U.S.A., modified the organizational structure of the denomination. One goal was to create greater participation in building the budget of the church and in setting priorities; a parallel concern was to establish increased accountability for the use of church funds. The new budget process removed policy setting power of the national Office for Planning, Budgeting, and Evaluation. The procedure for building a budget, spelled out in the church governance document, called for an elaborate process of collaboration and negotiation between national, regional, and district offices (general assembly, synods, and presbyteries).

Once the budget was set in place, national offices were given diminished room for flexibility, for they no longer were granted as much authority to determine priorities and to respond to emergencies as once was the case. This procedure reduced the likelihood that a board in the church hierarchy would allocate funds to radical groups or individuals who seek social change (as the Council on Church and Race had done for the legal defense of Angela Davis, a black militant involved in a highly publicized trial in the early 1970s).[10] But the policy also hampered the ability of the church leaders to offer aggressive leadership and to tackle important (and controversial) issues. Fry believes the church has been "trivialized," that the elaborated policy has tied the hands of the church and left it with only bland, marginally important issues to address as its social outreach. He is convinced that the church's sense of mission has been retarded due to an unwieldy bureaucratic process for building budgets and an excessive concern for consensus and harmony within the church. In this case, Fry thinks that the balance between accountability and flexibility has shifted so far in one direction (accountability) that a dilemma has turned into an outright dysfunction.

The Dilemma of Delimitation: Concrete Definition versus Substitution of the Letter for the Spirit

In the process of routinization, the religious message is translated into specific guidelines of behavior for everyday life. The general teachings about the unity of the universe or about the love of God must be translated into concrete rules of ethical behavior. If this is not done, the religious belief system may remain at such an abstract level that the ordinary person does not grasp its meaning or its importance for everyday living. The meaning of many of Jesus' teachings were not understood even by his disciples until he gave specific illustrations or elaborated through parables. In the ancient Hebrew tradition, the covenant that Abraham had made with God was comforting, but to understand the human obligations in it, specific ethical codes were spelled

---

[10]A member of the Communist Party in the United States, Angela Davis had been controversial as a professor at UCLA. In 1970 an effort to free two black prisoners and a black defendant resulted in a shoot-out in the Marin County, California, Courthouse, and the weapons used were found to be registered in Angela Davis's name. She was charged with kidnapping, conspiracy, and murder. She insisted that she was innocent, and her defenders believed that she could not get a fair trial in the political atmosphere of Marin County. Her black militance and her Communist Party affiliation had become as important in the pretrial publicity as her guilt or innocence. Eventually, she was acquitted of all charges.

out. The Torah, the first five books of the Hebrew Bible (the Christian Old Testament) is a record of this religious law.

However, in the process of translating the outlook of the faith into specific rules, something may be lost. Eventually, the members may focus so intently on the rules that they

The substitution of the letter for the spirit of a set of beliefs is illustrated in this linocut by Robert 0. Hodgell. Some religious people seem so intent on literal interpretation of the written word that the spirit of the faith seems to be lost; there seems to be little love, compassion, or joy in such religion. (Used by permission of R. O. Hodgell.)

lose sight of the original spirit or outlook of the faith. The religion may then degenerate into legalistic formulas for salvation and/or may become moralistic and judgmental in a way inconsistent with the original intent of the founder (O'Dea 1961). The legalism and ritualism of the late classical period of pharisaic Judaism provides one example. The fundamentalistic and rule-bound interpretations of Islam by the leading Shammai ayatollas of Iran provide another example; their posture is clearly inconsistent with the central thrust of Islam. The linocut print by Robert Hodgell illustrates his view of some segments of Protestantism in the United States. It expresses more eloquently than words the problem created when the letter of the religious ethical code becomes more important than the spirit of that code. The image could apply equally well to Islamic fundamentalists or to the way Reformed Jews feel about many Hasidic Jews.

Hence, the dilemma is created: the abstract moods, motivations, and concepts must be made concrete so that common laypeople can comprehend their meaning and implication for everyday life. However, by translating the spirit of the faith into specific moral rules and ritual requirements, the possibility is established that later generations may become literalistic and legalistic about those rules and may miss the central message.

The Dilemma of Power: Conversion versus Coercion

If a religious group is to stay together and sustain its common faith, conformity to the values and norms of the group must be ensured. Although occasional deviation from established norms may not threaten the group, most of the beliefs, values, and norms of the faith must be adhered to most of the time. In its early stages, the religious group is composed of members who have personally converted to the group. They feel a personal loyalty to the charismatic leader, they have had a nonrational conversion experience, or they have been motivated to internalize the faith through some other process. But later generations, who have grown up within the religious organization, may never have personally experienced anything that compelled them to accept the absolute authority of the faith in their own lives, or to accept the authority of the religious hierarchy to interpret the faith. They may be inclined to challenge official interpretations. Although such challenges can also come in the first generation, internalization of the authority structure is usually more complete in the first generation of believers than in later ones (O'Dea 1961).

To maintain the integrity of the organization and ensure consensus in their basic world view, religious organizations may resort to coercive methods of social control. Excommunication is one procedure. When Sonia Johnson, a Mormon, took a public stand in 1979 in favor of the Equal Rights Amendment, the Mormon hierarchy informed her that her stance was heretical. When she refused voluntarily to accept the position of the Mormon Church and the authority of its leaders, she was excommunicated. Likewise, other religious bodies have excommunicated members who fail to conform to basic doctrinal or ritual standards. Of course, in some periods of history, the unorthodox were subject to torture and death. Regardless of the specific methods used, the maintenance of conformity through coercion rather than conversion is significant. Conformity due to internalization of norms is much more powerful and lasting than the use of coercion, but voluntary internalization of the norms by all members is difficult to sustain. Therefore, an institutionalized religious organization may come to rely on coercive methods as a last resort to maintain conformity and consensus.

Edward Lehman (1985) points out that in democratic, pluralistic societies such as the United States, religious organizations have little coercive power over their members. In fact, it is the members who have some control over their churches; they may threaten to withhold financial support. Thus, churches in the modern world have much less clout to enforce and maintain their interpretations of the faith.

The Dilemma of Expansion: Rationalized Structure versus Communalism

In the early phases of development, much of the members' sense of commitment comes from the sense of belonging and the feeling of community. As we found in our section on conversion and commitment, a sense of belonging is a critical element in the commitment of members of new religious cults. But membership growth is also important; if the group fails to grow and expand its influence, the members' morale may waiver, and the sense of mission and destiny may fade. As the group does grow, it will soon reach the point when members do not all know each other, and it becomes necessary to develop rational structures and procedures for decision making. Hence, the process of institutionalization may undermine the sense of communalism (belonging). Affective commitment must then be reinforced by instrumental and moral commitment (see chapter 5). In fact, instrumental commitment may become primary, although it is based—consciously or unconsciously—on a cost-benefit analysis. Instrumental commitment heightens a person's sense of loyalty based on advantages accrued to the individual. This would seem to play into the dilemma of mixed motivation in a very direct way. When the individual's commitment hinges in large part on the question, "What's in it for me?" the problem of mixed motivation has become a reality.

Most religious groups establish local congregations that are relatively stable and that fulfill much of the need for affective commitment. However, David Bromley and Anson Shupe (1979) found this rational structure versus communalism dilemma to be one of the most significant facing the Unification Church in the mid-1970s. The original sense of communalism was being lost in the process of bureaucratization. The development of a rational structure was mandatory for the coordination of this large and growing organization. But as this happened, the close interpersonal caring and sharing that had attracted many persons into membership was beginning to wane. By creating permanent vocational opportunities within the organizational structure, Moon was able to reinforce the possibilities of instrumental commitment. People could develop their careers as expressions of commitment to the group. Moon also performed mass weddings, sometimes with hundreds of people married at one ceremony and to partners designated by Moon himself. This ensured endogamous marriages. It also meant that leaving the group would involve separation from one's spouse and (eventually) from one's children. In this way, Moon made the marriage bond a form of affective commitment to the group (Bromley and Shupe 1979). As this illustrates, it is possible to find alternative ways of generating the affective type of commitment. But the fact remains that when an organization expands to the point that a bureaucratic structure is needed, the affective commitment mechanisms will have to be transformed to account for the loss of communalism.

The fact that a group's growth means that members can no longer know all other members in itself means a change in the group's character. Growth also means that eventually the group must develop task specialization. As this happens, the common member does not know what is happening in all areas of the organization. Some individuals or special groups gain almost autonomous control over their own area or department, and they may use that platform to influence policies, budget allocations, and goals of the entire organization. As Ronald Johnstone puts it, "a bureaucracy, once formed, tends to take on a life of its own, initiates and implements policy partly of its own making, and may begin to direct the larger organization of which it is a specialized part in new directions" (1975: 110). Maintenance of the organization, avoidance of internal dissention, and enhancement of group solidarity become guiding norms in their own right (Lehman 1985).

Frequently, most lay members do not know who the leaders of their denominational church divisions are and are not even fully aware of policy decisions their church hierarchy makes. Nonetheless, those policies are implemented with the aid of donations by local churches. While common members provide the financial support, an elite group of people, unknown to most of the laity, decide how to spend it. This can be the basis of internal organizational conflict, especially if the elite supports causes that the laity oppose (e.g., civil rights, women's liberation, or liberationist movements in the Third World).

Institutional Dilemmas and Social Context

Milton Yinger (1961) points out that O'Dea's discussion of institutional dilemmas failed to specify the conditions under which the dilemmas are most and least likely to occur. Indeed, O'Dea suggests that the dilemmas are inherent, unavoidable, and inevitable. If they *are* inevitable, it seems clear that in some cases it may take several generations, and perhaps several centuries, to occur.

James Mathisen (1987) has analyzed the Moody Bible Institute in Chicago, tracing its 100-year history, with attention to how it has dealt with these institutional dilemmas. Several of the dilemmas appear not to have occurred, and the movement seems to have coped fairly effectively with most of the others. Mathisen's analysis highlights the fact that some social organizations and some social conditions may be more conducive than others to the occurrence of certain dilemmas.

It appears from Mathisen's study that the symbolic dilemma is less likely to occur in groups that stress intense emotional conversion experiences and that have strong mechanisms to sustain the plausibility of the world view and the symbol systems. Alienated or marginal groups in the society may also be less susceptible to this dilemma because the religious symbols may serve to enhance group boundaries. Conflict with outsiders provides a context in which symbols gain emotional force and relevancy for the members.

Likewise, the dilemma of delimitation (concrete definition versus substitution of the letter for the spirit) may be less of a problem in circumstances where the group perceives itself to be a persecuted or vulnerable minority group. Having a clearly defined set of "fundamentals" by which to measure faithfulness may become a source of strength for the group and may be defined as a virtue. Not only was this the case for fundamentalists running the Moody Bible Institute but also appears to be operative among Orthodox Jews in North America as well. Both groups are minority movements that are substantially concerned with maintaining clear boundaries between themselves and the larger society. If concrete definition sometimes does lead to a problem

Sun Myung Moon performs a mass marriage in 1982 at Madison Square Garden. The practice of mass weddings resulted in much negative publicity, but it served to enhance affective commitment of members as the religious group grew in numbers and became more impersonal and bureaucratic. (Ken Karp Photography.)

for the group, it is clear that this is not always the case.

The dilemmas of mixed motivation and of power may also be lessened in circumstances in which many commitment mechanisms are used. As we saw in chapter 5, commitment mechanisms heighten one's commitment to the needs and interests of the group by causing one to identify self-interest with group interests. This would lessen the likelihood of mixed motivation and would reduce the need for coercion as a means of social control. But these generalizations are at this point reasonable hypotheses that need to be tested empirically. Continued research is needed regarding the conditions under which the dilemmas are most and least likely to occur.

Dilemmas of institutionalization do plague organized religion, but the six dilemmas outlined in this chapter are not necessarily "inevitable," and it is clear that they need not be fatal. It appears that the dilemmas are more pronounced when the organization is a majority religious movement than when it is a minority protest movement preoccupied with tensions with the larger society.

Institutionalization as a Mixed Blessing

The process of institutionalization is a mixed blessing (or perhaps a necessary curse) for religion. If a new cult does not institutionalize, it is not likely to last long. The absence of routinization will mean that the group will expire with the death of the charismatic leader. The particular pattern of routinization will vary from group to group, and some organizations become more bureaucratic and centralized than do others. For example, some religious bodies have successfully routinized without establishing a professional clergy, while others have highly trained professionals as ministers and a hierarchy of area ministers, bishops, and archbishops. The student of religious organizations will find considerable variation in the extent and style of institutionalization, but some form of routinization is essential.

Of course, there are other reasons why religious bodies develop increasingly complex institutional structures that are decreasingly responsive to local congregations. One reason is

---

► **BOX 7.3**

The Subsystems of Religion and Their Linkages

As the symbolic dilemma shows, institutionalization obviously impacts the meaning system as well as the organizational structure. Likewise the dilemma of expansion demonstrates that the formal structure of an organization can affect the belonging system. If internal affective ties (the belonging subsystem) are especially strong or if external ties are weakened by conflict with nonmembers, we

also see that some of the institutional dilemmas are less likely to happen.

These phenomena vividly illustrate the intimate linkages and interdependencies between meaning system, structural system, and belonging system. Routinization impacts all three systems and is affected by the ties between the systems.

that such institutional expansion and organizational alliances are necessary if a group is to reach some of its goals. A single congregation may not be able to afford to sponsor a mission hospital in an impoverished country, so it joins with other churches in the denomination. But in creating such collaboration, the local congregation relinquishes its right to determine how the money will be spent. Such policies are made at another level: the denomination's board of discipleship or board of missions. Or, a group of local congregations from several denominations may unite to establish a low-income housing unit for the poor or the elderly, or may cosponsor an alcohol treatment center or a family counseling center for the community. Again, a board of directors is established to determine policy, and the local congregation loses some of its autonomy and control over its resources.

Other forces for ecumenical cooperation may strike even closer to home. For example, several denominations may develop a joint board for producing Sunday school materials. Such a cooperative venture reduces the cost for each of the denominations and allows them to hire highly trained specialists in religious education to design the curricula. In so doing, each denomination may get much higher-quality materials than it would if each congregation or each denomination tried to create its own. However, it does mean that the local congregation relinquishes some control over the content (Johnstone 1975). The board that directs policy is now interdenominational. These examples may help illustrate the fact that bureaucratization often helps groups achieve positive goals. Hence, religious groups are not just pushed into institutionalization for survival's sake. They are also "pulled" (attracted) into it in order to accomplish desired goals.

Despite the necessity of institutionalization, certain changes in the character of the group

occur in the process. Changes in motivation for membership; alienation from the symbol systems; development of unwieldy, bureaucratic structure in the organization; substitution of moralistic legal codes for the spirit of the original teachings; employment of coercion to ensure conformity and consensus within the group; and loss of a sense of communalism are some of the problems institutionalization generates. Avoiding these problems by avoiding institutionalization is simply not an option; rather, renewal movements, revivals, and other processes of regeneration are the means by which religious groups seek to overcome these dysfunctions. As we will see in chapter 9, the rebellion against routinization is one reason for the development of new sects. Much of the internal conflict and many of the schisms in denominations are due to the need for regeneration and a need to restate the faith in terms that are compelling to a new generation facing different problems of social meaning.

Even if a group goes through the process of institutionalization, it may face opposition from other groups and institutions in the society. Routinization is necessary, but not sufficient, to ensure survival. In the next chapter we turn to an analysis of resource mobilization and of processes that maintain plausibility of the world view.

Summary

Many religious movements appear to get started through the dynamism of a charismatic leader (Jesus, Mohammed, Sun Myung Moon, Ann Lee). The individual is viewed as an agent of God or perhaps as God incarnate (in the flesh). What that person says is held as true simply because he or she said it. However, Weber held that charisma is inherently unstable and if a group is to survive it must routinize. That is, it must develop norms, roles, and statuses; it must transfer the sense of awe from the individual personality to the teachings and the organization; and it must make provisions for succession of the leader when he or she dies. As these policies are spelled out and various statuses gain specialized job descriptions, the movement is taking its first steps toward institutionalization. Many decades later the group may be highly bureaucratized.

Some new religious groups are started by ideological leaders rather than charismatic ones. They are the interpreters of some scripture or other ideological source that is inherently authoritative. But even in cases where an ideological leader initiates a new religious group, routinization is essential if the group is to survive.

There may be other forces leading to institutionalization as well. Accomplishment of major goals calls for a high degree of organization and efficiency. For some goals to be achieved, alliances with other organizations may be required. This means the development of commissions, boards, and divisions to direct these projects.

Regardless of the cause of institutionalization, it brings many changes in the religious movement itself. Bureaucracies take on a life of their own, somewhat independent of the lay members, and tend to influence the workings of the whole organization. As we pointed out in chapter 4, this sometimes results in official and folk versions of the faith. Over time, the institutionalized religion is likely to face the dilemmas that routinization creates. Institutionalization is a necessity, but it has mixed consequences for the group.

CHAPTER EIGHT

Survival of Religious Movements: Mobilization of Resources and Plausibility of the World View

Institutionalization is necessary, but not sufficient, to ensure survival of a religious group. Institutionalization presumably aids in the provision of resources; but in this chapter, we look more closely at other factors that affect the ability of a group to control its environment and to attract money and volunteers. We also examine the way in which religious groups construct "plausibility structures" to make their world view seem uniquely realistic. A religious group will not survive for long unless the world view seems plausible (believable) to members.

Resource Mobilization and the Viability of Religious Movements

Proponents of the resource mobilization perspective[1] focus on the interaction between a group's organizational pattern, their world view, and their social and political environment. Unlike Rosabeth Kanter, John Lofland, James Downton, and others who maintain that viability depends primarily on the ability of the group to elicit commitment, resource mobilization theorists emphasize appropriate types of adaptation for specific types of religious movements and environments (Bromley and Shupe 1979).

The **resource mobilization perspective** maintains that the ability of any group to achieve its goals is limited by the self-interests of other groups and by various change-resistant forces. Hence, success can be realized only if the group is able to mobilize or activate resources in its own behalf. Such resources include financial support, political clout, favorable public attitudes (legitimacy), and the time

---

[1] Resource mobilization theory was actually developed by Mayer Zald and his associates. For a discussion of the resource mobilization perspective, see Mayer Zald and Roberta Ash (1966); John McCarthy and Mayer Zald (1977); and Mayer Zald and Michael Berger (1978). David Bromley and Anson Shupe will be discussed here because they have applied this perspective to religious organizations.

and energy of members. The resource mobilization perspective, then, stresses the interactive process between the religious group and the larger society. Internal organization, methods of recruitment, and formulation of doctrine are often profoundly affected by the response of the larger society to the group. The form and character of any religious group is a product of this interaction and is not solely a result of a sect's internal dynamics.

The problems of resource mobilization vary significantly for different types of groups, and one way of identifying these is to focus on the extent and level of change they seek to implement (Aberle 1966). Extent of change refers simply to the totality or partiality of change; level of change has to do with whether the change is personal or societal in nature.

The first type of group is the **alternative group**. Groups that stress alternative change are interested only in partial change in the individual. Some religious movements stress faith healing or place the emphasis on personal devotion and piety. The convert is to change his or her world view and behavior relative to one particular aspect of life, but change in political or economic views or in one's interpersonal relationships is considered unnecessary.

The second type of group is the **redemptive group**. It seeks total change in the individual. Changes in the organization of society are seen as secondary to personal conversion. In some cases, societal changes may even be considered utterly insignificant. The emphasis is on change of heart and mind: the remolding of personality.

The third type of group is the **reformative group**. This seeks partial change in the social structure. Change in individuals is considered insufficient; the society itself must be reformed. On the other hand, the society and culture are not viewed as utterly depraved. They simply need modification and fine-tuning.

The fourth group, the **transformative group**, seeks total change of the entire social structure. Moderate reforms are considered insufficient; a complete overhaul of all aspects of society and culture is mandated. David Bromley and Anson

▶ **BOX 8.1**

Religious Groups and Type of Transformation

		Level of Change	
		Individual	Societal
Extent of Change	Partial	Alternative	Reformative
	Total	Redemptive	Transformative

Shupe emphasize the totalistic nature of the expected change by referring to such groups as world-transforming movements. The Unification movement is an excellent example.

Most groups do not focus exclusively on individual or structural change. Frequently, a change at one level is seen as the precursor to change at another. Nevertheless, a primary emphasis on change at one level or the other is usually discernible.

The problems of resource mobilization for each of these types of groups are somewhat different. Those that have only minor impact on the loyalties and resources of individuals and that do not call for radical changes in the social order are much less likely to threaten the interests of others in society. Because of this, they are also less likely to meet with hostility and the stigmatizing labels of outsiders. As we found in chapter 5, groups that have not been stigmatized normally do not require isolation of members from nonmembers (Snow and Phillips 1980).[2]

Isolation of members from family ties can be a major cause of hostility toward new religious groups, and avoidance of this strategy can mean circumvention of a vicious cycle of stigmatization and defensive responses.

Furthermore, if no stigma is attached to the group and no hostility directed toward it, the group may be able to work cooperatively with conventional units of society, gain access to resources through many different persons in the society, and therefore not need to demand the total resources of its members. Because mobilization of resources by such groups is met with much less organized resistance, survival rates are somewhat higher. In fact, the major problem of resource mobilization may be simply one of stimulating enough commitment so that members do not become apathetic and withdraw their support. Conflict from outsiders does function effectively to strengthen in-group loyalty.

The Church of Christ, Scientist, which was begun in the 1860s, provides an example of a nonrevolutionary group that coexisted rather harmoniously with other social institutions. Mary Baker Eddy, the founder of the church, interpreted the central teachings of Christianity as guidelines for mental, physical, and spiritual health. She believed that disease, sin, and death are caused by mental error and can be overcome by right thinking. The world view was highly otherworldly and very individualistic. Her teachings did not threaten the social order. Rather, they called for changes in individuals. Furthermore, these changes did not require a radical break from one's family or from other nonmembers. The Christian Scientists received minimal stigmatization or hostility from outsiders (compared with world-transforming groups like the Moonies of our own day). In fact, their membership was and is composed largely of rather affluent and well-established people. Mobilization of financial resources has never been as severe a problem for the Christian Scientists as it has been for groups like the Hare Krishna (which demands total commitment) or the flying saucer cult (which has an idiosyncratic message).

Groups that stress alternative change (partial change of individuals) normally face the least amount of opposition from institutions or from individuals with affective ties to members. Redemptive groups (which seek total change of individuals) receive most of their opposition from individuals (especially family members) who have affective ties to the devotees. Because individuals have less power to apply against a group than does an institution, resource mobilization will be somewhat less problematic for redemptive groups than for

---

[2]However, groups that are highly *particularistic* (feel that salvation and truth can be attained only through membership in their own group) may weaken ties to nonmembers, regardless of whether their belief system is revolutionary or not.

transformative and reformative ones. Of course, if family members are sympathetic to the group or are themselves recruited, there may be little opposition to redemptive groups even from family members.

Reformative groups (which seek partial change of the social structure) also encounter opposition from institutions and persons with vested interests, but the opposition is not likely to be as intense or as widespread as that experienced by a radical group demanding total commitment of members. Transformative or world-transforming groups are likely to experience great resistance both from other institutions and from persons who have a vested interest in the status quo. Such groups demand not only total commitment of individuals but threaten the entire social structure with radical change. This may earn the group the label of "subversive."

The internal development of a religious group is therefore influenced by the type of change the charismatic leader espouses and by the response of the larger society to the movement. Because the world-transforming or transformative group is likely to experience the most severe conflicts with the larger society and to have the most problems with gaining legitimacy, it is appropriate to focus our attention on the resource mobilization problems in this type of group.[3] Bromley and Shupe have developed their theory specifically on the basis of their research on the Unification Church. The Moonies believe that the world as we know it is soon to end and that the new era will be structured under a world government apparently headed by the messiah, the Reverend Moon. This new government will be a form of theocracy (government

by God or by the agents of God—the clergy). Clearly, the world is to undergo a radical political reformation.

Bromley and Shupe (1979) point out that any group must choose a strategy for change from three possibilities: coercion, bargaining, or persuasion. The use of coercion by a world-transforming group is appropriate only if the group has access to substantial political or military resources. Otherwise, the group will be quickly crushed by defenders of the status quo. The bargaining strategy involves use of existing resources to exchange with outsiders so that outsiders are manipulated into the desired changes. Such a strategy is possible for reformative movements, which may use their buying power or political influence to further their cause. However, this strategy involves compromise and reciprocity. The world view and goals of the world-transforming group will usually not allow such compromise and cooperation with the existing structures. For a relatively small and powerless group that hopes to transform the world, persuasion is the only viable strategy available. Hence, all its resources must be mobilized to persuade people that the changes the group advocates are in the best interests of everyone. Box 8.2 relates the idea of resource mobilization explicitly to the issue of how open or closed a system is as discussed by systems theory.

The resources that a group has available are quite diverse. The first is a compelling ideology. The ideology of the world-transforming movement is characterized by its forecast of total, imminent, and cataclysmic change in the structure of society. Those who are prepared and help in this transformation will be exalted in the new era, and those who do not heed the message will be doomed to some horrible fate. The new era is envisioned as manifesting values and priorities that are very much in contrast with the depraved values of the current social order. The role of devotees in the new era is usually clearly defined by the ideology;

---

[3]Resource mobilization theory has also been applied to world-transforming groups more than it has to others. Hence, there is more information available using this theory to understand transformative groups than there is on other types of groups.

understandably, devotees are expected to have positions of power and prestige. Such an ideology can motivate members through its promise of awesome rewards and/or punishments. Furthermore, the day of transformation is viewed as so imminent that little time is left for preparation. This outlook can be a powerful spur to the mobilization of the personal resources (time, energy, money) of believers.[4]

Bromley and Shupe maintain that the leadership of world-transforming movements is characteristically charismatic. Because the source of authority is vested in the person of the leader, the entire structure of the organization tends to be pyramidal, from the leader and disciples down. This allows tremendous centralization of the decision-making process and

---

[4]Of course, the monumental goal of transforming the entire society may also cause disillusionment among

members if they perceive little accomplishment of—or even significant movement toward—their goal. Methods of dealing with this problem will be discussed in the following pages.

▶ **BOX 8.2**

Open versus Closed Systems and Mobilization of Resources

In chapter 3 we discussed the idea of open and closed social systems—a theoretical perspective that might help to clarify the issue of differences in how resources are mobilized. The tranformative movement is in opposition to the existing society, and tries to limit substantially any influence the larger society might have on the group. It filters "inputs" very carefully, symbolized in this diagram with the thick wall guarding against societal impact. Because the system does limit inputs,

it also limits the available resources and must mobilize internal resources more completely. Of course, sometimes the system has become closed in order to protect itself from external hostilities; by stigmatizing groups the conventional society sometimes causes them to become closed. More open systems, however, have a freer flow of ideas and resources with the larger society; therefore, they face different issues in generating resources for their survival.

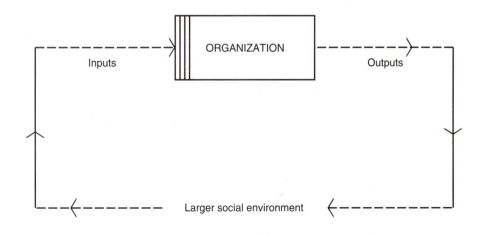

enhances the implementation of those decisions. Moreover, the unique authority of the leader even justifies control over the daily lives and personal concerns of members.

In terms of organization, the world-transforming movement usually has strong communal tendencies. This sense of familial bond and close affective ties enhances commitment. However, as the organization grows, a bureaucratic structure is established for more effective administration. To use resources wisely and efficiently, the organization must delineate lines of authority and areas of responsibility. This in turn tends to undermine the sense of community and the affective basis of relationships that are central to group commitment. This creates the dilemma of expansion, which was discussed in the previous chapter.

World-transforming movements must also engage in intensive socialization practices. Because the group hopes to instill values that are antithetical to those of the larger society, they must take the socialization of members seriously. Particularly, because a small number of people from the larger population are likely to be candidates for recruitment, the group must hold on to those members it does manage to interest in the movement. This intensive socialization is important in mobilizing and maintaining the personal resources of recruits.

These factors are critical in mobilizing and maintaining resources within the movement. But outside forces are also critical to the movement's viability. The first external factor is the environmental context. In social environments that have large numbers of alienated or discontented people, the ground is fertile for the growth of world-transforming movements. In social contexts that have few discontented members, such movements will not find many people receptive to their message about alienation and the need for social transformation. For the most part, world-transforming movements are not able to do much about creating favorable conditions, but they try to capitalize

on them when they do exist. They may also make adaptations in their message and their appeal if they move to new social environments with different sources of tension and dissatisfaction. Hence, world-transforming movements may make internal adjustments in order to exploit fully the resource of discontentment.

If transformation movements are to succeed through a strategy of persuasion, they must gain wide publicity. Social visibility is paramount to the achievement of their aims. However, if they are to gain converts, their visibility must be in a context of legitimacy. They must be viewed as unique and as worthy of attention, but they must also be considered noncontroversial and nonsubversive. In some cases, this is quite difficult to achieve. After all, their goal *is* subversive! They wish to undermine the present social order and replace it with one of their own.

This creates a serious dilemma for the group. Mobilization of resources means gaining general public approval and support, but the ideology demands an uncompromising opposition to the status quo. This means that the group must either conceal its real goals and purposes for a while (the Moonies called this "divine deception") or they must modify their ideology. For example, by suggesting that the present government has some ordained role in the transformation process, temporary cooperation with the current social order may be justified. Eventually, this may lead to more permanent accommodation to the values and standards of the larger society. The desire for legitimacy and the need to lessen public resistance are powerful drives for the movement. How a group resolves this dilemma will make a significant impact on subsequent developments in the organization and ideology.

Finally, the larger society may become aware of the revolutionary nature of the world-transformation movement and may impose measures to monitor or control the development of the group. The antiestablishment posture of the group may lead it to endorse unconventional and even illegal behavior. Formal legislation may be passed to limit the activities of the group, and ad hoc vigilante-style groups (e.g., deprogrammers) may be formed to undermine its work.[5] Clearly, such developments restrict the ability of the group to mobilize forces on its behalf.

The resource mobilization perspective makes an important contribution to the sociology of religion. It demonstrates that the viability of a group depends on more than the implementation of commitment mechanisms or a few simple steps of routinization. Resource mobilization theory requires a force-field analysis, an investigation of all the social forces that may be operating to advance or retard the success of the group. Depending on the extent and level of change advocated, there may be differing forces operating to resist the group's ambitions. The world-transforming movement is likely to experience the most severe resistance and face the most problematic dilemmas. However, the *response* of any new religious group to social resistance will largely determine its future. Not only will its viability be affected, but the group's composition, organization, and goals will be shaped by the decisions and compromises that are made. The resource mobilization perspective emphasizes that even internal affairs, such as the world view or belief system, are shaped in large part by interaction with the surrounding culture. Bromley and Shupe (1979) have demonstrated such changes within Moonie theology, and Thomas O'Dea's study of the Mormons (1957) showed similar theological accommodations in that group.[6]

Although routinization and mobilization of resources are both important, a group may also be unviable if its beliefs or world view are implausible, or if the culture changes so that the basis for establishing truth is modified. It is to this issue of plausibility that we turn next.

Plausibility of the World View

Another important factor in the survival of a religious group is the plausibility or believability of the world view. If everyday events or if scientific explanations seem to disprove the religious world view, the survival of the group may be threatened. If the belief system is viewed as implausible or unrealistic, it is unlikely to offer much sense of meaning and purpose in life. One widely respected sociologist of religion, Peter Berger, has devoted much of his writing to the exploration of **plausibility structures.** These are social interactions and processes within a group that serve to protect and sacralize the shared meanings and outlooks of the group.[7]

---

[5]Bromley and Shupe refer to the anticult deprogrammers as engaged in a modern-day form of witch-hunting. See Shupe and Bromley's book, *The New Vigilantes: Deprogrammers, Anti-Cultists and the New Religions* (1980).

[6]We might note here that only a historical analysis is capable of revealing these patterns. The ahistorical

procedure of classical functionalism could never reveal these modifications of world view. Hence, much of the sociology of religion research from the 1930s until the 1960s is lacking in this sort of analysis.

[7]It is worth noting that plausibility is an important issue for maintenance of any ideology, be it political, economic, or whatever. All social systems establish plausibility structures to reinforce belief in the status quo. In fact, Stuart Hills (1980) maintains that one of the problems in understanding deviance is that it is necessary to break through the "mystification" of conformity and deviance. He insists that all societies tend to mystify and label appropriately those behaviors that either support or threaten the status quo, thereby increasing the stability of the existing system by making conforming behavior seem uniquely moral and right. However, it is easy for people—including social scientists—to misunderstand much of deviant behavior because the plausibility structures that define deviance are so deeply rooted that they are taken for granted. In effect, Hills has taken Berger's concepts of the social construction of reality and the mystification of social structure and applied them to the field of criminology. This entire field of examining the social forces that cause people to accept the validity of social beliefs is known as the sociology of knowledge.

Much of chapter 4 was concerned with this issue, and the emphasis in chapter 5 on the importance of affective commitment in maintaining moral commitment (adherence to ideology) points to the same phenomenon. Belief systems, if they are to survive, must be rooted in a social base and reinforced through a sense of sacredness or absoluteness about the beliefs. Plausibility can be enhanced through a variety of mechanisms: reference groups committed to the belief system, dualistic belief systems, norms requiring that members engage in evangelism, a sense of profound respect or awe for the leadership, rituals that elicit a sense of awe, music that evokes strong emotions, emotionally laden symbols, and even especially beautiful and expansive architecture.

An understanding of the religious group as a reference group is particularly critical to any analysis of plausibility. Individuals are capable of accepting all sorts of strange beliefs if enough other people seem convinced. It is a basic maxim of symbolic interactionism that individuals look to others for a definition of the situation if they are uncertain themselves. When dealing with issues of the meaning of life, with the supernatural, and with the ultimate cause of perplexing events, ambiguity is a given.

Even if a plausibility structure exists, however, the belief system may be subject to disproof or may be counter to common sense. If a religious leader stakes his or her reputation on a specific time, date, and year when the end of the world will come, the movement may be in serious trouble the day after the predicted apocalypse.

But one should not assume that problems of plausibility are limited to doomsday groups. Wade Clark Roof maintains that liberal Protestantism is currently experiencing strains in theological plausibility. This is partially because the plausibility structures in liberal Protestant groups tend to be weaker, but the problem does not end there. Liberal Christians are inclined to accept scientific method and scientific knowledge as authoritative, and these are based on naturalistic explanations. Scientific causal analysis does not accept supernatural intervention as a factor. Laws of nature or natural factors are used to explain everything from the origin of the universe to an individual's mystical experience. For some liberal Protestants and Catholics, this naturalistic explanation is not a problem. They simply accept a remythologized meaning system (modernism), which suggests that God works through natural processes, including psychological ones. For others, scientific explanations seem to dismiss the need for belief in God. In fact, studies have shown that a small but significant percentage of American church members do not even believe in God (Roof 1978), or at least are unsure of God's existence (Glock and Stark 1966). For some people, scientific explanations threaten to make the religious view of reality implausible.

Even a book like this, with its psychosocial explanations of religious behavior, is threatening to many people. The type of analysis it presents may cause some readers to question the plausibility of their own faith. The tendency to view religious behavior through a naturalistic lens may trouble some readers, for we are approaching commitment and conversion through reference group theory rather than attributing these processes entirely to the Holy Spirit. Sociology provides a lens for viewing reality; it has its own assumptions and world view. Although we attempt to avoid either a theistic or an atheistic bias, some readers might consider the naturalistic mode of interpretation an attempt to debunk theism.

We cannot resolve these issues of plausibility here, but it is important to recognize that in a pluralistic society people are constantly exposed to meaning systems that seem to contradict their own. The most severe problems of plausibility occur for members of the world-transforming groups, who expect the transformation of the world imminently. What happens to the belief system when time drags on and the end does not arrive? We have already seen the mobilizing power that is inherent in millenialism, but how can such a view be sustained? Plausibility structures are important, but if one's religious group teaches that the millenium was to come on April 23, and this is May 1, something more than a reference group is needed to make the world view believable. If they are going to survive, world-transforming movements must develop belief systems that are self-validating.[8]

One of the important characteristics of the ideology of many sects and cults is **dualism,** the belief that reality is ultimately a battle between the forces of good and evil. Frequently, evil is personalized in the form of Satan, or the devil. Dualism is very functional in sustaining plausibility of an otherwise implausible world view. Because plausibility is essential for the survival of a group, dualism is often a significant factor in those groups that hold unconventional world views. In other words, groups that have a world view that contradicts the scientific and "commonsense" explanations are more likely to survive if they have a world view that is dualistic.

Lofland's description of the role of dualism in the Unification movement provides an interesting example. He articulates one of the central postulates of their world view, as follows:

> Anything that hinders or hurts [a member] or the group or an outsider who is assisting is an attack by Satan's spirits. Anything that helps a [member] or the group or an outsider who is assisting is an act of helping or leading by God's spirits (1977: 197).

Hence, "whether expectations are fulfilled or not, the believer cannot lose. He derives confirmation from any outcome" (Lofland 1977: 197). This dualism is not merely an interesting characteristic of many new religious movements in the United States; it is central to their appeal. Meredith McGuire emphasizes this point when she writes, "The tidiness and order of the dualistic interpretation of the world are part of the basic appeal of such movements. Dualistic figures of Good and Evil simplify the world for people who are overwhelmed by the ambiguity and complexity of modern life" (1992: 44). The sense of normlessness is crushed by the absoluteness of the answers that dualism provides.

Furthermore, once the dualistic perspective is adopted, it appears to be self-validating. Lofland explains that the Moonies fed on the conventional mass media to confirm their world view. When national and international events reflected unrest, deterioration, and disorganization, the devotees were jubilant. Surely this was evidence to everyone that the end was near! Surely this victory by Satan would convince people to repent and join the Unification cause. If a month went by when no tragedies occurred, this was because God was restraining Satan for some special reason:

> April had no new major crises because it was the month of Parent's Day, the [Moonie] equivalent of Christmas. God restrained both Satan and himself for the occasion, but they redoubled their efforts in May, and the stock market plummeted the week of May 21 (Lofland 1977: 200).

These interpretations were not limited to major world crises. Such news items as the collision of two ships or the suicide of a lonely forty-year-old secretary were confirmations of their world view. Not only does dualism offer a nice neat explanation of the meaning of events, but the world view can be constantly confirmed by viewing news events in its own light.

---

[8]For a fascinating study of a doomsday group that dissolved after its prediction failed, see Leon Festinger, Henry Riecken, and Stanley Schachter, *When Prophecy Fails* (1956).

Plausibility of Beliefs in the Greek Orthodox Church

In 1992, I traveled to Greece with a interdisciplinary team of scholars doing research on Greek culture. The focus of my work was plausibility of belief systems and legitimacy of the authority structure in the Greek Orthodox Church. The following observations are selections from my field notes—originally spoken into a small tape recorder.

The architecture of Orthodox churches contributes to plausibility by creating a sense of awe and mystery. Some of the churches in Greece are spectacular in their spaciousness; others, though less grand, display extensive art work, involve beautiful architectural design, and are imbued with the soft and eerie tones created by having light emitted almost exclusively from candles.

In Orthodox churches, the altar and chancel area are barred from vision by the laity. Only the clergy enter beyond the iconostasis, a panel separating the chancel from the rest of the sanctuary and covered with paintings (or icons). Only during worship are the central doors of the Iconostasis opened, thereby creating a sense of mystery about what happens and even what the altar region looks like. Much of the service, therefore, is shrouded in mystique. The very element of secrecy creates an aura of unquestionable authoritativeness.

Many more of the senses are used in Greek Orthodox worship than in most American Protestant services. Visual imagery is rich everywhere you look: there are icons, candles, and other kinds of symbols everywhere you look.

The auditory sense is stimulated by the rich baritone voices, which chant throughout the two-and-a-half-hour service. The only spoken word is the sermon, which lasts about five minutes. While there is little physical contact between the people, tactile sensory stimulation occurs in the kissing of various icons and relics. People light a candle for a deceased relative when they enter, then kiss one or more of the icons, paintings, or silver reliefs of Jesus or of a favorite local saint. The olfactory sense is activated by the incense blessing from the priest and by a pervasive smell of candle smoke (each candle is extinguished by an elder after it has burned for ten minutes or so, creating a constant smokiness). One begins to associate that smell with worship. The service concludes with communion—the taste of bread becoming a part of the overall sacred experience.

Following the service bread is available in the back of the church, and people stand around casually popping bits of bread in their mouths, like eating popcorn. Following some services, people also stand around with spoons eating a dry-grain mix from small paper bags. This occurs when a deceased person is honored at the service, the mix symbolizing everlasting life. So there is a definite element of taste stimulation involved in Greek Orthodox worship. One becomes very much aware of how exclusively auditory much Protestant worship is as one experiences the many dimensions of a Greek Orthodox service. Because many senses which are intimately related to memory and emotions are stimulated in worship, early socialization of religious ritual would be deeply embedded in the individual and definitions of what is normal and sacred would have strong affective roots.

Many Greeks cross themselves three times whenever they pass a church. It does not matter whether they are walking, driving a moped, or riding in a city bus; they symbolically acknowledge each church they pass. In some cases, particularly among the older people, there is a differential bowing of the head as well. This certainly appears to be a element of a plausibility structure in that there is a constant symbolic reminder of the sacredness of the church; it is so holy and revered that it deserves special recognition each time one passes. This appears to translate into an unquestioned authority of the church hierarchy.

Today in Athens I visited a very old church, probably built in the eleventh century. It was in very poor repair, and yet I noticed when I walked in there was a feel about it that was quite similar to a number of the other churches. As I began to analyze what that feeling was, I realized that it had largely to do with the sense of ancientness, of long-standing continuity. In some old churches the icons are now peeling and severely faded and blackened by the general soot of centuries of candlelight. Some of the icons were so blackened in this church, I couldn't even tell what the painting depicted. But these now-dark icons obviously had been there for generations— perhaps for 800 or 900 years. Their very existence for that long a period of time adds to the sense of permanence and

eternal truth they represent. William D'Antonio has made the same point regarding the Roman Catholic Church by suggesting that the very fact of change itself—initiated by Vatican II—has undermined plausibility for some Catholics. In the Greek Church, since the origins of the symbolic representations were unknown, the symbols and beliefs are "objectified" by centuries of former worshipers. Even the order of worship, the Orthodox liturgy, has remained unchanged for more than a thousand years. Who has the right to change it now? For many Americans, lack of change and adaptation suggests stagnation. Not so for the Greek Church.

On the other hand, Greek Orthodoxy nowhere displays the fervor—the intensity of commitment—that characterizes evangelical churches in America. Lack of options may create a monopoly, but competition for membership seems to contribute to vitality. The need to clarify one's own position vis-à-vis some other group can cause the group to articulate its position forcefully and with conviction—to make its belief system more believable to self and others. The strength of the Greek Orthodox Church in terms of plausibility may be the fact that its Truths are taken for granted; its message appears beyond need of justification. The weakness of the Greek Church may be precisely the same: its truths are taken for granted.

One element of the Greek Orthodox Church that creates a somewhat ambiguous effect on plausibility is the role of the clergy. On the one hand is

Continued

▶ **BOX 8.3**—*Continued*

their distinctive dress; they are draped in black from head to foot with a black head piece that apparently is the forerunner of the French chef's hat. The distinctive black attire, along with extremely bushy beards and rather long hair pulled up in an elongated bun at the back of the head, makes the priest look very different from anyone else. One senses a kind of deference to the authority and status of the priest. On the other hand, priests are a little bit suspect among Greeks (McNall 1974). They are, after all, paid in part by monies from the state because it is a state church. In the United States that is not true, but in Greece most of the funding comes from the government. Also, priests are not usually located in the local churches in which they grew up; they usually go to new regions. This means that the priest is neither one of the local folks nor one of the boys come back home, but is a kind of stranger in a kin-based peasant society. This social distance from priests is especially true out in the rural areas, where most folks have little education. (Nearly half of Greek villages are accessible only by donkey or by foot.) Because they are "strangers" and because they are on the public dole, so to speak, they are somewhat resented by the people. So we have interesting interplay when it comes to authority and sacred status of the priest; on the one hand the clothing adds an aura of au-

thority and specialness, but on the other hand there are other things that play against the unquestioned authority of this special role of priest. On balance, the social distance probably adds to the plausibility of the belief system; if these well-educated people say it is true, what lowly peasant would challenge the belief system? In highly educated America, it is a different story!

Religiously, Greek Orthodoxy totally dominates Greece. There simply is not much in the way of competition. The Greek Orthodox Church is not only the church of the state, but in terms of individual identity, being Orthodox is virtually synonymous with being Greek. While I did visit one Anglican church in Athens, those in attendance appeared to be entirely English-speaking foreigners. This means that plausibility structures are enhanced with a kind of "collective ignorance"; that is, the people simply don't seem to be aware that there are options—that there are religious alternatives. There is not the open market of supply and demand, of aggressive advertising, of consumer selection in the religious marketplace that exists in the United States. When only one path is offered, and that path is shrouded in mystery and made sacred in a variety of ways, plausibility of belief is not a serious issue.

Moonies often attend religious rallies of other groups in hope of finding seekers whom they might recruit. Being constantly exposed to other preaching would seem to be a poten-

tial threat to the plausibility structures of the Unification movement. However, Lofland reports that the opposite was the case. "If a church was ill-attended, people were falling away from the churches in these last days; if well attended, people were seeking for truth, but not finding it there. If it was housed in a new building, the church was resorting to external appearance to compensate for its inner death; if in an old building, people were falling away" (1977: 203). Furthermore, if a minister preached a message that in any way resembled a dualistic world view, that minister was viewed as a covert ally and was thought to be a convert secretly teaching the "Divine Principles" to Christians.

Of course, many other religious groups are also dualistic. The Jesus People, many Pentecostal and most fundamentalistic groups, and the Appalachian snake-handling cult (a folk version of Christianity) are a few examples of dualistic religious groups. In each of these cases, dualism provides for a simple plausibility process (Ammerman 1987). On the other hand, the expectation of a catastrophic end to the world in the near future has caused some doomsday prophets to set a specific date on which the Final Judgment will commence. A California-based group awaited The End in August of 1981. Followers of the fundamentalist preacher quit their jobs and sold all of their property as a sign to God of their faith. In the late 1970s, a number of preachers and laypeople, influenced by the writings of Hal Lindsey, expected the end of the world in the late 1980s. What happens to such groups when the predicted date passes?

In many cases, passage of the doomsday date results in the movement's collapse. However, the Unification Church has passed several critical dates established by the Reverend Moon. In these cases, the ideology was modified by simply proclaiming that the end of the world will come in several phases. The cataclysm that was expected was simply declared to have occurred—but in the unseen spiritual realm. Some Christian groups that predicted the end of the world have similarly modified their stance. In some cases, they simply set a

new date. However, only so many dates can come and go without group morale waning and religious plausibility declining. A more effective strategy is to proclaim that the new era is now in progress but that only the "saved" or the "elect" are able to see or experience the transformation. This has been the strategy of the Jehovah's Witnesses for whom the millennium began in 1914. In any case, basic dualism can continue to provide a simplistic and self-validating system of meaning.

Other plausibility mechanisms can also be used effectively to create apparently self-validating belief systems: When a body of scripture—whether it's the Koran, the Bible, or the Book of Mormon—is believed to be literally and absolutely true, passages testifying to the veracity of the contents may serve to reinforce the believer's conviction. All other forms of evidence (scientific or otherwise) can be readily dismissed if they contradict those scriptures. The sacred scrolls become the final authority on all things, and the sense of sacredness that surrounds that scripture makes anything in it seem plausible. In this case, the utter respect for the scripture serves as a self-validating plausibility structure.

Finally, Max Assimeng suggests that evangelism (efforts to convert others to the faith) may serve as a plausibility structure. Research on commitment mechanisms (chapter 5) suggests that investment of time and energy on behalf of any movement or organization will strengthen commitment. The very acts of trying to convert others to one's faith and to argue in favor of that faith serve to intensify loyalty. Assimeng adds to this the insight that groups that anticipate the end of the world sometimes become preoccupied with getting as many people as possible to join the movement (1986). This preoccupation tends to draw one's attention to the mundane requirements of recruiting members and away from careful analysis of the belief itself. Spreading the faith consumes one's energies, and increases in membership become

Some of the world's great cathedrals elicit a sense of awe and humility in the individual just through the effective use of space and the breathtaking beauty of the chancel area. Anyone entering the Salisbury Cathedral in Wiltshire, England, is likely to feel such awe. The architecture, by creating a mood, enhances the plausibility of belief in the transcendent power of God. (Georg Gerster/Comstock.)

both the central goal and the primary measure of validity of the faith. Each new recruit reinforces the commitment of the proselytizer. Hence, a requirement of evangelism for members of a group may enhance the plausibility of the world view for those members.

Close-knit reference groups and awe-inspiring rituals and symbols serve as important plausibility structures. But, the content of the belief system is also important. For those groups that reject the outlook of the dominant culture, dualism provides a world view that not only offers to explain the meaning of events but also provides a neat tautology (circular reasoning) that allows for self-validation of the world view. It is not surprising then that many of the new religious movements, especially the world-transforming ones that have managed to survive, are dualistic.

An Exercise in Application: The Development of the Shakers

The processes described in this and the previous chapter may become more meaningful to readers if applied to a single group. There are many studies of specific religious groups that students could use to exercise their skills in applying (and critiquing) these theories and concepts. In the following pages, I briefly outline the development of one religious group in North America so that readers can begin to identify these processes in a group.[9]

---

[9]The most widely cited scholar on Shaker life is Edward Deming Andrews. Although his publications on the group are numerous, students interested in reading more about the United Society will want to start with Andrews's book, *The People Called Shakers* (1963). For somewhat briefer accounts, see Mark Holloway (1966); William Kephart and William Zellner (l991); Charles Nordhoff (l966); or John Noyes (1966).

The United Society of Believers in Christ's Second Appearing—commonly known as the Shakers—was founded in England by Ann Lee. "Mother Ann," the illiterate daughter of a blacksmith, was born in 1736. When she was twenty-three years old, she—along with her family—joined an enthusiastic religious group derogatorily known in the community as the "Shaking Quakers." William Pitt was assuming political power at the time, and England was entering an era characterized by change and popular unrest. As so often happens, social change and upheaval spawned a number of religious movements (e.g., George Whitefield and the Wesleys were simultaneously producing a revival that resulted in Methodism).

The Shaking Quakers acquired their name because during worship services the members would fall into trances in which they would quiver and shake or manifest other frenzied behavior. Most people believed them to be "demented hooligans." They were sometimes attacked by mobs—which only solidified their commitment to each other and strengthened boundaries against outsiders. On a number of occasions, they were imprisoned for Sabbath breaking; their style of worship was considered indecent and even blasphemous.

While incarcerated in a Manchester jail in 1770 for just such an "offense," Ann Lee experienced a vision in which she witnessed "the original sin." She believed that the sexual act was the cause of all evil and suffering in the world. (She had always felt guilty about engaging in sex with her husband, and when her four children each died in childbirth, she was convinced that their deaths were divine judgments on her for her concupiscence.) She emerged from the jail with such conviction and sense of mission that she quickly emerged as the central leader of the Shaking Quakers. In fact, she was referred to as Mother Ann, and the woman who had previously led the group became known as "the female equivalent of John the Baptist." Mother Ann was believed to be Christ incarnate. Because God had come the first time in male form, it seemed only reasonable to the group that in the Second Coming Christ would be female.

Mother Ann was prone to visions. One such revelation compelled her to believe that the group was being called to America, and she and the Shakers emigrated in 1774. However, this strange group—which refused to bear arms and which had a British leader—was suspected of being a band of spies when the Revolutionary War broke out the following year. Furthermore, the insistence on celibacy among members was highly reminiscent of the requirements of the Catholic clergy. Many of the New England colonists therefore accused the Shakers of papalism—an especially derogatory label among bigoted Protestants. The Shakers were run out of many New England towns. In some cases, they were dragged to the edge of town by their hair. At one point, ten Shakers were jailed for their teachings. Their doctrine that married life was immoral clearly and directly challenged conventional society. Married persons who joined the group were required to separate. Such a policy earned the Shakers a label as "family breakers."

The Shakers again responded to the hostility by drawing more closely together, by developing a particularistic outlook (with high boundaries between "we" and "they"), and eventually by establishing communal societies so they could withdraw from contact with the larger society. Their imprisonment for their teachings also served another function: an otherwise little-known movement gained tremendous notoriety.

Shaker theology stressed a negative attitude toward humanity. People were viewed as inherently depraved, but salvation was possible if people would only confess their sins and reform their lives. The outlook—especially in the early years—was also highly dualistic, and

anything that opposed the group or its beliefs was identified as satanic. Perhaps the most novel aspect of Shaker theology was the insistence on God's bisexuality. God was believed to be both male and female, and was manifest in the bisexuality of all creation. (Hence, the explanation that, in the Second Coming, Christ would be in female form.) The Shakers rejected both the Christian doctrine of the Trinity and the belief in physical resurrection. The resurrection is not a future event, Lee insisted, but occurs to each individual at the time of confession and personal acceptance of "the new life." Salvation and resurrection were *individual* experiences.

Lee also stressed a return to primitive or Pentecostal Christianity with its five central principles: common property, celibacy, pacifism, separation of church from government, and belief in the power of spirit over physical disease. The last principle was the only one they felt they had not completely mastered. The insistence that the sexual act was the source of all evil and depravity in the world was a central Shaker doctrine, but it was not an uncommon sentiment in the eighteenth century. The fact that others in the culture shared this view allowed for group expansion. When social attitudes toward sexuality changed, the Shakers found recruitment of new members extremely difficult.

Upon entering the United Society of Believers, a person was required to make a total confession of his or her previous life. It was recognized that sometimes these confessions take several years to complete because a person may come only gradually to realize the full depravity of his or her former existence. When persons became a part of the group, they were also expected to engage in testimony and in seeking new converts.

Ann Lee died in 1784 after an intense two-year missionary tour of the eastern states. The Shakers had faced bitter opposition and many attempts to discredit them during this tour, but they had also gained many converts. The group was not yet living a communal life, but Ann Lee had predicted its necessity. Indeed, she had justified this requirement because of the precedent of the early church. If the group had not become communal, it may well have dissolved. The persecuted members needed a haven; they needed the emotional and financial support that a communal society could offer; and they needed the plausibility structure that intense social interaction would provide. Furthermore, given the resistance the group experienced, its members needed to mobilize personal resources. When the group did finally become communal, all possessions were given to the group or were sold and the money from the sale donated to the Shaker society. All members worked together, giving their skills, time, and energy in the service of the United Society of Believers.

But Ann Lee died before this communal society became a reality. Many converts fell away when the charismatic leader died, and even the faithful were nearly overcome with doubts and fears. But Ann had established James Whittaker (Father James) as her successor, and the passing of leadership occurred without major internal conflict. Whittaker had come from England with Ann Lee; his knowledge of her teachings and his outstanding ability as a speaker made him the generally acknowledged leader. But his own death came less than three years after Mother Ann's. He had dedicated the group's first meetinghouse in New Lebanon, New York, but the communal society was not yet in operation—nor had a procedure been established for choosing the next successor.

When the devotees gathered in the first assembly after Father James's death, the choice of leader loomed large. They waited prayerfully for divine inspiration, and eventually several members arose, each declaring that

the spirit of God had spoken: Joseph Meecham would be the new "chosen one." And it was Meecham who became the organizational genius in the United Society. He galvanized the followers into a unified band, established norms of behavior, and set up a central committee to make administrative decisions. Without the influence of Meecham, the Society would almost surely have collapsed (Andrews 1963).

One particular challenge that Meecham had to address was providing a stable economic base. However, once the communal society was established, it soon became highly productive. The Shakers were an extraordinarily resourceful people, having made, by some accounts, upward of 3,000 inventions during the course of their existence. Among their most notable were the flathead broom (such as you might use to sweep your porch), the common clothespin, a threshing machine, a turbine water wheel, the circular saw, the vacuum pan for evaporating liquids (eventually leading to evaporated milk), the first metal writing pens, and the first one-horse wagon used in this country (Andrews 1963). The Shakers refused to take out patents, and their ideas were often stolen and patented by others. But the group was able to support itself adequately because the inventions allowed for a high degree of efficiency in work.

Shaker worship services were emotional and spontaneous. They included speaking in tongues, singing, dancing, and frenzied seizures. In the early years, the services seemed chaotic to outsiders with each individual expressing religiosity in his or her own way (see Box 8.4). Later, the services became ritualized; complex group dances evolved which had a systematic pattern that many of today's marching bands might envy. Men marched or danced as one unit; women performed in an opposite unit. Positions of hands and feet were highly symbolic in those early days. Hands with palms up represented openness to the spirit of

► **BOX 8.4**

Observers' Descriptions of Shaker Worship

In the best part of their worship every one acts for himself, and almost every one different from the other: one will stand with his arms extended, acting over odd postures, which they call signs; another will be dancing, and some times hopping on one leg about the floor; another will fall to turning round, so swift, that if it be a woman, her clothes will be so filled with the wind, as though they were kept out by a hoop; another will be prostrate on the floor; another will be talking with somebody; and some sitting by, smoking their pipes; some groaning most dismally; some trembling extremely; others acting as though all their nerves were convulsed; others swinging their arms, with all vigor, as though they were turning a wheel, etc. Then all break off, and have a spell of smoking, and some times great fits of laughter.... They have several such exercises in a day, especially on the Sabbath....

When they meet together for their worship, they fall a groaning and trembling, and every one acts alone for himself: one will fall prostrate on the floor, another on his knees and his head in his hands; another will be muttering over articulate sounds, which neither they or any body else understand. Some will be singing, each one his own tune; some without words, in an Indian tune, some sing jig tunes, some tunes of their own making, in an unknown mutter, which they call new tongues; some will be dancing, and others stand laughing, heartily and loudly; others will be druming on the floor with their feet, as though a pair of drumsticks were beating a ruff on a drumhead; others will be agonizing, as though they were in great pain; others jumping up and down; others fluttering over somebody, and talking to them; others will be shooing and hissing evil spirits out of the house, till the different tunes, groaning, jumping, dancing, druming, laughing, talking and fluttering, shooing and hissing, makes a perfect bedlam; this they call the worship of God.

The Reverend Valentine Rathbun Sr.

About thirty of them assembled in a large room in a private house,—the women in one end and the men in the other,—for dancing. Some were past sixty years old. Some had their eyes steadily fixed upward, continually reaching out and drawing in their arms and lifting up first one foot, then the other, about four inches from the floor. Near the centre of the room stood two young women, one of them very handsome, who whirled round and round for the space of fifteen minutes, nearly as fast as the rim of a spinning-wheel in quick motion.... As soon as she left whirling she entered the dance, and danced gracefully. Sometimes one would pronounce with a loud voice, "Ho, ho" or "Love, love,"—and then the whole assembly vehemently clapped hands for a minute or two. At other times some were shaking and trembling, others singing words out of the Psalms in whining, canting tones (but not in rhyme), while others were speaking in what they called "the unknown tongue,"—to me an unintelligible jargon, mere gibberish and perfect nonsense. At other times the whole assembly would shout as with one voice, with one accord. This exercise continued about an hour....

This done, several of the young people, both men and women, began to shake and tremble in a most terrible manner. The first I perceived was their heads moving slowly from one shoulder to the other,—the longer they moved the quicker and more violently they shook. The motion proceeded from the head to the hands, and the whole body, with such power as if limb would rend from limb. The house trembled as if there were an earthquake. After this several young women embraced and saluted each other; two men embraced and saluted each other; a third clasped his arms around both, a fourth around them, and so on, until a dozen men were in that position, embracing and saluting. I did not observe any man salute or embrace a woman, or any woman a man....

Senator William Plumer

Source: Quoted in Edward Deming Andrews, *The People Called Shakers.* New York: Dover, 1963: 28–30. Used by permission.

God, and children[10] were trained to sit or dance during worship with palms heavenward. Eventually, the Shakers became rather rigid about their insistence on adherence to certain behavior patterns, many of which had originally been moral precepts or had served as symbolic gestures (see Box 8.5). However, the singing, dancing, and other emotional outlets during their ritual produced a tremendous feeling of group solidarity. The idea of continuing revelation seemed a real possibility to members when they saw it occur at their frequent worship gatherings. The highly emotional services and the intense group interaction created an extraordinarily strong plausibility structure.

However, the belief in continuing and spontaneous revelation eventually became a problem. Because anyone could have a revelation, the leaders had little control over the development of doctrine. The emphasis on spontaneity left the group open to all sorts of non-Shaker

---

[10]Some members had been married and had children prior to joining the group. This was one source of the children. In later years, the Shakers were also known for raising orphans (at a time before most communities had county homes for orphaned children).

proclamations. Eventually, each person who had a revelation was required to report it first to the executive committee of the Society, which would rule on whether the vision or insight was true or not. Only then would the whole society hear the message. This was certainly a cumbersome procedure, but it illustrates well the transformation that occurs after the charismatic leader has died and charisma is routinized. While Ann Lee lived, she had the authority to interpret other people's dreams or inspirations. The means of sustaining conformity and control is more complicated when such a leader passes from the scene.

At their peak in the 1830s, the Shakers had 6,000 members living in eighteen communities in the United States. Most of the settlements were in New England or in upstate New York, although there were also several Shaker villages in Ohio and Kentucky. As social attitudes toward sexuality changed in America, the Shakers did not compromise their stance that sexual expression is the root of all evil. It became increasingly difficult to recruit members to this celibate society, for this central belief no longer seemed plausible to many Americans. Furthermore, the fiery passion for evangelism had faded over the generations. The group was no longer able to

---

▶ **BOX 8.5**

Excerpts from Shaker "Orders and Gifts" (Posted in the Sisters' Retiring Room)

Every person must rise from their beds at the sound of the "first trumpet," kneel in silence on the place where you first placed your foot when getting out of bed. No speaking in the room unless you wish to ask a question of the sister having the care of the room, in that case whisper. Dress your right arm first. Step your right foot first. At the sound of the "second trumpet," march in order, giving your right side to your superior. Walk on your toes. Fold your left hand across your stomach. Let your right hand fall at your side. March to your workshop in order. No asking unnecessary questions.

Source: Quoted in Mark Holloway, *Heavens on Earth,* 2nd ed. New York: Dover, 1966: 73.

mobilize the energy and resources of a substantial number of people. The motivations for membership had gradually been transformed. Most of the new members by the turn of the century were orphans who had been raised within the Shaker society. They had been socialized as Shakers rather than joining as committed converts. Today only a few Shakers live in Shaker Village at Sabboth Day Lake, Maine.[11] In the early 1990s,

[11]There are several historic Shaker villages that have been kept up by historical societies, but only Sabboth Day Lake is still occupied by Shakers.

the four surviving elderly women were joined by four younger people who adopted the Shaker way of life.

Summary

Routinization of charisma is important, but it is not the only contributing factor in the continued existence of a group. To survive, the group must also gain access to basic resources and gain members' commitments of time, energy, and finances. In short, it must acquire a niche in the society. Because its claim on resources

THE SHAKERS IN NISKAYUNA.— RELIGIOUS EXERCISES.

Shaker Ring Dance. Shaker worship was originally emotional and spontaneous. Eventually, highly ritualized dances in group formations evolved as part of the liturgy—with the men as one unit and women as another. The two groups engaged in highly choreographed dance steps; in the "ring dance" the men and women merged into a series of concentric circles. In most of these dances, even the position of hands was viewed as symbolic of an inward spiritual attitude. There was little room for spontaneous emotional expression; the entire religion had become routinized. (Photo from Shaker Museum and Library, Old Chatham, N.Y. Used by permission.)

may conflict with those of other groups and institutions, the group must keep from being crushed or crowded out by other groups. If the religious ideology calls for a radical political transformation, it may be defined as subversive and may be opposed through political and legal channels. Understanding of the continued existence or the collapse of the group may call for a force-field analysis. In other words, one must understand the social forces that oppose the group and the forces mobilized by the group to protect its interests. The viability of the group may depend on its ability to mobilize resources on its behalf.

Finally, continued existence of the group depends on its ability to make its world view seem plausible. Clifford Geertz's definition of religion, discussed in detail in chapter 1, stresses the importance of plausibility structures even in the definition:

> A religion is a system of symbols which acts to establish powerful, pervasive, and long-lasting moods and motivations in [people] by . . . formulating conceptions of a general order of existence and . . . *clothing these conceptions in such an aura of factuality that . . . the moods and motivations seem uniquely realistic* (Geertz 1966:4, my emphasis).

Symbol systems, rituals, close-knit reference groups, and other mechanisms, which make the belief system seem "uniquely realistic," are called "plausibility structures." Besides the development of plausibility structures, some groups develop a world view that seems to be self-validating. Dualism (the belief in a good spiritual force that opposes an evil force) is such a belief system. Everyday experiences, when interpreted through dualistic assumptions, can appear to validate those very assumptions. Although circular reasoning is used, many people view their system as "proven" by everyday events. Other methods may be used to maintain plausibility, but if the religion is to survive, the world view it sets forth must seem uniquely believable and even compelling.

Survival of a religious group, then, depends on a basic level of routinization, an ability to mobilize resources in its behalf and defuse forces that oppose it, and an ability to maintain the plausibility of the world view. Groups cope with each of these issues in a variety of ways; hence, there are many types of religious organizations. In the next chapter, we explore types of religious groups and what sociologists look for in trying to understand any particular religious movement.

CHAPTER NINE

Analysis of Religious Groups and the Evolution of Religious Organizations

We have already seen in this book that religious groups vary a great deal and undergo significant changes in the process of development. To conduct research on religion and make generalizations about religious behavior, social scientists have categorized groups with significant similarities into types, comparing and contrasting characteristics of churches, sects, denominations, and cults. Max Weber called such groupings **ideal types.** By this he did not mean that they were "the best" or somehow preferable, but only that these classifications exist entirely in the world of ideas. If there are seven typical characteristics of a dysfunctional family, the ideal type would list all seven of these. However, most troubled families may have some combination of five or six of the features. As Milton Yinger points out, this procedure of referring to ideal types has shortcomings. "Classifications are in one sense arbitrary. They oversimplify the data by disregarding what are held to be minor differences in order to emphasize what are thought to be major similarities. They are constructs of

the mind, not descriptions of reality" (Yinger 1970: 251).

Generalizations about any social behavior can be made only by comparing and contrasting phenomena that are in some respects similar. However, it is essential that the conception of various types be as clear, precise, and accurate as possible. Otherwise, the concepts themselves may cause confusion, misunderstanding, and faulty generalizations. Some sociologists think that the concepts of church, sect, and denomination have produced just such confusion; they have been used in a variety of ways by various researchers, and there is no consensus about the meaning of the terms. Nonetheless, many scholars continue to try to clarify these terms because they feel that they continue to be valuable as analytical tools. As we explore the way in which terms such as *church, sect, denomination,* and *cult* have been used, it is important to keep in mind that they provide only one of many possible ways to organize the data and to think about religious groups. But they also represent the predominant mode of comparing religious groups in recent decades.

The goal of this chapter is to help students know what to look for when analyzing any specific religious group. What is it that the sociologist finds significant in analyzing religious groups? The concepts explored in the following pages may be useful in making generalizations about various types of religious groups (nomothetic approach), or they may be helpful in trying to describe the unique dynamics of any particular group (ideographic approach).

The Church-Sect Typology

Early Formulations

Most discussions of the church-sect typology begin with the work of Ernst Troeltsch and his teacher, Max Weber.[1] Weber emphasized that the **sect** is an exclusive group. To be a member, one must meet certain conditions such as adherence to a particular doctrine or conformity to particular practices (like adult baptism or abstinence from alcohol). Membership in the sect is voluntary, limited to adults, and involves a commitment by the members. The **church,** on the other hand, is viewed as an inclusive group that encourages all members of the society to join and that requires less specific commitment and conformity (Weber 1963). Members are frequently born into the group rather than choosing it. See Box 9.1 for a

discussion of how this distinction relates to open systems theory.

Troeltsch, who wrote much more extensively on this topic and who is widely cited, included Weber's defining criteria but expanded the concept to include many other factors. For Troeltsch, the central characteristic of the church is its acceptance of the secular order—including even reproduction of the secular stratification system within the church. In short, the church "compromises" Christian values and makes accommodations to the secular society. The sect, on the other hand, tends to reject the social order and to maintain a prophetic ministry. While this was his central emphasis, Troeltsch's model was a multidimensional one, with no fewer than nine distinguishing characteristics of church and of sect. (See Table 9.1 for the traits Troeltsch's associated with each.)

Troeltsch also described another type of religious group that has received less attention by scholars. He described **mystics** as that cadre of loosely associated individuals who emphasize nonrational personal experience as the cornerstone of religion. More recent scholars have called this mystic movement a "cult" (Becker 1932; Nottingham 1971; McGuire 1981). We will return to a discussion of the concept of cult later. At this point, it is interesting merely to note that Troeltsch was aware that some religious expressions did not seem to fit on his continuum from sect to church.

The generalizations drawn by Troeltsch in 1911 were significantly influenced by the particular location and era in which he studied. This is true, of course, of all sociological research, and it is important for the researcher to be aware of both cultural and historical bias. Troeltsch was well aware that his generalizations were limited to Christian European culture. He was interested in describing the correlation of factors that characterized religious groups there and at that time. He suggested

---

[1]It is unfortunate that sociologists have tended to use Troeltsch's definition of church and sect, for Weber's use of the terms actually seems to have greater utility for today. Weber's distinction is simpler and is based on sociological rather than theological criteria. Nonetheless, we discuss Troeltsch because his formulations have so profoundly influenced later developments in church-sect typology.

The Sect and the Church as Closed and Open Systems

Several times in this book we have discussed the idea of open and closed social systems. While most of the scholars discussed in this chapter do not use this particular language in explaining the difference between church and sect, the model can be useful. Most church-sect typologies essentially depict the church as an open system, with fairly free flow of influence *into* the larger society (outputs such as symbols, benevolent actions, definitions of morality, and so forth) and *from* the larger society (inputs such as new members, ideas from education, science, and business fields, predominant economic attitudes and assumptions, and even reproduction of the secular system of social stratification—with high-income professionals more respected as church members and more likely to be elected to church offices). The danger of openness for the church is that "the salt may lose its flavor"—the uniqueness of the religious perspective may be endangered as the church becomes just another social club. No religious group can allow this to happen, so all religious groups do *some* filtering of inputs. Nonetheless, the filter used by churches allows much to pass through it.

The sect chooses to protect its uniqueness at all costs, barricading itself against the secular culture and very carefully screening any in-puts. It is a much more closed system, though few systems can be totally closed and still survive. They need members and resources and even technology to enhance efficiency provided by the larger society. The sect allows inputs, but these inputs must pass through a very fine filter. The danger of this choice is that the group may risk becoming so isolated that its message may seem anachronistic and irrelevant to the larger society. The closed system also risks stagnation as little that is new or innovative can enter the system.

It is useful to think of open and closed systems not as categorically different types, but as opposite ends on a continuum. Any given religious group can be closer to one end than the other. As you read the section discussing various theorists' ideas of sects, denominations, and churches, it may be helpful to keep in mind the idea of more open and more closed social systems. Further, each group may make different choices as to what kinds of things are threatening: some will find certain economic ideas incompatible with their world view; others will reject modern technologies; still others may find definition of sexual morality or scientific theories especially threatening. Finally, keep in mind that open and closed systems each have their own advantages—and their own problems.

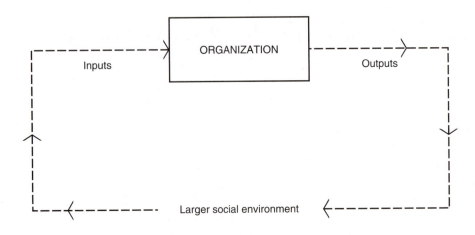

▶ **TABLE 9.1**

Characteristics of Sects and Churches as Delineated by Troeltsch and Niebuhr

The Sect	The Church
1. Volitional membership (emphasis on adult conversion and commitment).	1. Membership largely on the basis of birth (emphasis on religious education of children).
2. Exclusive membership policy—closely guarded.	2. Inclusive membership—may coincide with national citizenship or geographic boundaries.
3. Particularism—judgmental attitude toward those who do not accept the one true path; self-image that of the "faithful remnant" or the "elect."	3. Universalism—acceptance of diversity and emphasis on the brotherhood and sisterhood of all humanity.
4. Small faithful group.	4. Large, bureaucratic organization.
5. Salvation achieved through moral purity, including ethical austerity or asceticism.	5. Salvation granted by the grace of God—as administered by church sacrament and church hierarchy.
6. Priesthood of all believers; clergy de-emphasized or nonexistent; lay participation high.	6. Leadership and control by highly trained professional clergy.
7. Hostile or indifferent to secular society and to the state.	7. Tendency to adjust to, compromise with, and support existing social values and social structures.
8. Fundamentalistic theology—only the original revelation is an authentic expression of the faith.	8. Either orthodox or modernist theology—formulations and interpretation of the faith in later periods of history are legitimate in their own rights.
9. Predominently a group of lower-class persons or those otherwise socially disfranchised. (Worldly prestige is eschewed and spiritual or charismatic qualities become the basis for internal stratification.)	9. Membership composed of upper- and middle-class people, but with professional classes controlling most leadership positions. (Stratification of the society is reflected within the church.)
10. Informal, spontaneous worship.*	10. Formal, orderly worship.*
11. Radical social ethic—emphasizing the equality of all persons and the necessity of economic equality.*	11. Conservative social ethic—justifying the current socioeconomic relationships.

* Stressed by Niebuhr but not by Troeltsh.

that many of the correlations he was identifying might not apply to American Christianity.

One shortcoming of Troeltsch's study is that he does not give us many clues as to what social conditions are likely to generate which kinds of groups. A second problem, in terms of contemporary utility of the typology, is that he has suggested a correlation of many variables, some sociological, some theological. These particular constellations of factors may have been present in European Christian groups up until the beginning of the twentieth century, but we see many religious groups today that combine these factors in different ways (Knudsen et al. 1978).

Recent attempts to revise the typology have hinged largely on which one or two sociological factors should be the determining ones in the identification of a sect or a church. Theological differences, on the other hand, are sometimes used to distinguish different subtypes of sects or denominations (Wilson 1970). The lasting contribution of Troeltsch is his suggestion that a religious group may move from sect to church as the group assimilates to the surrounding culture. His scheme stimulated significant refinements by Niebuhr and others.

A Process Approach

The next major attempt to develop the church-sect typology was undertaken by H. Richard Niebuhr in his work *The Social Sources of Denominationalism* (1957). Niebuhr's work is important, for he elaborated Troeltsch's suggestion that the sect and the church are stages or points in the development of a religious group. He clearly placed these concepts in a framework of religious group evolution and added a new type, the denomination. He also moved beyond Troeltsch by identifying factors, including internal structural characteristics of a group, that cause it to move from one end of the continuum to the other.

Like Troeltsch, Niebuhr viewed the difference between sect and church as hinging on compromise and assimilation. At the outset of his book he wrote, "Denominationalism [involves] . . . a compromise . . . between Christianity and the world. . . . It represents the accommodation of Christianity to the caste-system of the world" (1957: 6). He believed the division of the Christian churches into different (and often exclusive) denominations was rooted in socioeconomic inequalities and ethnic prejudices and was therefore contrary to the core teachings of Christianity. As Niebuhr put it, "The inequality of privilege in the economic order appears to contain a fundamental denial of the Christian principle of brotherhood" (1957: 8–9). Hence, accommodation of religious ethics to accept secular prejudices and inequities is an implicit rejection of Christian values. For Niebuhr the emergence of the "church" is caused by a deterioration of Christian social ethics and adoption of secular definitions of human value. The reemergence of a sect is an attempt to recapture and reassert the Christian concern for social justice and equality.

Niebuhr stressed that the existence of different denominations is not due to mere ideological differences, as is often believed. He asserted that religious ideology is often used to justify economic self-interests and pointed out that groups from different social classes tend to develop different theological outlooks. The stratification of society invades both the social organization of Christianity and its theology.[2] The real source of the schism, however, is *social,* not theological.

Over a period of time, the tendency of Christian groups is to assimilate the values and perspectives of the secular world. This is a tendency toward the church type of religious

---

[2]We will take a closer look at the relationship between religion and social class and religion and racism in chapters 10 to 12.

group. On the other hand, the disfranchised often recognize the compromises of the faith and call the faithful back to radical commitment. This sectarian reaction is a means of renewal and revitalization of the faith. Niebuhr also pointed out that sectarian zeal seldom lasts more than a generation. The first generation of sect members stress adult conversion and commitment, but they also establish religious education programs for their children. Eventually, the children are accepted into full membership on the basis of their knowledge of the faith (memorized Bible passages and so on). Personal conversion and dramatic life changes are de-emphasized. Often the later generations also experience upward social mobility and are no longer disfranchised. The sect gradually institutionalizes at the same time it assimilates secular outlooks. In emphasizing the process of evolution, Niebuhr developed the sociological use of the term **denomination,** another type of religious group that represents a midpoint in the continuum between sect and church (Figure 9.1).

For Niebuhr, the key to understanding the movement from sect to denomination is the development of religious education programs. First, the focus on education reflected a departure from the emphasis on an abrupt change of life through conversion. Religion could be taught; it was not solely the result of a spontaneous and emotional conversion experience. Second, in most sectarian groups, the development of religious education programs represented the first stages of institutionalization. Impersonality and orderliness (lack of spontaneity) were marks of the trend to denominationalism, and both of these were normally results of institutionalization. This was even reflected in the tendency to a more sober, literate, intellectual, and orderly style of worship as opposed to the emotional expressiveness of sectarian worship. Hence, Niebuhr viewed the emergence of Sunday schools as an important benchmark in the movement toward becoming a denomination, but it was only one of several indicators of routinization.

Like Troeltsch, Niebuhr's formulation assumed a high level of correlation between many diverse factors. Although his description may have been accurate for many religious groups of his day, we can point to many that have some features of the sect and some of the denomination. For example, many of the more emotional, conversion-oriented Christian groups of today (born-again Christians) de-emphasize the importance of a trained professional clergy as necessary to transmit the grace of God; they downplay the necessity of orderliness and solemnity in worship; and they stress the centrality of a personal conversion experience. Yet, many of these same groups are not radicals who object to the stratification system and speak forcefully on behalf of the poor. Many of them support the current

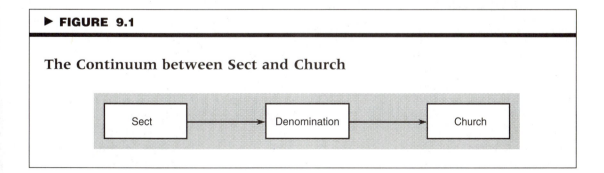

▶ **FIGURE 9.1**

The Continuum between Sect and Church

Sect → Denomination → Church

economic system (the status quo) and defend the national values of the United States; they are well acculturated.

Niebuhr would probably assert that they are not manifestations of early Christianity, but further forms of compromise: they fail to restore the original *social ethic* of Christianity. So the problem of Niebuhr's church-sect model is the problem of all ideal types: a significant number of groups do not seem to fit *all* the characteristics of any one type. Which characteristics are most important in classifying a group?

Moreover, some religious groups do not seem to fit Niebuhr's sequential model—with new groups returning to the purity of the original faith, and then gradually assimilating to the dominant culture. Several scholars (Cohen 1983; Steinberg 1965) have analyzed the emergence of Reform Judaism from Orthodox Judaism as a reform group resembling the church model. Reform Judaism did not represent a protest against the "perversion of true religion" and did not call for a return of the "old ways." Rather, it represented a fuller acculturation or modernization of the faith. This new group was rejecting what members considered an excessive tie to the past on the part of the parent body. The reforming body sought greater assimilation—in effect, more openness as a system. Likewise, Mauss and Barlow (1991) document the shift in Mormonism in recent years *away* from assimilationism and toward a deliberate religious traditionalism, an evolution opposite that predicted by Niebuhr. Therefore it is important to remember that Niebuhr describes the predominant trend, but the sequential evolution of sect-denomination-church and revolution back to sect is not universal.

Single-Variable Models

Various sociologists have continued to clarify the concepts of sect and church and to identify factors that contribute to the formation of one type of group as opposed to another. Some have suggested that a value conflict with the dominant society should be the central criterion that distinguishes the sect (Johnson 1963; Stark 1967; Stark and Bainbridge 1985). According to this view, all sects are countercultures (Stark 1967). The insistence on reducing the church-sect typology to one defining characteristic is an attempt to clarify the use of the term and to avoid a confusing typology that does not always correspond with social realities. There is a definite need for increased precision in the use of these terms. In short, there has been a recent movement toward simpler conceptualizations, as originally suggested by Weber.

Benton Johnson suggests: "A church is a religious group that accepts the social environment in which it exists. A sect is a religious group that rejects the social environment in which it exists" (1963: 542). Using this single criterion, the classification of a group will not depend on its intrinsic qualities (extent of institutionalization, emphasis on conversion and voluntary adult commitment, etc.). Rather, classification of a group would depend on the nature of its relationship to the larger culture in which it resides. Johnson points out that the use of this criterion involves a shift in the classification of some groups. For example, the Roman Catholic Church has always been considered the best example of a church. In the United States, the Catholic Church has represented a minority group that has sometimes been at odds with the predominant values and policies of the country. Johnson would suggest that, in the United States, Catholics are more toward the sectarian end of the continuum.

One problem with this criterion has to do with determining which value conflicts are so significant as to warrant classification as a sect. The "dominant value system of the United States" includes many different values, attitudes, and beliefs. These various values may themselves be found independent of one another. For example, no one who studies the Church of Jesus Christ of Latter-day Saints (Mormons) can fail to notice the emphasis on hard work, the importance of the family, individualism, and national loyalty. Yet, there are significant ways in which the Mormons have deviated from cultural values of this country. Although most of the above-mentioned values were part of the value orientation of this group in the nineteenth century, Mormons also endorsed the practice of polygyny (one man with two or more wives). Non-Mormon neighbors and the federal government were firmly opposed to this policy. The conflict between the Mormons and Gentiles at one point became violent. In 1857 President James Buchanan commissioned federal troops to move into Utah, and the resultant skirmishes are referred to as the Utah Mormon War (O'Dea 1957).

Is conflict over one value perspective (such as polygyny) enough to classify a group as sectarian, or must there be conflict in several major areas? Or, is it merely the *intensity* of the conflict that is the defining factor? Of course, intense conflicts may also rise over issues other than value orientations or religious beliefs. In fact, much of the prejudice against Mormons was due to conflict over scarce resources and valued lands. The problem was not strictly a conflict of value orientations, but one over who would possess what *both* groups valued. Johnson, and more recently Rodney Stark and William Bainbridge, would recognize a group as a sect if it is in *intense conflict* with its larger social environment. But students should recognize that conflict and harmony are not always mutually exclusive. A group may be in consensus with the dominant culture on some issues and in intense discord on others.

Perhaps the most significant difficulty with this value-conflict criterion is highlighted by Johnson himself. Many groups commonly recognized as sects actually socialize in dominant-

society values. Although they seem to be in conflict with the dominant society, many holiness sects are alternative modes of enculturating people in the values of the dominant society (Johnson 1961). Johnson writes, "It may well be that one of the most important functions of the conversionist bodies in the United States, both now and historically, has been to socialize potentially dissident elements—particularly the lower classes—in the dominant values which are our basic point of reference. The differences sociologists have seen between the Protestant 'churches' and the Protestant 'sects' may be matters of taste, rhetoric, and expressive symbolism . . . far more than they are matters of basic value orientation" (1963: 547). Yet, some sectarian groups, like the Old Order Amish, do provide an alternative value orientation that does not lead to eventual acculturation. The use of value conflicts with the dominant culture is one way to distinguish sects from churches, but this defining criterion is not without its shortcomings.

Several sociologists have emphasized that social conflict is a variable within sects rather than their defining characteristic. With sects enhancing either conflict or assimilation, conflict with the society hardly seems an appropriate defining characteristic of sects and churches. Andrew Greeley (1972) and Geoffrey Nelson (1968) both argue that the most salient and most measurable characteristic of sects is the complexity of organization—the degree of routinization. In any event, the trend is toward a simplified definition of church and sect (e.g., see Knudsen et al. 1978).

Yinger's Model

Like many contemporary scholars, Yinger holds that Troeltsch's concept of church and sect includes too many variables, many of which are not highly correlated in actual groups. Unlike Johnson, he prefers to use several factors in defining sects, denominations, and churches. Yinger suggests three social factors[3] that seem to him to be central, and he establishes a helpful model that lends insight into types of groups and their evolution. The three defining criteria suggested by Yinger are:

1. The degree to which the membership policy of the group is exclusive and selective or open and inclusive.
2. The extent to which the group accepts or rejects the secular values and structures of society.
3. The extent to which, as an organization, the group integrates a number of local units into one national structure, develops professional staffs, and creates a bureaucracy (1970: 257).

Yinger points out that in actual cases, the first two variables are very closely correlated. Those groups that reject secular values are likely to be exclusive and selective in their membership policies—indications of a closed social system; those groups that accept secular values are likely to be inclusive and open in their membership—indications of an open social system.

By using the first two factors as one component and the extent of institutionalization as the other, Yinger develops a model that suggests several different types of groups (Figure 9.2). This two-dimensional model is capable of showing a progression from sect to church, but it also demonstrates that increased institutionalization may occur somewhat independently from membership policy and from the acceptance of secular values. There are pressures (discussed in chapters 7 and 8) that cause groups to evolve generally from the types in the lower left side of the grid toward those in

the upper right side. Nonetheless, the rate, the direction, and the extent of this evolution is not inevitable. Whether a group stabilizes as an "established sect" or continues to acculturate to the stage of "institutional denomination" or "ecclesia" has to do with the group's belief system. A group that focuses on the sin and salvation of individuals will acculturate rather easily. Sects whose primary concern is social evils and injustices—reformative and transformative movements—are more likely to become established sects and may never become ecclesiastical or denominational bodies (Wilson 1970; Yinger 1970).

Two types of religious organizations do not fit this schema. The first is the shamanistic religion of many nonindustrialized societies. The religion is universally held by all members of that society. It does not pose values that are antithetical to the secular values, for it serves as a sort of glue that helps unify the culture. On the other hand, religion in such a culture is not highly institutionalized. Yinger calls such a religion a "Universal Diffused Church," for it is diffused through the culture rather than being specialized and maintaining its own autonomous organization. The second case that does not fit is the Universal Institutionalized Church, which most perfectly fits Troeltsch's description of the church. This is best exemplified by the highly institutionalized Roman Catholic Church of the Middle Ages. It was universal in that no other religion had a significant influence in Europe; national boundaries and religious loyalties were therefore coextensive, with Roman Catholic Christianity playing a major factor in the culture of medieval Europe.

These two exceptions highlight an important fact: The existence of sects and denominations is a phenomenon of pluralistic societies. In fact, scholars have maintained that the pure form of "Church" described by Troeltsch is impossible in a democratic and pluralistic society. Likewise, the Universal Diffused Church

---

[3]Yinger is explicit about using social factors—and not theological ones—so his model will have potential application for non-Christian groups.

► **FIGURE 9.2**

Yinger's Schema, Types of Religious Organizations (adapted)

Low   I. Inclusiveness of membership   High
             II. Extent of acceptance of societal values

High 4. Null	Rare (Seventh-Day Adventists)	Institutional denomination (The Church of God)	Institutional ecclesia (Episcopal Church)
3. Null	Established or institution-alized sect (Old Order Amish)	Diffused denomination (Beachy Amish Mennonite)	Diffused ecclesia (Christian Scientist)*
2. Sect movement (the Bruderhof)	Established lay sect (Amana Church Society)	Rare	Rare
1. Charismatic sect (The Way)	Null	Null	Null

III. Extent of organization, complexity, and distinctiveness of the religious structures

Low

Measurement of III. above.

	Are local religious units integrated into a national organization?	Are there religious professionals?	Is there a bureaucratic structure?
4. Most complex	yes	yes	yes
3.	yes	yes	no
2.	yes	no	no
1. Least complex	no	no	no

*The Church of Jesus Christ, Scientist, has a bureaucratic structure but no professional clergy. This church does not seem to fit the nomenclature of diffused ecclesia, but it does fit two of the three criteria of institutionalization.

Source: Adapted from J. Milton Yinger, *The Scientific Study of Religion*. New York: Macmillan, 1970: 261–62. Used by permission.

Sects Have Been Identified by a Variety of Defining Characteristics

	Max Weber	Ernst Troeltsch	H. R. Niebuhr	Benton Johnson	Geoffrey Nelson	Andrew Greeley	J. Milton Yinger	Rodney Stark and William Bainbridge
1. Volitional membership (emphasis on adult membership, personal conversion experience, high level of commitment)	X	X	X					
2. Exclusive membership policy (membership closely guarded and expulsion practiced for violation of norms)	X	X	X			X	X	
3. Particularism (belief that only members of the in-group are saved)		X	X					
4. Lack of complex organization (local group with no national organization or bureaucratic structure)	X	X	X		X	X	X	

No.	Characteristic					
5.	Belief that salvation is achieved through moral purity (including ethical austerity or asceticism)	X	X			
6.	Clergy role de-emphasized or nonexistent (lay participation high; priesthood of all believers stressed)	X	X		Sub-sumed under 4	
7.	Conflict with host society (rejection of secular values; hostile or indifferent to the state)	X	X	X	X	X
8.	Fundamentalistic theology (only the original revelation is the authentic expression of the faith)	X	X			
9.	Lower-class or disfranchised group (group membership composed primarily of socially disadvantaged persons)	X	X			
10.	Informal, spontaneous worship (expectation of spontaneous, emotional expression of faith in corporate worship)		X			
11.	Radical social ethic (emphasizing the equality of all persons and the necessity of economic equity)	X	X			

is a phenomenon of only very simple and homogeneous societies; it is not found in complex and heterogeneous ones.

I have found Yinger's conceptualization to be particularly helpful, for he reduces the number of variables to be considered while he shows how several different types of groups can emerge. The primary value of his schema is in identifying several possible patterns in the evolution of groups.

A Lack of Consensus

In short, some sociologists insist that the concepts of sect and church can be useful tools of analysis only if the criteria for defining them are greatly simplified. Others feel that church-sect theories have become such a hopeless hodgepodge of definitions and variables that the terms themselves have no real meaning or utility (Goode 1967; Murvar 1975; Greeley 1972). Still others persist in using multidimensional definitions of sects and churches but describe any particular group only with the adjectives "sectlike" or "churchlike." Using this procedure, a group may be called churchlike if it conforms to *most* of the specified characteristics of a sect (Demerath 1965; Winter 1977). Rather than describing pure types, these scholars simply attempt to describe groups as being closer to the sectarian or the ecclesiastical end of a continuum.

In chapter 10, I report some interesting findings using this multivariable approach to identifying sectlike groups, but the consensus seems to be emerging that sect and church concepts should be identified with no more than three factors and perhaps with no more than one. There is no consensus on which factor should be *the* determining factor for identifying sects and churches. In any case, *students of religion should be sure they understand how* sect *and* church *or* sectlike *and* churchlike *are defined and measured in any specific study they read.*

Social Conditions That Generate Each Type of Group

We might summarize this discussion of churches, denominations, institutionalized sects, and sects by reviewing the factors that seem to cause the emergence of new groups. Niebuhr pointed to four factors. First, when Christian denominations begin to ignore the original concern of the faith for poverty and inequality, sectarian groups are likely to arise. As members of those sects (who are disproportionately from the lower classes) begin to achieve some affluence, the sect begins to accommodate secular values and becomes comfortable with the status quo. The group begins to denominationalize. Those persons who are still economically disfranchised are likely to break again from the group and reject social inequality as contrary to the original ethic of the faith. Or, to put it in other terms, the poor may reject worldly affluence—defining it as depraved—and seek otherworldly compensation. By affirming asceticism and condemning the comforts of this world, the sect tends to alienate persons who are affluent (Stark and Bainbridge 1985). One cause of sectarianism, then, is the existence of social inequality.

Second, Niebuhr pointed out that some groups are expressions of ethnic values and national loyalties. In such cases, the belonging function operates to separate German Methodists from other Methodists and Italian Catholics from Irish Catholics. One recent analysis of sectarian movements concludes that approximately 21 percent of American sects were founded almost entirely on the basis of racial or ethnic identity (Stark and Bainbridge 1985: 132). On the other hand, the fact that ethnic and religious groups are mutually reinforcing in North America may explain why religious participation is so much higher and religious groups so much stronger than in Europe (Roof and McKinney 1987). The sense of ethnic belonging, then, has been a source of division within Christendom (Greeley 1972; Marty 1972; Nelsen and Nelsen 1975; Niebuhr 1957).

Third, Niebuhr pointed out that churches and denominations become bogged down in bureaucratic structures. Some sect movements are expressions of a desire for religious groups that are smaller, more informal, and less under the control of a professional clergy. Individuals may become alienated by the institutional constraints and formalized structures of large denominations. Sectarianism then is sometimes an expression of rebellion against complex organizational structure.

Fourth, he believed that sectarian movements are sometimes spawned by a desire for more spontaneity and more emotional expression in worship. Worship in the denominations tends to become formal, orderly, and highly intellectual. Niebuhr pointed to both internal and external factors in the emergence of new religious groups.

Of course, sectarian schisms can also occur over seemingly trivial issues. Max Assimeng (1986) points out that Seventh-Day Adventists split from other Adventists largely over the issue of whether the Sabbath should be on Saturday or Sunday.

Whether and how a sect develops into a denomination also depends largely on how the larger society responds to this new group. If the values of the dominant culture the sect challenges are central ones, if the host culture does not have a tradition of religious freedom and tolerance, and if the strategy of the sect is aggressive militance (rather than avoidance and withdrawal), the group will either be crushed or will reinforce its antiestablishment posture. If the group does survive, its acculturation is likely to be very slow. In fact, such a group may remain forever an established sect. On the other hand, if the dominant cultural values the sect rejects are tangential; if there is a tradition of religious tolerance in the host culture, and if the strategy by which the sect mobilizes its resources is inoffensive, the group may accommodate and become acculturated rather quickly. The movement from sect to denomination is determined in large degree by outsiders' response to the group (Redekop 1974).

In a comparison of Protestantism in the United States and Canada, Harold Fallding (1980) suggests that separation of church and state also contributes to the emergence of sects. Canada, with state-established religion, has generated far fewer religious sects than has the United States and has historically shown a greater trend toward denominational mergers. The struggle for religious liberty and disestablishment from government structures may unwittingly result in intensification of boundaries between groups and an environment conducive to religious innovation and independence.

As we discovered in the previous chapter, the internal belief system of the group is another factor important in the evolution of a group. If a sect's definition of evil and corruption is individualistic (matters of personal decision making and individual determination), then acculturation and accommodation is likely. If evil is considered to be social in nature, if the structures of the society are defined as incompatible with religious values, then the group is less likely to denominationalize. The Quakers (Society of Friends) have a very strong social ethic. Although they are not really persecuted in contemporary American society, Quakers remain an institutionalized sect. In this case, the resistance to denominationalizing is internal (based in their own social ethic) rather than external (Yinger 1970).

Brian Wilson (1959) has identified several different types of sects, depending on their theological orientation. Using his classifications, he points out that some types of sects are more likely to denominationalize than are others. He maintains that groups that have a theological orientation encouraging a simple ascetic lifestyle are more likely to generate an affluent membership. Affluence often leads to accommodation. Those sects that do not stress asceticism are slower to accommodate.

But an even more important point is made by Wilson when he demonstrates that the movement toward denominationalism is largely a function of an expanding economy. As members become more affluent, they tend to acculturate to the values of the dominant society and lose their fervor for revolution or reform. Because opportunities for upward mobility are most likely in a climate in which the economy is growing, the state of the economy may affect the likelihood of a group becoming a denomination or stabilizing as an institutionalized sect. Stagnant economics are more likely to generate rather permanent sects.

The formation and evolution of any group is the result of many interacting processes: the social standing of members, ethnic factors, survival forces that impel a group to institutionalize, responses of outsiders to the group and its message, the belief system of the group, and the state of the economy in the host society. Both internal and external forces determine its evolution.

Thus far, however, we have discussed only the development of sects, institutionalized sects, denominations, and churches. How does the term cult fit into all of this?

The Cult (or NRM)

The term *cult* is currently used by sociologists in two distinct ways and by the popular media in yet a third way. Sociologists feel that the popular usage has terribly misconstrued and distorted a useful sociological concept. The popular media and many anticult movements define a cult as a religious group that holds esoteric or occult ideas, is led by a charismatic leader, and uses intense and highly unethical conversion techniques. (See the discus-

sion in chapter 5 of the charges of mind control or brainwashing in new religious movements.) The group is almost always depicted as totalitarian, capable of bizarre actions, destructive of mental health of members, and a threat to conventional society. The tag "cult" is often used in this context as a stigmatizing label intended to discredit a group rather than as a nonjudgmental technical term that describes a social unit. This concept of cult is explicitly rejected by sociologists of religion, but such media use has managed to cause confusion about new religious movements and about the very concept of "cult."

One way sociologists currently use the term emphasizes the lack of internal discipline and the loose-knit structure in the cult. This is an attempt to elaborate Troeltsch's mysticism category and to rename it as a "cult." Following Howard Becker's formulation (1932), the cult is seen as an urban, nonexclusive, loosely associated group of people who hold some esoteric beliefs. They are kindred spirits who have some common views relative to one particular aspect of reality, but such persons may also belong to other, more conventional, church groups. The presence of a charismatic leader is common but certainly not necessary. The Spiritual Frontiers Fellowship provides an example. It is a group of people who believe firmly in life after death and in various forms of parapsychology. They emphasize spiritual healing, the power of mind over matter, and the possibility of communication with the dead. They hold occasional workshops and lecture/seminar programs to expand their understandings and to inspire one another to deeper belief in the power of the spirit. Much of the membership consists of professional people who are well educated, belong to mainline denominations, and do not think of themselves as esoteric "kooks." The group has no charismatic leader; in fact, authority is at a minimum.

Commitment to such groups is nondemanding, and membership is likely to be transient.

The chief defining characteristics of the cult are the loose structure and the lack of application of the world view to all aspects of life. A number of sociologists use this approach in defining cult (Becker 1932; Hargrove 1979; McGuire 1981; Nottingham 1971).

The second sociological approach is to define the cult as the beginning phase of an entirely new religion. The group may be loosely structured or it may demand tremendous commitment, but it must provide a radical break from existing religious traditions. This approach to identifying the cult is also used by a number of sociologists (Glock and Stark 1965; Stark and Bainbridge 1985; Yinger 1970; Nelson 1968; Johnstone 1975). Although both of these definitions have their advocates, the latter approach seems to be emerging as the more common one and seems to me to provide a more helpful analytical tool. Note, however that several sociologists now recommend that the meaning of the term has become so muddled and tainted by media misuse that it should be abandoned entirely. Because of the misunderstanding, many sociologists now use the phrase **new religious movements** (or **NRMs**) in place of "cult" (Richardson 1993). I have tended to use the phrase *new religious movement* through much of this book, but since the word *cult* is still frequently used, students should be aware of its proper sociological meanings.

Perhaps some new term is also needed to identify the quasi-religious movements that have little or no sense of group identification or cohesion—the groups Troeltsch called mystics. Stark and Bainbridge (1985) refer to these groups as either audience cults or client cults, depending on the type of appeal. **Audience cults** involve use of mass-media appeals—advertisements, direct mail, and other publicity to promote a lecture circuit, a series of workshops, or sale of books or tapes on esoteric or occult topics. Supporters of such movements are essentially consumers and not members.

Spiritual Frontier Fellowship, astrology magazines, *Fate* magazine, and *Science of Mind* are examples of audience cults and their media. **Client cults** tend to involve relationships based more on a patient-therapist model. Adherents to client cults seek help in specific areas: psychological adjustment, contact with the dead, forecasts of the future, medical miracles, and so forth. Scientology, est, transcendental meditation (TM), Silva Mind Control, and palm readers are examples of client cults.

Both audience and client cults involve very loose bonds between members and little sense of group identity. Stark and Bainbridge point out that these groups are really forms of magic rather than nascent religious groups. They are concerned primarily with manipulating nonempirical forces in the service of specific this-worldly needs. Genuine cult movements, on the other hand, are religious movements in that they address issues of ultimate meaning and purpose in life. Occasionally, audience or client cults may evolve into cult movements (TM and Scientology appear to have been undergoing such a transition), but our treatment of cults in this chapter focuses on religious cults that spawn new religious movements. Client and audience cults are, at best, only quasi-religious phenomena.

In an effort to distinguish cults from sects, Stark and Bainbridge write:

> Because sects are schismatic groups, they present themselves to the world as something old. They left the parent body not to form a new faith, but to reestablish the old one, from which the parent body had "drifted." Sects claim to be the authentic, purged, refurbished version of the faith. . . . Whether domestic or imported, the cult is something new vis-à-vis the other religious bodies of the society in question. If domestic—regardless of how much of the common religious culture it retains—the cult adds to that culture a new revelation or insight justifying the claim that it is different, new, "more advanced."

Imported cults often have little common culture with existing faiths; they may be old in some other society, but they are new and different in the importing society (1985: 25–26).

This emphasis distinguishes a cult from a sect in that the latter attempts to renew or purify the prevailing religion of the society, whereas the cult introduces a new and different religion. Sometimes it is difficult to determine whether a religious movement is attempting to renew or replace the traditional religion, for a new religion often tries to gain legitimacy and acceptability by exaggerating its continuity with existing faiths. Nonetheless, the issue of whether a group is trying to purify or to replace the traditional religion of a society is central to this concept of cult. Yinger, after his careful development of the sect-denomination-ecclesia grid, turned to a discussion of the cult:

> [Some religious groups] do not appeal to the classical, the primitive, the true interpretation of the dominant religion, as the sect does, but claim to build *de novo*. The term *cult* is often used to refer to such new and syncretist movements in their early stages. It often carries the connotations of small size, search for a mystical experience, lack of structure, and presence of a charismatic leader. They are similar to sects, but represent a sharper break, in religious terms, from the prevailing tradition of a society (1970: 279).

New religious movements often place researchers in awkward situations as the latter seek access to the group and the group struggles for legitimation in the society. This is discussed in Box 9.2. The Unification Church provides an interesting example of an NRM. The members of this group believe that Sun Myung Moon is the Messiah. They accept his doctrine that Jesus was supposed to have been the Son of God, but that he failed in his mission and got himself killed. Jesus provided a partial salvation (purely spiritual), but he failed to redeem the social, economic, and political structures of this world. Because

Jesus failed in the total task that was assigned to him, God has now blessed and empowered the Reverend Moon to fulfill this divine role. Obviously, such a doctrine is a sharp break from traditional Christianity. While the organizational structure and the conflict with the predominant societal values cause the Moonies to appear to be a sect, the development of a new and unique religious doctrine distinguishes them from the sects. To gain legitimacy and acceptance, however, the Unification Church has downplayed these radical doctrines and has stressed its endorsement of traditional American values (anticommunism, importance of family life, etc.).

The early period of the Church of Jesus Christ of Latter-day Saints provides another example. Although they believe that Jesus was the Messiah and they believe in the Bible, Latter-day Saints also have a second book that they hold as sacred scripture. The new scripture (The Book of Mormon) came from Joseph Smith's "translation" of some golden plates, which he found in upstate New York. Smith taught that prophets in the early Americas had made a written record of messages from God and of the visit that Jesus made to this continent. The last of these prophets buried the written record on golden plates, and Smith was told in several visions where to find them and how to translate them.

The Mormons emphasize that they are a branch of Christianity, but many of their theological innovations are not accepted as Christian doctrine by other Christian groups (such as the belief that unmarried individuals do not attain the celestial kingdom, the highest of their levels of heaven, or the belief that those married in the temple will remain married in the afterlife). It seems fair to say that at least the early Mormons were an example of a cult, a new religious movement, rather than a case of sectarian reform (Johnson and Mullins 1992; Shipps 1985; Stark 1984). Whether it is driven by a desire for legitimacy or is a reaction to gross misrepresentations of their faith,

---

► **BOX 9.2**

Researching the New Religions

Doing research on new religious movements raises logistic problems of how to establish rapport and gain access to the groups. But perhaps the ethical dilemmas involved in studying these groups are even more troubling for the researcher. Two sociologists who have experienced these problems firsthand share their perspectives with us.

Most Americans have learned about new religious movements (NRMs), popularly called "cults," not through direct personal experience but through media reports. The media often has painted these groups as sinister and secretive. Recall the numerous stories by journalists who "infiltrated a cult compound" and "escaped" with an expose of "life in a cult." Most recently we were informed that the only way government officials were able to obtain information about the Branch Davidians was to infiltrate undercover agents into the community. In most cases the reality is far less sensational. NRMs do vary considerably in their openness to nonmembers, and like corporations and government agencies, are likely to limit access by outsiders wanting inside or sensitive information.

There are various reasons for this reticence. One is that NRMs have granted the media access only to conclude that journalists betrayed their trust. Another is that groups think that ousiders will not understand them. They feel that revealing the revolutionary truths they possess without a proper foundation simply opens them up to ridicule. Finally, these groups all perceive themselves to be engaged in a world-saving mission; taking time out to give interviews to social scientists has very low priority unless it serves some function for their mission.

We have studied the three groups—Unification Church ("Moonies"), International Society for Krishna Consciousness (Hare Krishnas), and The Family (formerly called the Children of God) which precipitated the cult conflict that began in the 1970s and has waxed and waned ever since. Why did these NRMs allow us to study them firsthand? What did they expect in return?

NRMs grant researchers access for several common reasons. One is that members often believe that if you get to know them and listen to their message you will convert. (Anthropologists call this "going native.") This, of course, is very rare, but in a few cases it has happened. Since we did not convert, what we had to offer was an understanding of their beliefs and ability to speak their language, which they interpreted as a second-best alternative of sincere interest and acceptance. Another reason is that groups sometimes use sociologists as a status symbol; they boast to potential converts that the movement must be important—after all, they are being studied by social scientists! Most commonly in recent years, groups have opened themselves up to sociologists because they hope for a more "objective" hearing than they have received from journalists. These NRMs seek reciprocity when they become embroiled in public controversy. Each has come to us asking us to take their side in a dispute, serve as an information source to whom they can refer journalists or governmental officials, and even to testify in court cases. When this happens, we move from walking a tightrope between professional responsibilities and fairness to research subjects to an even more complex task of balancing professional norms, NRM expectations, and the public interest.

David G. Bromley and Sydney Newton
Virginia Commonwealth University

many Mormons reject the NRM designation (Barlow 1991). But the same was true of the initial decades of Christianity; the first Christians tended to think of their group as a faction of Judaism rather than the beginnings of a new religion. The difference is that Christianity eventually made a clean break and developed on its own path quite independent of its parent group; Mormons have in some ways moved closer to traditional Christianity in the twentieth century rather than asserting independence and stressing differences. Is the modern-day church of Latter-day Saints just another denomination of Christianity, or a new religion based on Christianity? I tend to think they are moving toward the latter and that seems to be the dominant interpretation (Shipps 1985; Stark 1984; Warner 1993), but the issue remains controversial, especially among Mormon scholars.

Although the issue of whether a group is initiating a new religion is the central one in defining a cult, there are several other characteristics that are common in cults. While sects often place a strong emphasis on the authority (perhaps even literal authority) of scripture, NRMs frequently stress mystical, psychic, or ecstatic experiences. There is not a categorical difference between the two groups on this, but NRMs seldom use previously existing scriptures as a sole source of truth. In fact, it is not uncommon in the United States for cults to generate their own scriptures. The Mormons are one example, and the Unification Church has also been generating a written record that seems to be taking on the aura of sacred scripture. This penchant for scriptural basis is probably caused by the scriptural (written record) orientation of American culture. Cults in other cultures do not ordinarily generate new scriptures. Hence, if the traditional religion emphasizes the role of scripture, the cult is likely to develop its own alternative form of "written word."

Another pattern that prevails in many new religious movements is the centrality of a char-

ismatic leader. A charismatic leader is a person who is believed to have extraordinary insights and powers (discussed in chapter 7). Such a person is attributed with certain divine qualities, and is believed to have direct and unique contact with the supernatural. It is the unique insights of these individuals that are the basis for the alternative faith. Although most cults are clearly founded by such charismatic leaders, some sociologists believe that cults can also develop in a more spontaneous way—through "spontaneous subcultural evolution" (Bainbridge and Stark 1979). Such cults, like the groups that focus their faith on the saving power of unidentified flying objects (UFOs), are usually more loosely structured and more democratic. They have no identifiable charismatic figure, but stigmatization and hostility by outsiders may force adherents to draw more closely together and raise boundaries against outsiders. Such groups usually start out as nonreligious subcultures but may eventually emerge into esoteric cultic groups with a world view and ethos that contradicts those of the dominant society (Nelson 1968; Bainbridge and Stark 1979). Hence, Bainbridge and Stark believe that there are really three different ways in which cults may emerge: through the process of spontaneous subcultural evolution; through the dynamic leadership of a charismatic leader who genuinely believes in the veracity of his or her teachings;[4] or through the leadership of a charismatic "entrepreneur" who sees religion as a money-making

---

[4]Bainbridge and Stark make a value judgment about these leaders by referring to them as "psychopathic characters." I prefer to avoid labeling all of these leaders with a pejorative term. Some of them do seem to be "psychopathic," but others are merely protesting the "sick side" of American culture and may be more mentally healthy in many respects than those who perpetuate the status quo. By allowing only two categories of charismatic leaders (conscious manipulators and "sincere" psychopaths), Bainbridge and Stark introduce an unwarranted value judgment.

scheme. (Some "charismatic leaders" do indeed seem to be con artists who are manipulating religion as a means of gaining power and wealth.) Social scientists are therefore not in agreement on the necessity of a charismatic leader in the formation of a cult.

Externally, the sect and the cult look much alike, although cults tend to appeal to the middle and upper classes, while sects appeal to the lower classes (Stark 1986). But both rebel against the predominant cultural values, both lack trained professional leaders and a bureaucratic structure, and both insist on a stringent membership policy that requires sig-

nificant commitment (although the cult may not require this in its very earliest stage of development). The cult, like the sect, is also capable of institutionalization. In fact, some institutionalization is necessary if the group is to outlive its founder. The evolution of sects and cults is comparable as indicated in Figure 9.3.

This diagram, while oversimplifying the process, does suggest the parallel manner in which these two types of groups may evolve. If we allowed for the two-dimensional analysis Yinger proposes (Figure 9.2), we would have a more accurate picture: Institutionalization and accommodation to secular values do

▶ **FIGURE 9.3**

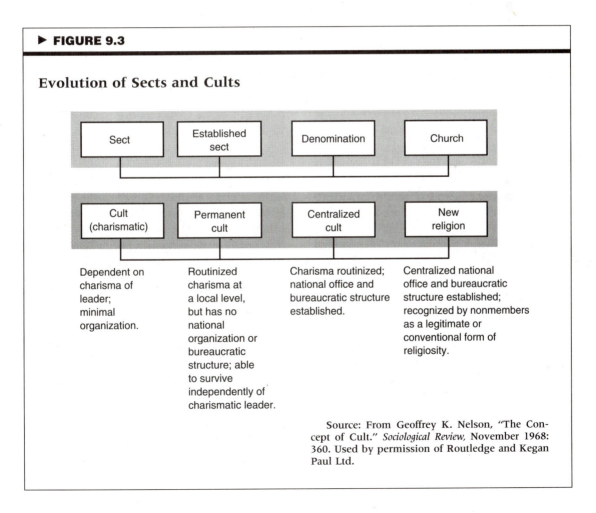

Evolution of Sects and Cults

Sect	Established sect	Denomination	Church

Cult (charismatic)	Permanent cult	Centralized cult	New religion

Dependent on charisma of leader; minimal organization.

Routinized charisma at a local level, but has no national organization or bureaucratic structure; able to survive independently of charismatic leader.

Charisma routinized; national office and bureaucratic structure established.

Centralized national office and bureaucratic structure established; recognized by nonmembers as a legitimate or conventional form of religiosity.

Source: From Geoffrey K. Nelson, "The Concept of Cult." *Sociological Review,* November 1968: 360. Used by permission of Routledge and Kegan Paul Ltd.

not necessarily occur at the same rate. Sects and NRMs, then, tend to evolve along parallel lines.

To understand fully the evolution of a sect or cult, however, we must give attention to the hostility toward the group by traditional religious groups in the society and to the strength of the desire for legitimacy within the new group. In other words, we must take into account the pressures at work on a group as it attempts to mobilize its resources and to counter opposition to its existence. Bainbridge and Stark (1979) insist that hostile forces may cause a sectarian group to evolve into a cult; as its beliefs are modified to define its separateness, it develops a unique world view. They refer to the People's Temple of Jonestown as an example of this sect-to-cult movement.

With this added variable that affects the development and self-image of a group, our view of sect and cult emergence becomes more complex (Figure 9.4).

A central point here illustrated by Nelson's model is that both sects and cults lack organizational complexity and both reject at least some of the values of the secular society. However, the sect views its role as one of purifying the traditional faith by calling members back to what are believed to be core principles. Cults represent the nascent stages of the development of a new or a syncretistic religion. Other factors may affect the evolution of a sect or a cult, but the institutionalizing and accommodating tendencies frequently cause sects to become denominational in form. The cult usually either

---

▶ **FIGURE 9.4**

Social Forces and Sect—Cult Transformation

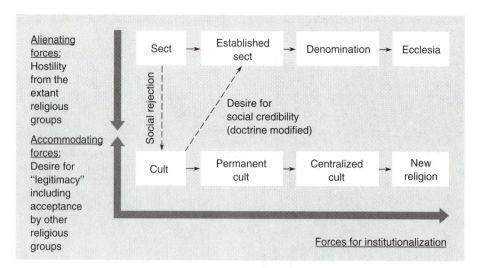

Source: From Geoffrey K. Nelson, "The Concept of Cult." *Sociological Review,* November 1968: 360. Used by permission of Routledge and Kegan Paul Ltd.

dies out or institutionalizes into a new religion. The debate discussed above regarding whether Mormonism is a new religious movement or another denomination of Christianity is an argument about how that group has evolved.

Clearly, no one diagram is capable of demonstrating the many factors that affect the evolution and development of a particular religious group. This one looks at sects and cults from a slightly different lens than does the one developed by Yinger. It is not possible graphically to combine all the complexity of both models, but Figure 9.5 is an attempt to synthesize these two perspectives into a three-dimensional or cube model. It emphasizes the fact that the force-field on any religious movement involves three different types of pressures, and as each group chooses strategies to cope with each set of dynamics, the evolution of the group is affected. If we were to name each stage or position within this model, we would have sixty-four "types" of religious groups. Such a process seems useless, for my real purpose here is to focus on the field of forces at work on groups rather than creating another typology.

If all of this seems terribly complex, it is because the evolution of religious groups *is* complex. Various scholars have focused on different aspects of religious group evolution and therefore have defined such terms as *sect, cult,* and *church* in alternative ways. This is an important point for the new student of religion to bear in mind when reading a study that discusses sects and cults. Readers should always be sure they understand how a given author defines his or her terms and how those terms were operationalized or measured.

Stark and Bainbridge have added another important dimension to our understanding of cult development. Using demographic data on church affiliation in various regions of North America and comparing these data with information on location of cult headquarters and on highest concentrations of cult memberships,

Stark and Bainbridge (1985) conclude that where traditional religious organizations are weak, NRM formation is highest. Where religious tradition is strong and church membership is high, cult formation is less common. The West Coast region, from southern California to northern British Columbia, has the lowest levels of church membership and the greatest incidence of cult success on the continent. These scholars believe that secularization breeds cult development; they insist that secularization involves a vacuum in which certain human needs are left unmet. If churches are not strong enough to satisfy those needs, cults will arise to fill that vacuum. Their thesis will be explored in more detail in chapter 14, but we note here that sects are more likely to form than are cults if traditional forms of religion are well established.

Theories about sect-to-church transformations are generalizations about how this change normally occurs. It may or may not be precisely descriptive of the process as it occurs in a specific group a reader chooses to study. Furthermore, such terms as *sect, cult, established sect,* and *denomination* are normally not ones that can be permanently assigned to a group. They simply describe organizational characteristics of a group at a particular moment in its history. With this in mind, church-sect theory can enable us to describe the normal process of organizational change in religious collectivities. References to churchlike or sectlike groups also allow us to identify similarities of religious style among certain religious groups and differences in character with others at any given time. One recent development in church-sect theory is the use of such adjectives as *sectlike* and *churchlike* to describe the religiosity of individuals—regardless of the groups to which those individuals belong (Demerath 1965). This has yielded fruitful insights, but students encountering such a study should be sure they understand how *churchlike* and *sectlike* were operationalized.

▶ **FIGURE 9.5**

The Force-Field of Religious Groups: A Three-Dimensional Model

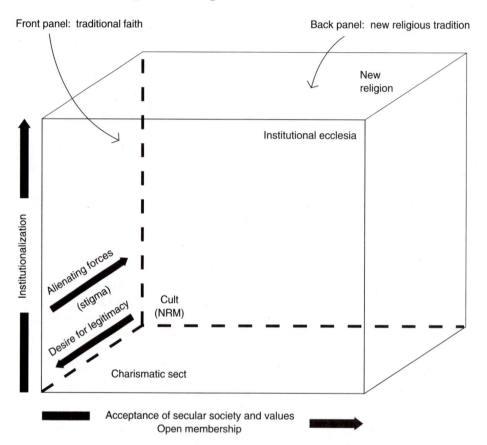

Front panel: traditional faith

Back panel: new religious tradition

New religion

Institutional ecclesia

Institutionalization

Alienating forces (stigma)

Desire for legitimacy

Cult (NRM)

Charismatic sect

Acceptance of secular society and values
Open membership

It may help to understand this diagram if you again familiarize yourself with Yinger's model in Figure 9.2. Imagine the front panel of this cube as Yinger's schema, depicting evolution from charismatic sect to institutional ecclesia. The back panel would be similar, but would represent evolution from the charismatic cult to a new religious tradition. The alienating and accomodating forces from the traditional religions in the society, represented in Figure 9.4, are depicted here as forces that could move a group from sect toward cult (front panel to back panel) or vice versa. Thus, the forces in the evolution of the group represent three types of choices regarding organization and environment that groups must make—hence the diversity of types of groups that exist at any one time. This must be seen as a dynamic model, however, with groups moving over time from one position to another.

In short, if one seeks to generalize about how most groups evolve and the stages they go through, the concepts of church, sect, and denomination can be helpful. However, if one seeks to understand a specific group, one must learn that group's characteristics on each issue. One must discover various dimensions of the group, including theological orientation, relationship with the secular society, amount of formality of the ritual ("high church" being very formal, elegant, and decorous and "low church" being informal, unpretentious, and spontaneous), appeal of the ritual (with a "Dionysian" appeal to emotions or an "Apollonian" appeal to reason), and the extent of organization (the complexity of the structure; whether there are official clergy and whether the clergy are formally trained; and the relative restrictiveness of membership policy). Other elements may also be included in this analysis (Greeley 1972). Looking at each issue separately rather than constructing a typology is sometimes called "choice point analysis" (O'Dea 1968; Winter 1977). Because these elements do vary somewhat independently of each other, analyzing these dimensions without reference to sectlike or churchlike categories can sometimes be very useful.

A Restructuring of American Religion?

Denominationalism, the organizational pattern of congregations being linked through centralized coordinating bodies, has served for several centuries as the core organizational structure for dominant Euro-American religions.[5] Whether the group be Lutheran, Latter-day Saints, Reformed Jews, or Roman Catholics, some overriding authority is granted to and considerable loyalty of members is directed toward a larger formal association. The nature of these organizations differ, some being very democratic and some being very hierarchical and centralized, but they have long been a central feature of organized religion in North America.[6]

At least one highly respected sociologist of religion thinks that that pattern has been changing in the latter half of the twentieth century, and especially since the 1960s. Robert Wuthnow argues, in *The Restructuring of American Religion* (1987), that religion in the United States is experiencing a dramatic shift rooted in special interest groups. Since early in the nineteenth century, special interest groups have operated alongside of denominations, crossing boundaries and providing for joint efforts between various groups. The American Bible Society (founded in 1816) was followed in that century by such groups as the American Sunday School Union, the Women's Christian Temperance Movement, the Anti-Saloon League, the American Anti-Slavery Society, and the YMCA. People of diverse religious affiliations banned together to address some problem or provide some service.

The twentieth century has seen a continuation of the spawning of special interest groups, with religiously motivated people mobilizing associations across denominational lines to public and professional issues: war and peace, abortion legislation, world hunger, civil rights, changes in gender roles, business ethics, and the recruitment activities of cults. The Full Gospel Business Men's Fellowship, the Christian Legal Society, the Moral Majority, the Fellowship of Christian Athletes, and Clergy

---

[5]Native American religions do not conform to this pattern, nor do some underground religious groups such as those practicing Wicca (witchcraft).

[6]Readers interested in the finer points of denominations as organizations and in an alternative typology of religious organization should see Scherer (1988).

and Laity Concerned about War are only a few examples of special interest groups for whom religion is intrinsically tied to social and political issues.

Until the 1970s, says Wuthnow, the members of these organizations still felt primary loyalty to their denominations and it was the churches, as such, which defined their core values and their sense of morality. The special interest groups were secondary in their sense of belonging and identity. However, the 1970s and 1980s brought intense conflicts over abortion policy, the Vietnam War, changing gender roles, definitions of sexual morality, and the role of religion in public schools and in public life. Wuthnow believes that the nation has polarized into conservative and liberal camps, each with their own sets of special interest groups. Members of each camp may belong to the same church, so that the church is split and is no longer able to claim the moral authority or elicit the deep loyalty necessary to define meaning and to sacralize values. The deeper loyalty, he says, is going to the interest groups, and these interest groups are growing remarkably in both numbers of groups and in memberships.

This may undermine the structure of religion in the United States, so that religious conservatives from various denominations who are adherents of, say, The Christian Voice, may find that that group elicits more loyalty and does more to provide a sense of identity and belonging than do the individual denominations to which they each belong. Wuthnow believes the face of religion in the United States is fundamentally and probably permanently changed by these special interest groups. Denominations, he believes, are no longer the central structural element of American religion.[7]

Robert Wuthnow's assessment is based on some sweeping interpretations of history, and it remains a controversial thesis. It does provide a new way of thinking about the shifts that appear to be occurring in American religion. It will no doubt be the basis for much research and interpretation for some years to come.

Summary

In attempting to classify different styles of religious groups, Weber and Troeltsch described different types of religious groups. Troeltsch's description of the sect and the church was more multidimensional than were Weber's. Niebuhr elaborated the typology even further by defining the denomination and discussing several added variables that he believed were correlated with the types. He also generalized about the typical mode of religious group evolution—from sect to denomination to church and back to sect. This began several decades of theorizing and generalizing about each type of religious group. The conceptions of church and sect had been transformed from purely descriptive tools to theory-building ones.

The lack of precise correlation of the many variables in multidimensional formulations led to changes in church-sect theory. One recent move has been to simplify the number of factors that are used to distinguish a sect from a denomination or church. Some scholars suggest using a single variable (Johnson; Greeley); others (such as Yinger) use two or three variables and identify several subtypes of religious groups (charismatic sect, established sect, diffused denomination, institutionalized denomination, etc.). This procedure has contributed

---

[7] Stephen Warner (1993) adds that church membership switching itself is increasingly based on this liberal/conservative dichotomy. This may be seen as

further evidence of the importance of this split in the Christian community.

to the identification of alternative paths of religious group evolution, depending on the independent rates at which a group may institutionalize and accept the values of the dominant society. Such approaches describe a multilinear process of group evolution rather than the unilinear evolution depicted by Niebuhr. Some social scientists continue to utilize the multidimensional conception of sects and churches, recognizing that few groups will fit all criteria. In this case, a group that fits most of the typical characteristics for a sect or a church is described as sectlike or churchlike. It is critically important therefore that students recognize how any given author has defined and measured "sect" or "church" in any particular study.

The concept of cult has also been added to the types of religious groups. Although the concept of cult has been used in various ways by different scholars, I have (with Nelson, Yinger, Bainbridge and Stark, and others) distinguished the cult as a new (or imported) religious movement in a society (also sometimes called an NRM to avoid the stigma of popular usage given to "cult"). This type of group is differentiated from the sect that rep-

resents the regeneration of a traditional religion in that society. The cult, like the sect, goes through processes of institutionalization and modification. But if it survives and eventually gains legitimacy in the society, the cult is viewed as a new religion rather than as a denomination of existing religions. As in the case of the sect, many social forces affect the development of the cult and shape its style and character. Extent of institutionalization, pressures to be part of the traditional religious tradition (and therefore a legitimate religion in the society) coupled with possible rejection and stigmatization by the traditional religions, and extent to which the group seeks to be an open social system that accepts dominant cultural values are just three of the key factors shaping evolution of a sect and cult.

Although the dominant Euro-American religion has been organized for several centuries primarily through denominationalism, Robert Wuthnow believes that special interest groups have now become so important in American religion that they are at least as important as denominational stuctures in shaping religious values, attitudes, and beliefs of Americans.

Religion and
Social Inequality

In the next four chapters we examine the interactive relationship between religion and the social structures and processes of the larger society. These chapters are designed to illustrate the sociological method of analysis; they are certainly not exhaustive treatments of the influence of religion on other social structures.

One of the important elements of social structure is the stratification system.

In chapter 11 we explore ways in which one's theology influences one's posture toward the existing structures: affirmation, resignation, or active rebellion. But first we must explore the relationship between one's position in the stratification system and one's religious orientation. Chapter 10 explores the interrelationships between socioeconomic status and religiosity.

CHAPTER TEN

Religion and Social Stratification: Interactive Process

One of the most important factors in shaping the life chances and life experiences of people is economics. In this chapter we explore how socioeconomic circumstances affect religion and how religion, in turn, impacts economic behavior. We begin by investigating the role of religion as a causal variable that affects one's economic behavior.

Religion and Economic Behavior: Religion as a Causal Variable

Weber's Protestant Ethic Thesis

Among the important factors determining the social status of individuals in any society are the economic behavior of those individuals and the nature of the economic system itself. The question that has interested many scholars has been: To what extent does religion affect economic behavior? The landmark study on this issue has been Max Weber's seminal work, *The Protestant Ethic and the Spirit of Capitalism,* for it has generated an incredible amount of research and discussion.

Weber's study was undertaken in response to two issues. First, he was interested in the relationship between religion and economic activity. This study was one of a series of comparative studies of religion and its effects on economic development (Weber 1951; 1952; 1958b; 1963).[1] In the first sentence of chapter 1 of *The Protestant Ethic,* Weber points out that Protestants tend to be more affluent than Catholics and to occupy the higher-status positions in virtually all industrialized societies. He was interested in the relationship between religious affiliation and social stratification, including the differential effects of various faiths.

Second, Weber wished to address a larger theoretical issue. He hoped to provide a corrective

---

[1]These comparative studies included investigations of Confucianism and Taoism, Hinduism and Buddhism, and ancient Judaism. Weber's interest was in the way religious beliefs encourage or discourage the development of rational business enterprise.

to the simple economic determinism of Karl Marx. Marx had maintained that one's economic status was the principal determining factor in all behavior. He felt that it was fruitless to try to understand human behavior as an expression of values, ideals, or beliefs. Marx believed that beliefs and values are a *result* of economic forces, that one's ideas and ideals act to justify one's economic fortunes—or to compensate one for a lack of economic fortune. Religion served to justify and sacralize the current social arrangements. Because of this, it helped reinforce the status quo and served to retard change. For Marx, values, beliefs, and ideals do not serve as primary causal forces; they are secondary factors that result from economic forces.

Marx recognized that beliefs—including religion—could serve as *proximate* causes, even as he insisted that they are not *ultimate* causes. He acknowledged that humans are active agents and that beliefs organize and propel one's action. It was for this reason that he stressed the importance of the working class changing from "false consciousness" to "class consciousness." He also emphasized that religion often served as an opiate of the masses—again revealing his awareness of the role of beliefs and ideas on action. Without ignoring this awareness, it is also accurate to say that Marx believed ideas are powerfully conditioned by material (or economic) circumstances. Economic forces were viewed as the principal factors in shaping human behavior; ideas, values, and beliefs were only proximate influences and were themselves largely shaped by economic forces. Religion, which deals in values, ideals, and beliefs as its primary currency, was viewed as a relatively unimportant force, at least for those interested in the principal factors that cause social change or ultimately shape human behavior.

Some writers have claimed that Weber's study was intended as a direct refutation of Marx, but this clearly was not the case. Weber agreed with Marx's contention that economic self-interests have a powerful effect on the beliefs and values of people. Yet, Weber viewed this position as only a partial truth. He insisted that while economics can affect religion, religion can also affect economics. In fact, he held that Protestantism (especially Calvinism) was a significant force in the formation of capitalism as an economic system. Rather than being a refutation of Marx, Weber viewed his study as a modification or corrective to the overly simplistic analysis by Marx. Although he accepted Marx's view that people behave in ways that enhance their own self-interests, Weber felt that perceptions of self-interest were not limited to the economic realm. A religious self-interest (e.g., concern over salvation) could also motivate people.

In *The Protestant Ethic and the Spirit of Capitalism,* Weber attempted to identify how religious beliefs and self-interests had affected economic behavior. In focusing on the Protestant "ethic," he was really referring to the overall perspective and sense of values of Protestantism. He felt that the breakthrough from the feudalistic to the capitalistic economic system was substantially enhanced by this particular world view. In sum, he felt that ideas could be important factors that facilitate social change, including changes in the economic system.

For capitalism to thrive, several conditions had to be met. There had to be a pool of individuals with the characteristics necessary to serve as entrepreneurs. They had to be individualistic and had to believe in the virtues of hard work and of simplicity of lifestyle. Protestantism tended to create a supply of such people. Although economic self-interests create such people today, Weber maintained that the original pool was formed largely by people motivated by religious beliefs and self-interests.

One of the primary concerns of people in the fifteenth and sixteenth centuries was their eternal salvation. One way to be assured of salvation was to serve God directly. If one was called by God to the priesthood or to holy orders in a monastery, one seemed to have a better chance of eternal salvation. But Martin Luther developed a different concept of divine service. He stressed the priesthood of all believers and insisted that one could be called by God to a variety of occupations that served humanity. This new concept of a calling is referred to as the **doctrine of vocation,** for the word *vocation* means calling. According to Luther's teachings, one may be called to many types of secular positions, as well as to the priesthood. Because secular positions were also viewed as service to God, any form of work could be a means of expressing one's faith. Hard work became a way of serving and glorifying God. Idleness or laziness, by logical extension, came to be viewed as a sin. Although Luther initiated this concept of vocation and held to it in principle, it was the Calvinists who fully implemented it. In fact, John Calvin even suggested that when a person was hard at work, he or she was most in the image of God.

Industriousness was an essential quality for the emergence of a class of entrepreneurs, and this quality was a central virtue among Calvinists. But it was not enough for people simply to develop an ethic of hard work. The rational investment of earnings was also critical. The Protestant emphasis on asceticism and on delayed gratification served to enhance this aspect of capitalistic enterprise. Asceticism was a major theme in the preaching of a number of reformers, for the pleasures of the world (gambling, drinking, secular forms of entertainment, and luxuries) were all viewed as sinful and evil. God required a simple, even austere, lifestyle. Calvin even described self-discipline as the "nerves of religion"; hence, self-denial became a central virtue. This denial of present desires was accomplished because of the principle of **delayed gratification.** Believers were willing to forgo pleasures now

for the promise of much greater rewards in the future. In the case of reformers, the future rewards were anticipated in the afterlife. Nonetheless, the principle of delayed gratification is an important one for the development of economic capital in *this* world. In fact, Weber defines capitalism as the systematic investment of time and resources with the hope of significant returns in the future (profits). The idea of denying one's immediate desires in the hope of a greater return in the future was basic to both Calvinism and to capitalism.

Among many of the early Protestants—and especially among Calvinists—hard work was a moral and religious duty; but because income from one's industriousness was not to be spent on luxuries or sensual pleasures, the only thing to do was to invest it. Among Methodists and certain other Protestant sects, excess income was to be given to the poor.[2] But according to R. H. Tawney (1954), the Calvinists felt that people who were impoverished were poor simply because they were lazy.[3] Not wishing to contribute to this wickedness, Calvinists were not inclined to donate much of their income to the needy. Most of their profits were available for investment. This created a situation in which increased amounts of capital were available in the society and economic growth was enhanced.

Other characteristics of Calvinism were also significant. One of the important doctrines in Calvin's theology was that of **predestination.** According to this doctrine, God has already decided who is saved and who is damned. One's fate is predetermined, and there is really

---

[2]John Wesley's economic ethic was "*earn* all you can, *save* all you can, and *give* all you can." He was extraordinarily hardworking and ascetic in his own lifestyle, but he gave nearly three-fourths of whatever he earned to the poor or for the establishment of churches and schools. Hence, he did not accumulate great wealth.

[3]This generalization applies to the Calvinists—the followers and successors of Calvin—much more than to Calvin himself. Calvin's own teaching stressed generosity (Calvin 1952).

nothing a person can do about it. This doctrine might easily have resulted in a sense of fatalism, despair, and despondency. But in this case, people coped with their anxiety about whether they were saved by acting as if they were. Of course, this would not improve their chances, but any impious or un-Christian behavior would only ensure to themselves and others that they were damned. Righteous behavior would not earn a person a position in heaven, but one's behavior was believed to be an outward sign of one's eternal status. Being righteous, thrifty, hardworking, and ascetic was a way of hedging one's bets. When so much was at stake, it seemed foolish to take chances.

Furthermore, this predestined state placed one in a position of radical individualism. One was not saved because of anything others did or because of the groups one belonged to. One was strictly on one's own in this matter of salvation. Weber writes: "In what was for the man of the age of the Reformation the most important thing in his life, he was forced to follow his path alone to meet a destiny which had been decreed for him from eternity. No one could help him. . . . In spite of the necessity of membership in the true church for salvation, the Calvinist's intercourse with his God was carried on in deep spiritual isolation" (1958a: 104–7).

Because an attitude of rugged individualism was important for the entrepreneur, the sense of religious individualism provided a compatible outlook. In fact, Weber suggests that the religious individualism may have partially predated and thereby contributed to the attitude of economic individualism. Economic individualism, in turn, means that individuals make rational economic decisions based on their own self-interests. Once capitalism is formed, according to Weber, it is capable of sustaining its own individualistic motivations. But he suggests that religious self-interests

and beliefs may have contributed to the original formation of capitalism.

Finally, Calvin taught that regardless of one's eternal salvation, everyone is to glorify God and to work for the creation of a Divine Kingdom on earth. In fact, Calvin emphasized that the proper aim of humanity is not personal salvation but the glorification of God through the sanctification of this world. This focus created a strong this-worldly component to the theology, for one's labors in transforming this realm—the here-and-now—were the best indicators of one's devotion to God. Later Calvinists (Puritans) reinforced the inner-worldly (or this-worldly) element even further by suggesting that one's socioeconomic status was an indicator of one's spiritual grace and eternal destination. Delayed gratification and asceticism became increasingly this-worldly and rational (i.e., based on concrete self-interest).

Due to certain beliefs, then, fifteenth-century Europe was supplied with an increasing supply of capital for investment and a pool of individuals who had the values and attitudes appropriate to becoming entrepreneurs. Although these characteristics were not sufficient to bring on the development of capitalism, they were necessary, and Weber believed that religion had contributed to the formation of the capitalistic system of economics by supplying these characteristics. He maintained that a religious outlook had influenced the economic behavior and financial fortunes of individuals (Protestants becoming more affluent than non-Protestants) and also had contributed to the development of a new economic system. Contrary to Marx, Weber felt that religion was capable of being a cause of economic conditions—not just a result.

Weber's thesis has been highly controversial and has generated a large number of essays and research projects. Some scholars have argued that Calvinism had little to do with the development of capitalism. Some insist that the beginning of colonialism (with its influx of new capital resources) and changes in postmedieval technology sparked the advent of capitalism. Others emphasize the fact that capital was available for entrepreneurs through Jews and through Catholic bankers in urban areas. In these cases, the concurrent rise of capitalism and Protestantism is seen as a simple coincidence (Samuelsson 1961). The outlook described as the Protestant ethic is viewed as insignificant—or at least its uniqueness to Protestants is denied.[4]

Other writers have basically agreed with Weber but have suggested modifications in his thesis. For example, R. H. Tawney (1954) suggests that most contributions of Protestantism to the development of an individualistic and laissez-faire economic system were entirely latent. He points out that in the Middle Ages, the Catholic Church held usury (lending money for interest) to be on a par with adultery and fornication.[5] Not only was lending money at interest considered immoral, but prosperity itself was viewed as a source of spiritual corruption. Both of these attitudes were carried over to various extents in the teachings of the reformers.

Luther, who represented a rural peasant orientation, was particularly opposed to self-interested individualism and to laissez-faire policies. Furthermore, he felt that it was immoral to make money through investments, lending, or any form of speculation. He held to a labor theory of value—the idea that one

should be rewarded financially only in proportion to the labor one actually performs.

Calvin, on the other hand, was much more urban and secular in background and orientation. Although he was no defender of laissez-faire capitalism, he did believe that capital investment was essential to a healthy economy. Hence, he insisted that there was nothing inherently evil about investing or lending money at moderate interest. However, he did insist that no interest should be charged the poor, and he put strict ethical guidelines on economic activity. He also remained deeply suspicious of the spiritual effects of economic prosperity. At one point he commented, "Wherever prosperity flows uninterruptedly, its delight corrupts even the best of us," and at another time he suggested that "prosperity is like rust or mildew." In fact, Calvin's distrust of the influences of money is revealed in his considerable ambivalence about usury. One English clergyman who studied Calvin's theology commented that "Calvin deals with usury as the apothocarie doth with poyson" (cited by Tawney 1954: 94). It seems clear that at the manifest level both Protestants and Catholics believed that "the spirit of capitalism is foreign to every kind of religion" (Samuelsson 1961: 19).

Tawney grants that Protestantism may have unconsciously contributed to the early development of capitalism, but even as it did so, the reformers were preaching against certain practices that were later taken for granted as an integral part of the free-enterprise system. In fact, he insists that the massive accumulations of wealth that were acquired by later industrialists were not the result of the Protestant ethic or of thriftiness. Such capital was acquired by unscrupulous exploitation of people and resources and by manipulating speculations that were euphemistically called "opportunities." Tawney agrees with Weber that Calvinistic theology and ethics (such as recognizing the

---

[4]Those interested in detailed critiques of Weber's Protestant ethic thesis will want to see Tawney (1954), Winthrop Hudson (1949), Amintore Fanfani (1936), H. M. Robertson (1959), Robert Green (1959), and Kurt Samuelsson (1961).

[5]It was for this reason that the Jews were looked to as sources of capital; they were willing to lend money at interest because usury was not defined as immoral within the Jewish tradition.

legitimacy of capital investment) contributed to the advent of the free-enterprise system, but he feels that early Protestant ethics were quite incompatible with the free-for-all capitalism of the eighteenth, nineteenth, and even twentieth centuries. Moreover, he felt that capitalism would probably have made its entrance even without the contribution of Protestantism. Calvin's endorsement of investment was viewed by Tawney as largely an accommodation to existing forces.

This brings us to another critique, the view that rather than causing asceticism, individualism, and a work ethic, Calvinism was simply an agreeable theology to those who already held these values and attributes. According to this position, people became Calvinists because Calvinism justified and even sacralized beliefs, behaviors, and outlooks that those people already practiced. The lonely individual risk of salvation paralleled the financial risks of venturesome entrepreneurs. We will return to this issue of **elective affinity** (the attraction of persons to a religious world view because it justifies one's self-interests and one's current outlook) in the next chapter.

Empirical Research

There have been many efforts to prove or disprove Weber's thesis through empirical research in the modern world. In order to provide insight into how sociologists try to test rather abstract theories, I will report in some detail on one widely cited research project, a study undertaken by Gerhard Lenski in suburban Detroit. He conducted in-depth interviews with 656 people—Protestants, Catholics, and Jews. He attempted to test the Weberian thesis in several ways. First, he asked people to rank the following in order of importance in a man's job:

1. Receiving a high income.
2. Having no danger of being fired (job security).

3. Being able to work short hours and having lots of free time.
4. Having chances for advancement.
5. Feeling that one's work is important and provides a sense of accomplishment (Lenski 1963: 89).

Although items 1 and 4 reflect the popular usage of the term *Protestant ethic,* Lenski points out that only item 5 is consistent with the original concept of vocation and Weber's treatment of the Protestant ethic.

Lenski found that Catholics were somewhat more likely to respond with 2 or 3 as first choices, while Protestants more often responded with 5. Part of the difference may have been due to the fact that Protestants were more highly represented in the professional classes, while Catholics were largely in the working class. But even when he held social class constant, he found a difference between Protestant and Catholic answers. The differences between the groups were not large (54 percent of Protestants versus 44 percent of Catholics responded with statement 5), but Lenski held that they were still significant. Jews ranked second in the number of positive responses to the fifth statement (48 percent) and ranked the highest on the number of positive answers on items 2 and 4. Lenski insisted that the differentials between groups, especially between Protestants and Catholics, were shrinking as more ethnic groups (largely Catholic) were being acculturated into the American value system.[6]

As a second means of measuring the Protestant ethic, Lenski sought to ascertain the attitudes of people toward installment buying.

---

[6]He also believed that black Protestants—who ranked lowest on the Protestant ethic scale—were affected in their attitudes largely by racial discrimination and the legacy of slavery. Hence, he felt that secular social forces were more responsible for their socioeconomic status and their economic outlooks than was their Protestant heritage.

Installment buying (have now, pay later) seemed to Lenski to be the utmost rejection of the principle of delayed gratification. A critical attitude toward installment buying would be a position consistent with the Protestant ethic. Again, Lenski found white Protestants more critical of installment buying and more in tune with the Protestant ethic than Catholics—but only by about 5 percent. Interestingly, Jews were the most in tune with the Protestant ethic, being most highly critical of installment buying (56 percent versus 44 percent for white Protestants).

As a third means of assessing the impact of religion on economic attitudes and behavior, Lenski compared active church members with nominal members (members in name only). He found that the sons and daughters of devout Protestants were more likely to be upwardly mobile than were the sons and daughters of nominal Protestants. Conversely, he found that the sons and daughters of active Catholics were more likely to be downwardly mobile than were the children of marginal Catholics. This, he suggests, provides evidence of the contrary influences of Protestantism and Catholicism on socioeconomic behavior. (There were not enough Jews in the sample to permit a reliable analysis on this item.) Although Lenski used other means to operationalize and measure economic attitudes and behavior, he essentially felt that the evidence strongly supported the Weberian thesis:

> With considerable regularity the Jews and white Protestants have identified themselves with the individualistic, competitive patterns of thought and action linked with the middle class, and historically associated with the Protestant Ethic or its secular counterpart, the spirit of capitalism. By contrast, Catholics and Negro Protestants have more often been associated with the collectivistic, security-oriented, working-class patterns of thought and action historically opposed to the Protestant Ethic and the spirit of capitalism (1963: 113).

Subsequent researchers, especially the Catholic priest Andrew Greeley, have come up with findings quite contrary to Lenski's. Greeley's research suggests no significant difference between Protestants and Catholics in concepts of vocation or in upward mobility. In fact, some of the evidence indicates more upward mobility for Catholics than for Protestants. The conflict between these two sociologists and their partisans has been intense on this issue. Although Lenski and Greeley have been the primary spokespersons for the contrasting positions, numerous others have conducted research too.

First, sociologists have not been able to agree on the question of whether Protestants do, in fact, tend to have higher social status than Catholics. Three studies indicated that Protestants generally do (Lenski 1963; Crowley and Ballweg 1971; Porter 1965); four indicated no differences (Cohen 1985; Gockel 1969; Goldstein 1969; and Mueller 1971a); one found Catholics to have higher status (Mueller and Lane 1972); and one found that liberal Protestants had higher status than Catholics but that fundamentalist Protestants did not (Morgan et al. 1962).

Many more studies have been done on status mobility of persons from various religious groups, and the results are equally mixed. Seven studies found Protestants to be more upwardly mobile than Catholics (Lenski 1963; Mayer and Sharp 1962; Crowley and Ballweg 1971; Jackson et al. 1970; Organic 1963; Weller 1963; Goldstein 1969); one found that Catholics had higher mobility (Alston 1969). Ten found no differences in mobility when such important variables as educational level and ethnicity were held constant (Featherman 1971; Mueller 1971a; Schuman 1971; Warren 1970; Greeley 1963, 1969a; Kohn 1969; Glenn and Hyland 1967; Lipset and Bendix 1959; and Mack et al. 1956).

One difficulty is variations in the way various scholars have operationalized social

mobility; two researchers reported higher social mobility for Protestants if one defined
mobility solely in terms of occupation; but if
one used other factors (such as education, income, and achievement orientation), the results
showed little difference.[7] A second problem is
that none of the studies distinguish clearly between current and previous religious affiliation
of respondents. Hence, there is no control that
would clearly identify religious affiliation as
cause or as consequence of social mobility.
Third, most studies do not distinguish between
Protestant denominations—they are all lumped
together.[8] Weber's thesis never suggested that
all forms of Protestantism equally enhance upward social mobility of believers, but only
those with a particular world view or set of
values (a strong work ethic, emphasis on asceticism, and an individualistic thrust). One of
the more recent studies suggests that in contemporary America Mormons, Seventh-Day
Adventists, Holiness Pentecostals, and Christian Reformed provide higher levels of economic motivation than do most other Protestant denominations—which makes sense given
the strong ascetic thrust of each of these denominations (Cohen 1985). Weber also never
maintained that it was only Protestant Christians who might hold those views.

The matters of whether modern-day Protestants manifest the characteristic outlooks of the
Protestant ethic more than do Catholics and
whether it makes any difference in socioeconomic standing is still not satisfactorily answered for many sociologists. For many others,
it seems to be a moot point. If evidence presented by Lenski and others proved to be ac-

curate, it would offer some plausibility to Weber's thesis, but it would clearly not prove it.
On the other hand, if present-day Catholics are
more upwardly mobile than are Protestants, we
would not have disproved the possible effects
of a Protestant ethic at the time capitalism was
coming into predominance. Moreover, the rational pursuit of wealth (spirit of capitalism) is
so thoroughly secularized in the Western world
that it has become independent of any one religious tradition. Weber himself had pointed
out that the spirit of capitalism had quickly
secularized and gained a standing independent
of any theological impetus.

Finally, Weber's study was not intended as
a narrow contrast of Protestants and Catholics,
with an implication that only Protestants were
capable of developing the outlook of the entrepreneur. Weber was suggesting that *any* sacred
milieu that stressed certain values and
outlooks—individualism, asceticism, and an
ethic of hard work—was conducive to the
development of capitalism and to the affluence
of those holding those views. He only asserts
that historically Protestant reformers developed those values somewhat earlier than did
the Catholic Church. In short, an empirical
study in contemporary society does not prove
or disprove a theory about the role of religion
in a previous era.

Regardless of whether Protestantism contributed to the rise of capitalism, the idea that
one's beliefs may affect one's economic standing is still popular. Many commentators besides Weber have suggested that when a broad
concept of vocation combines with asceticism,
the result is an increased likelihood of affluence for members of that group. John Wesley,
the founder of Methodism, pointed this out
with some alarm, for he felt that economic
affluence was one of the most corrupting forces
to spiritual growth:

> How then is it possible that Methodism . . .
> though it flourishes now as a green bay tree,

---

[7]For reviews and interpretations of the various studies cited here, see Gary Bouma (1973), Stan Gaede
(1977), and James Riccio (1979).

[8]One exception to this is recent research by Michael
Homola, Dean Knudson, and Harvey Marshall (1987),
which found significant differences between various
groups of Protestants and between various Roman
Catholic ethnic communities.

should continue in this state? For the Methodists in every place grow diligent and frugal; consequently they increase in goods. Hence they proportionately increase in pride, in anger, in the desire of the flesh, the desire of the eyes and the pride of life. So, although the form of religion remains, the spirit is swiftly vanishing away.

Is there no way to prevent this—this continual decay of pure religion? We ought not to prevent people from being diligent and frugal; we must exhort all Christians to gain all they can, and to save all they can; that is, in effect, to grow rich. What way then can we take, that our money not sink us into the nethermost hell? (1943: 208).

Likewise, Liston Pope (1942) found that asceticism and a theological concept of hard work in holiness sects were factors in the economic development of southern mill towns. One can see a similar phenomenon at work among Black Muslims. Ghetto blacks who were once impoverished began to have somewhat improved economic circumstances when they lived under the severe Muslim asceticism and the Islamic insistence that all work should be for the greater glory of Allah. These cases suggest that certain outlooks can be conducive to economic prosperity. However, there are many factors in the economic development of any group, and one would be foolish to maintain that any one set of beliefs is capable of single-handedly changing one's economic fortunes (Cohen 1985).

The Amish are a case in point. In Amish culture, asceticism and hard work are among the most important virtues. Clearly, they have a strong Protestant ethic. The Amish are generally pretty comfortable financially, and they usually have some savings. However, they are certainly not what one might call wealthy by normal American standards. Their refusal to use modern technology and to harness efficient forms of energy (gasoline engines, electricity, etc.) means that there are substantial limits to their productive capacity.

At the outset of the Protestant Reformation, the reformers had to establish standards for assessing the morality of social behavior. They upheld the Bible, and not the church hierarchy, as the standard against which all behavior was measured. As mentioned previously, for most Protestants, anything that was not specifically forbidden in the Bible (especially in the New Testament) was acceptable. For the followers of Jacob Amman, anything that was not expressly endorsed in the Bible was forbidden. Because the Bible does not say it is acceptable to depend on electricity, motor cars, tractors, telephones, or other such innovations, they are *verboten*. The Amish have refused to use most modern technological innovations.

So even if a group has a Protestant ethic, its members will not necessarily become highly affluent. Their access to natural resources, their access and willingness to use technology and other efficient sources of energy, and the economic opportunities available to that group within the larger social structure all affect economic development of the group and its members. No amount of asceticism and work ethic among black Americans will fully counteract the structural discrimination they experience. A profound work ethic combined with an emphasis on asceticism may contribute to affluence, but they are certainly not sufficient to bring prosperity. Box 10.1 suggests a causal model of factors that can lead to high socioeconomic status.

Although many sociologists question the effectiveness of the Lenski study—or of any contemporary empirical research—in proving or disproving the Weber thesis, the study can still be very instructive to the sociology student. First, it demonstrates how sociologists go about measuring and testing a theory in a survey method of research. Students can get some notion of how sociologists attempt to infer sets of values without asking direct questions about such abstract concepts as delayed gratification. Furthermore, Lenski's study is important in that it uncovered some other interesting correlations between religion and economic behavior.

First, Lenski found that people who were "devotional" in their religious orientation were more likely to be influenced by their faith in economic and political matters than were those who were "orthodox." Devotionalism was assessed by inquiring of the respondents whether they prayed at least once a day to ask God for personal guidance and direction. Those who answered positively were considered "devotionalists." Denominational orthodoxy was assessed by asking the following six questions:

▶ **BOX 10.1**

Model of Religious Influence on Socioeconomic Standing

Weber's thesis claims that religion may sacralize and instill certain values and attitudes that enhance high social mobility. Calvinism, he believed, led to certain values and beliefs— among them a work ethic and asceticism— that contributed to social mobility. These beliefs, he asserted, are contributing factors but are neither necessary nor sufficient in themselves to ensure upward social mobility. This path model of causality suggests a few of the variables that may influence social status either positively or negatively.

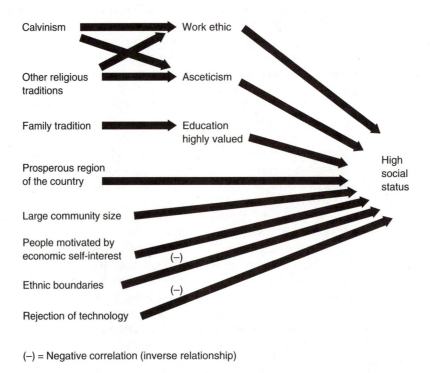

(−) = Negative correlation (inverse relationship)

1. Do you believe there is a God, or not?
2. Do you think God is like a Heavenly Father who watches over you, or do you have some other belief?
3. Do you believe that God answers people's prayers, or not?
4. Do you believe in a life after death, or not; if so, do you also believe that in the next life some people will be punished and others rewarded by God, or not?
5. Do you believe that, when they are able, God expects people to worship Him in their churches and synagogues, *every* week, or not?
6. Do you believe that Jesus was God's only Son sent into the world by God to save sinful men, or do you believe that he was simply a very good man and teacher, or do you have some other belief? (Lenski, 1963: 56).

Affirmative answers to all of these questions were necessary for a person to be considered orthodox. Orthodoxy reflects an intellectual commitment, whereas devotionalism is more behaviorally oriented (i.e., prayer). One might expect that most persons who are high on the orthodoxy measure might also be high on devotionalism, but this was not the case. Lenski found that the two varied rather independently. Although the two orientations are not logically contrary, neither are they highly correlated empirically (Lenski 1963).

Lenski found that those who were high on orthodoxy tended to compartmentalize life into discrete categories: family life, religion, economics, and so on. On the other hand, devotionalists are more likely to view religion as the lens through which all of life is understood and are therefore more likely to apply their faith to everyday life. (See illustration in Box 10.2.) Religion had much more effect on the economic and political attitudes of devotionalists than it did on the orthodox. This is

most interesting in that a person's overall world view appears more important than his or her specific beliefs.[9]

Second, Lenski attempted to measure whether religion affected people through institutional affiliation and by participation at services or through reference group factors (having most of one's friends and one's spouse from the same religious orientation). One might expect associational and communal involvement to be rather highly correlated, but the correlation was far from perfect. In fact, Lenski suggests that there was "almost no relationship" between them (1963: 24). Lenski was especially interested in those cases in which the correlation was very low: persons who attended worship services regularly and participated in the institutional life of the church but who had a majority of friends from other denominations or were married exogamously; and persons who were *not* active in the institutional church but who married endogamously and retained friendships that were religiously homogeneous. He concluded that religion may influence a person either through a formal structure or through an informal network of friends, but overall communal involvement appears to be the more important variable. However, he also found instances in which the two had differential effects—one contributing, for example, to racial tolerance and the other to racial bigotry. It is important for the student of religion to remember that religion can affect behavior and attitudes through many different channels.

Religious Ethics and Economic Action

Thus far we have pointed to unconscious or indirect ways in which religiosity affects people's economic action. But religion can also

---

[9]This is one reason I stressed the broader concept of world view in my definition of religion (see chapter 1).

affect the economic behavior of individuals directly—through "moral boycotts." In such cases, definitions of morality and immorality by religious groups are significant in that these groups use their economic clout to influence nonmembers and to coerce them into moral behavior.

In the late 1960s, the National Catholic Conference for Interracial Justice initiated an organization called Project Equality. Many Protestant churches also joined this effort and it is now an interdenominational organization. Member churches are asked to contact all companies and suppliers who do business with

---

▶ **BOX 10.2**

Narrow-Scope and Broad-Scope Religion

A person's world view can compartmentalize life into separate and discrete realms, with little sense of integration among the various areas. Religion, then, may be simply one of many areas of life—one that lacks much relevance for everyday life. Clifford Geertz (1968) calls this approach "religion with a narrow scope." Others have a more integrated outlook, in which religion gives meaning and direction to all other areas of life. This latter approach means that religion has a broad scope. The research shows that orthodox Christians tend to have narrow-scope world views, wheras devotionalists are more likely to have unitary, broad-scope world views. The *official* posture of all religious groups and denominations is that religion should have a broad scope.

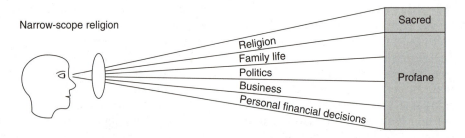

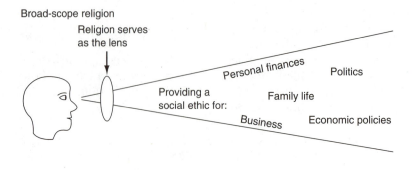

the church and ask them to develop affirmative action policies in hiring. An affirmative action policy, as originally conceived, simply requires that when there is a job opening the employer takes affirmative or positive steps to ensure that discrimination does not occur unintentionally. If an employer goes to a local employment agency when job openings occur, that employer may not be purposefully discriminating. But if there is discrimination in housing and if the employment bureau is in an all-white suburb, then only white middle-class people may find out about the opening. A more qualified candidate may fail to obtain the job due to lack of information about it. Hence, *unintentional* discrimination would have occurred, and Project Equality wants to eliminate that possibility.

In the case just given, an employer would contact not only the employment agency in that suburb, but would also notify offices in the minority sections of town. If one were seeking a new college graduate, the employer would contact not only the well-known universities that are predominantly white, but would also make a special effort to notify the placement offices at predominantly black colleges. This would ensure that qualified minorities would know about the job and would have an equal chance to apply. The most qualified candidate would then be hired. (Affirmative action is sometimes confused with job quotas or with favoritism to minority candidates. Both quotas and racial goal programs are viewed by some people as reverse discrimination.)

With the Project Equality program, if a business, service company, or supplier refuses to adopt an affirmative action program, churches cease doing business with the company and encourage church members to patronize other firms. Project Equality annually prints a *Buyer's Guide*, listing companies that have affirmative action/equal opportunity hiring policies and encourages church people to reward these companies with their business. It is difficult to establish how much economic impact this policy actually has, but use of financial resources to influence social policies is a continuing issue for churches.

Some congregations that have endowment funds have invested in certain companies so they could attend stockholder meetings and insist that the corporation no longer make certain types of weapons (nerve gas, napalm, neutron bombs, etc.) or that companies cease their cooperation with and implicit support of oppressive governments in the Third World. For example, prior to the recent democratic reforms in the Republic of South Africa it was observed that making investments in and paying taxes to that government helped stabilize the national economy of South Africa and thereby perpetuated its racist economic and political system. Some churches insisted that American corporations withdraw from investment in those countries that violate human rights (Seidman 1979). By 1986, Leon Sullivan, a black Baptist minister, had pledges from churches and church members calling for divestment in South Africa amounting to 40 billion dollars in potential investment monies (Lincoln and Mamiya 1990). In this way, churches have used their economic clout to influence social policies and to create what they believe to be a more just society. (Box 10.3 explores another inplication of religious values in international economic affairs.)

Of course, there is often disagreement about what the moral issues are. The examples above are the types of issues that more liberal congregations are likely to address, for social and economic justice is frequently defined as the central issue in Christian social ethics for many liberals. Some conservative groups have defined sexual innuendo on television to be of central import, and they have proposed boycotts against companies that sponsor shows they have defined as immoral. Other groups have focused on other issues, but the procedure is similar. Critics of this strategy for bringing change have suggested that the use of economic power as coercion and as a means of establishing policies that one considers moral is inappropriate in a pluralistic society. The procedure itself is challenged as morally questionable. Students may want to discuss whether the use of institutional resources to bring change is justifiable. Regardless of one's position, the fact remains that religious definitions of morality and the strategies of religious groups to attain a moral or "good society" have affected the economic behavior of many individuals.

In conclusion, religious orientation can affect economic behavior. There is evidence, however, that religion is more likely to affect one's behavior if it takes the form of a single, overall world view than if it represents only one of several ways of looking at things. Because their religious views permeate virtually all aspects of their lives, devotionalists are more influenced by their religious views than are those who are orthodox. Furthermore, the evidence suggests that religion influences the economic and political views of individuals more through participation in informal com-

munal networks than through participation in the formal structure. Regardless, the sacralization of specific values or outlooks may affect one's economic behavior. While one's religious perspective may not be sufficient to change one's socioeconomic position, it may contribute to such a change.

Social Class and Religious Involvement: Religion as a Dependent Variable

Whether one accepts Weber's explanation of causality, the fact remains that denominational affiliation is correlated to social class. The pattern of religious affiliation by social class is demonstrated in Table 10.1. Taken as a whole, no denomination is class-exclusive. However, at a local level, congregations tend to be more class-segregated than denominations as a whole. In other words, a large downtown Baptist church in a southern community may have a large percentage of upper- and middle-class people from that town. On the edge of town, a smaller Baptist church may be attended

---

▶ **BOX 10.3**

Religion and Global Economics

One of the key developments in the sociology of religion in the past decade has been the study of religious implications of the global system of economic interdependence. As the case of religious groups boycotting businesses investing in South Africa illustrates, religious groups can have a profound impact in international economics and politics. When religiously motivated people lobby the U.S. Congress or the Canadian Parliament to apply political or economic sanctions against other

countries, the *religious* values and attitudes in one country become an *economic* factor in another. Likewise, in certain Arab countries conservative Islamic attitudes define American consumerism as intrinsically evil. This both limits those economic markets for multinational corporations and influences international political relations between countries. The impact of religion on economics is not limited to its influence on the behaviors of individuals.

almost entirely by working- and lower-class persons. Likewise, the Congregational churches (United Church of Christ) in big cities in the northeast tend to draw the more highly educated population. But in a small town in upstate New Hampshire, where only two or three churches serve the community, the Congregationalists may draw heavily from the lower- and middle-class population. Probably no local congregation is totally class-exclusive, and some congregations are relatively well integrated in terms of class. Nevertheless, the tendency is for local congregations to be somewhat more segregated by social class than Table 10.1 indicates.

There are many reasons for the correlation between social class and denominational affiliation. We discussed one explanation in the previous section: the belief system of some denominations may enhance the members' likelihood of worldly success. A second explanation deals with the relationship of the theology to the secular order. Some theological orientations endorse the present social order as ordained by God (a modern-day version of the divine right of the king); others insist that religion has little or nothing to do with the social order and that religious ethics is concerned only with personal motives and intentions. In either of these cases, members of the privileged classes would not find their self-interests being threatened. On the other hand, some religious groups (such as the Bruderhof) define affluence as the root of evil and glorify the life of poverty and self-denial. Still others attack the social order and advocate a restructuring of the socioeconomic system (much like the radical reformation of the Anabaptists).[10] In these groups, members of the privileged

classes might find themselves very uncomfortable, whereas the lower classes would find either solace or hope for the future. In this case, class differences between denominations would be due to elective affinity; people choose a religious group that fits their own socioeconomic circumstances (Stark and Bainbridge 1985). We explore this view more thoroughly in the next chapter.

A third reason for class differentials may be a simple matter of like-seeking-like. Those of similar educational level may be drawn by common interests, common speech patterns, and other homogeneous characteristics. A highly educated person may not return to a church in which the minister demonstrates little scholarship and uses bad grammar. The visitor simply feels uncomfortable. Likewise, a person with little education may feel alienated and lost in a church where the minister delivers a scholarly sermon based on tightly argued logic. Such a sermon may seem utterly irrelevant and uninspiring to the visitor. Moreover, when people move to a new community, they sometimes join churches that are attended by their colleagues at work. This pattern of affiliation is based on the tendency to associate with people who are in some respects similar. Common socioeconomic background is one factor in this feeling that others are somehow similar.

A fourth explanation is based on this like-seeking-like concept. This view suggests that as people move from one social status to another they tend to change their religious affiliation. Hence, advocates of this explanation take a position precisely opposite of the Weberian thesis. Rather than suggesting that religious beliefs may cause social mobility, these theorists insist that changes in religious affiliation frequently *follow* changes in social status. This is so because people are more comfortable with persons of the same socioeconomic standing or because they are using religious

---

[10]For a more detailed treatment of the social ethics of specific groups or of specific eras, see Ernst Troeltsch (1931), Richard Niebuhr (1951), and George Forell (1966).

▶ **TABLE 10.1**

Socioeconomic Profiles of American Religious Groups

Religious Group	Median Annual Household Income	Percent College Graduates
Jewish	$36,000	46.7
Unitarian	$34,800	49.5
Agnostic	$33,300	36.3
Episcopalian	$33,000	39.2
Eastern Orthodox	$31,500	31.6
Congregationlist	$30,400	33.7
Presbyterian	$29,000	33.8
Disciples of Christ	$28,800	39.3
Buddhist	$28,500	33.4
Hindu	$27,800	47.0
Catholic	$27,700[†]	20.0[*]
NRMs	$27,500	40.6
No religion	$27,300	23.6
Churches of Christ	$26,600	14.6
Lutheran	$25,900	18.0
Christian Science	$25,800	33.1
Mormon	$25,700	19.2
"Protestant"	$25,700	22.1
Methodist	$25,100	21.1
Muslim	$24,700	30.4
Seventh-Day Adventist	$22,700	17.9
Assemblies of God	$22,200	13.7
"Evangelical"	$21,900	21.5
Nazarene	$21,600	12.5
Jehovah's Witnesses	$20,900	4.7
"Christian"	$20,700	16.0
Baptist	$20,600	10.4
Pentecostal	$19,400	6.9
Brethren	$18,500	11.4
Holiness	$13,700	5.0

Source: Barry A. Kosmin and Seymour P. Lackman, *One Nation Under God: Religion in Contemporary American Society.* New York: Harmony Books, 1993. © 1993 Seymour P. Lackman and Barry A. Kosmin. Reprinted by permission of the publisher.

[*]Educational levels for Roman Catholics vary substantially depending on ethnicity, with those who have been in this country longer generally ranking higher than more recent Catholic immigrants. For example, Irish Catholic had a mean educational score of 12.7 years, while Spanish-speaking Catholics had a mean educational level of 10.3 years in 1976 (Roof 1979).

[†]Income levels for Roman Catholics vary substantially depending on ethnicity, with those who have been in this country longer generally ranking higher than more recent Catholic immigrants. For example, in 1976 the mean income for English and Welsh Catholics was $12,900; for Irish Catholics it was $11,940; for Italian Catholics it was $11,275; and for Spanish-speaking Catholics it was $7,860 (Roof 1979).

affiliation as a way of reinforcing their upward social mobility. (See the discussion of religious switchers in chapter 5.)

This explanation is a controversial one. Hart Nelsen and William Snizek (1976) studied this theory of "musical pews," using data from a national sample. They concluded that there is no evidence to support the idea that denominational switching follows social mobility. Frank Newport (1979), using data from previous studies combined with new survey information from the National Opinion Research Center, insists that his evidence does support the theory that denominational switching follows social mobility. More empirical evidence is needed and perhaps a more sophisticated treatment of variables is necessary. It may well be that this explanation holds for some types of groups or for some types of people, but not for others. At this point, our tools of analysis are still too crude to make firm generalizations.

Finally, class differences in denominational affiliation may sometimes be explained by matters of history and ethnicity. In this country, the Episcopalians, Congregationalists, and Presbyterians are the denominations that have been established for the longest period of time. Christian Science—also a high-status denomination—was founded more recently, but it was founded in this country and is not a product of recent immigration. Lutherans, who occupy higher status in certain European countries, represent somewhat more recent arrivals in this country. The highest-status positions were already occupied, and the German and Scandinavian immigrants have had to work their way up the social ladder from the bottom. Persons from these ethnic backgrounds are also located in more rural areas of the United States. Hence, they tend to rank lower on such status indicators as educational level, income, and occupational prestige. Likewise, the Roman Catholic population includes many Irish, Italian, and Hispanic Americans whose immigrating ancestors date back only one or two generations. These original immigrants had to accept unskilled labor positions. Their descendants have only gradually been integrated into higher-status positions. They have not had the same period of time to accumulate family fortunes. Jews are the notable exception to this pattern. They are, for the most part, relatively recent immigrants, but they have obtained higher socioeconomic status than one might expect for fairly recent arrivals (Roof and McKinney 1987).

Perhaps even more important than denominational affiliation by social class, however, is the research that has focused on ways in which one's social class seems to affect one's style of religiosity. In chapter 1 we discussed some of the ways in which religiosity has been operationalized. Some of the early studies on religion and social class used attendance as the prime indicator of religious commitment. Because upper-class people tend to be more regular in church attendance, it appeared that the upper and middle classes were considerably more "religious" than were the lower classes. When researchers began to use multidimensional measures of religiosity, a rather different pattern emerged. Yoshio Fukuyama (1961) found that among Congregationalists, people who ranked high in socioeconomic status also scored highest for church attendance[11] and for religious knowledge (biblical teachings and the theological orientation of the denomination). On the other hand, lower-class members scored higher on devotionalism (personal religious experience, daily prayer, etc.) than did higher status Congregationalists.

---

[11]Virtually all studies in the 1950s, 1960s, and early 1970s found that church attendance was higher among those with high socioeconomic status. However, four later studies challenged this assumption—claiming that socioeconomic status has very little effect on attendance at religious services (Mueller and Johnson 1975; Davidson 1977; Alston and McIntosh 1979; Roof and McKinney 1987).

Steven Cohen (1983) reports similar differentials among Jews. Highly educated Jews were more likely to have institutional affiliation and participation at the synagogue but were less likely to observe private family rituals (Jewish devotionalism) than were lower-class Jews. Family income was also positively correlated to institutional affiliation but negatively to private family observances.

N. J. Demerath III (1965) and Rodney Stark (1972) added further insights on the relationship between social class and style of religious commitment. Demerath did an in-depth case study of one denomination (Lutheran) and followed it with survey data from four other denominations for comparison (Congregationalists, Presbyterians, Disciples of Christ, and Baptists). He began by distinguishing two types of religiosity: churchlike and sectlike. Churchlike religiosity was operationalized in terms of attendance at Sunday worship services, participation in parish activities, and involvement in secular civic organizations. (The rationale for the last one was that sectarians usually withdraw from worldly organizations and reject the current social order, whereas churchlike people viewed civic involvement as an expression of one's faith.) Sectlike commitment was operationalized in terms of the number of close friends in the congregation (communal involvement), extent to which the religion provided aid and direction for everyday living, and disapproval of the minister's participation in community affairs.[12]

---

[12]The validity of this last item as an indicator of sectlike religion may be questioned. Clergy from sectlike groups are often involved in community affairs, but affairs of a different sort than their mainline counterparts. Not many sectarian ministers would join conventional civic clubs such as the Rotarians, but they may be involved in antimilitary movements (a number of "sectarian" groups are pacifist) or in local efforts to close an X-rated movie theater.

Demerath found that within any given denomination, an individual's style of religiosity is highly correlated to his or her socioeconomic status. More important, Demerath suggests that members of different social classes who belong to the same church may be active in different ways and may have quite different needs met by the same organization. The higher a Lutheran's social status, the more likely he or she is to participate in churchlike ways. The lower the social status, the more likelihood there was of sectlike participation. The same pattern held for the other four denominations as well. Table 10.2 shows the percentages of people for each social class and in each denomination who rated high on churchlike commitment.

Stark used a somewhat different procedure. He did not begin by defining which patterns were characteristic of churchlike or sectlike commitment, but simply looked for correlations and patterns. He found that participation at religious rituals, a high degree of religious knowledge, and high involvement in voluntary church organizations and activities were strongly correlated to high socioeconomic status. He then suggested that these three dimensions of religiosity are generally indicative of churchlike commitment. On the other hand, he found that orthodoxy (actually biblical literalism), reports of having had a religious experience, personal devotionalism (such as daily prayer), communal involvement (reports that most close friends are members of the same church), ethicalism (application of religious principles to everyday life), and particularism (belief that only members of one's own denomination will be saved) are inversely related to socioeconomic status (Stark 1972). Stark notes that high-status church members participate to a greater degree in those activities that reinforce their respectability and confirm their worldly success. Lower-class persons are religiously active in ways that will offer comfort and solace and will provide compensations for one's lack of worldly success. Stark (1972) and Demerath (1965) independently conclude that differences in religiosity between the social classes are not ones of *degree* of involvement so much as ones of *kind* or *style* of involvement.[13]

Several other empirical studies using various measures of churchness and sectness have also found both churchlike participation and sectlike participation within each denomination—and have found socioeconomic status to be the critical variable affecting a member's orientation (Dynes 1955; Winter 1977).[14] Further, the bulk of empirical research on social status and religiosity suggests that persons with high status are more likely than lower-class persons to be committed at an instrumental level—through investment of time and money in the formal struc-

ture (Estus and Overington 1970). Lower-status persons are more likely than higher-status persons to be committed at the affective level— through close friendship networks.[15]

In short, expressions of religious commitment tend to be significantly affected by socioeconomic status in a variety of ways. Not only do people of different social classes tend to affiliate with different denominations, but members of the same denomination who are of different socioeconomic status tend to participate in the life of the church in different ways and for different reasons. Furthermore, the overall socioeconomic level of a local congregation affects the style of religiosity of that group,[16] and members may be affected in their religiosity as they conform to the norms of

---

[13]Those interested in the finer points of this field of research should see James Davidson (1977), Jere Cohen (1985), and Wade Clark Roof and William McKinney (1987).

[14]One study in the late 1980s indicates that the divergence in styles of religiosity between social classes seems to be lessening. Styles of religiosity may be moving in the direction of greater convergence (Roof and McKinney 1987).

---

[15]At this point, there is little evidence on differences in moral commitment—commitment to the belief system itself—because the belief systems are articulated differently. For a discussion of types or levels of commitment, see chapter 5.

[16]Predominant socioeconomic status is, of course, not the only important factor in shaping a congregation's style of religiosity. The educational background and the personality characteristics of the minister are also extremely important, and regional, denominational, and ethnic factors may have important impacts on congregational style.

▶ **TABLE 10.2**

Percentage of Those High in Churchlike Involvement

Denomination	Individual Status			
	Upper	*Middle*	*Working*	*Lower*
Congregationalists	65	62	46	34
Presbyterians	67	55	45	36
Disciples of Christ	73	63	55	42
Baptists	67	54	37	32
Lutherans	51	45	32	24

Source: N. J. Demerath III, *Social Classes in American Protestantism*. Chicago: Rand McNally, 1965: 87, 118. Used by permission.

their local congregation (Davidson 1977). Socioeconomic status is certainly not the only factor affecting one's style of religiosity, but it is an important one.

In conclusion, we might add that several recent studies indicate that the link between social class and religiosity may be weakening in the latter part of the twentieth century. Nancy Ammerman (1987) studied a fundamentalist church in New England and found it comprised largely of affluent middle-class people; Mary Jo Neitz (1987; 1990) met many lawyers and business executives at charismatic prayer group meetings in Chicago; and Stephen Warner (1988) found a substantial number of professionals among devotionalist-oriented evangelicals in California. Other scholars have also found the link of Pentecostalism and fundamentalism to lower-class status to be changing rapidly, and religious statuses within religious groups to be less tied to one's socioeconomic position in society than was true in the past (McGuire 1982; Warner 1993). The connection between socioeconomic status and style of religiosity *may* be weakening as the twentieth century comes to a close.

Summary

Religion is correlated to socioeconomic status as both dependent and independent variables. According to Weber's thesis, one's values and one's world view may contribute to one's rise or decline in the socioeconomic system. If one

is taught a sacred ethic that requires hard work and simple living, this may enhance eventual accumulation of wealth. However, other social conditions must be present for such social mobility to take place. The debate continues on the importance of a particular theological orientation in the formation of capitalism. In the modern world, the most that can be claimed is that certain religious values and perspectives may serve as *contributing* factors to upward mobility. Theological orientation is neither necessary nor sufficient.

Religion is also very much influenced by the socioeconomic circumstances of its adherents. People in the lower classes tend to have different styles of religiosity than do coreligionists of the upper classes. This variation shows up not only between denominations serving different socioeconomic groups but also between people of different socioeconomic status within the same denomination.

Religion both influences and is influenced by the socioeconomic system. At this point, the strong consensus among social scientists is that economics is the more powerful variable. In other words, a person's religiosity is significantly affected by his or her position in the stratification system. The effects of religion on the socioeconomic behavior of most people is considerably less pronounced. The Marxian perspective is that economic self-interests affect religion more than religion affects economic behavior. Much to the chagrin of many religious people, the empirical evidence tends to support this view.

CHAPTER ELEVEN

Social Stratification and Religious Ideology

In chapter 10 we began to explore the relationship between religion and socioeconomic status. But an important issue regarding religion and social status remains: How does theology serve as a social ideology appropriate to one's economic circumstances? The underlying questions are these: How is the religion of the affluent different from that of the poor? What are the social consequences of the religions of the affluent and of the disfranchised for social change or social stability? And how does the religion of the disfranchised affect the larger society? Does it always act to justify the status quo? Or, does religion sometimes inspire oppressed people to militant resistance and advocacy of change? We address these questions in this chapter.

Theology as Social Ideology

Early in this study, we discovered that one of the functions of religion is to address issues of meaning. When people experience suffering or encounter injustices, they want to know why—or why me? Why is it that the good often seem to encounter suffering and hardship, while the evil seem to flourish like the green bay tree? On the other hand, when a family member or a good friend meets tragedy or death, people sometimes question, Why couldn't it have been I? The arbitrariness of suffering causes people to want an explanation; the world should make sense—it should have some ultimate meaning. If these events do not make sense, then life somehow seems a cruel joke. Any belief system that attempts to explain the reasons for evil, suffering, and injustice by placing them in a divine master scheme is referred to as a **theodicy**.

In trying to make sense out of the world and out of human experience, religious ideologies frequently provide explanations for the inequalities that exist in the social system. Sometimes religious beliefs endorse the current social system as established under divine will. For example, the present social arrangements may be viewed as God's divine plan, or the structures of this world may be viewed as a testing ground established by God to determine the truly faithful. Alternatively, the structures of this world may be viewed as the province of an evil force (e.g., Satan). This latter view is more likely to be found among lower-class religious groups. Because lower-class persons are more likely to experience frustrations with the existing social system and to feel it is unjust, they are likely to have a rather different theodicy. Max Weber maintains that the lower their social class, the more likely people are to adhere to an otherworldly religion (1963).

The theodicies of the lower classes are essentially "theodicies of despair" or "theodicies of escape," whereas theodicies of the upper classes tend to be those of "good fortune." People who are socially oppressed and who are experiencing a great deal of suffering need some explanation of a deeper justice or a deeper meaning that will ultimately prevail. In many lower-class religious groups, financial affluence is defined as the root of avarice and as a sign of evil. Human experience is divided into worldly and spiritual realms, and attachment to the latter requires a rejection of worldly success. This rejection makes economic deprivation much easier to bear, for poverty is espoused as a noble choice; it is made a virtue. In fact, a frequent text for preachers in lower-class Christian sects is the saying by Jesus, "It is easier for a camel to go through the eye of a needle than for a rich man to enter the Kingdom of Heaven." The saying is likely to be understood literally and as applicable to the present day. (In affluent churches, this saying is often treated as a comment directed specifically at the rich young ruler Jesus was addressing or strictly at the rich people of that day and age. Its application to today's world is minimized.)

Other devices can also be used to make deprivation and suffering meaningful. When the ancient Hebrews were exiled from their homeland and were made slaves of the Babylonians, their plight seemed hopeless, and many of them felt their God had forsaken them. These people awaited a Messiah who would rescue them and take them back to their homeland. (The expectation of a Messiah was a distinctly Jewish theodicy.) The Messiah, they believed, would be a military general who would show forth the power of God with his mighty leadership. But the Messiah did not come. Eventually, a prophetic genius came along who reformulated the theodicy. He insisted that the ultimate victory would come not through military might but by the ability to endure suffering. The suffering of the Jews was part of God's master plan to provide salvation to all of humanity. The Messiah was recast as a "suffering servant." Suffering was not meaningless; indeed, it was a high calling. Release from the suffering would come in Yahweh's time—only after the divine purposes had been fulfilled. The idea of being a chosen people was preserved by being redefined. Rather than being chosen for privilege, the Jews were chosen for service. They were handpicked to be God's tools to transform the world. Jews have been persecuted and oppressed for 2,500 years, yet their theodicy of suffering has sustained them and held them together. Second Isaiah (Isaiah 40–55) was the first to articulate a theodicy for their oppression.[1]

This provides only one of many possible examples of religious groups that recast their theology and world view to fit their social circumstances. Groups that are composed of members of the privileged class also develop theodicies to justify their good fortune. As Weber puts it, "the fortunate is seldom satisfied with the fact of being fortunate. Beyond this one needs to know that one has the right to good fortune, . . . that one 'deserves' it" (1963: 107). Elizabeth Nottingham elaborates:

---

[1]Theodicies of disprivilege are discussed in more detail later, in the section on religion and minority status.

Almost equally important for a society [as a theodicy of disprivilege] is a morally acceptable explanation of its successes. Since a successful society often enjoys its worldly accomplishments at the expense of less fortunate peoples, its members are frequently driven to find a moral formula that will not only provide positive meaning for their own good fortune but also will help diminish any guilt they feel about the less happy situation of other groups (1971: 126).

One reason for differential denominational affiliation by social class may be that the theodicy of one denomination may have a better fit with the needs and concerns of those in certain circumstances. Weber referred to the tendency for members of certain social and economic groups to be drawn to certain religious beliefs as "elective affinity" (1946). Hence, Weber himself recognized that during the reformation many people whose fortunes were rising may have been drawn to Calvinism. John Calvin's emphasis on individualism and his refusal to condemn usury as intrinsically evil may have attracted upwardly mobile people. This could be seen as a modification by Weber of his earlier suggestion that Calvinist beliefs caused upward mobility. No doubt Weber would assert that both processes are at work; upward social mobility and Calvinistic beliefs were mutually reinforcing.

As we found in chapter 3, Karl Marx believed that economic self-interests are the driving forces of social behavior. He was convinced that the economic self-interests of the rich—those who own the industries and corporations—caused them to develop a religious view that justified their wealth and alleviated any sense of guilt. Because those with wealth and power can do much to control the belief systems of the society, Marx viewed religion as a system that sacralized the current forms of inequality and even oppression. For conflict theorists, theodicies of privilege are not so innocent as to be called an "elective affinity." They are, instead, insidious tools of the "haves" that "mystify" the true causes of inequality and serve to keep an unfair social system in place.

Whether the theodicy of privilege simply attracts the affluent because of compatibility with their own circumstances (a functional perspective) or is a consciously developed instrument of the wealthy to help them maintain their privileged position (a conflict theory view), the theologies' virtues and vices of the different socioeconomic groups do tend to be different. Liston Pope (1942) found that for lower-class Protestant mill workers in North Carolina the world is a battlefield where God and Satan struggle for each individual soul. The sacrificed "blood of Jesus" and Bible reading by the faithful are the critical elements that allow God to be victorious in any given situation. Richard Niebuhr (1957) has further pointed out that the lower-class concept of the deity is one of a comforter, protector, and savior. The role of God is to "take care of His people."

The chief decisions that control the lives of unskilled laborers occur at a level that they cannot control directly. They are often bystanders as the owners of corporations close plants, move factories to new locations, and make other decisions that profoundly shape the lives of wage laborers. Likewise, Pope found that mill workers viewed their role in the supernatural realm as one of observer, cheerleader, and marginal supporter. The battle is viewed as one between superpowers (God and the devil), and it is largely the action of a third party (the sacrifice of Jesus) that will determine the outcome. This passive-observer posture is typical of lower-class religiosity, especially for those groups stressing a theodicy of escape. A content analysis of hymns used in lower-class congregations illustrates the emphasis on dependency, alienation from this world, and blood sacrifice. Notable also is the negative concept of human character and of one's self evaluation ("such a worm as I"). (See Box 11.1 for examples.)[2]

According to Pope, alienation from upper-class values was also expressed in lower-class concepts of immorality, for upper-class forms

of entertainment are typically viewed as vices. Niebuhr also stressed the social ethic inherent in lower-class expressions of Christianity. It is not only the individual who needs saving but also the whole social system. The current social arrangements are often viewed as unjust and inequitable; hence, they are in need of redemption and transformation. In fact, sin is not just thought of as wrong actions but as a "state of being" that is all-pervasive. Sin is a depraved condition that infects both the individual soul and the fabric of society. Today this seems especially true of black churches and

---

[2]Of course, the hymnals of the various denominations carry many of the same hymns. In analysis of differences in hymns, two factors can be viewed as significant: the character of hymns that are *not* common to upper- and lower-class hymnals and differences between denominations in the popularity of those hymns that *are* common to all of the hymnals.

▶ **BOX 11.1**

Hymns in Churches of the Less Affluent

In lower-class and working-class churches, the hymns frequently depict the world as a place of suffering and hardship, and the inherent worth of the individual is viewed rather dimly ("Naught of good that I have done"; "a worm such as I"). Sin is viewed as a state of being rather than as a specific action. A major focus is comfort in this world combined with hope for the next. Finally, the decisive action which determines one's changes is not accomplished by the individual, but by some external force or action (the sacrificial blood of Jesus).

"Nothing but the Blood"

What can wash away my sin? Nothing but
   the blood of Jesus;
What can make me whole again? Nothing
   but the blood of Jesus.
Oh! precious is the flow That makes me
   white as snow;
No other fount I know, Nothing but the
   blood of Jesus.

Nothing can for sin atone, Nothing but
   the blood of Jesus;
Naught of good that I have done, Nothing

but the blood of Jesus.

Oh! precious is the flow That makes me
   white as snow;
No other fount I know, Nothing but the
   blood of Jesus.

This is all my hope and peace, Nothing
   but the blood of Jesus;
This is all my righteousness, Nothing but
   the blood of Jesus.
Oh! precious is the flow That makes me
   white as snow;
No other fount I know, Nothing but the
   blood of Jesus.
(Baptist hymn)

"A Gathering in the Sky"

There'll be a great gathering in the sky
When all of God's children get home.
We'll join the happy millions as they sing
There around the great white throne;
I'm speaking of a big tent meetin'
Where we never shall say good-bye.
I'm longin' for the day
When I hear my savior say
There's a gathering in the sky.

the churches of the very poor. It is less true of white working-class churches.

Another characteristic of lower-class churches, pointed out by Niebuhr, is a high degree of emotionalism in the worship services. One explanation of this is that religious liturgies may provide an emotional outlet for frustrations and humiliations experienced in the society. Weston LaBarre discusses the extreme emotionalism in snake-handling churches of the Appalachian hills. The members are impoverished, many having only a few years of formal education. Some are illiterate. Although their religious life involves shouting, dancing, seizures, and trances, these people are not more emotional in everyday life than any other Americans. LaBarre comments that for these poor folks of rural Tennessee and Kentucky, "their church is the only place where they can freely and spontaneously feel and act out their feelings" (1962: 174).

In the upper classes, economic prosperity is defined as a blessing of God or even as a sign of divine favor. Moreover, members of the upper classes are accustomed to controlling their own destinies. Their outlook stresses individual accomplishment, a positive assessment of their ability to change things in this world, and a high valuation of individual

One by one we passed through the valley dim,
Our load seems hard to bear;
But I'm going to a great reunion,
Where people's not afraid of prayer.
There'll be a lot of old time singing,
Somewhere up there on high.
It seems I can hear them saying
There's a gathering in the sky.
(Rural Appalachian hymn)

"Remember Me"

Alas! and did my Savior bleed? And did my Sov'reign die?
Help me, dear Savior, Thee to own, And ever faithful be;
Would He devote that sacred head, For such a worm as I?
And when Thou sittest on Thy throne, Dear Lord, remember me.

Was it for crimes that I have done, He hung upon the tree?
Help me, dear Savior, Thee to own, And ever faithful be;
Amazing pity! Grace unknown! And love beyond degree!

And when Thou sittest on Thy throne,
Dear Lord, remember me.
(Nazarene hymn)

"No One Understands Like Jesus"

No one understands like Jesus, He's friend beyond compare;
Meet Him at the throne of mercy, He is waiting for you there.
No one understands like Jesus, When the days are dark and grim:
No one is so dear as Jesus—Cast your ev'ry care on Him.

No one understands like Jesus, Ev'ry woe He sees and feels;
Tenderly He whispers comfort, And the broken heart He heals.
No one understands like Jesus, When the days are dark and grim;
No one is so dear as Jesus—Cast your ev'ry care on Him.
(Country-and-western hymn used in independent Baptist and Methodist sects)

Religions of the affluent tend to be very orderly and decorous in their ritual (high church), and the theology is very logical or cognitively oriented (Apollonian). The formal garb and demeanor of Pope Paul VI and Athenagores (Patriarch of the Greek Orthodox Church) in this photograph illustrates this pattern. The religious ritual of the disfranchised is more often spontaneous or lacking in a formal order (low church), and the appeal is more emotional and expressive (Dionysian) than logical—rational. (Ara Guler/Magnum.)

The photograph above depicts a worship service of Appalachian snake handlers, a sect of very poorly educated and impoverished Americans located in the hills of Kentucky, West Virginia, and Tennessee. While worshipers pass copperheads and rattlesnakes back and forth or drape them around their bodies during worship, others usually sing, dance, play instruments, or pray "in tongues" (glossolalia). This photograph is of Rev. C.H. Bunn in a Durham, North Carolina, worship service. (Charles H. Cooper.)

initiative. In fact, Niebuhr suggests that the American middle and upper classes[3] character-ize the deity as "energetic activity" and as a

---

[3]Niebuhr focused on the characteristics of what he called the middle-class churches—but because he was juxtaposing them against the lower-class churches, it is clear that he was describing the religious tendencies of all nonpoor—including both middle and upper classes.

being who expects the same sort of productive activity from humanity. "The conception of God which prevails in bourgeois faith is that of dynamic will" (Niebuhr 1957: 84). This set of values is vividly illustrated by the hymns that are sung in upper- and upper-middle class churches (see samples in Box 11.2).

Equally important is the way in which conventional secular norms and values are

▶ **BOX 11.2**

Popular Hymns in Affluent Denominations

In upper- and middle-class churches, the hymns frequently express a positive value of this-worldly activity, an affirmation of individual self-worth, a high valuation of individual initiative and accomplishment, and a sense that persons are in charge of their own destinies. In one of these hymns, Jesus is depicted as an *example* to humankind rather than as a bloodied sacrificial Lamb. Furthermore, the saints of God are depicted in one hymn as common folks rather than as a highly committed elect.

"O Brother Man, Fold to Thy Heart"

O brother man, fold to thy heart thy
    brother;
Where pity dwells, the peace of God is
    there;
To worship rightly is to love each other,
Each smile a hymn, each kindly deed a
    prayer.

Follow with reverent steps the great
    example
Of him whose holy work was doing good:
So shall the wide earth seem our Father's
    temple,
Each loving life a psalm of gratitude.
(Congregational hymn)

"I Sing a Song of the Saints of God"

I sing a song of the saints of God
Patient and brave and true,
Who foiled and fought and lived and died
For the Lord they loved and knew
And one was a doctor, and one was a
    queen,
And one was a shepherdess on the green:
They were all of them saints of God,
And I mean, God helping, to be one too.

They loved their Lord so dear, so dear,
And his love made them strong;

And they followed the right, for Jesus'
    sake,
The whole of their good lives long.
And one was a soldier, and one was a
    priest,
And one was slain by a fierce wild beast:
And there's not any reason, no, not the
    least,
Why I shouldn't be one too.

They lived not only in ages past,
There are hundreds of thousands still:
The world is bright with the joyous saints
Who love to do Jesus' will.
You can meet them in school or in lanes,
    or at sea,
In church, or in trains, or in shops, or at
    tea;
For the saints of God are just folk like me,
And I mean to be one too.
(Episcopal hymn)

"Rise Up, O Men of God"

Rise up, O men of God!
Have done with lesser things;
Give heart and soul and mind and
    strength
To serve the King of kings.

Rise up, O men of God!
His Kingdom tarries long;
Bring in the day of brotherhood
And end the night of wrong.

Rise up, O men of God!
The Church for you doth wait,
Her strength unequal to her task:
Rise up, and make her great!

Lift high the cross of Christ!
Tread where His feet have trod.
As brothers of the Son of Man,
Rise up, O men of God.
(Presbyterian hymn)

embraced in upper-class churches. Pope points out that in the mill town he studied, the concepts of sin in the affluent uptown churches emphasize failure to pay one's debts, participating in "shady business activities," failure to live up to one's contracts or agreements, and lack of involvement in social and civic obligations. Pope also found that upper-class church members were more likely to view religion as a specialized sphere of life. Religion is generally viewed as a good and leavening force in society, but upper-class citizens believed that religious organizations should not meddle in political or economic matters.[4]

Niebuhr also pointed to the narrowing of the scope of religiosity among the affluent, indicating a transformation in the concept of Christian morality. In the process, the conception of sin is changed in a very fundamental sense—a sense much more important than simply a matter of upper-class churches defining different behaviors as sinful. Whereas the lower-class churches focus on sin as a state of being, the middle-class churches limit their concept to the plural "sins"—specific actions or personal characteristics. In the middle classes, "sin is not so much a state of soul as a deed or a characteristic; it is not so much the evil with which the whole social life and structure is infected as it is the personal failure of the individual" (Niebuhr 1957: 85).

In middle- and upper-class churches, individuals are encouraged to cultivate a sense of

self-worth and self-esteem; members do not often sing on Sunday morning about an Amazing Grace that "saved a *wretch* like me" or about how the blood of Jesus was shed "for a *worm* such as I." Such negative self-images are characteristic of lower-class hymnology where the conception of sin is more pervasive. The upper-class churches are likely to respond positively to such theologians as Harvey Cox when he writes of sin: "I believe a careful examination of Biblical sources will indicate that humanity's most debilitating proclivity is *not* pride. It is *not* the attempt to be more than human. Rather it is sloth, the unwillingness to be everything humanity was intended to be" (1964: xi).

As one reviews the hymns in Boxes 11.1 and 11.2, one can see this difference in emphasis. These distinctions are not a categorical or exclusive difference between upper- and lower-class churches. Clearly, there is wide variation of religious expression and theology within denominations and between persons of the same social class. Niebuhr and Pope describe trends and attempt to make us aware of the fact that socioeconomic status does affect religiosity in important ways.

The specific issues have changed since Niebuhr and Pope published their findings in the mid-twentieth century, but differences continue between the churches of the privileged and those of the lower and working classes. In the United States, the churches of the less affluent are also those that are normally identified as "conservative churches." They include Southern Baptists, Churches of Christ, Nazarenes, Pentecostal and Holiness sects, Assemblies of God, Churches of God, Adventists, Jehovah's Witnesses, and miscellaneous evangelicals and fundamentalist groups. Conservative white Christians tend to define the moral issues of our day as secular humanism, which includes the ban on prayer in the schools, the teaching of evolution (and not creationism) in the schools; changing roles of

---

[4]As we noted earlier, Gerhard Lenski found the same pattern in his study of religion in Detroit: upper-class people were more likely to be theologically orthodox and to categorize religion as a realm separate from economics and politics. Lower-class persons were more likely to be devotionalists and were more likely to apply their religion to everyday life. The sociology student should be cognizant, however, that this generalization refers to a statistically significant difference that exists between the groups; there is clearly not a categorical difference between the classes in these matters.

women; the new morality (which includes nonmarital sexual behavior), legalization of abortion, and tolerance of homosexuality and of "homosexual rights"; increases in the divorce rate; and tolerance of pornography.

The most affluent churches in the United States are also those that are most theologically and ethically liberal: Unitarian, Episcopalian, United Church of Christ, and Presbyterian. (Methodist, Lutheran, Disciples of Christ, Northern Baptist, and reformed churches serve as a middle-class buffer and are often referred to collectively as "moderate Protestants.") The moral issues of our day for these churches—at least as identified by their clergy and their official denominational boards and agencies—tend to be war and peace issues; protection of the environment; social justice (especially the elimination of institutionalized discrimination against women and minorities); and the lack of tolerance of those who are different, including those from other cultures, those with different sexual orientations, and those with different definitions of morality. Pluralism and tolerance seem to be the central moral themes of the churches of privilege in the latter decades of the twentieth century (Roof and McKinney 1987).

The bar graphs in Figure 11.1 illustrate the divergence in attitudes toward the "new morality" and toward "tolerance" of civil liberties. The measurement of civil liberties here specifically assessed attitudes toward atheists, while the new morality was measured in terms of support for unrestricted legal abortions, permissive attitudes toward nonmarital sexual relationships, and nonjudgmental attitudes toward sexual relations between two adults of the same sex. On both graphs, a score of zero (at the center of the graph) represents the national norm. Scores to the right represent permissive (liberal) attitudes, and those to the left represent restrictive (conservative) attitudes. The differences of opinion shown in the figure reflect variations in definitions of the "real" issues of our day.

The churches of the less affluent define moral relativism as evil. They stress absolutism and obedience to rules. Of course, we might acknowledge that people in lower- and working-class jobs usually find that obeying rules of the workplace and adhering to the instructions of the employer or supervisor are qualities that are central to success on the job. Lack of conformity can have serious consequences, and parents socialize their children to develop those attitudes and behaviors that they believe will serve their children well in life (Bowles and Gintis 1976; McLeod 1987). Further, if one works in an occupation where brute strength is essential and often gets the job done, one may look for clear, decisive, and forceful solutions to religious problems as well (Batson and Ventis 1982).

For the churches of the affluent, relativity is valued, and lack of tolerance of other perspectives or values is condemned. Those forces that limit individual opportunity (e.g., institutional racism and sexism) and curb individual freedom in decision making are more frequently viewed as evil or as evidences of a sinful world. In the churches of the well educated and the well heeled, conventionalism for its own sake is often shunned.

It is important to note that many of the people in these churches are paid to be divergent thinkers—to be creative and to solve problems. They often manage organizations and are frequently rule makers. They will not do well in their fields if they merely obey rules. They must respect divergent or nonconformist thinking because creativity and innovation are often necessary to solve new problems. Acknowledgment of ambiguity and utilization of careful analysis of problems are essential (Batson and Ventis 1982; Bowles and Gintis 1976). It is not surprising then that their conception of good and evil embraces tolerance of differences and condemns rigidity, absolutism, and conventionalism. These people also are self-conscious about socializing their children to develop those characteristics that they believe will help them in the world of work. Their experience tells them that critical thinking, creativity, and even a streak of independence are valuable characteristics.[5]

Social class variations are found among other world religions as well. For example, Hinduism in the upper classes of India conforms much more to the official religion of that faith; it is monotheistic and stresses concepts of transmigration of souls (reincarnation). The lower classes have a sort of Hindu folk religion, which is polytheistic. Lower-class Hindus tend to identify Hindu statues as gods in themselves (rather than as symbols), and they believe in heaven and hell rather than in reincarnation. In fact, in some areas, the folk Hinduism of the lower classes can hardly be recognized as Hinduism at all (Noss 1949).

In each society where members of several social classes share a common religion, the faith tends to be modified and reinterpreted to fit the needs and the values of each socioeconomic group. It is difficult to say which socioeconomic group is most faithful to the religious teachings. In the United States, various studies have shown that upper-class church members tend to have much more accurate knowledge of the official teachings. However, lower-class members tend to be more willing to apply their faith to everyday life—including all realms. Perhaps this is why Ernst Troeltsch insisted that the "sects" of the lower classes and the "churches" of the upper classes each accurately depicted certain biblical teachings and core themes while they each distorted

other central concepts. The important point for our purposes is to recognize that one's social status and one's economic self-interests do tend to affect one's theodicy and hence one's world view and one's style of being religious. As Box 11.3 points out, the theodicy of a religious group and the social conditions in a society can also affect the spread of a religion into that society.

Of course, this discussion would be incomplete if we pointed merely to economic self-interest as a determinant of religious ideologies. An important and interesting phenomenon in today's world is the fact that many denominations whose members are affluent have directly and rather aggressively challenged the structures of inequality and privilege. For example, Congregationalists, Presbyterians, Methodists, Episcopalians, and Catholics all have commissions or task forces on racism, poverty, and social inequities. These task forces do not just attack the problem at an individual level; they challenge the very structure of society and point to systemic causes of poverty and racism. They issue statements calling for change—sometimes for radical change—in the basic social and economic structures of society.

Many of the liberal positions taken by the National Council of Churches and by various denominational boards, of course, have not been supported by a majority of the lay constituencies of the churches (Hadden 1970; Jenkins 1977). These controversial policies have been formulated and approved by highly trained professionals who are insulated from direct contact with conservative laity. Craig Jenkins (1977) suggests that because these religious professionals are not paid in proportion to their level of training their major sense of occupational satisfaction comes from their sense of mission—the sense that they are involved in a moral issue of great importance and that they are making a significant contribution to its resolution. The fact that they

---

[5]The middle-class churches (including moderate Protestants and Roman Catholics) include professionals, managers, and self-employed persons along with laborers.

▶ **FIGURE 11.1**

Social Attitudes of Members of Various Religious Groups

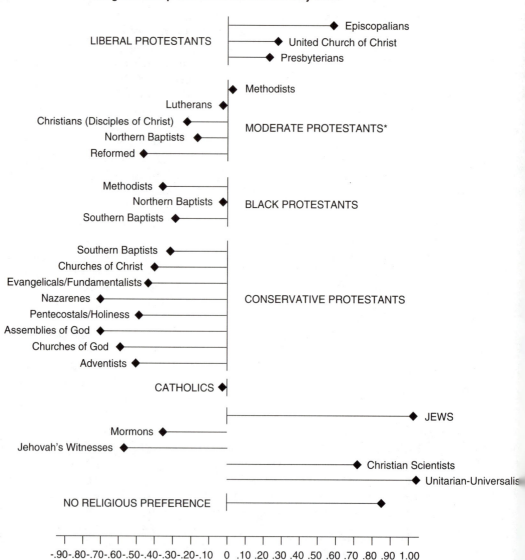

Religious Group Scores on the New Morality Scale

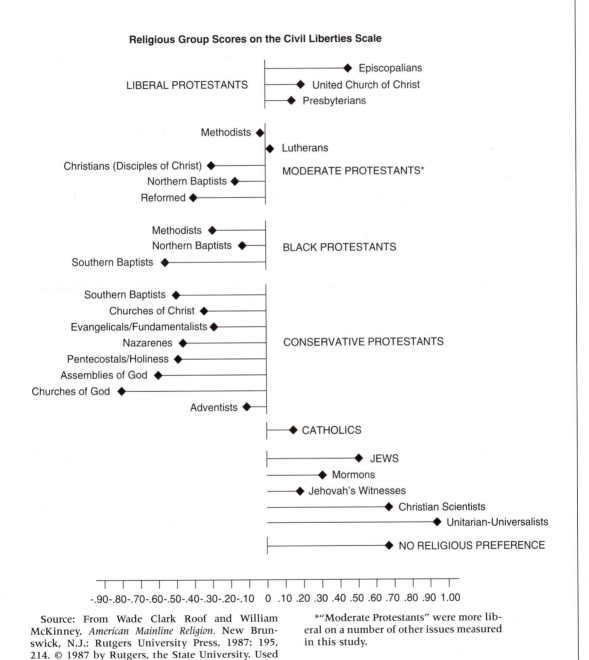

Religious Group Scores on the Civil Liberties Scale

LIBERAL PROTESTANTS
◆ Episcopalians
◆ United Church of Christ
◆ Presbyterians

Methodists ◆
◆ Lutherans
Christians (Disciples of Christ) ◆
MODERATE PROTESTANTS*
Northern Baptists ◆
Reformed ◆

Methodists ◆
Northern Baptists ◆   BLACK PROTESTANTS
Southern Baptists ◆

Southern Baptists ◆
Churches of Christ ◆
Evangelicals/Fundamentalists ◆
Nazarenes ◆   CONSERVATIVE PROTESTANTS
Pentecostals/Holiness ◆
Assemblies of God ◆
Churches of God ◆
Adventists ◆

◆ CATHOLICS

◆ JEWS
◆ Mormons
◆ Jehovah's Witnesses
◆ Christian Scientists
◆ Unitarian-Universalists

◆ NO RELIGIOUS PREFERENCE

-.90 -.80 -.70 -.60 -.50 -.40 -.30 -.20 -.10 0 .10 .20 .30 .40 .50 .60 .70 .80 .90 1.00

Source: From Wade Clark Roof and William McKinney, *American Mainline Religion*. New Brunswick, N.J.: Rutgers University Press, 1987: 195, 214. © 1987 by Rutgers, the State University. Used with permission.

*"Moderate Protestants" were more liberal on a number of other issues measured in this study.

work for causes that are *not* in their own self-interest is part of their professional identity and serves to enhance their self-esteem. Because these officials are somewhat removed from the local congregations and have a good deal of autonomy, they are able to develop programs that may not be supported by their affluent and often conservative constituency.

However, bureaucratic control by liberal clergy is only part of the reason that denomi-

national boards of middle-class churches have championed causes of the poor, for there are also many relatively affluent church members who are highly supportive of programs—denominationally sponsored or otherwise—that challenge the status quo. This concern for the disprivileged among affluent congregations appears to be stimulated by religious teachings. The prophets of the Bible consistently called for social justice as the primary

---

▶ **BOX 11.3**

Theodicies, Social Conditions, and the Spread of a Religion to Other Cultures

The ability of a religion to spread to other cultures may be affected by the nature of its theodicy. Most religions in the world are limited to a particular tribe or nation of people. The theodicy is articulated in terms of what is good and bad solely for that one group. The chosen people imagery of the ancient Hebrews (prior to Second Isaiah) tended to view good and evil strictly in terms of the fortunes of their own group. This highly ethnocentric view was repeated in the American doctrine of Manifest Destiny in the nineteenth century. Many Americans held the view that it was the divine will that the United States dominate "underdeveloped people" (such as Native Americans) in order to "civilize" them. This doctrine justified incredible exploitation of Native Americans in this country and tragic colonialism abroad. The ideology obviously was only intended for one group, Anglo-Americans. The earlier English doctrine of "white man's burden" (the responsibility of whites to "take care of" nonwhite people who supposedly could not take care of themselves) is another example of a secularized theodicy.

Religions that focus on tribal ancestors or that define good and evil solely in terms of the self-interests of one nation are not likely to spread and become world religions (ones that are found around the world and in a variety of cultures). Only when the theodicy addresses conditions common to all of humanity will the religion be acceptable in other cultures. The sense of universalism—the idea that the victory over pain, suffering, injustice, and death is appropriate and available for all people—is a first step in a religion diffusing to other cultures. For Christianity, this was implemented by Saint Paul. But even after the religion is articulated in universalistic terms, its spread will be affected by the compatibility of the religious outlook with the values and outlooks in the host culture. One factor in this compatibility is the economic circumstances of the group in question. If the people are impoverished, oppressed, disfranchised, or otherwise in despair, a theodicy of escape is much more likely to take hold. If the people in question are affluent or are otherwise comfortable with their position and their circumstances, a theodicy of despair will not likely have great appeal. The spread of any religion to other cultures is limited in part by the fit between its theodicy and the social conditions of the people hearing the message.

indicator of true religious expression, and this theme is frequently developed in the adult education materials of the Catholic Church and most mainline Protestant denominations. James Wood (1981) has found that congregations will often act collectively in ways that members would reject individually. This is largely because the clergy are able to call on beliefs that are commonly held but that do not coincide with the self-interests of the members. In the context of a group that they view as important, these members will support policies and actions that they might otherwise oppose.

An ethical or prophetic theme is also central to the Reform branch of Judaism. Although Jews are generally among the more affluent members of American society, they have often championed the cause of blacks and other minorities. For example, Jews were instrumental in founding the National Association for the Advancement of Colored People (NAACP) and the National Urban League, two organizations that have had crucial roles in fighting for equal rights for African Americans.

Likewise, migrant farm workers (predominantly poor Mexican Americans) have received support from affluent Christian and Jewish congregations, which send financial aid to the United Farm Workers and encourage church members to participate in boycotts of grapes, lettuce, and other products. The boycotts end only after wages are increased, conditions improved, and a union contract is signed. However, this usually means increases in the cost of the produce. In other words, affluent church members knowingly boycott goods with the ultimate result that they must pay higher prices. Such behavior is not in the narrow self-interests of these affluent individuals, yet they persist in this behavior because they are convinced that it is the moral thing to do.

The point I wish to make is that while the theology of a group has a tendency to be shaped by the group's economic circumstances and self-interests, the causal relationship can run the other way. Theological teachings can cause people to behave in ways that one might not expect from looking only at their socioeconomic circumstances. Religious teachings can become a tool for justifying one's self-interests, or they may cause one to advocate positions that run counter to one's own economic interests. The reasons for this lie in theodicies that people adopt. In the following section, we will see that a theodicy may mobilize people to action, or it may encourage accommodation and passivity.

Religion and Minority Status

Is Religion an Opiate for the Oppressed?

A good deal of recent sociological research has focused on the religion of the disprivileged. This has been stimulated by a debate over the role of religion for the poor: Does it act as an opiate of the masses, or does it inspire the dispossessed to militancy? Karl Marx maintained the former, that religion gave the poor a feeling of solace and a hope of compensation so that they would not rebel. They were, in essence, drugged. Those who hold to this position insist that religion serves as a tool of control for the dominant economic class and ethnic group. Critics have maintained that when European missionaries went to regions that were later colonized, they had the Bible while the natives had the land. When the missionaries left, the natives had the Bible, and the Europeans had the land (Marx 1967). Although examples of this view that religion is a tool of exploitation abound, they neither provide proof nor establish causality.

Other researchers point to contrary data, such as the facts that most civil rights leaders have been members of the clergy and that as many as 60 percent of the members of the

Congress of Racial Equality (a civil rights group) are weekly church attenders. Many historical analyses have also found that black religion was frequently a motivating force in slave revolts, for religion asserted the intrinsic human worth of slaves (Lincoln and Mamiya 1990; Wilmore 1972). Scholars from several disciplines have used a variety of research methods to clarify the relationship between religion and activism regarding social injustices. Our treatment in this section focuses on the function of religion in minority groups—specifically ethnic minorities.[6]

One landmark empirical study of the effects of religion on blacks in the United States was conducted by Gary Marx (1967). Using a sample survey method of research, Marx discovered that blacks who were members of higher-status (and predominantly white) denominations were more likely to be militant in their civil rights positions than were those from lower-class churches or sects (including exclusively black churches and sects). A militant black was defined as one who actively and consistently opposed discrimination and segregation.[7] Percentages of blacks who were militant for each denomination were as follows: Episcopalian, 43 percent; United Church of Christ, 42 percent; Presbyterian, 36 percent;

Catholic, 36 percent; Methodist, 28 percent; Baptist, 25 percent; and sects and cults, 15 percent (Marx 1967: 99). For most scholars, the fact that blacks in lower-class churches were more passive was not really unexpected; but the evidence that blacks in *entirely black congregations* were more passive than blacks in predominantly white congregations was something of a surprise to many sociologists.

Gary Marx also correlated several measures of religiosity to civil rights militance. He found that infrequent church attendance and indifference to religion were positively correlated with militancy. Eighteen percent of those who attended church more than once a week were militant, while 32 percent who attended less than once a year were activists (Marx 1967: 101). When asked how important religion is to the person, 22 percent of those who said "extremely important" were militant, while 62 percent of those who answered "not at all important" were militant (Marx 1967: 100). Marx also found that orthodoxy was inversely related to militancy.[8] When he combined these factors into an overall index of religiosity, he found a negative relationship between religiosity and militance. Furthermore, the finding held even when he kept certain key variables constant: age, sex, denomination, and region of the country in which the respondent was raised (see Table 11.1). Marx concluded that there apparently is an "incompatibility between piety and protest."

Seymour Lipset, by doing a cross-cultural political analysis, has come to a similar conclusion but offers an added dimension to Gary Marx's investigation. He maintains that rigid fundamentalism and dogmatism are based on

---

[6]The sociologist uses the term *minority* to refer to groups that have less power to control their destiny than do others. It does not mean the group is necessarily smaller in numbers. (Blacks constitute three-fourths of the population of the Republic of South Africa, but they are still referred to as a minority group.) In the United States, women, homosexuals, the disabled, and the elderly are often referred to by sociologists as minority groups. In suggesting that we will be focusing on ethnic minorities, I wish to make clear that we will not be treating these other groups in this section.

[7]Gary Marx asked seven questions to determine attitudes toward civil rights policy. Only those who answered with activist responses to at least six of the questions were considered militant. Those who gave activist responses on three, four, or five questions were classified as "moderates." Those who took activist responses on two or fewer were called "conservatives."

[8]The way in which Marx operationalized orthodoxy may be open to some question. He used three items to measure orthodoxy: having no doubt about the existence of God, about the existence of the devil, and about the existence of the afterlife. The second of these is not accepted by all Christian denominations as a central tenet of faith or as "orthodox."

the same underlying personality characteristics, attitudes, and dispositions as political radicalism. In fact, he insists that the most radical political movements often have developed from seedbeds of religious fanaticism. However, he also points out that religious fanaticism and political fanaticism tend to serve as functional alternatives; one usually finds only one or the other at any given time (Lipset 1960: 107–8). In this respect, his finding supports that of Marx. Lipset's study adds a new insight, however, because of its diachronic (historical) methodology. He found that in certain circumstances religious groups

▶ **TABLE 11.1**

Militancy Related to Religiosity by Age, Sex, Place of Upbringing, and Denomination (percent militant)

	Very Religious		Quite Religious		Not Very Religious		Not at All Religious	
	%	N	%	N	%	N	%	N
Age:								
18–29	20	(25)	28	(110)	35	(55)	43	(37)
30–44	22	(54)	31	(161)	37	(59)	53	(58)
45–59	21	(63)	21	(117)	24	(33)	52	(21)
60+	13	(67)	11	(96)	26	(19)	*	
Sex:								
Women	18	(133)	21	(286)	32	(76)	42	(38)
Men	20	(76)	28	(199)	33	(90)	52	(86)
Where raised:								
Deep South	16	(122)	19	(255)	25	(61)	38	(29)
Border states	29	(49)	28	(104)	31	(42)	54	(35)
Non-South	16	(38)	32	(126)	41	(63)	60	(52)
Denomination:								
Episcopalian, Presbyterian, or Congregationalist	17	(12)	39	(23)	46	(13)	58	(12)
Catholic	10	(10)	31	(49)	40	(20)	54	(28)
Methodist	35	(23)	20	(76)	36	(28)	50	(12)
Baptist	17	(161)	23	(325)	30	(101)	46	(68)

Source: Gary Marx, *Protest and Prejudice: A Study of Belief in the Black Community.* New York: Harper & Row, 1967, © 1967 by Anti-Defamation League of B'nai B'rith. Reprinted by permission of HarperCollins Publishers, Inc.

Note: The percentage in each category represents those in that category who are militant. For example, of those who are between the ages of 18 and 29 and are "very religious," 20 percent are militant. Of those respondents who are between the ages of 18 and 29 and are "not at all religious," 43 percent are militant. The number in parentheses is the number of respondents in that category.

*Three out of six respondents scored as militant.

may be the spawning ground for political militancy, but in the process of development, these militant groups frequently become less religious (at least in the traditional sense of the word). The sample survey method used by Marx would not indicate this type of pattern, for it focused on attitudes at one given time period.

Eric Lincoln and Lawrence Mamiya (1990) also point out that regardless of the belief system, African American religious structures have enhanced resistance to subjugation. They insist that churches can empower people simply by establishing stable institutions, fostering networks, and forging a sense of common identity in suppressed peoples. Regardless of the intent of the religious group, those interested in change are able to use the networks and sense of common interest to mobilize a social movement. Since religious bodies were the first black organizations locally and the first national institutions, they contributed to social activism and sense of potency irrespective of intent. Religious institutions spawned various types of protest organizations by providing networks, leadership training in organizational management, and an overall sense of organizational competence. This sort of contribution by religion to the civil rights movement is not assessed by Gary Marx's survey research.

Other sociologists have challenged Gary Marx's findings more directly by questioning the accuracy of his data on black religion. Follow-up studies have indicated a much more varied effect of black religiosity. Hart Nelsen, Thomas Madron, and Raytha Yokley (1975) have provided empirical data that demonstrate that black religion sometimes does stimulate social change. In two other studies, Larry Hunt and Janet Hunt (1977) and Hart Nelsen and Anne Nelsen (1975) found that, regardless of denominational affiliation, blacks who are churchlike in their religiosity are more likely to be inspired to militancy than

are blacks who are sectlike. When this variable is held constant, the inverse relationship between militancy and church attendance disappears. Hans Baer (1984) points out that even these analyses deal crudely with the data, for "sectarian" movements themselves are not all the same. Some black "sects" are highly militant, while others—such as the black spiritual movement—encourage passivity. A more in-depth understanding of the world view or the theodicy of a subjugated group is necessary before one can predict passivity or militance.[9]

Theodicies and Levels of Activism

The world view of many sectarian groups is otherworldly. The reality or at least the importance of this world is denied except for its function as a testing ground. Only the faithful will be saved and will reach heaven in the afterlife; only the true believers will have "pie in the sky in the sweet by and by" (as it is sometimes referred to affectionately by believers and derisively by skeptics). This afterlife experience is expected to commence for each individual immediately after death. This sort of otherworldly religion is frequently associated with passivity in this-worldly affairs. Members of the dominant social groups are usually more than happy to have their subordinates believe that vindication will come only after death. Slave owners in this country often had that sort of doctrine preached to their slaves and coupled it with warnings that the saved would be those who lived out their status in this world without causing any trouble.

Another sort of world view is eschatological. In the eschatological world view, the ultimate victory over suffering and death will

[9]Baer's work on mainstream black denominations, however, causes him to conclude that those churches also tend to support the existing structures of society and to discourage militant stands.

commence at some future time in history. Eschatology may take either of two forms: progressivism or millenarism. Furthermore, millenarism sometimes has a subtype known as apocalypticism.

In the progressive view, the day of perfection will be reached when God and humanity have worked together to attain it. This involves a gradualistic concept of social evolution. The view is based on the idea that God is the creator and rules over the earth. God's master plan is for the evolution of the world into an ever more humane, just, and Godly kingdom (the Kingdom of God on earth). But it is believed that God will not establish this without human effort and participation. According to this evolutionary eschatology, trust in God is often equated with trust in the goodness of God's creation. Believers are to look for signs of God at work in this world and are to become actively involved in the material world. Progressive eschatology was characteristic of much of the Social Gospel movement in the United States at the turn of the century. In a somewhat modified form, this sort of outlook—with its positive view of this world—continues to be a force in many mainline denominations and is the predominant view of Reformed Jews.[10] The progressive view of history is depicted in Figure 11.2.

Another form of eschatology, **millenarism**, assumes that the transformation of the world will be sudden rather than gradualistic and

will be inaugurated primarily by supernatural powers. Norman Cohn, a historian who has done extensive comparative studies of millenarism, points to five defining characteristics of these movements. The millenarian vision is

1. Collective, in the sense that it is to be enjoyed by the faithful as a group.
2. Terrestrial, in the sense that it is to be realized on this earth and not in some otherworldly heaven.
3. Imminent, in the sense that it is to come both soon and suddenly.
4. Total, in the sense that it is utterly to transform life on earth, so that the new dispensation will be no mere improvement on the present but perfection itself.
5. Accomplished by agencies which are consciously regarded as supernatural (1964: 168).

The word *millennium* means a thousand years and refers to the new era to come. Although the term originates from the New Testament prediction (in the Book of Revelation) that Jesus will return and rule for 1,000 years, the word is also used to refer to non-Christian groups with this sort of world view. Hence, millenarians are those people who await a future event by which the Kingdom of God or the new era will begin. Many millenarian Christians have their own life-after-death scenario. This involves a bodily resurrection of the dead at the time the new Kingdom begins. This is a rather different concept from the belief that eternal life for an individual begins immediately after death and that the spiritual world is coexistent with the material one. Nonetheless, many people hold some combination of both beliefs and are not much troubled by the need for coherence and consistency in their theodicy.

The concept of salvation for millenarians, then, is time-oriented, terrestrial (although life on earth in the new era will be quite different

---

[10]Actually, this-worldly eschatology is the predominant theodicy in the Hebrew and Christian Bibles. In the entire Jewish Bible (the Christian Old Testament), the idea of life after death is mentioned only four times. Salvation was expected to be this-worldly and was anticipated within history. God was thought to be in charge of creation and of history, both of which were viewed as good. The idea of the soul, as something separate from the body, that would live on after the material body died was an idea introduced by the Greeks and is found in later rabbinical writings and in the Christian New Testament.

from present life on earth), and collective (rather than individualistic). Although the transformation will ultimately be accomplished by supernatural forces, humans do have an active and important role in preparing the way. Life in this world is viewed as a time of suffering and of being tested, but the new era will mean the advent of a new social order where justice prevails.[11]

For disadvantaged groups, the millenarian view offers great hope for the future. (See Box 11.4.) Frequently, groups that hold this view are highly emotional in their religious expression and become fanatical in their efforts to inaugurate the new Kingdom. Hence, it is not uncommon for millenarian groups to precipitate active revolt against the established authorities. Yonina Talmon writes:

[11]Each of these theodicies (salvation in an afterlife, progressive eschatology, and millennial eschatology) are within the mainline tradition of Christian theology and are given different emphasis by various denominations. For example, one study revealed that 94 percent of the Southern Baptists felt that Jesus would definitely return

to earth some day. By contrast, only 13 percent of the Congregationalists fully believed in that prediction (Stark and Glock 1968). This is one reason that the procedure of operationalizing orthodoxy only in terms of one of these views and then assuming that those who are more orthodox are also more religious is suspect.

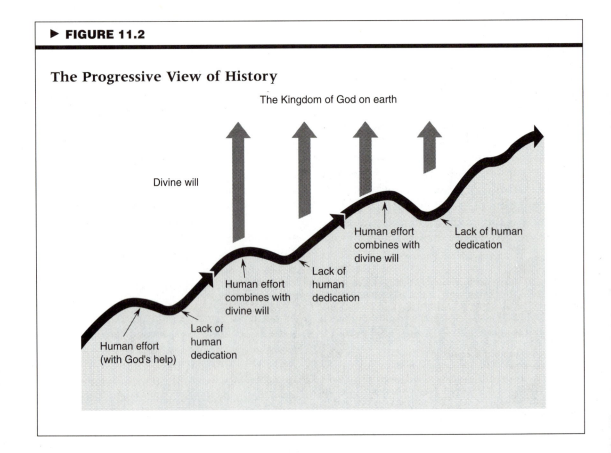

▶ **FIGURE 11.2**

The Progressive View of History

Comparative analysis seems to indicate that, generally speaking, the more extremely millenarian a movement is the more activist it is. . . . There seems to be a correlation between the time conception of each movement and its position in the passivity-activity continuum.

Movements which view the millennium as imminent and have a total and vivid conception of redemption are, on the whole, much more activist than movements which expect it to happen at some remote date. . . . It would seem that truly great expectations and a sense

---

► **BOX 11.4**

Milleniarian Anticipation Expressed in Hymns

These two hymns express vividly the revolutionary and earthly expectations of the millennial vision. The first stresses the collapse of the present social order and the destruction of kingdoms. The second expresses a mood of waiting until the supernatural does its work. Compare the messages to those in the hymns in Boxes 11.1 and 11.2.

"Jesus Comes"

Watch ye saints with eyelids waking, Lo,
   the pow'rs of heav'n are shaking;
Keep your Lamps all trimmed and
   burning, Ready for your Lord's
   returning.
Lo! He comes, lo! Jesus comes; Lo! He
   comes, He comes all glorious!
Jesus comes to reign victorious, Lo! He
   comes, yes, Jesus comes.

Kingdoms at their base are crumbling,
   Hark, His chariot wheels are rumbling;
Tell, O, tell of grace abounding, Whilst the
   seventh trump is sounding.
Lo! He comes, lo! Jesus comes; Lo! He
   comes, He comes all glorious!
Jesus comes to reign victorious, Lo! He
   comes, yes, Jesus comes.

Nations wane, tho' proud and stately,
   Christ His Kingdom hasteneth greatly;
Earth her latest pangs is summing, shout,
   ye saints, your Lord is coming!
Lo! He comes, lo! Jesus comes; Lo! He
   comes, He comes all glorious!

Jesus comes to reign victorious, Lo! He
   comes, yes, Jesus comes.

"Our Lord's Return to Earth Again"

I am watching for the coming of the glad
   millennial day
When our blessed Lord shall come and
   catch His waiting Bride away
Oh! my heart is filled with rapture as I
   labor, watch and pray
For our Lord is coming back to earth
   again.
Oh! our Lord is coming back to earth
   again,
Yes, our Lord is coming back to earth
   again,
Satan will be bound a thousand years,
We'll have no tempter then,
After Jesus shall come back to earth again.

Then the sin and sorrow, pain and death
   of this dark world shall cease
In a glorious reign with Jesus of a
   thousand years of peace;
All the earth is groaning, crying for that
   day of sweet release,
For our Lord is coming back to earth
   again.
Oh! our Lord is coming back to earth
   again,
Yes, our Lord is coming back to earth
   again,
Satan will be bound a thousand years,
We'll have no tempter then,
After Jesus shall come back to earth again.

of immediacy enhance the orientation to active rebellion while postponement of the critical date and lesser expectation breed passivity and quietism (1965: 527).

Talmon points out that millenarism has enjoyed popularity at all levels of society at one time or another. The theodicy of the Unification Church is millenarian, yet the members have been recruited substantially from relatively affluent middle- and upper-middle-class families. This provides a contemporary example of millenarism that is not rooted in economic dispossession. Nonetheless, it has normally been a religion of deprived groups—oppressed peasants, the poorest of the poor in cities and towns, and populations of colonial countries. The millennial outlook usually develops as a reaction to especially severe hardships and suffering. Talmon writes: "Many of the outbursts of millenarism took place against a background of disaster—plagues, devastating fires, recurrent long droughts that were the dire lot of the peasants, slumps that caused widespread unemployment and poverty and calamitous wars" (1965: 530). In most cases, millenarism is a phenomenon of ethnic groups that have endured sustained subjugation. The predisposing factor is the gap between the socioeconomic expectations of a group and their actual ability to satisfy their needs.

For example, when simple tribal societies encounter complex ones and the people in the simpler society are attracted by advanced technologies and tools, there are generated enormously inflated expectations without an adequate development of institutional means for their satisfaction. This was the case in the Cargo cult of Melanesia where exposure to an American military base caused poor indigenous peoples to feel frustrated with their own lack of possessions. Their response was to develop a mystical cult around a flag pole. They believed that if they cracked the mystical marching code of the soldiers, an airplane

loaded with cargo for the natives would arrive. The discrepancy between desire and reality is often bridged by millenarian hope. The millennial hope, in turn, sometimes leads to action.

One can also see the correlation of millenarism with "relative deprivation" in the American lower-middle class. For example, Ohio lost many jobs and some of its population in the late 1970s as industries moved to states where energy costs would be less (the Sun Belt). When this combined with the impact of the economic recession of the early 1980s, many people lost jobs. Furthermore, the predictions for the future were gloomy, and many working- and middle-class people began to doubt the American dream of prosperity and plenty in the future. It is noteworthy that at the same time there was a substantial growth of millenarism in southern Ohio.

One must be wary of simplistic generalizations about the kind of social behavior millenarism generates. Some modern millenarian movements are ineffective in their change strategies because they employ mystical methods to bring change; for others the millennium is too distant to motivate members to militancy. Nonetheless, the overall tendency is for millenarians to be activists. Sometimes the activism is directed at the social system and has an empirical likelihood of bringing change. This is what Anthony Wallace called a "rational strategy" (see chapter 7). If people believe that they are responsible to God for helping overthrow the present social order, their concept of religious duty may, in fact, stimulate social reform.

Unlike the progressivists who see the present order as good and getting better, millennial movements usually seek total transformation of this world—which they view as unjust or even inherently evil. Many groups that begin with a rational approach become progressively more strategic and more rational (more secular?) if they begin to meet with success. This is illustrated by the tendency, which

Lipset described, for religious movements to spawn radical political movements and the political movements, in turn, to lose much of their religiosity (Lipset 1960). Of course, for sociologists who insist that a world view may be religious without being supernaturalistic, these secular political movements are no less religious than their predecessors. They simply have this-worldly and rationalistic systems of faith.

To complicate matters further, there are actually two types of millenarism. **Postmillenialism** holds that Christ will come to reign over the earth, but only *after* humans have prepared the way. This is sometimes thought to involve a 1,000-year period of justice and peace prior to Christ's arrival. Obviously, this stimulates this-worldly activism and is what has been described so far.

The other type of millenarism is common among the most destitute—those who feel utterly vulnerable in relationship to another group of people. This form emphasizes much more strongly the idea that the world is evil and controlled by Satan. Contrary to the evolutionary eschatology, this view describes human history as being on a hopelessly downward spiral. Ironically, this depressing circumstance is viewed as a sign of hope because it indicates that the end is near. God will intervene in history and bring forth the new era. Nothing humans can do will significantly alter the course of history. The believer can only be ready for the day of judgment, preparing his or her own soul and perhaps engaging in mystical ritual action, such as dancing around a fire (the Ghost Dance), marching around a flag pole (the Cargo cult), or spreading the word until everyone is informed of the noble story (Seventh-Day Adventists and Jehovah's Witnesses). This extreme form of millenarism is called **apocalypticism,** or **premillenialism** (see Figure 11.3). This latter phrase means that Christ will come before the 1,000-year period of justice, peace, and divine rule.

Within Christianity, apocalypticism is normally based on a literal interpretation of the Book of Revelation. Its utter rejection of the present age and present world disallows any attempt to bring change. For this reason, it usually leads to passivity in terms of the social structure. Groups or individuals are more likely to adopt this posture and this world view if they are powerless and utterly despairing.[12] If some hope exists of social change through human action, the group or individual is more likely to develop a rational strategy.

Christianity, then, has within it several theodicies, which in numerous ways are quite different. Some congregations and some denominations stress one of them exclusively. Most congregations have some people who do not believe in a Second Coming or in an imminent end to the world; rather, they believe in a spiritual world that is coexistent with this world and that is attained by individuals if they have a right relationship with God. Others do not believe in life after death, at least not immediately after death; rather, they expect the millennium to occur sometime in the future. Many Christians believe a little bit in each of these outlooks, but have no coherent explanation of how the views fit together.[13] The important point is that, depending on which world view is stressed among an oppressed minority group, one may expect very different levels of activism or militance. Those whose hope lies in a

---

[12]This does not mean that *only* the destitute will develop such a world view, but they are more likely to be inclined in this direction than are those in other socioeconomic circumstances.

[13]Lack of logical coherence or consistency is not uncommon; many people hold more than one world view, even though those world views may be contradictory in many respects. Melford Spiro (1978) points out that some Chinese say devotions at both Taoist and Buddhist temples; some Japanese worship the gods of both Shinto and Buddhism; certain Singhalese pay homage to both the Hindu *deva* and the Buddhist Gautama; and many Burmese Buddhists believe firmly in the Thirty-Seven Nats (the folk religion of Burma). In many cases, the outlook on life of two theodicies is utterly different, yet local people claim allegiance to both world views.

coexistent spiritual world that is attained by individual means are frequently passive. Those who hold an apocalyptic view are also usually passive. However, millenarians are frequently activist and militant. For them, religion is not an opiate; it is the inspiration that gives them hope, provides them with vision, and shores up their courage. The progressive view, with its suggestion that the present social system is already a good one and is constantly improving, has little appeal to the oppressed. This view is frequently held by social activists in more affluent religious groups.

Judaism also has within it several theodicies. Reform Jews await a "messianic age," which they believe will be established by combined human and divine effort. Orthodox Jews hold to a belief in a coming Messiah who will bring the Kingdom of God into being, will reunite the Jews, and will rebuild the temple. This millenarian view has been especially emphasized in times of Jewish history when oppression of Jews was most severe. A belief in resurrection from the dead was introduced to the Hebrews through the Persians nearly 2,000 years ago and is now part of the messianic expectation as well. Another theodicy—the belief in life after death in heaven or purgatory[14]—was also introduced by

---

[14]Jews believe that no soul is so evil that it deserves a permanent condemnation. Hence, they have no concept of hell. The worst that can happen to an utterly evil person is that his or her soul will cease to exist and the person will not be remembered among the living. A person who has lived a life that is less than holy may spend up to eleven months in purgatory, but is eventually united with God. Jewish theology spends much less time on speculations about the nature of the afterlife than does Christian theology.

▶ **FIGURE 11.3**

The Apocalyptic (Premillenial) World View

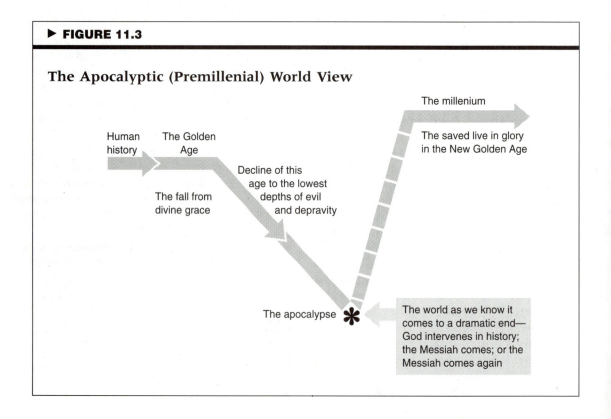

the Greeks. Orthodox Jews affirm this doctrine as well, even though it represents quite a different theodicy from the more this-worldly messianic expectation. Conservative Jews vary a great deal from one congregation to another in which of these theodicies they emphasize.

Reform Judaism (at least in its official form) does not accept the beliefs in resurrection or in heaven and purgatory. Its members are messianic, but they anticipate a messianic age—a time of peace and justice—which will be inaugurated due to the work of God and of many people. They do not expect a single individual to arrive who will solve the world's problems. The confidence of Reform Jews that human action can be effective in bringing significant change is itself a product of a people who are not destitute and powerless. The social circumstances of Reform Jews has allowed for and encouraged this modification of the traditional theodicy. Likewise, the theodicy has justified and encouraged social activism. The Reform branch of Judaism is often noted for being especially prophetic and activist in its attention to social and political change.

The Jews have been subjugated and persecuted throughout much of their history, and the theodicies that they have developed have usually been ones of disprivilege. Sometimes the theodicies have motivated Jews to militancy and activism (such as the times of the escape from Egypt and the Maccabean revolt), and sometimes they have called for passivity—waiting for the Messiah. There can be little doubt, however, that these theodicies have served to bond the Jews together and have helped to sustain them through incredible hardships.

What we have found is that oppressed people frequently adhere to a world view that is either otherworldly or is millenarian; the answer to life's frustrations is sought in a transformed future or in a different realm of existence. Given the subjugation of women throughout the history of the Western world,

the role of women in millenaristic movements is especially interesting. Cohn (1964) points out that millennial movements are common when there is a substantial group of wealthy, leisure-class women who are without social function or prestige. He points out that a number of millennial reformers during the Reformation were able to survive because they were sheltered and supported by women of the nobility. These women were experiencing extreme status inconsistency; they had high social status in terms of wealth and family political prestige, yet as individuals they had no respected function and could demand little personal prestige or respect. Because of their subordination and their boredom, medieval women of the leisure classes were likely to support millenarians whose primary constituencies were the economically and politically dispossessed.

Weber (1963) also noted that women showed a great receptivity to all religious prophecy except that which is exclusively military in orientation. He emphasized that prophets challenge the status quo and are usually rather egalitarian in their relationships with women. Jesus and Buddha are both cited as examples of charismatic figures who ignored many traditional gender-role norms. Weber also pointed out that egalitarianism of the sexes rarely survives beyond the earliest stages of the sect's existence. Routinization almost always has meant a return to traditional roles. The point here is that at least two outstanding scholars have suggested that women are disproportionately attracted to the type of religious experience that normally appeals to the very poor.

Most empirical studies have not shown significant differentiation in religious outlooks between men and women, but this may be due to a dearth of research on the issue. We certainly know much more about differences in religiosity between members of different social and economic groups than we do about differences in religiosity between men and women. Weber's and Cohn's comments are suggestive of an area of research that deserves our attention: Are women, because of their subjugated position in society, more likely than men to be otherworldly or millenarian? Do men and women differ in other matters of religiosity?[15]

One conclusion can safely be drawn from our foregoing discussion: The experience of social and political disprivilege can have a significant impact on one's world view and on one's style of religious expression. Likewise, the world view and sacred ethos of a group may have a significant effect on how its members respond to the experience of social and political subordination. To understand better the workings of religion in the experience of a specific subjugated group, let us turn to a brief overview of religion in the African American experience.

Religion in the African American Community

The vast majority of African Americans who are religiously affiliated are members of a Methodist or a Baptist denomination. In fact, well over 80 percent of the black Christians in this country are members of one of the seven largest independent black denominations of Baptists and Methodists (Lincoln and Mamiya

1990; Roof and McKinney 1987).[16] Nonetheless, one must be cautious about making generalizations about black religion or the black church of the United States, for there is tremendous diversity of religious expression among blacks. There is a strong local autonomy emphasis in the independent black denominations, and this means that local churches within the same denomination may vary considerably in theology and in style of ritual. Of course, there is also wide variation in the white denominations, but these denominations tend to be somewhat more centralized. The localistic bias of black churches tends to facilitate local variations and to exaggerate intradenominational diversity.

Gayraud Wilmore (1972) points out that in Cincinnati in the 1930s only 10.6 percent of the population was black, but black churches accounted for 32 percent of all churches in that city. Similar figures reveal the same pattern in Detroit and Philadelphia. Wilmore cites these crude figures as illustrations of the high degree of divisiveness and separation that exists in the black religious community. Perhaps the most important variation in black religiosity is that due to socioeconomic standing. The lower-class churches are characterized by emotionalism and fundamentalism, and the minister is unlikely to have had any formal theological training. On the other hand, the religious expression

---

[15]We do know that women attend religious services more than men and that they are more likely to report that their faith influences everyday life, but the few studies that have been done show little difference in belief systems (Argyle and Beit-Hallahmi 1975; Batson and Ventis 1982; Hoge and Roozen 1979; Sloane and Potvin 1983; Roberts and Davidson 1984). One study did find that men who are less machoistic in their outlooks and values are more likely to be religious (Thompson 1991).

[16]Roof and McKinney estimate the current rate at 85 percent, and since Niebuhr found that the figure was 88 percent in 1929, it appears that little change has occurred in the past sixty years. The seven largest black denominations include three Methodist ones (the African Methodist Episcopal, the African Methodist Episcopal Zion, and the Christian Methodist Episcopal) and four Baptist associations (National Baptist Convention, National Baptist Convention, U.S.A., National Baptist Convention of America, and the Progressive National Baptist Convention). There are also four additional independent black Baptist denominations, but they are quite small. For more information and a history of these black churches, see Lincoln and Mamiya (1990).

of the black professional class is quite similar to the religiosity of the white middle class. It is characterized by orderly and rational worship conducted by a well-educated and theologically trained minister. Beyond the variations of Christianity in the black community, there also exist a large number of black religious cults. Yet, regardless of variations within the black community, we can still safely say that black religiosity tends to be more emotional in character than white religiosity.

We are able to discuss the existence of black religion as a distinct phenomenon in large part because the vast majority of African Americans do belong to all-black churches. This is not due to theological differences but to the caste-like nature of American society relative to African Americans. During the time of slavery, black Christians were required to occupy the balcony while whites were seated on the main floor. This allowed slave owners to keep track of their slaves and ensure that religious meetings were not used to incite rebellion. Gradually some "trusted" black preachers were allowed to meet separately with slaves to have religious services. This was virtually the only official leadership role allowed black slaves, and it is not surprising that the African American pastor enjoyed tremendous prestige and occupied the primary leadership position in the black community for more than two centuries (Lincoln and Mamiya 1990).

However, it was free blacks who actually founded the first independent all-black denominations.[17] In Philadelphia two African American clergymen, Richard Allen and Absalom Jones, started the African Methodist

Episcopal Church in 1794, and a group of free blacks in New York started the African Methodist Episcopal Zion Church in 1820 (Wilmore 1972). The segregation in the white churches was unbearable for free blacks. To Allen and Jones, it seemed to be a direct contradiction of the Christian faith. Furthermore, predominantly white denominations were very little concerned about the needs of African Americans. The ability of all-black churches to minister effectively to the social and religious needs of their people resulted in a tremendous increase in the membership of these denominations and eventually in the spawning of others. The result is that most black Christians have continued to this day to worship in segregation from white Christians. As one theologian has put it, "Sunday morning at 11 o'clock is the most segregated hour of the week in America" (Winter 1962). It is precisely this separateness that makes it possible to speak about black religion and the black church as a distinct entity.

The Unique Character of the Black Christian Experience

There are two different schools of thought regarding the origins and central character of African American religion. One group of scholars believes that the conversion of blacks was a final step in obliterating any remnant of African culture among the slaves. The experience of being torn from their homelands and their families and being involuntarily relocated on a new continent was a stunning experience for the first generation of African Americans. Furthermore, slaveholders frequently had policies that blacks from the same African culture or who spoke the same African language were not to be placed on the same plantation. Hence, no common language, religion, or culture could enhance communication and solidarity among

---

[17]The first black Baptist churches predate the Methodist ones—in 1758 the African Baptist or "Bluestone" Church was founded in Mechlenberg, Virginia, but the Baptists did not organize a denominational network or structure until long after the African Methodist Episcopal and African Methodist Episcopal Zion churches were established.

slaves. In fact, members of enemy societies were sometimes thrown together in the most unhappy of circumstances.

At first, the white masters refused to allow their slaves to be preached to, for most Christian denominations maintained that a Christian could not own another Christian. Hence, if a slave converted, the master would either have to give up his or her own church mem-

African American religion is often highly expressive in character. The debate rages whether the emotionalism, rhythmic cadence, and other characteristics of the religion are a function of the fact that black Christianity in North America typically serves the needs of disprivileged people, or of an ethnic survival from the religious and cultural patterns in Africa. (Leonard Freed/Magnum.)

bership or would have to free the converted slave. For this reason, slave owners prohibited proselytization. Because many Christian missionaries wanted to preach to the Africans, they gradually compromised their position: conversion did not automatically require manumission. Eventually, slave owners found that religion could be a powerful tool for controlling slaves, for they could use the aura of sacredness to reinforce desirable behavior patterns: submissiveness, industriousness, and obedience. By providing blacks with a world view that is profoundly otherworldly, slave owners hoped to replace the last vestiges of African hopes for freedom with a sacred system that the whites could control.

E. Franklin Frazier (1957, 1963) and Arthur Fauset (1944) first developed the thesis that the Christianization of blacks was the final step in the deculturation of Africans. However, they also pointed out that these African converts used the imagery of Christianity to forge a religious expression appropriate to their own needs. In this view, Christianity became functional for the slaves in that it established a common base for unity and solidarity among otherwise disparate peoples. This view of African American religiosity stresses the fact that slave religion was a synthesis of white religion and black experience, and it developed its own unique character and history. The emotionalism that is characteristic of African American churches is attributed to the fact that it was mostly Baptists and Methodists who evangelized the slaves. Because the revival-meeting style of those denominations is highly enthusiastic and emotional, it is not surprising that black Christianity was also revivalistic. Furthermore, poorly educated and economically impoverished groups are frequently more emotional in religious expression than are more educated and affluent coreligionists. This would also add to the highly emotional tenor of African American religion (Baer 1984).

Other scholars, such as Melville Herskovits (1958), Gayraud Wilmore (1972), Joseph Washington (1972), Peter Williams (1980), and Eric Lincoln and Lawrence Mamiya (1990), have insisted that slave religion was influenced by certain patterns of religiosity that are common to many African religious ceremonies. According to Herskovits, the tendency to turn to religion rather than to political action to alleviate frustrations is typical of African cultures. Moreover, the rhythm and motion that characterize the singing, preaching, and congregational responses in black churches is also common in Africa. Hence, the style of religiosity of the black church is viewed as a survival of previous cultural patterns in much the same way that the sentence structure of the black dialect is viewed by linguists as a survival of African languages. The specific religious belief systems are granted to be a product of the new world and of contact with white missionaries, but the mode of expression is viewed as uniquely African.

The debate continues between those holding each of these views with some efforts having been made at synthesis (Glenn 1964). We cannot expect to resolve the issue here, but I do want to highlight the significance of the alternative views. For those who deny that African culture had any real influence on slave religiosity, the characteristic features of the African American church are thought to originate in socioeconomic subordination. If this view is correct, the emotionalism of black religiosity may fade, even in all-black churches, as members of those congregations improve their socioeconomic standing.[18]

On the other hand, black religiosity will continue to have a different flavor from white religiosity if the difference is rooted in ethnic differences that are preserved in segregated religious organizations. There is empirical evidence to support both views, but I do not believe that one can fully understand the religiosity of the first slaves without some understanding of their previous experiences of religion. Through the transmission of religion from one generation to the next, the remnants of African religiosity have been passed down to the contemporary black church. Only history will be able to answer the question about whether assimilation to white American culture and changes in socioeconomic status will result in a more subdued and rationalized religious style among blacks. My own expectation is that the unique, expressive style of the black church will continue.[19]

Regardless of the causes of black religious patterns, there is a consensus that black religion in the United States does have a unique character (Cone 1972; Johnstone 1975; Lincoln and Mamiya 1990; Washington 1964, 1972; Wilmore 1972; Winter 1977). In fact, Washington refers to black Christianity in the United States as a form of folk religion. First of all, the Christianity that was preached to blacks was a truncated and manipulated version of Christian theology; it was designed to help pacify and compensate them for their inferior position in life (see Box 11.5). Furthermore, religion

---

[18]The assumption here is that religious emotionalism is an expression of socioeconomic deprivation (a thesis discussed earlier in this chapter and in chapter 9). According to this argument, emotionalism will give way to middle-class forms of religiosity—which are more cerebral and more subdued—as blacks achieve economic affluence. A second line of argument is that, although the origins of black religious emotionalism

were due to socioeconomic subordination, the pattern is now institutionalized and will continue independently of economic changes among blacks.

[19]It is interesting to note that middle-class black theologians, such as James Cone and Gayraud Wilmore, continue to support the emotionalism of the black church. Although they are not personally impoverished, they do not conform to the subdued style of worship of white churches. Most black preachers—despite their economic standing—take pride in the distinctiveness of black preaching and the emotional expressiveness in black worship services.

became the means by which slaves could express their frustrations and their hopes—both of which emanated from their subordinate standing in society. Other scholars point out that all world religions adapt to local needs and that while African American Christianity has its unique character, it is no different than other expressions of Christianity in adapting a local flavor. Like Christianity in Poland, Brazil, or Anglo America, African American Christianity has both folk elements and strong universalistic themes (Lincoln and Mamiya 1990).

Religion of the Oppressed and Coded Messages: The Black Spiritual

One of the characteristic expressions of this African American religiosity was the black spiritual. Surprisingly, few African American spirituals were Christological; in fact, many do not even mention God (Wilmore 1972). The message of most spirituals was an expression of hardship and a hope of freedom. Those spirituals that do focus on Jesus stress his suffering, his experience of being scorned, and his role as liberator. Some spirituals were based on biblical stories (such as "Joshua Fit the Battle of Jericho"), but many were commentaries on contemporary events. "Oh, Lord, What a Morning, when the Stars Begin to Fall" emerged right after Nat Turner's insurrection (1831) when slaves were under the tightest scrutiny. The slaves hoped for that day when the apocalypse would come, the revolution would be successful, and the sky would fall on whites. Washington insists that slaves used the vocabulary of white ministers and the Bible and that whites believed the slaves were being socialized in the values that owners wanted. But content analysis of these hymns, combined with reports from former slaves on the role of the spirituals, has suggested a different interpretation. Washington writes,

> The popular view that Negro spirituals are of Christian origin is based upon the preponderance of otherworldly themes, Biblical words, and the instruction and messages of the missionaries. These were the tools the Negroes had at hand, but this view assumes the credulity of the slave. It overlooks the awareness of Negroes that religion was methodically used to hold them in check, and their capacity to use it for other purposes than worship. Thus, the distinction between spirituals

---

▶ **BOX 11.5**

Excerpts from a Catechism for American Slaves

These questions from a catechism designed for slaves illustrate the way Christianity was twisted to serve the interests of the powerful group. Indeed, if black slaves had any accurate understanding of Christianity it would be surprising. Several denominations established special catechisms for slaves which were, at best, truncated interpretations of the faith.

Question: What did God make you for?
Answer: To make a crop.
Question: What is the meaning of "Thou shalt not commit adultery?"
Answer: To serve our heavenly Father, and our earthly Master, obey our overseer, and not steal anything.

Source: Gayraud S. Wilmore, *Black Religion and Black Radicalism.* Garden City, N.Y.: Doubleday, 1972.

being forged from materials presented by Christians and forged from the Christian faith itself is essential . . . (1964: 218).

Scholars have found that many spirituals were, in fact, "code songs" that communicated one thing to blacks, while white masters sat by—content that their slaves were getting a heavy dose of otherworldly religion. For example, the spiritual "Let Us Praise God Together, on Our Knees," which is included in the hymnbooks of many mainline white denominations and many sects, was actually a call to a secret meeting of slaves at dawn. The chorus of that spiritual is as follows: "When I fall on my knees *with my face to the rising sun*, Oh, Lord, have mercy on me." Likewise, when a slave working in the fields began singing "Steal away, steal away home; I ain't got long to stay here," he or she was indicating this-worldly intentions to other slaves. Participation of the other slaves in the chorus was a way to wish the person well and a promise to try to cover for the slave's absence as much as possible. Some of the spirituals were rather thinly veiled codes, such as the one that went

I am bound for the promised land;
I am bound for the promised land;
Oh who will come and go with me?
I am bound for the promised land!

"Canaan, Sweet Canaan" did not point only to an otherworldly realm, but it referred to Ohio, Indiana, Illinois, and even Canada. Similarly, references to the Jordan River usually meant the Ohio River. "Swing Low, Sweet Chariot" provides an example. When the underground railroad was ready to take another group of escapees north, blacks could let others at a worship gathering know about it without giving themselves away to white attendants who came to ensure that nothing subversive happened at these religious gatherings. Someone would begin to sing, with great emotion,

I looked over Jordan [the Ohio River] and
    what did I see;

Coming for to carry me home;
A band of angels [Harriet Tubman or another
    conductor of the underground railroad]
        Coming after me;
Coming for to carry me home [freedom]
Swing low [deep into the South] Sweet
    Chariot [the underground railroad]
Coming for to carry me home.

The slaves at those worship services understood the symbolism and double meanings very well (Cone 1972).

In some cases, it is hard to know whether a particular spiritual was otherworldly in its meaning or a code song. Some spirituals, like "When the Saints Go Marching In" had a definite otherworldly character. Other songs had a here-and-now double meaning, but they were not necessarily calls to action. A biblical theme was being rehearsed, but contemporary characters were clearly identified with historical figures in the story. The spiritual "Go Down, Moses" emerged at the time when Bishop Francis Asbury of the Methodist Church was instrumental in formulating anti-slavery planks in the Methodist code of discipline. Asbury had himself referred to South Carolina as "Egypt" when he had been there to preach (Washington 1964) and that theme was expressed in the chorus of this popular hymn:

When Israel was in Egypt's land, let my
    people go;
Oppressed so hard they could not stand, Let
    my people go.
Go down, Moses, way down in Egypt land;
Tell old Pharaoh, Let my people go.

Oh let us all from bondage flee, let my
    people go;
And let us all in Christ be free, let my people
    go.
Go down, Moses, way down in Egypt land;
Tell old Pharaoh, let my people go.

It doesn't take much imagination to figure out who represented "Moses," "the Israelites," and the "Egyptians" in the eyes of those slaves.

The use of religious language for coded communication is certainly not a new phenomenon, for there are other reports of oppressed people communicating in a similar manner. Most biblical scholars believe that the Apocalypse (the Book of Revelation) was a coded message from John the Elder (a prisoner on the Island of Patmos) to his people in the churches of Asia Minor. At that time, one was required to worship the emperor of Rome. Because Christians refused to do so, they were persecuted. The Book of Revelation is an encoded book that is very difficult to translate because many of the symbolic meanings of that day have been lost. An understanding of the double meanings requires fluency in Aramaic and Greek. The book was not destroyed by the Romans, for they viewed it as a harmless fantasy about another world. They never recognized the political references that abound in the book and that served as a resounding criticism of Rome.

Likewise, an acquaintance of mine was a minister in Cuba during and after the revolution in that country. He told me that he occasionally preached against certain policies of Fidel Castro, but he always did so in code, using the language of the Book of Revelation and other seemingly otherworldly references from Pauline epistles. As he put it, "I had to be careful, for I never knew when a visiting soldier might be in the congregation who might report me for subversive political comments. However, my people knew what I was talking about."

All of this simply serves as a warning against facile generalizations regarding the otherworldliness of the religion of the oppressed. Of course, some blacks did understand Christianity in other-worldly terms, and it served to compensate them and to discourage any rebellion in this world. They believed they would get their just deserts in the next world. The important point here is that slave religion was not a simple adoption of white Christianity; it was a reworked Christianity that had its own character, style, and outlook. Much of the black church today has been influenced by this heritage. Even where the message is otherworldly, political issues have never been entirely foreign to black churches. Most black Christians today feel that it is utterly appropriate to use the church for political purposes: 92 percent of African American clergy surveyed nationally support the idea of churches expressing their opinions on social and political questions, 91 percent of black laity believe it is appropriate for clergy to participate in civil rights protests, and nearly a third of the black churches house civil rights organizations and/or voter registration programs (Lincoln and Mamiya 1990). In another study, 30 percent of the black ministers interviewed said it is proper for a minister to tell parishioners how to vote (Johnstone 1975). While the African American church has gone through a period of quietism in the middle and later part of the twentieth century, it has historically been more involved in political affairs than its white counterpart (Lincoln and Mamiya 1990; Wilmore 1972).[20]

The Leadership Role of the African American Minister

One reason the African American church has been involved in political matters has been the fact that the black preacher was the main spokesperson for the African American community. During the period of slavery, the role of plantation preacher was often the only leadership role afforded southern blacks. Hence, it became a position of considerable prestige within the black community. Following emancipation, this position continued to be the most important leadership role; the black

---

[20]This recent period of quietism may be what is reflected in Gary Marx's research, which was cited earlier.

preacher became the spokesperson for the community and the liaison between the dominant white class and the subordinate black one. Because whites often owned the buildings where blacks worshiped and held other clubs over the black community, the black preacher had to be sensitive to the interests of both whites and blacks. This liaison role was certainly not just religious in character; it was often explicitly political.

The preacher's role as the central spokesperson for the community has largely survived to this day. The African American church has served since emancipation as the heart of that ethnic community. It has sponsored social and cultural affairs, established insurance programs for members who did not qualify for insurance under white-controlled corporations, started schools and colleges to educate young people, sponsored political debates held in the church sanctuary, initiated economic recovery and growth programs for African Americans, and generally served as a community center. In fact, Gunnar Myrdal called the African American church a "community center par excellence" (1944: 938). The preacher was the person who gave impetus to most of these programs and thus came to be highly esteemed in the community.

Because the preacher held a position that afforded leadership opportunities and offered status in the community, his was a highly coveted position. Hence, there have often been young would-be preachers waiting in the wings to have their chance to preach and start their own congregations. Perhaps this is another reason for the large number of small black churches, each with its own semiautonomous preacher. The ministry was attractive to energetic African Americans because other professions were essentially closed to them. However, there has been a significant decline over the past fifty years in the ratio of blacks in the ministry per 10,000 people in the population as increasing numbers of African Americans enter law, medicine, politics, and other professions (Glenn 1964). The black minister no longer holds a monopoly on leadership and status as was once the case. Nonetheless, the preacher still holds a more substantial position within the African American community than does his or her white counterpart. It is noteworthy how many African American political figures have begun their careers as ministers. Jesse Jackson and Andrew Young are among the better-known politician-preachers on a long list of such leaders.

Partially because of the acceptance by the black community of clergy being involved in political affairs, ministers were able to gain ready acceptance as civil rights leaders. Martin Luther King Jr. provides a particularly good example. King's civil rights speeches were constructed and delivered in the style of African American preaching. His nonviolent resistance strategy of the 1950s and 1960s required resistance to injustice but forbade participants from using violence. He insisted that blacks would change social structures by appealing to the conscience of the nation and by economic boycotts. If a white police officer struck a black protestor, African Americans were to resist the temptation to strike back. They were instructed to turn the other cheek and to love their enemies. They were told to hate injustice but not the person who perpetuated it. They were taught that love would be the weapon by which opponents would be transformed. The mixture of religious teaching and political action did not seem at all inconsistent to King's followers, for they were used to African American preachers also being political figures.

It is hard to imagine how the many rallies that King led could have remained nonviolent without the influence of religious teachings. Moreover, when people's homes and churches were being bombed and rallies were dispersed by police officers swinging billy clubs, religion served to shore up the courage and conviction of the people, for they were assured that God was on the side of justice and ultimate victory was certain. Some African American critics of nonviolence felt that King's religion was another form of opiate and that blacks should fight back. Nonetheless, there is little doubt that the civil rights movement of the 1950s and 1960s gained much of its impetus from a black Baptist preacher—Dr. Martin Luther King Jr. Clearly, the role of the minister has been a central one within the African American community.

The role of the pastor was not the only leadership role that the black church has afforded. In a society where African Americans have often held menial and low-status jobs, the roles of elder, deacon, Sunday school superintendent, or choir leader have provided leadership opportunities and respected positions in the community. Often these positions have been given exalted and lengthy titles. Such roles in exclusively black denominations enhance the self-esteem of individuals who have rather humble standing in the larger society (Baer 1984).

Black Sects and Cults

African American religion in the United States has also included many black sects and cults. There are a great variety of them, each emerging out of the common black experience of subjugation, but each offering its own unique characteristics (Washington 1964, 1972; Wilmore 1972; Lincoln 1973; Fauset 1944). Two of the best-known African American cults were Father Divine's Peace Mission and the Nation of Islam (Black Muslims). The Father Divine movement started in 1932 when a man by the name of George Baker opened a mission in Harlem. He took the name of Major J. Devine and quickly gained notoriety by distributing alms among poor blacks. He taught that God is everywhere, everything, and everyone, and eventually his followers came to believe that

Devine was God incarnate. Baker then came to be known as Father Divine. Under his direction, the mission developed into a communal living settlement and maintained extremely high standards of cleanliness and of morality. Although the group was highly ascetic in character, the emphasis was not otherworldly. It was directed toward changing the socioeconomic system. The strategy of change focused primarily on benevolences rather than radical political changes. Because of its moderate stand, it did not incur the opposition of powerful white organizations. The movement spread across the country and was one of the larger African American cults in the United States.

The Lost/Found Nation of Islam was more radical in its outlook and has had considerable influence in many of America's prisons—where much of the proselytization took place. The movement started in the summer of 1930 when an Arab peddler, known as Wali D. Fard, came to the ghetto of Detroit. He sold silks and other materials and preached that black people in Africa and the Middle East were Islamic, not Christian. Christianity was depicted as the religion of the white people with a white God and a white savior. Being a Christian was equated with worshiping white people and was described as the white society's way of duping blacks into subordinate roles.

Fard insisted that whites are incapable of telling the truth, and he sought to tell the real story of black civilization in Asia and Africa. He told fantastic stories about black culture on other continents. All African Americans were viewed as Muslims in their origins and were referred to as the "Lost Tribe of Shebazz." Many African Americans were delighted with this stranger's stories of sophisticated and advanced black culture and his insistence on black superiority. It provided a basis for a sense of dignity and pride, which was often denied to poor ghetto blacks. Furthermore, the preacher's claim of Arab heritage lent credibility to his claims of firsthand knowledge of Africa and Arabia.

Fard developed a substantial following—estimated at 8,000 adherents. One of his devotees was a dynamic African American whom Fard renamed Elijah Muhammad. (Muslims refuse to accept the names they received from slavery and accept a new name when they join the Islamic temple.) When Fard mysteriously disappeared in 1934, Elijah Muhammad was named Minister of Islam. One of Muhammad's main disciples, in time, was Malcolm X.

The Black Muslims originally insisted that only black people could join. As a political-religious group, the Muslims experienced their heyday in the 1960s. Malcolm X became the primary spokesperson and gained national attention as a militant civil rights leader, being among the first to stress "black pride" and "black is beautiful" as central themes. Propelled by his forceful and articulate speeches, the Muslim movement grew rapidly. Attention was also focused on the Muslims when such notable sports personalities as Muhammad Ali and Kareem Abdul-Jabbar converted to the Nation of Islam.

The Muslims have been a religious group that is as thoroughly political as it is religious. For them, the distinction between politics and religion is meaningless. They explicitly reject any otherworldly views, so the socioeconomic-political structures of this world are of central importance to their view of "salvation." In fact, the ultimate goal of the original Nation of Islam was an autonomous and separate black nation in the United States. (Whites, they believed, belong in Europe.) The Muslims advocated a program of social, economic, and political segregation of blacks from whites. Because the "original man" was declared by Allah to be black, whiteness meant a lack of purity and truth. In short, whiteness was a sign of evil.

The Islamic world did not recognize the legitimacy of the original Muslim theology. In terms of official Islamic orthodoxy, the teachings of the Lost Nation of Islam were heretical. In short, the Lost Nation of Islam was a folk religion (see chapter 4), which had grown out of the experience of black America (Washington 1972). But to call such a movement a folk religion is not to denigrate its importance as a religious movement. Indeed, the Black Muslims may well be one of the most important religious developments in twentieth-century American religion. Because of the ascetic teachings, the emphasis on industry and hard work, and the extreme sacrifice and devotion to the cause, the Lost/Found Nation mobilized a significant amount of financial and personal resources on its behalf. And because of high levels of internal discipline, Muslim ministers have also been able to deliver a significant block of votes to politicians. By acting as a unified front, they were able to make their presence felt in the larger society (Lincoln 1973).

Malcolm X formally broke with Muhammad in 1964 after a trip to Mecca. On that trip he learned that the teachings of the Black Muslims were quite different from Orthodox Islam. He established the Muslim Mosque, Inc., that same year, but was assassinated in 1965. Before he died he repudiated the views of whites as intrinsically evil and introduced a movement toward a more orthodox Islamic faith. When Elijah Muhammad died in 1975, Warith Deen Muhammad became the new leader of the Nation of Islam. He has modified doctrine and has changed the name of the group twice; it is now known as the American Muslim Mission. This mission is recognized in the Islamic world as a branch of orthodox Sunni Islam and has a North American membership estimated at 100,000. A splinter group of about 20,000 continues to call itself the Nation of Islam and is led by Minister Louis Farrakhan. Farrahkan continues the black separatist teachings of Wali Fard and Elijah Muhammad (Lincoln and Mamiya 1990).

In earlier chapters, we discussed the fact that sectarian movements are more common among socially and economically disfranchised groups. Because blacks in this country are disproportionately represented in this category, it is not surprising that African American religion is characterized by a large number of sectarian movements. Nonetheless, movements like the Black Muslims and the Father Divine Mission comprise a relatively small percentage of the church-affiliated blacks in this country. One interesting phenomenon, however, is the trend toward more this-worldliness in mainline black churches.

African American Religion: Present Themes and Future Trends

James Cone and Gayraud Wilmore are two of the outstanding black theologians of our day, and they both stress the eschatological theme in Christianity and de-emphasize the otherworldly one. Cone and Wilmore are perhaps the best known of a core of black theologians who have been articulating a "liberation theology," an emphasis on social and economic liberation at some future time in history. Otherworldliness is viewed by Cone, especially, as an opiate to black people. The true world view of Christianity, according to these theologians, is eschatological. In fact, a Christianity that is not supportive of black power is viewed as no Christianity at all. Liberation theologians insist that because Jesus was an advocate for the poor and the oppressed, so also must all true Christians be. This sort of Christianity would certainly incline believers toward militancy rather than passivity. It is noteworthy that Cone finds a rejection of otherworldliness and an endorsement of eschatology (millenarism) to be a first step in making the black church an effective tool of social and political change.

African American religion includes a wide diversity of styles and emphases. However, religion in the black community is more highly emotional than is most white religios-

ity, it places a heavy emphasis on freedom and equality (either in the next world or at a future time in history), and it is characterized by a distinctive rhythm in singing, preaching, and congregational responses. Some of the distinctiveness of black religion is probably due to survivals from African religion. Much of it is also due to white racism and to the distinctive place that African Americans have held in the stratification system of American society (Baer 1984).

Even a brief look at the African American church is enough to illustrate the fact that the religion of any group is affected by the socioeconomic status of its members. Furthermore, the outlook the religion fosters may motivate people to seek change, or it may enhance acquiescence. If African American theologians who teach at major seminaries—scholars like Cone and Wilmore—are any indication of what the future will be, black ministers are likely to continue to be more politically involved than their white counterparts. Moreover, if these theologians do set a course for the black church (and that is a big "if"), then the black church is likely to be increasingly an inspiration to social and economic militancy rather than an opiate. Only time will tell. However, one empirical study published in 1990 indicates that while many African American pastors are interested in instilling ethnic pride and identity, the majority are not actively asserting liberation theology, as such, in their preaching (Lincoln and Mamiya 1990).

Summary

In providing meaning in life, theology must address the real issues that face people. Because the problems of meaning in people's lives are different for the affluent and the disfranchised, it is not surprising that theodicies are different. The theodicy of privilege tends to justify one's good fortune, whereas theodicies of despair tend to provide certain psychological compensations for and a sense of victory over one's adversities. Even the basic values and sense of morality tend to be different. Those in occupations where obeying rules is fundamental to success are more comfortable with religious systems that are precise and absolute about moral expectations. Those who are in fields where creativity and divergent thinking are the keys to occupational success are more comfortable with relativity, ambiguity, and open-endedness in systems of meaning.

Religions of the disfranchised can either cause passivity and inaction in the face of social injustice, or they can inspire people to work for change. Theologies that are either otherworldly or apocalyptic (premillennial) tend to cause passivity, whereas postmillennial theologies tend to inspire activism.

African American religion provides an interesting example. Slave Christianity often inspired change and was used to transmit coded messages for escape, despite the efforts of slave owners to control slaves with religion. Further, the black church has often provided roles and leadership opportunities that enhanced self-esteem. African American pastors often became the central leaders in civil rights struggles and were the obvious spokespersons for the African American community in the political arena. This opportunity for leadership by the black pastor made the role so attractive that a number of aspiring charismatic blacks started their own sects and cults as channels to gain prestige and power within their own community.

Clearly, religion is correlated to socioeconomic status, and theology often serves as an ideology that is appropriate to one's economic circumstances.

Religion and Prejudice: Racism and Sexism

In chapter 11 we explored the effects of minority status on the religious outlook of people. In this chapter and the next, we turn the tables and explore the relationship between religion and the attitudes of members of the dominant group. This allows us to gain a more holistic view of the relationship between religion and social power. There is a second reason for exploring religion and prejudice: The investigation also allows us to see the complex ways in which religion can affect people by exerting influence as a reference group, as a belief system, or as an institution.

This analysis is limited to a discussion of the influence of Christianity. The decision to focus only on one religious tradition is based on three considerations. First, it is possible to go into more depth if we limit the scope of our application. This section, like the entire book, is designed to show students how sociologists of religion attack a particular problem; the goal is to illustrate how sociologists study religion rather than to provide comprehensive data on all religions. By focusing on the tools the sociologist uses for analysis and on the interrelationship of variables, the reader should have an idea about how the sociologist would approach the relationship between religion and prejudice in any religious group. Second, my own background and research in Christian theology and ethics allow me to offer a more comprehensive analysis in this tradition than in others. Third, most of the recent empirical studies on religion and prejudice have concentrated on prejudice among Christians.

CHAPTER TWELVE

Religion and Prejudice: Christianity and Racism

As we learned earlier, religion involves meaning, belonging, and institutional subsystems, each related in complex ways to the others. Sometimes these subsystems can be working at cross-purposes, with some contributing to bigotry while others combat it. So religion is related to ethnic prejudice in complex ways. Furthermore, secular forces and conflicts are often the prime cause of prejudice and discrimination, and religion, as the system of meaning, is used to justify existing inequities. Religious forces may be either cause or effect of antipathy.

The discussion in this chapter is directed to an understanding of racial bias. Religion can contribute to other types of ethnic prejudice (such as anti-Semitism), and these forms of prejudice are commented on but not explored in detail. In the following chapter we explore the relationship between religion and gender prejudice.

Empirical Findings

In the 1950s empirical studies showed that church members were more racially prejudiced than nonmembers. Despite the fact that Christianity claimed to enhance fellowship and love among people, the research indicated a correlation between Christianity and bigotry. A number of explanations were formulated to interpret this phenomenon. Some scholars attempted to identify factors in the belief system of Christianity that might contribute to prejudice. Others felt that the correlation was spurious, that both prejudice and church membership resulted from some third factor. But the whole debate changed significantly as more sophisticated and refined data were gathered.

In the 1960s several survey studies revealed that, although church members are more prejudiced than nonmembers, the most active church members were less prejudiced than any other group. The earlier studies had lumped together all members without regard to level of commitment or amount of participation in the life of the church. Because there are larger numbers of marginal members in most churches than there are active members, the statistics were weighted heavily in the direction of marginal member attitudes. The evidence now shows that infrequent church attenders are more prejudiced than nonattenders but that frequent attenders are the lowest of all on scales of prejudice (Allport 1966; Gorsuch and Aleshire 1974; Perkins 1983, 1985). In one study of nonracist respondents, the assertion that racism is incompatible with their religious beliefs was the most frequently cited reason for liberal attitudes toward others (Tamney and Johnson 1985).

This finding of low levels of prejudice only among the highly committed led to several theories and hypotheses. One of the first asserted that some church members are intrinsically religious and others are extrinsically religious (Allport 1966). **Intrinsically religious** people join churches because their faith is meaningful to them in and of itself. Such people are committed at what Rosabeth Kanter would call the "moral level" (see chapter 5). The meaning functions of religion are central for them. Individuals who are **extrinsically religious** tend to join churches because of secular advantages. Those who join because of status factors, for example, would be considered extrinsically religious. To use Kanter's formulation of types of commitment, we might say that people who are committed primarily at the instrumental and/or affective levels would be extrinsically religious. The belonging, identity, and status functions are especially important to them. Gordon Allport insisted that persons who were intrinsically religious score low on measures of racial prejudice, while persons who are extrinsically religious score high.

As research continues on this issue, it becomes obvious that the variables affecting the relationship between religion and prejudice are complex. For example, several scholars have found that the specific theological orientation of church members was very important (Hadden 1970; Quinley 1974; Roof and McKinney 1987). Fundamentalists are likely to oppose civil rights for blacks, much more so than those of other theological persuasions. Theological liberals are most sympathetic to granting equal rights to minorities, followed by the neoorthodox and then by the conservatives. One recent study even found that intrinsically religious Seventh-Day Adventists are *more* prejudiced than extrinsics (Griffin et al. 1987). These findings suggest that it is not enough to know whether a person is intrinsically religious; one must also understand something about the nature of the meaning system itself before correlations can be predicted.

Two other approaches to the correlation have indicated that other factors may be responsible for the correlation between religion and prejudice. For example, it is possible that prejudice and dogmatism (especially in the form of fundamentalism) are both results of personality factors. We explore this possibility later when we discuss simple dualism in the world view and how that relates to both prejudice and dogmatism.

Another interesting explanation suggests that prejudice and religious orthodoxy may both be products of social overconformity. Richard Gorsuch and Daniel Aleshire (1974) maintain that nonchurch membership and very active membership are both deviations from the American social norm. Hence, they offer the explanation that racial tolerance and level of church involvement both result from an individual's willingness to be a cultural deviant. The key to the relationship, they believe, may be in identifying what factors cause a person to take a stand different from the crowd (Gorsuch and Aleshire 1974).

In an earlier study, Allport (1966) had found that the *most* prejudiced people were those who were "indiscriminately proreligious." That is, they agreed with all statements that were in any way supportive of religion, including those that contradicted one another. The desire to be generally proreligious, but without giving much thought to the

For some Americans, religious conviction *is* closely related to racism and even serves to sacralize white supremacy. Above, Ku Klux Klan members display the American flag and a burning cross—the latter historically a symbol of terrrorism as it signaled to blacks that if they did not obey the norms of white superiority, they would be lynched on the nearest tree. The KKK identifies God with racial differentiation and white supremacy. (UPI/Bettmann Photo.)

specifics, might be construed as a tendency to conformism.

In his study of religion and social attitudes, Jeffrey Hadden concluded that for the laity, religious beliefs and social beliefs operate relatively independently (1970). For clergy, theological values were more closely related to social values. Some scholars have concluded from this that religion has little influence on the everyday life of people. Others have continued to search for differences among religious people to explain the differential effect of religion on people's everyday attitudes. In the remainder of this chapter, we explore the possibility that religion may simultaneously contribute both to tolerance and to bigotry.

Racism as a World View

The belief that some categories of human beings are biologically or genetically less human than others is actually a modern phenomenon (Kelsey 1965; Jordan 1968; Mosse 1978). Of course, people throughout history have believed that those who had different values, beliefs, or styles of life were stupid or inferior. Ethnocentrism (prejudice based on differences in cultures) is a universal phenomenon. One can also find occasions in history when "outsiders" have been excluded because they were not of the same lineage. But the articulation of a systematic philosophical and "scientific" statement that divides humans into higher and lower orders of being has been given credence only since the eighteenth century (Jordan 1968; Mosse 1978).[1] George Kelsey (1965) has

done an incisive analysis of the modern racist world view and its fundamental difference from the basic world view of Christianity.

The important characteristic of racism is that a person's inherent worth is judged on the basis of his or her genes. The philosophical foundations of racism are naturalistic: "Persons are understood in terms of that which is below themselves—the elements of the world, their animality, specifically their genes. To find out who people are and the quality of their life, we must inquire into their ancestry. . . . The question of who a person is, is answered in his or her genetic structure" (Kelsey 1965: 56).[2] Persons who are racist feel superior to or of greater worth than someone who has a different genetic structure (different skin color, hair color, facial features, etc.). In other words, their sense of worth is centered on their genes.

At this point, it is instructive for the reader to recall the definition of faith provided by Richard Niebuhr (quoted in chapter 1). Niebuhr

---

[1]The origins of racism are difficult to pinpoint with precision, for the emergence of the concept was gradual. The first systematic effort to classify all humanity into distinct groups based on physical characteristics was conducted by Francois Bernier in 1684. The first to place humans into a pseudoscientific ranked order (the chain of being) was Carolus Linnaeus in the 1730s. Many other efforts to develop a "scientific"

system of racial classification ensued. Contributions to the idea that humans could be classified and valued according to physical characteristics were offered by such writers as David Hume in 1748, Johann Friedrich Blumenbach in 1775, Johann Kaspar Lavater in 1781, Christian Meiners in 1785, Peter Camper in 1792, Joseph Gall in 1796, and Charles White in 1799. Meiners was the first to suggest that civilization would decline because of interracial marriages and the degeneration of the white race. The full systematic articulation of modern racial thinking did not occur until the 1850s. In that decade three major tracts were published that formulated the chief tenets of contemporary racism: Robert Knox, *Races of Men* (1850); Carl Gustav Carus, *Symbolism of the Human Form* (1853); and Comte Arthur deGobineau, *Essay on the Inequality of Human Races* (1853–55). deGobineau is commonly cited as the "father of modern racism." Regardless of whether one identifies the beginnings of racism with the Linnean chain of being (1730s), with the more careful articulations of the late 1700s, or with the systematic pseudoscientific statement by deGobineau (1850s), racism is a relatively modern construct in the Western world. For an analysis of the history of modern racism, see Winthrop D. Jordan's *White Over Black* (1968) and George L. Mosse's *Toward The Final Solution* (1978).

[2]I have modified some nouns, verbs, and pronouns in order to make the language sexually inclusive.

says that whatever provides one with a sense of worth and meaning is properly termed one's "god." Elsewhere, Niebuhr talks of faith as "trust in that which gives value to the self" (1960b: 16). In fact, the term *worship* refers to a celebration of the center of worth or the center of all other values. Literally, the word *worship* means a state or condition of worth. Kelsey cites Niebuhr's definition of faith and goes on to explain how racism serves as a faith or world view. He writes, "The racist relies on race as the source of his [or her] personal value. . . . Life has meaning and worth because it is part of the racial context. It fits into and merges with a valuable whole, the race. As the value-center, the race is the source of value, and it is at the same time the object of value" (Kelsey 1965: 27). In fact, the logical means to improve humanity is, from this perspective, selective genetic breeding and maintenance of the purity of the superior race.

Kelsey goes on to discuss the world view of Christian theology. The source of personal worth for the Christian is not found in his or her biological nature but in one's relationship with God. In this sense, Christian theology has allowed for only one distinction between persons, that between the regenerate and the unregenerate. The means of saving or improving human life is not through biological controls but through divine grace. Humans have worth because of their relationship with that which transcends them, not because of something they inherit through their genes. By contrast, racism assumes some segments of humanity to be defective in their essential being and thereby incapable of full regeneration (Kelsey 1965). The assumed defect is not one of character or spirit but a defect of creation: biologically "they" are less human.

Of course, many persons in American society are racist and still consider themselves Christian. Kelsey suggests that such persons are, in fact, polytheists; they worship more than one god. The question is, Which center of worth pre-

dominates in any given situation? Such persons do not have a single world view that gives unity, coherence, and meaning to life. Most of them are unaware of and unconcerned with theological contradictions in their outlook, or the fact that they are actually polytheists.

The official position of all major denominations in the United States is that Christianity and racism are mutually exclusive. Racism is viewed as a form of idolatry (worship of a false god) that is utterly incompatible with Christian theology. The line of argument generally follows the same pattern Kelsey outlined. Yet, despite the fact that racism and Christianity involve assumptions that are logically contradictory, the two ideologies have historically existed together and even been intertwined. Let us investigate some of the ways that Christendom may have unconsciously contributed to racist thinking.

Sources of Racial Prejudice in Christianity

Christianity may have unwittingly contributed to racism through its world view (meaning factors), its reference group influences (belonging factors), or its organizational strategies (institutional factors). In the following pages, we explore how each of these types of factors may be conducive to the formation and/or the persistence of racism.

Meaning Factors

We will explore four meaning factors in Christianity that may have affected the development and persistence of racism, but first it is necessary to make a distinction between types of racism. In his psychohistory of white racism, Joel Kovel (1970) identifies two types of racist thinking. **Dominative racism** is the desire by some people to dominate or control members of another group. It is usually expressed in attempts to subjugate members of the out-group. This is the sort of racism that histori-cally has been predominant in the southern United States. White slave owners, for ex-ample, would live and work in close proxim-ity to African Americans, even assigning black women to nurse and care for their children. White men also visited slave row for sexual purposes. Whites did not mind associating with blacks on a daily basis and having con-tact with them—as long as blacks knew their place! They were not to get "uppity" or self-assertive.

This sort of racism is quite different from the racism of the North. Here the racism was of the aversive variety. **Aversive racism** is ex-pressed in the desire to avoid contact with African Americans rather than the desire to subjugate them. In fact, northerners have often been quite moralistic about the dominative racism of the South, while they were system-atically restricting blacks to isolated neighbor-hoods and ghettos. Part of the reason that school desegregation has been more problem-atic in the North than in the South is that aversive racism has resulted in more isolated housing patterns. Therefore, desegregation has required a more significant cost. Meanwhile, with the weakening of dominative racism in the South in recent decades, some evidence suggests an increase in aversive racism there.[3]

Most measures of racism have not con-trolled for these two types of racism. A study by Frank Westie (1965) did turn up findings that would suggest high levels of aversive racism. He got much higher levels of prejudi-cial answers to questions where close personal contact was required (living next door to a black family or inviting a black couple to a

dinner party). Today, few Americans think it is acceptable to discriminate against a person on the job because of the color of her or his skin. Yet data gathered in the 1980s suggest that among white Americans 60 percent oppose open-housing laws that would permit African Americans to be neighbors, and 34 percent favor or at least would not object to laws that would *prohibit* interracial marriage (Roof and McKinney 1987). We do not really have good empirical data on how much difference there is between dominative and aversive racism in American attitudes. I do know that many stu-dents in my classes have felt that domination of another person was wrong, but by the end of the course have admitted aversive feelings they had not previously recognized.

Moral Perfection and Color Symbolism
The distinction between dominative and aversive racism is significant because Christian thought may sometimes contribute to aversive racism even while it fights against dominative racism. Several scholars have pointed to the role of Protestant pi-etism in the formation of racism. Gayraud S. Wil-more has suggested that certain strains of Protes-tant theology placed heavy emphasis on the moral purity and perfection of the "saved." The desire for moral purity was especially strong among New England Puritans and later among the Per-fectionists. An important aspect of this puritanism was the desire to avoid contact with anything that was evil or could be polluting.

Wilmore relates this to the cultural symbol-ism of European and American society. Per-haps this is most vividly seen in the color symbolism of the European languages, which is especially noticeable in English. For ex-ample, prior to the sixteenth century, the defi-nition of *black*, according to the *Oxford English Dictionary,* included the following:

> Deeply stained with dirt; soiled, dirty; foul. . . . Having dark or deadly purposes, ma-lignant; pertaining to or involving death,

---

[3]In some cases, a person may hold to both domina-tive and aversive racism, and the two types of racism may be mutually reinforcing. For analytical purposes here, I will focus on the distinctions between the two.

deadly; baneful, disastrous, sinister. . . . Foul, iniquitous, atrocious, horrible, wicked. . . . Indicating disgrace, censure, liability to punishment, etc.[4]

In discussing this phenomenon, historian Winthrop Jordan goes on to say, "Black was an emotionally partisan color, the handmaid and symbol of baseness and evil, a sign of danger and repulsion. Embedded in the concept of blackness was its opposite—whiteness. . . . White and black connoted purity and filthiness, virginity and sin, virtue and baseness, beauty and ugliness, beneficence and evil, God and the devil" (1968: 7). Even much of the art work of this period showed the devil as dark-skinned and the saintly figures as white. This color symbolism cannot be traced particularly to Christian teachings, but Christian responses to persons with dark skin may have been influenced by this symbolic association.

Wilmore insists that areas of the United States that were especially influenced by Puritanism and Perfectionism are more likely than other areas to have strong aversive racism. Pietism—in many forms—emphasized moral purity. Ownership of slaves was often condemned by these groups because it might compromise the moral righteousness of the owner. However, many of these same pietists did not want to have to associate with these dark-skinned people. Although the source of the feelings was probably only partially conscious to the individuals, they often felt that blacks were unclean—in body and in soul. They simply wished to avoid contact. Dominative racism was condemned, aversive racism was not.

Laurens Van Der Post (1955) has a slightly different interpretation of the role of perfectionistic or puritanist theology. He suggests that the desire for inner purity—and the re-

fusal to admit anything negative in oneself—caused pietists to "project" evil onto blacks.

This statue of Mary and baby Jesus is at the front of the sanctuary in Our Lady of the Sioux Church at the St. Joseph Indian School in Chamberlain, South Dakota. Jesus and Mary are clearly Native American, and the crucifix behind the altar at this same chapel has a Christ on the Cross who looks very much like a Sioux. Europeans and Americans have done the same thing, making images of Jesus with white skin, classical Greek features, and even straight blonde hair and blue eyes. Jesus was obviously Semitic and no doubt had rather dark skin and other Jewish features. But many people are more comfortable with religious heroes who look like themselves. (Photo from St. Joseph's Chapel Indian School, Our Lady of the Sioux.)

---

[4]Current English dictionaries retain many of these pejorative meanings in their definitions of "black."

His interpretation focuses on projection, but it also suggests that obsession with moral purity and innocence contributed to racism.

Jordan (1968) has shown that, among some of the religious groups that opposed slavery, the opposition was based largely on concern for how slaveholding might corrupt the soul of the owner. In this case, the ultimate goal is the purity and righteousness of the dominant group member more than concern for minority group members who were suffering. For example, one of the primary reasons for the abolitionism of Quaker John Woolman in the mid-1700s was that slaveholding created a feeling of superiority and pride in the owners. At that time, pride was considered the most heinous of sins. Because slave owning caused pride, it was a source of evil. It was domination of another group that was the central problem. By 1776 the Society of Friends were excommunicating any Quaker who owned slaves (Jordan 1968).

The Quakers were more effective than most groups at setting up programs to educate African Americans and to provide them with resources for economic independence. Their stance against dominative racism was unparalleled among religious groups. Yet, very few blacks ever became members of the Society of Friends. No doubt this was partially because the quiet, contemplative style of worship practiced by the Friends was so unlike the emotional and enthusiastic style of African religious ritual. The emotional expressions of the Baptists and Methodists were more similar to the type of religious expression familiar to people of African ancestry. Beyond this, blacks may have felt unwelcome in many Quaker congregations; Quaker pietism may have created an unconscious aversive form of racism among some members of this group. This may be part of the reason for an almost total lack of African American converts. Quakers may have been intense about ending domination, but less so about establishing associational ties by

including African Americans within their own group (Jordan 1968). Wilmore's thesis is that Christian groups may have combated dominative racism even while they unwittingly contributed to aversive racism.

The Protestant emphasis on moral purity or perfection is perhaps the most important unwitting contributor to the formation of racist attitudes among American Christians. But this doctrinal emphasis contributed primarily to one type of racism and only in the context of certain other cultural attitudes and structural circumstances. Pietism in modern America may not have the same effect. There are other aspects of Christian thought, however, that may contribute to the persistence of racism in American society.

Freewill Individualism and Failure to Recognize Institutional Discrimination Rodney Stark and Charles Glock, among others, have pointed to the importance of the Christian emphasis on free will. The doctrines of sin and salvation are based on the assumption that humans are free and responsible beings. After all, if a person was entirely predetermined in his or her behavior, one could not hold him or her responsible or guilty for an act. Guilt implies freedom of choice, with the wrong choice having been made by an individual. The concept of individual freedom is also the foundation of such socioeconomic concepts as rugged individualism. In this latter case, each individual is viewed as getting his or her just deserts in society because one's circumstances are considered a result of personal choices, lifestyle, and willingness to work hard. As Stark and Glock put it, "Christian thought and thus Western civilization are permeated with the idea that [people] are individually in control of, and responsible for, their own destinies. If I am really the 'captain of my soul' and 'the master of my fate,' then I have no one but myself to thank or blame for what happens to me" (1969: 81).   This doctrine is significant in race relations because many conservative Christians put the blame for disadvantage on those who are disadvantaged. Although there is no evidence that the doctrine of freewill individualism contributes to the *formation* of prejudicial attitudes, it may disincline those who are affluent to help those who have been subjugated to poverty and discrimination (Stark and Glock 1969). The doctrine reinforces the attitude that those who are down and out are probably getting their just deserts. And—the reasoning goes—if those who are impoverished are not receiving their due, they will better themselves without the help of anyone. Persons who hold such a view are not likely to want to change the institutional structures of society that systematically discriminate. In fact, they are not likely to recognize the existence of institutional discrimination at all. **Institutional discrimination** refers to policies that discriminate against members of a particular group. Frequently, this is not intentionally directed against members of a particular group, but because members of that group are disproportionately represented in a certain status, they are disproportionately affected.

One example of intentional institutional discrimination is the California Anti-Alien Land Act of 1913, which specified that foreign-born individuals could not own farmland unless they were American citizens or were eligible to become citizens. This in itself does not seem to discriminate unduly against any particular group. However, Congress had previously passed a law that specified that people of Japanese origin were not eligible for citizenship. Likewise, the literacy tests that required a person to be able to read and write before they were allowed to vote in certain southern states in the 1950s were disproportionately disfranchising to blacks. African Americans were not the only ones who could not vote. Nor were *all* blacks prohibited. But there is no question that illiteracy was higher in the African American community and that African Americans were disproportionately affected.

Sometimes discrimination in one institution affects discrimination in another. This is called **systemic discrimination**. For example, discrimination in education has often led to discrimination in the job market. Because African Americans, Native Americans, and Hispanics have poorer educational backgrounds (with poorly funded and staffed schools in their neighborhoods), they do not meet the job qualifications for the better-paying jobs in our society.[5] The employer is not purposefully discriminating against members of these ethnic groups, but the net effect is that Native Americans and Hispanics are underrepresented in the professional positions in our society. Institutional or systemic discrimination is discriminatory in effect, even if not in intent.[6]

The important point here is that those who hold to a strong doctrine of rugged individualism usually deny the existence or importance of institutional discrimination. Stark and Glock found that those who hold to traditional Christian doctrines of total freewill, individual responsibility, and moral retribution (punishment for lack of adherence to moral standards) are more likely to believe in rugged individualism and are less likely to work for the reduction of institutional discrimination. These religious traditionalists often maintain that the only factor necessary to reduce inequality between groups is to teach minority persons to be more responsible for their own lives.

---

[5]The percentage of various ethnic groups in the United States not having completed high school are as follows: Mexican Americans, 56 percent in 1991 (40 percent having not completed 8th grade); African Americans, 33 percent in 1991; Native Americans, 49 percent as of 1989. This is compared to a figure of 20 percent for white Anglos. At the other end of the scale, 22.3 percent of white Americans have completed college, compared to 6.2 percent of Mexican Americans, 7.7 percent of Native Americans, and 11.5 percent of African Americans (U.S. Census Bureau 1991, 1992).

[6]Students who want to explore more fully the subtle workings of institutional discrimination may want to see *Discrimination American Style*, by Joe R. Feagin and Clairece Booher Feagin (1986).

Hence, a particular religious belief (freewill individualism) is correlated to other beliefs (such as rugged individualism) and the entire set of beliefs contributes to apathy about racial discrimination. Clearly, we have no proof that the religious beliefs come first and cause belief in rugged individualism or cause complacency. In fact, it is likely that these beliefs simply justify complacency rather than cause it. They allow people to ignore structural inequality and to benefit from inequality without feeling guilty about it. The religious beliefs do not contribute to the formation of racism, but they do contribute to its persistence.

The "Miracle Motif" and Resignation to the Status Quo   Religious people may also allow racism to persist because of adherence to a "miracle motif" (Stark and Glock 1969: 85). A **miracle motif** is the expectation that God will bring change only when the divinely appointed time arrives. It includes a belief that change will occur without the benefit of human resources. Hence, working for change is viewed as futile. Because the matter is viewed as being in God's hands, the miracle motif does not inspire members to work for change. Insofar as religious people adhere to this outlook, they are likely to encourage the persistence of racial discrimination by their own lack of action. Fortunately—from the standpoint of combating racism—the miracle motif is far from universal in the Christian community.

Particularism and Antipathy to Outsiders   Another set of religious beliefs is also correlated with certain kinds of prejudice. This set revolves around the assumption that one's own religion is uniquely true and legitimate and that all others are false. Only members of one's own group are expected to be saved. Glock and Stark (1966) refer to this orientation as **particularism**.[7] Not all religious people are particularistic. However, some groups teach that persons who are members of any other denomination or any other faith are damned. Glock and Stark (1966) found that among Christians particularism is highly correlated with anti-Semitism. It is also highly correlated with antipathy toward atheists and agnostics. However, they did not find a correlation between particularism and racial prejudice (Stark and Glock 1969). This is no doubt due to the fact that both blacks and whites in the United States are predominantly Christian.

Particularism would be expected to contribute to racial prejudice in social settings where boundaries between racial and religious groups are coextensive. In other words, in societies where members of one racially identifiable group is Christian and members of another physically identifiable group are Moslems, particularism may contribute to antipathy between them. Hence, particularism is a potential contributor to racial prejudice in certain circumstances, and it was definitely operative in the formation of racism in this country—before blacks were converted to Christianity (Jordan 1968). However, particularism does not currently seem to be a factor in antiblack sentiment in the United States.[8]

---

[7]Particularism is a form of ethnocentrism—a concept that may be more familiar to sociology students.

[8]Because particularism does contribute to certain kinds of prejudice, a good deal of attention has been given to assessing its relation to hatred of Jews. There are several Christian doctrines that, if narrowly defined, may lead to a particularistic view. Gordon Allport, for example, points to the doctrine of election as a belief system that may contribute to bigotry (1966). The doctrine of election is the belief by some people that they are God's chosen people. The issue is whether this doctrine is interpreted as election for service and responsibility or election for salvation. Some charismatics, fundamentalists, and born-again Christians emphasize that only those who have experienced the Holy in exactly the way they have are eligible for salvation. Others of these groups may view their religious experience as a unique call to serve humanity; they do not interpret the concept of election in particularistic terms. When the doctrine of election is interpreted in terms of exclusive salvation, it is highly correlated to particularism. Whether it is a cause, as Allport suggests, remains to be established by empirical research.

Despite the fact that official Christianity manifestly opposes racism and encourages a sense of the brotherhood and sisterhood of humankind, certain beliefs may have the effect of increasing certain kinds of prejudice.[9] This brings us to the second process by which religion may contribute to prejudice: reference group loyalties and we-they categories of thought.

Belonging Factors

Religion may contribute to prejudice through its sense of community and the feeling of belonging. As the religious community becomes a major reference group, people want to conform to the norms of the community in order to feel accepted. Furthermore, as they begin to identify closely with the group, they develop a sense of "us" and "them." In fact, we discovered in chapter 5 that the creation of strong group boundaries was one technique used to enhance commitment to a religious group (see the discussion of Kanter's theory of commitment, especially affective commitment). Now we explore three factors that relate in-group loyalties and norms to prejudice.

Informal Group Norms   The informal community of believers that provides individuals with a sense of belonging is a very important part of religion. However, the community develops unwritten norms and expectations—some of which may conflict with official religious policy. In an attempt to conform, members may adhere to the informal norms of the community rather than to the official policy of the formal religious organization. It is noteworthy that Gerhard Lenski (1963) found that communal members (who are influenced

through the belonging function) were much more likely to be racially prejudiced than were associational members (who were either morally or instrumentally committed). Informal norms and values of the community may be contrary to the official ones, but they may be vigorously enforced through informal sanctions (Lenski 1963). A group of Lutheran laity at a Sunday afternoon picnic may tell ethnic jokes or may subtly reinforce negative images of blacks, regardless of the minister's sermon that morning to the contrary. The reference group norms are often more powerful in influencing behavior than are the idealized norms in the ideology.

Group Boundaries and Identification with the In-Group   Another major theory of racial and ethnic prejudice is based on the tendency of people to accept those who are similar to them and to be suspicious of anyone who is defined as "different." This view of the cause of prejudice is sometimes called the we-they theory, perhaps best illustrated by an empirical study conducted by Eugene Hartley (1946). Hartley used a variation of the Bogardus Social Distance Survey, an instrument designed to measure prejudice toward various ethnic groups. A list of ethnic groups is provided and respondents are asked to rate the closest relationship that they would be willing to have with a member of that group. Seven categories are provided, ranging from "would marry a person who is a member of this group" and "would be willing to have a member of this group as a best friend" to "would allow only as visitors to my country" and "would exclude from my country entirely."

Hartley adapted the Bogardus instrument by adding three fictitious groups: Danireans, Pireneans, and Wallonians. Using a random sample of college students at eight northeastern universities, he attempted to measure the correlation between prejudice toward blacks and prejudice toward these fictitious groups. Hartley found a high level of prejudice toward

---

[9]There is one other belief system or outlook that may contribute directly to prejudice: dualism. However, I wish to delay our discussion of dualistic world views and prejudice until certain other theoretical foundations are set forth.

these three nonexistent groups: more than half of the respondents expressed a desire to avoid contact with these people and some respondents wanted them expelled from the country. Moreover, nearly three-fourths of those who were prejudiced against blacks and Jews were also prejudiced against Pireneans, Wallonians, and Danireans. He used these data as evidence that prejudice is not caused by stereotypes (stereotypes are rigid and largely erroneous images of a particular group or category of people). After all, no one has a negative stereotype of a group that does not exist. The negative feelings of respondents toward Danireans, Pireneans, and Wallonians were based on the fact that these groups sounded unlike the respondents. That is, their negative reaction was based on a simple issue of whether the people sounded similar to or different from the respondents; the name Pireneans sounded more like one of "them" than one of "us" (Sherif 1976). Many other empirical studies by social psychologists have supported this we-they theory of the causes of prejudice.

One of the most important functions of religion, as we have seen at several points in this book, is to provide a sense of belonging, a sense of group identity, a sense of we. To add to this, a number of Christian groups place a strong emphasis on particularism (discussed in the previous section). Such a belief would tend to add to the in-group sense of superiority and to the distinction between "us" and "them." The belonging function of religion, then, is capable of contributing to antipathy.

The development of religiously based we-they prejudice is especially likely in situations where racial boundaries and religious boundaries are coextensive. The importance of its influences is illustrated by several empirical studies that show higher levels of prejudice against those with differing belief (e.g., atheists or Jews) than against those of another race (blacks) (Rokeach et al. 1960; Rokeach 1968; Smith et al. 1967; Byrne and Wong 1962;

Byrne and McGraw 1964). But if "they" practice a different religion and also look different, the exclusionary tendencies are reinforced even further.

The white Christians who encountered blacks from the fifteenth to the eighteenth centuries were meeting people who were different on several counts. In fact, in the eighteenth century, the words *white, Christian,* and *civilized* were used by many European writers as synonyms for "we," while the terms *black, heathen,* and *savage* were used interchangeably with "they" (Jordan 1968). At that point, much of the denigration of blacks was because they were not Christians. We-they religious distinctions, then, may have contributed to the formation of racial prejudice, even if these factors are not a primary cause of racial prejudice today. Nonetheless, one can see the application of religio-racial we-they categories in contemporary Ku Klux Klan literature and in various types of anti-Semitic materials.

An Alternative Perspective on the Causes of We-They Boundaries   At this point, it is helpful to return to a theoretical perspective discussed earlier in this text: cognitive structuralism. This offers an interesting alternative interpretation. In chapter 6 we explored the cognitive structuralist theory of moral and intellectual development. This perspective, based on the earlier work of Jean Piaget, maintains that the human mind grows through sequential stages. Cognitive structuralists insist that all humans go through the same steps but that a person can freeze at any one stage. Lawrence Kohlberg, for example, identifies three levels of thinking (which translated, might be called egocentric, ethnocentric, and universalistic thinking), and he specifies two stages at each level (see chapter 6 for more detail). Other cognitive structuralists have conducted research on the overall world view or mode of perceiving the world of college students as they move through stage 3 (interpersonal sharing—loyalty to one's own group), stage 4 (social maintenance—loyalty to the authority structures of one's community and one's nation), and stage 5 (social contract—protection of the rights of all people, regardless of whether they are members of one's own in-group). William Perry (1970) identifies nine "positions" or modes of perception and elaborates them in much more detail than Kohlberg spelled out in his scheme. Karen Kitchener (1986) suggests seven substages.[10] We do not have the space here to explore each of these positions in detail, but these scholars offer some interesting insights into we-they thinking.

Perry and Kitchener have found that people who are in stage 3 according to Kohlberg's classification[11] are extremely dualistic in their thinking. They see "right" and "wrong" as absolute categories and have little sense that moral decision making can be highly ambiguous, with many shades of gray. People with this outlook tend to view authority figures, absolute truth, and rightness as closely aligned with one another. Furthermore, all three are synonymous with "we." On the other hand, wrongness and "they" are viewed as identical. Group loyalty at this stage is so strong that it is unthinkable that "we" could be anything but right. Furthermore, the absoluteness of right and wrong categories contributes to highly dogmatic thinking. Perry calls this outlook "simple dualism."

Through the challenge of the educational process and through cognitive dissonance created in the classroom, the subjects began to recognize the ambiguities of human history and the shades of meaning that can be applied to human behavior. They moved into a position of complex dualism (similar to Kohlberg's stage 4, social maintenance) and eventually to relativism and to universalistic commitment. The important point here is that some students perceived the world in terms of simple dualism, and those who were dualistic saw every issue in terms of "we" and "they." This would suggest that *any* belief system or ideology is likely to be perceived and interpreted by some people in categorical terms. It may not be the belief system or the reference group per se that causes the prejudicial outlook, but rather the cognitive mode of organizing and interpreting experience. Insofar as some people view all things as categorically right or wrong and insofar as those persons view right as synonymous with "we" and wrong as synonymous with "they," a fertile ground is tilled for prejudice and antipathy. This suggests that a dualistic world view—regardless of specific religious content—is likely to be related to prejudice. It also suggests that religious particularism may be effect rather than cause. Finally, it offers an explanation for the apparent high correlation between dualism, dogmatism, and prejudice.[12] One recent empirical test has

---

[10]Perry does not discuss his research in relation to Kohlberg's stages. His research is on students and how their thinking patterns change during their four years of college. He engaged in an inductive exploration of the patterns of perception of these students and only then tried to interpret the data and develop a theory. Kitchener's work is a continuation and refinement of Perry's scheme. Nonetheless, one cannot help but see the correlations of their "positions" with Kohlberg's stages. Hence, I have taken the liberty to discuss Perry's findings in relation to Kohlberg's stages rather than present an entirely new paradigm at this point.

[11]Stage 3 thinkers see right as what is popular with one's closest associates. The primary motive is to be popular and to be accepted by one's in-group.

[12]At this point, we lack the hard empirical evidence that might demonstrate a correlation between religious dualism and prejudice, largely because dualism has not been operationalized and studied in relationship to various measures of prejudice. However, we do know that Christian fundamentalists are somewhat more racist than other Christians and they are much more likely to be prejudiced toward Jews and atheists. Because fundamentalists tend to be dualistic (i.e., the "children of light" versus the "children of darkness"), the correlation between dualism and prejudice would seem to have some empirical support. However, the correlation between fundamentalism and dualism is far from perfect, and the nature of causality in this matter is not firmly established.

found that stage of faith development (using Fowler's model) is a strong predictor of prejudice against members of any "out-group." (The interpretation of causality between reference group and structural theories is compared in Figure 12.1.) Of course, some religious traditions reinforce this tendency to dogmatic intolerance of others by emphasizing the absoluteness of their doctrine and the unquestionable stature of their authority figures (either clergy or charismatic leaders). In fact, questioning the tradition or the correctness of

an authority has sometimes been equated with a lack of faith and a decline in status within the group. If one takes the structuralist paradigm seriously, this would mean that many religious groups try to eliminate the very cognitive dissonance that would lead to intellectual growth and to a reduction in we-they thinking.

To summarize, the belonging functions of a particular religion may enhance antipathy toward others in several ways. First, the informal community may develop norms that

▶ **FIGURE 12.1**

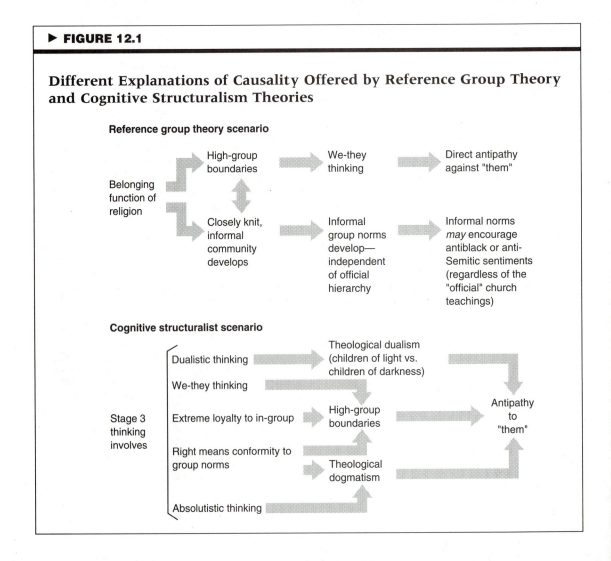

Different Explanations of Causality Offered by Reference Group Theory and Cognitive Structuralism Theories

Reference group theory scenario

Belonging function of religion → High-group boundaries → We-they thinking → Direct antipathy against "them"

Belonging function of religion → Closely knit, informal community develops → Informal group norms develop—independent of official hierarchy → Informal norms *may* encourage antiblack or anti-Semitic sentiments (regardless of the "official" church teachings)

Cognitive structuralist scenario

Stage 3 thinking involves:

Dualistic thinking → Theological dualism (children of light vs. children of darkness)

We-they thinking

Extreme loyalty to in-group → High-group boundaries

Right means conformity to group norms → Theological dogmatism

Absolutistic thinking

→ Antipathy to "them"

encourage discrimination, despite the official position of the church. Second, the development of high boundaries between groups can reinforce we-they categories of thought. On the other hand, cognitive structuralists suggest that we-they thinking may be a *result* of persons being in stage 3 ethical thinking—with its simple dualism, its intense group loyalty, and its dogmatic and particularistic outlook. This view suggests an alternative interpretation of the initial cause. I present this structuralist view so that students can see how a new theoretical perspective can totally change the kinds of questions one raises and the assumptions one makes about causality. Regardless of one's theoretical perspective, religion is known to be related to prejudice insofar as it creates and/or sanctifies we-they thinking.

Institutional Factors

Religion as an institutional structure can affect social behavior somewhat independently from the belief system or the reference group factors. This is perhaps best illustrated by a study of the clergy of Little Rock, Arkansas, in the midst of a major racial crisis.

Ernest Campbell and Thomas Pettigrew (1959) studied the role of Protestant ministers in the school desegregation controversy in 1957. Consistent with other findings, they found that ministers of small working-class sects were supportive of segregation and that most of the clergy of mainline denominations were sympathetic to integration. However, very few of the ministers of mainline denominations spoke out or got actively involved in the conflict. The official positions of their denominations, their professional reference system (other mainline clergy), and their own personal convictions supported integration. Yet, they did not take a prophetic stance, which one might expect.

When they did speak out, it was often in generalities, with references to "deeper issues," or with other techniques that would

prevent anyone from taking offense (or from taking their statements too seriously). Social psychologists use the term *aligning actions* to refer to statements that modify the meaning of other statements or actions. When the clergy in Little Rock did discuss the racial crisis with their congregations, they would usually preface their remarks with a comment that softened the impact of the stance. An ethical view can be moderated and made more palatable when a minister begins by saying something such as this: "Everyone has to make up his or her own mind on moral questions. My opinion is simply the opinion of one person, and there is certainly room for other views." Such statements allowed ministers in Little Rock to speak briefly to the issue of segregation without raising too much opposition or offending people too deeply. Members of the congregation were, in effect, invited to ignore the comment or to view it as one opinion among many.

Other clergy used the "exaggerated Southerner technique," stressing their own deep roots as Southerners and their ancestors' positions as plantation owners. Having said this, a few brief comments would be offered on the values of desegregation or at least of peaceful action. Again, the effort was to avoid being cast as an outsider or as a subversive. This technique, like the first, allowed ministers to feel that the issue had been addressed and that a prophetic stance had been maintained. Hence, they could avoid feeling guilty for having ignored the issue. They felt they had not compromised their principles.

Those clergy who spoke out in favor of desegregation used aligning actions such as these. By doing so, ministers avoided becoming isolated and alienated from their congregations, but they also made it easier for congregations to take their ministers less seriously. Moreover, few clergy spoke out against segregation—even with the use of aligning actions.

One reason that the clergy avoided discussing segregation was because their congregations overwhelmingly supported it. Because their congregations were important reference groups to the pastors, they were caught between reference groups (the professional reference and the congregational one). Furthermore, many held to the position that "you can't teach those you can't reach." They insisted that if members of the congregation were offended by the minister's position, then later opportunities for education and change would be lost. Such factors were no doubt part of the reluctance of clergy to take a strong stand, but the most important factors were institutional in character.

Although the official statements of most denominations condemn segregation, the working propositions of the church bureaucracies are such that rewards come to those who do not "rock the boat." Concepts of success in the ministry are related to growth in membership and in church finances. The addition of a new educational wing on the church or the need to build a new and much larger church building are often viewed as signs that the pastor must be doing something right. Moreover, ministers often view harmonious, satisfied congregations as evidence of success. The minister whose church is racked with conflict and is declining in membership is certainly not a prime candidate for promotion to a larger church. Whether the minister is part of an episcopal system (where a bishop appoints clergy to a congregation) or of a congregational system (where a pulpit committee from the local church seeks out a pastor to hire), a reputation for controversy and uncompromising conscience is not an asset. The minister who wants to advance in his or her career keeps the congregation united, the funds flowing, and the membership stable and/or increasing.

This process provides an excellent illustration of Thomas O'Dea's "dilemma of mixed motivation." Clergy were torn between two motivations: being faithful to the prophetic teachings of the church on the one hand and enhancing their careers by doing that which is necessary to be "successful" on the other. Many felt that they would work on one of the goals first (building their careers) and would later take on the hard task of speaking their consciences forthrightly. Yet some observers were skeptical of such a strategy. One Little Rock minister who did speak out had this to report:

I talk to the young ministers and I ask them why they aren't saying anything. They say no one will listen to them, they aren't known and their churches are small. But wait, they say, until we get big churches and are widely known. We won't be silent then. Then I turn to the ministers in the big churches and I listen to them trying to explain why they have done so little. Their answer is a simple one; they say they have too much to lose. Only recently, one such man said to a group I was in, "I've spent seventeen years of my life building up that church, and I'm not going to see it torn down in a day" (Campbell and Pettigrew 1959: 120–21).

A complex set of factors plays on a minister and affects decision making. Some of these factors may create pressure that calls for contradictory behavior. Just understanding the belief system of a religion is by no means sufficient to understanding the behavior of religious persons. In the case of racial bigotry in Little Rock, the official position of most denominations called for prophetic forthrightness by the clergy, but at the same time they provided concrete rewards (promotions to bigger churches) for taking the road of least resistance. In effect, the institutional procedures operated to reward those who were restrained in their comments or even complacent about the entire matter. The silence by the clergy, in turn, created an environment in which it seemed that everyone shared the same view. Conformity to norms of prejudice was easy, for few people were saying anything to create cognitive dissonance or to challenge the reference group norm. In such a case, religion is *not* a factor in *causing* prejudice, but in failing to oppose prejudice forthrightly, the churches *contributed* to the *continued existence* of racism.

A study by Harold Quinley (1974) found similar patterns among Protestant clergy in California. He explored variables affecting the willingness of ministers to take prophetic stands on controversial social issues. The region and the era were more conducive to social activism than was Little Rock, Arkansas, in the 1950s, so it is not surprising that a higher percentage of Protestant clergy were involved in social issues. Twenty-five percent of the clergy studied by Quinley had an activist ministry, and 5 percent were even willing to risk arrest to express their convictions. The issues in California were civil rights legislation, the Vietnam War, and organization of farm workers. Quinley found that support for prophetic ministry depended on at least three variables: the relative liberalism or conservatism of the congregation, the liberalism or conservatism of the denominational leaders, and the organization of the denomination (congregational, presbyterian, or episcopal). He did find, however, that regardless of denominational polity, congregational members have more control over most minister's actions than do the denominational hierarchy. While the hierarchy may control appointments and removals from office in episcopal systems (with a bishop) and in presbyterian organizations (in which denominational leaders and the local church share in decision making), the local congregation controls salary in virtually all Protestant denominations. So support from a powerful and like-minded denominational hierarchy could enhance the tendency to have a prophetic ministry, but local congregations frequently had a moderating effect on the liberalism of clergy. As Quinley concludes, "Despite a very liberal hierarchy in most Protestant denominations, most parish ministers believe that their careers would suffer if they became

overly involved in controversial public issues" (1974: 284). Ethical convictions regarding civil rights and other matters were often muted in California, as well as in Little Rock, by institutional factors. These same forces were also found to be at work among clergy during racial conflicts in Rochester, New York (Martin 1972), and in Boston (Thomas 1985).

Of course, religious institutions are also very capable of using their influence to combat racism. For example, the Roman Catholic Church was instrumental in starting a program known as Project Equality (discussed in chapter 10). This involved churches using their buying power to reduce racial discrimination by requiring all their suppliers to adopt affirmative action policies. Some businesspeople became angry with their church for such coercion and cut off their pledges, and some local churches discontinued the activity because of this response. Nonetheless, many national church offices remained members of Project Equality (as did some local congregations). This suggests only one of many ways in which churches have used their corporate influence to bring change, particularly at the level of the national denominational office. In fact, several studies have indicated that the more insulated the official church hierarchy is from the local congregation, the more likely they are to emphasize egalitarian stances. Southern Catholics, for example, have been less likely to discriminate than members of congregationally based Protestant churches in the South. This has been largely because bishops, who are not directly responsible to the local congregation, have been willing to advocate strongly the official church posture (Beck 1978; J. Wood 1970, 1981).

My point is that institutional factors may work to enhance racial prejudice and discrimination or to combat it. But just knowing the official position of the denomination does not give the whole picture. Just as the religious belief system may have countervailing influences within it, so also may the religious institution provide motivations and influences that run counter to the official doctrine. It is simplistic to say that religion contributes to bigotry or it contributes to tolerance. First, it is necessary to know what interpretation of Christianity one is talking about: pietist, fundamentalistic, orthodox, liberal, and so on. Second, any given religious group may be contributing to tolerance in some respects while contributing to exclusivity and prejudice in other ways. The meaning, belonging, and institutional subsystems that comprise religion may work at cross-purposes. Our discussion of the countervailing influences of religion here has been only illustrative of the process. A comprehensive analysis would take another book in itself.

Our focus on ways that religion sometimes contributes to bigotry is only part of the picture. Religious prejudice is frequently an expression of other conflicts within the society at large. That is, religious prejudice is frequently effect rather than cause.

Social Conflict and Religious Expression: The Conflict Perspective

It often happens that religious prejudice is actually a reflection of larger social conflicts rather than their cause. In this case, religion may be acting purely as a justification for discriminatory behavior; the out-group is defined as spiritually inferior so that members of the in-group do not feel guilty about their blatantly unjust behavior. This perspective is an important contribution of the Marxian theory of social conflict. Marxian analysts look to nonreligious causes of prejudice, although they recognize the role of religion in maintaining social inequities.

Perhaps the most important theory of racial and ethnic discrimination is that which insists that prejudice and discrimination are caused by conflict over scarce resources. Some items in any society are scarce and nondivisible or nonsharable (or at least are viewed as such). The best jobs, the best housing, the best educational opportunities (admittance into a professional school), and social status are examples of items that are viewed as scarce and over which there may be conflict.

Three variables are central in discrimination and prejudice (Noel 1968; Vander Zanden 1983). First, when two groups are in conflict over some scarce resource, the likelihood of prejudice is very high. It is interesting to note the increase in anti-Arab sentiments in this country after the energy crisis began in the 1970s (with Arabs controlling oil resources). Second, when the two groups in conflict have differences that are highly visible physically (skin color, facial features) or culturally (dress, language, beliefs), prejudice and discrimination are even more likely to occur. Symbolic distinctions between groups allow for strong feelings of "we" and "they." Third, where one of the groups has more power to control access to scarce and valued resources, discrimination and prejudice are nearly universal. The more powerful group uses its power to control the resources. It then develops stereotypes of the out-group in order to justify discriminatory behavior and to make that behavior seem morally right. Religion is frequently a part of this moral justification.

An important point here is that prejudice and discrimination are enhanced if the groups in question differ not only in their economic interests but also in their physical appearance, their language, their culture, and their religion. In cases where two groups differ in all of these ways, it is common for the conflict to be justified and highlighted in religious terms. Native Americans were freely exploited and their lands taken from them because they were "heathens" who needed to be "civilized" (which usually meant "Christianized").

Likewise, many southern states had laws that forbade conversion of slaves during the early period of the slave trade. The slave owners were afraid that, if blacks held the same religious beliefs as whites, owners would be forced to free their chattel. Once this idea passed, justification for discrimination came to be based more intensely on color than on religious affiliation.

The central point is this: When lines of differentiation between people in racial characteristics, cultural backgrounds, language, religious orientations, and economic self-interests are coextensive and mutually exclusive, antipathy is likely to occur (Farley 1988). Although religion is one cause, it is not necessarily the primary cause. However, religion may be used as the primary justification for hostility. After all, if "they" are immoral heathens and infidels who are damned by God, treating them with something less than respect seems quite reasonable and moral. It must therefore be recognized that what seems on the surface to be religious prejudice may, in fact, be caused by conflicts between groups that seek control over the same scarce resources. The source of the conflict is primarily economic.

The conflict in Northern Ireland represents a situation in which economic, religious, and ethnic boundaries are coextensive. The Protestants are the landowners and are of Scottish descent. The Catholics tend to be poor laborers who are fiercely loyal to the concept of an independent and united Ireland. The conflict is referred to as one between Protestants and Catholics, but religion is not the sole or even the primary cause of the conflict. The medieval crusades of Christians against the Moors were also justified on religious grounds, but the conflict was rooted in economic and ethnic interests as well.

In social circumstances, where members of an ethnic group are not necessarily of the same social class or the same religious group, the likelihood of religiously based prejudice is reduced. Likewise, where members of a particular religious group do not share the same ethnic background or economic interests, the likelihood of prejudice is somewhat diminished, and religious justifications for discriminatory behavior are also reduced. Hence, religion often acts to reflect larger social conflicts. The student of religion must be wary of overgeneralizing about religion as a cause of social conflict. In any given situation, religion may well be a cause of conflict, but each case must be evaluated in terms of the specific social setting and the specific world view of the religious group.

Summary

Christianity may contribute in subtle ways to the development and persistence of racism and other ethnic prejudice, even if its official posture mitigates against such prejudice. Although there are differences between members of different denominations and between theological liberals and conservatives, for the most part, the most religiously committed people tend to rank lower on scales of racism than less active members or than those disaffiliated with religion. Further, the logic of Christian theology is such that racism is really incompatible with Christianity; racism is, in fact, a theology with its own internal logic and value structure. But despite all this, Christianity has sometimes contributed, even unwittingly, to the formation and continued existence of racism.

First, aversive discrimination may have been unconsciously fostered through a meaning system that linked concern with purity to color symbolism (with blackness associated with evil). Other beliefs emphasizing individual autonomy and free will may also have contributed to the persistence of racism because of a failure of Christians to recognize the realities of systemic or institutional racism.

Second, prejudice may be passed on through the we-they boundaries and through informal norms of the community. The belonging function of religion can be a source of exclusivity and hostility.

Finally, formal institutional structures may contribute to the *persistence* of prejudice by rewarding behaviors other than prophetic ministry. Ministerial or organizational definitions of success may reward (with promotions and professional advancements) those whose style is noncontroversial and unobtrusive.

In short, the three subsystems of religion may sometimes work at cross-purposes, contributing simultaneously to tolerance of others and to bigotry.

Not only is Christianity capable of contributing to racial prejudice but religious prejudice is also often a reflection of larger conflict in the society. This is especially true if color lines, socioeconomic stratification, political parties, and religious boundaries are coextensive and mutually exclusive. In any case, our discussion points to the interactive relationship between religious values and the social conditions at large. We have also found that religions are themselves complex entities that can have many countervailing forces within them.

Religion and Prejudice: Christianity and Sexism

Women's groups that are committed to changing gender roles and attitudes have often charged that religion perpetuates traditional role expectations of men and women. Historically, many groups have refused to ordain women—barring them from the major leadership position in the church. A few denominations continue to maintain this position today. Recent studies have suggested that this is not only true of the established churches; women have often been singled out and accused of sexual weakness, sinfulness, and impurity in the new religious movements as well (Jacobs 1987). Some pagan religious traditions, such as Wicca, have a much more positive attitude toward the feminine, with female gods and leadership positions for women. But as John Hawley concludes, "Theological appreciation of the feminine does not necessarily lead to a positive evaluation of real women" (1986: 235). In the following pages, we explore the role of religion in sacralizing gender stereotypes and roles.

To keep the scope of this chapter manageable, we again focus primarily on the relationship between Christianity and gender prejudice. Although the coverage is not comprehensive of all religious traditions, students should be developing skills in analysis and should gain a sense of how sociologists approach the issue for any religious tradition. We begin by exploring the empirical evidence about whether organized religion really does stigmatize women and legitimate male dominance.

Empirical Findings

We have much less empirical research available on religiosity and sexism[1] than we have on religion and racial attitudes. Most of the

---

[1]Sexism refers to any behavior that discriminates against a person because of sex and any ideology that maintains that one sex is intrinsically and immutably superior to the other. We will be dealing in this chapter primarily with ideologies or belief systems that define women as inherently inferior. Sex bias may be manifested in either of two related concepts: rigid *gender-role expectations* or *concepts of gender*. Gender roles are tasks that are assigned to males or females. Concepts of

studies available contrast church members with nonmembers, or they compare gender-role attitudes between denominations. Nonetheless, researchers have turned up some interesting findings. We can say that generally those who are nonaffiliated tend to score lower on measures of sexism than those who are church members (Bayer 1975; Dempewolff 1974; Henley and Pincus 1978; Lipman-Blumen 1972; Martin et al. 1980; Mason and Bumpass 1975; McMurry 1978; Meier 1972; Tedlin 1978). But unlike the studies of religion and racial prejudice (in which the most active church members were least prejudiced), the most active church members in the United States have been found to be most likely to hold sexist attitudes (McMurry 1978; Lehman 1985; Roof and McKinney 1987). Interestingly, the correlation does not seem to hold in Canada. The religiously devout appear no more likely than other Canadians to hold traditionalist views of gender roles, although our data are very limited for that country (Bibby 1987a).

One study in the United States compared the effects of thirteen different variables on gender role traditionalism and found religious affiliation to be the most important single factor in predicting gender attitudes (Martin et al. 1980). Individuals who are fundamentalistic in their religious orientation are more likely than other religious persons to insist that women "stay in their place" (Hesselbart 1976; Thornton and Freedman 1979). Further, there are significant variations between denominations, with active members of liberal denominations (United Church of Christ, Episcopal, and Presbyterian) less traditional than inactives in these churches and far less traditional than conservative Protestants (Southern Bap-

tists, Evangelicals, Fundamentalists, Pentecostals, Nazarenes, and Adventists). Indeed, in every American religious group *except* the liberal denominations,[2] level of church activity was positively correlated to gender-role traditionalism (Roof and McKinney 1987).

Another study used the distinction between intrinsic and extrinsic religious orientations, which Gordon Allport had used in studying racial prejudice, and applied it to a study of sex bias. However, in the case of sexism, it was intrinsic religiosity (valuing religious experience for its own sake and not because of secondary rewards) that correlated with prejudice (Kahoe 1974). Furthermore, one's present religiosity and affiliation have been found to be more important predictors of gender-role attitudes than one's childhood religious orientation (Lipman-Blumen 1972; Welch 1975). The bulk of this research suggests that there might be something about Orthodox Christian theology that contributes to sexist attitudes. Such a finding would indicate that the relationship between religion and prejudice is quite different in the cases of racism and sexism. Let us explore the factors that seem to contribute to gender bias among Christians.

Sources of Sexism in Christianity

As with racial prejudice, we will investigate three ways that religion may be related to sex bias: meaning factors, belonging factors, and institutional factors. These three dimensions are explored because, as we have seen, religion is a set of ideas about life, a reference group that provides a sense of belonging, and an

gender are ideas about the innate personality characteristics and capacities of the "normal" female (femininity) or of the "normal" male (masculinity). Gender roles are usually justified on the basis of gender concepts.

[2]Liberal denominations in this analysis included liberal and moderate white denominations (e.g., Presbyterians, Episcopalians, United Methodists, American Baptists, Christian Church), mainstream black Protestants, Roman Catholics, and Jews.

organization with established roles, rules, and bureaucratic structures.

Meaning Factors

One might expect that George Kelsey's thesis on Christianity and racism being philosophically incompatible might apply to sexism as well. After all, Christian theology has stressed that one's worth is not founded in one's chromosomes but in one's relationship to God. Basing one's sense of self-worth on gender rather than on skin color would seem to be no less a form of idolatry. Indeed, logic would seem to require such a position. However, the history of sex bias is much longer than that of racial bias. Sexism is not a modern phenomenon; it is deeply rooted in the religious and philosophical traditions of the Western world. Sexual differences have been viewed as creations of God, and sexual inequality has frequently been viewed as God-ordained. Hence, the meaning system has often reinforced gender roles (tasks designated as "women's work" or "men's work") and concepts of gender (concepts of "masculinity" or "femininity"). Because sexism is so much a part of the history of the Western world, it is appropriate that we briefly explore sex-role attitudes in Western philosophical and religious thought. Obviously we can only scratch the surface in the space we have here, but it is instructive to note some of the views held at various points in history by influential religious and philosophical thinkers and by religious bodies.

A Historical Overview of Gender Attitudes in Western Christianity   Because of the increase of women theologians and biblical scholars, more attention has been given in recent years to gender-role and gender assumptions in the Old and New Testaments. Familiarity with the original Hebrew, Greek, and Aramaic has allowed women scholars to find patterns that were previously overlooked.

For example, the Hebrew language has two different words that have commonly been translated as *man*. One of these, *'adham,* is a generic term that refers to all of humanity. The other word, *'ish,* refers specifically to males. Because both terms have been translated into English as *man,* some of the subtle implications are lost in the translation. The passage in the first chapter of Genesis that says that God created man is written with the term *'adham.* Hence, it would read "God created humanity in his own image, male and female he created them." Here the scriptures are less sexist than some people assume when they are limited to English versions (Bird 1974; Trible 1979).

Elsewhere it is clear that the scripture was written for males, as in the books of law (Bird 1974). The legal code is divided into apoditic law (moral commandments) and casuistic law (case law). The apoditic law is written primarily to men in that the literary voice and the examples are relevant to males. The Tenth Commandment provides a good example: "You shall not covet your neighbor's house; you shall not covet your neighbor's wife, or his manservant, or his maidservant, or his ox, or his ass, or anything that is your neighbor's." Not only does the passage specify *wife* rather than the more general term *spouse,* but the wife is included in a list of property that was owned exclusively by men. Furthermore, the Hebraic second-person pronoun, which we translate as *you,* had masculine and feminine forms (similar to the way our third-person pronoun has masculine and feminine forms: he and she). In the Ten Commandments, as in most of the apoditic law, the masculine form of the second-person pronoun was used. Clearly, the community was being addressed only through its male members. Note as another example the audience that is being addressed in Exodus 22:22–24: "You shall not afflict any widow or orphan. If you do ... then your wives shall become widows and your children fatherless."

Similar assumptions are part of the casuistic law, in which punishments for committing proscribed acts are spelled out. Most casuistic law begins with the formula "If a man does X, then. . . . " But the term *man* here does not translate as the generic term *person,* for it is the masculine term *'ish* that is used. In those instances in which laws were articulated for women, they often served to remind them of their inferior position. Women were defined as unclean during their menstrual period and were unfit to enter the temple for seven days after the birth of a son. By comparison, women were unclean for fourteen days after the birth of a daughter! Such contamination was not normally associated with the natural bodily processes of men.

Of course, attitudes toward women are not consistent in the Old Testament, for it was written over a period of many centuries and contains many types of literature. The Book of Proverbs, for example, depicts women as sources of great wisdom. But the overall effect is clearly that women have a subordinate position. Even much of the symbolic action is limited to males; the primary symbolic act that represents the covenant with God is circumcision. Hence, only men could be ritually inducted into the covenanted community of God's people. Clearly, there were elements of intrinsic sexism in the early biblical period. Such attitudes are taken particularly seriously today by those Christians who accept the totality of the Bible as literally true.

Of course, Christian thought has been more than just a continuation of Judaism; historically, it represented a synthesis of Hebrew and Greek world views. Many of the early theologians drew heavily from Greek philosophers. The Greek tradition was actually more explicitly sexist than was Hebrew culture. Aristotle's biological and political sciences, for example, depicted free Greek males as the embodiment of rationality. Such rationality was to be the ruling force in the good society, and the "spirit people" (males) were obligated to subjugate the "body people"—slaves, barbarians, and women (Ruether 1975). Furthermore, Aristotle taught that every male seed should normally produce its own image in another male. Females were the result of an accident or aberration in the womb in which the lower material substance of the female womb subverted and warped the higher characteristics of the male. Women, clearly, were viewed as defective human beings (Ruether 1975).

Even before Aristotle, the common belief was that reason and affectivity were mutually exclusive and were associated with good and evil, respectively. Plato had taught that the sexual act lowered people to the frenzied passions characteristic of beasts. The world of nature and of natural impulses was viewed as depraved and corrupted, whereas reason was viewed as the path to true goodness and spirituality. Moreover, reason was identified with males; passion and natural creation (in the form of childbirth) were associated with females.

This sort of dualistic world view is characteristic of nearly all philosophical systems in classical Greece. Religious historian Rosemary Ruether (1975) maintains that such **hierarchical dualism**[3] is universally associated with sexist thinking (Shields 1986). Women are invariably associated with the "lower" processes and with worldliness. Women are viewed as the cause of passion and are believed to be preoccupied with it; furthermore, they are identified with worldly creation because of their biological function in childbirth. Ruether insists that dualistic thinking—in

---

[3]Hierarchical dualism refers to any belief system that divides all of life into two distinct realms, one of which is higher than the other (this world/other world, darkness/light, carnality/spirituality, reason/emotion, etc.).

which the empirical world is defined as evil and the spiritual world is viewed as good—may have an inherent sexist bias. Ruether maintains that much of the sexist bias in Christian history comes from the Greek, not the Hebrew, legacy. She writes that, unlike Christianity and Greek philosophy, "Hebrew religion, especially in its preexilic period, is not a religion of alienation that views nature as inferior or evil" (1975: 187). (We will return to the relationship between dualism and sexism in the next section.)

The New Testament Gospels depict a much more positive view of women (Ruether 1975; Parvey 1974). Jesus himself violated many of the gender-role taboos of his day. He allowed women to join his traveling group (Luke 8:1–3) and encouraged them to sit at his feet and learn (traveling and studying with a rabbi were viewed as very improper for women in that day). Jewish law also defined any woman with a flow of blood as unclean and polluting, and it forbade any Jewish male from speaking alone to a woman who was not his wife. Jesus deliberately disregarded both taboos (Mark 5:25–34; Matthew 9:20–22; Luke 8:43–48; John 4:27). He frequently contrasted the faithlessness of the religious leaders with the profound faith of poor widows and outcast women. In that day, unattached women were considered suspect and were to be avoided. His comments would certainly have been insulting and sacrilegious to many people (Luke 4:25–29).

Even his own ministry was modeled after the role of women, for Jesus taught that the role of the faithful was not one of glory and fame but of service. He capped his ministry by washing the feet of his disciples, a task normally assigned to women or servants, and at the time of his greatest disappointment outside the gates of Jerusalem, he described himself as feeling like a "mother hen"—an interesting analogy because of its feminine connotation. Finally, after Jesus had been killed, it was only the

women followers who remained faithful. Other examples could be used, but few scholars question that the Gospels are among the least sexist books in the Bible.

If the Gospels were remarkable for their lack of sexism, the New Testament epistles are another matter. Many people have a view of Saint Paul as one of the world's worst misogynists. He ordered women to obey their husbands, he told them not to speak in church, and he held to the old Hebrew belief that women serve men and only men could serve God. Much has been written on these passages; they are frequently used today in conservative congregations to reinforce traditional roles. However, there are numerous references to women preachers who were sent by Paul or who accompanied him. In actual practice, he did not prohibit women from leadership roles.

Paul was a complex personality who often lacked consistency among his theology, his social teachings, and his behavior. It was Paul who asserted that in Christ, "there is neither male nor female." The society in which he lived was much more extreme in its sexism, and by comparison he appears liberal (Parvey 1974). For example, some Christians of that day were much influenced by Gnostic philosophy and attempted to synthesize it with Christian doctrine. Some of these Gnostics taught that women were not worthy of becoming Christians, at least not unless they first became males.[4] The Gnostic Gospel of Thomas (which was never accepted as part of the biblical

---

[4]Some recent works have attempted to depict Gnosticism as a profoundly feminist religious tradition (e.g., Pagels 1979). But Gnosticism was not a unified movement or philosophy. Some Gnostics appear to be very sympathetic to women, but others are clearly hostile, viewing sexuality and women as intrinsically evil. One must be wary of sweeping statements about gender images within Gnosticism as though it were a single, coherent philosophical tradition (Williams 1986).

canon) stated boldly, "For every woman who makes herself male shall enter the kingdom of heaven" (cited in Bullough 1973: 113). It was this sort of influence from Greek philosophy that Paul combated in stating that in Christ there is no distinction between men and women.

Despite Paul's efforts, this ancient Greek view that women are defective humans found its way into the scriptures. Vern Bullough points to this when he concludes, "the most misogynistic statements in the scriptures appear not in the Epistles of Paul but in the Apocalypse (the Book of Revelation)" (1973: 103). In that book, John the Elder describes the procession of the redeemed as a company of virgin *men* "who have not been defiled with women." Obviously, women were viewed as lesser beings who were not capable of being saved.[5] The influence of Gnosticism can be clearly seen in this final book of the New Testament. In the context of this extreme antipathy to women in the larger culture, Paul appears quite liberal on the gender issue.

While he rejected Gnostic misogynism, Paul was the one who emphasized so heavily the sin of Adam and Eve, and he clearly believed that the responsibility for original sin lay with Eve. The implication is that women are an easier mark for the forces of evil. Interestingly, the idea that Eve introduced original sin is discussed only in the first few chapters of Genesis; it is never mentioned again in the Old Testament. Yet, centuries later this was to become a major theme in the teachings of many Christian evangelists and theologians. Tertullian, one of the early church fathers, picked up on this theme and continually re-

minded women that each one of them was an Eve, "a devil's gateway." He held women responsible for being "the first deserter of the divine law" and wrote to them, "You are she who persuaded him who the devil was not valiant enough to attack. You destroyed so easily God's image, man. On account of your desert—that is, death—even the Son of God had to die" (cited by Bullough 1973: 114). Hence, women were held responsible for the crucifixion! At a much later time, Martin Luther also emphasized that a woman was responsible for the Fall. Although he generally opposed ridicule of women in public, he did on one occasion follow his comments on the story of humanity's Fall with the directed observation, "We have you women to thank for that!" (cited in Bullough 1973: 198). So it was that the Adam and Eve story became a much more important justification of misogynism in Christian history than it ever was in the ancient Hebrew tradition.

Although the story of the Fall and the guilt of Eve became a justification for sexist attitudes, such scholars as Ruether have pointed to dualist theology as a more basic cause. When the world view separates the world into two distinct realms, with the worldly realm governed by the passions and being inherently evil and with the heavenly realm governed by rationality and being inherently good, women and men are commonly identified as beings of one or the other of these realms. Such dualistic theology also frequently associates the sexual drive as worldly, ruled by passion, and evil. As a cause of sexual arousal in men, women have often been identified with the evil, worldly, and passionate side of the polarity. This occurs because men usually have the power to apply the labels of good and evil and to make their labels stick.

Saint Augustine, a theologian who has influenced Christian thought for centuries, held to the Platonic view that passion was evil and that the sexual act lowered humans to the

---

[5]It is noteworthy that early Christianity was not dualistic (O'Dea, 1966). In fact, the Book of Revelation was held to be heresy by many church leaders for the first few centuries of Christendom. It was excluded from the Canon until a vote by church leaders at the Provincial Council in A.D. 392 made it an official part of the Christian scriptures (Weaver 1975).

frenzied and unthinking level of beasts. Hence, he taught that when the sexual act was performed it should be done without emotion or feeling. The man was to plant his seed in the woman with the same dispassion as a farmer sowing seeds in the furrow of a field. So appalled by passion was Saint Augustine that he held the male erection to be the essence of sin. He waxed at some length and in horrified disgust about the "hideous" and uncontrollable (irrational) nature of the male erection. But if the erection was the essence of sin, it was clear who was responsible for causing it: women! (Ruether 1974c: 16465). In fact, this sort of projection of sexual lust on women and a general view of women as temptresses was so common among Christian theologians that Bullough concludes: "Sometimes it almost seems as if the church fathers felt that woman's only purpose was to tempt man from following the true path to righteousness. . . . Many of the church fathers seemed to find it difficult to follow their ascetic ideals and obviously felt the task would have been somewhat simpler if women did not exist" (1973: 98).

Because sexual activity was viewed as corrupting (if not outright evil), a life vow of chastity was considered a more holy mode of life. But Ruether has studied the rationale for virgin lifestyles in the early church and has found a consistent pattern: virginity caused women to *rise above* their (innately evil) natures, but it caused men to *fulfill* their (innately good) natures (Ruether 1974c). Further, celibacy was *one* Christian lifestyle for men. For women it was the *only* path to holiness. In fact, Augustine and Jerome suggested that for women the choice between childbearing and celibacy was a choice between shame and glory (Bullough 1973). Eventually, the feeling that sexual activity was depraved and evil led to a new doctrine about the birth of Jesus. Because Jesus was to have been born of an uncontaminated womb, Mary herself came to

be viewed as a source of purity. In the medieval period, the doctrine of immaculate conception was articulated. According to this doctrine, Mary was herself born without original sin; hence, her womb was a sinless environment. Clearly, the obsession with sex as evil was reaching extreme proportions.

One can also see the increase in misogynism at the time of the Protestant Reformation as it is manifested in Christian art. For many centuries, the Prince of this world (Satan) was sculpted as a handsome, attractive man as viewed from the front. As one walked around the statue, one would see that the back was a hollow shell, eaten by worms, frogs, and snakes. The imagery was powerful in its condemnation of this-worldly values. In the fourteenth century, however, the image of this-worldliness became "Frau Welt," a beautiful and alluring young woman from the front. But again, the back side of the figure was decayed and infested with snakes, frogs, rats, and other vermin. The image of evilness and worldliness had become female (McLaughlin 1974). Furthermore, the physical attraction of a beautiful woman was identified with baseness and corruption. This trend in Christian art was expressed in both Protestant and Catholic circles.

Sexism continued in the Protestant Reformation. The Protestant reformers abolished the requirement of celibacy among the clergy and reemphasized the childbearing role as a holy vocation, and one might expect that this would result in a lessening of sexism. Nonetheless, sexism can be seen in the writings of Martin Luther, John Calvin, John Knox, and other prominent reformers. In fact, *The First Blast of the Trumpet against the Monstrous Regiment of Women* was published by Knox in 1558 and stands to this day as one of the most misogynistic statements in Christendom. Moreover, the removal of Mary as a primary religious figure of adulation left Protestantism without a major saint or model who was female (Douglass 1974; Ruether 1975).

The Feminization of Christianity Although women were viewed for centuries as spiritually more vulnerable than men and as a source of evil influence, an interesting shift occurred in America in the nineteenth century. As opposed to the sternness and harshness of eighteenth-century American Christianity, the sentimentality of the nineteenth century was clearly more "feminine" in tone. Barbara Welter, who refers to this as the "femininization of American religion," writes "When . . . a more intuitive, heartfelt approach was urged, it was tantamount to asking for a more feminine style" (1976: 94). Welter points out that the most popular hymns written at that time stressed passive and accepting roles. Such hymns as "Just As I Am, Without One Plea," "To Suffer for Jesus Is My Greatest Joy," and "I Need Thee Every Hour" illustrate a pattern in hymnody of exalting dependency, submissiveness, and a willingness to suffer without complaint as Christian virtues. These were also viewed as feminine characteristics and as feminine virtues in nineteenth-century American culture. In contrast, the ideal characteristics of the male were embodied in the aggressive, independent, self-sufficient industrialist. This transformation of American religion was perhaps most noticeably seen in the imagery of Jesus. In the eighteenth century, he had been viewed as the stern taskmaster and as the exalted ruler of God's kingdom. In the nineteenth century, the major characteristics attributed to Jesus were loving self-sacrifice, tenderheartedness, and willingness to forgive those who injured him.[6]

Given the mixed signals that men were receiving about masculine and Christian virtues, it is not surprising that male church attendance dropped off and religion came to be viewed as a woman's concern. As depicted in almost any popular novel or sermon of that day, women were more spiritual, more noble, and more generous than men. As Welter put it, "Womanhood was believed to be, in principle, a higher, nobler state than manhood, since it was less directly related to the body and was more involved with the spirit; women had less to transcend in their progress" (1976: 95). Religion also came to be viewed as less rational (Ruether 1975). Rationality was associated with science, technology, and industry, all of which were male-dominated spheres. Women were now viewed as more religious than men and as the transmitters of morality, but still not as highly rational. The clergy, who were still almost entirely male, were sometimes viewed as naive, unknowing, and incapable of understanding business practices. As religion was feminized, the leaders of the church were also attributed with feminine virtues and vices (Ruether 1975).[7]

Although women came to be seen as more spiritual, this happened at a time when religion was having decreased influence on the affairs of the world. Commerce and politics were increasingly secular and governed by principles of secular rationality. At the very time when women were being identified with religiosity, religion was being demoted to a less influential position in society. In fact, the feminization of religion may have occurred precisely because religion was being dislodged from direct access to political power; it was becoming identified as a concern of the home and of the individual. This loss of social

---

[6]Research in the latter half of the twentieth century has found that girls are more likely to view God as loving, comforting, and forgiving, while boys tend to view God as a supreme power, forceful planner, and controller (Batson and Ventis 1982; Cox 1967; Wright and Cox 1967).

[7]Interestingly, some of the very popular evangelists in the early part of the twentieth century, Billy Sunday most notable among them, depited Jesus using very tough, macho imagery. Sunday once described Jesus as "the greatest scrapper that ever lived" (Hofstadter 1963: 116). The trend to a more meek and mild Jesus is far from uniform over the past century.

power was equated to taking on a more feminine role in society. To state it in its most negative form, to be religious was to be unknowing, lacking in power, and guided by naive sentimentality rather than by realism and reason. The stereotypes of women as irrational and emotional had remained constant, but the role of religion in society—and hence its image—had changed significantly.

Research in the early 1990s indicates that persons—male or female—who have more "feminine" value orientations (valuing feelings and expressiveness) tend to rate higher in various measures of religiousness than persons of either sex who have more "masculine" (instrumental) orientations. In fact, gender orientation in one's values is a better predictor of religiousness than is the sex of the person (Thompson 1991). At least in the contemporary United States, religion continues to have feminine overtones, despite the

fact that it has often been less than sympathetic to women.

Interpreting the Relationship Between Ideology and Sex Bias   We have explored several ways in which religious ideology has been related to gender roles and concepts of gender. What is needed at this point is more empirical evidence to validate the hypotheses set forth here, especially on Ruether's theory of a relationship between dualism and sexism. There is some empirical evidence that lends support to Ruether's thesis. Fundamentalist Christians are frequently dualistic in their theology; they also score much higher than other Christians on measures of sex bias. A correlation appears to exist. On the other hand, fundamentalist groups and Christian sects have proportionally more clergywomen than do the mainline denominations, despite the fact that they tend to be more dualistic. Dualism and

---

► **BOX 13.1**

In the Late Twentieth Century, Religion Remained More Important to Women Than to Men

How important would you say religion is to your own life?

	Very Important (%)	Fairly Important (%)	Not Very Important (%)
Men	45	35	19
Women	64	27	9

Are you a member of a church or synagogue?

	Yes (%)	No (%)
Men	63	37
Women	74	26

Did you happen to attend church or synagogue in the last seven days?

	Yes (%)	No (%)
Men	33	67
Women	46	54

The *superchurched* (church members who say religion is very important to them and who attended church in the past week)

Men	23%
Women	38%

Source: From The Gallup Poll, *The Gallup Report: Religion in America*. Princeton, N.J.: The Gallup Organization, 1987: 13,36,39,41.

sexism may be closely related, but there appear to be other variables at work which we have not yet clarified. One such variable appears to be the extent of institutionalization of a group; generally speaking, the more complex the religious organization, the less likelihood of women being ordained. (Ordination of women is explored later in this chapter.)

Continued research is also needed on the reasons why church members in all but the most liberal churches rate higher on sexism scales than do nonmembers, and why active members seem to be more sexist than inactive members. One explanation is that the long history of sexism in theology has carried over into the present day and that, unlike racial bias, sex bias has been intrinsic in Orthodox Christian theology. (The exception of the liberal churches can be explained by the fact that their theology has assimilated much more of the orientation and values of the secular culture.)

Another thesis suggests that religious sexism operates more implicitly. This explanation maintains that contemporary theological language may have a subtle psychological effect that contributes to sex bias. Some congregations are attempting to do away with the use of male nouns and pronouns in reference to God, the exclusive use of male terms in church hymns, and male pronouns in liturgies and prayers. Empirical evidence on the effects of these patterns is as yet inconclusive, primarily because the research on these topics is in its infancy.

In chapter 12 we discussed William Perry's (1970) thesis regarding simple dualism in the world view of some people and how that might relate to racist categories of thought. Superficially, his theory seems to support Ruether's claim, for dualism does seem to be related to sexism. The dualistic thinking of some of the most misogynistic ancient philosophers illustrates the point.

Pythagorus viewed the universe as divisible into two opposing principles: light versus darkness, odd versus even, right versus left, good versus evil, and male versus female. Light, odd, right, good, and male were in one category; dark, even, left, evil, and female were in the other (Bullough 1973). Likewise, Saturnius, a Gnostic leader, believed that God had created two kinds of people, the wicked and the good. He believed that men represented the good and women the inherently evil (Bullough 1973). Philo, the Hellenistic Jewish writer, insisted that the world was made up of two realms: the created world dominated by sense perception and feelings and the heavenly realm characterized by rationality. Women were defined as inferior because they were people of this world (oriented to feelings and the senses). Men, on the other hand, were people of the heavenly realm because they represented the rationality of the soul. Progress, according to this view, meant giving up the female gender! (Bullough 1973).

In each of these cases, we-they thinking is related to antipathy toward women. Perry's theory, however, suggests a different causal sequence. It may be that dualistic ideology is not the cause of sexism (as Ruether suggests) but merely a correlate. In other words, it may be that persons in a particular stage of intellectual development (simple dualism) are likely to hold a certain type of theology (dualistic) and are likely to be highly sexist. Cognitive structuralism may offer an alternative view about which is cause and which is effect. On the other hand, it may be that dualistic theology and simple dualism—as a cognitive mode of understanding the world—are mutually reinforcing and *together* contribute to sexism.

Continued research is needed. At this point we can only conclude that Christianity has a long history of sex bias, which has continued into many present-day congregations. In many cases, this sexist bias appears to have been transmitted through the meaning system. However, there may be other patterns of religious behavior that are equally important or even more important than beliefs in maintaining gender prejudice.

Belonging Factors

When members of conflicting ethnic or racial groups also belong to different religious groups, the likelihood of religiously based prejudice increases. However, in most religions in the industrialized world, men and women are not utterly segregated. Men and women are members of the same families and are members of the same religious organizations. Hence, it might seem that we-they distinctions would not occur. Nonetheless, the distinction of "we" and "they" between male and female is often given sanction in religious groups. Among Orthodox and Hasidic Jews, men and women sit separately during worship. The same pattern has prevailed among certain Protestant groups in the United States, such as the Shakers and the Old Order Amish. Such religiously sanctioned segregation of the sexes would seem to reinforce we-they distinctions that are part of the larger culture: males and females are viewed as different species.[8] Belonging has to do with a particular sex group.

Another case of sexual segregation has been the Roman Catholic practice of maintaining monasteries and convents for male and female devotees. Originally, this practice was designed to maintain celibacy, for the celibate life was viewed as more holy. However, it was only celibate males who articulated theological doctrine. It was those same celibate males who sometimes felt sexual desires and who blamed women for creating these "unholy" feelings. Clearly, a form of aversive prejudice developed toward women and exacerbated the dominative patterns that already existed. Hence, the segregation of men and women may have contributed to we-they distinctions and to primary identification with the sex group. Because it was men who developed the formal theological positions of the church, the we-they social pattern may have been an important factor in the development of explicitly sexist theology.

Of course, sexual segregation was not an entirely negative factor for many of the women in the convents. They were able to work in jobs that otherwise would have been denied to women. Because they were free of childbearing and childrearing responsibilities, they could devote their lives entirely to careers (teaching, nursing, etc.). Moreover, many nuns advanced to positions of organizational leadership and responsibility within the convent that would have been denied them in the larger secular society. Hence, the effects of such segregation were mixed: some women gained freedoms and opportunities otherwise unavailable, but the system may also have heightened sexism among the men by highlighting we-they distinctions.

Further, informal norms within the religious community may cause people to adhere to prejudicial attitudes in order to feel accepted—regardless of the position of the church hierarchy or of official denominational theology. To feel included—a sense that one belongs—one may feel compelled to laugh at jokes about women and to accept the prevalent attitudes and norms regarding the proper place of women. The social sanctions for not conforming to informal norms and expectations can be much stronger than those associated with violation of the official norms of the denomination. The penalty for ignoring the informal, unwritten standards is social exclusion; the reward is a sense of belonging. The official position of the denomination frequently lacks such immediate and concrete reinforcements. Hence, the informal culture of the group and the desire to belong may be more important in shaping attitudes than the group's formal or official posture.

The belonging function of religion, then, may enhance sex bias in several ways. Insofar as the religious outlook stresses the fact that

---

[8]Actually, Shaker women had a more egalitarian position than did their sisters in the secular culture. In this case, the segregation of the sexes was to help maintain the policy of celibacy.

males and females are utterly different, the sense of "we" versus "they" may be heightened and the sense of belonging may be tied to sex group rather than to faith community. This may lead to suspicion and prejudice. Beyond this, the informal community that provides the sense of belonging may have informal norms that foster sexism. This leads to the next major way in which religion may enhance

Barbara Harris, wearing the vestments of a Protestant Episcopal bishop, gives her blessing to the crowd after being consecrated in 1989 as the first female bishop in the 400-year Anglican tradition. Ordination of women is an important issue because when women are in leadership positions and involved in formulation of the official theology, there is much less likelihood of misogynistic policies and ideologies. (Reuters/Bettmann.)

sex bias—the formal organizational structure itself.

Institutional Factors

Perhaps the most vexing problems of religious prejudice toward women lie in institutional patterns. After a study of Christianity and Islam, Bullough concludes, ". . . regardless of what a religion teaches about the status of women, or what its attitudes toward sex might be, if women are excluded from the institutions and positions which influence society, a general misogynism seems to result" (1973: 134). We have already seen that denigration of women became part of the theological system (meaning system) of Western Christianity. This would not likely have occurred if women had been in positions to formulate and shape the official theology of the church. For this reason, denial of ordination becomes a significant issue. Furthermore, as long as a significant distinction is made between clergy and laity and as long as the clergy are looked up to as leaders, as those most in tune with God and as the legitimate messengers of God, the denial of ordination to women affirms their inferior position among the "people of God."

Many women scholars believe that ordination of women is a key issue: "By this exclusion the church is saying that the sexual differentiation is —for one sex—a crippling defect which no personal qualities of intelligence, character, or leadership can overcome" (Daly 1970: 134; see also Ruether 1975). When the Church of Jesus Christ of Latter-day Saints (Mormons) refused to ordain blacks, it was widely recognized as a statement about the inferiority of black people.[9] Yet, some of the same denominations that were critical of the Mormons have opposed ordination of women.

---

[9]The Mormon Church began to ordain African Americans in 1978.

In this latter case, the argument that denial of ordination was a statement of inferiority was vigorously denied. Most of the theologically trained women seeking ordination have not found the denial convincing. Furthermore, the lack of women in leadership positions can subtly influence attitudes, especially of small children. The absence of women in important positions often communicates to children— much more vividly than any words to the contrary—the social inferiority of females.

The reasons for exclusion of women from ordination are noteworthy. Some scholars trace this exclusion back to Saint Paul who, in keeping with the contemporary attitude toward women, wrote that women were not to speak in church. However, I have already pointed out that he did not vigorously follow that policy himself. At least one historian has traced the original restriction on ordination to Constantine. When Christianity became the official religion of the Roman Empire, it came under some of the cultic attitudes then prevalent. Specifically, religious leaders were to maintain ritual purity. Because women were viewed as unclean at particular times of the month because of natural biological processes, they were unfit for ministry (Ruether 1975). And because males dominated the priesthood and formulated the theology, women were continually defined as unfit. In fact, in the thirteenth century, Thomas Aquinas adopted Aristotle's view that women are defective males—biologically, morally, and intellectually. He held that the male seed should normally result in another male. Only if the mother's blood caused a defect in the fetus did the child result in a "misbegotten male" (a female). Hence, he reasoned that only men could fully represent Christ (the perfect human being) in the ministry. Such a rationale would not likely have occurred if women had been part of the hierarchy all along. But the fact is that they were not, and given the belief that females were less human (basically and irre-versibly defective), it is somewhat surprising that women were allowed even to be baptized. Total exclusion of women from religious participation is not unknown in the world.

Nonetheless, most major denominations have recently accepted women for ordination, and the official church pronouncements reject sexism and endorse equality for women at all levels. One recent study has even indicated a willingness by rather large majorities of church members to have a clergywoman (Lehman 1981). Despite all this, few theologically trained women are receiving appointments to large congregations. They continue to be placed in positions as assistant ministers, as directors of religious education, or as the sole minister in small, struggling congregations that have very low salary scales. If the official position of these church hierarchies is that women are equally competent and should be placed in positions of leadership, why is this not happening? The answer seems to lie in the inherent biases and goals of complex organizations.

Edward Lehman Jr. (1981) approaches the issue of women in the ministry from the resource mobilization perspective. Once an organization is in existence, it tends to take on characteristics and needs of its own, the most important being viability. If the organization is to survive, it must mobilize and control critical resources: the financial support of members, the skills, time and energy of members, members' compliance with role requirements, and so on. However, in such voluntary organizations as churches, people must be convinced rather than coerced into compliance. Members who are not convinced can simply withdraw their support from the organization. (See the discussion on the dilemma of power in chapter 7.) Part of the problem for voluntary organizations is that members experience few negative consequences for *not* participating. Political and economic organizations control many basic resources, so one can be severely incapacitated by refusing to play by the rules. It is the lack of coercive control that makes commitment mechanisms so important for voluntary organizations (see the discussion of commitment in chapter 5). Regardless, the leaders and committed members of an organization will hold the survival of that organization to be the highest priority. This sort of built-in value system tends to play against women in the ministry.

Although Lehman's research on American Baptist churches indicated that a majority of church members had no objection to having a woman minister, three-fourths of them believed that "most church members" were opposed to having a woman pastor. Furthermore, the more active a member was in the life of the church, the more likely he or she was to be negative about the idea of a woman minister. The primary concern was that having a woman as minister would cause controversy and conflict, and such conflict might result in members leaving the church or withholding financial support. Because this sort of action could threaten the continuation of the entire organization, the controversy is studiously avoided. In virtually all churches, the pulpit committee or search committee is elected from representative areas of the church life. In almost all cases, the members of the committee are chosen from among the most active members in the church—people who have made an investment in the church and care about its health and survival. Hence, pulpit committees normally have a built-in bias to avoid anything that might threaten its vitality or viability, including conflict.

Lehman found that churches that were growing were the least likely to consider a clergywoman. He also found that the larger the congregation, the more resistance there was to having a woman as a senior minister (Lehman 1985). Where things were going well, members saw little reason to risk everything on a potentially divisive action. So the churches that were "healthiest" from an organizational standpoint were least likely to accept a woman pastor. The churches already in serious trouble, with declining enrollment and dwindling financial resources, had little to lose in accepting a clergywoman. In fact, their members often reasoned that it was better to have a first-rate clergywoman than a second-rate clergyman. And because women have harder times finding positions, they will more often accept lower-paying appointments than will equally qualified men.

Although the official position of the denomination may encourage local churches to accept women in positions as senior pastors, organizational concerns regarding viability often play against that. The local congregation is simply more interested in promoting and maintaining its cohesiveness and stability than in responding to denominational resolutions. When denominational statements are perceived as being in conflict with local congregational needs, there is seldom much question about which will prevail in the end (Lehman 1981). Yet, the fear of declining membership and reduction in giving was not justified. Lehman (1985) found that the advent of a clergywoman to a church actually brought substantial increases in giving, attendance, and membership.

Virtually all denominations have some sort of executive minister who is responsible for a geographic region. These area ministers or district superintendents are supposed to act as "pastors to the pastors" and implement official church policy. Furthermore, these organizational functionaries are usually the ones to whom pulpit committees go when they seek a new minister and to whom ministers appeal when they desire a move. The specific organizational pattern and the official titles vary from one denomination to another—as does the amount of authority of these officials over the congregations in their district. Although the role and job descriptions vary, one expectation remains rather constant: A major function of officials in this position is to maintain harmony in the congregations. Furthermore, an area minister may appear to be doing a poor job if a large number of congregations in that area withdraw from the denomination or radically reduce their pledges to the national organization. To be recognized as successful and to be a candidate for career advancement, the regional official must cultivate intrachurch harmony. The institutional reward system tends to favor caution. Although most of the executives of the American Baptist churches Lehman interviewed felt that clergywomen were just as competent as clergymen, they also shared the perception that laypeople would balk at the placement of a woman pastor. Their tendency was to avoid rocking the boat. So although these executives were charged with responsibility for implementing official church policy, they often did not press potentially controversial issues. Lehman writes, "An important theme in these patterns is the executives' role of maintaining organizational viability, especially in the local churches" (1981: 114).

The problem of organizational maintenance has continued to be a critical factor in resistance to the appointment of clergywomen. In subsequent studies of lay members of four denominations in England (Lehman 1987a) and of the Presbyterian Church in the United States (Lehman 1985), concern for the harmony and vitality of the organization and anticipation of destructive conflict over the appointment of a female minister was the primary barrier to appointment of a clergywoman. However, Lehman did find that, in the Presbyterian church of the 1980s, denominational placement personnel are more sympathetic to the placement of women and were less likely to be fearful of local backlash. Further, as congregations have more contact with clergywomen, resistance does decline significantly (Lehman 1985). Attitudes and behaviors are changing, but they are changing slowly.

Meanwhile, seminaries are educating increasing numbers of women. Because the number of male applicants to seminaries has declined in the past two decades and because the average level of academic ability of male candidates has also declined, the tremendous increase in women theology students[10] has allowed theological schools to continue without lowering their standards. In effect, this same organizational need—survival—has driven many seminaries to admit women to preministerial programs. Once granted a degree, however, women have difficulty finding a suitable appointment, and seminaries at this point do not have adequate organizational structures or sufficient influence on local churches to place their graduates.

The major issue of this section is how the ordination of women and their placement may perpetuate assumptions of female inferiority in our culture. The lack of women in positions of church leadership may affect the way people think about males and females. This is especially likely to influence the thinking of children, as I mentioned earlier. Furthermore, the lack of women in the hierarchy has allowed explicit sexism to be expressed by theologians and to go unchallenged by anyone with similar credentials.

The current trend (at least as it is expressed in the official resolutions of most major denominations) is in the direction of ordaining and appointing clergywomen. Some denominations continue to deny ordination to women, the most notable example being the Roman Catholic Church. Perhaps the first Protestant

---

[10]Lehman reported a 570 percent increase of women Master of Divinity students in one decade in Baptist seminaries (1981: 114).

denomination in North America to ordain women was the African Methodist Episcopal Zion church in 1898 (Lincoln and Mamiya 1990). The last Protestant denomination to ordain women was the Protestant Episcopal Church in 1976.[11] But as we have seen, even in those denominations that have been more aggressive in endorsing ordination of women, clergywomen have a hard time gaining positions in larger churches, unless they settle for an assistantship or a directorship of religious education. The problem is not one of outright prejudice as much as one of organizational goals and assumptions taking precedence over other considerations. In short, the church has been guilty of institutional sexism. Clergywomen have encountered an "invisible ceiling," which limits their opportunities. The ceiling is invisible because it is an indirect result of policies and attitudes within the church.

One fact is highlighted by this exploration of institutional factors: Religion is both a world view (set of beliefs, attitudes, and outlooks) and an institution in society. Understanding religious behavior can never be limited to one or the other. As an organization in society, religious bodies are often influenced by purely organizational considerations. In many ways, the organizational considerations take precedence. Hence, a strictly philosophical analysis of belief systems can never provide anything more than a partial analysis of religious behavior. It is precisely the interplay between social forces and belief systems that fascinates the sociologist of religion.

The central theme of this unit thus far has been that Christianity has often contributed to

---

[11]The only schism in the Episcopalian Church occurred in 1976, largely over the ordination of women. Other divisive issues included adoption of a new prayer book and advocacy of certain social policies by the Protestant Episcopal Church. The splinter group—which does not ordain women—is known as the Anglican Church of North America.

sex bias through its meaning system, its belonging and identity functions, and its institutional reward systems. Many denominations are currently trying to reverse these trends, but the countervailing forces of sexism are deeply embedded. But there is more to this web of behaviors than the fact that religion may have caused or contributed to gender prejudice. It is also true that religion may sometimes simply be the arena in which larger social conflicts are expressed and justified. In this case, religion is primarily a reflection of conflict rather than a cause. A number of scholars feel that this perspective is more helpful in understanding the witch-burning craze of Europe.

Social Conflict and Religious Expression: The Conflict Perspective

We discussed earlier the fact that racial prejudice is often caused by deeper economic conflicts between groups and is then justified on religious terms. Obviously, both sexes are represented in each social class, ethnic group, and religious organization in the Western world. Nonetheless, Marxian conflict theory can be useful in understanding religious expressions of sexism. When social tension and conflict are at a peak, especially in the economic arena, the conflict may find expression in the religious realm. For example, in traditional patriarchal societies, beliefs in the innate avarice and pollution of women are related to women gaining independence from men (Douglas 1966; Gluckman 1965). One anthropologist has also pointed out that belief in evil female witches almost always occurs when women are attaining economic independence from males (Hoch-Smith 1978). In other words, negative religious views of women frequently develop at precisely those times when men are losing the economic advantages of having a subordinate female class to serve their needs.

Mary Nelson has explored the foundations of the European witch burnings of the fifteenth to eighteenth centuries and has found the Marxian conflict perspective to be particularly helpful in understanding this phenomenon.[12]

Interestingly, belief in the existence and efficacy of witchcraft was for many centuries considered a pagan superstition, an illusion or fantasy that originated in dreams. Until the thirteenth century, the belief that there was such a thing as a witch was considered by church officials to be superstitious nonsense (Bullough 1973; Nelson 1975; Ruether 1975). It is true that sorcery was practiced by some Europeans—a legacy of pre-Christian folk religion.[13] Herbs and potions were used to cure illnesses and to ward off evil spirits. This folk religion affirmed the existence of all sorts of supernatural forces and evil spirits that inhabit the earth, and a sorcerer was often used to ward off misfortune. The Christian missionaries and church hierarchy believed that as local communities were Christianized, such magical fears and beliefs would disappear. In fact, when inquisitors in the thirteenth century began to run out of heretics to prosecute, they appealed to the Pope to let them extend their jurisdiction to sorcery. But Pope Alexander IV held to the official church position that witchcraft and sorcery were illusions. The appeal was denied; the Pope would not have church officials prosecuting something that didn't even exist except in the minds of the superstitious. At an earlier time, Charlemagne had imposed the death penalty for killing a supposed witch (Clark and Richardson 1977). Nonetheless, by 1426 the church would be punishing as a heretic anyone who even used the services of a "witch" (Nelson 1975).

During the period from 1400 to 1700, between 500,000 and 1 million people were burned as witches (Ruether 1975; Nelson 1975). Most of these victims were women. In fact, the loss of lives was so staggering that it has been referred to by some scholars as a holocaust. Hugh Trevor-Roper reports that "in twenty-two villages 368 witches were burnt between 1587 and 1593, and two villages, in 1585, were left with only one female inhabitant apiece" (1967: 16). This sort of massive attack on women represents a kind of genocide, but one that focuses on one sex rather than on an ethnic or religious group. Perhaps *gynocide* is a more appropriate term.

A number of scholars have sought to address the question, Why were women identified as witches? This is not the case in all cultures. In fact, in many hunting-gathering and agricultural societies, witches are exclusively males. Witchcraft carries a prestigious and highly protected status in these societies, and women are frequently excluded from the ranks entirely. Nonetheless, in Reformation Europe it was overwhelmingly women who were tried as witches. In Germany and France, more than 80 percent of those burned or drowned as witches were women, and in some areas of the continent women comprised well over 90 percent of the victims. In England 92 percent of those convicted and put to death were women, and in Russia the figure was 95 percent (Larner 1984; Ben-Yehuda 1980).

It was not until 1484 that Pope Innocent VIII issued a bill making witchcraft a form of heresy and empowering inquisitors to eradicate this cancer from Christendom. Two Dominican

---

[12]Witch-hunts were substantially tools for the suppression of women, and that theme is developed on the following pages. But other factors were at work as well. Readers interested in exploring some of these other factors may want to see Nachman Ben-Yehuda (1980) and Christina Larner (1984) for good overviews of the literature.

[13]There is much disagreement about whether modern Wicca is an ancient religion that can be traced back to prehistoric times. Margaret Murray (1921) set forth the thesis that witchcraft is an ancient religion. Others have challenged this thesis, claiming that witchcraft as a religion was largely a countercultural response to the repressive climate of the witch-hunt hysteria (see Adler 1986: 3–70).

priests, armed with this authority, wrote a book that became the handbook for witch-hunters. *The Malleus Maleficarum (The Witches' Hammer)* by Jakob Sprenger and Henry Kramer became a classic statement of misogynism as it articulated the reasons why women were witches. The importance of this book cannot be overestimated for it was widely circulated—being one of the first books printed on the recently invented printing press (Ben-Yehuda 1980).

The authors claimed that the term *female* came from the word *femina,* which meant "lacking in faith." The basic premise of the *Malleus* was that witches are pawns of the devil and that the devil recruits his agents through carnal lust. As they put it in the *Malleus,* "All witch-craft comes from carnal lust, which in women is insatiable." In fact, the inquisitors taught that witches ride broomsticks at night to "black Masses" in which they fornicate with the devil and feast on roasted children (Nelson 1975).

It appears that the distinction made be-tween witches (which henceforth were strictly female) and wizards or warlocks (which were the male counterpart) was a product of this period. It was only the female practitioners of witchcraft who were believed to be duped by carnal lust. Because women were viewed as fickle, feeble in intelligence, spiritually weak, and innately carnal, they were considered to be much more vulnerable to Satan than men. Furthermore, because the devil was viewed as male, it was clear that his paramours would be female. As Ruether puts it, "the devil was a strict heterosexual!" (1975: 97). Clearly, the most evil sort of sorcerers were (female) witches, for only they engaged in sex with the devil. Hence, even the application of different terms for male and female sorcerers (wizard or warlock versus witch) had a sexist foundation.

From the *Malleus* it was clear that witches were dangerous for three reasons: They took away men's generative powers (both economic and sexual); they killed infants, frequently while the babes were still in the womb; and they indulged in sexual intercourse with no goal of childbearing but for the pure gratification of sexual lust. Surprisingly, Nelson sug-gests that all three of these charges against women had some foundation in reality.

Witch-hunts always seem to arise at times of profound social upheaval, which was certainly the case in Europe during the period in ques-tion. "The development of an industrial system of producing goods and urban living patterns made the medieval family structure obsolete and required changes in the makeup of the labor force. Both of these new conditions made it nec-essary for women to step outside their tradi-tional social roles" (Nelson 1975: 343). The property-holding function of the medieval fam-ily made it necessary for women primarily to bear male heirs and to maintain the household. But commercialization required people to move to the city, and cash income became increasingly important; in some cases, it was necessary for wives to seek work. As women entered the labor force, they entered into direct competition with men for jobs. In so doing, they did "threaten the generative force" of some men. Many women engaged in sorcery or became midwives be-cause, in a society that did not offer women many job opportunities, these activities did pro-vide a source of income. But these midwives and herbalists were taking business that otherwise would have gone to male doctors. So it was not only laboring-class males whose economic gen-erative powers were threatened.

Second, because families could not afford to support members who did not work, women were expected to marry when they came of age. Unmarried daughters either joined con-vents or had to fend for themselves. Many young men at this time joined trade guilds in order to make a living, but most guilds had regulations forbidding apprentices from mar-rying until they were well established in the trade. This usually meant they were in their thirties or forties before they could marry. For this reason, there were many young women who could not find husbands, had difficulty finding a job that would support them, and yet were on their own. Some of these women found employment and displaced men from their work; others turned to prostitution. In the latter case, they "participated in sex with no eye to childbearing and for the sole purpose of satisfying the sexual drive" (albeit of the male partner!).

Finally, the economically marginal family in the city found children to be a tremendous financial liability. Various forms of birth control were used, including coitus interruptus and abortion. There is also some evidence that infanticide increased significantly. This meant that "babies were being killed, many of them while still in the womb" (abortion).

The events that so alarmed witch-hunters were to some extent occurring, and women came to be blamed for these things. Nelson insists that women were not merely scapegoats, they were in fact competing with men for jobs. It is noteworthy that witch-hunters accused primarily women who were independent of men—widows, divorcees, and never-marrieds—and women who deviated from the established norms—midwives, healers, and individuals who were considered very wise. The witchcraft hysteria was a religious expression of larger social conflicts: conflict regarding gender roles, the role of the family in society, the morality of contraception, and priority rights of one sex to employment. In the midst of these social conflicts, two forces emerged to entice women to return to the traditional role. One was the great increase in the veneration of the Virgin Mary. Mariolatry became a cultic obsession as she was made a model of traditional female virtue. Second, fear of being accused of witchcraft caused women to think twice before they deviated from accepted

norms of proper female behavior (Nelson 1975; Ben-Yehuda 1980).

Remnants of pagan sorcery did exist in Europe during the time of the witch-hunt hysterias, but they appear to have existed before and after as well. Only an understanding of the tensions caused by social upheaval can adequately explain the impetus behind the massacre. On the other hand, recent research on collective behavior makes it clear that social tension is necessary but not sufficient to cause a collective movement (Smelser 1962). Such factors as a conducive "generalized belief system" must be present.

Ruether picks up on this insight and insists that the general belief system of postmedieval Europe must be taken into account in understanding the witch-hunts. She maintains, with Murray (1921) that pagan sorcery practices did exist and were commonly used by village folk. There also existed a folk belief in supernatural forces and spiritual beings that could be controlled through magic. Because women tend to be more involved in folk religion and folk magic than men (largely because women have been denied full access to official religion), women were much more vulnerable to charges of witchery (McGuire 1981). But perhaps the most important shared belief was the view that women were more carnal than men. The theology of the day was one of ascetic dualism: the self-denying children of light were in perpetual conflict with the lascivious children of darkness. And ascetic Christianity identified carnality with femaleness and spirituality with maleness (Ruether 1975). This assumption allowed the easy association of evil and witchcraft with women. If an understanding of ideology is not enough to explain the witchcraft hysteria, neither is the existence of social tension sufficient in itself. It was the combination of the world view *and* the tensions involved in the changing social structure (in gender roles, economics, and family structures)

► **BOX 13.2**

Excerpts from *Malleus Maleficarum*

. . . Since women are feebler both in mind and body, it is not surprising that they should come under the spell of witchcraft. For as regards intellect, or the understanding of spiritual things, they seem to be of a different nature from men; a fact which is vouched for by the logic of the authorities, backed by various examples from the Scriptures. Terence says: Women are intellectually like children. . . .

But the natural reason is that she is more carnal than a man, as is clear from her many carnal abominations. And it should be noted that there was a defect in the formation of the first woman, since she was formed from a bent rib, that is, a rib of the breast, which is bent as it were in a contrary direction to a man. And since through this defect she is an imperfect animal, she always deceives. . . . And it is clear in the case of the first woman that she had little faith. . . . And all this is indicated by the etymology of the word; for Femina comes from Fe and Minus, since she is ever weaker to hold and preserve the faith. And this as regards faith is of her very nature.

Therefore a wicked woman is by her nature quicker to waver in her faith, and consequently quicker to adjure the faith, which is the root of witchcraft. . . .

If we inquire, we find that nearly all the kingdoms of the world have been overthrown by women. . . . Therefore it is no wonder if the world now suffers through the malice of women.

And now let us examine the carnal desires of the body itself, whence has arisen unconscionable harm to human life. Justly may we say with Cato of Utica: If the world could be

rid of women, we should not be without God in our intercourse. For truly, without the wickedness of women, to say nothing of witchcraft, the world would still remain proof against innumerable dangers. . . .

Let us consider another property of hers, the voice. For as she is a liar by nature, so in her speech she stings while she delights us. Wherefore her voice is like the song of the Sirens, who with their sweet melody entice the passers-by and kill them. For they kill them by emptying their purses, consuming their strength, and causing them to forsake God. . . .

To conclude. All witchcraft comes from carnal lust, which is in woman insatiable. See Proverb 30: There are three things that are never satisfied, yea, a fourth thing which says not, It is enough; that is, the mouth of the womb. Wherefore for the sake of fulfilling their lusts they consort even with devils. More such reasons could be brought forward, but to the understanding it is sufficiently clear that it is no matter for wonder that there are more women than men found infected with the heresy of witchcraft. And in consequence of this, it is better called the heresy of witches than of wizards, since the name is taken from the more powerful party. And blessed by the Highest Who has so far preserved the male sex from so great a crime: for since He was willing to be born and to suffer for us, therefore He has granted to men this privilege.

Source: Jakob Sprenger and Henry Kramer, *Malleus Maleficarum,* ed. and trans. by Montague Sommers. New York: Benjamin Blom, 1970: 44–47. (Originally published in 1486.)

that allowed for this religiously sanctioned holocaust.[14]

There are three major explanations for the decline of the witch hysteria. Trevor-Roper (1967) has maintained that witchcraft declined because of a general scientific enlightenment that made belief in witches implausible. This approach assumes that the movement died when belief was undermined. Clark and Richardson suggest that the witchcraft hysteria came to an end because a new male-female equilibrium was established so that men were no longer threatened by new gender-role relationships: "If the persecution of witches was rooted in male anxiety about the sexual power of women, an anxiety that burst forth in persecution as the old patriarchal culture was disintegrating, then the witch craze would end only as women attained a new status and men began to find themselves relatively secure with it" (1977: 120).

A third view is that charges of witchcraft had come to be used as a blatant form of secular political exploitation. Although most victims were poor, this explanation suggests that enterprising judges in the seventeenth century occasionally accused rather wealthy people of witchcraft because the judges were allowed to keep all property confiscated from witches (Currie 1968; Nelson 1975; Ruether 1975). According to this interpretation, witch-hunts came to an end when the self-interests of the powerful were threatened. Political structures were modified so that local judges lost their unchecked capacity to exploit people for their own benefit (Nelson 1975). This view is illustrated in the way the brief witch hysteria

(1692) of Salem, Massachusetts, came to an abrupt halt; when powerful and prestigious members of the community were accused as witches they used their influence to stop it (Erikson 1966; Bonfani 1971).[15] Less powerful members of the society had not been able to shed the label of "witch" so easily.

Recent research, however, challenges this latter theory as it applies to Europe. Although such economic motivation may have been at work in a few cases in Germany, prosecutions were more often a burden on local authorities, and in most cases the victims remained poor and elderly women (Midelfort 1972; Larner 1984).

Witch-hunts never became as massive nor were the penalties as severe in England during the period of time when witch-hunts prevailed in southern and central Europe. This may have been in large part because women already had a more secure and independent role in England than in the rest of Europe. Some scholars insist that Puritanism—although far from a champion of women's rights by today's standards—gave women a more independent and respected position than did other religious traditions of the day. Although punishment of supposed witches did occur in England and was sometimes initiated by Puritans, the

---

[14]There were no doubt other conducive factors as well. Larner (1984) insists that the rationalization of the legal-criminal justice system and the invention of the printing press were contributing factors. Ben-Yehuda adds that anxiety caused by European plagues heightened the anxiety or tension of people, making them more susceptible to hysteria.

---

[15]The causes of the witch hysteria of Salem are somewhat different from those of the three-century-long hunt in Europe. In Massachusetts twenty people were hanged or pressed to death (fourteen of whom were women), and 150 others were being held in prison when the hysteria abated. The hysteria had lasted only one year, and within four years colonialists were holding yearly fasts to repent for their behavior. In 1709 the General Court also ordered a small payment to surviving victims as a redress of damages. The general atmosphere of skepticism combined with a threat to the interests of the powerful to bring this movement to an end. However, misogynistic theology was not the central theme in the American hysteria. In fact, based on a study of sermons and inspirational literature, Laurel Ulrich (1980) suggests that Puritan New England between 1668 and 1735 was much less sexist than Europe at the time of the witch-hunts. The Salem witch-hunts are better explained by theories of collective hysteria.

Changes in Gender Roles and the Contemporary Satanism Hysteria

Since the early 1980s, rumors, sensationalized press reports, and unsubstantiated assertions on talk shows have fueled fears of satanic cults that supposedly engage in ritual abuse, animal mutilation, and even human sacrifices of babies or innocent youth. There is not space here to discuss the overwhelming evidence that no such massive satanic activity is taking place, but most sociologists and investigators at the Federal Bureau of Investigation agree that what is really occurring is a mass hysteria akin in many ways to the witch-hunts of yesteryear. (Those interested in more detailed discussions of purported cases of satanic cults and satanic abuses and the lack of evidence of these will want to see Richardson, Best, and Bromley 1991; Lanning 1989; Shupe 1991; and Wright 1993.)

David Bromley (1991), one of the first sociologists to investigate the satanic cult hysteria, has concluded that, like the witch-hunts, the sources of the anti-Satanism movement reside in structural tensions within the society; furthermore, in both cases the stressors involve changing women's roles. He notes that when people continue to assert the reality of an event (e.g., the existence of massive numbers of satanic cults abusing children) despite overwhelming evidence to the contrary, one must look to structural tensions and system-based anxiety as the cause of the continuing hysteria.

Bromley points out that American society is characterized by two kinds of relationships: (1) **covenantal ties** involving caring, commitment, nurturance, bonding, and self-sacrifice on behalf of others, and (2) **contractual ties** governed by impersonal transactions based on mutual exchange, negotiation over resources and exchange, and pursuit of self-interest. The former is characteristic of familial and religious institutions; the latter is characteristic of economic, managerial, governmental, and bureaucratic settings. The covenantal realm also seems to be shrinking, and the contractual dimension expanding and taking over many functions traditionally defined as covenantal.

Most legal cases that include accusations of satanic abuses have involved day-care centers and other child-care facilities (Bromley 1991). As gender roles have changed and women have started working outside the home, an important shift has occurred in the United States: a covenantal task—the care and nurture of children—has been subsumed in the contractual domain. People are being paid in a market exchange to provide a nurturing environment for children. This has created enormous anxiety in Americans, with surveys showing widespread feelings of guilt and discomfort about the new trend of leaving young children in the care of "hired hands." Anxiety about care of children has come out in a distorted and mystified expression: accusations of Satanism and urban legends about danger to innocent youth (especially blue-eyed and blonde-haired virgins, the cultural paradigm of innocent vulnerablility).

In the case of witchcraft, charges against women as witches were distorted and mystified; but it is true that women were engaging in some behaviors that resembled those attributed to witches—competing with men, engaging in sexual activity for nonprocreative purposes, and ending pregnancies with abortions. Likewise, while the accusation that there is an epidemic of child-abusing satanic cults seems entirely unfounded, it is true that the care of children generally in our culture has been compromised, and some children may be in jeopardy. The solution proposed by many anti-Satanists is to try to entice women to return to the traditional role of mother and homemaker, a remedy reminiscent to that enforced by the witch-hunters in medieval Europe.

Ironically, another solution proposed by anti-Satanists is to impose further governmental regulations on child-care facilities. The irony is that this imposes still more contractual control over a covenantal function: bureaucratic solutions to regulate the love, care, and nurturance of children (Bromley 1991).

social climate was such that changes in gender roles were not viewed as such a dire threat to the interests of men (Anderson and Gordon 1978).

All this points to the effects of social processes on religious behavior and attitudes. Marxian theorists suggest that religious discrimination is often merely an expression of deeper economic and political conflicts. Social conflict between men and women over jobs and family roles was central in the witch-hunt holocaust that was sanctioned by the Christian Church. However, without the presence of a world view that made this discriminatory action toward women seem right and just (i.e., consistent with the laws of the universe), it is unlikely that it would have taken place.

Summary

Although the contributions of Christianity to racism were for the most part subtle and indirect, Christianity has fostered sexism much more directly. Except for the most liberal churches in the United States, traditional images of women are correlated to high levels of church activity and religiosity. Christianity has contributed to prejudice against women in a variety of ways. First, women have been conceived as subordinate citizens in the meaning systems of most religions and philosophies of the Western world, and Christianity is no exception. Second, prejudice is passed on through we-they boundaries established by some churches and by informal norms of the community. Finally, formal institutional concerns, such as concern for maintenance of the health and vitality of the local church, can predispose lay leaders against having a clergywoman. When women are not in leadership roles, it can contribute to a perception of inferiority of women, especially in the eyes of children. More important, if women are not ordained and in leadership positions, there is a greater likelihood that the meaning systems will develop with a strong bias against women.

One cannot make generalizations about Christianity as a whole on any of these characteristics. Some Protestant Christian groups, for example, have been remarkable for their lack of prejudice. The Shakers believed in a female Christ figure (Mother Ann Lee), and the Christian Scientists were founded by a female charismatic leader (Mary Baker Eddy). Nor can one conclude that sexual segregation of men and women into monasteries and convents in the Roman Catholic tradition was always bad for women. It did allow for leadership roles otherwise denied to women.

The foregoing discussion should serve to illustrate the complex way in which any given religious body can have countervailing influences. This is precisely why the sociologist who studies religion is not satisfied simply with an investigation of official beliefs of a denomination or world religion or even a study of the beliefs of the common folk. Religion can influence human behavior in a variety of ways.

Although Christianity has sometimes been a cause of prejudice, religious prejudice is often a reflection of larger conflicts in the society. We saw this clearly in the case of the incredible witch-hunt hysteria in postmedieval Europe. The Church was the formal sponsor of this holocaust, but the real issue behind the conflict was the change occurring in gender roles as the society moved from a feudal to a commercial economic system. Clearly, religious values and behaviors are intertwined with social conditions in the larger society.

Social Change and Religious Adaptation

One of the realities of the modern world is social change. Some changes occur so rapidly that we can observe them over a few years. Others are long-term and have been so gradual that individuals hardly see any change within their own lifetimes. Religion can be a source of stability and certainty in times of change, but some people also claim that if religion does not change with the times, it will become alien to the lives and experiences of the people. In these last three chapters, we explore ways in which religion has responded to shifts and modifications in the larger society.

In chapter 14 we discuss a long-term change that has profound implications for religion: modernization, or secular-ization. In chapter 15 we investigate a more recent and quite rapid change: the utilization of modern mass-media technology for religious purposes. As we explore the impact of televangelism, we will see that adaptation of religion to the surrounding culture is not just a matter of liberal religion assimilating to the culture; conservative evangelical Christianity has also been undergoing modification. In chapter 16 we explore evidence of some alternative forms of religion that seem to be emerging in our rapidly changing society and that may be replacing traditional expressions of religion. In chapter 17 we consider the religious implications of globalization—the trend toward the world becoming "one place."

CHAPTER FOURTEEN

Secularization: Religion in Decline or in Reformation?

I n earlier chapters we discussed the role of myth and explored the importance of world view in religion and in the society at large. Until the nineteenth century, religion—in virtually every society—fundamentally shaped the world view of the entire culture. But in the modern world, other forces come into play, especially the advent of science as an institution, the greater sophistication of technology, and the higher levels of formal education in the general population. The scientific method becomes the arbitrator of truth. Further, other institutions in the society appear to become less dependent on religious legitimization.

Industrialized societies tend to generate their own world views, independent of religious myths and symbols, and these secular world views may even begin to shape the traditional religious systems of belief. This may spell conflict not only between religious groups and the larger society but also within religious groups themselves.

Conceptualizations of Secularization

There seems to be some consensus that secularization is of considerable import, but there are a number of models emphasizing different processes. We have little agreement on the core elements that constitute secularization, what causes it, and what effects it might have. One point of agreement seems to be that traditional religious symbols are no longer a unifying force for industrialized society. The modern empirical scientific world view has replaced the miraculous religious world view. Truth and knowledge are gained through double-blind, crossover studies rather than through visions or religious intuition. People look to science and technology to solve problems. As a means of compensating, religionists have developed systematic theologies that are logical, coherent, and rational. Mythology has given way to empiricism, both in the secular world and within religion itself.

Another point of agreement is that this change of world view has been accompanied by structural changes in society, with institutions (family, government, economics, religion, education, science, health care, etc.) becoming separate and differentiated bodies, and with various institutions gaining greater autonomy from domination by religion. While there is general agreement that institutional transformation occurs, theorists disagree over the issue of whether institutional change is the cause or the effect of the metamorphosis in world view, or is the defining characteristic of secularization. Considering the points of agreement, we might define **secularization** as transformation of a society to a more rational, utilitarian, and empiricist outlook on life and a reduction in supernaturalistic explanations. This modification of world view is normally accompanied by organizational changes involving greater institutional differentiation and autonomy in the society. When the same sort of transformation occurs *within* a religion—either in the form of a theology which emphasizes logical reasoning and acceptance of scientific method and discoveries, or as an organizational change using rational, utilitarian business practices in running the institution, it is sometimes called **modernism**.

That a process of change has taken place in the world view and social organization of the Western world is unquestioned.[1] How to understand and evaluate it is more problematic. A number of writers feel that this spells the decline of religion. (Some report this with

delight; others are aghast.) Several social scientists are alarmed that it could mean a collapse of the entire society. Still others maintain that it is a healthy process that will strengthen the influence of religion. They acknowledge religious change but do not see this change as decline. In any case, a change in the foundations of the world view of Western culture is at stake. To provide some sense of the secularization debate, we will begin by exploring the issues as outlined by several key theorists who represent very different points of view.

Secularization as Religious Decline: Loss of Sacredness and Decline of Social Consensus

Peter Berger (1967, 1979) is very much alarmed by the process of secularization. He sees this process as having many adverse effects on individuals and on the society as a whole. Berger defines secularization as "the process by which sectors of society and culture are removed from the domination of religious institutions and symbols" (1967: 107). The function of religion in providing unifying symbols and a unifying world view is extremely important in Berger's view. He insists that a society's *constructed world* (his term for world view) is very fragile. It must be protected by being clothed in an aura of sacredness. The critically thinking empiricist allows that nothing is sacred; that is, nothing is beyond study and question. The world construction of the scientist is based on causality and logic. Because individual thinking is valued, the scientifically oriented society allows and even encourages a plurality of world views. In fact, Berger asserts that "the phenomenon called pluralism is a social-structural correlate of the secularization of consciousness" (1967: 127). But he implies that pluralism is not necessarily a good thing. A multiplicity of world views may make all world views seem relative. None of them can be taken as absolute

---

[1]Secularization has different effects in different cultures and even on different religions in the same society. For a discussion of political and other sociocultural variables, see Martin 1969, 1978. For a discussion of secularization in Judaism, with its emphasis on orthopraxy (conformity to ritual and ethical behaviors) rather than orthodoxy (conformity to beliefs), see Sharot 1991. The focus of this discussion will be on secularization theory as it applies to Christian churches, especially on the North American continent.

and above doubt (1979). This has fostered an "acute crisis" for individuals by creating a sense of anomie. This lack of meaningfulness in life can be extremely disorienting to individuals. Berger insists that the introduction of critical thinking about one's world view "was bought at the price of severe anomie and existential anxiety" (1967: 125).

The dysfunctions of allowing pluralism of world views and of reducing the realm of the sacred is not limited to individuals. Pluralism also poses threats to the stability and workability of the entire society. Berger is a functional or consensus theorist in the fullest sense of the word. He believes that commonly held beliefs, values, and symbols are the glue that hold a society together. He maintains that a society cannot long exist without a discoverable core of common purposes. Religion has always played this role, and Berger is alarmed that the absolute and uncompromising imperative of religion has been relativized. "Religion no longer legitimates the world. Rather, different religious groups seek, by different means, to maintain their particular subworlds in the face of a plurality of competing subworlds" (1967: 152). Because of this, individuals become aware of the fact that there are a plurality of possible religious views—each potentially legitimate—from which they must choose. The fact that one consciously selects a religious orientation (rather than being compelled by the conviction that there is only one possible view) automatically makes the choice relative and less than certain. Berger does not view the current situation as one in which the individual is free to choose—simply an option now available to individuals. Rather, each person *must* choose; that is, one is coerced into doing so. The net effect is a diminishing of the power of religion in the lives of people. To use Clifford Geertz's phrase, it is the difference between holding a belief and being held by one. Berger laments that "religious traditions have lost their character as overarching sym-

bols for the society at large, which must find its integrating symbolism elsewhere" (1967: 153).

Berger concludes that religion must either accommodate, "play the game of religious free enterprise," and "modify its product in accordance with consumer demand," or it must entrench itself and maintain its world view behind whatever socioreligious structures it can construct (1967: 153). A religious group that takes the first course tends to become secularized from within and to lose its sense of transcendence or sacredness. It focuses on "marketing" the faith to a clientele that is no longer constrained to "buy." In the process, the faith may be severely compromised and changed. If it fails to accommodate, the religion may be charged with being an "irrelevant" minority faith that does not respond to the needs of the society. As a religious conservative, Berger strongly supports the "entrenchment option."[2]

The causes of secularization are many. Berger points out that some of the causes lie within the Judeo-Christian outlook itself. Old Testament theology acted to despiritualize the world. Only God was sacred, and the world was not viewed as being inhabited by spirits. The world was given to humanity to use. This outlook allowed an attitude to develop that God's people have the responsibility to manipulate and control resources. Humanity was instructed to have dominion over the earth, and this attitude allowed for the later development of science and technology (Berger 1967). Another possible factor in this secularization process may have been the institutional

---

[2]Berger's own theological conservatism has shaped his perception of religion and its relationship to society. This is not necessarily a criticism of Berger, for the same can be true of any social scientist who studies macro trends in religion. Facts are interpreted through some paradigm, some overriding explanation of how things are. Hence, one's own religious posture tends to shade one's view of the potential threat or benefit of secularization (Johnson 1979).

specialization of religion. The concentration of religious activities and symbols in one institutional sphere automatically defines the rest of society as "the world"; it becomes the profane realm removed for the most part from the jurisdiction of the sacred (1967). By enabling the growth of science and technology and by limiting the scope of religion to a particular institution, Judeo-Christian religion may itself have promoted secularization.

Berger believes the causes of secularization are complex; he also believes the effects are potentially destructive. The unifying power of religious symbols and the integrating function of a common religious world view are very important for social stability. The lack of a single world view, couched in sacred symbols and an aura of absoluteness, is Berger's fundamental concern. Hence, he believes that secularization—the removal of many sectors of society and culture from the domination of religious institutions and symbols—is a critical process in the relationship between religion and modern society.[3]

Other scholars have also stressed religious decline. Thomas O'Dea, for example, maintains that secularization involves a transformation of nonrational religious experience into language in the form of myths, and eventually to a systematizing of beliefs in logical, rational terms. For him it is the move two steps away from the awe-filled mysteries of nonrational experience to the abstractions of rationality and analysis that is the core of secularization. Myths themselves are necessary preservers of the primal religious experience, but are a step

removed from real religion. Any further move away from direct supernatural encounter represents decline.

The systematic and modernistic theologies of Paul Tillich and Henry Nelson Weiman, for example, use logic and the insights of the empirical sciences to reflect on the meaning of human experience; they do not necessarily begin with Bible stories. These liberal theologians view God as the source of creation, human experience, and knowledge. For this reason, *all* human experience is appropriate for theological reflection, not just certain religious stories. Scientific evidence is considered a legitimate starting point for theologizing. Furthermore, a norm of logical consistency and coherence is foremost in most philosophical theologies and becomes a measuring stick for truth. Such theologies are rational meaning systems; they sometimes involve recasting biblical perspectives so that they are consistent with the modern scientific world view. For O'Dea, these theologians have missed the point of experiential religion—personal encounter with the supernatural. Rationality, when applied to religion, is simply a symptom of decline.

Max Weber's thesis that ascetic Protestantism had contributed to the rationalization of economics and other spheres of social life is important here. According to Weber, this rationalization process allowed bureaucratic structures to develop in the Western world. O'Dea, following Weber, concludes that the rational, ascetic, this-worldly character of Protestant Christianity—the Protestant ethic—had much to do with the secularization of Western culture. Theology becomes highly rationalized and systematic only with the development of a professional clergy, an element of institutional differentiation, and specialization. It is the religious elite who are intent on internal theological coherence and consistency. O'Dea points out that the Mormon Church, which has no

---

[3]Garrett and Robertson (1991) suggest that the historic link between modernization and indifference to religion was a European phenomenon. They argue that decline in religious commitment in the Western countries may have been a function of unique forces at work at that particular place and period rather than an intrinsically antireligious characteristic of modernization itself.

full-time professional clergy, has not significantly rationalized its belief system. So O'Dea and Berger both think that Protestant Christianity had within it the seed that caused its own demise. But central to their thinking and that of a number of other writers is the idea that secularization equals waning of religion (Wilson 1966; 1976).

Secularization as Religious Evolution and Development: Increased Complexity of Thought and Greater Religious Autonomy

Talcott Parsons (1964) and Robert Bellah (1970c) have treated secularization as part of the increasing complexity and diversity of modern industrial society. Religion, both as institution and as individual belief system, has become increasingly differentiated from the rest of society. According to Parsons and Bellah, it has simultaneously become more of a private affair. However, they do not see this as a negative change. The possibility of consciously choosing one's religious outlook, rather than being given a theology, may make religion more important to the individual. Parsons insists that Christianity may still have a great effect on Western society; after all, the institutions of the Western world were developed by people who were under the influence of the Christian ethos and the Christian world view. Moreover, private religiosity will continue to affect public behavior; ultimate values cannot help but affect an individual's "system of action." In this view, much of the influence of religion will be unconscious: "Modern man, working in a large corporate structure that is infused somewhat by Christian ideas, with himself directed somewhat by the Christian ethic, may be behaving religiously a good deal of the time, though the fact that he is influenced by religion may not be immediately clear to him because the influence is both indirect and implicit" (Greeley 1972: 134).

Bellah would agree with Berger that religious institutions exert less direct influence on secular institutions than in the past. But he explains this change as a process of religious evolution rather than decline. A more detailed discussion of this concept of religious evolution might help readers grasp Bellah's view of the contemporary religious scene.

It is necessary first to understand Bellah's definition of religion and his treatment of evolution. Bellah defines religion as "a set of symbolic forms and acts which relate [persons] to the ultimate conditions of [their] existence" (Bellah 1970: 21). Obviously Bellah uses a very inclusive definition of religion, and his focus is on the evolution of symbols. The increase in the complexity of symbols is correlated with an increase in the complexity of social organization. Through this process of evolution, religion is able to do more than reaffirm the present social structure; it can challenge the current norms and values of the secular society and offer an alternative culture. Hence, the latter stages of evolution represent an increased autonomy of religion relative to its social environment. Bellah does not suggest that the evolutionary process is inevitable, irreversible, or unidirectional. He simply suggests a general trend of increasing differentiation of religion from the rest of the society.

Bellah has posited five stages in the evolution of religion: primitive religion, archaic religion, historic religion, early modern religion, and modern religion. The most simple form —**primitive religion**—is exemplified by the Australian aborigines. The symbol system of this type of group focuses on a mythical world, and that mythical world provides a model for understanding the real world. The mythical world is peopled by spirits, but the spirits are not greater than humans. Through ritual, people identify with these mythic or spiritual beings. There are no separate or distinctive religious roles, social structure, or organization.

Religion is an undifferentiated part of the culture; hence, it serves to unify the culture and enhance the stability of the social structure. Religion does not serve as a lever for social change.

In **archaic religion,** the spiritual beings have more power and influence than in primitive religion. They are more than models, as they are attributed with power and authority in their own right; they are capable of actively influencing everyday life. Hence, prayer, sacrifice, and other means of communication are established to make contact with these superhuman beings. The development of differentiated religious roles and organizations occurs, but those roles and organizations are still under the control of the political hierarchy. Religion still functions primarily to sanctify the status quo. In fact, the close relationship between religious and political systems is sometimes manifested in a form of divine kingship. Families with high political status usually control the higher-status religious roles as well. The world view is essentially monistic, with the energies of the gods focused on the realm of existence in which humans live. In other words, the religion is essentially this-worldly. The religious symbol system is still not autonomous from the secular symbol system; hence, the religious world view does not offer an alternative to that of the predominant culture.

The distinguishing characteristic of **historic religion** is that the religious realm is entirely different from that of the secular realm. Historic religion truly emphasizes the distinction between sacred and profane worlds. This dualism usually leads to a rejection of the empirical world and its values in favor of the divine realm. Historical religion is otherworldly in the fullest sense of the word. Its emergence is a significant development because at this stage religion becomes more than tribal loyalty. Historic religions affirm the existence of a single God who is God of all peoples and all tribes.

Furthermore, the concept of a separate and independent realm of existence involves the articulation of an alternative model of what the world really is and what is expected of humans. A tension between the religious culture and the secular culture is now possible as each demands the loyalties of the individual. A differentiated religious organization also emerges as a separate institutional structure. As a somewhat autonomous entity, both institutionally and in terms of symbol systems, religion becomes a source of social and cultural change. Political actions may be judged by standards the political authorities do not control.

Early modern religion carries forth a similar pattern in the dualism of the world view and in the autonomy of religious institutions. However, the negative view of the empirical world is modified. While salvation is still viewed as a reward in another realm, one's salvation is worked out through one's personal relationship with God and one's personal demonstration of faithfulness in this world. Bellah traces the beginning of early modern religion to the Protestant Reformation. The Protestant reformers de-emphasized the mediating role of the religious organization and stressed the "priesthood of all believers." Hence, salvation became a matter of individual responsibility and of ethical action in this world. Loyalty and devotion to God was viewed in terms of the conduct of everyday life rather than frequency of attendance at a religious ritual.[4] This emphasis meant that secular institutions (law, education, politics) became appropriate arenas for expressing values and attitudes that one derived from a religious view of the world. Religion may provide an alternative view of the world and establish the

---

[4]This raises some interesting questions about the measures of religiosity that view religious action strictly in terms of church attendance and view application of religion to everyday life as a variable.

motive for change, but other institutions may be used as power bases to initiate the change. The society is characterized by increased tension and conflict as various groups seek to establish their concept of the good society or of the Kingdom of God on earth. Religion has become a more private affair in the sense of not being controlled or determined by public officials, yet the arena for expressing one's religious values has become the arena of public policy and social ethics.

Modern religion is a phenomenon that Bellah believes is currently emerging, although he is quick to point out that the nature of this stage and even its existence are somewhat speculative. Bellah suggests that we are currently undergoing a transformation of religion that involves further privatization and less organizational control. He maintains that new forms of religiosity are emerging. The new form of religious expression is characterized by a breakdown in the dualistic view of the world (with its two realms of existence). This is being replaced by a grounding of religion in ethical life in this world. The world view is less otherworldly but still involves a symbol system that "relates persons to the ultimate condition of their existence." In this sense, he views the world view as profoundly religious. Bellah writes, "The analysis of modern [humanity] as secular, materialistic, dehumanized, and in the deepest sense areligious seems to me fundamentally misguided, for such a judgement is based on standards that cannot adequately gauge the modern temper" (1970: 40). The attempts by several key social scientists to discover "invisible religions" is in keeping with this emphasis on new forms of privatized religion (Luckmann 1967; Yinger 1969, 1977; Wuthnow 1973, 1976b).[5]

Religious evolution is seen by Bellah as an increase in the complexity of symbol systems and in the complexity of the organization of society.[6] The later stages of the evolutionary process allow individuals to make choices about which world view they will accept. Furthermore, individuals have more autonomy in being able to think for themselves and create their own system of meaning. This allows for greater freedom, and in this sense may be viewed as an advancement for humankind. Several researchers have pointed out that the idea of a "religious marketplace" can mean inexhaustible variety rather than watering down and marginalizing of religion (Finke and Stark 1992; Stark and Bainbridge 1985; Warner 1992). As Stephen Warner (1993) puts it, when it comes to religious commitment, achievement may be far superior to ascription.

Parsons and Bellah each treat secularization as the process by which religion has become a private matter, and they believe that such secularization is taking place. However, if secularization is referred to as a process by which religion decreases in importance and by which it has less influence on one's world view and on social behavior, then Bellah and Parsons would deny that secularization is occurring. Differentiation of world views and pluralization of the culture is evaluated in positive terms. It represents progression of society rather than regression and dissolution.

It has been the group that Berger accuses most of having secularized religion—the theological

---

[5]This notion of privatized religion will be explored more completely in chapter 16.

[6]Bellah's theory of religious evolution must be understood within the confines of his operational definition of evolution. Bellah stresses increased differentiation and complexity as the essence of evolution. The natural sciences stress variation and selective retention as the key elements in evolution—factors on which Bellah does not elaborate in his essay. For this reason, some social scientists question whether Bellah's theory is truly evolutionary. Readers should be cautioned that evolution is used in a very specialized way by many scientists and social scientists, whereas others use the term rather freely to describe the emergence of increasingly complex forms from simpler ones. For a comparison and contrast of biological and sociocultural concepts of evolution, see Gerhard Lenski and Jean Lenski (1978).

liberals—who have been most actively involved in "social concerns" struggles (civil rights, antiwar movements, etc.). Although these movements are themselves not always explicitly religious, many participants are motivated by theological convictions. Many theological liberals have de-emphasized the concept of the sacred but have emphasized that all of life is to be understood in theological terms. Hence, they have broadened the scope of religion,[7] even while accepting a rational, empirical understanding of the world. Such theologians as Harvey Cox have celebrated the secularization of religion as a healthy sign (1965). Liberal theologies tend to reformulate the tradition so that it will be in harmony with the most recent scientific findings and other humanistic values in contemporary society. In this sense, liberal or modern theologies tend to be intentional in assimilating the religion to the larger society. Bellah and Parsons have personally identified with this more liberal strain of theology, and they are not inclined to think of it as less religious or as a sign of the decline of religion.

One difficulty with the theory of secularization presented by Parsons and Bellah is that it is developed on such a high level of abstraction that it is virtually impossible to prove or disprove. Their theory represents a complex analysis of the evolution of symbol systems and of the relationships between symbol systems and "action orientations." The theory is significant and deserves attention, but there is no way to measure or test it empirically. Hence, one cannot validate or invalidate the theory with the kinds of hard evidence most social scientists prefer.

---

[7]Berger strongly opposes this sort of broadened scope of religion. He insists that religionists have no business bringing theology into the arena of politics (Berger 1981). Yet he defines the narrowing of the influence and scope of religion as secularization and decline.

Secularization and Its Correlates: The Common Themes

These models provide some sense of the differences in perspectives on the secularization process. As we have seen, one of the areas of conflict is the emphasis on "decline of religion" as a defining element. Robert Bellah and Milton Yinger insist that religion in North America is not declining, it is simply changing. They can assert this, in part, because of the definition of religion they use: reduction in supernaturalism is not equated to reduction in religion. What is needed is a nonevaluative definition of secularization—one which includes the concerns of the various authors but is not based on a single definition of religion.

Let us turn, then, to an overview of commonalties in various models. While emphases vary, there are several elements that are shared by nearly all secularization models (Tschannen 1991). The first two are typically viewed as either cause or effect of one another:

1. a rational, utilitarian, and empirical/scientific approach to decision making, so that the world becomes "disenchanted," and

2. institutional differentiation and increased autonomy of various institutions from religious domination.

Some scholars think changes in thinking patterns or "consciousness" were primary and caused institutional changes, others stress structural changes causing change of outlooks.

Another element is also tied closely to the first one, but places more emphasis on meaning systems *within* religious ideologies:

3. decrease in otherworldliness or supernaturalism.

Whether reduction of supernaturalism represents a decline of religion depends on whether a belief in the supernatural is part of one's definition of religion. Using reduction of supernaturalism as a defining criterion of secularization—rather than "religious decline"—allows us to speak of degrees of secularization, it avoids the supposition that secularization is an irreversible process, and it allows the study of naturalistic and philosophical theologies without assuming that they are less religious. This criterion neither presupposes a definition of religion nor makes a value judgment about secularization as harmful to religion. Some scholars have even suggested that this single factor should be used as the sole criterion in defining "secularization," with the other factors as causes (Johnson 1979). In any case, these are the three core elements most commonly identified as the secularization process.

There are a number of other factors that also occur as correlates of the secularization process, but a debate rages as to which are causes and which are effects:

1. Cultural and religious pluralism in the society
2. Loss of the overall sacralizing role of the culture by religion
3. Increase in the "rational mentality" of individuals, involving openness to new ways of doing things and new ways of thinking that are not based solely on tradition
4. Increase in the "rationality of organizations": emphasis on rational (utilitarian)

▶ **BOX 14.1**

The Attack by Conservative Christians on Secular Humanism: A Conflict Theory Perspective

Most of the discussion of secularization in this chapter has followed a line of argument that has dominated thinking in sociological and theological circles. However, an alternative sort of perspective is provided by conflict theory. The following will provide a conflict theory analysis of the antisecular and antipluralistic movement in United States.

Some religious groups have been very vocal in denouncing the trend in American society toward pluralism and away from public expressions of religiosity. The outcry by some groups about the banning of prayer in the schools is one example. In these cases, pluralistic policies are attacked as **secular humanism**—a term that carries loaded meanings of atheism and antigodliness. Conflict theorists point out that the objections are coming primarily from conservative Protestants—not Jews, Catholics,

Muslims, or members of other groups. It was generally not the faith of these latter groups that was being expressed in public gatherings. Meanwhile, some Protestants feel there is a decline of religion because their own religion is no longer being voiced in "nonreligious" settings. A conflict theory analysis would point to this outcry against pluralistic policy as a thinly veiled conflict over power and prestige in the society. For the conflict theorist, groups act in their self-interests; many times these groups will define anything that threatens the power and prestige for their own group as degenerate or immoral. The conflict theorist may view the popular discussions of pluralism and secularization as part of a larger power-play by Protestants as they seek to sustain their position of privilege in American culture and society.

decision making based on the internal needs of each organization

5. Increase in rationality of economic systems, with each person or family pursuing their own interests
6. Increase in the complexity of symbol systems
7. Privatization of religious beliefs
8. Marketing of religion in a competitive environment
9. Decline in the sphere of influence of religion
10. Decline in religious practice and belief

The latter item is again controversial. Many scholars are not convinced that this is even a correlate of secularization (Greeley 1972; Hadden 1987; Finke and Stark 1992; Warner 1993). Indeed, at least one scholar thinks that *failure* of religion to modernize—failure to adapt to the secular trends—is a sure formula for religious decline (Tamney 1992).

Is Secularization a Pervasive and Unstoppable Force?

The question of whether religion is an overpowering and inevitable force has been debated heatedly. Most treatments of secularization have argued that secularization is the most powerful and pervasive process in the modern world. Indeed, it is often treated as the defining characteristic of the modern world and is viewed as an unstoppable trend. But in one of the most important recent analyses of secularization, Rodney Stark, William Bainbridge, and Roger Finke challenged the conventional wisdom, and they are being joined by a number of other scholars as well (Hadden 1987; Warner 1993). Indeed, the idea that secularization is *not* inevitable now seems to have become the conventional position, at least in the United States (Sharot 1991; Tschannen 1991).

Stark and Bainbridge begin by defining supernaturalism as the central characteristic of religion. They also define secularization as the decline of supernaturalism and the growth of scientific empiricism. Hence, they view religion and secularization as opposites. They acknowledge that secularization has been an extremely important process in the modern world, but they also believe that secularization is "self-limiting." They insist that "the sources of religion are shifting constantly in societies, but . . . the amount of religion remains relatively constant" (Stark and Bainbridge 1985: 3). So although these two scholars maintain that secularization is antithetical to religion, they believe it does not necessarily spell a decrease of religion in the society. Their thesis deserves a more complete discussion.

Stark and Bainbridge begin with the observation that "humans seek what they perceive to be rewards and try to avoid what they perceive to be costs" (1985: 5). They continue by pointing out that some rewards are scarce and unequally distributed within society and some desired rewards (such as life after death) may not be available from the society at all. When humans do not have access to desired rewards, they seek compensators. "A **compensator** is a belief that a reward will be obtained in the distant future or in some other context which cannot be immediately verified" (1985: 6).

Social inequality means that some people in the society—the affluent—can satisfy most of their material wants and needs with empirically available methods. Those who are at the lower end of the socioeconomic hierarchy may desire compensation for their lack of ability to meet their material needs, including everything from food and shelter to health care. Compensators that address needs that could be satisfied through empirical means but are denied because of scarcity or social competition are referred to as *specific compensators*.

Supernaturalism that is geared exclusively to specific compensators is a form of magic (discussed in chapter 1). It is a type of "supernatural technology," a method of manipulating nonempirical forces in the service of this-worldly needs. Stark and Bainbridge believe that religion, properly understood, deals only with *general compensators*. But they also point out that most religious organizations in the past and a great many in the present offer a mixture of general and specific compensators. Religious groups are being discredited, they believe, because empirical scientific methods are disproving many specific compensator claims (such as faith healings of physical disabilities and illnesses). This creates a problem of plausibility for many religious groups. Doubts about the ability of supernatural methods to satisfy empirical needs have caused skepticism about the plausibility of religious claims to satisfy general needs (e.g., hope for life after death). Stark and Bainbridge insist that science will ultimately drive out magic because modern science and technology prove more effective in addressing this-worldly needs. But science can never replace religion per se because empirical methods are incapable of addressing nonempirical (spiritual) needs (1985).

These "rationale choice" theorists also maintain that the effectiveness of the scientific view of the world has created a problem for many traditional religious organizations. People in modern societies have come to depend increasingly on scientific empirical methods as sources of validation rather than on supernatural explanations (see Box 14.2). Many religious leaders have coped with the scientific revolution by lowering tension with the secular (this-worldly) culture: they adopt a more secular perspective. They develop a theology that is consistent with scientific empiricism, often by shying away from supernaturalism altogether. In the seventeenth century, European scientists like Galileo were forced by the Christian Church to recant their findings,

but "in this century it has been the religious intellectuals, not the scientists, who have done the recanting" (Stark and Bainbridge 1985: 434). But when religious organizations abandon supernaturalism, they are only able to offer very weak general compensators (Stark and Bainbridge 1985; Finke and Stark 1992).

Stark, Bainbridge, and Finke believe this abandonment of supernaturalism is a serious mistake: "Simply because human societies have the blessings of advanced science does not mean that they are free from existential anxieties [about the meaning of life] or from the desire for rewards that remain unobtainable" (Stark and Bainbridge 1985: 434). The result of all of this is not a society of empirical secularists who eschew any sense of supernaturalism but a revival of new expressions of religion. These come in the form of renewals of traditional faiths (sects) or in the formation of entirely new religious movements (cults).

These scholars offer several types of evidence in support of their claim that supernaturalism is, in fact, not declining in North America. First, many secularization theorists have argued that one bit of evidence of declining religiosity in modern industrialized societies is the number of people who, when asked their religious preference, indicate "none." But Stark and Bainbridge point out that further analysis of religious "nones" indicate that most of them are not secular empiricists. They frequently accept unconventional supernaturalism in the form of astrology, transcendental meditation, yoga, or some other form of other-worldly compensation. Second, in the region of the continent where traditional forms of religion are weakest (the Pacific Coast), secular humanism does not abound; cults do. They develop precisely to fill the vacuum of general (supernatural) compensators.

Third, Stark and Bainbridge cite evidence that atheism or agnosticism in one generation is very often followed by reaffirmation of religious conviction in the next generation (1985). The movement away from supernaturalism and toward a purely secular outlook is not an inevitable process that spells a substantial and long-term decline of religion. The inability of secularism to provide general compensators (a sense of meaning in life, the hope for an afterlife, etc.) means that it is self-limiting. Secularization does not mean a decline of religion, but it does mean a *reformation* of traditional religions and the spawning of new religious movements.

This view directly contradicts that of many modernization theorists, for whom cult formation is part of the secularization process. These writers believe that cult formation is part of the pluralization and trivialization of religion that occurs as we enter an era of religious entrepreneurship and the individualization of faith. Stark and Bainbridge believe cult formation is the opposite of, and occurs as a *response* to, secularization.

Reading the Trends in Religious Commitment

As we have seen, social scientists differ widely in their interpretation of current trends and in their projections of the future of American religion. Some believe that religion has undergone a recent resurgence. Others see a tremendous decline in the face of secularization. Still others maintain that religion is neither growing nor declining but undergoing transformation. We turn now to the empirical data itself and how these data have been interpreted.

▶ **BOX 14.2**

Scientific Discovery and the Plausibility of Religious Claims

Magical explanations about how to gain a desired reward (or avoid a damaging cost) will tend to be discredited by scientific test and to be discarded in favor of scientifically verified explanations. This tendency has serious consequences for religions that include a significant magical component. Consider the case of the lightning rod. . . . For centuries, the Christian church held that lightning was the palpable manifestation of divine wrath and that safety against lightning could be gained only by conforming to divine will. Because the bell towers of churches and cathedrals tended to be the only tall structures, they were the most common targets of lightning. Following damage or destruction of a bell tower by lightning, campaigns were launched to stamp out local wickedness and to raise funds to repair the tower.

Ben Franklin's invention of the lightning rod caused a crisis for the church. The rod demonstrably worked. The laity began to demand its installation on church towers—backing their demands with a threat to withhold funds to restore the tower should lightning strike it. The church had to admit either that Ben Franklin had the power to thwart divine retribution or that lightning was merely a natural phenomenon. Of course, they chose the latter, but, in so doing, they surrendered a well-known and dramatic magical claim about the nature of the supernatural. Such admissions call into question other claims made by a religion, including even those that are eternally immune from empirical disconfirmation.

Source: From Rodney Stark and William Sims Bainbridge, *The Future of Religion.* Berkeley: University of California Press, 1985.

Resurgence of Religion in the United States and Canada?

Those who maintain that a major religious revival is under way in the United States point to the rejuvenation of evangelical Christianity and to the rise of new religious movements. For example, the born-again movement has gained a great deal of media attention in recent years. A Gallup Poll in 1986 indicated that 45 percent of Protestants and a third of the total American public identify themselves as born-again Christians (The Gallup Poll 1987: 29). These figures suggest that more than 50 million Americans attest to some sort of personal religious experience or personal commitment.[8] Among Canadians, 50 percent report having had a personal religious experience, and gross church membership in Canada has continued to increase every decade (Bibby 1987a). While skeptics of the resurgence have pointed to a decline in church building programs, supporters of this view point out that extraordinary increases in spending for mass-media evangelism show a shift of priorities in spending, not a decline. Indeed, the expansion of religious programming on television (sometimes called "the electronic church") has been remarkable. However, an increase in programming does not automatically signal a growth in new believers or a deepened commitment to the faith by present members. (In chapter 5 we discussed different types of commitment and the fact that financial giving may occur independently of commitment to an ideology.)

Others, such as Stark and Bainbridge, suggest a growth of religion in North America in the form of nontraditional religious movements—the cults or new religious movements (NRMs). The emergence and expansion of these groups in the past two decades indicate to some observers an intense search for meaning. While traditional religious organizations and ideologies may have failed to provide it for many, these new religious movements show that religion has been regaining interest.

No one knows the number of members in most NRMs (the groups and their detractors both tend to exaggerate substantially the number of followers). But a survey by George Gallup resulted in an estimate that about 6 million people are involved in transcendental meditation, 3 million in mysticism, and 2 million in groups of Eastern origin, such as Zen. Even without inclusion of fairly large and socially legitimized new religious movements, such as Christian Scientists and Mormons, over 40,000 persons per million in the U.S. population identified with a cult in the early 1980s. By contrast, an analysis of U.S. census data from 1926 suggests that cults were far less popular.[9] Including figures on Theosophy, Liberal Catholics (an offshoot of Theosophy), Divine Science, Bahai, Spiritualism, Swedenborgianism, and the very large Christian Science movement, only about 2,000 Americans per million were identified with NRMs in the 1960s (Stark and Bainbridge 1985). Both figures may be biased a bit by the fact that some persons may affiliate with more than one of these movements, but clearly the percentage of the population interested in new religious groups has risen dramatically in this century and especially in recent decades. It appears that some young Americans seem to be opting

---

[8]Actually, the term *born-again* is a broad one that includes many types of experiences. Depending on the group, being born again may entail a personal religious experience, an adult baptism, glossolalia (speaking in tongues), or a gradual experience of deepened commitment. For example, 33 percent of the teenage respondents in the Princeton sample reported being born-again, but 27 percent described being born-again as a gradual process of deepened religious commitment and only 6 percent pointed to a specific, sudden experience (Princeton Religion Research Center 1980: 70).

---

[9]The U.S. Census Bureau discontinued its practice of gathering data on religious groups in 1926, so we do not have recent Census Bureau information available.

for a new form of religion rather than opting out of religion altogether.

One other source has caused some observers to believe that traditional religiosity has undergone a revival. According to data reported on denominational membership, the conservative denominations (Southern Baptist, Nazarene, Assembly of God, etc.) are the ones that are growing, and the moderate and liberal denominations (Episcopal, United Church of Christ, United Methodist, United Presbyterian, etc.) are declining (see Box 5.4 in chapter 5). Dean Kelley, an official of the National Council of Churches, maintains that people have been switching to more conservative denominations because the latter seem more certain of their claims to truth and because they require a strict and uncompromising commitment (sacrifices and investments). Other researchers, using better controls on their data, have challenged this thesis. They report that most switching is from conservative denominations to more liberal ones and from liberal ones to "no religion" (Newport 1979). These researchers grant that conservative denominations have been growing more rapidly than liberal ones, but they insist that the increase in crude numbers has been due to higher birth rates among the more conservative denominations. (For more detail, refer to the discussion of religious switchers in chapter 5.)

There are some signs of renewed religious intensity in North America, much of which took social scientists by surprise. But a large number of social scientists claim that these are still small minority movements or temporary aberrations in an overriding trend of religious decline.

Decline of Religion in the United States and Canada?

Those who maintain that religion is in a declining pattern point to drops over the past several decades in the percentage of the population who are formally members of a congregation and the percentage attending religious services on a weekly basis (see Figures 14.1 and 14.2). The trend is clearly downward. Of course, these indexes only show institutional expressions of religion, not religion as a world view. Church membership tends to be a particularly poor measure of personal religiosity (Demerath 1965). Church attendance is a somewhat better indicator, but it is correlated highly to some dimensions of religiosity (religious knowledge, doctrinal orthodoxy) and not to others (reports of personal religious experience, devotionalism, ethicalism, and communal involvement). But affiliation and attendance are not the only items that have suggested a decline in the influence of religion. In recent years, fewer people respond positively when asked whether they think religion is increasing its influence on everyday life. Furthermore, the number of people who report that they believe in life after death or that they have "no doubts about the existence of God" has also declined.

An interesting difference occurs between the United States and Canada, however, and deserves our attention. The drop in membership in the United States has paralleled the decline in weekly attendance at worship. In Canada the drop in church attendance has been stunning, but membership has remained constant at nearly 90 percent for at least four decades (Bibby 1987b). Reginald Bibby believes that Canadians may be developing a more casual attitude toward religion and that the scope of religion for Canadians has narrowed and become compartmentalized. He writes, "What a majority of Canadians appear to engage in is 'religion à la carte'—a belief here, a practice there, a Sunday service, a baptism, a wedding, a funeral" (Bibby 1987a: 264). Although Canadians are not abandoning their religion, the pattern does seem to represent a decline in the overall potency of religion in Canadian society.

As we have seen, many social scientists have written about the process of secularization, which most scholars seem to feel is antithetical to religion or at least to traditional forms of religion.

There are, however, a few sociologists who have recently sought to disrupt this consensus. One of these dissenters, Andrew Greeley (1969b, 1972) insists that no long-term decline has taken place. Although there may be some recent drops in affiliation from the extraordinary high of the 1950s, church affiliation and church attendance is far ahead of historical averages for the nation as a whole. There is evidence to support his position; historians claim that in 1800 less than 10 percent of the population belonged to churches and only about 20 percent [10] attended religious services

[10]Winthrop Hudson estimates church membership at one out of fifteen members of the population, with attendance at about three times that number. Membership was very low because it was highly restricted. Church membership as a percentage of the population increased partially because criteria for such membership were relaxed. However, even using present-day definitions of religious affiliation, Hudson (1973) claims only about 40 percent of the population would have identified themselves as church members. Such a figure is far below contemporary figures in the United States.

▶ **FIGURE 14.1**

Percentage of Adults Attending Church on an Average Week (Based on Those *Saying* They Attend)

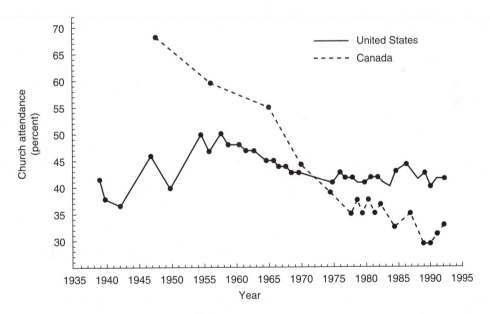

Source: Adapted from Benson Y. Landis, ed., *Yearbook of American Churches*. New York: National Council Press, 1965; Constant H. Jacquet Jr., ed., *Yearbook of American and Canadian Churches*. Nashville: Abingdon Press, 1987; and Princeton Religion Research Center, *Religion in America* 1992–93. Princeton, N.J.: Princeton Religion Research Center, 1993, and Gallup Canada, Inc.

(Hudson 1973). By 1850 only 16 percent of the population were members of religious organizations. Recent exhaustive research on American church membership in 1776 is very convincing in supporting the claim that in the "good old days" of colonial America, church membership was about 10 percent (Stark and Finke 1988; Finke and Stark 1992) (see Figure 14.3).

Greeley (1972; 1989) interprets any reversal in church growth patterns since the 1950s as part of a normal cycle or a response to specific events. But he even doubts that a really

▶ **FIGURE 14.2**

Church-Synagogue Membership in the United States, 1937–1990 (Based on Those *Saying* They Are Members)

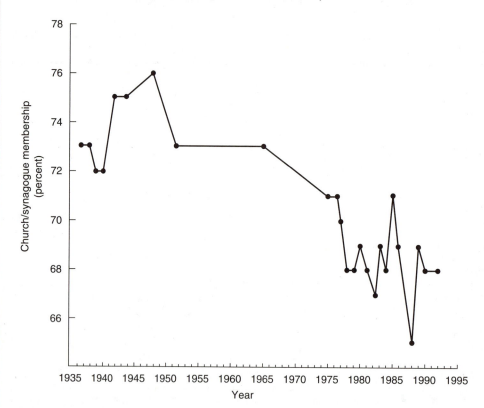

Source: The Gallup Poll, *The Gallup Report: Religion in America.* Princeton, N.J.: The Gallup Organization, 1987.

Note: These figures indicate those who claim church membership in a sample survey. However, respondents sometimes report that they are members of a particular denomination even though the local congregation no longer has that person on its active membership roles.

significant downturn in religious involvement has taken place at all. He argues that there has been a decline in some dimensions of religiosity and an increase in others. For example, in his 1972 study he found that among Protestants there was a decrease in the number of people who believed in heaven but a small increase in the number that prayed three times a day or more. Among Catholics he found a small decrease in the number that prayed three times a day or more but a net increase in participation in church activities. Among Jews he found a substantial decline in the number

that believed in God or in life after death, but a significant increase in active synagogue involvement. In all three groups, fewer people reported that religion was important in their own life, but in all three there was an increase in the percentage who engaged in weekly Bible reading. His 1989 analysis indicated small increases in daily Bible reading among Americans, combined with declines among American Catholics in acceptance of papal authority and in financial donations to churches. (The latter seem to be responses to Vatican II rather than to secularization trends.) We might

---

▶ **FIGURE 14.3**

Church Membership as a Percentage of the U.S. Population, 1776–1990 (Based on Denominational Reports of Membership)

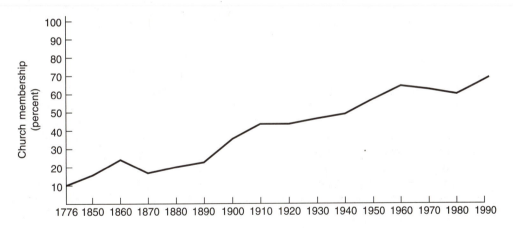

Sources: Benson Y. Landis, ed., *Yearbook of American Churches.* New York: National Council Press, 1965; and Constant H. Jacquet Jr., ed., *Yearbook of American and Canadian Churches.* Nashville: Abingdon, 1987, 1991.

Note: While short-term statistical figures seem to indicate a tremendous decline in church membership (see Figures 14.1 and 14.2), the long-term figures make the downturn of the sixties and

seventies appear slight. These long-term statistical figures must also be evaluated with caution. Prior to the 1920s, some churches counted only the heads of families as members and others counted only adult members. Some denominations now report all baptized members—including infants. Note also the difference in self-reports and denominational reports of church members for the years 1936–1979 as reported in Figure 14.2 and this figure.

add that while trends may be downward in some areas, overall survey responses to traditional religious questions indicate a highly religious America: 94 percent believe in God, 71 percent believe in life after death, and only 10 percent list "none" when asked about religious preference (Princeton Religion Research Center, 1990).

Moreover, Greeley suggests that religion is less important to people in that they don't think about it all of the time or when making everyday decisions. But it does provide a sense of ultimate meaning in life, and it establishes an important sense of belonging and fellowship. In this role as a significant reference point, religion may have more influence over the individual's behavior than it did as an abstract set of beliefs and principles. (As we found in chapter 10, communal processes usually are more important factors in affecting behavior than are affiliational ones.) Greeley insists that exclusive loyalty to religious ideology—in which all of one's attitudes are scrutinized for their consistency with religious doctrine—is a phenomenon that has been rare in the history of human religions (Greeley 1972).

As for faith in the principles of science, declines in otherworldliness, and a waning sense of the sacred, Greeley sees little among the common laity. Secularization, if it exists at all, is a phenomenon of religious elites (the clergy, theologians, and religious officials). Even among graduate students at twelve of the top universities in the United States, where one would expect the most secularization, Greeley reports that only a modest decline in religious affiliation has taken place. He insists that minor downturns in several indexes of religiosity have caused many sociologists to make sweeping generalizations about a long-term and pervasive pattern. He believes this interpretation has grossly exaggerated the facts. We might also add that any drop that has occurred in church membership is exclusively a phenomenon of white America; membership has not declined

in any of the seven black denominations in the United States (Lincoln and Mamiya 1990) nor have surveys indicated secular attitudes among African American Christians (Jacobson, Heaton, and Dennis 1990).

Several other scholars have offered other data that challenge the thesis that religion is caught in a long-term process of decline. Dean Hoge and David Roozen (1979), Robert Wuthnow (1976c), and Rodney Stark and Roger Finke (1988) agree with Greeley that the downturn is short-term. They insist that short-term trends cannot be explained by long-term processes (such as secularization). Hoge and Roozen explain growth and decline trends with several interacting variables. They point out that social and cultural changes in the larger society (values, beliefs, socioeconomic conditions, etc.) can affect patterns of religious affiliation and membership. These are referred to as *contextual factors.* However, to understand growth and decline of any given denomination or local congregation, one must also understand the effects of *institutional factors,* which may either mobilize people or alienate them. They point out that the membership factors in churches are affected by national contextual factors (wars or economic recessions), local contextual factors (a natural disaster or a plant closing), national institutional factors (those in a denominational hierarchy), and local institutional factors (those in a local congregation). Church membership and attendance in the nation at any given time is influenced by these factors—and at any given time there are likely to be countertrends that strengthen or weaken church ties in various denominations and in various regions of the country (Hoge and Roozen 1979). These counterforces explain the irregularity of church membership patterns as the force-field changes from time to time.

Daniel Rigney, Richard Machalek, and Jerry Goodman (1978) have also found irregular variation in religiosity. Using longitudinal data on seven measures of religiosity, they found a long-term pattern of decline in some areas (e.g., annual contributions to religious organizations and to charities as a percentage of all per-capita expenditures, religious books published as a percentage of all books), a pattern of long-term increase in one area (church membership as a percentage of the total population), and irregular variation in others (percentage reporting regular church attendance, church construction as a percentage of all construction). They conclude that there are clearly countervailing forces at work in American religiosity and that secularization is "not a unitary process." However, one factor pervades all attempts to discern long-term trends in religiosity, an unfortunate lack of reliable and comparable historical data (Rigney et al. 1978). Even some of the very contemporary data used to interpret trends are being challenged, as Box 14.3 indicates.

Conclusions

By way of summary, we can point to three important issues that affect one's interpretation of the data: one's definition of religion, one's interpretation of the privatization factor, and one's understanding of the youth factor. For many scholars who hold to a substantive definition of religion (religion as a belief in the supernatural), religion seems to be in decline.[11] For those who use a functional definition (religion as that which provides a sense of meaning in life), religion is changing but is not necessarily declining. Most of the statistical data that indicate a decline in religiosity and a rise in secularization are based on a substantive definition of religion. A decline in orthodoxy is viewed as a decline

[11]Stark, Bainbridge, and Finke are the notable exceptions to this generalization.

▶ **BOX 14.3**

Church Attendance Rates in the United States

For scholars arguing that the United States is not secularized and is, indeed, the most religious country in the world, one of the strongest points of evidence is polling data showing that more than 2 out of 5 Americans attend church each Sunday (Princeton Religion Research Center 1993). But three researchers have recently raised questions about the accuracy of that data. They reasoned that if over 40 percent of the population were actually attending church each Sunday, the numbers and financial resources of many denominations would not be dwindling so severely.

By actually comparing survey data—in which people respond to a question of whether they have attended church in the past seven days—with an actual head count of people in church, Hadaway, Marler, and Chaves (1993) conclude that the actual church attendance each Sunday is only about half of what the polls indicate. Their study focuses primarily on a single county in Ohio, but other nationwide evidence available on Roman Catholics corroborates their findings.

The problem with opinion polls, say the researchers, is that many people feel they should attend church more often—they think others expect that of them—and so they respond affirmatively. In religious behavior, even more than other areas of human life, there may be an especially large gap between what people *say* they do and what they really *do*.

If this finding holds up under further research—that is, if only about 20 to 25 percent of Americans do attend church each week—many scholars will need to rethink their theories, or at least base their arguments on different data.

in religiosity, and orthodoxy is often measured with questions about belief in the devil, in the virgin birth of Jesus, and in Jesus' ability to walk on water. Among Catholics, belief in the infallibility of the Pope in matters of faith and morals is often a criterion of orthodoxy and hence of religiosity. The assumption behind these measurement devices is that religion and science are antithetical. Hence, a move from a fundamentalist or conservative theological stance to a liberal one is interpreted as a decline in religiosity—an interpretation most liberals would reject.

Much of the survey data is based on the idea that religion must be otherworldly. Those who do not believe in life after death are said to be less religious. Parsons (1964) and Weber (1963) have insisted that religion is not necessarily otherworldly. Hence, a decline in otherworldliness is not necessarily an indication of a decline in religiosity. Theologian Harvey Cox is an interesting example. He claims that secularization is the fulfillment of a central biblical theme: liberation from superstition and from animism (the belief that all material objects have spirits). A profound this-worldly orientation is deeply biblical, he asserts. A number of liberal theologians concur with this view. For these religious scholars, secularization and religiosity are not antithetical; an increase in one is not interpreted as a decline in the other. The point I wish to make here is that some of the data that have shown declines in religiosity have measured only certain expressions of religiosity.

The tendency to measure religiosity in terms of adherence to specific beliefs is clearly understandable, for we have seen that religious systems tend to "freeze" their world views and encapsulate them in beliefs that are supposedly immutable. But as societies change, these beliefs can come to be implausible or irrelevant. It is interesting to note the emergence of process theology among the religious elite at a time in which social change seems to be the only certainty. One of the fundamental principles of process theology is that change is indisputable,

inescapable, and eternal. Not even God is viewed as immutable and absolute, but rather as changing and evolving. Even the deity is "in process." Many observers view this as a further accommodation to society and as evidence that religion is losing ground—even within its own ranks—to the secular world view.

The accommodation of a religious world view to be compatible with the larger culture and structural realities is certainly not new and is not necessarily evidence of a decline. Few people would describe the theology of John Calvin as antithetical to religion, yet his system of belief accommodated Christian thought to the emergence of capitalism (discussed in chapter 10). Few view Second Isaiah as less religious than his predecessors, even though he accommodated the Hebrew theodicy to account for the secular exigencies of the exile. Sociologists who define the accommodation of contemporary religious beliefs to secular social realities seem to be placing a value judgment on our contemporary transition, which they would not think of doing to earlier transitions.

A second issue in interpreting religious trends has to do with how one understands the process of the privatization of religion. Sociologists from a wide range of perspectives (Berger, Luckmann, Parsons, Bellah) have maintained that religion has increasingly become a private, individual affair. Each individual is able to choose his or her religious orientation from a wide range of religious "entrepreneurs." Religious beliefs are not taken for granted—appearing unquestionable and embedded in the very nature of reality. The modern citizen can choose his or her form of religiosity. Berger and his followers view this as hazardous for religion.[12] Parsons, Bellah, Stark, Finke, and Bainbridge see it as a healthy sign.

---

[12]In his earlier work (1967), Berger suggested that privatization is disastrous for both traditional forms of religion and for society as a whole. His more recent work (1979) suggests certain offsetting advantages of individualized religion. But despite certain benefits, individualization continues to be viewed by Berger as a threat to *traditional* forms of religiosity.

Related to this privatization is the fact that religion comes to have an ever narrower scope of direct influence. With the differentiation of institutions and the specialization of functions of these institutions, religion is seen—at least by some scholars—as having less impact on the society as a whole. In other words, increasing numbers of people have a multiple narrow-scope world view rather than a single integrated wide-scope world view. This assertion that religion has a narrowed scope is still at the stage of hypothesis. We have no hard empirical data by which we can compare contemporary world views with historical outlooks. Furthermore, those who use a functional definition of religion may insist that the "real" religion of a people is that which has scope. One's real system of meaning may be something other than traditional doctrines that one affirms only verbally. According to this definition of religion, a person's "real faith" is always manifest in his or her daily life—even if he or she does not consciously call that faith "religion."

If it can be established that there is an increase in multiple narrow-scope world views, another interesting possibility occurs: Traditional religion may be undergoing simultaneous revival and decline. Geertz (1968) discusses the difference between force and scope in religion. **Religious force** refers to the intensity with which people hold their beliefs, **religious scope** to the influence of one's religious symbols and ideas on other areas of life. It is possible (and again, this is hypothesis) that the increase in born-again and charismatic movements represents an increase in force of traditional religiosity for some Americans, but that traditional religiosity is simultaneously declining in scope. Students may want to explore their own assumptions about what it means to be religious. Can religion exist without scope? Or, are those belief systems something other than the true meaning system of individuals? Does the current growth of traditional religiosity represent an increase in force

but not in scope? How would a sociologist go about proving or disproving this thesis? How would you design a research model?

Finally, any interpretation of religious trends must come to terms with the youth factor. The increases in the 1970s of those reporting "no religion" were largely younger members of the adult population. Some observers have felt that this bodes ill for religion because young people would not be sustaining the churches in a few years and would not be raising their children in a religious context. Hence, the major form of recruitment—procreation and religious socialization within the home—would not be sustaining the churches in future decades. Other observers have pointed out that religious inactivity in the teens and early twenties is not a new phenomenon. It is a normal developmental process most generations have experienced. Most people, by their early to mid thirties, join churches and see that their children get some religious training. This generation, it is claimed, will be no different.

Still others claim that the religious apostasy of the current generation is due to the unique experiences in young adulthood which these individuals have endured. Americans who are just now approaching forty grew up in an atmosphere of political assassinations (John Kennedy, Martin Luther King Jr., Robert Kennedy), radical politics, the Vietnam War, and the Watergate scandals. All these events occurred when this generation was at an impressionable age. The effects of these events on this particular age group may be lasting. The group may have developed—with more frequency than most generations—a larger number of cynical personalities or larger numbers of individuals who seek political solutions to problems. The group of young people who were born ten years later may have been less aware of the events of the 1960s and may be more inclined to involvement in traditional religious organizations (Newport 1979; Perrin 1989; Wuthnow 1976c).

The data provided in the table in Box 14.4 seems to offer some measure of support to this latter interpretation, although readers should be warned that in a sample of just over 2,000 respondents, broken down by age, the number in each category is so small (150 to 250) that the percentages should be read with great caution (The Gallup Report 1987: 20).[13]

Most interesting, however, is the fact that the cohort of Americans who were in their teens during the 1960s do not appear to be returning to traditional churches at the rate of those born a decade earlier. Two recent studies using national data also concluded that older baby boomers are starting to return to churches, though still not in numbers that match those of their own parents (Hadaway and Marler 1993; Roozen, McKinney and Thompson 1990).

On balance, there does appear to be a recent reduction in traditional forms of religion, at least among whites. But even among this group, current affiliation and attendance patterns continue to remain ahead of their levels for colonial days and for the early 1800s—in what were supposed to have been the "good old days" of high levels of religious commitment.

---

[13]Most recent surveys do not indicate the large increase for those over age fifty, nor the sharp decline for the eighteen-to-nineteen and twenty-to-twenty-four year-old groups that appear in this sample.

▶ **BOX 14.4**

"No Preference" in Religion as a Correlate of Age (United States)

The proportion of people responding "no preference" when questioned about their religious preference has increased significantly since the 1960s. In 1967, 2 percent of the population responded with this answer. By 1979, 8 percent expressed no preference. In 1980 and again in 1987, the number was 7 percent. Most of the increase was related to age because it is mostly young adults (ages eighteen to thirty-two) whose religious involvement fades. The debate is whether the current group of young adults lived through social upheavals that permanently affected their sense of religiosity or whether—like their elders—they will also join churches as they age. Part of the increase from 1967 to 1979 in "no preference" may be due to the fact that the very large number of people who were born during the baby boom (1947–1960) were in their late teens, twenties, and early thirties during that period. Some of the baby boom people are still in that age group; by the early 1990s, those born during the "birth dearth" (late 1960s and early 1970s) become predominant in that critical age range. This is a partial explanation for the decline in the overall figures for "no preference."

	Percentage	
Age	1980	1987
18–19	11	3
20–24	14	7
25–29	13	8
30–34	11	12
35–39	8	11
40–44	6	9
45–49	6	9
50–59	4	7
60–69	4	8
70 and older	3	12
Total population	7	7

Source: Gallup Report, 1980. Reported by the Princeton Religious Research Center, 1981; and Gallup Poll, 1987. Data provided by the Roper Center for Public Opinion Research.

Summary

Secularization has been viewed by sociologists as one of the most powerful forces in the modern world. But there are marked differences in what are considered the core characteristics of secularization, and in the causes and effects of the process. Berger has defined it as loss of sacredness; O'Dea has treated it as increased rationalization of the society and of theology. Both view secularization as causing a decline in religion. Parsons and Bellah view secularization as evolution, as an increased sophistication in religious symbolism and religious structures. They understand secularization as involving change in religious world views but not necessarily as decline in religion.

By looking at commonalties in secularization theories, we find three core elements: (1) a rational, utilitarian, and empirical/scientific approach to decision making and to truth, so that the world becomes "disenchanted"; (2) institutional differentiation and increased autonomy of various institutions from religion; and (3) decrease in otherworldliness or supernaturalism. Several other factors are correlated with these three elements either as causes or effects. Whether secularization entails a decline in religion may depend in part on whether one uses a substantive or functional definition of religion, since not all scholars view supernaturalism as central to religion.

Stark and Bainbridge agree with Berger and O'Dea that secularization is antithetical to religion. But they do not think that religion is therefore necessarily declining. They are convinced that secularization is "self-limiting" and is not an inevitable and overpowering force. They believe that magic, or supernatural solutions for this-worldly problems, will fade as secular scientific empiricism replaces it. But religion, properly understood, addresses general needs that cannot be solved by this-worldly methods.

Interpretation of statistical evidence regarding religious growth or decline in North America has also been controversial. Part of the disagreement depends on whether one looks at trends of the past few decades or longer-term patterns. Beyond that, low levels of religious involvement by young adults have been variously interpreted. This pattern may mean lean times ahead for many American denominations, but low levels of participation by young adults have been characteristic of every generation. Although disaffection seems higher among "baby boomers," some of these people are returning to churches. Further, the "birth-dearth" generation born during the late 1960s and early 1970s may not be quite as disaffected from religion. A general decline in traditional expressions of religion occurred from the 1950s to the early 1980s. But the evangelical movement shows a countertrend to even this pattern. And overall levels of religiosity are much higher now than in colonial days and are higher than many other parts of the world.

Clearly, if secularization is occurring, it is happening primarily among those with a more liberal theological orientation. Indeed, liberals are often explicit about making the theology relevant to the contemporary world and do not apologize for the fact that religion needs to be continually reformed in light of social and cultural changes. In the next chapter, however, we will see that adaptation of theology is also at work in some elements of the evangelical movement. And if secularization includes use of rational economic/business practices in running religious organizations, televangelism may be an example of secularization par excellence.

► **CHAPTER FIFTEEN**

Televangelism: The Marketing of Religion

O ne of the important ways in which change occurs is through the introduction of new technology, and few technological innovations have been more significant than the introduction of mass media, especially television. We do not have space here to explore the effects of this new technology on the society at large, but surely no one will contest the premise that television has had important impact on the society at large. But television does not impact only the secular society. The past four decades have seen the introduction of television and other electric media as tools of evangelism and of commitment maintenance. The crude numbers are impressive. By the end of the 1980s, there were a reported 1,370 radio stations owned and operated exclusively for religious programming and more than 220 religious television stations. Three Christian networks broadcast twenty-four hours a day to a nationwide audience (Hadden and Shupe 1988). (Terminology for referring to religious use of the media is discussed in Box 15.1.)

The use of television for religious broadcasting has a number of implications. For one thing, the electronic media greatly expands the potential audience for any evangelist. As Billy Graham once pointed out, ". . . in a single telecast, I preach to millions more than Christ did in His entire lifetime" (1983: 5). The expansion of the audience of a preacher means that an evangelist can gain considerable national following and can mobilize tremendous resources. Pat Robertson's Christian Broadcasting Network and related enterprises alone reported an income of $230 million at its peak in 1986 (Hadden and Shupe 1988). Such resources have never before been accessible to a single minister or a single church.

Indeed, access to the airwaves is itself an important resource, one that has been the source of considerable conflict. Television ministry is dominated almost entirely by those with a very conservative orientation, although that has not always been the case. Insofar as television is a homogenizing medium that significantly influences the character of the national culture, this may mean an important conservative influence on the culture and a powerful evangelical thrust to Christianity in North America.

Given its size and potential influence in the culture, televangelism might be of intrinsic interest to us. But a deeper issue is at stake here. We have already seen that institutionalization creates certain dynamic forces that have an influence and direction of their own. This is no less true of the mass-media religious industry. The medium of television and the forces of the media organization lead to goal displacement and even to a transformation of the message itself. Some critics believe that the message of televangelists is a truncated and profoundly revised theology. They charge that televangelist theology accommodates, often unwittingly, to secular materialism, that the need to raise enormous amounts of money becomes a driving force in the nature of the religious programming, and that the resultant need to "market" Christianity means that the theology is modified to fit popular demand. The medium, television, comes to transform the message itself. In chapter 14 we saw that liberal theology often celebrates secularization and consciously assimilates the faith to be relevant to the surrounding culture. But in this chapter, we find that liberal religion is not the only one that adapts to the culture. Some conservative evangelicals may be accommodating to the culture even as they rail against it. These will be among the underlying issues we explore as we investigate this innovation to religion in North America.

The Control of Television Ministry by Evangelicals

Television ministry in the late twentieth century has been dominated almost exclusively by evangelicals who have built vast electronic empires. One cannot understand the structure of television ministry or the domination by the religious right without an understanding of the historical background.

The Foundations: A Marketing Perspective

Razelle Frankl (1987) has shown that the structure of modern television "parachurches"

▶ **BOX 15.1**

Religion, Technology, and Terminology

Several terms have been used to refer to the use of sophisticated electronic media to spread religious beliefs. The term *electronic church* involves the use of the entire range of electronic communications to build a following; this includes broadcasting, videotaping of sermons, personalized word processing to communicate in an apparently intimate manner with viewers who write or call, phone-in responses to broadcast questions, use of high-speed computers, and so forth. All these media are used to create a feeling of intimacy and the sense of being part of a church family. The term *electronic church* has been used more by those outside the industry, sometimes with derision. Hence, those within the industry prefer the term *electric church:* They favor a play on words that acknowledges their use of electric media and also suggests that television evangelism has an electrifying or inspiring effect on viewers. The term *televangelism* is limited specifically to television ministries (and not radio programming). Televangelism does include, however, talk show formats, worship services, variety shows, and other programming with an explicitly religious content.

are a logical extension of the contributions of three great revivalists: Charles Grandison Finney (1792–1875), Dwight L. Moody (1837–1899), and Billy Sunday (1862–1935). Charles Finney, often called "the father of modern revivalism," published a book in 1835, *Lectures on Revivalism of Religion,* which became the "how-to" manual for generations of evangelists. The most important element of Finney's work is that he believed that conversion was not merely a mystical process of the Holy Spirit, but that it could be stimulated or manipulated by careful planning and use of various techniques. The revival was demystified, and the process for converting people was institutionalized (Frankl 1987). Finney not only stressed the importance of using any means, but chided preachers for not being more scientific—for not using cause and effect to promote religion in any way possible. Frankl goes so far as to suggest that this conviction that religious experience can and ought to be rationally calculated and that any means is justified to convert people is at the root of the schism between evangelicals and mainline denominational religion.

It is certainly ironic that modern evangelism was founded on empirically based principles of cause-effect manipulation because the religious right today is frequently skeptical of the social sciences. But Finney was so oriented to the pragmatic—to "whatever works"—that he had little patience for theoretical discussions or for philosophical debates about whether ends justify means (Frankl 1987).

Conversion of sinners, for Finney, became the measure by which all ministers and all techniques were to be judged. He thereby replaced the conventional standards for calculating ministerial success. The importance of this change is illustrated if we compare this posture to that of an earlier evangelist. Jonathan Edwards, along with other leaders of the Great Awakening, believed that a religious revival was sent by the Holy Spirit and was

truly a sacred event. It would never have occurred to him that he was manipulating or orchestrating the event. He was simply to preach the gospel. The number of conversions or lack thereof was not a criterion for evaluating his performance as a minister. Finney, on the other hand, was to argue that conversion "is not a miracle or dependent on a miracle in any sense. . . . It is purely a result of the right use of constituted means" (McLoughlin 1978: 125).

By operating outside the realm of official denominations or local churches, Finney also created the first independent "parachurch." Edwards and others in previous revivals were based in local churches and had denominational connections. Finney and later revivalists operated more as religious entrepreneurs. Likewise, contemporary televangelism empires operate as independent parachurches (Hadden and Shupe 1988).

The model of an independent revivalist organization is central to the structure of televangelism. This structure and the idea of using the most modern technology and the most sophisticated media available to stimulate conversions are the legacy of Charles Finney.

Dwight Moody differed from Finney in his theology, but he was clearly Finney's successor in terms of contributions to urban revivalism. Moody adopted most of Finney's rational model of evangelism and added a marketing perspective. Moody was the consummate businessman who developed a complex division of labor to ensure careful management of resources and precise execution of revivals. He also persuaded members of the business community to underwrite the cost of local revivals. Although Finney's philosophy of managing the conversion process had a lasting impact, Moody's contribution was in management of a complex organization and management of public image in the media. Further, Moody's expanding parachurch eventually spun off other institutions, such as the Moody Bible Institute, a process that has become virtually compulsory for the modern televangelist.

Evangelists had to learn to apply principles of management to the evangelistic enterprise if they were ever to create the television empires that operate today. Moody provided a model and trained a generation in how to build and maintain such an organization (Frankl 1987; Hadden and Shupe 1988).

Billy Sunday inherited the contributions of these earlier evangelists and built on them. A former professional baseball player, Sunday was the great showman. As Jeffrey Hadden and Anson Shupe put it, "Sunday was undoubtedly the most colorful preacher in American history. In contrast to Finney's logical argument or Moody's calm persuasive style, Sunday was all emotion. His behavior often bordered on the outrageous. But it was great entertainment.... He would skip, gyrate, slide, and do cartwheels. He would stand on chairs, peel off layers of clothing as he worked himself into a lather, and do burlesque style imitations" (1988: 45). Sunday's emphasis on high-energy entertainment clearly was the precursor to both Jimmy Swaggart's enthusiasms and the more decorous variety shows developed by other televangelists.

But Sunday's contribution was not only showmanship and commercialism. He was also an organizational genius whose model of success was drawn from the business world. He calculated the "efficiency" of revivals by determining the cost per convert. In so doing, he further separated revivalism from denominational Protestantism and created a model of

Urban revivalists Charles Finney, Dwight Moody, and Billy Sunday set the stage for a marketing approach to Christianity. Depicted above is a Moody revival at Agricultural Hall in London. (Photo courtesy of the Moody Bible Institute Library.)

"scientific management in the pulpit" (Frankl 1987:145). This application of cost-benefit analysis to managing revivals is clearly seen in the operations of televangelism. As Frankl puts it, "Just as [Billy] Sunday demonstrated his effectiveness by counting the number of converts and calculating the cost at $2.00 a soul, the leaders of the electric church measure their success by audience size and market penetration" (1987: 81). While Finney evaluated the "success" of a minister based on the number of converts, Sunday evaluated the minister on a basis of cost efficiency per convert. This further extension of marketing principles to evangelism was a necessary prerequisite for the development of the televangelism empires (Frankl 1987). This application of utilitarian business principles to religion raises interesting questions about evangelical secularization, as Box 15.2 makes clear.

The combined contribution of these three evangelists was the model of a freestanding institution with scientific management in the pulpit, dynamic showmanship, and the goal of conversion of the masses through use of the most effective techniques. As such, revivalism became available to anyone with the energy and skills to build such an organization (Frankl 1987). As an autonomous professional who built his own career, "[the revivalist's] role was more akin to that of an entrepreneur than a churchman" (Frankl 1987: 145). So too, the televangelist builds an independent organization, defines his or her own goals, obtains his or her own financial resources, and manages his or her own empire—all independent of denominational controls. These parachurches have boards of directors, but the members of the board are handpicked by the star of the show and seldom do more than rubber stamp what the founder proposes.

In essence, the televangelist organizations are like the revivalist organizations in being small "fiefdoms" or oligarchies (governed by an elite). This is a structural factor that made possible the scandals of the late 1980s.

The first three televangelists built directly on the contributions of earlier revivalists and are the logical successors of urban revivalism. These first three were Billy Graham, Oral Roberts, and Rex Humbard. Graham never has established a weekly program, and his televised programming has remained in the format of a worship service or a revival. But he was the first evangelistic fundamentalist to gain national recognition. Much of his early notoriety was because of an editorial directive from publisher William Randolph Hearst who sent a simple memo to the editors of his nationwide chain of newspapers: "Puff Graham." Graham made the most of the subsequent publicity and became a role model for younger evangelists. And his career linked the fundamentalist tradition to the new media of television and radio. Eventually, he came to be a spiritual adviser to a number of U.S. presidents. With this step into television ministry, writes Frankl, "this religious tradition [of fundamentalism], which had lost much of its credibility in the aftermath of the Scopes trial, gained new legitimacy and recognition" (1987: 74).

Graham remains the "dean of televangelists," but he was never one to be a great innovator. Oral Roberts became a showman, introducing a variety of formats, using a wide range of entertainment forms, and showing the value of flexibility of material to meet changing markets. Most important, however, Roberts discovered that if a televangelist wants to raise money the key is to build buildings and devise outlandish projects. He discovered that people will contribute far more money to build a university or a hospital than they will to buy airtime. The excess money brought in for building projects can then be diverted to other projects such as broadcasting costs. This is a principle soon learned by nearly every other

---

▶ **BOX 15.2**

Secularization within Evangelical Circles

Evangelicals and sociologists both tend to identify secularization with theological liberals and their rational/empirical theologies. The tendency is to view liberal churches as open systems, incorporating perspectives and values from the larger culture, and to view conservatives as maintaining closed systems that resist input. Clearly it was the liberals who have embraced evolutionary theory of origins, and evangelicals have preserved the creation story as authoritative.

While there is an element of truth to this view that liberals are the assimilators, it is also an oversimplification. Rational/utilitarian approaches to organizational decision making is often defined as one of the components of the secularization process. The ideas of using empirically tested methods for conversion, of marketing religion for maximum appeal, and of success defined in terms of "cost efficiency

per convert" all indicate an extremely high application of "organizational rationality" to revivalism. In short, even the great urban revivalists, such as Dwight Moody and Billy Sunday, embraced some aspects of secularization.

The point is not that secularization is bad or good, nor that one group is more secular than another, but that all groups are bound to be influenced by the larger culture—to adapt, reject, and modify aspects of secular society. Sometimes the very act of rejecting the outside world causes innovation as a group defines itself in opposition to the larger society. Both liberals and conservatives have opened the door to certain influences of the dominant culture and to the secularization process. They have, however, made very different decisions about where to draw the line between the "essentials" of the faith that cannot be compromised and those elements of the culture that can be adopted.

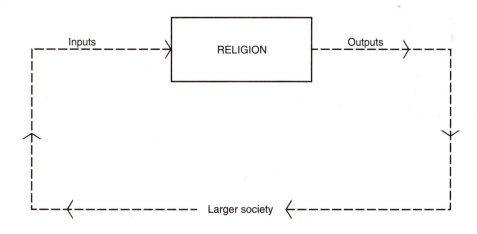

televangelist. With the oligarchical structure of the organization, Roberts and others could make such transfers without challenge.

Rex Humbard was the third of the original televangelists with nationwide programming. Humbard contributed two innovations. First, he created an intensely personal style, using a family format (telling stories to his gathered children and to the audience who became part of his family), sharing personal troubles, and airing feelings publicly. Humbard often cried on television and would bare his soul for his national audience. Whatever else this process did, it was highly profitable as people responded with their hearts to a person they had come to know intimately—more intimately than members of their own church. Later on, other televangelists also found that open displays of emotion build intense audience loyalty.

Second, Humbard built a cathedral especially designed and equipped for broadcasting. Graham and Roberts initially simply brought cameras into their existing services. But Humbard invested in the most sophisticated modern

Oral Roberts was the first televangelist to experiment with diverse formats and to extend Billy Sunday's use of entertainment to the new medium. Roberts was also the first to discover that building projects raise enormous amounts of money. Here Roberts's son Richard appears with the Oral Roberts University Singers in an upbeat program that blends evangelism and patriotism while publicizing the opening of the City of Faith Medical Center in Tulsa, Oklahoma. (Photo courtesy of the Oral Roberts Evangelistic Association.)

technology; he also established television effects as the highest priority in the architecture and decor of the cathedral.

Other televangelists have developed their own distinctive styles, theological orientations, and formats. But each has built on these early foundations. Without these foundations, televangelism empires would probably not exist. On the other hand, while the factors discussed so far all contributed to the growth of televangelism, they are not sufficient to explain the domination of religious television by the evangelical community.

Changes in Federal Communications Commission Regulations

Until 1960 most religious television programming in the United States was sponsored by one of the mainline denominations. The most popular weekly religious television show with a national audience in the 1950s was "Life Is Worth Living," featuring Roman Catholic Bishop Fulton J. Sheen. And the majority of local and regional religious broadcasting was sponsored by various liberal Protestant churches. To understand the change to evangelical dominance, one must understand the role of the Federal Communications Commission (FCC).

The FCC is the agency of the U.S. government that regulates radio and television broadcasting. The FCC does not determine program content, but it establishes cultural guidelines for good taste and respectability and provides rules regarding "the public interest."[1] Among

the regulations of the FCC is a requirement that each station provide a certain percentage of its broadcast time for public-interest broadcasting, known in the industry as "sustaining time." This involved free broadcast time for civic announcements, public health information, and so forth. Religious programming was explicitly included as qualifying for sustaining time.

Until 1960 religious groups could broadcast either by paying for commercial time or by qualifying for free sustaining time. The FCC held that commercial time bought by religious organizations could not be a substitute for "sustaining time" donated in the public interest. Broadcasters still had the obligation of providing free time. The networks turned to the Federal Council of Churches of Christ (now called The National Council of Churches) to provide the religious programming. This association allocated the time to its member groups—mainstream religious organizations. Small sects and independent religious associations who wanted to broadcast—including almost all fundamentalist and Pentecostal groups—usually had to pay for it.[2] Among conservative evangelicals, only the very popular Billy Graham was able to gain access to gratis time. In 1960 the picture changed dramatically.

In 1944 a group of 150 evangelical broadcasters had banded together to form an alliance called the National Religious Broadcasters (NRB). This group petitioned the networks to reconsider their policies and lobbied the FCC about the distribution of airtime. Eventually, the NRB was able to persuade the FCC that evangelicals were being treated unfairly. In 1960 the FCC ruled that no important public

---

[1]In other countries broadcasting is considered a cultural resource rather than a profit-making industry. The type of controls and regulations are more complete, but access to airwaves is actually greater. Where broadcasting is funded by advertising and airtime is competitive, market factors determine programming. The cost of broadcasting increases in this competitive market and access to airtime becomes more difficult (Frankl 1987).

[2]There were also limits on acceptance of paid evangelical programming—limits which had arisen to bar from the airwaves several evangelists who preached a message of anti-Semitism and of bigotry toward immigrants and other "outgroups" (Hadden 1993).

interest is served by distinguishing between gratis airtime and commercial programming, as long as they addressed the same needs (Frankl 1987; Hadden and Shupe 1988).

This new policy allowed networks to count religious programming that was paid for as fulfilling their public-interest requirement. The practice of providing free airtime to churches faded very quickly. Mainline churches were less highly motivated to focus their energies on trying to convert others, were not willing to put forth the enormous amounts of money necessary for commercial broadcasting, and did not have the organizational structures in place to move quickly into this new market. But evangelical parachurch organizations were so postured, and many other freelance organizations quickly emerged. Within a decade, religious television programming was dominated by conservative Christian groups. As cable television emerged, evangelicals had the structures in place to capitalize on the new developments (Frankl 1987). Indeed, Pat Robertson accurately anticipated the impact of cable and satellite communications systems and had his technology in place to broadcast through these mediums before most of the country was technologically ready (Peck 1993).

The virtual monopoly of religious television by the new religious right is thus the result of several factors coming together at the right time. Independent religious organizations with a strong marketing orientation are especially well suited to televangelism. Such organizations are part of the legacy of revivalists Charles Finney, Dwight Moody, and Billy Sunday. Changes in federal policy allowed for these organizations to flourish in a changing television industry. The result is that the new religious right has harnessed a powerful resource. Indeed, viewed from the standpoint of resource mobilization theory, evangelicals effectively mobilized the resources to take control of the religious television industry, and that industry is now a resource that they plan to use to further strengthen their position in North America.

The Televangelism Audience

The importance of televangelism as a resource to shape the larger culture depends in part on the nature of the audience: How large is the audience, and who is watching? Clearly, televangelists have the potential for an extensive audience. At the height of his ministry, Rex Humbard's program alone was broadcast by 650 stations, was carried in eighteen countries, and was translated into seven languages (Hadden and Swann 1981). But the size of the actual viewership of religious television programming has been a matter of considerable debate.

Audience Size

The high estimate for the electronic church is 130 million viewers; the low is 10 million. Televangelists tend to exaggerate the size of their audiences, while their detractors tend to underestimate. And even the "hard data" are difficult to interpret. Nielsen and Arbitron ratings indicate how many televisions are turned on and to which channels. But they do not necessarily tell us whether anyone is in the room or is paying attention. They fail to indicate which viewers are duplicates (i.e., watch more than one religious program). They do not tell us whether those television sets were turned to that channel for five minutes or for the duration of the program. And they tend not to measure programming on cable television—where the bulk of televangelism now appears.

Pollsters who ask people whether they watched religious television in the past month tend to get very different figures (much higher) than those produced by Arbitron and Nielsen. But surveys leave it up to the viewer to decide what is religious programming (they may be including a movie with a religious theme), and they allow respondents to recall their behavior from the past month (which may or may not be accurate) (Gerbner et al. 1984; Hoover 1987; Hadden and Shupe 1988).

While we really do not know exactly what the viewership is for televangelism, several efforts have been made to control for the many variables and the different sources of information. Stewart Hoover (1987) has concluded that 20 to 25 million Americans watch religious television per month. In any given week, he estimates about 13 million viewers. Hadden and Shupe believe that the top ten television programs alone involved an unduplicated average of 34 million households in any given week and as many as 68 million in a month (1988). This latter figure would mean that about 40 percent of all Americans watch religious television at least once a month, and 21 percent watch weekly.[3]

Some scholars are convinced from their own studies that viewers are watching simply because they are bored or alienated from commercial television and find the televangelists an amusing alternative (Adelman 1987). Others suggest that many viewers turn on religious television for very short periods of time (five or six minutes) before switching to other channels (Hoover 1987). Clearly, not all viewers are committed; only 8 percent of the viewers sent money to television evangelists in a twelve-month period in 1987 (The Gallup Report 1987).

But those who do send money tend to increase their levels of commitment: by sending money they make an investment and develop a sense of commitment to the organization. The top televangelists bring in tens of millions of dollars each year to finance their programs and their projects (medical centers, universities, etc.). Although the numbers of viewers of televangelism are less than the viewership of the Phil Donahue program (Hadden and Swann 1981), the electronic church does have a committed core who provide a base of support for some truly enormous empires. Anyone who dismisses televangelists as marginal kooks (as the media have often done) is making a serious mistake (Hadden and Shupe 1988; Peck 1993).

Audience Composition

Another issue concerning the televangelism audience has to do with who regularly views and supports the electronic church. First, it appears that televangelism is mostly a phenomenon of the United States. A 1958 Gallup Poll indicated that at that time 29 percent of Canadians were regular patrons of religious broadcasts. By 1985 that figure had dropped to only 4 percent! (Bibby 1987a). This pattern seems to be consistent with the lack of growth of conservative evangelical Christianity generally in Canada.

Second, viewers of televangelism tend to already be evangelical in orientation. One rationale often given by televangelists for using television is to fulfill "the great commission" of Christ to spread the gospel. The idea is that television allows preachers to reach people who might otherwise never have heard of Christ. Yet empirical evidence suggests that televangelism has little persuasive impact in terms of converting degenerates; most viewers are already sympathetic to the basic philosophy (Gaddy 1984). This is not to say that religious broadcasting is insignificant; it serves as a reinforcer and a plausibility structure for those already committed.

---

[3]Hadden and Shupe's estimate places more validity in the figures produced by polls than those produced by Nielsen and Arbitron, whereas Hoover argues that the polling procedure overestimates viewership.

Third, patrons of religious television tend to be the disfranchised and lower-status members of society (Frankl 1987; Gaddy and Prichard 1985). They are older, less well educated, poorer, more likely to be female, and more likely to be black than the larger population or than mainline denominations tend to be. Jeffrey Hadden and Charles Swann (1981) report that between two-thirds and three-fourths of the viewers of syndicated programs are fifty years of age or older. But this could be deceiving. The evangelical population as a whole in the United States is younger than the average for mainline denominations, and as the "baby boomers" age, the market for televangelism may increase significantly (Hadden and Shupe 1988). Except for Robert Schuller's "Hour of Power," the electronic church also procures much of its support from the South (Hadden and Swann 1981; Gaddy and Prichard 1985).

But each of these generalizations must be treated with caution. The demographic summaries have been part of the reason that many commentators have viewed televangelism as a marginal and inconsequential phenomenon. The general demographic summary overlooks the fact that evangelicalism, including fundamentalism and charismatic Christianity, has expanded in the past two decades to become common in the middle class. Although the majority of supporters of televangelism are low income and poorly educated, the patrons of the television evangelists span the socioeconomic spectrum.

Theological Orientation and Televangelism Viewership

It is important at this point to emphasize that there is considerable difference in the religious orientation and appeal of various televangelists. Consequently, one can expect their audiences to be rather different. Robert Schuller's

"possibility thinking" is most in harmony with the values and perspectives of the middle class. He stresses the traditional theme of God's love, but he plays much less on a theme of innate depravity of humans than most evangelists, and he emphasizes individual initiative, goal setting, and perseverance as the most Godly of values. Likewise, Pat Robertson's "700 Club" is based on rational argumentation and an endorsement of this-worldly prosperity. Robertson is witty, urbane, and articulate. Humans are not intrinsically evil, but they have made some bad decisions. Correcting one's course and being responsible for one's self are core themes; middle class individualism is affirmed (Peck 1993). It is not surprising that these two televangelists would draw a better educated, more affluent, and more achievement-oriented following than most of the evangelists. Max Weber's concept of "elective affinity" would cause us to predict such a pattern.

Most other televangelists are either fundamentalist or charismatic in orientation. Yet many readers may not realize the intensity of the conflict between adherents of these groups—and even within these groups. Many evangelicals have charged other evangelicals with being heretics, or at least with lacking the essentials of the Christian faith.

Fundamentalism arose at the turn of the century, largely in reaction to modernism and biblical criticism. It took its name from a series of ninety articles that began to appear in 1910 in a twelve-volume publication called *The Fundamentals.* This volume insisted on the inerrancy of scripture and on a literal interpretation of the Bible. The movement was also premillenial (apocalyptic) and was characterized by a defensive and strident tone and an intense anti-intellectualism. This was even more the case following the Scopes trial over the teaching of evolution in the public schools in 1925. Emphasis among fundamentalists is on correct belief. Many fundamentalists place so much emphasis on biblical authority that they deny the validity of continuing revelation from God in our own day.

In the period following World War II, a neofundamentalism emerged. While stressing right doctrine and biblical inerrancy, the new fundamentalism rejected the isolationism, the strident tone, and the anti-intellectualism of the earlier fundamentalism. Some even adopted a postmillenial theology, believing that the 1,000-year reign of Christ would come only after humans had created a foundation on earth. This approach is more activist and more optimistic, and neofundamentalism became more acceptable to the middle class. Fundamentalism began to lose its nearly exclusive association with the lower classes (although middle-class literalists prefer the term *biblical inerrantists*). Intense conflict sometimes occurred between old-guard fundamentalists and neofundamentalists, with the former claiming that the latter were "sell-outs." Jerry Falwell describes himself as a fundamentalist, but Bob Jones, a member of the old guard, describes Falwell as a heretic, a liberal, and "the most dangerous man in America" (cited in Hadden and Shupe 1988: 78). Likewise, Billy Graham has been attacked by archfundamentalist Carl McIntyre for compromising the "true faith." The most popular fundamentalist televangelists today are actually neofundamentalists.

In contrast to the emphasis on doctrine and right belief, charismatics and Pentecostals believe in the "gifts of the spirit" as the marks of the Christian. These gifts include healing, prophecy (which here means predictions of the future), miracles, and "speaking in tongues" or *glossolalia*. Charismatics and Pentecostals stress the importance of a firsthand experience of God and believe strongly in the continuing revelations of God to true Christians. Many Pentecostals also stress biblical

inerrancy (including the authenticity of the biblical story of creation), but their primary focus is not on doctrine per se: Experiencing the Holy Spirit is central. The charismatic movement differs from Pentecostalism mostly in organization and socioeconomics. Pentecostals tend to have their own denominations, are lower socioeconomic-status churches, and often have a strong strain of anti-intellectualism. People who call themselves charismatics are more often members of mainline denominations (Episcopal, Roman Catholic, Presbyterian, etc.), are relatively affluent, and do not adopt the strident anti-intellectualism of Pentecostalism (McGuire 1982; Hadden and Shupe 1988).

Among the televangelists, Jimmy Swaggart is Pentecostal, anti-intellectual, and very emotional in his presentations. Affluence is not glorified—as it is among most televangelists. The message is clearly one that is more widely received among the less well educated and the poorer segments of society. Pat Robertson ("700 Club") is charismatic, but the message is much more compatible with middle-class values. Affluence is embraced as God's gift, and while the thrust of the message is conservative socially and theologically, the tone is not stridently anti-intellectual. Indeed, the talk-show format presents arguments primarily in a rational way and Robertson's authority rests in large part on his image as an articulate and knowledgeable commentator on world affairs (Peck 1990).

Conflicts between fundamentalism and Pentecostalism mean that many viewers do not cross over and watch both types of televangelists. At this point, there is little available research on the socioeconomic characteristics of specific religious television programs. But the audience appeal of some shows would seem to draw a more highly educated and more affluent audience than others (Peck 1993). Viewers of religious television programming are clearly not a homogeneous group.

Criticisms of the Electronic Church

Televangelism has come under heavy criticism for several reasons and from a number of quarters. Former evangelist Charles Templeton, who was himself involved in the production of religious television programming, assesses contemporary televangelism in this way:

> Television Christianity is an undemanding faith; a media apostasy that tells listeners that to become a Christian all they have to do is "believe." ... The offerings, [extracted] mostly from the poor, the elderly, and lonely women, amount to millions of dollars annually. Few of these dollars are used to give succour to the needy, to put food in empty bellies or to help the helpless and dispossessed.... There are, among the host of televangelists, exceptions to those I have described, but they are a minority.... On balance I think the contemporary television evangelist is deleterious to society (cited in Bibby 1987a: 36).

No less a figure than Billy Graham (1983) has spoken out against abuses, the most severe of which he believes is the constant harangue for money. But the most common complaint of critics has been that televised Christianity erodes support for local churches.

Does Televangelism Undermine Commitment to Local Congregations?

The most consistent and most strident attacks on televangelism have come from mainline denominations and from the National Council of Churches. And the primary conflict has been over resources: money and members. The first concern here is that significant numbers of people may stay home and watch televised worship services rather than attending their local church and being active in other ways. Televangelism is feared by mainline churches as an alternative to church activity and therefore as a threat to the viability of local congregations.

But research shows that the gratifications one receives from watching a televised worship service are different from those gained by attending worship services. Among those who are regular viewers of television, experiencing solemnity and atmosphere, praying to God, experiencing God's presence, feeling forgiven for sins, demonstrating solidarity with Christian values, and getting a sense of distance from the worries of everyday life are all facilitated more by attending worship services in a local church than by watching religious television (Petterson 1986). Indeed, viewers of religious television attend church more frequently than nonviewers, and only one viewer in seven reports watching services on television rather than attending church (Wuthnow 1987). Or, to view the matter from another perspective, comparing active church members to nonmembers shows that "actives" are the primary patrons of televangelism (Gerbner et al. 1984; Hadden and Swann 1981; Stacey and Shupe 1982). Only 3 percent of religious television viewers report a decrease in local church involvement, and content analysis of religious programs shows that local churches are mentioned regularly and local church attendance is encouraged (Gerbner et al. 1984). Bibby finds the same pattern in Canada, with religious television serving for most viewers as a supplement to church attendance rather than as a substitute (1987a). Only among the very elderly is religious television a substitute.[4]

The second issue, of course, is whether financial contributions to television evangelists

---

[4]Two empirical studies report findings contrary to the bulk of the research, each suggesting a negative relationship between local church involvement and televangelism viewership (Gaddy and Prichard 1985; Korpi and Kim 1986). Gary Gaddy and David Prichard found this negative relationship to exist only among Protestants.

are replacing support to local churches. Most of the research indicates that money given to religious television programs are not in lieu of contributions to churches. They are donations made over and above the local church pledge and do not normally involve a decline in local church contributions. Only one study indicates some pattern of decline in contributions, but only for those who have found religious television a satisfying alternative to Sunday morning church services (Korpi and Kim 1986). This population is primarily the very elderly or others who find it difficult to get out of the house to attend services (Petterson 1986). A 1987 Gallup Poll lends support to this interpretation, showing that while 4 percent of all Americans surveyed sent money to a televangelist, 7 percent of those over the age of sixty-five did so (*The Gallup Report* 1987).

It seems clear that the charge of mainline denominations, that televangelism is siphoning off support for the local church in terms of both "bucks and bodies," is unfounded. Regular viewers of religious television programming tend to treat such programming as a supplement to church activity and as a healthy alternative to the fare offered by commercial television. Although there may be some dent in the coffers of local congregations because of televangelism, the impact appears to be quite small.

Does the Medium Transform the Message?

Televangelism empires are institutions, and like any other institution, they face dilemmas that can compromise the original mission of the organization. We have already learned that, once created, institutions tend to develop an existence and momentum of their own. The need to maintain the organization itself may lead to goal displacement, and eventually even the ideology (or, in this case, the theology) of the group may be modified.

According to Frankl, the structure and content of religious television is transformed so that it is no longer based on the intrinsic logic of the message but on extrinsic, rationally calculated needs of the economic system that produces the show. "The age range and predominant sex of the audience must be determined [through market analysis]. . . . This information influences program content. . . . The decisions, then, concern matching the program to the desired audience" (1987: 81). This is the logical but extreme consequence of the marketing of religion. "No longer driven by the charisma and zeal of the urban revivalist, these television programs are driven by the rational-legal authority of the television industry" (1987: 146).

One problem is that the medium of television does not lend itself well to complex analysis and rational debate. It is an entertainment medium that calls for rapid-moving programming, which will keep the audience attentive and will disincline viewers from switching channels. Content must be simple, fast-paced, and entertaining. The message itself thus often has to be truncated to meet the market needs of the media. Content analyses of religious television programs suggest that three basic themes run through the messages of most successful televangelists.

First, the "preacher must relieve viewers of ambiguity in spiritual, ethical, and moral matters. He must communicate the impression of absolute certainty" (Hadden and Swann 1981: 101). Along with this, successful televangelists must avoid challenging the viewer's existing faith and are best served if they avoid complex issues of theology and present only the bare rudiments of the faith. By providing only the broadest and simplest outlines, viewers can read their own specifics into what is being said.

Second, a simple message of "the benefits of a positive attitude toward life" has powerful appeal. Robert Schuller's "possibility thinking" is among the most explicit in this focus, but all televangelists soon find that the message that is successful and sells well is "If you would just let God be in charge of your life, everything would be super A-OK" (Hadden and Swann 1981: 102). Suffering and pain are seldom addressed, except to point out that adversities are abnormalities that will vanish when one adopts utter faith in God.

Third, most televangelists eventually adopt the message that looking out for oneself is all right: human selfishness, properly viewed, is not a sin. God wants you to have whatever you want. Oral Roberts perhaps comes closest to equating personal desires with God's will—and both with the success of *his* ministry. But Rex Humbard, Pat Robertson, and Jim and Tammy Bakker have been very eager to communicate the same message. The title of one of Humbard's books is illustrative: *Your Key to God's Bank.* The idea that God wants you to have whatever you desire is certainly very far removed from the ascetic theme that has been fundamental to Christianity for centuries. Certainly, self-denial was always an intrinsic part of the message of urban revivalism.

But this endorsement of desire and of affluence works well because it can be tied to religious fund-raising. As Hadden and Shupe put it, "Most televangelists end up at a common point: the Gospel of Prosperity. God *wants* you to be financially prosperous and content. . . . [Further] God works on a principle of reciprocity. The more money you send to Him [presumably through their own televangelism organization], the more God will return materially on your investment" (1988: 131). A passage from Robertson's book *The Secret Kingdom* illustrates:

> If we want to release the superabundance of the kingdom of heaven, we first give. . . . I am as certain of this as of anything in my life. If you are in financial trouble, the smartest thing you can do is to start giving money away. . . . Your return, poured into your lap,

will be great, pressed down and running over (cited in Hadden and Shupe 1988: 131).

These are elements of a message that "sells" well in terms of large audience viewership. The message is popular. But it also sells well in terms of fund-raising. (An exception to this Gospel of Prosperity theme among televangelists is discussed in Box 15.3).

To understand this transformation of the message of Christianity to one that fits the market, it is important to understand the unique relationship that all televangelists have with their audience. While commercial television sells advertising to support each program, televangelists sell Jesus, the program itself, and usually a major project (e.g., a university, a medical center, or a Christian amusement park) (Hadden and Shupe 1988). When commercial television programs break for an advertisement, there is usually a psychological distance between the sponsor's product and the main characters of the show. But for religious broadcasters, preaching, entertaining, and selling are all intertwined. Fund-raising in support of the program becomes part of the message, with all the moral imperative of the faith itself. Having no outside product to sponsor the show, evangelists end up begging for money, hawking their own books and tapes, and designing elaborate projects that will stimulate giving. In a book published before scandals of the late 1980s rocked televangelism, Hadden and Swann concluded, "Not since Vatican officials sold papal indulgences—written protection against the wages of sin—has there been such a public marketing of Christian favors. And never, surely, has religion found a mass market like TV's many-channeled auction block" (1981: 104).

Billy Graham himself has warned televangelists against allowing fund-raising to dominate airtime and permitting the medium of television to distort the message (1983). Yet content analyses have suggested that some television preachers have turned as much as a fourth of the show over to fund-raising, and Oral Roberts was forced to devote nearly the entire program to solicitation (Frankl 1987; Hadden and Shupe 1988). As two scholars investigating televangelism have recently concluded, "Fund-raising has virtually become the tail that wags the dog, even to the point of dominating . . . the theologies of some of the televangelists" (Hadden and Shupe 1988: 133).

To summarize, the marriage of Christian message with television has meant changes in the message itself. The medium requires a simplified message, and the survival of the organization requires behaviors that will bring in large amounts of money to keep the organization going. In the process, the message of Christianity undergoes scrutiny for its marketability and is modified accordingly. Although televangelists insist that television is simply God's tool to be used to send his message, television has profoundly affected the message itself.[5] Hadden and

Swann conclude: "The irony of the electronic churches is that although they mean to transmit a message . . . that is unchanging through the ages, they may simply be transmitting blips—blips packaged in ways that satisfy immediate needs . . . but have little relationship to a major world religion that has survived two millenia" (1981: 185).

Frankl summarizes the transformation that the media has made of the message thus: "The effect has been so profound that, after thirty years of television, we now have [a] hybrid organization. In creating this hybrid, the second parent, television, has transmitted a far more dominant set of genetic codes than did the first parent, urban revivalism" (1987: 97). Televangelism illustrates once again that institutions, once created, take on a life of their own—with goals, motivations, and measures

---

[5]Of course, not all televangelists have modified the content of their shows to the same extent Frankl suggests from her content analysis of the big eight televangelists with weekly programs (Jimmy Swaggart, Jim Bakker, Robert Schuller, Oral Roberts, Rex Humbard, James Robison, Jerry Falwell, and Pat Robertson) that Pat Robertson has strayed the furthest from the traditional message of urban revivalism. Of active televangelists, Jimmy Swaggart and Robert Schuller remain the closest to the traditional message (Frankl 1987).

▶ **BOX 15.3**

Exceptions to the Gospel-of-Prosperity Theme

It is important to note that some televangelists, Jimmy Swaggart the most notable among them, have continued to preach a world-negating theology accompanied by asceticism and a rejection of prosperity. Swaggart's appeal is also extremely emotional, experiential, and highly interactive with the audience—all in the tradition of urban revivalism. While Pat Robertson characterizes himself as a Christian broadcaster, Swaggart defines himself as a "country preacher." Not surprisingly, Swaggart's program appeals much more to the less affluent and the socially disfranchised. Interestingly, Swaggart's major fund-raising theme is a call for help in fulfilling the "great commission" to spread the gospel. This is in contrast to Robertson's individualistic appeal that giving to God (or God's agents) will enhance one's own self-interests, including one's financial interests. While Swaggart has made some adaptations of religion to fit the medium of television, his transformation of Christian theology has been far less sweeping than that of Robertson (Peck 1993).

of success that may be very different from those originally conceived by the founders.

Insofar as televangelists are a major resource for the spread of conservative Christianity and insofar as the message of televangelism has undergone adaptation, we might expect a ripple effect to occur in which much of evangelical Christianity is influenced by these changes. Clearly, televangelists are the most visible spokespersons for neofundamentalism and charismatic Christianity. Modifications in the message of evangelical faith illustrate the fact that assimilation to the culture and adaptation to larger social changes are not solely processes of liberal religion or "modern theology." Conservative religion also modifies its message in accord with the society in which it is found, including in some cases, a great deal of emphasis on this-worldly rewards.

Televangelism Scandals and the Future

In the mid-1980s, scandals rocked the world of televangelism and threatened the credibility and financial base of the entire industry. In March 1987, under financial pressures that could destroy his entire empire, Oral Roberts announced that God had informed him that his life would be taken if he could not raise $8 million by the end of the month. Roberts appealed to his audience and even went public in the secular media to proclaim that God was not fooling, that if donors did not respond by sending in donations for the completion of his latest project, God would strike the televangelist dead. Referred to in the secular media as "ransom money," Roberts's appeal was the first such threat of its kind used to raise funds. The entire scheme created a good deal of skepticism in the eyes of most of the public as Roberts's action came to be viewed as a major scam.

Before the action in Tulsa, Oklahoma, had played itself out, another crisis was unfolding

for another empire in Heritage U.S.A., South Carolina. At the headquarters of the PTL ("Praise The Lord" or "People That Love") network, Jim Bakker announced that he would step down, at least temporarily, as president of the PTL and turn the helm over to televangelist Jerry Falwell. Bakker had been involved in an extramarital affair several years earlier with a church secretary and had paid hundreds of thousands of dollars of PTL funds in blackmail money to keep her from telling all. The sex scandal was only the first shock wave. Bakker's resignation was accompanied by a claim that another televangelist, later identified as Jimmy Swaggart, was trying a power play to take over the PTL network. This led to a series of counter charges by several televangelists and some very ugly press regarding the jealousies and power politics within televangelism's inner sanctum.

But the sex scandal and the unveiling of petty jealousies and power politics among televangelists were only the tip of the iceberg. As Falwell tried to unravel the financial mess at the PTL and as the press began to probe, it became clear that the Bakkers had lived in phenomenal luxury, receiving nearly $2 million in salary in 1986 and hundreds of thousands more in benefits and perks. In addition, millions of dollars of PTL funds had been allocated annually to the Bakkers and others in the organization as "special bonuses." No fewer than forty-seven separate checking accounts had been discovered in the first few days of Falwell's takeover, and the financial records were in a shambles (Hadden and Shupe 1988). The net effect was that televangelists began to be viewed by much of the public as con artists who were more interested in raising money and living in luxury than in the traditional values of asceticism and unselfish commitment to the spreading of the gospel.

One of the most virulent in his attacks on Jim Bakker was fellow Assemblies of God minister Jimmy Swaggart. Swaggart had never preached the "Gospel of Prosperity" as Bakker had, and he was outspoken about this distortion of the gospel, but his attacks on Bakker's sexual immorality were even more intense. Then in the spring of 1988, Swaggart himself admitted that he also had sinned. He had been photographed entering a hotel with a prostitute by a colleague of Bakker. The hypocrisy of Swaggart's attacks on Bakker—less than one year previous to the unearthing of his own impropriety—were exploited widely in the mass media.

The net effect of these scandals was devastating to the credibility of televangelists and their organizations. Under the leadership of Billy Graham and more recently of Jerry Falwell, televangelists have made some efforts to address the structural problem that made the scandals possible in the first place.

As we have already seen, the most successful televangelism programs are like the revivalist organizations in being oligarchies (governed by an elite) (Hadden and Shupe 1988). But whereas part of the offering of revival meetings was connected to local churches and communities, "this is not the case with televangelists. . . . Funds are used at each preacher's personal discretion without any meaningful accountability to the viewers who support him. Consequently, although fundraising appeals are still based on old-time religion, their goals have been profoundly altered" (Frankl 1987: 141–42). The Bakker tragedy could not have happened if televangelism empires were not oligarchies that permit individual entrepreneurs enormous freedom to do as they wish with the income (Hadden and Shupe 1988). In short, the structure of televangelism organizations have created a situation conducive to abuse.

Recognizing this problem and fearing government regulation, televangelistic associations have begun to establish procedures for reporting financial matters and ensuring accountability to the public. This move could restore some of the confidence that was lost,

but at this point there is little monitoring of televangelists' compliance with the code of ethics established by the national Religious Broadcaster's Ethics and Financial Accountability Commission. If the current prime time preachers are unable to reestablish credibility with the public, surely other aspiring preachers will attempt to fill the gap in the competitive market. Televangelism has become such an important power base and such an essential resource of the New Right in the United States that both religious and political conservatives will fight hard to sustain its overall vitality.

One of the leading sociological scholars interested in televangelism thinks that the problems facing the industry are deeper than the scandals and include problems beyond lack of regulation. Jeffrey Hadden (1993) insists that even without the scandals, viewership for any given program was likely to drop. We will explore only two of the inherent dilemmas which he discusses. First, Hadden believes that the enormous expansion of religious broadcasting had reached a point of market saturation. During the expansion of new stations and new Christian broadcasting companies, there were new opportunities for preachers and producers of religious programming to enter the arena. But eventually a limit of interested "customers" was reached. Rather than expanding the base of viewers, various programs were beginning to compete with each other. As new programs emerged, existing ones experienced a decline in the average number of viewers per program. Some stations then encouraged bidding wars for airtime. As costs increased, some overextended companies had to cut back dramatically in their syndications. The scandals simply hit at a time of market vulnerability: from 1986 to 1992, the number of households watching religious broadcasting dropped by 37 percent, and deep cuts had to be made.

A second problem for the industry, according to Hadden, was the explicitly political character of some of the religious programming. Many people who are evangelical and support certain religious views of Pat Robertson's, as one example, are loyal Democrats and are more liberal than he on social issues (international relations, policy on racial relations, and so forth). Involvement by a religious leader in politics runs the risk of alienating many viewers. Between 1985 and 1988, when he was running for president, Pat Robertson lost 52 percent of his viewership (Hadden 1993). Regardless of whether one's politics are liberal or conservative, one is likely to lose support when religion is mixed with political views. This is all the more likely when televangelists depend heavily on lower socioeconomic groups (who tend to be liberal on many economic policies) and the televangelists support conservative capitalistic policies.

In any case, what is at stake in domination of religious broadcasting is the ability to define the meaning of national events, shape American civil religion, and ultimately legitimate political views of the right or the left. For conservatives, televangelism has been an extremely valuable resource in their effort to influence American moral values and social policies. They will likely do whatever they can to restore the credibility of their television ministries. Anyone who believes that the scandals of the 1980s were a death knell to televangelism or to the New Christian Right has severely underestimated the resilience of the industry and the movement.

Summary

The early period of television broadcasting was dominated by the mainline denominations, but the picture changed in 1960. Part of the change is due to a ruling by the FCC that television networks could count commercial (paid-for) religious programming as fulfilling their public-interest time requirement. They were no longer required to provide free "sustaining time," time that had been allocated to denominations belonging to the Federal Council of Churches of Christ. Evangelicals were postured to move quickly into the new broadcasting market because of the legacy of three urban revivalists: Charles Finney, Dwight Moody, and Billy Sunday. The legacy of urban revivalism included an emphasis on using any techniques or any technology available to stimulate conversions, a tradition of building independent parachurch organizations in which the revivalist had control and flexibility to adapt to new markets and to spin off new projects, an endorsement of showmanship and entertainment in the pulpit, and a business-marketing approach to religion and to defining ministerial success. Early televangelists built on the principles of urban revivalism and made further adaptations appropriate to the medium of television.

Televangelism has become a multimillion-dollar industry, which serves as a major resource of conservative Christian groups. Evangelicals claim to reach many unchurched and nonreligious people, but research shows that the listening audience is composed of those already evangelical in orientation. Although viewers span the socioeconomic spectrum, they tend to be disproportionately older, poorer, less well educated, and more likely to be female than the population at large. Viewership does appear to vary from one program to another, depending on the socioeconomic status of the viewers and "elective affinity" to the message of a given preacher.

Leaders of mainline churches have feared that the electronic church siphons committed members away from local churches, but this claim is contradicted by the empirical evidence. Viewers of religious television are more likely than nonviewers to attend church regularly, and donations to televangelism programs for the most part appear to be in addition to normal church pledges. Religious television programming is a supplement rather than a substitute and appears to serve as an additional plausibility structure for the already committed.

Perhaps the most serious charge by critics of televangelism is that the medium transforms the message. First, because televangelism requires a fast-paced and uncomplicated message so that viewers do not change the channel, the theology of televangelism becomes simplistic and truncated. Further, the need for enormous amounts of money to cover broadcasting costs means that televangelists must constantly sell their own programming and beg for funds. The theology comes to be transformed because a message that "sells well" is adopted. Ultimately, most televangelists adopt some form of the Gospel of Prosperity, stressing that God wants viewers to have everything they want and that a way to ensure receipt of all of God's blessings is to give—preferably to that televangelist's organization. Eventually, the endorsement of desire and self-gratification becomes so pervasive that the message bears little resemblance to that of traditional urban revivalism. This message is popular, however, and brings in enormous donations that sustain the program and its spin-off organizations (hospitals, colleges, Christian amusement parks, etc.).

Clearly, conservative Christianity is susceptible to change as it adapts to the social and cultural climate of the larger culture.

In the 1980s, several scandals rocked the world of televangelism. The sex scandals of Jim Bakker and Jimmy Swaggart were far less devastating to most religious television empires than were the revelations of transfers of funds from one project to another (with no accountability to anyone), the incredible lavish lifestyles of some televangelists, and the "ransom money" fundraising technique of one televangelist. Credibility of many evangelists was challenged as the public began to perceive them as con artists involved in a scam to enrich themselves. Despite this public opinion, most televangelists are more properly viewed as people who were originally well intended but who have been caught in the dilemma of mixed motivation.

The future of evangelical broadcasting is not necessarily dim. Religious television programming is an important tool of conservatives aspiring to influence public policy and to shape the moral and religious character of North America. Indeed, televangelism is such an important resource that conservatives will likely do everything possible to restore the credibility of religious broadcasting.

Alternative Forms of Religion

A number of social scientists maintain that religion in contemporary North America is undergoing significant transformation as new forms of religion are emerging. Some of these new forms are nontheistic, and some even lack a supernatural dimension. For this reason, many sociologists prefer to call these processes "quasi-religious phenomena" or "functional alternatives to religion." Regardless of what one calls them, these value perspectives provide many people with a sense of purpose in life and with a center of worth (which is the etymological basis for the word *worship*). When any ideology or value system becomes a meaning system—one that defines the meaning of life, death, suffering, and injustice—it usually takes on a sacred cast in the eyes of the adherents.

Sometimes we are so familiar with these sacred meaning systems in our own culture that we are only partially conscious of them; we take them for granted as a part of the way things are. Some sociologists who use a functional definition of religion seek to discover these value perspectives that underlie American culture and that serve as a world view or a faith system. This requires a distinction between what people *say* they value or believe and what their *behavior* reveals about their values or beliefs. When someone thinks he or she should believe something is desirable (e.g., daily exercise) but fails to act on that belief, phenomenologists refer to the belief as a velleity rather than a value. A value is something a person feels is so important that she or he takes action on it. The acid test of value, according to this perspective, is action. (We discussed the difference between a value and a velleity in chapter 1.) In the same way, some social scientists have sought to go beyond the verbal affirmations of people regarding their religion to discover the actual faith systems or meaning systems of Americans. In the following pages, we explore three types of meaning systems that serve as alternative forms of religion or quasi-religious dimensions of American culture.

Civil Religion

Emile Durkheim maintained that all cultures have a religious dimension. In fact, Durkheim believed that religion represents a sanctification of society and that the true object of worship is society itself. The sense of sacred imperative was viewed as essential to social maintenance because it convinces people to do that which they might not want to do. They become willing to make sacrifices on behalf of the larger society and set aside their individual self-interests. Moreover, the sense of sacredness provides a source of social unity and harmony; Durkheim viewed a set of common values as mandatory for a society's survival. Not all these assumptions are shared by most contemporary sociologists, but many do believe that there is a religious dimension to all cultures.

In many societies, the sense of unity and common meaning is provided by a traditional religion. If a single religion is held by an overwhelming proportion of the population, it may serve as a source of national unity, and religious officials may explain the fortunes and misfortunes of the nation in terms of the traditional religious symbols and values. However, in a religiously heterogeneous society, no one religious group can serve this function. In fact, religious groups may become sources of civil conflict and hostility rather than harmony and unity. In a pluralistic society, something other than traditional religions must serve as a basis for social consensus and for defining the meaningfulness of national activity (Cole and Hammond 1974). Hence, pluralism requires a new meaning system—which becomes sacralized and serves as a form of religiosity.

Such national religions are referred to by social scientists as *civil religions.* (The term was originally coined by Jean Jacques Rousseau.) Stated more formally, civil religion is the set of beliefs, rites, and symbols that sacralize the values of the society and place the nation in the context of an ultimate system of meaning. This system of meaning can be a supplementary one that complements the traditional religiosity of citizens, or it may become a primary source of devotion and commitment in itself.

Socially, civil religion serves to define the national purposes in transcendent terms and acts as an expression of national cohesion. In short, it offers a nondenominational theodicy for the nation.

Civil Religion in the United States

In the United States, civil religion is expressed through myths, rituals, national holidays (holy days), celebrations of the lives of national "saints," visitations to national "shrines," and sacred treatment of national symbols. The mythology of American civil religion began early in the nation's history. In the speeches of some of the first presidents and in sermons of some of the colonial preachers, America was treated as the "promised land." In fact, in his second inaugural address, Thomas Jefferson explicitly compared the founding of the new nation to the founding of Israel, and Europe was defined as the contemporary Egypt—from which God's people had fled. This began a long process of myth development that has grown through the past 200 years. The belief in the American Dream, the American Way of Life, and the fundamental goodness of America is expressed with reference to a supernatural blessing: "America, America, God shed His grace on thee, and crown thy good with brotherhood from sea to shining sea." Hymns such as these evoke a profound sense of reverence, for they express a deeply ingrained mythology.

Civil religion is also expressed through the rituals that take place on such "high holy days" as Memorial Day, the Fourth of July, and presidential inauguration days. The ceremonials on these days express central American values and inspire a feeling of unity and a sense of transcendence (greater purpose). The meaning of the nation is believed to transcend individual lives and is important in understanding the significance of contemporary events. The effort to stop Hitler and "make the world safe for democracy" provides one example. More recently, the space shuttle program and moon landings provided a sense of national accomplishment and collective identity.

National ceremonies tend to emphasize the transcendent purpose of the nation. Most such celebrations occur around national shrines, which are themselves capable of eliciting a feeling of awe—for they symbolize both the ideals of the nation and the sacrifices made on the nation's behalf. Examples of national shrines are the Washington and Lincoln Memorials in Washington, D.C., the Capitol, the Tomb of the Unknown Soldier, war cemeteries, and the birthplaces or burial sites of American presidents. In an excellent analysis of the symbolism of a Memorial Day celebration in an American town, Lloyd Warner discusses the unifying quality of these rituals and symbols: "The cemetery and its graves become the objects of sacred rituals which permit opposing organizations, often in conflict, to subordinate their ordinary opposition and to cooperate in expressing jointly the larger unity of the total community through the use of common rites for their collective dead" (Warner 1953: 24–25).

Because some sociologists view these ceremonials as the central expression of civil religion, content analyses of speeches and newspaper articles on Memorial Day and the Fourth of July and analyses of central themes in presidential inaugural addresses have become an important means of studying this phenomenon (Toolin 1983). There are also other national holidays, but they tend to be of somewhat lesser significance as expressions of civil religion: Thanksgiving (which George Washington first made a national holiday in 1789 so that citizens might thank God for the blessings of this land and this nation), Presidents' Day (birthday celebrations for Washington and Lincoln), and Labor Day (a time to celebrate the accomplishments of American labor and the upward social mobility provided for Americans through the labor movement).

The paramount sacred object in this religion is the American flag. The importance of this symbol can be seen not only in the prescribed handling of the flag (see Box 4.2 in chapter 4) but also in the intensity of the outrage when the stars and stripes are "desecrated"—treated inappropriately.

Daily recitation of the pledge to the flag by schoolchildren became a major theme of George Bush in the 1988 presidential election. Particular national heroes, or saints, also serve as focal points for veneration and myth development. Washington and Lincoln are the most important and most widely recognized "saints," and are paid homage on Presidents' Day. For some people, Presidents Jefferson, Wilson, Franklin Roosevelt, or Kennedy are key figures. Sometimes folk heroes (like Betsy Ross, Daniel Boone, or Charles Lindberg), business tycoons (who symbolize the rags-to-riches mythology), and military heroes (who symbolize courage and a willingness to sacrifice for the nation) are given honored status and held up to children as exemplary of the American Way. In many quarters, Martin Luther King Jr. has become a saint of the civil religion because of his efforts to apply the motto "freedom and justice for all" to all Americans. These national "saints" serve as inspirations and as behavioral models, much as Saint Francis, Mother Seton, or Saint Teresa of Avila do in the Christian tradition.

Many observers of this American civil religion have been appalled by it, labeling it as idolatry or as "American Shinto."[1] But Robert Bellah, the most widely cited scholar investigating civil religion in the United States, has argued that this phenomenon needs our careful attention no less than any other form of religiosity. Bellah has focused primarily on

---

[1]Shintoism is a Japanese religion (the state religion prior to 1945) that involves worship of ancestors and ancient heroes, a glorification of national accomplishments, a deification of the emperor of Japan, and a profound reverence for nature.

references to God or to the transcendent realm in the Declaration of Independence, Washington's Farewell Address, the inaugural addresses of various presidents,[2] and other formal speeches made at times of transition or times of crisis (e.g., Lincoln's Gettysburg Address and John Winthrop's landing sermon before the Pilgrims debarked from their ship at Salem). Bellah finds that references to God and to the transcendent mission of the United States are pervasive in these formal addresses. Even our pledge of allegiance mentions that we are a nation "under God" and our currency is stamped with "In God We Trust." But this religiosity is clearly *not* Christianity. Civil religion is limited to affirmations that members of any denomination or sect can accept—including non-Christians. Although this public theology has a distinctly Protestant style to it and is much influenced by the Protestant ethic, it is not a form of Protestant Christianity.

Bellah claims that the civil religion has gone through three major trials, which have called for refinement and revision in its theology. The first major crisis was the Revolutionary War. Out of that testing of will and purpose emerged the imagery of Washington as a Moses who led us out of bondage. The Judeo-Christian imagery of God working in history was and is the clear paradigm for our civil theology. The second major crisis was the Civil War. The imagery of the Gettysburg Address sets the stage for this next phase of civil theology. Lincoln consistently used rebirth imagery in his ode to "these honored dead." He repeatedly used phrases such as "brought forth," "conceived," "created," and "a new birth of freedom." Not long after he delivered that speech, Lincoln himself became "our martyred President," who "gave the last full measure of devotion." Bellah points out that the

theme of sacrificial giving of one's life was indelibly written into the civil religion. Lincoln became the martyr who gave his life so that the nation might live—an interesting repetition of the Christian theme of a martyred savior.

Bellah (1975) insists that the United States is now in the midst of its third time of crisis. Part of the crisis stems from events of the past two or three decades: ambiguity about the mission of the United States in a world of poor nations, the schism in the nation over the Vietnam War, and the cynicism about American politics that resulted from government scandals in the 1970s and 1980s (Watergate, the Iran-Contra scandal, and the prosecution of many government officials for various illegal activities). But the crisis is more deeply rooted than would seem from looking only at current affairs. In a more recent study, Bellah and his colleagues point to a long-term collapse of the sense of covenant and the commitment to the common good (1985).

In colonial days, says Bellah, a legal and economic system was devised that would protect the rights of the individual to pursue his or her own self-interests. But a moral ethos counterbalanced narrow selfishness by proclaiming the obligation to act in the public interest. This moral climate was reinforced by two sources: the biblical concept of covenant with God and the secular republican political philosophy that called forth commitment to the common good. He documents the self-sacrifice of many of the founders of the country, even while they defended the legal right of individuals to act in their own self-interest. Without this moral tone and sense of obligation, unfettered self-interest would destroy both the cohesion and the spirit of goodwill within the country. An endorsement of individualism, says Bellah, must be countered with some sense of obligation to the larger community. Bellah and his coauthors believe that both the republican spirit and the sense of covenant have so deteriorated over the past

---

[2]Every president has made reference to God or to divine will and divine guidance in an inauguration ceremony.

two centuries that the nation now faces a national crisis. A revival of civil religion is needed. But the nature of that civil religion—the way we define the meaning of the nation and the core values that unite us—will be of critical importance in the development of the American character in the next century.

The role of civil religion is not only that of curbing individual self-interest; it also must provide moral guidelines for the country as a whole. Bellah insists that "without an awareness that our nation stands under higher judgment, the tradition of the civil religion would be dangerous indeed" (1970b: 185). It would be dangerous because it would serve only to sanctify the status quo and the current social structures, regardless of whether they are just. He denies that the conservative function is the only role of civil religion in the United States. American civil religion is also prophetic; that is, it proclaims judgment on the United States when it fails to live up to its creed. The ideals of the nation provide a foundation for criticism and improvement. For example, Martin Luther King Jr. delivered a critical speech about his hopes for the nation, and it proved deeply moving to the American people because his dream was "deeply rooted in the American Dream" (see Box 16.1). According to Bellah, civil religion guards against governments doing whatever they want to do and then sanctifying their actions; civil religion provides a standard of judgment for national policy.

Prophetic and Priestly Versions

Martin Marty (1974) has pointed out that civil religion can be either prophetic or priestly. **Prophetic** religion tends to challenge the status quo and call the faithful to change behaviors in accord with ethical concerns. **Priestly** religion tends to provide comfort and stability, often by legitimating and sacralizing the present system.

While it may provide a basis for judgment and correction, civil religion has often served simply to endorse the status quo. In this case, the nation is not "under God"; rather the name of God is simply used to sanctify the actions of the nation. Bellah recognized the same phenomenon when he contrasted the inaugural address of John Kennedy in 1961 with that of Richard Nixon in 1973. Bellah claims that Nixon's version of civil religion was one in which God gave blessing and sanction to the actions of the United States but seldom called the nation to task. Kennedy's speech beckoned the nation to a higher calling that only God would ultimately judge. Hence, just as there are several theological interpretations of Christianity, so also are there several interpretations of American civil religion. This creates an interesting irony, for precisely those symbols and beliefs that are supposed to unite the country often become the basis of conflict. Advocates of civil rights for blacks and members of the Ku Klux Klan both appeal to the American Way and to quasi-religious American values in defense of their stance. Likewise, both advocates and opponents of other social movements have based their stance on a version of the American civil religion for this serves as the legitimizing ideology of any movement.

One might conclude from all of this that liberal civil religion is prophetic, whereas the civil religion of conservatives is priestly. This is not always the case. The new religious right in the United States has its own agenda for moral reform and is very intense about calling the nation back to a covenant with God. Some members of the Christian right have been very ethnocentric in their rhetoric, and this may cause some commentators to mistake their position as priestly. But Jeffrey Hadden and Anson Shupe (1988) point out that the national covenant theme is deep and strong in the preaching of televangelists such as Pat Robertson, Jerry Falwell, Jimmy Swaggart, and Oral Roberts. Because they have nationwide audiences, these televangelists are important in formulating the conservative vision of the

United States and served to legitimate the conservative political reforms of Ronald Reagan and George Bush.[3] But this vision of the

[3]Of course, endorsements by Presidents Reagan and Bush of Falwell and others, in turn, gave these televangelists legitimacy with the public.

United States is not just priestly. The new Christian right is enraged at the direction of the country. The removal of prayer from public schools, the legalization of abortion, the "new morality" in sexual behavior, and problems of family instability are among the issues that conservatives see as central to the covenant with God.

▶ **BOX 16.1**

I Have a Dream

Martin Luther King's "I Have a Dream" speech, delivered at the March on Washington in 1963, is a major formulation of American civil religion. Although King was a Baptist preacher, he appealed not to values that are uniquely Christian, but to ones that would be compelling to Americans of any religious stripe. He quotes scripture only once, and that was from the Old Testament—thereby appealing to Jews as well as to Christians. This speech provides an example of the prophetic role of American civil religion.

I say to you today, my friends, that in spite of the difficulties and frustrations of the moment, I still have a dream. It is a dream deeply rooted in the American dream.

I have a dream that one day this nation will rise up and live out the true meaning of its creed: "We hold these truths to be self-evident: that all men are created equal."

I have a dream that one day on the red hills of Georgia the sons of former slaves and the sons of former slaveowners will be able to sit down together at the table of brotherhood. . . .

I have a dream that my four little children will one day live in a nation where they will not be judged by the color of their skin but by the content of their character.

I have a dream today. . . .

I have a dream that one day every valley shall be exalted, every hill and mountain shall be made low, the rough places will be made plains, and the crooked places will be made straight, and the glory of the Lord shall be revealed, and all flesh shall see it together.

This is our hope. This is the faith with which I return to the South. . . . With this faith we will be able to work together, to pray together, to struggle together, to go to jail together, to stand up for freedom together, knowing that we will be free one day.

This will be the day when all of God's children will be able to sing with new meaning "My country 'tis of thee, sweet land of liberty, of thee I sing. Land where my fathers died, land of the Pilgrim's pride, from every mountainside, let freedom ring."

And if America is to be a great nation this must become true. So let freedom ring. . . .

From every mountainside, let freedom ring.

When we let freedom ring, when we let it ring from every village and every hamlet, from every state and every city, we will be able to speed up that day when all of God's children, black men and white men, Jews and Gentiles, Protestants and Catholics, will be able to join hands and sing in the words of that old Negro spiritual, "Free at last! Free at last! Thank God almighty, we are free at last!"

Source: C. Eric Lincoln, *Is Anybody Listening to Black America?* New York: Seabury. 1968: 65–66 (abridged).

For the new Christian right, the covenant calls for maximum freedom for the individual and for a strong and autonomous family. For liberals, protection of equality of all citizens and care for those unable to care for themselves are central responsibilities of the covenant. Liberals, then, call for more government regulation to prevent discrimination against any group of people and more support to the poor and the disfranchised. As Richard Neuhaus (1984) points out, the sin of government for the liberals is the sin of omission—it fails to do what it ought to have done. But conservatives tend to view the best government as one that leaves the people alone and lets them make their own decisions. All the regulation and interference, sometimes under the guise of "support," is viewed as an infringement. Government does things that conservatives think it should not do and forbids individuals from doing things that conservatives think they ought to be free to do: praying in school, owning handguns, hiring whom they want, and so forth. The sin of government for conservatives is a "sin of commission." Sins of commission are always experienced as more of an intrusion on one's self than sins of omission, and that is no less true in this case. So, as Neuhaus puts it, "In very everyday ways [conservatives] feel assaulted by liberal government as liberals do not feel assaulted by conservative government" (1984: 34). As a consequence, the new Christian right is angry.

Televangelists tend to be among their most powerful spokespersons because they articulate a conservative civil religion and proclaim it from a national platform—religious television broadcasting. The civil religion that they set forth is one with a prophetic ring, but many liberals fail to hear it as prophetic because it plays a different tune than does their own prophetic call to arms. Clearly, conservative and liberal approaches to civil religion call for and legitimate very different types of governmental policies.

Official and Folk Versions

Not only does American civil religion have prophetic and priestly versions, but it also has official and folk versions. Will Herberg (1955) undertook a study of American religiosity in the 1950s and claimed that Protestants, Catholics, and Jews in the United States were all worshiping the American Way of Life. Herberg found Americanism to provide the most important set of values and to serve as the most central faith system for most Americans. He maintained that the core beliefs of the traditional religions (such as belief in Jesus Christ as the Son of God) were only peripheral in the lives of most church members. The central sacred system of beliefs was the American Way of Life. Herberg's interest was not primarily in formal pronouncements of presidents at their inaugurations or in civil religion as it is expressed in formal documents (such as the Declaration of Independence). This would reflect the official version of civil religion at a given time period. Herberg instead focused on the everyday values and sense of sacredness of the common American.

Other scholars interested in the folk version of American civil religion have done content analyses of Fourth of July newspaper editorials (Thomas and Flippen 1972) or such popular events as the "Honor America Day" sponsored by Billy Graham and Bob Hope (Streiker and Strober 1972) or the programming content of televangelism programs (Hadden and Shupe 1988). Still others have distributed questionnaires to a random sample of the population to determine their attitudes and beliefs (Wimberly 1976; Wimberly et al. 1976; Wimberly and Christianson 1981). In each of these cases, the studies tapped the civil religiosity of the common folk rather than the official aspirations of the nation as articulated by presidents or by formal documents.

Clearly, civil religion is complex and multifaceted. At the risk of oversimplifying, we can identify at least four types of civil religion: official-prophetic, official-priestly, folk-prophetic, and folk-priestly. However, folk versions of civil religion are usually priestly in character.

Civil Religion and Social Integration

Many nations have spawned a civil religion because of its role in uniting a pluralistic country. A fundamental part of building a new nation is the development of a common ethos or set of values and loyalties. Furthermore, the new political system must be justified and sacralized. Civil religion is not a phenomenon limited to American life (Coleman 1970; Markoff and Regan 1981; McGuire 1981). In some cases, civil religion may be established by a national government that tries to abolish traditional religiosity and replace it with national loyalties and a transcendent meaning to the nation. The Soviet Union provides one example of this type of secular civil religion. In other cases, civil religion is not expected to replace the traditional religion, but is designed as an added dimension to existing religions. This style is illustrated in the requirement of the Roman Empire that, besides their own god or gods, all subjects had to worship the emperor. A variety of systems of civil religion can be found—some sponsored by traditional religion, some in conflict with it—but all pluralistic societies seem to have an element of "national religiosity."

A number of scholars believe that, although many Americans attend churches and have memberships in traditional religious groups, the central meaning system of these people is Americanism (their "true" religion). For these people the flag is a more important symbol of their religion than is the Star of David or the cross, and the Fourth of July is a more celebrative and meaningful holiday than Easter or Passover. This sort of analysis is by no means limited to social scientists. The theologian H. Richard Niebuhr was emphatic in his insistence that nationalism was a greater threat to Christianity than atheism.

But for many Americans, two systems of faith seem to operate simultaneously, sometimes complementing, sometimes conflicting with each other. Most of the time, Americans are probably no more aware that they hold two rather different meaning systems than are the Burmese who hold to both Buddhism and the folk religion of the Thirty-Seven Nats or the Chinese who say devotions at both Taoist and Buddhist temples. There is a strain toward coherence and logical consistency in the world view of most people, but in any given instance the strain may be large or small. Students should never underestimate the capacity of humans to overlook or ignore incoherence and logical inconsistency in their meaning systems. Nor should they overemphasize the cognitive aspects of religion at the expense of affective dimensions. People will often hold to a meaning system because it makes them feel like an accepted member of the group or because it helps them feel significant. Logical consistency is often of secondary importance. More important, social integration may sometimes be acquired at the expense of personal integration.

Regardless of one's personal evaluation of civil religion, the student of religion must keep in mind that it serves functions for the individual and for the society as a whole. American civil religion provides a sense of ultimate meaning to one's citizenship. It causes people to feel good about themselves as participants in the nation. It is not likely to disappear soon from the American scene. Besides simple survival, the particular style and character of American civil religion in the future is important, for civil religion may be influential in shaping the course of the nation. As for the personal religiosity of most Americans, some blend of traditional and civil religiosity is likely to continue.

Invisible Religions

Several other scholars have stressed the individualization of religion—the way in which each individual in modern society constructs his or her own meaning system by drawing from many popular philosophies. Perhaps the most important work developing this thesis is that by Thomas Luckmann (1967). Luckmann uses an extraordinarily broad definition of religion, referring to religion as the "symbolic universes of meaning" that infuse all of life with a sense of transcendent purpose. He emphasizes world view as an elementary and universal manifestation of religion (1967). In this respect, Luckmann's definition of religion is similar to other functional definitions (Yinger, Geertz). But rather than limiting religion to macrosystems of meaning—meaning systems that address death, suffering, and injustice—he seeks to understand world view at all levels of generality and specificity. He insists that "no single interpretive scheme performs the religious function. It is rather the world view as a whole, as a unitary matrix of meaning" that defines one's identity and

---

▶ **BOX 16.2**

Operationalizing Civil Religiosity

Most studies of civil religion have relied on content analyses or participant observation studies. In studies where a survey method is used, the researcher must operationalize civil religiosity. It is not easy to formulate questions that reveal both official and folk versions of civil religion in both their priestly and prophetic forms. The items below have been used to operationalize civil religion—with a five-point scale ranging from strongly agree to strongly disagree. Some questions, such as 6, are asked in such a way that a positive response would imply a rejection of civil religiosity—for civil religion endorses religious pluralism in the nation. Students may want to try formulating their own series of questions that might measure the civil religion dimension of respondents.

1. America is God's chosen nation today.[*]
2. To me, the flag of the United States is sacred.[*]
3. Human rights come from God and not merely from laws.[*]

4. If our government does not support religion, government cannot uphold morality.[*]
5. We should respect the President's authority since his authority is from God.[†]
6. National leaders should not only affirm their belief in God but also their belief in Jesus Christ as Lord and Savior.[†]
7. God can be known through the experience of the American people.[†]
8. The founding fathers created a blessed and unique republic when they gave us the Constitution.[†]
9. America is a "promised land" to immigrants.[‡]

[*]From Ronald C. Wimberly and James A. Christenson, "Civil Religion and Other Religious Identities." *Sociological Analysis,* Summer 1981: 93.
[†]From Ronald C. Wimberly, Donald A. Clelland, and Thomas C. Hood, "The Civil Religious Dimension: Is It There?" *Social Forces,* June 1976: 893.
[‡]From Adam Gamoran, "Civil Religion in the Schools." *Sociological Analysis,* Fall 1990: 247.

serves as one's religious orientation (1967: 55–56). In essence, he points to personal identity as "a form of religiosity" (1967: 70). A person's sense of identity—his or her values, attitudes, dispositions, and sense of self-worth—are part of his or her rcligiosity because all these are related to feelings about what makes life worth living. These are "invisible" forms of religion in that they do not have the social manifestations one normally associates with religion.

This is certainly a broad definition. Many social scientists have objected that it makes everything religious—or makes nothing at all specifically religious. They make an important point. The aspect of this definition that I find intriguing is that Luckmann has defined religiosity in a way very compatible with that of a number of twentieth-century theologians. Richard Niebuhr, Paul Tillich, and a number of other modern theologians have strongly resisted the idea that one's faith or one's religiosity is expressed primarily through cognitive beliefs. Rather, they insist that one's faith is most fully manifested in everyday assumptions, in actions, and even in personality structure. Hence, Niebuhr and Tillich seek to discover one's "real" center of worth by exploring the issue of what one ultimately trusts. Given the fact that some of the most widely acknowledged theologians (whose trade is meaning systems) have defined religiosity similarly to Luckmann, his formulation deserves our attention.

Luckmann believes that as society has become increasingly complex, and as institutions have specialized their sphere of influence, traditional religions have had an influence over a decreasing range of human behavior and thinking. Combined with this is the tendency of traditional religions to freeze their systems of belief so as to make them seem more eternal, absolute, and unchanging. At the same time, technological, political, and economic changes have continued to occur; indeed, in the modern Western world, change occurs at ever increasing rates. Luckmann maintains that this has caused traditional forms of religion to become irrelevant to the everyday experiences of the common person. He denies that this represents a decline of religiosity. The common person is as religious as ever, but the religiosity of the laity has taken on new forms. Luckmann insists that claims of a decline in religiosity are due to the fact that sociologists have usually asked questions that measure only traditional religiosity (church affiliation and attendance, belief in traditional doctrines, frequency of prayer, and so forth).

Privatization: "Do-It-Yourself Religion"

In the modern world, people derive their sense of meaning by drawing on a wide range of popular philosophies. Each of these competes for the loyalties of the citizen, who is basically a consumer at the marketplace. The product which each popular philosopher is selling is a world view—with its own center of worth or system of values and its own definition of what makes life worth living. Popular religious tracts, *Playboy* magazine,[4] psychological theories expressed in best-selling books and magazines, and underlying themes and values in popular television programs can all affect a person's sense of the meaning of life and one's individual "philosophy of life."

Other organizations, social movements, or businesses also compete in the philosophy-of-life marketplace. Libertarianism is a political movement that exalts the rights of the individual to seek his or her own self-interests without interference. The prime formulator of libertarianism was the late Ayn Rand, whose

---

[4]*Playboy* is very explicit about expressing a consistent philosophy and set of personal values in its stories and editorials. Unrestricted personal expressiveness and the desirability of substantial economic affluence are among those values most worthy of a person's effort.

newsletter was faithfully read by believers and whose public addresses packed houses with enthusiastic followers. Rand stressed individual initiative and the survival of the fittest and believed that altruism was the worst sort of vice. Selfishness, if one followed the logic of her argument, was the most exalted virtue and would ultimately lead to the best type of society. At the opposite end of the political spectrum, Marxism offers a coherent outlook on life and a constellation of values that promises to bring a better life in the future through collective action and collective consciousness. Each of these social movements offers a philosophy of life and a set of values that compete with traditional religions in defining the meaning and purpose of life.

Even business enterprises, like Amway Corporation, seek to motivate by stressing the primacy of financial independence, the ultimate value of free-enterprise economics, and the rewards of close friendship with other distributors. In fact, the regular Amway weekend regional rallies can be analyzed as plausibility structures (see chapter 8) that operate to reinforce the believability of the values and outlook presented by the corporation. **Privatization** of religion involves each individual developing a personalized meaning system or philosophy of life by drawing from many sources in modern life, including secular media, the traditional religions and popular televangelism programs.

In their analysis of mainline religion in the United States, Wade Clark Roof and William McKinney conclude that "the enemy of church life in this country is not so much 'secularity' as 'do-it-yourself religiosity' " (1987: 56). For many Americans, religious authority lies in the individual rather than in the Bible, the church tradition, or the church hierarchy. Each person is expected—even required—to pick and choose what they believe to be true. This has two consequences. First, some religious leaders begin to "market religion." (One example of this was explored in chapter 15.) A second consequence is that religion comes to be viewed as a matter of "opinion," which can be easily modified or discarded. The idea of religious conviction comes to be replaced with the more noncommittal notion of "religious preference" (Roof and McKinney 1987).

Reginald Bibby suggests that the same process is very much at work in Canada. Canadians do not switch denominations very often but have begun to treat their religion as casually as a menu choice in a restaurant: "Canadians are still eating in the restaurants [i.e., mainline denominations]. But their menu choices have changed. . . . [Many] are opting only for appetizers, salads, or desserts [funerals, weddings, and baptisms], rather than full course meals [of full commitment and weekly Sunday worship]. The minimum charge has been lifted—it is now possible to skip the entree page altogether" (Bibby 1987a: 133–34). Bibby also believes that such privatized religion is very vulnerable because it lacks the sanction and support of a group and carries with it no plausibility structures.

It may be recalled that Talcott Parsons and Robert Bellah view the privatization process as a good and healthy sign, while Peter Berger points to the phenomenon as evidence of a decline in religion (discussed in chapter 14). While Luckmann does not see the process as indicative of a decline in religion, neither does he view it as a particularly healthy trend. When individuals must construct their own meaning systems, those systems may seem less eternal and less compelling. The individual may therefore experience anomie or normlessness. Further, those who do construct a sustainable meaning system often develop one that is so privatized that it offers meaning only to the individual—ignoring the larger social structure. Because many privatized meaning systems in modern society exalt the autonomy of the individual (self-realization, individual social and geographic mobility, etc.), the locus of meaning is in the individual biography (Luckmann 1967). With this locus of meaning, individuals are not likely to make sacrifices on behalf of the larger society. If this orientation continued indefinitely, the needs of the society itself would go unmet. For this reason, the privatization of religiosity could be unhealthy in the long run for the larger society.

Hence, Luckmann insists that religiosity is not declining in the modern world; it is undergoing transformation. An alternative form of religiosity has been developing—a form that does not look like religion to many people because it lacks the institutional structures and the conventional dogmas characteristic of traditional religions. Luckmann insists that an alternative form of religiosity is emerging and that it needs to be understood as a modern manifestation.

Luckmann's thesis has drawn a great deal of attention. Several attempts have been made to measure the relative influence of traditional religious views and other "popular" meaning systems in personal philosophies of life. The results are mixed: Richard Machalek and Michael Martin (1976) found evidence to support Luckmann's thesis regarding invisible religions; Hart Nelsen and his colleagues (1976) did not. William Bainbridge and Rodney Stark (1981) studied lay attitudes toward traditional religious doctrines and found that they may not be as impotent and irrelevant to the average citizen as Luckmann implies. On the other hand, Robert Wuthnow (1973) found substantial variations in the personal theologies of seminary students—many departing significantly from traditional Christian theology. In any case, most social scientists would grant that the meaning systems of most Americans seem to be somewhat eclectic, with traditional religiosity, patriotism, and other value systems converging. At the present time, we do not know for sure whether this phenomenon is any more common in the modern world than it was in past eras. Furthermore, our tools of analysis are at present so crude that it is difficult to make

significant generalizations about privatized systems of faith in North America. We might note, however, that two scholars studying African American Christianity have concluded that privatization is primarily a white church phenomenon, being little evidenced in the black church (Lincoln and Mamiya 1990).

Readers may find it interesting and worthwhile to reflect on their own sense of meaning and their own system of values. Do all your values evolve out of a traditional religion? Most of them? Some of them? What other sources have affected your outlook on life? What about the sense of meaning and the personal values of your friends and acquaintances? Does it make sense to you to refer to personalized systems of meaning as a form of religiosity? Why or why not? Do you agree with Niebuhr when he says that whatever provides one with a sense that life is worth living is his or her god and that one's center of values is what one truly worships? Is it essential for a meaning system to address the meaning of death in order for it to be called religion? These are important issues that have divided sociologists in their approaches to studying religion and in their generalizations about religious trends in this country.

Quasi-Religious Movements

Loosely integrated societies—in which the intensity of commitment to cultural tradition is low—are more likely than tightly integrated ones to generate cults and other nontraditional social movements (Stark and Roberts 1982). So it is not surprising that in the United States—a pluralistic and rather loosely integrated society—there are many new religious and quasi-religious movements. Some of these movements hold rather esoteric beliefs; others are based on concepts from popular psychology and from the "human potential" movement. Among the quasi-religious movements that we discuss in this section, none attracts a large following, and most do not attempt to articulate a comprehensive world view that explains the meaning of death, suffering, and injustice. Nonetheless, they have collectively affected a significant segment of the North American population—especially in urban areas.

Quasi-religious movements are cultlike in character, and many sociologists have treated them as cults.[5] However, in chapter 9, I defined a cult as a new religious movement that offers a world view, theodicy, or set of beliefs that departs significantly from traditional religious groups. If a group or movement does not provide a world view that addresses the issues of suffering, death, and injustice, it is not a religion and therefore not a cult in the sense that we have used that word. Nonetheless, there are social movements and organizations in the United States and Canada that address themselves to issues of world view, transcendence, or ultimate fulfillment in at least partial ways. Like the invisible religions Luckmann discusses, these outlooks and beliefs can affect the world view of adherents and their overall state of religiosity. Furthermore, some of these movements continue to elaborate their perspectives on life and eventually do develop theodicies and evolve into full blown new religious movements. Some are closer to becoming NRMs than others, but at this point it will suffice to identify them collectively as quasi-religious movements.

One such orientation is astrology, a set of beliefs about impersonal forces in the universe that profoundly influence human life on earth. These forces can be "read" or predicted through an understanding of the stars. The zodiacal sign under which a person is born is thought to influence significantly (or even determine) one's personality structure and one's thinking processes. Astrology is not a new phenomenon, nor is it limited to any particular age group. It is not organized around a particular group of people (there is no church), there is no ordained clergy or other sanctioned leadership hierarchy, and there is no formal doctrine. Yet, certain principles and beliefs, which are transmitted through books and word of mouth, are common to those who believe in astrology.

A surprisingly high number of Americans believe in astrology. According to a study conducted in San Francisco, approximately 10 percent of the respondents reported that they are "firm believers" (Wuthnow 1976a: 158). Many others follow the horoscopes printed in newspapers, know their zodiac sign and the characteristics of persons under that sign, and "half-believe" in the efficacy of astrology (i.e., they are not fully converts, but they remain open to astrology and believe that there is probably something valid about it). In fact, only 4 percent of those interviewed in the San Francisco study were "firm disbelievers."

In Canada, Bibby has found that 5 percent of the population firmly believe in astrology, and another 44 percent remain open to the possibility that it is true. He found that fully 77 percent of those polled read their horoscopes at least occasionally (Bibby 1979).

Astrology is sometimes integrated into the world views of persons who are members of mainline religious groups. Their religiosity is a synthesis or blend of a traditional religion and astrology. For others who are not active in traditional religious groups, astrology may play a more significant role in their overall world view.[6] One study found that astrology seems to serve as an alternative to conventional

---

[5]As we found in chapter 9, cults have been defined in a number of ways. Those who have followed the tradition of Howard Becker in defining cults as religious movements with little sense of group coherence or group cohesion are likely to view these movements as cults. Stark and Bainbridge call such phenomena "audience cults" or "client cults" (1980a).

---

[6]Among those who are in mainline religious groups, the fatalism and predestination emphasis of astrology may be countered somewhat by Jewish or Christian perspectives.

religion for some people—especially marginal or subjugated members of society: the poorly educated, nonwhites, females, the unemployed, the overweight, the unmarried, the ill, and the lonely (Wuthnow 1976a).

Another form of quasi-religious movement has focused more on the development of untapped human capabilities. Transcendental meditation, Silva Mind Control, Scientology, and est are examples of this type of movement. Transcendental meditation is a meditation technique that bears some resemblance to yoga. Its advocates insist that it is not a new religion, and practitioners include both people who are active in traditional religious groups and those who are by traditional measures nonreligious. Some persons use this technique as a means of relaxation; others seek to tap the "cosmic consciousness" that is the ultimate source of energy in the universe.

Transcendental meditation was started in the late 1960s by a Hindu teacher, Maharishi Mahesh Yogi. It involves chanting a *mantra*—a word, phrase, or sound which is given to each recruit. A mantra is not to be shared with others, but chanting one and concentrating exclusively on it offers one a channel to inner bliss. Transcendental meditation masters maintain that such social problems as war, poverty, crime, and racism would disappear if everyone would engage in transcendental meditation. They maintain that if everyone were in tune with the cosmic consciousness such problems would not exist. People would be more relaxed and more able to fulfill their cosmic purposes (Needleman 1970). Transcendental meditation claims it is not a religion but only a discipline of meditation. While it was founded by a Hindu leader, it is used by some Christians and by persons unaffiliated with any religious group. One poll has suggested that approximately 4 percent of the American public practice transcendental meditation (Princeton Religion Research Center 1980). While this is a small percentage of the population, it does mean that a much larger number

of people are involved in transcendental meditation than in any of the religious cults that received so much attention in the 1980s.

Silva Mind Control, Scientology, and est are movements that are very highly organized and have an internal stratification system. All three are related to popular psychology and parapsychology (belief in clairvoyance, telepathic communication, and psychic healing), and all three are based on education models. Silva Mind Control offers to train people in "psychic powers," while Scientology and est offer to help people become "clear" and to maximize their human potential. The more courses one takes, the higher one moves in the stratification system of the group. This, of course, enhances instrumental commitment, for one makes a financial investment (the courses are not cheap) and begins to rise in the system of respectability and esteem within the group (Bainbridge and Stark 1980b; Bainbridge 1978; Wallis 1977). Some observers view these movements as essentially business enterprises (the courses are substantial sources of income) that sell a popular psychology/self-help product. They do seem to operate on the fringes of both religion and popular psychology. However, Scientology is very explicit about its claim to be a religious movement,[7] and est has increasingly moved in the direction of claiming access to ultimate truth. (Werner Erhardt, the founder of est, started out in Scientology and later formed his own group. Many of the teachings of est and much of the jargon are borrowed from Scientology.)

Some writers have attempted to formulate an eclectic philosophy that purports to synthesize these diverse orientations into a unitary—

---

[7]The original movement started by Ron Hubbard was called Dianetics and was set forth as a science. In 1955 Hubbard recast his theories as a religion by incorporating into the Founding Church of Scientology. This was presumably to differentiate his system from empirical investigation so that it could not be disproven by other scientists (Bainbridge and Stark 1980b).

but very diffuse—movement called the New Age movement. Proponents such as actress Shirley MacLaine and writer Marilyn Ferguson (1987) have claimed that a compelling new religion is emerging from these movements and from scientific sources. The most systematic statement for this perspective is Ferguson's book *The Aquarian Conspiracy*. New Age theology is very mystical (intuitive) in its source of knowledge, but it also blends "human potential" psychology, "holistic medicine," process philosophy, and—from the natural and social sciences—general systems theory. Some advocates of New Age thought are theistic, but by no means do all adherents believe in a deity. The New Age movement does seem to have a strong supernatural spirituality as a common core. Ferguson insists that this emerging form of spirituality has no organization but is an unplanned and uncoordinated groundswell that amounts to a "conspiracy." Because it has no organization and takes so many forms, the New Age movement seems to be entirely in the eye of the beholder. But because its advocates are very process-oriented (denying any absolute answers in life) and because they so fully embrace humanistic values, the New Age theology has become a favorite point of attack for Christians who adhere to biblical inerrancy.

The quasi-religious movements discussed here are only illustrative of a number of such movements that offer inner peace, ultimate fulfillment, spiritual expansion, or insights into the "truth" about human existence. Meher Baba, Spiritual Scientists, Association for Research and Enlightenment, Spiritual Frontiers Fellowship, and I Ching are only a few of the many other religious movements one might explore. Whether some of these are actually new religions may be debatable, but they do seem to represent a form of spirituality that might influence traditional religiosity or serve as an alternative mode of religion. For example, a person may use transcendental medi-

tation to relax, to get into deeper touch with his or her inner self, or to tap a cosmic source of energy. Yet, that person may not consider this activity "prayer" and may not respond positively to other traditional measures of religiosity (doctrinal orthodoxy, church attendance, etc.). Likewise, a person who believes in astrology may not be religious in traditional ways, but he or she may have a world view that offers to explain the meaning (or at least the cause) of events. Any empirical studies of religiosity that attempt to explain current trends and likely patterns for the future must take into account the possibility that religiosity is not declining, but is changing in both form and substance.

The nature of religiosity in North America does seem to be changing somewhat. World views of both Canadians and Americans, including those who are active in traditional religious groups, appear to be somewhat more this-worldly (or secular, if you prefer that term). There also seems to be less willingness to assent to traditional doctrines. This may very well be a sign of an increase in the privatization of religiosity and an increase in syncretistic world views. At this point, we have little comparative data for firm generalizations. The meaning systems of people have, no doubt, always been characterized by a good deal of syncretism, but because of changes in access to the mass public due to television and other mass media, self-help groups, and others espousing their own philosophy of life probably have more influence on common citizens than in earlier eras. This may account for more individuality in meaning systems.

Whether this is a trend that will have unfortunate consequences for the society as a whole remains to be seen. The trend may have negative effects for the established churches: If fewer people feel committed to the theology that traditional religions espouse, it could involve a decrease in commitment to those organizations. On the other hand, privatization may bestow other offsetting benefits to the society—and perhaps even to religious organizations. Predictions at this point are highly speculative. The recent downturn in traditional forms of religiosity may be the beginning of a pattern, but at present the attendance levels at conventional churches are much higher than they were in Puritan days and are higher than other industrialized nations in the modern world.

My own interpretation is that religion is not in a declining phase—but readers should remember that I use a broad definition of religion. Systems of meaning that offer to explain the meaning of human events through a world view, an ethos, and a system of symbols are not likely to disappear. However, certain traditional views and certain established religious institutions may well decline in their influence. Whether the reader views this change of religiosity as a decline in religion will be determined largely by his or her operational definition of religion.

Summary

In rapidly changing societies, religion sometimes takes on unconventional forms. One of the most widely studied of these is civil religion—a meaning system that explores the ultimate significance of the nation. In pluralistic societies in which no one religion can serve to sacralize the existing social arrangements and provide a common core of values, a civil religion emerges to fill that void. In the early period of U.S. history, the civil religion focused on the United States as the "promised land" with George Washington as the mythical Moses. At the time of the Civil War, the nation faced a crisis, and a new mythology emerged. This time the slain Lincoln became the "savior" of the nation who "gave his life that the nation might live." National heroes such as Washington and Lincoln serve as "saints" in the civil religion.

Some scholars think that we currently face a crisis period. For Bellah, the crisis is due partially to pervasive cynicism about the integrity of the nation's leaders and ambivalence about the United States' role in the world. Combined with this is a nearly unfettered pursuit of self-interest by Americans and the loss of commitment to civic duty or the common good. The new Christian right also believes that the United States has broken the covenant with God, but sees the problem as rooted more in removal of prayer from the schools, the legalization of abortion, the decline of family stability, and the invasion of individual autonomy by government. Although civil religion normally serves as the glue that helps bond the country together, conflict over civil religion in the United States has become a source of significant dissension.

Civil religion can have both prophetic and priestly forms. It can judge the nation for not living up to its high ideals, or it can simply sacralize the nation and the powers-that-be. It can also appear in official form (as articulated by presidents and official documents) or in folk versions (as popularized by common people).

A second approach to alternative religions focuses on "invisible" or "privatized" expressions of religiosity. Individuals may create their own systems of meaning, compiled from the philosophies expressed in popular religious tracts, best-selling pop psychology books, popular television programs, or independent political organizations of the far left or far right. Such privatized religion is often vulnerable because it lacks a plausibility structure, and it often is relevant only to one individual. Privatized religions frequently lack concern for the larger social system. Some commentators, such as Canadian scholar Reginald Bibby, see "do-it-yourself religion" as the foremost threat to traditional religions.

A third alternative form of religion in the modern world is the quasi-religious movements.

Astrology, transcendental meditation, Silva Mind Control, Scientology, est, and the New Age movement are among these. They each attempt to explore supernatural forces and/or philosophies of life that can bring greater fulfillment.

Some scholars believe that these alternative forms of religion mean that religion is not so much declining in North America as changing in significant ways. New forms are emerging and old forms are taking on modified form. Religion in North America clearly does adjust and adapt to the larger society of which it is a part.

Religion and Globalization

A consistent theme throughout this text has been that religion is a complex system that is involved in complex interrelationships with other structures and processes of the society. The meaning system, for example, is composed of an interplay of rituals, myths, and symbols, all of which reinforce a world view and a sacred set of moods and motivations. That meaning system, in turn, is only one subsystem of the larger system we call the religious system. This larger system is made up of meaning, belonging, and structural (institutional) systems, all of which are interrelated in complex and sometimes contradictory ways. We found, for example, that the vested interests of officials in the institutional system may cause them to behave in ways that run counter to the meaning system—as occurs when denominations refuse to promote clergy-women to large and successful churches or when clergy are not promoted when they speak out against racism.

Religion, in turn, is part of a larger system, the nation, and is in interaction with economic, health care, political, and educational institutions. Sometimes these interactions are mutually supportive and integrative, and sometimes they are conflictual.

The nation as a macro system, in turn, relates to yet a larger system: the world system of interdependent nations, involving transnational division of labor and mutual dependence for needed resources and products. In this web of networks, subsystems can impact larger systems in important ways: for example, economic collapse in a country can affect not only that nation, but the interaction of that nation with other nations. The processes in a more macro system can also shape processes in smaller systems: a multinational trade treaty or decisions made by the United Nations may profoundly affect the internal dynamic of a country's economy and therefore the economic circumstances of a family.[1]

---

[1]Although this model seems to assume a structural-functional perspective, let me be quick to emphasize that while I assume structural interdependence and interaction, I do not assume harmony and integration in the system. Open systems theory recognizes that the system is open, dynamic, changing, and racked with conflicts over self-interests between groups.

This chapter will briefly explore the role of religion in the largest of networks—as the entire world increasingly takes on the characteristics of a social system. We will find that even at this level, what religions *say* may differ in important ways from what they actually *do*.

The Globalization Process

During the past century and a half, and more especially during the past fifty years, societies around the world have been undergoing a radical transformation; each society and nation has become less an isolated and autonomous unit. The process, called **globalization,** has involved the entire world becoming "a single sociocultural place" (Robertson 1989). This change involves several interdependent processes: (1) a structural interdependence of nation-states, (2) a synthesis and cross-fertilization of cultures as societies borrow ideas, technologies, artistic concepts, mass media procedures, and definitions of human rights from one another, (3) a change in socialization to a broader inclusiveness of others as being "like us" and to a sense of participation in a global culture, and (4) an increase in individualism, accompanied by a decrease in traditional mechanisms of control, such as strong clan and family ties (Robertson 1989).

There are several theories of global interdependence and transformation. One of the most widely discussed perspectives in the 1980s and 1990s has been "world systems theory," developed in large part by Immanuel Wallerstein (1974, 1979, 1984). This perspective, sometimes also referred to as "dependency theory," is based on a Marxian or conflict model. Affluent industrial societies based on a capitalistic economy are referred to as the *core* of the world economy. Poor nonindustrialized societies are viewed as part of the *periphery.* These peripheral countries typically have narrow, export-oriented economies, based largely in providing raw materials to the industrialized countries. They import manufactured products and in the process develop enormous debts to the richer nations. As a result they become highly dependent on the developed countries. They remain poor not because of lack of resources or hard work, but because they are exploited by the "haves" who control capital and technology (Shannon 1989).

Wallerstein's world systems theory says little about religion. On the one hand, it assumes that secularization is an unstoppable force, and that religion is a relic destined for decline. Thus, religion does not deserve much attention (Robertson 1992; Simpson 1991). The prime movers of social behavior are thought to be economic. Like most neo-Marxian theories, when religion *is* discussed, it is often viewed simply as a mechanism by which the affluent preserve their power and keep the poor in their place. Ironically, as we shall see, some religious movements use world systems theory to explain poverty in poor countries, despite the theory's indifference to religious variables.

An alternative view of globalization is set forth by Roland Robertson, whose perspective takes cultural values and norms more seriously as determinants of social processes. Robertson is convinced that religion is an important player in the global transformation process. Since he gives more consideration to the role of religion, we will explore his sociocultural theory in more depth in this chapter. However, those interested in global inequality issues should continue to be aware of the insights offered by Wallerstein relative to how power is used to serve the self-interests of the "haves" of the world.

According to Robertson, globalization has been influenced by religion and has impacted religion in important ways; it has been both a dependent and independent variable relative to religion. The topic of globalization is itself a complex issue, and as with other issues in this book, we can only illustrate some of the issues and demonstrate how sociological perspectives can be applied to the globalization process. Our discussion here will explore the emergence of global theologies, the impact of globalization on traditional religions, and the role of religions in international politics.

The Emergence of Global Theologies

One interesting religious development during the past 120 years is the increase of global perspectives in the theologies and ethical systems of major world religions. Contemporary religious groups often stress the idea that the world is a single place and that all humans are children of the same God. Rather than stressing differences based on ethnicity or race, contemporary world religions often combat bigotry with affirmations of the fundamental similarity of people everywhere. The World Council of Churches, as well as many Christian denominations, have sponsored a variety of programs aimed at health care, hunger relief, and amelioration of suffering caused by natural disasters. Prior to the twentieth century, outreach programs were limited mostly to proselytizing. And for the thousand years prior to the eighteenth century, remarkably few efforts had been made to reach out to persons in other cultures (Hunter 1983; Lee 1992; Meyer 1988; Vidler 1961). While these examples draw upon Christianity, global inclusiveness seems to be a modern world trend in other world faiths as well.

Religions often construct images of the oneness of the world in their myths (Simpson 1991), the modern imagery of the "global village" being one example advanced by the World Council of Churches. The image itself creates a view of a closed, close-knit, interdependent, communal society (Turner 1991a). Perhaps it is because of unifying images that religion often serves as a basis for unity and

integration even where language differences might separate. Members of the same religious tradition often feel a bond and are inclined to cooperate with others perceived as "like us" when the two might as easily have adopted a posture of animosity.

Some social scientists believe this change in the direction of accommodation and tolerance of other religious traditions is itself a result of increased global interdependence (Lee 1992; Meyer 1988). As we are forced to trade and interact with people in other parts of the world who control resources we need, it soon becomes clear that judgmental attitudes implying their inferiority—and an accompanying self-righteous posture regarding our own moral and spiritual values—are dysfunctional. Thus, since about 1875, many Christian theologians and church leaders have offered conciliatory attitudes towards other Christian churches and toward other religions. As Lee writes, "Rather than authority based solely in the Bible, there was now a new stress on the authority of personal religious experience. Instead of viewing the world as static, liberals accommodated new scientific views by attributing divine purposes to the newly evident evolutionary dynamism of nature and history" (1992: 131). Likewise, liberal theologies suggested that God may speak to people through other religious traditions, and that while Christianity may be the fullest and most complete expression of God's Truth, it was not the only path to Truth. Christianity is depicted as "different only in degree from other religions" (Cauthen 1962: 24).

More recent liberal formulations even hesitate to assert that Christianity is the fullest and most complete expression, for that implies a superiority/inferiority posture that continues to offend members of other traditions. Many theologians and church leaders now simply assert that Christ is the way they personally came to know God, either affirming or remaining mute on the matter of whether other faiths are equally valid paths to God.

It is noteworthy that these very liberal or "tolerant" religions are usually strongest in precisely those areas characterized by cultural diversity and most involved in international transactions. Urban areas, coastal trade centers, and other "crossroads" of cultures and people are more likely to generate such outlooks than rural areas where the people rarely encounter much heterogeneity.

If this shift in theology was a result of globalization, it also resulted in countertheologies and reactions which will be discussed later. But the trend toward greater tolerance on the part of the mainstream denominations was clear. The change in the position of the Roman Catholic Church during the twentieth century has been dramatic. In 1910 Pope Pius X required all Roman Catholic clergy and teachers to sign an "antimodernist oath." By the 1950s Pope Pius XII acknowledged truth and goodness outside of Christianity, and in an encyclical, *Evangelii Praecones,* asserted that rather than attacking other religions as evil when evangelizing, the gospel should be assimilated into whatever is "good and honorable and beautiful" in existing religions.

The controversial Vatican II of the 1960s opened the door even further to viewing other religions as "colleagues with similar problems" rather than as enemies (Sheard 1987). So it is that the indigenous religion among Pueblo Indians in the Southwest of the United States—once brutally suppressed with acts of terrorism and torture and strictly forbidden by church and state—is now becoming blended into Roman Catholic Christianity. Zuni artist Alex Seowtewa is painting murals of Kachina dancers on the upper walls of the Catholic church in Zuni, New Mexico. This is done with the blessing and cooperation of the Catholic officials; it is mostly Zuni Kiva leaders and Kachina dancers who feel that their religion is being compromised and that a sacrilege is being perpetrated.

Sometimes the impulse to modify the group's theology or system of ethics can come

from internal dynamics within a religion. As the membership composition of a religious group changes, with a marked increase in membership in one region, there may be theological ramifications. The Roman Catholic Church, an international organization whose historic development and population base was European, is now undergoing transition from a first world (industrialized, capitalistic countries) to a third world (poor, nonindustrialized nations) entity. Catholicism is experiencing enormous growth in South America and Africa, causing the population makeup of the membership of the church to shift (Budde 1992).

As its membership majority has shifted from the Northern to the Southern Hemisphere, many Catholic theologians and priests have supported one or another version of liberation theology.[2] Liberation theology tends to be highly critical of capitalistic economic systems and to view the world through the lens of conflict theory, championing the cause of those exploited by the capitalistic world system. The major cause of poverty in the third world is not identified as slow adoption of industrialization, but as neocolonial *exploitation* by the affluent nations of the world. Such direct attacks on capitalism as a system, attribution of sinister motives to the policy makers of developed countries, and legitimation of movements antithetical to the interests of affluent capitalists are bound to create tensions between the church and Western leaders.

This created an interesting dilemma for the Roman Catholic Church; it is placed in a position of choosing between defending the self-interests of the poor, the new and very sizeable constituency of the church, or sacralizing the interests of the affluent capitalistic countries which have been its historic constituency. Further, the "we" within the church now includes people from a vast array of cultures, races, and

---

[2]Liberation theology tends to draw heavily on world systems theory for its analysis of poverty.

regions of the globe. The Church is itself increasingly multicultural. While Roman Catholicism is the most vivid example of these internal transformations, other Christian denominations are also experiencing substantial ethnic diversity.

The trend toward interreligious accommodation, the inclination to define other religious ·groups as fellow travelers, the desire for "dialogue" and discovery of common ground with other religions, and internal cultural diversity all compel churches to accept pluralism as a positive value. Indeed, whether within the church or external to it, embracing pluralism appears to be a critical first step toward accommodation of diverse peoples and alternative social systems. Those who believe that globalization is an unstoppable trend would interpret increased religious tolerance as the inevitable wave of the future.

On the other hand, a few evangelical Christian groups have tried to develop their own version of globalized theology, and these models do not emphasize pluralism and diversity. In a study of the conservative Faith movement in Sweden and the United States, Coleman (1993) found that specialization of roles by various national groups was emphasized. Interdependence was recognized, but there was no particular expectation of equity, unification, and homogenization of peoples and cultures. The point that this study makes is that "globalization cannot be regarded as an internally homogeneous, inexorable phenomenon" (Coleman 1993: 371).

Globalization will no doubt take many forms and result in a wide array of efforts to define its meaning and delineate the appropriate form of its evolution. Religious groups will likely make many attempts to define what global interdependence should look like. The one generalization that seems fairly certain is that religions can no longer ignore global interdependence and the fact that the world is becoming "a single sociocultural place." Theologies of the major world religions will likely be permanently affected by the expansion of vision to include the entire world.

Impact of Globalization on Traditional Religions

The interdependence of the world has long been a factor in shaping religious movements. Robert Wuthnow (1980) argues that much religious change, including even the Protestant Reformation, has been caused by international processes. We do not have space for a long-term overview here, so we will limit the discussion to the modern world. Globalization in the past century has involved at least three important processes that impact religion: modernization or secularization of social structures and cultures, introduction of advanced and complex communication technologies, and demographic migration patterns.

Diffusion of Modernization and Religious Response

In chapter 14 (Secularization) we learned that secularization involves (1) a rational, utilitarian, and empirical/scientific approach to decision making, so that the world becomes "disenchanted" or de-spiritualized and (2) institutional differentiation and increased autonomy of various institutions from religious domination. Ability of a society to function effectively in the interdependent world system requires "modernization." As societies modernize (become more westernized) religious institutions are often relegated to a less encompassing role in social life. Religious organizations begin to provide services that are perceived as "optional" (Turner 1991). Joseph Tamney (1992) describes this as "selective religiosity." Official religious pronouncements compete with efforts by the state to define acceptable social behavior and the individual is free to select which religious pronouncements to follow.

As governments become more concerned about "quality of life" issues and expand the scope of their concerns, they begin to encroach on the traditional realm of religion (Shupe and Hadden 1989). Religious groups traditionally had monopolistic control over education, stability and health of marriage ties, preparation for and grief following death, and the provision of charities to help the destitute. But in the modern world, those services are increasingly provided by "helping" or "service" professionals paid by governments (Turner 1991b). And governments increasingly become embroiled in disputes over issues of morality, justice, and meaning as they promulgate norms governing a very wide range of behaviors (Shupe and Hadden 1989). As we globalize, international organizations begin to fulfill some of these same functions. We now have more than 500 international organizations and an emerging international law that defines boundaries of acceptable behavior in everything from commerce to human rights (Lechner 1991; Berman 1991).

Moreover, the utilitarian and rational pursuit of self-interest in the political and economic realms has divorced these arenas from religious norms. Turner (1991) points out that distribution of resources is no longer tied directly to honor, chastity, or loyalty, as it once was. The result is that adultery, divorce, adolescent disobedience of parents, premarital sexual activity, and other traditionally forbidden religio-moral behaviors are not visited with economic sanctions. Religious norms lose their clout, and the realm of religious influence is focused more narrowly.

Another way to conceptualize this is to think of rational-utilitarian ties between people, ones stressing mutual self-interests and negotiation of resources in the interaction, as "contractual" relations. This is in contrast to "covenantal" relations: emotive-expressive ties, based on bonding, shared values, and sense of commitment to specific other persons. The latter represent familial and religious relationships, while the former are more characteristic of bureaucratic, governmental, and economic affiliations. David Bromley and Bruce Busching (1988) and Bryan Turner (1991) have developed arguments that the covenantal realm is shrinking in the face of expanding contractual ties. This is a global trend and it provides a profound threat to most traditional religions.

A number of scholars point out that the rise of religious fundamentalism[3] and other legalistic, literalistic, and rigid revitalistic movements in the twentieth century is not a process unique to a single religious tradition or society. Therefore it cannot be interpreted simply in light of local or national events, nor in terms of characteristics of a given religion. Its cause, they assert, is global (Robertson 1989; Turner 1991a; Wuthnow 1980). Whether the revivalism or "fundamentalism" be Islamic, Japanese Buddhist, Hasidic Jewish, Evangelical Christian, or Malaysian Dukway, the cause appears to be reaction against global modernization (Shupe and Hadden 1989; Davidman 1990). The formation of these movements is interpreted as being rooted in several features of the globalization process.

First, the pluralism and relativity of a diverse world is threatening to traditions that always protected the absoluteness of norms and values (Robertson 1989). Bryan Turner points out that the whole idea of alternative lifestyles being tolerable is offensive to those who are so certain that they alone know "the Truth" (Bryan Turner 1991b: 162). Second, fear of economic interdependence on other peoples

---

[3]These movements are, in essence, what we earlier called revivalistic movements, which attempt to restore legitimacy to the traditional world view of a people—often combining ethnic traditions and religious beliefs in an absolute and uncompromising dogma. Since recent literature has called these movements "fundamentalist" because of their rigid posture, I have occasionally used the term in this broad sense here.

—some of whom are very different and are viewed as undependable—stimulates a desire to reassert autonomy and, at least symbolically, to proclaim one's uniqueness (Robertson 1985). Fundamentalism or rigid revivalism is in large part an attempt to reestablish isolation and independence from the world system.

Third, fundamentalism represents a reaction against the institutional differentiation that is so characteristic of modernization. Ironically, the blending of Islamic fundamentalism with governmental functions is much more a twentieth century phenomenon than a historic one (Turner 1991a, 1991b). It represents a desire to merge institutions in reaction to the Western pattern of differentiating institutions. Shi'ite fundamentalists (Moslems) do not want religion removed from other spheres of life, and they react by forging an even closer marriage between religion and other societal functions. In essence, these are nativistic movements reacting against changes that they identify as neocolonialism. They are convinced—with good cause—that the acceptance of globalism involves ethnocide, the death of their traditional culture. Fundamentalism is an attempt to defend their culture.

Fourth, fundamentalisms are sometimes counteractions against religious reforms themselves. As Iran underwent modernization in the mid-twentieth century, official Islam in that country underwent reformulation, becoming liberated from folk versions and emphasizing a universalistic monotheism. It also embraced aspects of secularization, including changing roles for women and economic reform that eventually left Iran highly dependent on the United States and other Western nations. But modernization of the country resulted in some economic dislocations and a degree of "cultural wobble." As conservatives rejected modernism in favor of traditionalism, they also rejected the new interpretation of Islam. Rather than returning to polytheistic folk versions of the faith, conservatives forged

a literalistic and uncompromising interpretation of Islam (Turner 1991a, 1991b). Official Islam as it was taught by the elites was seen as having sold out to westernization; it was depicted as a traitor religion that abandoned traditional roots.

While the examples used here have been mostly of Islamic fundamentalism, the argument of many social scientists is that these movements are occurring across religious traditions, and that they represent reclaiming of authority over a sacred tradition. This religious tradition "is to be reinstated as an antidote for a society [astray] from its cultural moorings" (Shupe and Hadden 1989: 111). The ultimate cause for the straying is the process of globalization.[4]

Worldwide revivalistic movements are not the only type of religious reaction attributed to global modernism. An alternative response to institutional differentiation and the narrowing scope of religious influence, according to Robertson (1989) and Turner (1989; 1991b), is privatization of religion. Since religions with a universal message are not linked closely to a specific ethnic group or geographic region, and since religious institutions have been moved to the periphery of social life, individuals are freer to formulate their own theology, their own meaning system. Thus, global trends toward diversity and institutional autonomy may be linked to the rise in individualization of religion (discussed in chapter 16), as well as to the formation of fundamentalist movements. In the face of global interdependence, liberals may tend toward privatization of religion, while conservatives tend to institute movements proclaiming absolute and infallible answers to questions of meaning and morality.

---

[4]Rather than viewing secularization as an unstoppable force, then, Robertson, Hadden, Shupe, and several other scholars cited in this chapter suggest that secularization often results in renewed religious fervor and the birth of new types of religious movements.

Religion and the Globalization of Communication Technologies

As we discovered in chapter 15 (on televangelism), communications technologies can have a powerful impact on religion. These technologies are not entirely "value neutral." Anthropologist Conrad Kottak, for example, found in a longitudinal study[5] of the impact of television on Brazil that the net effect was a homogenizing and standardizing of the culture. Values, language usage, and attitudes were affected in the direction of a more singular national culture (Kottak 1990). Some sociologists maintain that the same process is occurring globally, with the norms being set by secularized Western societies (Robertson 1992; Turner 1991b).

Much of the television programming that is aired around the world is produced in the United States, and a good deal of the rest of it is created in developed Western societies—Europe, Canada, and so forth. Not only does the programming press cultures of the world toward common aspirations and lifestyles, but the advertising that finances the broadcasts often explicitly seeks to instill nonascetic, consumer-oriented values (Turner 1991b). Radio programming, whether under the auspices of Radio Free America or of religious evangelicals from North America, also communicates a very Western view of the world. As one might expect, this can provide a very direct threat to traditional religions which have often had a monopoly on setting moral standards and on defining and defending traditional values.

This does not mean that non-Western traditional religions have disdained modern mass media. Bryan Turner points out that mass communication has been used effectively by Islamic leaders to communicate their message. Because of the availability of mass media,

official monotheistic Islam has spread to the hinterlands where folk versions of Islam or non-Islamic local deities had prevailed. A more standard and universalistic interpretation was disseminated by new communications technologies. But the same medium that disseminated orthodox interpretations of Islam also introduced Western consumerism and diffused Western values. Moslems are therefore divided on whether these technological wonders have been a bane or a blessing (Turner 1991b). The fundamentalists are more likely to attack the media with its intrusive consumerism, while the orthodox leaders have tended to see the benefits of the new media.

Of course, other economically productive technologies have also been adopted in many parts of the world, carrying with them values of economic efficiency, more effective exploitation of resources, utilitarian valuation of the natural world, and a positive attitude toward change. As Garrett and Robertson (1991: xii) put it, "The most remarkable thing about the international embrace of technology is that modern humanity has agreed with Christianity that we have a right, indeed a duty, to change the world." Technologies of various sorts, having been imported from the Western world or having been stimulated by Western example and competition, have pushed relentlessly toward social change. Since religious groups often sacralize and protect traditions, the existing religions often either feel besieged or are forced to adapt and to develop some form of "process theology" that embraces change. In either case, religion is affected.

World Population Patterns and Religious Consequences

Yet another way in which global trends may influence religion is through demographic changes. The twentieth century has seen massive amounts of human geographic mobility. The improved communication technologies mentioned above have brought new awareness

---

[5]This study spanned several decades, beginning shortly after the first introduction of television to Brazil.

of other parts of the world and other opportunities. Advanced transportation technologies, on the other hand, have allowed more people to move to new locations than at any time in human history. And with the economic transformations of an interdependent world come forces that push people out of rural areas and pull them into urban ones.

Some of the increased migration in the twentieth century has been cross-continental. Changes in U.S. immigration laws in 1965 allowed for increased immigration into North America. Much of this immigration was from non-European regions of the world, especially Asia. With these new immigrants came many new religious traditions. Gordon Melton, a specialist on new religious movements (NRMs), insists that part of the increase in the number of NRMs in North America is simply a function of high global immigration rates (Melton 1993). These newcomers to American soil bring with them their religious traditions. The very presence of these alternative religious traditions adds to the diversity of the "religious marketplace" in North America. Berger, as we learned in chapter 14, believes that religious pluralism is itself deleterious to religion as anomie is created and religious plausibility undermined.

Beyond international migration, however, is the worldwide trend to urbanization. Urbanization of a society has a number of consequences, not the least of which is to increase the number of educational institutions and the overall educational level of the people. As religious elites come together in seminaries and other educational settings, they can begin to formulate more systematic theologies and standardize norms within the faith. Arjomand (1989) maintains that increased density of population and the concentration of elites stimulated an insistence on orthodoxy within Islam that had never been central to that tradition. Readers may recall from earlier chapters that Islam has typically put more emphasis on behavior (orthopraxy) than on belief, and it

has historically allowed for considerable local adaptation. Urban centralization contributes to standardization. Increased literacy of the common adherents of the faith is also bound to impact interpretations of doctrine.

Religion, then, can be influenced in important ways by global trends. The global spread of a rational-utilitarian world view, of institutional differentiation of religion from other spheres, of communication technologies, and of urbanization and international migration have impinged on religion. All three subsystems of religion can be affected: the institutional structure and its tie to other institutions in the society, the sense of religious belonging as a source of personal identity, and the meaning system which tries to make sense of people's experiences and establish norms of behavior. Before we conclude this look at religion in a global context, however, we need to consider ways that religious groups and movements may impinge on international relations.

The Role of Religion in International Politics

Religious groups themselves are often multinational conglomerates of sorts. Some religious organizations have international constituencies. Others may have memberships concentrated in one nation, but sponsor benevolent and evangelical programs that span the globe. By reaching into other parts of the world, religious organizations develop vested interests, sympathies, and responsibilities to adherents that may bring it into conflict with one or more governments.

We have already discussed the fact that the Roman Catholic Church is an international body that must be sympathetic to the circumstances of people in many nations. It cannot align itself with the economic and political interests of one nation or set of nations without risking the alienation of tens of millions of members in another part of the world. But there are other ways in which multinational religious organizations can be involved in social and economic policies of a nation.

In Poland during the 1970s and 1980s, the Polish people often felt colonized by a foreign power—the Soviet Union. The Communist government in Poland was extremely unpopular and the people had no real way to make the government more responsive to their needs. In a survey conducted in 1983, only 3 percent of the respondents felt that the government and the Communist Party represented the interests of the Polish people. By contrast, 60 percent identified the Catholic Church and the Pope as protecting Polish interests (Tamney 1992: 33).

Joe Tamney (1992) reports that the Catholic Church became a real power broker in negotiations between unions and the government. Indeed, he reports that bishops sometimes themselves took on a role akin to a union leader, and in so doing became major players in the political future of the country. Since those bishops were ultimately responsible to the Pope and had a source of support external to the nation, they experienced a good deal of independence. Clergy supported by a state church, one financed with tax dollars, would not likely have the same freedom to challenge the government. The global nature of the Catholic Church influenced the role bishops could play in the Polish situation.[6]

The locus of control of a religious hierarchy (national versus cross-national) can influence the power of religious officials in our complex global environment. On the other hand, the vitality of religion is frequently connected to its functions for ethnic identity or for the mobilization of political power of an ethnic or regional group (Turner 1991b). Interestingly, the Polish conflict supports this interpretation as well: people vigorously supported the Catholic Church because the parish became a better symbol of national and ethnic identity than the government. Poland is an especially intriguing case in that a single religion tended to be identified with national pride and culture, but that religion was global in its power base. That combination provided an exceptionally strong base for challenging governmental policies (Tamney 1992).

This role of religion in solidifying ethnic identity may be even more important for religions in pluralistic societies, where supernatural sanction of one's own culture helps to fend off anomie. Nonetheless, the conclusion that a confluence of religion and ethnic group interests is important to religious vigor raises serious questions about the capacity of religion to unite people across these boundaries. Can a religion that advocates tolerance and diversity, and downplays we-they polemics, have vitality? In a local community seeking divine legitimation of its own values, religious ambivalence and nonspecificity is not appreciated.

Religious groups often are faced with a dilemma (Robertson 1989). Church officials may choose to embrace the emerging global culture, acknowledge and celebrate global economic interdependence, and foster greater tolerance and open-mindedness toward those who are "different." The alternative course would be to intensify the solidarity between the religion and the national or ethnic group and to stress the differences between "us" and "them." The latter course is likely to buoy the numbers of adherents. Although virtually all religions give lip service to a desire for world peace, and although world peace requires greater tolerance and understanding between people, an institution is actually rewarded

---

[6]Being a religion that crosses over national boundaries can also be a source of suspicion in some circumstances. Roman Catholics were traditionally suspected of lacking national loyalty in the United States; they were derisively called "papists." Likewise, Jews have often been accused of maintaining dangerous, subversive ties because of their international networks with others who share their faith.

with increased numbers and additional resources if it takes the path of identifying with ethnic pride. The institutional reward system may actually work *against* openness to diversity. Despite meaning system proclamations in support of peace and tolerance of others, the drive for institutional survival may entice religious leaders to follow a path leading to popularity and membership growth. Those religions that do not choose this path may dwindle in numbers and risk their continued viability.

In chapters 3 and 16 we discussed Durkheim's idea, elaborated in recent years by Robert Bellah, that societies—especially pluralistic ones—need a common core of sacred symbols, values, and beliefs to enhance social integration and to provide an overarching system of meaning. The world has no such universal system, no myths, rituals, and symbols that powerfully unite the people of the world. While many world religions have become more tolerant to others, there is no prospect in the near future that any one religion will become dominant worldwide and be capable of fulfilling this role. And there is no global civil religion that at this point can fill the void. (The religious diversity and composition of the world are set forth in Table 17.1.)

Not only does the globe lack a comprehensive and unifying meaning system, the planet is actually populated by religions that have historically each claimed exclusive access to divine truth. Bryan Turner writes, "It is difficult to imagine how one can have several universalistic, global, evangelistic religions within the same world political space. How can one have mutually exclusive households within the world cultural system?" (1991a:179).

It is not just social coherence that is at stake. In the midst of a pluralistic world, with extraordinarily powerful self-interests inclining nations and societies to conflict, world organizations such as the World Court and the United Nations lack the legitimated authority that civil religion can provide (Berman 1991;

Meyer 1980; Robertson 1989, 1991; Simpson 1991). Without some sacralization of their authority, such bodies find it very difficult to make their policies binding.

Religion is often closely linked with ethnic exclusiveness. Among many Jews, and especially among Hasidic Jews such as this teacher at the yeshiva, religion and ethnic identity are merged thoroughly. Pariah peoples (outcast minority groups which survive over time as ethnic islands in dominant societies) must build strong boundaries between themselves and the larger culture to prevent assimilation and extinction. Jewish kosher laws regarding food preparation, Gypsy rules about spiritual cleanliness, Amish practices of shunning deviants who violate their strict code of behavior, and unusual clothing or hairstyles worn by group members all serve as ingenious mechanisms to preserve the culture and the religion, but they also establish barricades between people that hamper unity at another level. (Cornell Capa/Magnum.)

It is noteworthy that at least two of the new religious movements, the Unification Church (the "Moonies") and the amorphous New Age movement, both propose elements of a global theology (Robertson 1985). They each set forth the rudiments of a global civil religion. The Moonies see the world eventually united under the theocratic leadership of Reverend Moon, a distinctly undemocratic model. Some people think the New Age religion is a universalistic faith that might unify diverse people. The New Agers posit a more democratic

---

▶ **TABLE 17.1**

Religious Membership around the Globe

Religious diversity characterizes the world religious situation. The question is whether these many religious traditions contribute to the unity of all humanity, or will be a source of divisiveness and conflict. The following gives some idea of the proportions of the world's population adhering to various religious traditions.

Religion	Membership (in millions)	Percent of world population
Total Christian	1,833.0	33.4
Roman Catholic	1,025.6	18.7
Protestant	373.7	6.8
Eastern Orthodox	170.4	3.1
Anglican	74.9	1.3
Other Christian	188.4	3.4
Islam	971.3	17.7
Hinduism	732.8	13.4
Buddhism	314.9	5.7
Chinese folk religions (including Taoist)	187.1	3.4
New religious movements	143.4	2.6
Tribal religions	96.6	1.8
Sikh	18.8	0.3
Judaism	17.8	0.3
Shamanism	10.5	0.2
Confucianism	6.0	0.1
Baha'i	5.5	0.1
Jainism	3.8	0.1
Shintoism	3.2	0.1
Other religions	18.6	0.3
Atheists	240.3	4.3

Source: Robert Famighetti, editor, *World Almanac and Book of Facts.* Mahway, N.J.: World Almanac, 1994, pp. 727–28.

international interdependence in which all people are members of a single, egalitarian, global network. Yet the New Age movement is as caught in polemics as any other religion. It hardly appears, at this point, to be able to unify various religions and people of the world. Regardless of whether either of these theologies is at all adequate for a global vision, it is a sign of the times that there is a felt need for a meaning system that encompasses the entire world.

Of course, many other sociologists insist that the primary "glue" that unites most modern societies is not common beliefs and values anyway. Economic interdependence, technological linkages between social units, and bureaucratic processes provide the primary coherence, they argue (Turner 1991b; Wallerstein 1974, 1984). For these scholars, a global civil religion is unnecessary. Readers may want to give thoughtful consideration to their own position: Are certain common values and beliefs important to an integrated and well-functioning society? Does global harmony and genuine cooperation require some global religion? If so, how will this affect existing world religions? If not, what does the lack of importance of global religion say about the role and the vitality of religion in the future?

Even if a global meaning system is not essential, this does not mean that religious groups will cease to be players in the multinational economic ties that are developing. The rejection of modernization by uncompromising revivalistic groups (whether Islamic, Christian, or Buddhist) impacts international economic networks (Shupe and Hadden 1989). Since these networks are increasingly based on capitalistic principles of pursuing self-interests, without restraint by emotional ties or ideologies, many religious groups will mobilize to disrupt and oppose the networks and the invasive values they bring with them. Western nations that lead the impetus to globalization may be "demonized" by revivalistic groups, and intense animosity may be directed toward American individuals, companies, products, and policies. Further, these international economic ties occasionally present a direct financial threat to the religious group, as outsiders begin to provide products or services that the religious group uses to support its operation. So whether it is a source of global unification or of resistance to that process, religion is likely to be an important variable in the evolution of the world system.

Religious movements and institutions can have an impact on international processes in other ways, too. American televangelists have sometimes expanded their "markets" by broadcasting programs abroad. In doing so they diffuse a very Americanized version of Christianity. When this message is not warmly received by indigenous governments, these evangelists sometimes jam the message into the country with a high-kilowatt station located in a nearby country. As Jeffrey Hadden (1991) points out, these "pirate broadcasters" assume that God's law and purposes (which they are sure they alone know) stand above the laws of mortals. They will not be dissuaded by local officials or national leaders if they feel they are called to evangelize a country.

Often these televangelists are Americans, and rather ethnocentric and culturally insensitive Americans at that. According to Hadden, the bad feelings generated by this aggressive promulgation of a religious tradition can create diplomatic tensions and conflicts. Other highly sensitive negotiations between the target country and the United States may be jeopardized (Hadden 1991).

Of course, religious groups from developed countries are also frequently involved in benevolence programs directed toward impoverished areas of the world. These programs have the potential to enhance goodwill between countries, but occasionally the manner in which assistance is provided can be demeaning to the recipient nation or people. If the latter occurs, the net result could be hostile feelings rather than ones of mutual respect and appreciation.

Whether the concern is international bigotry, prospects for economic cooperation and trade, a struggle for human rights and justice, or a desire for world peace, religious groups are likely to be important players in the outcome. Religion affects international relations and is affected by global trends. As in all other social processes, religion is both a dependent and independent variable.

Summary

Religion is not only itself a complex social system, with internal processes that are sometimes integrative and sometimes contradictory and conflictive, but it is one part of the larger national and global macro systems. Religion can both affect and be affected by the globalization processes.

Globalization involves several interdependent processes: structural interdependence of nation-states, synthesis and cross-fertilization of cultures as a modern secularized global culture emerges, a change in socialization to a broader inclusiveness of others as being "like us," and an increase in individualism and reduction of traditional mechanisms of social control. While world systems theory uses conflict theory to stress economic interdependence, Robertson's globalization perspective stresses cultural patterns, including religion.

Theologies of world religions have been influenced by this globalization trend. As people have traded and become increasingly interdependent, liberal theologies have emerged that view other religions as colleagues with similar problems and allow the possibility that other traditions may also offer insights into divine truth. Further, shifts in the membership composition of religious organizations with global constituencies can cause a shift in theological views and ethics, as occurs with the anticapitalist liberation theology of Roman Catholics in third world countries. The Catholic Church finds itself in a dilemma as to whether it should sacralize the social system of its traditional constituency, the affluent Western world, or of its rapidly growing population in the southern hemisphere. In any case, global perspectives seem to be emerging in the theologies of many groups, as diverse groups try to make sense of this new and compelling social reality.

Globalization impacts religion in a number of ways. The emerging global culture is a highly secularized one stressing a rational-utilitarian outlook on the world and calling for institutional differentiation of religion from other spheres. This means that "covenantal relations," characterized by love, commitment, and sacrifice on behalf of others is shrinking as the self-interested utilitarian "contractual relations" of government and economics expand. New communications technologies and worldwide population patterns—urbanization and international migration—have made these trends even more pervasive. In reaction to this and to the compromises to modernism made by liberal theologies, a pattern of rigid and uncompromising revivalistic movements have developed in religions around the world. These revivalistic or "fundamentalist" religions attempt to reclaim sacred authority over a society and culture, combatting ethnocide of their culture by the press of global homogeneity. Some sociologists, then, believe that fundamentalist movements are a result of worldwide trends, not local factors.

Many scholars believe that social systems need either a unifying religious system or a "civil religion." The entire world has no single set of sacred symbols, beliefs, and values that unify all people and that legitimate the growing number of global institutions designed to reduce conflicts and meet human needs. These scholars feel that the lack of any legitimating and solidifying sacred system is a problem in the prospects for world peace.

No other institutions are so explicit about their commitment to peace as religious ones. Christians, for example, claim to follow the "Prince of Peace" and most other world religions give voice to the need for peace. Yet the often exclusive claim to truth and the incredibly powerful we-they sentiments they generate often belie their presumed commitment. If it is peace they want, religious groups often only want it on *their* terms. Once again in this text we learn that if we want to understand religion in society, we must look beyond the official creeds. Just as religion may verbally oppose racism, yet support it in other ways , so

also religion may undermine the conditions that would lead to peace even as it proclaims commitment to it.

Religion is, indeed, a complex phenomenon. It is composed of many parts and is itself one component of yet larger systems. It may contribute to integration or to schism; it may give voice to one set of values, yet undermine those values in other ways; it may elicit the most noble and caring qualities of persons, or it may foster the most hateful and narrow-minded forms of bigotry. Whatever else one may conclude about religion, it is a multifaceted, dynamic, and always interesting part of our social system and of our most intimate personal lives. Its role in the emerging world system is no less intriguing and important.

The Sociological Perspective on Religion: A Concluding Comment

S ociology seeks to understand the social processes of religion. Because the discipline is limited to empirical investigation, it does not address the truth or falsity of a religious system. The researcher adopts a posture of at least temporary agnosticism. Nonetheless, explanations of cause and effect are offered with only empirically identifiable causes being noted. Hence, the effect is apparently to dismiss any supernatural causes. Sociology offers only one lens or one vantage point for understanding religious processes, and it tends to operate within the confines of that vantage point. Other disciplines and other vantage points can offer other insights.

Furthermore, the interpretations of causality that are presented in this book represent the current understandings of sociologists, and the social sciences remain ever open to new data and new perspectives. Like Clifford Geertz's Javanese informants, social scientists are willing to accept a new interpretation if it seems more plausible and if the data support it. The discipline will continue to develop, and new data may prove or disprove theories about religious behavior that now seem plausible. Methods of data collection and data interpre-

tation are constantly being challenged and reassessed. Even the naturalistic bias of empiricism—with its stance of temporary agnosticism—is being challenged in some quarters. This naturalistic bias has caused some scholars to posit an alternative assumption; they have attempted to formulate empirical research procedures and sociological theories that assume the reality and efficacy of the supernatural (Garrett 1974; Poloma 1982a). It remains to be seen whether these efforts will bear fruit or are futile attempts to overcome the innate limitations of an empirical discipline.

Regardless, the meaning of a transcendent dimension of life for individuals can never be fully grasped through objective, scientific study. Margaret Poloma (1982b) insists that scientific empiricism is itself a world view and that the determinism of the social sciences can dull one's sensitivity to the mystical, intuitive, symbolic-imagistic side of life.[1] Milton Yinger states the case eloquently:

---

[1]Robert Wuthnow (1976b) has also treated social science as a world view or an invisible religion. Those interested in pursuing this issue will want to see Michael Polanyi (1946, 1949) as well.

No one would claim that the analysis of paint, painter, and patron exhausts the meaning of art; we are becoming cautious about making equivalent claims for the analysis of religion. The scientist must realize that propositions derived from objective study do not exhaust the meaning of things (1970: 2).

Social psychologist James Vander Zanden (1987) points out that our five senses are limited to certain sensations. We know that there are wavelengths of light that we cannot see and frequencies of sound we cannot hear. Yet we do not deny that they exist. Scientists have now demonstrated that some creatures have sensory capabilities not even available to humans. Birds, for example, are sensitive to changes in barometric pressures and to the earth's magnetic fields, and they can detect high-frequency waves produced by magnetic storms and auroras. Vander Zanden concludes that we must never forget the limitations of our empirical senses: scientists must approach all forms of knowledge with a healthy dose of humility.

With Milton Yinger and Thomas O'Dea, I remain convinced that neither theism nor atheism is inherently unsophisticated. Both are assumptions about the nature of the world that deserve our respect.

The purpose of this text has been neither to destroy the faith of believers nor to make believers out of skeptics. The purpose has been to help readers gain insight into the complexity of religion and the relationship between religion and society. In the process, the views of readers (including their world views) may have been changed or modified. Sometimes the insights of social scientists are unsettling, for they challenge our assumptions about reality. But that is the nature of the search for truth—the seeker must be willing to follow the data wherever they lead. Certainly sociology does not offer the *whole* truth about religion or about any aspect of human life, but sociological investigation can contribute to a *holistic* understanding of human experience—including religious experience. As I suggested in chapter 2, sociological study of religion cannot be proven to be directly beneficial to religious faith, but surely ignorance is more harmful in the long run than is disquieting knowledge. Likewise for nonbelievers, ignorance of this phenomenon—which is so important to many people—leaves a gap that prevents a holistic understanding of human behavior.

Future contributions to the understanding of religion will likely require two characteristics: uncompromising academic rigor and an honest recognition of the limitations of our current knowledge. Certainly, there is much that we do not know about religion and about religious behavior. I only hope that my own fascination with the sociology of religion has been contagious to the readers, and that this brief introduction will serve only as the beginning of a continuing study.

Bibliography

Aberle, David F.
1966   *The Peyote Religion Among the Navaho.*
        Chicago: Aldine.

Adelman, Robert
1987   "Why Do People Watch Religious
        TV? A Uses and Gratifications
        Approach." *Review of Religious Research*
        (December): 199–210.

Adelman, Robert, and Kimberly Neuendorf
1987   "Themes and Topics in Religious
        Television Programming." *Review of
        Religious Research* (December): 152–74.

Adler, Margot
1986   *Drawing Down the Moon: Witches,
        Druids, Goddess-Worshippers and Other
        Pagans in America Today,* revised and
        expanded ed. Boston: Beacon Press.

Alba, Richard D.
1976   "Social Assimilation among
        American Catholic National-Origin
        Groups." *American Sociological Review*
        (December): 1030–46.

Alba, Richard D., and Ronald C. Kessler
1979   "Patterns of Interethnic Marriage
        Among American Catholics." *Social
        Forces* (June): 1124–40.

Allport, Gordon W.
1950   *The Individual and His Religion.* New
        York: Macmillan.
1966   "The Religious Context of
        Prejudice." *Journal for the Scientific
        Study of Religion* (Fall): 447–57.

Alston, Jon P.
1969   "Occupational Placement and
        Mobility of Protestants and
        Catholics, 1953–1964." *Review of
        Religious Research* (Spring): 135–40.

Alston, Jon P., and William Alex McIntosh
1979   "An Assessment of the Determinants
        of Religious Participation." *The
        Sociological Quarterly* (Winter): 49–62.

Ammerman, Nancy
1980   "The Civil Rights Movement and the
        Clergy in a Southern Community."
        Sociological Analysis (Winter): 339–50.
1987   *Bible Believers: Fundamentalists in the
        Modern World.* New Brunswick, N.J.:
        Rutgers University Press.
1990   *Baptist Battles: Social Change and
        Religious Conflict in the Southern Baptist
        Convention.* New Brunswick, N.J.:
        Rutgers University Press.

Anderson, Alan, and Raymond Gordon
1987   "Witchcraft and the Status of
        Women—The Case of England."
        British Journal of Sociology (June):
        171–84.

Anderson, Charles
1970   *White Protestant Americans.* Englewood
        Cliffs, N.J.: Prentice Hall.

Andrews, Edward Deming
1963   *The People Called Shakers,* new
        enlarged ed. New York: Dover.

Anti-Defamation League of B'nai B'rith
1993   *1992 Audit of Anti-Semitic Incidents.* New
        York: Anti-Defamation League of
        B'Nai B'rith.

Argyle, Michael, and Benjamin Beit-Hallahmi
1975   *The Social Psychology of Religion.* Boston:
        Routledge & Kegan Paul.

Arjomand, Said Amir
1989   "The Emergence of Islamic Political
        Ideologies." Pp. 109–123 in *The
        Changing Face of Religion.* Edited by

James A. Beckford and Thomas Luchmann. London: Sage.

Arnold, Eberhard, and Emmy Arnold
1974   *Seeking for the Kingdom of God: Origins of the Bruderhof Communities.* Edited by Heini and Annemarie Arnold. Rifton, N.Y.: Plough.

Assimeng, Max
1987   *Saints and Social Structures.* Jema, Ghana: Ghana Publishing Co.

Baer, Hans A.
1984   *The Black Spiritual Movement: A Religious Response to Racism.* Knoxville: University of Tennessee Press.
1988   "Black Mainstream Churches: Emancipatory or Accomodative Responses to Racism and Social Stratification in American Society?" *Review of Religious Research* (December): 162–76.

Bainbridge, William Sims
1978   *Satan's Power: Ethnography of a Deviant Psychotherapy Cult.* Berkeley: University of California Press.

Bainbridge, William Sims, and Rodney Stark
1979   "Cult Formation: Three Compatible Models." *Sociological Analysis* (Winter): 283–95.
1980a   "Client and Audience Cults in America." *Sociological Analysis* (Fall): 199–214.
1980b   "Scientology: To Be Perfectly Clear." *Sociological Analysis* (Summer): 128–36.
1981   "The Consciousness Reformation Reconsidered." *Journal for the Scientific Study of Religion* (March): 1–15.

Balch, Robert W.
1980   "Looking Behind the Scenes in a Religious Cult: Implications for the Study of Conversion." *Sociological Analysis* (Summer): 137–43.

Balch, Robert W., and David Taylor
1976   "Salvation in a UFO." *Psychology Today* (October): 58–66, 106.
1977   "Seekers and Saucers." *American Behavioral Scientist* (July/August): 839–60.

Ballantine, Jeanne H.
1993   *The Sociology of Education,* 3d ed. Englewood Cliffs, N.J.: Prentice Hall.

Barker, Eileen
1984   *The Making of a Moonie: Brainwashing or Choice?* New York: Basil Blackwell.

Barlow, Philip L.
1991   *Mormons and the Bible: The Place of the Latter-Day Saints in American Religion.* New York: Oxford University Press.

Barnes, Douglas F.
1978   "Charisma and Religious Leadership: An Historical Analysis." *Journal for the Scientific Study of Religion* (March): 1–17.

Barnouw, Victor
1982   *An Introduction to Anthropology: Ethnology,* 4th ed. Homewood, Ill: Dorsey Press.

Baroja, Julio Caro
1964   *The World of the Witches.* Chicago: University of Chicago Press.

Barrish, Gerald, and Michael R. Welch
1980   "Student Religiosity and Discriminatory Attitudes Toward Women." *Sociological Analysis* (Spring): 66–73.

Batson, C. Daniel
1975   "Rational Processing or Rationalization? The Effect of Disconfirming Information on a Stated Religious Belief." *Journal of Personality and Social Psychology* (July): 176–84.
1977   "Experimentation in Psychology of Religion: An Impossible Dream." *Journal for the Scientific Study of Religion* (December): 413–18.
1979   "Experimentation in Psychology of Religion: Living with or in a Dream?" *Journal for the Psychology of Religion* (March): 90–3.

Batson, C. Daniel, Stephen J. Naifeh, and Suzanne Pate
1978   "Social Desirability, Religious Orientation, and Racial Prejudice." *Journal for the Scientific Study of Religion* (March): 31–41.

Batson, C. Daniel, and W. Larry Ventis
1982   *The Religious Experience: A Social-Psychological Perspective.* New York: Oxford University Press.

Bayer, Alan E.
1975   "Sexist Students in American Colleges: A Descriptive Note." *Journal of Marriage and the Family* (May): 391–96.

Beck, Marc
1978   "Pluralist Theory and Church Policy Positions on Racial and Sexual Equality." *Sociological Analysis* (Winter): 338–50.

Becker, Howard
1932   *Systematic Sociology.* New York: Wiley.

Beckford, James A.
1985   *Cult Controversies: The Societal Response to the New Religious Movements.* London: Tavistock.

Beckford, James A., and Thomas Luckmann, eds.
1989   *The Changing Face of Religion.* London: Sage.

Bedell, Kenneth B.
1993   *Yearbook of American and Canadian Churches, 1993.* Nashville: Abingdon.

Bellah, Robert N.
1970a   "Christianity and Symbolic Realism." *Journal for the Scientific Study of Religion* (Summer): 89–96.
1970b   "Civil Religion in America." Pp. 168–215 in *Beyond Belief: Essays on Religion in a Post Industrial World.* New York: Harper & Row.
1970c   "Religious Evolution." Pp. 20–50 in *Beyond Belief: Essays on Religion in a Post Industrial World.* New York: Harper & Row.
1974   "American Civil Religion in the 1970's." Pp. 255–72 in *American Civil Religion.* Edited by Russell E. Richey and Donald G. Jones. New York: Harper Row.
1975   *The Broken Covenant: American Civil Religion in Time of Trial.* New York: Seabury Press.

Bellah, Robert N., and Frederick E. Greenspahn, eds.
1987   *Uncivil Religion: Interreligious Hostility in America.* New York: Crossroad.

Bellah, Robert N., Richard Madsen, William M. Sullivan, Ann Swindler, and Steven M. Tipton
1985   *Habits of the Heart: Individualism and Commitment in American Life.* Berkeley: University of California Press.

Belth, Nathan C.
1979   *A Promise to Keep.* New York: Times Books.

Benedict, Ruth
1934   *Patterns of Culture.* Boston: Houghton Mifflin.

Ben-Yehuda, Nachman
1980   "The European Witch Craze of the 14th to 17th Centuries: A Sociologist's Perspective." *American Journal of Sociology* (July): 1–31.
1985   *Deviance and Moral Boundaries: Witchcraft, the Occult, Science Fiction, Deviant Sciences and Scientists.* Chicago: University of Chicago Press.

Benz, Ernest
1964   "On Understanding Non-Christian Religions." Pp. 3–9 in *Religion, Culture, and Society.* Edited by Louis Schneider. New York: Wiley.

Berger, Peter L.
1961   *The Noise of Solemn Assemblies.* Garden City, N.Y.: Doubleday.
1963   "Charisma and Religious Innovation: The Social Location of Israelite Prophecy." *American Sociological Review* (December): 940–50.
1967   *The Sacred Canopy.* Garden City, N.Y.: Doubleday.
1969   *A Rumor of Angels.* Garden City, N.Y.: Doubleday.
1974   "Some Second Thoughts on Substantive Versus Functional Definitions of Religion." *Journal for the Scientific Study of Religion* (June): 125–33.
1979   *The Heretical Imperative.* Garden City, N.Y.: Anchor Press.

1981   "The Class Struggle in American Religion." *The Christian Century* (February): 194–200.

Berger, Peter L., and Thomas Luckmann
1966   *The Social Construction of Reality.* Garden City, N.Y.: Doubleday.

Bergson, Albert
1980   *Studies of the Modern World-System.* New York: Academic Press.

Berman, Harold J.
1991   "Law and Religion in the Development of a World Order." *Sociological Analysis* (Spring): 27–36.

Berry, Brewton, and Henry L. Tischler
1978   *Race and Ethnic Relations,* 4th ed. Boston: Houghton Mifflin.

Bestor, Arthur
1957   *Backwoods Utopias,* 2d enlarged ed. Philadelphia: University of Pennsylvania Press.

Bianchi, Eugene C., and Rosemary Ruether
1976   *From Machismo to Mutuality: Essays on Sexism and Women-Men Liberation.* New York: Paulist Press.

Bibby, Reginald W.
1978   "Why Conservative Churches Really Are Growing: Kelley Revisited." *Journal for the Scientific Study of Religion* (June): 129–38.
1979   "Religion and Modernity: The Canadian Case." *Journal for the Scientific Study of Religion* (March): 1–17.
1987a   *Fragmented Gods: The Poverty and Potential of Religion in Canada.* Toronto: Irwin.
1987b   "Religion in Canada: A Late Twentieth Century Reading." Pp. 263–67 in *Yearbook of American and Canadian Churches, 1987.* Edited by Constant H. Jacquet Jr. Nashville, Tenn: Abingdon Press.

Bibby, Reginald W., and Merlin B. Brinkerhoff
1973   "The Circulation of the Saints: A Study of People Who Join Conservative Churches." *Journal for the Scientific Study of Religion* (September): 273–83.

1992   "On the Circulatory Problems of Saints: A Response to Perrin and Mauss." *Review of Religious Research* (December): 170–75.

Bird, Frederick, and Bill Reimer
1982   "Participation Rates in New Religious Movements and Para-Religious Movements." *Journal for the Scientific Study of Religion* (March): 1–14.

Bird, Phyllis
1974   "Images of Women in the Old Testament." Pp. 41–88 in *Religion and Sexism.* Edited by Rosemary Radford Ruether. New York: Simon & Schuster.

Black, Alan W.
1985   "Theological Orientation and Breadth of Perspective on Church Members' Attitudes and Behaviors: Roof, Mol, and Kaill Revisited." *Journal for the Scientific Study of Religion* (March): 87–100.

Bonfani, Leo
1971   *The Witchcraft Hysteria of 1692.* Wakefield, Mass: Pride.

Botting, Heather, and Gary Botting
1984   *The Orwellian World of Jehovah's Witnesses.* Toronto: University of Toronto Press.

Bouma, Gary D.
1973   "Beyond Lenski: A Critical Review of Recent Protestant Ethic Research." *Journal for the Scientific Study of Religion* (June): 141–55.
1980   "Keeping the Faithful: Patterns of Membership Retention in the Christian Reformed Church." *Sociological Analysis* (Fall): 259–64.

Bowles, Samuel, and Herbert Gintis
1976:   *Schooling in Capitalist America.* New York: Basic Books.

Bringhurst, Newell G.
1981   *Saints, Slaves, and Blacks: The Changing Place of Black People Within Mormonism.* Westport, Conn: Greenwood Press.

Brinkerhoff, Merlin B., and Reginald W. Bibby
1985   "Circulation of the Saints in South America: A Comparative Study." *Journal for the Scientific Study of Religion* (March): 39–55.

Bromley, David G.
1991   "Satanism: The New Cult Scare." Pp. 49–72 in *The Satanism Scare.* Edited by James T. Richardson, Joel Best, and David G. Bromley. New York: Aldine de Gruyter.

Bromley, David G., and Bruce C. Busching
1988   "Understanding the Structure of Contractual and Covenantal Social Relations: Implications for the Sociology of Religion." *Sociological Analysis* (December): 15S–32S.

Bromley, David G., and Phillip E. Hammond, eds.
1987   *The Future of New Religious Movements.* Macon, Ga: Mercer University Press.

Bromley, David G., and Anson D. Shupe Jr.
1979   *Moonies in America: Cult, Church and Crusade.* Beverly Hills, Calif: Sage.
1980   "The Tnevnoc Cult." *Sociological Analysis* (Winter): 361–66.
1981   *Strange Gods: The Great American Cult Scare.* Boston: Beacon Press.

Buber, Martin
1958   *Hasidism and Modern Man.* Edited and translated by Maurice Friedman. New York: Harper Row.

Buck, Robert Enoch
1993   "Protestantism and Industrialization: An Examination of Three Alternative Models of the Relationship between Religion and Captialism." *Review of Religious Research* (March): 210–24.

Budde, Michael, L.
1992   *The Two Churches: Catholicism and Capitalism in the World System.* Durham, N.C.: Duke University Press.

Bull, Malcolm
1989   "Seventh-Day Adventists: Heretics of American Civil Religion." *Sociological Analysis* (Summer): 177–87.

Bullough, Vem L.
1973   *The Subordinate Sex: A History of Attitudes Toward Women.* Urbana: University of Illinois Press.

Bultmann, Rudolf
1958   *Jesus Christ and Mythology.* New York: Scribner.

Butterfield, Stephen
1985   *Amway: The Cult of Free Enterprise.* Boston: South End Press.

Bynum, Caroline Walker
1986   " '. . . And Woman His Humanity': Female Imagery in the Religious Writing of the Later Middle Ages." Pp. 257–88 in *Gender and Religion.* Edited by C. W. Bynum, S. Harrell, and P. Richman. Boston: Beacon Press.

Bynum, Caroline Walker, Stevan Harrell, and Paula Richman
1986   *Gender and Religion: On the Complexity of Symbols.* Boston: Beacon Press.

Byrne, Donn, and Carl McGraw
1964   "Interpersonal Attraction Toward Negroes." *Human Relations* (August): 201–13.

Byrne, Donn, and Terry J. Wong
1962   "Racial Prejudice, Interpersonal Attraction, and Assumed Dissimilarity of Attitudes." *Journal of Abnormal and Social Psychology* (October): 246–53.

Calvin, John
1952   *Golden Booklet of the True Christian Life.* Translated by Henry J. Van Andel. Grand Rapids, Mich: Baker Book House.

Campbell, Ernest Q., and Thomas F. Pettigrew
1959   *Christians in Racial Crisis.* Washington, D.C.: Public Affairs Press.

Cannon, Walter B.
1942   " 'Voodoo' Death." *American Anthropologist* (April): 169–81.

Carden, Maren Lockwood
1969   *Oneida.* New York: Harper & Row.

Carr, Leslie G., and William H. Hauser
1976   "Anomie and Religiosity: An
        Empirical Re-Examination." *Journal
        for the Scientific Study of Religion*
        (March): 69–74.

Carroll, Jackson, Barbara Hargrove, and Adair T.
    Lummis
1981   *Women of the Cloth.* New York: Harper
        & Row.

Carroll, Jackson, and Wade Clark Roof
1993   *Beyond Establishment: Protestant Identity
        in a Post Protestant Age.* Louisville:
        Westminster/John Knox.

Cauthen, Kenneth
1962   *The Impact of American Religious
        Liberalism.* New York: Harper & Row.

Chalfant, H. Paul, Robert E. Beckley, and C.
    Eddie Palmer
1981   *Religion in Contemporary Society.*
        Sherman Oaks, Calif: Alfred.

Chambers, Patricia Price, and Paul H. Chalfant
1978   "A Changing Role or the Same Old
        Handmaidens: Women's Role in
        Today's Church." *Review of Religious
        Research* (Winter): 192–97.

Christ, Carol P., and Judith Plaskow, eds.
1979   *Womanspirit Rising: A Feminist Reader in
        Religion.* New York: Harper & Row.

Clark, Elizabeth, and Herbert Richardson, eds.
1977   *Women and Religion.* New York: Harper
        & Row.

Cleage, Albert B., Jr.
1968   *The Black Messiah.* New York: Sheed
        and Ward.

Clinebell, Howard J.
1965   *Mental Health Through Christian
        Community.* Nashville, Tenn:
        Abingdon Press.

Cohen, Jere
1985   "Protestant Ethic and
        Status-Attainment." *Sociological
        Analysis* (Spring): 49–57.

Cohen, Steven M.
1983   *American Modernity and Jewish Identity.*
        New York: Tavistock.

Cohn, Norman
1964   "Medieval Millenarism: Its Bearing
        on the Comparative Study of
        Millenarian Movements." Pp.
        168–81 in *Religion, Culture, and Society.*
        Edited by Louis Schneider. New
        York: Wiley.
1975   *Europe's Inner Demons.* New York:
        Basic Books.

Cole, William A., and Phillip E. Hammond
1974   "Religious Pluralism, Legal
        Development, and Societal
        Complexity: Rudimentary Forms of
        Civil Religion." *Journal for the Scientific
        Study of Religion* (June): 177–89.

Coleman, Simon
1993   "Conservative Protestantism and the
        World Order: The Faith Movement in
        the United States and Sweden."
        Sociology of Religion (Winter): 353–73.

Coleman, John A.
1970   "Civil Religion." *Sociological Analysis*
        (Summer): 67–77.

Collins, John J.
1978   *Primitive Religion.* Totowa, N.J.:
        Littlefield, Adams.

Commission for a New Lutheran Church
1984   *Where Are the Lutherans?* Minneapolis:
        Augsburg.

Comte, August
1880   *General View of Positivism,* 2d ed.
        Translated by J. H. Bridges. London:
        Reeves and Turner.

Condran, John G., and Joseph B. Tamney
1985   "Religious 'Nones': 1957 to 1982."
        Sociological Analysis (Winter): 415–24.

Cone, James H.
1969:   *Black Theology and Black Power.* New
        York: Seabury Press.
1970   *Liberation.* Philadelphia: Lippincott.
1972   *The Spirituals and the Blues.* Westport,
        Conn: Greenwood Press.

Conway, Flo, and Jim Siegelman
1978   *Snapping: America's Epidemic of Sudden
        Personality Change.* Philadelphia:
        Lippincott.

Coriden, James A., ed.
1977   *Sexism and Church Law.* New York:
        Paulist Press.

Cornwall, Marie
1987   "The Social Basis of Religion: A Study
        of Factors Influencing Religious Belief
        and Commitment." *Review of Religious
        Research* (September): 44–56.

Coser, Lewis A.
1954   *The Functions of Social Conflict.* New
        York: Free Press.
1967   *Continuities in the Study of Social Conflict.*
        New York: Free Press.

Council on Interracial Books for Children
1982   *Fact Sheets on Institutional Racism.* New
        York: Council on Interracial Books for
        Children.

Cox, Edwin
1967   *Sixth Form Religion.* London: SCM
        Press.

Cox, Harvey
1964   *On Not Leaving It to the Snake.* New
        York: Macmillan.
1965   *The Secular City.* New York: Macmillan.

Cross, Whitney R.
1950   *The Burned Over District: The Social and
        Intellectual History of Enthusiastic Religion
        in Western New York, 1800–1850.* Ithaca,
        N.Y.: Cornell University Press.

Crowley, James W., and James A. Ballweg
1971   "Religious Preference and Worldly
        Success." *Sociological Analysis*
        (Summer): 71–80.

Currie, Elliot P.
1968   "Crimes Without Victims: Witchcraft
        and Its Control in Renaissance
        Europe." *Law and Society Review* (3):
        7–32.

Daly, Mary
1968   *The Church and the Second Sex.* New
        York: Harper Row.
1970   "Women and the Catholic Church."
        Pp. 124–38 in *Sisterhood Is Powerful.*
        Edited by Robin Morgan. New York:
        Vintage Books.

D'Antonio, William, James Davidson, Dean
    Hoge, and Ruth Wallace
1989   *American Catholic Laity in a Changing
        Church.* Kansas City, Mo: Sheed and
        Ward.

Darley, J. M., and C. Daniel Batson
1973   "From Jerusalem to Jericho: A Study
        of Situational and Dispositional
        Variables in Helping Behavior."
        *Journal of Personality and Social
        Psychology* (July): 100–108.

Davidman, Lynn
1990   "Accomodation and Resistence to Mo-
        dernity: A Comparision of Two Con-
        temporary Orthodox Jewish Groups."
        Sociological Analysis (Spring): 35–51.

Davidson, James D.
1975   "Glock's Model of Religious
        Commitment: Assessing Some
        Different Approaches and Results."
        Review of Religious Research (Winter):
        83–93.
1977   "Socio-Economic Status and Ten
        Dimensions of Religious
        Commitment." *Sociology and Social
        Research* (July): 462–85.
1985   *Mobilizing Social Movement
        Organizations.* Storrs, Conn: Society
        for the Scientific Study of Religion.

Davidson, James D., and Dean D. Knudsen
1977   "A New Approach to Religious
        Commitment." *Sociological Focus*
        (April): 151–73.

Davis, Kingsley
1949   *The Human Society.* New York:
        Macmillan.

Davis, Rex, and James T. Richardson
1976   "The Organization and Functioning
        of the Children of God." *Sociological
        Analysis* (Winter): 321–39.

Dawson, Lorne
1990   "Self-Affirmation, Freedom, and
        Rationality: Theoretically Elaborating
        'Active' Conversions." *Journal for the
        Scientific Study of Religion* (June):
        141–63.

DeJong, Gordon F., Joseph E. Faulkner, and Rex H. Warland
1976   "Dimensions of Religiosity Reconsidered: Evidence From a Cross-Cultural Study." *Social Forces* (June): 866–90.

Demerath, N.J., III
1965   *Social Class in American Protestantism.* Chicago: Rand McNally.

Dempewolff, J. A.
1974   "Some Correlates of Feminism." *Psychological Reports* (April): 671–76.

Deutscher, Irwin
1966   "Words and Deeds: Social Science and Social Policy." *Social Problems* (Winter): 235–54.
1973   *What We Say, What We Do.* Glenview, Ill: Scott, Foresman.

De Vaux, Roland
1961   *Ancient Israel,* 2 vols. New York: McGraw-Hill.

Ditman, Keith S., Max Hayman, and John R. B. Whittlesay
1962   "Nature and Frequency of Claims Following LSD." *Journal of Nervous and Mental Disease* (April): 134, 336–52.

Dolan, Jay P.
1975   *The Immigrant Church: New York's Irish and German Catholics, 1815–1865.* South Bend, Ind: Notre Dame University Press.

Doress, Irvin, and Jack Nusan Porter
1978   "Kids in Cults." *Society* (May/June): 69–71.

Douglas, Mary
1966   *Purity and Danger.* London: Routledge and Kegan Paul.
1968   "Pollution." Pp. 336–41 in *International Encyclopedia of the Social Sciences, Vol. XII.* Edited by David Sills. New York: Macmillan and Free Press.

Douglass, Jane Dempsey
1974   "Women and the Continental Reformation." Pp. 292–318 in *Religion and Sexism.* Edited by Rosemary Radford Ruether. New York: Simon & Schuster.

Downton, James V., Jr.
1979   *Sacred Journeys: The Conversion of Young Americans to Divine Light Mission.* New York: Columbia University Press.
1980   "An Evolutionary Theory of Spiritual Conversion and Commitment: The Case of Divine Light Mission." *Journal for the Scientific Study of Religion* (December): 381–96.

Dunlap, Knight
1946   *Religion: Its Function in Human Life.* New York: McGraw-Hill.

Durkheim, Emile
1965   *The Elementary Forms of the Religious Life.* Translated by Joseph Ward Swain. New York: Free Press. (Originally published in London: George Allen and Unwin, 1915.)

Duska, Ronald, and Mariellen Whelan
1975   *Moral Development: A Guide to Piaget and Kohlberg.* New York: Paulist Press.

Dynes, Russell R.
1955   "Church-Sect Typology and Socioeconomic Status." *American Sociological Review* (October): 555–60.

Ebaugh, Helen Rose Fuchs, and Sharron Lee Vaughn
1984   "Ideology and Recruitment in Religious Groups." *Review of Religious Research* (December): 148–57.

Eddy, Mary Baker G.
1886   *Science and Health with Keys to the Scriptures,* 19th ed., revised. Boston: Published by the author.

Edwards, Jonathan
1966   *Jonathan Edwards: Basic Writings.* Edited by Ola Elizabeth Winslow. New York: New American Library.

Eichler, Margrit
1972   *Charismatic and Ideological Leadership in Secular and Religious Millenarian Movements: A Sociological Study.* Ph.D. dissertation, Duke University. Ann Arbor, Mich: University Microfilms.

Eister, Allan W.
1967   "Toward a Radical Critique of Church-Sect Typologizing." *Journal for the Scientific Study of Religion* (April): 85–90.

Eliade, Mircea
1959   *The Sacred and the Profane: The Nature of Religion.* Translated by Willard R. Trask. New York: Harcourt, Brace World.

Elias, Nicholas M.
1984:   *The Divine Liturgy Explained.* Athens: Astir Publishers.

Enslin, Morton S.
1930   *The Ethics of St. Paul.* New York: Harper & Row.

Erikson, Erik H.
1963   *Childhood and Society,* 2d ed. New York: Norton.

Erikson, Kai
1966   *Wayward Puritans.* New York: Wiley.

Estus, Charles, and Michael A. Overington
1970   "The Meaning and End of Religiosity." *American Journal of Sociology* (March): 760–78.

Evans-Prichard, E. E.
1937   *Witchcraft, Oracles, and Magic Among the Azande.* Oxford, England: Clarendon Press.

Fabian, Stephen Michael
1992   *Space-time of the Bororo of Brazil.* Gainesville: University Press of Florida.

Fallding, Harold
1980   "An Overview of Mainline Protestantism in Canada and the United States of America." Pp. 249–57 in *Yearbook of American and Canadian Churches, 1980.* Edited by Constant H. Jacquet Jr. Nashville, Tenn: Abingdon.

Famighetti, Robert, ed.
1993   *World Almanac and Book of Facts, 1994.* Mahway, N.J.: World Almanac.

Fanfani, Amintore
1936   *Catholicism, Protestantism, and Capitalism.* New York: Sheed and Ward.

Farber, I. E., Harry F. Harlow, and Louis Jolyon West
1951   "Brainwashing, Conditioning, and D. D. D. (Debility, Dependency, and Dread)." *Sociometry* (December): 271–83.

Farley, John E.
1988   *Majority-Minority Relations,* 2d ed. Englewood Cliffs, N.J.: Prentice Hall.

Fauset, Arthur H.
1944   *Black Gods of the Metropolis.* Philadelphia: University of Pennsylvania Press.

Feagin, Joe R., and Clairece Booher Feagin
1986   *Discrimination American Style.* Malabar, Fla: Krieger.

Featherman, David L.
1971   "The Socioeconomic Achievement of White Religio-Ethnic Sub-Groups: Social and Psychological Explanations." *American Sociological Review* (April): 207–22.

Fenton, John H.
1960   *The Catholic Vote.* New Orleans: Hauser.

Ferguson, Marilyn
1987   *The Aquarian Conspiracy.* Los Angeles: J. P. Tarcher.

Festinger, Leon, Henry W. Riecken, and Stanley Schachter
1956   *When Prophecy Fails.* New York: Harper & Row.

Fichter, Joseph
1954   *Social Relations in the Urban Parish.* Chicago: University of Chicago Press.

Fichter, Joseph H., ed.
1983   *Alternatives to American Mainline Churches.* New York: Rose of Sharon Press.

Findlay, Alexander
1948   *A Hundred Years of Chemistry,* 2d ed. London: Duckworth.

Finke, Roger, and Rodney Stark
1986   "Turning Pews into People: Estimating 19th Century Church Membership." *Journal for the Scientific Study of Religion* (June): 180–92.
1988   "Religious Economies and Sacred Canopies: Religious Mobilization in American Cities, 1906." *American Sociological Review* (February): 41–49.
1992   *The Churching of America, 1776–1990: Winners and Losers in Our Religious*

Economy. New Brunswick, N.J.:
Rutgers University Press.

Fisher, Miles Mark
1953   *Negro Slave Songs in the United States.*
New York: Citadel.

Fitzgerald, Frances
1981   "A Reporter at Large: A Disciplined,
Charging Army." *The New Yorker*
(May 18): 53–141.

Forell, George W.
1966   *Christian Social Teachings.* Minneapolis:
Augsburg.

Foster, Thomas W.
1984   "Separation and Survival in Amish
Society." *Sociological Focus* (January):
1–16.

Fowler, Floyd J.
1977   *1975 Community Survey: A Study of the
Jewish Population of Greater Boston.*
Boston: Combined Jewish
Philanthropies of Greater Boston.

Fowler, James W.
1981   *Stages of Faith.* San Francisco: Harper
& Row.

Fox, William S., and Elton F. Jackson
1973   "Protestant-Catholic Differences in
Educational Achievement and Persistence in Schools." *Journal for the Scientific Study of Religion* (March): 65–84.

Frankl, Razelle
1983   "Charisma and Old Time Religion in
the Electric Church." Paper presented
at the annual meeting of the Society
for the Scientific Study of Religion.
Knoxville, Tenn.
1987   *Televangelism: The Marketing of Popular
Religion.* Carbondale: Southern
Illinois University Press.

Frankl, Viktor E.
1962   *Man's Search for Meaning,* revised ed.
New York: Simon & Schuster.
1967   *Psychotherapy and Existentialism.* New
York: Simon & Schuster.

Frazier, E. Franklin
1957   *Negroes in the United States,* revised ed.
New York: Macmillan.

1963   *The Negro Church in America.* New
York: Schocken Books.

Fredman, Ruth Gruber
1981   *The Passover Seder.* Philadelphia:
University of Pennsylvania Press.

Fry, John R.
1975   *The Trivialization of the Presbyterian
Church.* New York: Harper & Row.

Fukuyama, Yoshio
1961   "The Major Dimensions of Church
Membership." *Review of Religious
Research* (Spring): 154–61.

Gaddy, Gary
1984   "The Power of the Religious Media:
Religious Broadcast Use and the Role
of Religious Organizations in Public
Affairs." *Review of Religious Research*
(June): 289–302.

Gaddy, Gary, and David Prichard
1985   "When Watching TV Is Like
Attending Church." *Journal of
Communication* (Winter): 123–31.

Gaede, Stan
1977   "Religious Affiliation, Social
Mobility, and the Problem of
Causality: A Methodological Critique
of Catholic-Protestant Socioeconomic
Achievement Studies." *Review of
Religious Research* (Fall): 54–62.

Galanter, Mark, Richard Rabkin, Judith Rabkin,
and Alexander Deutsch
1979   "The Moonies: A Psychosocial Study
of Conversion and Membership in a
Contemporary Religious Sect."
American Journal of Psychiatry
(February): 165–70.

The Gallup Poll
1987   *The Gallup Report: Religion in America.*
Princeton, N.J.: The Gallup
Organization.

Gamoran, Adam
1990   "Civil Religion in America's Schools."
Sociological Analysis (Fall): 235–56.

Garrett, William R.
1974   "Troublesome Transcendence: The Supernatural in the Scientific Study of

Religion." *Sociological Analysis*
(Autumn): 167–80.

Garrett, William R. and Roland Robertson
1991   "Religion and Globalization: An
Introduction." Pp. ix–xxiii in *Religion
and Global Order*. Edited by Roland
Robertson and William R Garrett.
New York: Paragon.

Geertz, Clifford
1957   "Ritual and Social Change: A
Javanese Example." *American
Anthropologist* (February): 32–54.
1958   "Ethos, World View and the Analysis
of Sacred Symbols." *The Antioch
Review* (Winter): 421–37.
1966   "Religion as a Cultural System." Pp.
1–46 in *Anthropological Approaches to
the Study of Religion*. Edited by
Michael Banton. London: Tavistock.
1968   *Islam Observed: Religious Development in
Morocco and Indonesia*. Chicago:
University of Chicago Press.

Gerbner, George, Larry Gross, Stuart Hoover,
Michael Morgan, Nancy Signorilli, Harry
Cotugno, and Robert Wuthnow
1984   *Religion and Television*. Philadelphia:
University of Pennsylvania and The
Gallup Organization.

Gill, Sam D.
1982   *Native American Religions*. Belmont,
Calif: Wadsworth.

Gilligan, Carol
1982   *In A Different Voice*. Cambridge, Mass:
Harvard University Press.

Glazer, Nathan
1957   *American Judaism*. Chicago: University
of Chicago Press.

Glenn, Norval
1964   "Negro Religion and Negro Status in
the United States." Pp. 623–39 in
Religion, Culture, and Society. Edited by
Louis Schneider. New York: Wiley.

Glenn, Norval D., and Ruth Hyland
1967   "Religious Preference and Worldly
Success: Some Evidence from
National Surveys." *American
Sociological Review* (February): 73–85.

Glock, Charles Y.
1959   "The Religious Revival in America."
Pp. 25–42 in *Religion and the Face of
America*. Edited by Jane Zahn.
Berkeley: University of California
Press.

Glock, Charles Y., ed.
1973   *Religion in Sociological Perspective: Essays
in the Empirical Study of Religion*.
Belmont, Calif: Wadsworth.

Glock, Charles Y., and Rodney Stark
1965   *Religion and Society in Tension*. Chicago:
Rand McNally.
1966   *Christian Beliefs and Anti-Semitism*. New
York: Harper & Row.

Gluckman, Max
1965   *Politics, Law, and Ritual in Tribal Society*.
Oxford, England: Basil Blackwell.

Gmelch, George J.
1971   "Baseball Magic." *Transaction* (June):
39–41, 54.

Gockel, Galen L.
1969   "Income and Religious Affiliation: A
Regression Analysis." *American
Journal of Sociology* (May): 632–47.

Goen, C. C.
1970   "Fundamentalism in America." Pp.
85–93 in *American Mosaic*. Edited by
Phillip E. Hammond and Benton
Johnson. New York: Random House.

Goldman, Ronald
1964   *Religious Thinking from Childhood to
Adolescence*. New York: Seabury Press.
1965   *Readiness for Religion*. New York:
Seabury Press.

Goldscheider, Calvin, and Alan S. Zuckerman
1984   *The Transformation of the Jews*. Chicago:
University of Chicago Press.

Goldstein, Sidney
1969   "Socio-Economic Differentials
Among Religious Groups in the
United States." *American Journal of
Sociology* (May): 612–31.

Goode, Erich
1967   "Some Critical Observations on the
Church-Sect Typology." *Journal for the*

Scientific Study of Religion (April): 69–77.

Gorsuch, Richard L., and Daniel Aleshire
1974   "Christian Faith and Ethnic Prejudice: A Review and Interpretation of Research." *Journal for the Scientific Study of Religion* (September): 281–307.

Graham, Billy
1983   "The Future of T.V. Evangelism." *TV Guide* (March): 4–11.

Greeley, Andrew M.
1963   *Religion and Career: A Study of College Graduates.* New York: Sheed and Ward.
1969a "Continuities in Research on the Religious Factor." *American Journal of Sociology* (November): 355–59.
1969b *Religion in the Year 2000.* New York: Sheed and Ward.
1970   "Comment on Educational Expectations." *American Sociological Review* (September): 917–18.
1971   *Why Can't They Be like Us?* New York: Dutton.
1972   *The Denominational Society.* Glenview, Ill: Scott, Foresman.
1974   *Ethnicity in the United States.* New York: Wiley.
1981   "Catholics and the Upper Middle Class: A Comment on Roof." *Social Forces* (March): 824–30.
1989   *Religious Change in America.* Cambridge, Mass: Harvard University Press.

Green, Charles W., and Cindy L. Hoffman
1989   "Stages of Faith and Perceptions of Similar and Dissimilar Others." *Review of Religious Research* (March): 246–54.

Green, Robert W., ed.
1959   *Protestantism and Capitalism: The Weber Thesis and Its Critics.* Boston: Heath.

Greil, Arthur L., and David R. Rudy
1984   "What Have We Learned from Process Models of Conversion? An Examination of Ten Case Studies." *Sociological Focus* (October): 305–23.

Griffin, Glenn A., Richard L. Gorsuch, and Andrea Lee Davis
1987   "A Cross-Cultural Investigation of Religious Orientation, Social Norms, and Prejudice." *Journal for the Scientific Study of Religion* (September): 358–65.

Gusfield, J. R.
1963   *Symbolic Crusade: Status Politics and the American Temperance Movement.* Chicago: University of Chicago Press.

Hadaway, Christopher Kirk
1978   "Life Satisfaction and Religion: A Reanalysis." *Social Forces* (December): 636–43.
1980   "Denominational Switching and Religiosity." *Review of Religious Research* (Supplement): 451–61.

Hadaway, C. Kirk, and Wade Clark Roof
1979   "Those Who Stay Religious 'Nones' and Those Who Don't: A Research Note." *Journal for the Scientific Study of Religion* (June): 194–200.

Hadaway, C. Kirk, and Penny Long Marler
1993   "All in the Family: Religious Mobility in America." *Review of Religious Research* (December): 97–116.

Hadaway, C. Kirk, Penny Long Marler, and Mark Chaves
1993   "What the Polls Don't Show: A Closer Look at U.S. Church Attendance." *American Sociological Review* (December): 741–52.

Hadden, Jeffrey K.
1969   *The Gathering Storm in the Churches.* Garden City, N.Y.: Doubleday.
1987   "Religious Broadcasting and the New Christian Right." *Journal for the Scientific Study of Religion* (March): 1–24.
1991   "The Globalization of American Televangelism." Pp. 221–244 in *Religion and Global Order.* Edited by Roland Robertson and William R. Garrett. New York: Paragon.
1993   "The Rise and Fall of American Televangelism." *The Annals of the American Academy of Political and Social Science* (May): 113–30.

Hadden, Jeffrey K., and Razelle Frankl
1987   "Star Wars of a Different Kind: Reflections on the Politics of the Religion and Television Project." *Review of Religious Research* (December): 101–10.

Hadden, Jeffrey K., and Raymond C. Rymph
1973   "Social Structure and Civil Rights Involvement: A Case Study of Protestant Ministers." Pp. 149–62 in *Religion in Sociological Perspective*. Edited by Charles Y. Glock. Belmont, Calif: Wadsworth.

Hadden, Jeffrey K., and Anson Shupe
1988   *Televangelism: Power and Politics on God's Frontier*. New York: Holt.

Hadden, Jeffrey K., and Anson Shupe, eds.
1986   *Prophetic Religions and Politics*. New York: Paragon.
1989   *Secularization and Fundamentalism Reconsidered*. New York: Paragon.

Hadden, Jeffrey K., and Charles K. Swann
1981   *Prime Time Preachers: The Rising Power of Televangelism*. Reading, Mass: Addison-Wesley.

Hammond, Phillip E.
1987   "Cultural Consequences of Cults." Pp. 261–73 in *The Future of New Religious Movements*. Edited by David G. Bromley and Phillip E. Hammond. Macon, Ga: Mercer University Press.

Hammond, Phillip E., Luis Salinas, and Douglas Sloane
1978   "Types of Clergy Authority: Their Measurement, Location and Effects." *Journal for the Scientific Study of Religion* (September): 241–54.

Hammond, Phillip E., and Kirk R. Williams
1976   "The Protestant Ethic Thesis: A Social Psychological Assessment." *Social Forces* (March): 579–89.

Hargrove, Barbara
1979   *The Sociology of Religion*. Arlington Heights, Ill: AHM Publishing.

Hartley, Eugene L.
1946   *Problems in Prejudice*. New York: King's Crown Press.

Hartman, Warren J.
1976   *Membership Trends: A Study of Decline and Growth in the United Methodist Church, 1949–1975*. Nashville, Tenn: Discipleship Resources.

Haugk, Kenneth
1976   "Unique Contributions of Churches and Clergy to Community Mental Health." *Community Mental Health Journal* (12): 20–28.

Hawley, John Stratton
1986   "Images of Gender in the Poetry of Krishna." Pp. 231–56 in *Gender and Religion*. Edited by C. W. Bynum, S. Harrell, and P. Richman. Boston: Beacon Press.

Hay, David, and Ann Morisey
1978   "Reports of Ecstatic, Paranormal or Religious Experience in the U.S. and Great Britain—A Comparison of Trends." *Journal for the Scientific Study of Religion* (September): 255–68.

Henley, Nancy M., and Fred Pincus
1978   "Interrelationship of Sexist, Racist and Homosexual Attitudes." *Psychological Reports* (February): 83–90.

Herberg, Will
1955   *Protestant-Catholic-Jew*. Garden City, N.Y.: Doubleday.
1974   "America's Civil Religion: What It Is and Whence It Comes." Pp. 76–88 in *American Civil Religion*. Edited by Russell E. Richey and Donald G. Jones. New York: Harper & Row.

Herren, John, Donald B. Lindsey, and Marylee Mason
1984   "The Mormon Concept of Mother in Heaven: A Sociological Account of Its Origins and Development." *Journal for the Scientific Study of Religion* (December): 396–411.

Herskovits, Melville
1958   *The Myth of the Negro Past*. Boston: Beacon Press.

Hesselbart, Susan
1976   "A Comparison of Attitudes Toward Women and Attitudes Toward Blacks

in a Southern City." *Sociological Symposium* (Fall): 45–68.

Hesser, Gary, and Andrew J. Weigert
1980   "Comparative Dimensions of Liturgy: A Conceptual Framework and Feasibility Application." *Sociological Analysis* (Fall): 215–29.

Hills, Stuart L.
1980   *Demystifying Social Deviance.* New York: McGraw-Hill.

Himmelstein, Jerome L.
1986   "The Social Basis of Antifeminism: Religious Networks and Culture." *Journal for the Scientific Study of Religion* (March): 1–15.

Hoch-Smith, Judith
1978   "Radical Yoruba Female Sexuality: The Witch and the Prostitute." Pp. 245–67 in *Women in Ritual and Symbolic Roles.* Edited by Judith Hoch-Smith and Anita Spring. New York: Plenum Press.

Hoch-Smith, Judith, and Anita Spring, eds.
1978   *Women in Ritual and Symbolic Roles.* New York: Plenum Press.

Hofstadter, Richard
1963   *Anti-Intellectualism in American Life.* New York: Vintage.

Hoge, Dean R.
1981   *Converts, Dropouts, Returnees: A Study of Religious Change Among Catholics.* New York: Pilgrim Press.

Hoge, Dean R., and Jackson W. Carroll
1973   "Religiosity and Prejudice in Northern and Southern Churches." *Journal for the Scientific Study of Religion* (June): 181–97.
1975   "Christian Beliefs, Nonreligious Factors, and Anti-Semitism." *Social Forces* (June): 581–94.
1978   "Determinants of Commitment and Participation in Surburban Protestant Churches." *Journal for the Scientific Study of Religion* (June): 107–28.

Hoge, Dean R., and David A. Roozen
1979   *Understanding Church Growth and Decline, 1950–1978.* New York: Pilgrim Press.

Holloway, Mark
1966   *Heavens on Earth,* 2d ed. New York: Dover.

Homans, George C.
1941   "Anxiety and Ritual: The Theories of Malinowski and Radcliffe-Brown." *American Anthropologist* (April): 164–72.

Homola, Michael, Dean Knudsen, and Harvey Marshall
1987   "Religion and Socioeconomic Achievement." *Journal for the Scientific Study of Religion* (June): 201–17.

Hood, Ralph W.
1970   "Religious Orientation and the Report of Religious Experience." *Journal for the Scientific Study of Religion* (Winter): 285–91.
1978   "The Usefulness of the Indiscriminately Pro and Anti Categories of Religious Orientation." *Journal for the Scientific Study of Religion* (December): 419–31.

Hoover, Stewart M.
1987   "The Religious Television Audience: A Matter of Significance, or Size?" *Review of Religious Research* (December): 135–51.

Hostetler, John A.
1980   *Amish Society,* 3d ed. Baltimore: Johns Hopkins University Press.

Hudson, Winthrop S.
1949   "Puritanism and the Spirit of Capitalism." *Church History* (March): 3–17.
1973   *Religion in America,* 2d ed. New York: Scribner.

Hunt, Larry L., and Janet G. Hunt
1977   "Black Religion as Both Opiate and Inspiration of Civil Rights Militance: Putting Marx's Data to the Test." *Social Forces* (September): 1–14.

Hunt, Richard A.
1972   "Mythological-Symbolic Religious Commitment: The LAM Scales." *Journal for the Scientific Study of Religion* (March): 45–52.

Hunter, James Davidson
    1983   *American Evangelicalism.* New
            Brunswick, N.J.: Rutgers University
            Press.

Jackson, Elton F., William S. Fox, and Harry J.
    Crockett Jr.
    1970   "Religion and Occupational
            Achievement." *American Sociological
            Review* (February): 48–63.

Jacobs, Janet
    1987   "Deconversion from Religious Move-
            ments." *Journal for the Scientific Study of
            Religion* (September): 294–308.

Jacobs, Jerry
    1971   "From Sacred to Secular: The
            Rationalization of Christian
            Theology." *Journal for the Scientific
            Study of Religion* (Spring): 1–9.

Jacobson, Cardell K., Tim B. Heaton, and Rut-
    ledge M. Dennis
    1990   "Black and White Differences in
            Religiosity: Item Analysis and a
            Formal Structural Test." *Sociological
            Analysis* (Fall): 257–70.

Jacquet, Constant H., Jr., ed.
    1969   *Yearbook of American and Canadian
            Churches.* New York: National Council
            Press.
    1980   *Yearbook of American and Canadian
            Churches.* Nashville, Tenn: Abingdon.
    1982   *Yearbook of American and Canadian
            Churches.* Nashville, Tenn: Abingdon.
    1987   *Yearbook of American and Canadian
            Churches.* Nashville, Tenn: Abingdon.

James, Janet Wilson, ed.
    1980   *Women in American Religion.*
            Philadelphia: University of
            Pennsylvania Press.

James, William
    1958   *Varieties of Religious Experience.* New
            York: New American Library.
            (Originally published in 1902.)

Jenkins, J. Craig
    1977   "Radical Transformation of
            Organizational Goals." *Administrative
            Science Quarterly* (December): 568–86.

Jewett, Paul K.
    1980   *The Ordination of Women.* Grand
            Rapids, Mich: Eerdmans.

Johnson, Benton
    1961   "Do Holiness Sects Socialize in
            Dominant Values?" *Social Forces*
            (May): 309–16.
    1963   "On Church and Sect." *American
            Sociological Review* (August): 539–49.
    1979   "A Fresh Look at Theories of
            Secularization." Paper presented to
            the American Sociological
            Association. Boston, August 27,
            1979.

Johnson, Martin, and Phil Mullins
    1992   "Mormonism: Catholic, Protestant,
            Different?" *Review of Religious Research*
            (September): 51–62.

Johnson, Paul E.
    1959   *Psychology of Religion,* revised and
            enlarged ed. Nashville, Tenn:
            Abingdon Press.

Johnson, Stephen D., and Joseph B. Tamney
    1985   "The Christian Right and the 1984
            Presidential Election." *Review of
            Religious Research* (December): 124–33.

Johnstone, Ronald L.
    1975   *Religion and Society in Interaction.*
            Englewood Cliffs, N.J.: Prentice Hall.

Jones, W. T.
    1972   "World Views: Their Nature and
            Their Function." *Current Anthropology*
            (February): 79–109.

Jordan, Winthrop D.
    1968   *White over Black.* Baltimore: Penguin.

Judah, J. Stillson
    1974   *Hare Krishna and the Counterculture.*
            New York: Wiley.

Kahoe, Richard D.
    1974   "The Psychology and Theology of
            Sexism." *Journal of Psychology and
            Theology* (Fall): 284–90.

Kanter, Rosabeth Moss
    1972   *Commitment and Community.*
            Cambridge, Mass: Harvard
            University Press.

Kearney, Michael
  1984   *World View.* Novato, Calif: Chandler and Sharp.

Kelley, Dean M.
  1972   *Why Conservative Churches Are Growing.* New York: Harper & Row.
  1978   "Comment: Why Conservative Churches Are Still Growing." *Journal for the Scientific Study of Religion* (June): 165–72.

Kelsey, George D.
  1965   *Racism and the Christian Understanding of Man.* New York: Scribner.

Kephart, William M.
  1991   *Extraordinary Groups: An Examination of Unconventional Life-Styles,* 4th ed. New York: St. Martin's Press.

Kilbourne, Brook, and James T. Richardson
  1989   "Paradigm Conflict, Types of Conversion, and Conversion Theories." *Sociological Analysis* (Spring): 1–21.

Kim, Hei C.
  1977   "The Relationship of Protestant Ethic Beliefs and Values to Achievement." *Journal for the Scientific Study of Religion* (September): 255–62.

King, Ursula
  1987   *Women in the World's Religions: Past and Present.* New York: Paragon.

Kitchener, Karen S.
  1986   "The Reflective Judgment Model: Characteristics, Evidence, and Measurement." Pp. 76–91 in *Adult Cognitive Development: Methods and Models.* Edited by Robert A. Mines and Karen S. Kitchener. New York: Praeger.

Kluckhohn, Clyde
  1972   "Myths and Rituals: A General Theory." Pp. 93–105 in *Reader in Comparative Religion: An Anthropological Approach,* 3d ed. Edited by William A. Lessa and Evon Z. Vogt. New York: Harper & Row.

Knudsen, Dean D., John R. Earle, and Donald W. Schriver Jr.

  1978   "The Conception of Sectarian Religion: An Effort at Clarification." *Review of Religious Research* (Fall): 44–60.

Kochman, Thomas
  1981   *Black and White Styles in Conflict.* Chicago: University of Chicago Press.

Koestler, Arthur
  1964   *The Act of Creation.* New York: Macmillan.

Kohlberg, Lawrence
  1971   "From Is to Ought." Pp. 151–284 in *Cognitive Development and Epistemology.* Edited by T. Mischel. New York: Academic Press.
  1980   "Educating for a Just Society: An Updated and Revised Statement." Pp. 455–70 in *Moral Development, Moral Education, and Kohlberg.* Edited by Brenda Munsey. Birmingham, Ala: Religious Education Press.

Kohn, Melvin L.
  1969   *Class and Conformity: A Study in Values.* Homewood, Ill: Dorsey Press.

Korpi, Michael F., and Kyong Liong Kim
  1986   "The Uses and Effects of Televangelism: A Factorial Model of Support and Contribution." *Journal for the Scientific Study of Religion* (December): 410–23.

Kosmin, Berry A., and Seymour P. Lachman
  1993   *One Nation Under God: Religion in Contemporary American Society.* New York: Harmony.

Kottak, Conrad Phillip
  1990   *Prime-Time Society: An Anthropological Analysis of Television and Culture.* Belmont, Calif: Wadsworth.

Kovel, Joel
  1970   *White Racism: A Psychohistory.* New York: Pantheon Books.

Kox, William, Wim Meeus, and Hart Harm't
  1991   "Religious Conversion of Adolescents: Testing the Lofland and Stark Model of Religious Conversion." *Sociological Analysis* (Fall): 227–40.

Kwilecki, Susan
  1988   "A Scientific Approach to Religious
          Development: Proposals and a Case
          Illustration." *Journal for the Scientific
          Study of Religion* (September): 307–25.

LaBarre, Weston
  1962   *They Shall Take Up Serpents: Psychology
          of the Southern Snake-Handling Cult.*
          New York: Schocken Books.
  1964   *The Peyote Cult,* enlarged ed. New
          York: Schocken Books.
  1972   *The Ghost Dance.* New York: Dell.

Land, Gary, ed.
  1987   *Adventism in America.* Grand Rapids,
          Mich: Eerdmans.

Landis, Benson Y., ed.
  1965   *Yearbook of American Churches.* New
          York: National Council Press.

Lanning, Kenneth
  1989   "Satanic, Occult, Ritualistic Crime: A
          Law Enforcement Perspective." *The
          Police Chief* (56): 62–83.

Larner, Christina
  1984   *Witchcraft and Religion; The Politics of
          Popular Belief.* New York: Basil
          Blackwell.

Leach, Edmund R.
  1972   "Ritualization in Man in Relation to
          Conceptual and Social
          Development." Pp. 333–37 in *Reader
          in Comparative Religion,* 3d ed. Edited
          by William A. Lessa and Evon Z.
          Vogt. New York: Harper & Row.

Lechner, Frank L.
  1991   "Religion, Law, and Global Order."
          Pp. 263–80 in *Religion and Global
          Order.* Edited by Roland Robertson
          and William R. Garrett. New York:
          Paragon.

Lee, Dallas
  1971   *The Cotton Patch Evidence.* New York:
          Harper & Row.

Lee, Gary R., and Robert W. Clyde
  1974   "Religion, Socioeconomic Status, and
          Anomie." *Journal for the Scientific Study
          of Religion* (June): 35–47.

Lee, Richard Wayne
  1992   "Christianity and the Other
          Religions: Interreligious Relations in
          a Shrinking World." *Sociological
          Analysis* (Summer): 125–39.

Lehman, Edward C., Jr.
  1980   "Patterns of Lay Resistance to
          Women in Ministry." *Sociological
          Analysis* (Winter): 317–38.
  1981   "Organizational Resistance to Women
          in Ministry." *Sociological Analysis*
          (Summer): 101–18.
  1985   *Women Clergy: Breaking Through Gender
          Barriers.* New Brunswick, N.J.:
          Transaction Books.
  1987a   "Sexism, Organizational Maintenance,
          and Localism: A Research Note." *Socio-
          logical Analysis* (Fall): 274–82.
  1987b   "Research on Lay Member's Attitudes
          Toward Women in Ministry: An As-
          sessment." *Review of Religious Research*
          (June): 319–29.
  1993   *Gender and Work: The Case of the Clergy.*
          Albany: State University of New
          York Press.

Lenski, Gerhard
  1963   *The Religious Factor,* revised ed. Garden
          City, N.Y.: Doubleday.

Lenski, Gerhard, and Jean Lenski
  1978   *Human Societies,* 3d ed. New York:
          McGraw-Hill.

Levine, Saul V.
  1984a   "Radical Departures." *Psychology
          Today* (August): 20–27.
  1984b   *Radical Departures: Desperate Detours to
          Growing Up.* San Diego: Harcourt
          Brace Jovanovich.

Lewis, James R.
  1986   "Reconstructing the 'Cult'
          Experience: Past Involvement
          Attitudes as a Function of Mode of
          Exit and Post-Involvement
          Socialization." *Sociological Analysis*
          (Summer): 151–59.
  1989   "Apostles and the Legitimation of
          Repression: Some Historical and
          Empirical Perspectives on the Cult

Controversy." *Sociological Analysis*
(Winter): 386–96.

Lifton, Robert Jay
1969 *Thought Reform and the Psychology of
Totalism: A Study of "Brainwashing" in
China.* New York: Norton.

Lincoln, C. Eric
1973 *The Black Muslims in America,* revised
ed. Boston: Beacon Press.
1974a "The Power in the Black Church."
Cross Currents (Spring): 3–21.

Lincoln, C. Eric, ed.
1968 *Is Anybody Listening to Black America?*
New York: Seabury Press.
1974b *The Black Experience in Religion.* Garden
City, N.J.: Doubleday.

Lincoln, C. Eric, and Lawrence H. Mamiya
1990 *The Black Church in The African
American Experience.* Durham N.C.:
Duke University Press.

Lipman-Blumen, Jean
1972 "How Ideology Shapes Women's
Lives." *Scientific American* (January):
33–42.

Lipset, Seymour
1960 *Political Man.* Garden City, N.Y.:
Doubleday.

Lipset, Seymour M., and Reinhart Bendix
1959 *Social Mobility in Industrial Society.*
Berkeley: University of California
Press.

Lofland, John
1977 *Doomsday Cult,* enlarged ed. New
York: Irvington.

Lofland, John, and Norman Skonovd
1981 "Conversion Motifs." *Journal for the
Scientific Study of Religion* (December):
7–85.

Long, Theodore E.
1986 "Prophecy, Charisma, and Politics:
Reinterpreting the Weberian Thesis."
Pp. 3–17 in *Prophetic Religions and
Politics.* Edited by Jeffrey Hadden and
Anson Shupe. New York: Paragon.

Luckmann, Thomas
1967 *The Invisible Religion.* New York:
Macmillan.

Luhman, Reid, and Stuart Gilman
1980 *Race and Ethnic Relations.* Belmont,
Calif: Wadsworth.

McCarthy, John D., and Mayer N. Zald
1977 "Resource Mobilization in Social
Movements: A Partial Theory."
American Journal of Sociology (May):
1212–39.

McCutcheon, Alan L.
1988 "Denominations and Religious Intermarriage: Trends Among White
Americans in the Twentieth Century."
Review of Religious Research (March):
213–27.

McGaw, Douglas B.
1979 "Commitment and Religious
Community: A Comparison of a
Charismatic and a Mainline
Congregation." *Journal for the Scientific
Study of Religion* (June): 146–63.
1980 "Meaning and Belonging in a
Charismatic Congregation: An
Investigation into Sources of
Neo-Pentecostal Success." *Review of
Religious Research* (Summer): 284–301.

McGuire, Meredith B.
1977 "Testimony as a Commitment
Mechanism in Catholic Pentecostal
Prayer Groups." *Journal for the
Scientific Study of Religion* (June):
165–68.
1981 *Religion: The Social Context.* Belmont,
Calif: Wadsworth.
1982 *Pentecostal Catholics.* Philadelphia:
Temple University Press.

McLaughlin, Eleanor Commo
1974 "Equality of Souls, Inequality of
Sexes: Women in Medieval
Theology." Pp. 213–66 in *Religion and
Sexism.* Edited by Rosemary Radford
Ruether. New York: Simon &
Schuster.

McLeod, Jay
1987   *Ain't No Makin It.* Boulder, Colo:
        Westview.

McLoughlin, William G.
1978   *Revivals, Awakenings, and Reform.*
        Chicago: University of Chicago Press.

McMurry, Mary
1978   "Religion and Women's Sex-Role
        Traditionalism." *Sociological Focus*
        (April): 81–95.

McNall, Scott G.
1974   *The Greek Peasant.* Washington D.C.:
        American Sociological Association.

McNamara, Patrick H.
1984   *Religion: North American Style,* 2d ed.
        Belmont, Calif: Wadsworth.

Machalek, Richard
1977   "Definitional Strategies in the Study
        of Religion." *Journal for the Scientific
        Study of Religion* (December):
        395–401.

Machalek, Richard, and Michael Martin
1976   "Invisible Religions: Some
        Preliminary Evidence." *Journal for the
        Scientific Study of Religion* (December):
        311–22.

Mack, Raymond W., Raymond J. Murphy, and
        Seymour Yellin
1956   "The Protestant Ethic, Level of
        Aspiration and Social Mobility: An
        Empirical Test." *American Sociological
        Review* (June): 295–300.

Malinowski, Bronislaw
1931   "Culture." Pp. 621–45 in
        *Encyclopaedia of the Social Sciences, Vol.
        IV.* Edited by Edwin R. A. Seligman
        and Alvin Johnson. New York:
        Macmillan.
1936   *The Foundations of Faith and Morals.*
        London: Oxford University Press.
1944   *A Scientific Theory of Culture and Other
        Essays.* Chapel Hill: The University of
        North Carolina Press.
1948   *Magic, Science, and Religion and Other
        Essays.* New York: Free Press.

(Reprinted, Garden City, N.Y.:
        Doubleday, 1954.)

Marett, R. R.
1914   *The Threshold of Religion.* London:
        Methuen & Co.

Markoff, John, and Daniel Regan
1981   "The Rise and Fall of Civil Religion:
        Comparative Perspectives."
        Sociological Analysis (Winter): 333–52.

Martin, David A.
1969   *The Religious and the Secular: Studies in
        Secularization.* London: Routledge &
        Kegan Paul.
1978   *A General Theory of Secularization.*
        Oxford, England: Basil Blackwell.

Martin, Patricia Yancey, Marie Withers Osmond,
        Susan Hesselbart, and Meredith Wood
1980   "The Significance of Gender as a
        Social and Demographic Correlate of
        Sex Role Attitudes." *Sociological Focus*
        (October): 338–96.

Martin, William
1972   *Christians in Conflict.* Chicago: Center
        for the Scientific Study of Religion,
        University of Chicago.
1979   "Hearts and Minds." *Texas Monthly*
        (September): 260–66.
1981   "Time of Repentance, Season of Joy."
        Texas Monthly (December): 218–24.

Marty, Martin E.
1972   "Ethnicity: The Skeleton of Religion
        in America." *Church History* (March):
        5–21.
1974   "Two Kinds of Civil Religion." Pp.
        139–57 in *Civil Religion in America.*
        Edited by Russell E. Richey and
        Donald G. Jones. New York: Harper
        & Row.

Marx, Gary
1967   *Protest and Prejudice.* New York: Harper
        & Row.

Maslow, Abraham
1964   *Religions, Values, and Peak Experiences.*
        Columbus: Ohio State University
        Press.

Mason, Karen, and Larry L. Bumpass
 1975 "U.S. Women's Sex Role Ideology, 1970." *American Journal of Sociology* (March): 1212–19.

Masters, Robert, and Jean Houston
 1966 *The Varieties of Psychedelic Experience.* New York: Rinehart & Winston.

Mathisen, James A.
 1987 "Thomas O'Dea's Dilemmas of Institutionalization: A Case Study and Reevaluation After Twenty-Five Years." *Sociological Analysis* (Winter): 302–18.
 1989 "Twenty Years After Bellah: Whatever Happened to American Civil Religion?" *Sociological Analysis* (Summer): 129–49.

Mayer, Albert J., and Harry Sharp
 1962 "Religious Preference and Worldly Success." *American Sociological Review* (April): 218–27.

Mead, Margaret, ed.
 1955 *Cultural Patterns and Technical Change.* New York: New American Library.

Mead, Sidney E.
 1974 "The Nation with the Soul of a Church." Pp. 45–74 in *American Civil Religion.* Edited by Russel E. Richey and Donald G. Jones. New York: Harper & Row.

Meier, Harold C.
 1972 "Mother Centeredness and College Youths' Attitudes Towards Social Equality for Women: Some Empirical Findings." *Journal of Marriage and the Family* (February): 115–21.

Melton, J. Gordon
 1993 "Another Look at New Religions." *Annals of the American Academy of Political and Social Science* (May): 97–112.

Menschung, Gustav
 1964 "The Masses, Folk Belief, and Universal Religion." Pp. 269–72 in *Religion, Culture, and Society.* Edited by Louis Schneider. New York: Wiley.

Merton, Thomas
 1968 *Social Theory and Social Structure.* New York: Free Press.

Meyer, John W.
 1980 "The World Polity and the Authority of the National-State." Pp. 109–37 in *Studies of the Modern World-System.* Edited by Albert Bergson. New York: Academic Press.
 1988 "The Evolution of a World Religious System: Some Research Design Ideas." Paper presented at the annual meeting of the Association for the Sociology of Religion, Atlanta, Ga.

Middleton, Russell
 1973 "Do Christian Beliefs Cause Anti-Semitism? A Comment." *American Sociological Review* (February): 33–52.

Midelfort, H. Eric
 1972 *Witch Hunting in Southwestern Germany, 1526–1684.* Stanford, Calif: Stanford University Press.

Miller, Robert T., and Ronald B. Flowas
 1977 *Toward Benevolent Neutrality: Church, State and the Supreme Court.* Waco, Tex: Baylor University Press.

Moberg, David
 1980 "Prison Camp of the Mind." Pp. 318–30 in *Society as It Is.* Edited by Glen Gaviglio and David E. Raye. New York: Macmillan.
 1984 *The Church as a Social Institution,* 2d ed. Grand Rapids, Mich: Baker Book House.

Moody, Edward J.
 1977 "Urban Witches." Pp. 427–37 in *Conformity and Conflict,* 3d ed. Edited by James P. Spradley and David W. McCurdy. Boston: Little, Brown.

Mooney, James
 1965 *The Ghost-Dance Religion and the Sioux Outbreak of 1890.* Abridged by Anthony F. C. Wallace. Chicago: University of Chicago Press.

Morgan, James N., Martin H. David, Wilbur J. Cohen, and Harvey E. Brazer

1962   *Income and Welfare in the United States.* New York: McGraw-Hill.

Morris, Brian
1987   *Anthropological Studies of Religion.* New York: Cambridge University Press.

Moseley, Romney M.
1978   *Religious Conversion: A Structural-Developmental Analysis.* Ph.D. dissertation, Harvard University.

Mosse, George L.
1978   *Toward the Final Solution: A History of European Racism.* New York: Harper & Row.

Muelder, Walter G.
1961   *Methodism and Society in the Twentieth Century.* Nashville, Tenn: Abingdon Press.

Mueller, Charles W., and Weldon T. Johnson
1975   "Socioeconomic Status and Religious Participation." *American Sociological Review* (December): 785–800.

Mueller, G. H.
1980   "The Dimensions of Religiosity." *Sociological Analysis* (Spring): 1–24.

Mueller, Samuel A.
1971a   "Dimensions of Interdenominational Mobility in the United States." *Journal for the Scientific Study of Religion* (Summer): 76–84.
1971b   "The New Triple Melting Pot: Herberg Revisited." *Review of Religious Research* (Fall): 18–33.

Mueller, Samuel A., and Angela V. Lane
1972   "Tabulations from the 1957 Current Population Survey on Religion: A Contribution to the Demography of American Religion." *Journal for the Scientific Study of Religion* (March): 76–98.

Munsey, Brenda, ed.
1980   *Moral Development, Moral Education, and Kohlberg.* Birmingham, Ala: Religious Education Press.

Murray, Margaret
1921   *The Witch-Cult in Western Europe.* London: Oxford University Press.

1952   *God of the Witches,* 2d ed. London: Oxford University Press.

Murvar, Vatro
1975   "Toward a Sociological Theory of Religious Movements." *Journal for the Scientific Study of Religion* (September): 229–56.

Myrdal, Gunnar
1944   *An American Dilemma.* New York: Harper & Row.

Nadal, Siegfried Fredrick
1954   *Nupe Religion.* London: Routledge & Kegan Paul.

Nason-Clark, Nancy
1987a   "Are Women Changing the Image of Ministry? A Comparison of British and American Realities." *Review of Religious Research* (June): 330–40.
1987b   "Ordaining Women as Priests: Religious vs. Sexist Explanations for Clerical Attitudes." *Sociological Analysis* (Fall): 259–73.

Neal, Marie Augusta
1975   "Women in Religion: A Sociological Perspective." *Sociological Inquiry* (December): 33–45.

Needleman, Jacob
1970   *The New Religions.* Garden City, N.Y.: Doubleday.

Neihardt, John G.
1961   *Black Elk Speaks.* Lincoln: University of Nebraska Press.

Neitz, Mary Jo
1987   *Charisma and Community: A Study of Religious Commitment within the Charismatic Renewal.* New Brunswick, N.J.: Transaction.
1990a   "Steps Toward a Sociology of Religious Experience: The Theories of Mihaly Csikszentmihalyi and Alfred Schutz." *Sociological Analysis* (Spring): 15–33.
1990b   "Studying Religion in the Eighties." Pp. 90–118 in *Symbolic Interaction and Cultural Studies.* Edited by Howard Becker and Michael McCall. Chicago: University of Chicago Press.

Nelkin, Dorothy
  1982   *The Creation Controversy: Science or Scripture in the Schools.* Boston: Beacon Press.

Nelsen, Hart M.
  1973   "Intellectualism and Religious Attendance of Metropolitan Residents." *Journal for the Scientific Study of Religion* (September): 285–96.

Nelsen, Hart M., Robert F. Everett, Paul Douglas Mader, and Warren C. Hamby
  1976   "A Test of Yinger's Measure of Nondoctrinal Religion: Implications for Invisible Religion as a Belief System." *Journal for the Scientific Study of Religion* (September): 263–68.

Nelsen, Hart M., Thomas W. Madron, and Raytha L. Yokley
  1975   "Black Religion's Promethean Motif: Orthodoxy and Militancy." *American Journal of Sociology* (July): 139–46.

Nelsen, Hart M., and Anne Kuesener Nelsen
  1975   *Black Church in the Sixties.* Lexington: University Press of Kentucky.

Nelsen, Hart M., and William E. Snizek
  1976   "Musical Pews: Rural and Urban Models of Occupational and Religious Mobility." *Sociology and Social Research* (April): 279–89.

Nelsen, Hart M., and Hugh P. Whitt
  1972   "Religion and the Migrant in the City: A Test of Holt's Cultural Shock Thesis." *Social Forces* (March): 379–84.

Nelson, Geoffrey
  1968   "The Concept of Cult." *Sociological Review* (November): 351–63.

Nelson, Mary
  1975   "Why Witches Were Women." Pp. 335–50 in *Women: A Feminist Perspective.* Edited by Jo Freeman. Palo Alto, Calif: Mayfield.

Neuendorf, Kimberly, and Robert Adelman
  1987   "An Interaction Analysis of Religious Television Programming." *Review of Religious Research* (December): 175–98.

Neuhaus, Richard John
  1984   *The Naked Public Square.* Grand Rapids, Mich: Eerdmans.

Newport, Frank
  1979   "The Religious Switcher in the United States." *American Sociological Review* (August): 528–52.

Newsweek
  1980   "A Tide of Born Again Politics." *Newsweek*, Sept. 15, 1980: 28–36.

Niebuhr, H. Richard
  1951   *Christ and Culture.* New York: Harper & Row.
  1957   *The Social Sources of Denominationalism.* New York: Meridian Books. (Originally published in 1929 by Henry Holt Company.)
  1960a   *Radical Monotheism and Western Culture.* New York: Harper & Row.
  1960b   "Faith in God and in Gods." Pp. 114–26 in *Radical Monotheism and Western Culture.* New York: Harper & Row.

Nietzsche, Friedrich
  1924   *The Birth of Tragedy.* New York: Macmillan. (Originally published in German in 1872.)

Noel, Donald L.
  1968   "A Theory of the Origins of Ethnic Stratification." *Social Problems* (Fall): 157–72.

Nordhoff, Charles
  1966   *The Communistic Societies of the United States.* New York: Dover.

Noss, John B.
  1949   *Man's Religions.* New York: Macmillan.

Nottingham, Elizabeth K.
  1971   *Religion: A Sociological View.* New York: Random House.

Noyes, John Humphrey
  1966   *Strange Cults and Utopias of 19th Century America.* New York: Dover.

Oates, Wayne E.
  1955   *Religious Factors in Mental Illness.* New York: Association Press.

O'Dea, Thomas F.
1957   *The Mormons.* Chicago: University of Chicago Press.
1961   "Five Dilemmas in the Institutionalization of Religion." *Journal for the Scientific Study of Religion* (October): 30–39.
1966   *The Sociology of Religion.* Englewood Cliffs, N.J.: Prentice Hall.
1968   "Sects and Cults." Pp. 130–36 in *International Encyclopedia of the Social Sciences,* Vol. 14. New York: Macmillan.

Ofshe, Richard
1980   "The Social Development of the Synanon Cult: The Managerial Strategy of Organizational Transformation." *Sociological Analysis* (Summer): 109–27.

Ogburn, William F.
1950   *Social Change.* New York: Viking Press.

Olsen, Marvin
1978   *The Process of Social Organization: Power in Social Systems,* 2d ed. New York: Holt, Rinehart, and Winston.

Organic, Harold Nathan
1963   *Religious Affiliation and Social Mobility in Contemporary American Society: A National Study.* Ph.D. dissertation, University of Michigan.

Ornstein, Robert
1972   *The Psychology of Consciousness.* San Francisco: W. H. Freeman.

Otto, Rudolf
1923   *The Idea of the Holy,* revised ed. Translated by John W. Harvey. London: Oxford University Press.

Pagels, Elaine
1979   *The Gnostic Gospels.* New York: Vintage Books.

Pahnke, Walter N.
1963   *Drugs and Mysticism: An Analysis of the Relationship Between Mystical Consciousness and Psychedelic Drugs.* Ph.D. dissertation, Harvard University.

Pargament, Kenneth, and June Hahn
1986   "God and the Just World: Causal and Coping Attributions to God in Health Situations." *Journal for the Scientific Study of Religion* (June): 193–207.

Parker, Robert Allerton
1935   *A Yankee Saint: John Humphrey Noyes and the Oneida Community.* New York: Putnam.

Parsons, Talcott
1955   *Essays in Sociological Theory,* revised ed. Glencoe, Ill: Free Press.
1964   "Christianity in Modern Industrial Society." Pp. 233–70 in *Sociological Theory, Values, and Sociocultural Change.* Edited by Edward Tiryakian. Glencoe, Ill: Free Press.

Parsons, Talcott, and Edward A. Shils, eds.
1951   *Toward a General Theory of Action.* Cambridge, Mass: Harvard University Press.

Parvey, Constance F.
1974   "The Theology and Leadership of Women in the New Testament." Pp. 117–49 in *Religion and Sexism.* Edited by Rosemary Radford Ruether. New York: Simon & Schuster.

Pavlos, Andrew J.
1982   *The Cult Experience.* Westport, Conn: Greenwood Press.

Peck, Janice
1993   *The Gods of Televangelism: The Crisis of Meaning and the Appeal of Religious Television.* Crosskill, N.J.: Hampton.

Perkins, H. Wesley
1983   "Organized Religion as Opiate or Prophetic Stimulant: A Study of American and English Assessments of Social Justice in Two Urban Settings." *Review of Religious Research* (March): 206–24.
1985   "A Research Note on Religiosity as Opiate or Prophetic Stimulant Among Students in England and the United States." *Review of Religious Research* (March): 269–80.

Perrin, Robin D.
1989   "American Religion in the Post-Aquarian Age: Values and Demographic Factors in Church Growth and Decline." *Journal for the Scientific Study of Religion* (March): 75–89.

Perrin, Robin D., and Armand L. Mauss
1991   "Saints and Seekers: Sources of Recruitment to the Vinyard Christian Fellowship." *Review of Religious Research* (December): 97–111.
1993   "Strictly Speaking . . . : Kelley's Quandary and the Vinyard Christian Fellowship." *Journal for the Scientific Study of Religion* (June): 125–35.

Perry, William G., Jr.
1970   *Forms of Intellectual and Ethical Development in the College Years.* New York: Holt, Rinehart Winston.

Petterson, Thorleif
1986   "The American Uses and Gratifications of T.V. Worship Services." *Journal for the Scientific Study of Religion* (December): 391–409.

Piaget, Jean
1950   *The Psychology of Intelligence.* London: Routledge & Kegan Paul.
1954   *The Construction of Reality in the Child.* New York: Basic Books.

Poblete, Renato, and Thomas F. O'Dea
1960   "Anomie and the 'Quest for Community': The Formation of Sects Among the Puerto Ricans of New York." *American Catholic Sociological Review* (Spring): 18–36.

Polanyi, Michael
1946   *Science, Faith, and Society.* Chicago: University of Chicago Press.
1949   "The Nature of Scientific Convictions." Pp. 49–66 in *Scientific Thought and Reality.* Edited by Fred Schwartz. New York: International Universities Press.

Poloma, Margaret M.
1982a   *The Charismatic Movement: Is There a New Pentacost?* Boston: Twayne.

1982b   "Toward a Christian Sociological Perspective: Religious Values, Theory and Methodology." *Sociological Analysis* (Summer): 95–108.

Pope, Liston
1942   *Millhands and Preachers.* New Haven, Conn: Yale University Press.

Porter, John
1965   *The Vertical Mosaic.* Toronto: University of Toronto Press.

Porterfield, Amanda
1987   "Feminist Theology as a Revitalization Movement." *Sociological Analysis* (Fall): 234–44.

Pratt, James Bissett
1964   "Objective and Subjective Worship." Pp. 143–56 in *Religion, Culture, and Society.* Edited by Louis Schneider. New York: Wiley.

Princeton Religion Research Center
1980   *Religion in America: 1979–80.* Princeton, N.J.: Princeton Religion Research Center.
1981   *Religion in America, 1981.* Princeton, N.J.: Princeton Religion Research Center.
1993   *Religion in America, 1992–1993.* Princeton, N.J.: Princeton Religion Research Center.

Quebedeaux, Richard
1987   "'We're On Our Way Lord': The Rise of 'Evangelical Feminism' in Modern Christianity." Pp. 129–44 in *Women in the World's Religions: Past and Present.* Edited by Ursula King. New York: Praeger.

Quinley, Harold E.
1974   *The Prophetic Clergy: Social Activism Among Protestant Ministers.* New York: Wiley.

Quinley, Harold E., and Charles Y. Glock
1983   *Anti-Semitism in America.* New Brunswick, N.J.: Transaction Books.

Radcliffe-Brown, A. R.
1939   *Taboo.* Cambridge, Mass: Harvard University Press.

Redekop, Calvin
1974   "A New Look at Sect Development."
        Journal for the Scientific Study of Religion
        (September): 345–52.

Riccio, James A.
1979   "Religious Affiliation and
        Socioeconomic Achievement." Pp.
        179–228 in *The Religious Dimension.*
        Edited by Robert Wuthnow. New
        York: Academic Press.

Richards, P. Scott, and Mark L. Davison
1992   "Religious Bias in Moral
        Development Research: A
        Psychometric Investigation." *Journal
        for the Scientific Study of Religion*
        (December): 467–85.

Richardson, James T.
1985   "Paradigm Conflict in Conversion
        Research." *Journal for the Scientific
        Study of Religion* (June): 163–79.

Richardson, James T., Joel Best, and David G.
        Bromley, eds.
1991   *The Satanism Scare.* New York: Aldine
        de Gruyter.

Richardson, James T., and Mary Stewart
1977   "Conversion Process Models and the
        Jesus Movement." *American Behavioral
        Scientist* (July): 819–38.

Richardson, James T., Mary White Stewart, and
        Robert B. Simmonds
1978   "Conversion to Fundamentalism."
        Society (May/June): 46–52.
1979   *Organized Miracles.* New Brunswick,
        N.J.: Transaction Books.

Richey, Russell E., and Donald G. Jones, eds.
1974   *American Civil Religion.* New York:
        Harper & Row.

Rigney, Daniel, Richard Machalek, and Jerry D.
        Goodman
1978   "Is Secularization a Discontinuous
        Process?" *Journal for the Scientific Study
        of Religion* (December): 381–87.

Robbins, Thomas
1969   "Eastern Mysticism and the
        Resocialization of Drug Users."
        Journal for the Scientific Study of Religion
        (Fall): 1308–17.

Robbins, Thomas, and Dick Anthony
1972   "Getting Straight with Meher Baba."
        Journal for the Scientific Study of Religion
        (June): 122–40.
1978   "New Religions, Families, and
        Brainwashing." *Society* (May/June):
        77–83.

Robbins, Thomas, and Dick Anthony, eds.
1981   *In Gods We Trust: New Patterns of
        Religious Pluralism in America.* New
        Brunswick, N.J.: Transaction Books.

Roberts, Keith A.
1992   "Ritual and the Transmission of a
        Cultural Tradition: An Ethnographic
        Perspective." Pp. 74–98 in *Beyond
        Establishment: Protestant Identity in a
        Post Protestant Age.* Edited by Jackson
        Carroll and Wade Clark Roof.
        Louisville: Westminster/John Knox.

Roberts, Michael K., and James D. Davidson
1984   "The Nature and Sources of
        Religious Involvement." *Review of
        Religious Research* (June): 334–50.

Robertson, H. M.
1959   *Aspects of the Rise of Economic Individual-
        ism: A Criticism of Max Weber and His
        School.* New York: Kelley & Millman.
        (Originally published in 1933.)

Robertson, Roland
1981   "Considerations from within the
        American Context on the
        Significance of Church-State
        Tensions." *Sociological Analysis* (Fall):
        193–208.
1989   "Globalization, Politics, and
        Religion." Pp. 1–9 in *The Changing
        Face of Religion.* Edited by James A.
        Beckford and Thomas Luchmann.
        London: Sage.
1991   "Globalization, Modernization, and
        Postmodernization: The Ambiguous
        Position of Religion." Pp. 281–91 in
        Religion and Global Order. Edited by
        Roland Robertson and William R.
        Garrett. New York: Paragon.
1992   *Globalization: Social Theory and Global
        Culture.* London: Sage.

Robertson, Roland, and William R. Garrett, eds.
1991   *Religion and Global Order.* New York: Paragon.

Robinson, John
1963   *Honest to God.* Philadelphia: Westminster Press.

Rochford, E. Burke, Jr.
1985   *Hare Krishna in America.* New Brunswick, N.J.: Rutgers University Press.

Rokeach, Milton, ed.
1968   "The Nature of Attitudes." In *Beliefs, Attitudes and Values.* San Francisco: Jossey Bass.

Rokeach, Milton, Patricia W. Smith, and Richard I. Evans
1960   "Two Kinds of Prejudice or One?" Pp. 132–68 in *The Open and Closed Mind.* Edited by Milton Rokeach. New York: Basic Books.

Roof, Wade Clark
1974   "Religious Orthodoxy and Minority Prejudice: Causal Relationship or Reflection of Localistic View." *American Journal of Sociology* (November): 643–64.
1976   "Traditional Religion in Contemporary Society: A Theory of Local-Cosmopolitan Plausibility." *American Sociological Review* (April): 195–208.
1978   *Commitment and Community.* New York: Elsevier.
1979   "Socioeconomic Differentials Among White Socioreligious Groups in the United States." *Social Forces* (September): 280–89.

Roof, Wade Clark, Christopher Kirk Hadaway, Myrna L. Hewitt, Douglas McGaw, and Richard Morse
1977   "Yinger's Measure of Non-Doctrinal Religion: A Northeastern Test." *Journal for the Scientific Study of Religion* (December): 403–8.

Roof, Wade Clark, and William McKinney
1987   *American Mainline Religion: Its Changing Shape and Future.* New Brunswick, N.J.: Rutgers University Press.

Roozen, David, William McKinney, and Wayne Thompson
1990   "The 'Big Chill' Generation Warms to Worship: A Research Note." *Review of Religious Research* (March): 314–22.

Rosewicz, Barbara
1985   "At Jerusalem Church, People Often Ignore Tenth Commandment." *Wall Street Journal,* April 5, 1985: 1, 5.

Rowley, Peter
1971   *New Gods in America.* New York: McKay.

Royle, Margorie H.
1987   "Using Bifocals to Overcome Blind Spots: The Impact of Women on the Military and the Ministry." *Review of Religious Research* (June): 341–50.

Ruether, Rosemary Radford
1974a   *Faith and Fratricide: The Theological Roots of Anti-Semitism.* New York: Seabury Press.
1974b   "The Persecution of Witches." *Christianity and Crises* (December 23): 291–95.
1974c   "Misogynism and Virginal Feminism in the Fathers of the Church." Pp. 150–83 in *Religion and Sexism.* Edited by Rosemary Radford Ruether. New York: Simon & Schuster.
1975   *New Woman, New Earth.* New York: Seabury Press.
1983   *Sexism and God Talk.* Boston: Beacon Press.

Ruether, Rosemary Radford, ed.
1974d   *Religion and Sexism.* New York: Simon & Schuster.

Ruether, Rosemary Radford, and Rosemary Skinner Keller
1981   *Women and Religion in America. Vol. 1: The Nineteenth Century.* San Francisco: Harper & Row.

Ruether, Rosemary, and Eleanor McLaughlin, eds.
1979   *Women of Spirit: Female Leadership in the Jewish and Christian Traditions.* New York: Simon & Schuster.

Runda, John, and John Seidler
1980   "Religion and Prejudice: New Evidence and a New Interpretation."

Paper presented to Society for the Scientific Study of Religion, Cincinnati, November 2.

Samuelsson, Kurt
1961   *Religion and Economic Action.* Translated by E. Geoffrey French. New York: Basic Books. (Originally published in Sweden in 1957.)

Sanua, Victor D.
1969   "Religion, Mental Health, and Personality: A Review of Empirical Studies." *American Journal of Psychiatry* (March): 1203–13.

Sapp, Gary L., and Logan Jones
1986   "Religious Orientation and Moral Judgment." *Journal for the Scientific Study of Religion* (June): 208–14.

Savage, C., W. W. Harman, J. Fadimann, and E. Savage
1963   "A Follow-up Note on the Psychedelic Experience." Paper presented at the annual convention of the American Psychological Association, St. Louis, May, 1963.

Schachter, Stanley
1964   "The Interaction of Cognitive and Physiological Determinants of Emotional State." Pp. 49–80 in *Advances in Experimental Social Psychology.* Edited by Leonard Berkowitz. New York: Academic Press.

Schachter, Stanley, and Jerome E. Singer
1962   "Cognitive, Social and Physiological Determinants of Emotional State." *Psychological Review* (September): 379–99.

Schachter, Stanley, and Ladd Wheeler
1962   "Epinephrine, Chlorpromazine, and Amazement." *Journal of Abnormal and Social Psychology* (August): 121–28.

Scherer, Ross P.
1988   "A New Typology for Organizations: Market, Bureaucracy, Clan and Mission, with Application to American Denominations." *Journal*

for the Scientific Study of Religion (December): 475–98.

Schmemann, Serge
1983   "New Soviet Rituals Seek to Replace Church's." *New York Times,* March 15, 1983: 1, 6.

Schneider, Herbert
1952   *Religion in 20th Century America.* Cambridge, Mass: Harvard University Press.

Schneider, Louis
1970   *Sociological Approach to Religion.* New York: Wiley.

Schneider, Louis, ed.
1964   *Religion, Culture and Society.* New York: Wiley.

Schneider, Louis, and Sanford M. Dornbusch
1958   *Popular Religion.* Chicago: University of Chicago Press.

Schreiber, William I.
1962   *Our Amish Neighbors.* Chicago: University of Chicago Press.

Schuman, Howard
1971   "The Religious Factor in Detroit: Review, Replication, and Reanalysis." *American Sociological Review* (February): 30–48.

Seidman, Ann
1979   "Why U.S. Corporations Should Get Out of South Africa." *Issue: A Quarterly Journal of Africanist Opinion* (Spring/Summer): 37–41.

Shannon, Thomas Richard
1989   *An Introduction to the World-System Perspective.* Boulder, Colo: Westview Press.

Shannon, William
1963   *The American Irish.* New York: Macmillan.

Sharot, Stephen
1991   "Judaism and the Secularization Debate." *Sociological Analysis* (Fall): 255–75.

Sheard, Robert B.
1987   *Interreligious Dialogue in the Catholic Church Since Vatican II.* Lewiston, N.Y.: Mellon.

Sherif, Carolyn Wood
1976   *Orientation in Social Psychology*. New York: Harper & Row.

Shields, David L.
1986   *Growing Beyond Prejudices: Overcoming Hierarchical Dualism*. Mystic, Conn: Twenty-Third Publishing.

Shipps, Jan
1985   *Mormonism: The Story of a New Religious Tradition*. Urbana: University of Illinois Press.

Shupe, Anson
1991   "A Comparison between the Satanist Scare in Indiana and Across the United States." Unpublished paper presented at the Symposium on New Religions, International Federation of Catholic Universities, Creighton University, Omaha, Nebraska (April).

Shupe, Anson D., Jr., and David G. Bromley
1978   "Witches, Moonies and Evil." *Society* (May/June): 75–76.
1979   "The Moonies and the Anti-Cultists: Movement and Countermovement in Conflict." *Sociological Analysis* (Winter): 325–34.
1980   *The New Vigilantes: Deprogrammers, Anti-Cultists, and the New Religions*. Beverly Hills, Calif: Sage.

Shupe, Anson, and Jeffrey K. Hadden
1989   "Is There Such a Thing as Global Fundamentalism?" Pp. 109–122 in *Secularization and Fundamentalism Reconsidered*. Edited by Jeffrey K. Hadden and Anson Shupe. New York: Paragon.

Shupe, Anson, and William A. Stacey
1982   *Born Again Politics and the Moral Majority*. New York: Mellen Press.

Simpson, John H.
1991   "Globalization and Religion: Themes and Perspectives." Pp. 1–18 in *Religion and Global Order*. Edited by Roland Robertson and William R. Garrett. New York: Paragon.

Singer, Margaret Thaler
1979   "Coming Out of the Cults." *Psychology Today* (January): 72–83.

Singer, Merrill
1988   "The Social Context of Conversion to a Black Religious Sect." *Review of Religious Research* (December): 177–92.

Sklare, Marshall, and Joseph Greenblum
1979   *Jewish Identity on the Suburban Frontier*, 2d ed. Chicago: University of Chicago Press.

Sloane, Douglas A., and Raymond H. Potvin
1983   "Age Differences in Adolescent Religiousness." *Review of Religious Research* (December): 142–54.

Smelser, Neil J.
1962   *Theory of Collective Behavior*. New York: Free Press.

Smith, Carole R., Lev Williams, and Richard H. Willis
1967   "Race, Sex, and Belief as Determinants of Friendship Acceptance." *Journal of Personality and Social Psychology* (February): 127–37.

Smith, Huston
1958   *The Religions of Man*. New York: Harper & Row.

Smith, Tom W.
1992   "Are Conservative Churches Growing?" *Review of Religious Research* (June): 305–29.

Snow, David A., and Cynthia L. Phillips
1980   "The Lofland-Stark Conversion Model: A Critical Reassessment." *Social Problems* (April): 430–47.

Soloman, Trudy
1981   "Integrating the 'Moonie' Experience: A Survey of Ex-Members of the Unification Church." Pp. 275–94 in *In Gods We Trust*. Edited by Thomas Robbins and Dick Anthony. New Brunswick, N.J.: Transaction Books.

Southwold, Martin
1982   "True Buddhism and Village Buddhism in Sri Lanka." Pp. 137–52

in *Religious Organization and Religious Experience*. Edited by John Davis. London: Academic Press.

Spickard, James V.
1991 "Experiencing Religious Rituals: A Schutzian Analysis of Navajo Ceremonies." *Sociological Analysis* (Summer): 191–204.

Spilka, Bernard, Ralph W. Hood Jr., and Richard L. Gorsuch
1985 *The Psychology of Religion*. Englewood Cliffs, N.J.: Prentice Hall.

Spilka, Bernard, Phillip Shaver, and Lee A. Kirkpatrick
1985 "A General Attribution Theory for the Psychology of Religion." *Journal for the Scientific Study of Religion* (March): 1–20.

Spiro, Melford
1966 "Religion: Problems of Definition and Explanation." Pp. 85–126 in *Anthropological Approaches to the Study of Religion*. Edited by Michael Banton. London: Tavistock.
1970 *Buddhism and Society*. New York: Harper & Row.
1978 *Burmese Supernaturalism*. Philadelphia: Institute for the Study of Human Issues.

Sprenger, Jakob, and Henry Kramer
1970 *Malleus Maleficarum*. Edited and translated by Montague Summers. New York: Benjamin Blom. (Originally published in 1486.)

Spretnak, Charlene, ed.
1982 *The Politics of Women's Spirituality*. Garden City, N.Y.: Anchor Press.

Stacey, William, and Anson Shupe
1982 "Correlates of Support for the Electronic Church." *Journal for the Scientific Study of Religion* (December): 291–303.

Staples, Clifford L., and Armand L. Mauss
1987 "Conversion or Commitment: A Reassessment of the Snow and Machalek Approach to the Study of Conversion." *Journal for the Scientific Study of Religion* (June): 133–47.

Stark, Rodney
1964 "Class, Radicalism, and Religious Involvement." *American Sociological Review* (October): 698–706.
1971 "Psychopathology and Religious Commitment." *Review of Religious Research* (Spring): 165–76.
1972 "The Economics of Piety: Religious Commitment and Social Class." Pp. 483–503 in *Issues in Social Inequality*. Edited by Gerald W. Thielbar and Saul D. Feldman. Boston: Little, Brown.
1984 "The Rise of a New World Faith." *Review of Religious Research* (September): 18–27.
1986 "The Class Basis of Early Christianity: Inferences from a Sociological Model." *Sociological Analysis* (Fall): 216–25.
1987 "How New Religions Succeed: A Theoretical Model." Pp. 11–29 in *The Future of New Religious Movements*. Edited by David G. Bromley and Phillip E. Hammond. Macon, Ga: Mercer University Press.

Stark, Rodney, and William Sims Bainbridge
1979 "Of Churches, Sects and Cults: Preliminary Concepts for a Theory of Religious Movements." *Journal for the Scientific Study of Religion* (June): 119–21.
1985 *The Future of Religion: Secularization, Renewal, and Cult Formation*. Berkeley: University of California Press.

Stark, Rodney, and Roger Finke
1988 "American Religion in 1776: A Statistical Portrait." *Sociological Analysis* (Spring): 39–51.

Stark, Rodney, Bruce D. Foster, Charles Y. Glock, and Harold E. Quinley
1973 "Ministers as Moral Guides: The Sounds of Silence." Pp.163–86 in *Religion in Sociological Perspective*. Edited by Charles Y. Glock. Belmont, Calif: Wadsworth.

Stark, Rodney, and Charles Y. Glock
  1968   *American Piety: The Nature of Religious Commitment.* Berkeley: University of California Press.
  1969   "Prejudice and the Churches." Pp. 70–95 in *Prejudice U.S.A.* Edited by Charles Y. Glock and Ellen Siegelman. New York: Praeger.

Stark, Rodney, and Lynne Roberts
  1982   "The Arithmetic of Social Movements: Theoretical Implications." *Sociological Analysis* (Spring): 53–67.

Stark, Werner
  1967   *Sectarian Religion. Vol. 2, The Sociology of Religion: A Study of Christendom.* New York: Fordham University Press.

Steinberg, Milton
  1947   *Basic Judaism.* New York: Harcourt, Brace World.

Steinberg, Stephen
  1965   "Reform Judaism: The Origin and Evolution of a 'Church Movement.' "*Journal for the Scientific Study of Religion* (October): 117–29.

Stempien, Richard, and Sarah Coleman
  1985   "Processes of Persuasion: The Case of Creation Science." *Review of Religious Research* (December): 169–77.

Stevens, Edward
  1974   *The Morals Game.* New York: Paulist Press.

Straus, Roger
  1976   "Changing Oneself: Seekers and the Creative Transformation of Life Experience." Pp. 252–73 in *Doing Social Life.* Edited by John Lofland. New York: Wiley Interscience.
  1979   "Religious Conversion as a Personal and Collective Accomplishment." *Sociological Analysis* (Summer): 158–65.

Streiker, Lowell, and Gerald Strober
  1972   *Religion and the New Majority.* New York: Association Press.

Suchman, Mark C.
  1991:   "Analyzing the Determinants of Everyday Conversion." *Sociological Analysis* (Supplement): S15–33.

Swatos, William H., Jr.
  1976   "Weber or Troeltsch? Methodology, Syndrome, and Development of Church-Sect Theory." *Journal for the Scientific Study of Religion* (June): 129–44.

Talmon, Yonina
  1965   "The Pursuit of the Millennium: The Relation Between Religion and Social Change." Pp. 522–37 in *Reader in Comparative Religion,* 2d ed. Edited by William A. Lessa and Evon Z. Vogt. New York: Harper & Row.

Tamney, Joseph B.
  1992   *The Resilience of Christianity in the Modern World.* Albany: State University of New York Press.

Tamney, Joseph B., and Steven D. Johnson
  1985   "Consequential Religiosity in Modern Society." *Review of Religious Research* (June): 360–78.

Tavard, George H.
  1973   *Women in Christian Tradition.* South Bend, Ind: University of Notre Dame Press.

Tawney, R. H.
  1954   *Religion and Capitalism.* New York: New American Library. (Originally published in 1924.)

Tedlin, Kent
  1978   "Religious Preference and Pro/Anti Activism on the Equal Rights Amendment Issue." *Pacific Sociological Review* (January): 55–66.

Tester, S. J.
  1987   *A History of Western Astrology.* Wolfeboro, N.H.: Boydell Press.

Thomas, Charles B., Jr.
  1985   "Clergy in Racial Controversy: A Replication of the Campbell and

Pettigrew Study." *Review of Religious Research* (June): 379–90.

Thomas, Michael, and C. C. Flippen
1972   "American Civil Religion: An Empirical Study." *Social Forces* (December): 218–25.

Thompson, Edward H., Jr.
1991   "Beneath the Status Characteristic: Gender Variations in Religiousness." *Journal for the Scientific Study of Religion* (December): 381–94.

Thornton, Arland, and Deborah Freedman
1979   "Changes in the Sex Role Attitudes of Women, 1962–1977: Evidence from a Panel Study." *American Sociological Review* (October): 831–842.

Tillich, Paul
1957   *Dynamics of Faith.* New York: Harper & Row.

Titiev, Mischa
1972   "A Fresh Approach to the Problem of Magic and Religion." Pp. 430–33 in *Reader in Comparative Religion: An Anthropological Approach,* 3d ed. Edited by William A. Lessa and Evon Z. Vogt. New York: Harper & Row.

Toolin, Cynthia
1983   "American Civil Religion from 1789 to 1981: A Content Analysis of Presidential Inaugural Addresses." *Review of Religious Research* (September): 39–48.

Trevor-Roper, Hugh
1967   "Witches and Witchcraft." *Encounter* (June): 13–34.

Trible, Phyllis
1979   "Eve and Adam: Genesis 2–3 Re-read." Pp. 74–83 in *Womanspirit Rising.* Edited by Carol P. Christ and Judith Plaskow. New York: Harper & Row.

Troeltsch, Ernst
1931   *The Social Teachings of the Christian Churches.* 2 vols. Translated by Olive Wyon, with an introduction by H. Richard Niebuhr. New York: Macmillan. (Reprinted. New York: Harper & Row, 1961; originally printed in German in 1911.)

Tschannen, Olivier
1991   "The Secularization Paradigm: A Systematization." *Journal for the Scientific Study of Religion* (December): 395–415.

Turner, Bryan S.
1991a   "Politics and Culture in Islamic Fundamentalism." Pp. 161–81 in *Religion and Global Order.* Edited by Roland Robertson and William R. Garrett. New York: Paragon.
1991b   *Religion and Social Theory.* London: Sage.

Turner, Jonathan H., and Alexandra Maryanski
1979   *Functionalism.* Menlo Park, Calif: Benjamin/Cummings.

Turner, Victor
1967   *The Forest of Symbols.* Ithaca, N.Y.: Cornell University Press.

Tylor, Edward B.
1958   *Primitive Culture,* Vol. II. New York: Harper & Row. (Originally published in London: John Murray, 1873.)

Ulrich, Laurel Thatcher
1980   "Vertuous Women Found: New England Ministerial Literature, 1668–1735." Pp. 67–87 in *Women in American Religion.* Edited by Janet Wilson James. Philadelphia: University of Pennsylvania Press.

Ungerleider, J. Thomas, and David K. Wellisch
1979   "Coercive Persuasion (Brainwashing), Religious Cults, and Deprogramming." *American Journal of Psychiatry* (March): 279–82.

U.S. Bureau of the Census
1991   *Statistical Abstract of the United States, 1991.* 111th ed. Washington D.C.: U.S. Government Printing Office.
1992   *Statistical Abstract of the United States, 1992.* 112th ed. Washington D.C.: U.S. Government Printing Office.

Van der Leeuw, Gerardus
1963   *Religion in Essence and Manifestation,*
        Vol. I. New York: Harper Torchbooks.

Van Der Post, Laurens
1955   *The Dark Eye in Africa.* New York:
        Morrow.

Vander Zanden, James W.
1983   *American Minority Relations,* 4th ed.
        New York: Knopf.
1987   *Social Psychology,* 4th ed. New York:
        Random House.

Vidler, Alec R.
1961   *The Church in an Age of Revolution, 1989
        to the Present Day.* London: Hodder &
        Stoughton.

Vogt, Evon Z.
1952   "Water Witching: An Interpretation of
        a Ritual Pattern in a Rural American
        Community." *Scientific Monthly*
        (September): 175–86.

Von Bertalanffy, Ludwig
1962   "General Systems Theory—A Critical
        Review." *General Systems Theory* (7):
        1–20.

Wagner, Melinda B.
1983   "Spiritual Frontiers Fellowship." Pp.
        45–66 in *Alternatives to American
        Mainline Churches.* Edited by Joseph
        H. Fichter. New York: Rose of Sharon
        Press.

Wald, Kenneth D.
1987   *Religion and Politics in the United States.*
        New York: St. Martin's Press.

Walker, Williston
1970   *A History of the Christian Church,* 3d ed.
        New York: Scribner.

Wallace, Anthony F. C.
1966   *Religion: An Anthropological View.* New
        York: Random House.
1972   "Revitalization Movements." Pp.
        503–12 in *Reader in Comparative
        Religion: An Anthropological Approach,*
        3d ed. Edited by William A. Lessa
        and Evon Z. Vogt. New York: Harper
        & Row.

Wallace, Carolyn M.
1986   "The Priesthood and Motherhood in
        The Church of Jesus Christ of Latter-
        Day Saints." Pp. 117–40 in *Gender
        and Religion.* Edited by C. W. Bynum,
        S. Harrell, and P. Richman. Boston:
        Beacon Press.

Wallace, Ruth
1975   "Bringing Women In: Marginality in
        the Churches." *Sociological Analysis*
        (Winter): 291–303.

Wallerstein, Immanuel
1974   *The Modern World System.* New York:
        Academic Press.
1979   *The Capitalist World Economy.* New
        York: Cambridge University Press.
1984   *The Politics of the World Economy.* New
        York: Cambridge University Press.

Wallis, Roy
1977   *The Road to Total Freedom: A Sociological
        Analysis of Scientology.* New York:
        Columbia University Press.

Walster, Elaine
1971   "Passionate Love." Pp. 85–99 in *Theo-
        ries of Attraction and Love.* Edited by Ber-
        nard I. Murstein. New York: Springer.

Warner, R. Stephen
1988:   *New Wine in Old Wineskins: Evangelicals
        and Liberals in a Small-Town Church.*
        Berkeley: University of California
        Press.
1993   "Work in Progress toward a New Para-
        digm for the Sociological Study of Re-
        ligion in the United States." *American
        Journal of Sociology* (March): 1044–93.

Warner, W. Lloyd
1953   *American Life: Dream and Reality.*
        Chicago: University of Chicago Press.
1961   *Family of God: A Symbolic Study of
        Christian Life in America.* New Haven,
        Conn: Yale University Press.

Warren, Bruce L.
1970   "Socioeconomic Achievement and
        Religion: The American Case." Pp.
        130–55 in *Social Stratification.* Edited
        by Edward O. Lanmann.
        Indianapolis: Bobbs Merrill.

Washington, Joseph R., Jr.
1964   *Black Religion.* Boston: Beacon Press.
1972   *Black Sects and Cults.* Garden City, N.Y.: Doubleday.

Waxman, Chaim I.
1983   *America's Jews in Transition.* Philadelphia: Temple University Press.

Weaver, Horace R.
1975   *Getting Straight About the Bible.* Nashville, Tenn: Abingdon Press.

Weber, Max
1946   *From Max Weber: Essays in Sociology.* Edited and translated by Hans H. Gerth and C. Wright Mills. New York: Oxford University Press.
1947   *The Theory of Social and Economic Organization.* Edited and translated by A. M. Henderson and Talcott Parsons. New York: Oxford University Press.
1951   *The Religion of China.* Translated by Hans H. Gerth. New York: Free Press. (Originally published in 1920–1921.)
1952   *Ancient Judaism.* Translated and edited by Hans H. Gerth and Don Martindale. New York: Free Press. (Originally published in 1920–1921.)
1958a   *The Protestant Ethic and the Spirit of Capitalism.* Translated by Talcott Parsons. New York: Scribner. (Originally published in 1904–1905.)
1958b   *The Religion of India.* Translated and edited by Hans H. Gerth and Don Martindale. New York: Free Press. (Originally published in 1920–1921.)
1963   *The Sociology of Religion.* Translated by Ephraim Fischoff. Boston: Beacon Press. (Originally published in 1922.)

Weigert, Andrew J., and Thomas L. Darwin
1970   "Secularization: A Cross-National Study of Catholic Male Adolescents." *Social Forces* (September): 28–36.

Weisman, Richard
1984   *Witchcraft, Magic, and Religion in 17th Century Massachusetts.* Amherst: University of Massachusetts Press.

Welch, Susan
1975   "Support Among Women for the Issues of the Women's Movement." *Sociological Quarterly* (Spring): 216–27.

Weller, Neil J.
1963   *Religion and Social Mobility in Industrial Society.* Ph.D. dissertation, University of Michigan.

Wells, Alan
1974   "Are Some Electronic Preachers Social Darwinists?" *Christianity Today* (October 21): 50.

Welter, Barbara
1976   "The Feminization of American Religion, 1800–1860." In *Dimity Convictions.* Athens: Ohio University Press.

Wesley, John
1943   *Selections from the Writings of the Rev. John Wesley, M.A.* Compiled and arranged by Herbert Welch. Nashville, Tenn: Abingdon Press.

Westie, Frank
1965   "The American Dilemma: An Empirical Test." *American Sociological Review* (August): 527–38.

Whitehead, Harriet
1974   "Reasonably Fantastic: Some Perspectives on Scientology, Science Fiction, and Occultism." Pp. 547–87 in *Religious Movements in Contemporary America.* Edited by Irving I. Zaretsky and Mark P. Leone. Princeton, N.J.: Princeton University Press.

Wilcox, Mary M.
1979   *Developmental Journey: A Guide to the Development of Logical and Moral Reasoning and Social Perspective.* Nashville, Tenn: Abingdon Press.

Williams, Michael A.
1986   "Uses of Gender Imagery in Ancient Gnostic Texts." Pp. 196–227 in *Gender and Religion.* Edited by C. W. Bynum, S. Harrell, and P. Richman. Boston: Beacon Press.

Williams, Peter W.
1980   *Popular Religion in America: Symbolic Change and the Modernization Process in Historical Perspective.* Englewood Cliffs, N.J.: Prentice Hall.

Williamson, Clark M.
1982   *Has God Rejected His People? Anti-Judaism in the Christian Church.* Nashville, Tenn: Abingdon Press.

Wilmore, Gayraud S.
1972   *Black Religion and Black Radicalism.* Garden City, N.Y.: Doubleday.

Wilson, Bryan R.
1959   "An Analysis of Sect Development." *American Sociological Review* (February): 3–15.
1966   *Religion in Secular Society: A Sociological Comment.* London: C.A. Watts.
1967   "The Pentecostal Minister: Role Conflicts and Contradictions of Status." Pp. 138–57 in *Patterns of Sectarianism.* Edited by Bryan R. Wilson. London: Heinemann.
1970   *Religious Sects.* New York: McGraw-Hill.
1976   *Contemporary Transformations of Religion.* Oxford: Clarendon Press.

Wilson, Gerald L., Joann Keyton, G. David Johnson, Cheryl Geiger, and Johanna C. Clark
1993   "Church Growth Through Member Identification and Commitment: A Congregational Case Study." *Review of Religious Research* (March): 259–72.

Wilson, John
1978   *Religion in American Society.* Englewood Cliffs, N.J.: Prentice Hall.

Wimberley, Ronald C.
1976   "Testing the Civil Religion Hypothesis." *Sociological Analysis* (Winter): 341–52.

Wimberley, Ronald C., and James A. Christenson
1981   "Civil Religion and Other Religious Identities." *Sociological Analysis* (Summer): 91–100.

Wimberley, Ronald C., Donald A. Clelland, and Thomas C. Hood

1976   "The Civil Religious Dimension: Is It There?" *Social Forces* (June): 890–900.

Wimberley, Ronald C., Thomas C. Hood, C. M. Lipsey, Donald Clelland, and Marguerite Hay
1975   "Conversion in a Billy Graham Crusade: Spontaneous Event or Ritual Action?" *The Sociological Quarterly* (Spring): 162–70.

Winter, Gibson
1962   *The Suburban Captivity of the Churches.* Garden City, N.Y.: Doubleday.

Winter, J. Alan
1977   *Continuities in the Sociology of Religion.* New York: Harper & Row.

Wood, James R.
1970   "Authority and Controversial Policy: The Churches and Civil Rights." *American Sociological Review* (December): 1057–69.
1972   "Personal Commitment and Organization Constraint: Church Officials and Racial Integration." *Sociological Analysis* (Fall): 142–51.
1981   *Leadership in Voluntary Organizations: The Controversy Over Social Action in Protestant Churches.* New Brunswick, N.J.: Rutgers University Press.

Wood, Ralph W., Jr.
1970   "Religious Orientation and the Report of Religious Experience." *Journal for the Scientific Study of Religion* (Winter): 285–91.

Wright, Derek, and Edwin Cox
1967   "A Study of the Relationship Between Moral Judgment and Religious Belief in a Sample of English Adolescents." *Journal of Social Psychology* (June): 135–44.

Wuthnow, Robert
1973   "New Forms of Religion in the Seminary." Pp. 187–203 in *Religion in Sociological Perspective.* Edited by Charles Y. Glock. Belmont, Calif: Wadsworth.
1976a   "Astrology and Marginality." *Journal for the Scientific Study of Religion* (June): 157–68.

1976b   *The Consciousness Reformation.* Berkeley: University of California Press.

1976c   "Recent Pattern of Secularization: A Problem of Generations?" *American Sociological Review* (October): 850–67.

1980   "World Order and Religious Movements." Pp. 57–75 in *Studies of the Modern World-System.* Edited by Albert Bergson. New York: Academic Press.

1981   "Two Traditions of Religious Studies." *Journal for the Scientific Study of Religion* (March): 16–32.

1987   "The Social Significance of Religious Television." *Review of Religious Research* (December): 125–34.

1988   *The Restructuring of American Religion: Society and Faith Since World War II.* Princeton, N.J.: Princeton University Press.

Yeaman, Patricia A.
1987   "Prophetic Voices: Differences Between Men and Women." *Review of Religious Research* (June): 367–76.

Yeatts, John R., and William Asher
1979   "Can We Afford Not to Do True Experiments in Psychology of Religion? A Reply to Batson." *Journal for the Scientific Study of Religion* (March): 86–9.

Yinger, J. Milton
1961   "Comment." *Journal for the Scientific Study of Religion* (October): 40–44.

1969   "A Structural Examination of Religion." *Journal for the Scientific Study of Religion* (Spring): 88–100.

1970   *The Scientific Study of Religion.* New York: Macmillan.

1977   "A Comparative Study of the Substructure of Religion." *Journal for the Scientific Study of Religion* (March): 67–86.

Yinger, J. Milton, and Stephen J. Cutler
1982   "The Moral Majority Viewed Sociologically." *Sociological Focus* (October): 289–306.

Zablocki, Benjamin
1971   *The Joyful Community: An Account of the Bruderhof.* Baltimore: Penguin Books.

Zaechner, R. C., ed.
1967   *The Concise Encyclopedia of Living Faith.* Boston: Beacon Press.

Zald, Mayer N., and Roberta Ash
1966   "Social Movement Organizations: Growth, Decay and Change." *Social Forces* (March): 327–41.

Zald, Mayer N., and Michael A. Berger
1978   "Social Movements in Organizations: Coup d'etat, Insurgency, and Mass Movements." *American Journal of Sociology* (January): 823–61.

Zaretsky, Irving I., and Mark P. Leone
1974   *Religious Movements in Contemporary America.* Princeton, N.J.: Princeton University Press.

Zygmunt, Joseph F.
1970   "Prophetic Failure and Chiliastic Identity: The Case of the Jehovah's Witnesses." *American Journal of Sociology* (May): 926–48.

Index

Credits

Short quotations within the main body of the text are used with permission of the sources noted below. Credits for boxed material, tables, figures, and other illustrations are noted on the pages on which the materials appear.

Berger, Peter L. 1967: *The Sacred Canopy*. Garden City, N.Y.: Doubleday. ©1967 by Peter L. Berger. Reprinted by permission of Doubleday & Company, Inc. **(Chapter 4, p. 102; Chapter 14, pp. 338–40.)**

Campbell, Ernest Q., and Thomas F. Pettigrew. 1959: *Christians in Racial Crisis*. Washington, D.C.: Public Affairs Press. Reprinted by permission of Public Affairs Press. **(Chapter 12, p. 306.)**

Geertz, Clifford. 1958: "Ethos, World View and the Analysis of Sacred Symbols." *The Antioch Review* 17:4 (Winter): 421–37. ©1958 *The Antioch Review*. Reprinted by permission of *The Antioch Review*. **(Chapter 3, p. 59; Chapter 4, pp. 99, 102, 104.)**

Geertz, Clifford. 1966: "Religion as a Cultural System." Pp. 1–46 in *Anthropological Approaches to the Study of Religion*. Ed. by Michael Banton. London: Tavistock Publications. Reprinted by permission of Tavistock Publications. **(Chapter 1, pp. 9–12.)**

Judah, J. Stillson. 1974: *Hare Krishna and the Counterculture*. New York: John Wiley & Sons. Reprinted by permission of J. Stillson Judah. **(Chapter 4, pp. 91, 95, 98; Chapter 5, pp. 117–18.)**

Kelsey, George D. 1965: *Racism and the Christian Understanding of Man*. New York: Charles Scribner's Sons. ©1965 George D. Kelsey. Reprinted by permission of Charles Scribner's Sons. **(Chapter 12, p. 295.)**

Lenski, Gerhard. 1963: *The Religious Factor*. Rev. ed. Garden City, N.Y.: Doubleday. ©1961 by Gerhard Lenski. Reprinted by permission of Doubleday & Company, Inc. **(Chapter 10, pp. 236, 237, 241.)**

Niebuhr, H. Richard. 1960: *Radical Monotheism and Western Culture*. New York: Harper & Row. ©1942, 1952, 1955, 1960 by H. Richard Niebuhr. Reprinted by permission of Harper & Row, Publishers, Inc. **(Chapter 1, p. 7–8.)**

Weber, Max. 1947: *The Theory of Social and Economic Organization*. Ed. and trans. by A. M. Henderson and Talcott Parsons. New York: Oxford University Press. ©1947, renewed 1975 by Talcott Parsons. Reprinted by permission of Macmillan Publishing Co., Inc. **(Chapter 7, pp. 161–63, 166.)**

Yinger, J. Milton. 1970: *The Scientific Study of Religion*. New York: Macmillan. ©1970 by J. Milton Yinger. Reprinted by permission of Macmillan Publishing Co., Inc. **(Chapter 1, pp. 6–9; Chapter 9, pp. 202, 210, 218; Epilogue, p. 414.)**